The USSR and the Muslim World

The USSR and the Muslim World

Issues in Domestic and Foreign Policy

Edited by Yaacov Ro'i

London
GEORGE ALLEN & UNWIN
Boston   Sydney

© Yaacov Ro'i, 1984
This book is copyright under the Berne Convention. No reproduction without permission. All rights reserved.

George Allen & Unwin (Publishers) Ltd,
40 Museum Street, London WC1A 1LU, UK

George Allen & Unwin (Publishers) Ltd,
Park Lane, Hemel Hempstead, Herts HP2 4TE, UK

Allen & Unwin, Inc.,
9 Winchester Terrace, Winchester, Mass. 01890, USA

George Allen & Unwin Australia Pty Ltd,
8 Napier Street, North Sydney, NSW 2060, Australia

First published in 1984
Second impression 1985

British Library Cataloguing in Publication Data

Ro'i, Yaacov
    The USSR and the Muslim world.
1. Soviet Union—Foreign relations—Islamic countries 2. Islamic countries—Foreign relations—Soviet Union
I. Title
327.47071   DK68.7.I/
ISBN 0-04-301171-3

Library of Congress Cataloging in Publication Data

Main entry under title:
    The USSR and the Muslim world.
"Based on papers given at a conference held by the Russian and east European research Center at Tel Aviv University in December 1980"— Acknowledgments.
Includes index.
1. Muslims—Soviet Central Asia—Congresses. 2. Near East—Foreign relations—Soviet Union—Congresses. 3. Soviet Union—Foreign relations—Near East—Congresses. 4. Afghanistan—History—Soviet Occupation, 1979—Congresses. I. Ro'i, Yaacov. II. Universitat Tel-Aviv. Makhon le-heker Berit ha-mo'atsot u-Mizrah Eropah. III. Title: U.S.S.R. and the Muslim world.
DK855.5.M8U85   1984   327.56047   83-25709
ISBN 0-04-301171-3

Photoset in 11 on 12 point Times by Grove Graphics, Tring, Hertfordshire and printed in Great Britain by Blackmore Press, Shaftesbury, Dorset.

Contents

Acknowledgments	ix
Abbreviations	xi
Introduction	xiii

Part One The Soviet Domestic Context: Socio-Political Aspects

1. National Symbiosis: Vitality, Religion, Identity, Allegiance *by Michael Rywkin* — 3
2. The Central Government and Peripheral Opposition in Khiva, 1910–24 *by Dov. B. Yaroshevski* — 16
3. Central Asian Political Participation and Soviet Political Development *by Steven L. Burg* — 40
4. Trends in the Soviet Muslim Population: Demographic Aspects *by Murray Feshbach* — 63
5. The Soviet Muslim Population: Trends in Living Standards, 1960–75 *by Alastair McAuley* — 95

Part Two The Soviet Domestic Context: Cultural and Ideological Aspects

6. The Significance of Increasing Bilingualism among Soviet Muslims *by Paul B. Henze* — 117
7. The Effect of the USSR's Language Policy on the National Languages of its Turkic Population *by Michael Bruchis* — 129
8. The Impact of the Islamic Fundamentalist Revival of the Late 1970s on the Soviet View of Islam *by Yaacov Ro'i* — 149

Part Three Foreign Policy Aspects

9. Soviet Central Asia: a Model of Non-Capitalist Development for the Third World *by Teresa Rakowska-Harmstone* — 181
10. Soviet Experience of Muslim Guerrilla Warfare and the War in Afghanistan *by Chantal Lemercier-Quelquejay and Alexandre Bennigsen* — 206
11. First Steps in Soviet Diplomacy toward Afghanistan, 1917–21 *by Michael Volodarsky* — 215
12. Soviet Policy and the Constraints of Nationalism in Iran and Afghanistan *by Marvin G. Weinbaum* — 226

13 Saudi Arabia's Attitude toward the USSR, 1977–80: Between Saudi Pragmatism and Islamic Conservatism *by Jacob Goldberg* 261
14 Dilemmas of Arab Communism: The case of the Syrian Communist Party, 1969–73 *by Dina Kehat* 272

Afterword 290
Index 293

Acknowledgments

This book is based on papers given at a conference held by the Russian and East European research Center at Tel Aviv University in December 1980 on 'The USSR and the Muslim world'. The editor wishes to take the opportunity to thank all those who made the conference possible: the United States Information Service (USIS); the British Council; the Jewish Community Foundation of Greater Montreal, Carleton University; the Inter-University Committee for Middle Eastern Studies; and, above all, Tel Aviv University. In particular, I should like to express my gratitude to Professor Yoram Dinstein, rector of Tel Aviv University, who took a personal interest in the conference. Without his encouragement the conference, and consequently also this present volume, would probably not have materialized. And last, but certainly not least, thanks are due to the staff of the Center, who gave generously of their time and assistance to make the conference a success, and to its editor, Philippa Shimrat (Lewis), for her valuable editorial help in preparing the book.

Abbreviations

ASSR Autonomous Socialist Soviet Republic
CPSU Communist Party of the Soviet Union
PDRY People's Democratic Republic of Yemen (South Yemen)
RSFSR Russian Socialist Federated Soviet Republic
SSR   Socialist Soviet Republic

Introduction

This volume does not claim to encompass the entire history of the USSR's relationship with the Muslim world, or the numerous political, economic, social and cultural aspects of that relationship. First, this could hardly be a feasible project for a single volume and, secondly, a great deal of excellent research work has already appeared on a wide variety of the topics involved.

The conference which generated this volume represented, however, a recognition that the topic — the USSR and the Muslim world — is one not only of increasing political significance but also of considerable intellectual interest. Its sponsors undertook to update some of the research on problems that seemed essential to understanding the issue at large, and to illuminate a number of other angles that had hitherto not been delved into. A number of the talks were indeed in the nature of preliminary reports and have therefore not been reproduced here. Those problems which were not discussed were omitted not because they were considered ancillary or irrelevant, but simply because it was not within the scope of a single three-day symposium to cover more ground than it did. The participants all expressed the hope that this first convention would be the predecessor of further, similar initiatives.

The main focus of both the conference and this volume is on the Muslim areas of the USSR itself which from the point of view of academic interest seem to constitute the most significant issue (quite apart from the possible political implications). The first chapter deals with the all-important question of the components of the Soviet Central Asians' national or collective consciousness. Who are they? Who do they feel they are? What distinguishes them from other Soviet citizens and particularly from the Russians and other Europeans who have settled in their midst in a coordinated effort to assimilate them? How do they feel about the Russians and their position of inferiority toward them? A significant part of the work on Soviet Muslims, in this and other volumes, dwells specifically on the Central Asians. Although they are not the only Muslims in the USSR, they comprise nearly 70 percent of the entire grouping and constitute a large, compact group that is technically the easiest to study. The polyglot population of Dagestan and the widely scattered Tatars and Bashkirs are much more elusive. Moreover, not having Union Republics, they do not have a national press that is available however, believes that even a growing use of Russian will not necessarily mean russification. The subsequent chapter shows how in practice the Soviets have actually russified the languages of their Muslim minorities, taking advantage of the greater suitability of Russian to the needs of both technology and communist construction.

The final chapter of Part 2 relates to the Soviet attitude to Islam and the disconcertment evident in Moscow at the revival of Muslim fundamentalism outside the USSR which, it is feared, must eventually resound inside the country. The entire attitude to Islam, seemingly embedded in Bolshevik theory, seems to have become a question of preferences in dealing with political exigencies at home, where Islam has in any case refused to die out although notably modified, and abroad where accommodation with the Islamic rebirth may bring the Soviet Union important benefits.

Another issue that connects domestic and foreign policy and also touches upon questions of ideology is Moscow's use of the Soviet Central Asian model in selling its regime and ideals to the Muslim world outside. Here, too, theory has been made to bend to policy requirements. The question is how far is Soviet Central Asia with all its relative material achievements attractive to Third World statesmen.

The other side of the picture is the Kremlin's application or non-application of lessons it learned, or should have learned, from its oppression of Muslim opposition in Central Asia in the first decade or so of Soviet rule, in its attempt fifty years later to subdue opposition in neighboring Afghanistan, the first foreign Muslim country that the USSR, for its own reasons, found necessary to bring under its sway through the use of force. Some of the problems involved are the topic of Chapter 10. It in turn is followed by a chapter that depicts the beginnings of Soviet diplomatic relations with Afghanistan – once more a story that helps understand later events.

The final chapter that deals with the USSR's Muslim neighbors looks at their needs and internal political developments. In particular, it shows how their relationship with the USSR is interlaced with their nationalism and nationalist factions. Can the USSR in fact accommodate itself to these nationalist trends in Iran and Afghanistan and can the local nationalists reach an accommodation, a *modus operandi*, with their powerful neighbor?

The volume closes with two chapters on the Arab world and its endless difficulties with the Soviet Union. Both deal with issues that have not traditionally been central to Soviet policy in the Middle East, but they are not only valid but also present large question marks for the future. The first, the question of Saudi Arabia's attitude toward the USSR, has become increasingly important to Moscow as it is pushed toward the periphery of the Arab world. (The seventies saw the USSR's estrangement from Egypt, its major ally in the region's heartland, and difficulties with other Arab countries with which it had sought partnership.) If the USSR can reach a working relationship with Riyadh, that will be a significant victory in its perpetual rivalry with Washington, which from the Soviet point of view is the pivot of its regional policies. It will also signify the Soviet Union's capability to take advantage of coinciding interests with any regional state irrespective of its ideological position and will bring it into the Persian Gulf. The second question is that of the Arab Communist parties' position *vis-à-vis* the Soviet Union. Can these parties present themselves as popular parties, faithful to the interests of their nations as they are popularly comprehended, if they serve the interests of a superpower which constantly appears as opposed to those interests? The possibility of these parties becoming an alternative to the Arab leaderships as partners of the USSR has also become an issue which the Soviet Establishment is re-evaluating in view of its growing problems with the Arab governments. The case of the Syrian Communist Party and its internal deliberations helps us comprehend the answer to yet another of the dilemmas which pervade Moscow's relations with the Muslim world.

PART ONE

The Soviet Domestic Context: Socio-Political Aspects

1
National Symbiosis: Vitality, Religion, Identity, Allegiance

MICHAEL RYWKIN

In its national perspective the Soviet Central Asian problem revolves around four main issues: the vitality, the religious solidarity, the identity and the allegiance of its native majority, all within the framework of welfare colonialism, which will be described below.

Vitality: Demographic

Vitality, first of all, signifies demographic vitality: young age pyramid, large and united families, rarity of divorce.

The Muslims of Soviet Central Asia are the fastest-growing group in all the Soviet Union. Even by republics, their gross reproduction rates in 1978–9 were 2·15–2·91 as opposed to 0·93–1·00 in the Slavic republics, the RSFSR, Ukraine and Belorussia. (It is worth noting that even these much higher rates denote a decrease as against previous figures, those of 1974–5, for example, having been 2·33–3·07 for the Central Asian Muslims as opposed to 0·98–1·08 in the Slavic republics.)[1]

Families of seven or more members living together are common: between 43·3 and 47·4 percent of families in Uzbekistan, Turkmenistan and Tadzhikistan as against 1·04 percent in the RSFSR (1979).[2] Unlike the Slavs, who aspire to Western material amenities, having children is still regarded by the Muslims as much more desirable than acquiring material possessions. This may be a survival from the old oriental tradition of valuing living 'possessions' (whether wives, children or domestic animals) or simply a genuine love for family life and children common to Muslim societies in general. Figures are revealing: an average Central Asian Muslim woman expects to have between 5·93 and 6·26 children as opposed to two children for the Russian woman.[3]

The youthfulness of the population is visible to casual observers, and statistical data confirm this impression. In 1970, children aged 1 to 5 belonging to the titular groups of the six Muslim republics of the USSR accounted for approximately one-half of the total within their own group, while Slavic children accounted for barely one-quarter of the total in the three Slavic republics.[4] Soviet sources calculate that by the year 2000 every second child born in the USSR will come from a Muslim family.[5]

The principal cause of the Muslim population explosion is the stability of the Muslim family. Divorce is rare, early marriage is frequent and women tend to stay home, which in turn allows them to have even more children. Grandparents are often present at home, facilitating their grandchildren's upbringing.[6] There is mutual respect between the generations and a sense of belonging to an extended family.

Favorable climatic conditions, lessening the demand for clothing, and covered living-space, heating, etc., are also helpful. Low population mobility, especially the rarity of outmigration to distant areas, and the resulting stability of traditional neighborhoods add to favorable conditions for raising children.

The importance attached to family life influences not only the size of the family. Under Soviet conditions a strong united family is the best defense against state interference in private life. Mutual trust within the family extends to relatives and friends and helps Soviet Muslims protect the privacy of their everyday lives from the unwelcome eyes of meddling local officials – something the Russians have a harder time achieving. Furthermore, Central Asian Muslims value everyday joys, need no vodka to forget their troubles, are not interested in theoretical problems and remain indifferent to 'isms' of any kind or shape as long as their family lives and daily pleasures remain unaffected. Their inner vitality is based on their epicurean nature and extended family cohesion, something difficult to control even for a Soviet-style state.

Vitality: Private Initiative

The vitality of a population also translates itself, under Soviet conditions, into profitable private plots, privately owned one-family houses, rich secondhand-goods markets, and a healthy ability to overcome bureaucratic control and red tape. This is very much the case in Central Asia, where the private sector is stronger than elsewhere in the Soviet Union, Transcaucasia aside. In 1979 over half of available urban housing in Uzbekistan and over one-third in Turkmenistan and Tadzhikistan were privately owned as opposed to about one-fifth in the RSFSR. Newly built housing completed in 1979 (both urban and rural) was 45 percent private in Uzbekistan, 51 percent in Tadzhikistan, 54 percent in Kirgizia and 58 percent in Turkmenistan as against 13 percent in the RSFSR, 35 percent in the Ukraine and 25 percent in Belorussia.[7] Given the recognized importance of housing as a factor determining Soviet living standards, these figures deserve more than passing attention.

Similar differences mark the relative importance of private-plot agriculture. Private-plot production of grain, fruits and berries, grapes, vegetables, meat, milk, eggs and wool accounts for a larger slice of the Uzbek total than of that of the USSR average. Thus, such basic staples as meat and vegetables produced privately account for 49 percent of Uzbek production against the USSR average of only 29 percent.[8] It is probable that both figures are scaled down as is generally the case with Soviet statistical data dealing with the private sector, but we have no reason to doubt the rough relationship between the two figures.

Private initiative is not limited to food. The Tashkent open-air market is almost legendary for its variety of merchandise, whether local, brought from European Russia or 'imported' from abroad. But what is especially remarkable is the extent of private dealings in the public sector, whether in the *kolkhoz*, the *sovkhoz*, the store or the factory. It is an open secret that private herds are camouflaged as *kolkhoz* cattle, kiosks sell privately processed goods when meager 'official' supplies are exhausted, cooperatives and consumer-goods factories work *na levo* ('on the side') on top of their regular production, theft and corruption are commonplace, and so on. True, all this also occurs elsewhere in the Soviet Union, from Minsk to Vladivostok, but Central Asia is way ahead, coming near to Transcaucasia in the importance of its private sector. This is made possible by the very nature of the Central Asian Muslim society: family unity, extended family ties, local friendships (*mestnichestvo*), ethnic-religious solidarity, all combine together to shield private dealings from the public (or, rather, governmental) eye. Russian society, being that of the ruling group, failed to develop inner defense mechanisms common to Georgians or Uzbeks, while Lithuanians or Latvians, for example, who possess such defense mechanisms, lack the shield of extended family (or tribal) ties which is difficult to penetrate, even by an outsider with the same ethnic background. As a result, private income accounts for less in an average Russian or Latvian family budget than in that of a Georgian or an Uzbek. How much less is hard to determine, as reliable data are, to a large extent, unavailable, but the general picture is common knowledge to anyone familiar with the matter.[9]

Vitality: Social Mobility

Muslim personal initiative is not confined to the private sector (which is, after all, limited) and to a variety of *na levo* deals. Upward social mobility is a fact. Muslims are on the offensive in the public sector, clamor for all kinds of 'affirmative actions'. They want jobs previously occupied by the European settlers, priority admissions to institutions of higher learning in their own republics, and even a degree of immunity for minor (and not so minor) violations perpetuated during the process of social ascendance. For the time being, Moscow tends to give in to all but the most damaging socio-economic demands, thus creating a situation where the accumulation of advantages gained by the native Muslim elite is eventually bound to reach a point where it will translate itself into a quantitative difference in the existing system of governance, and this in the Muslims' favor. But, as far as Moscow is concerned, such danger looms only in the future, while spreading education and integrating educated natives into the system are of immediate economic advantage to the USSR as a whole. It is thus in the education and promotion of trained native cadres that most progress is seen.

Educational advances are most visible and most stressed by Moscow. Percentages of 'titular nationalities' among scientific workers in the five Central Asian republics, Kazakhstan included, moved from the 6·4–16·9 percent range in 1947 to the 21·4–36·9 percent range in 1960 and to the 29·8–50·8 percent range in 1973.[10] Numerically, Central Asian scientific and technical cadres quadrupled between 1960 and 1975, while European settler cadres only doubled.[11]

Similar progress has been made in general high-school (as distinct from vocational) education. While in 1959 only fifty-nine out of every thousand Uzbeks received such education as against ninety-three among Russian settlers, by 1970 the figures were already 142 and 148, showing the closing of the gap.[12]

Figures alone, however, do not give us the full picture. Educational equalization of ethnic groups has been achieved to a large extent through special preferences given to Muslim students, in a manner resembling very much the priorities extended to Blacks in American schools and universities. They consist of favorable admission quotas, lowering of educational requirements, and easier grading (including quotas for failures), the goal being the speedy creation of a native intelligentsia which could be co-opted into the ruling Soviet elite, thus 'creaming' the most capable layer from the non-integrated Muslim mass.

Since the late 1950s, some Muslims have even managed to enter (albeit in limited numbers) the exclusive field of management of 'enterprises of all-Union importance' located on their territory. The number of Muslim managers of lesser enterprises grew much faster. The Muslim intelligentsia and the Muslim managerial class are needed to provide the numerically growing Muslim masses with cadres they can best relate to (culturally, linguistically, psychologically) – an essential condition for the economic development of the area. However, several difficulties have developed in the process:

(1) Russian and other European settlers resent the educational priorities granted to the natives and often view native managers as 'affirmative action' appointees with limited qualifications.
(2) The native managers, intellectuals and technicians who fully accept the advantages of their newly acquired positions are not automatically co-opted away from their ethnic groups. True, they deal with their Russian colleagues socially ('business is business') and look down on their less fortunate Muslim brothers (as was traditional in the area long before the Russian conquest), but otherwise show little 'acculturation' into the Russian-dominated Soviet elite.
(3) Owing to their different value system, many gifted Muslims do not even attempt to climb the same social ladder as the Russians, concentrating instead on more profitable, less bureaucratic fields. Some others combine career advancement with traditional occupations (e.g. they work in a Soviet office, but keep a stand on the *kolkhoz* market).
(4) Those Muslims who 'join the system' and achieve higher positions are often much more interested in the status symbols, prestige and appearance than in the actual responsibilities attached to the function, which are often relegated to Russian or other European assistants. This creates problems: the Russians who are left with the burden of doing the job without enjoying the prestige of official

status feel exploited, and the Muslims feel supervised by the assistants who are more trusted by Moscow and appointed by the central authorities, although sometimes a satisfactory and mutually profitable *modus vivendi* is found and the cooperation is successful.

The three components of Central Asian vitality – the demographic explosion, the successful survival of private initiative, and the progress achieved on the road to modernization – are not of the same origin. The demographic explosion has its source in a combination of religious and cultural factors with improved sanitation and medical advances introduced by the Soviet regime. Private initiative, to the contrary, has survived despite Soviet efforts to curtail it; and modernization, although pursued by the regime for the sake of socio-economic progress, is becoming a source of competition between fast-growing Muslim cadres and well-entrenched Russian settlers. Furthermore, all the three components of Muslim vitality bear the imprint of, and reinforce the role played by, the Muslim faith in shaping the future of the area.

Religion

A key component of Muslim vitality in Soviet Central Asia is the continued importance of Islam. The religious factor can only partially be measured in standard terms (percentage of believers, attendance of mosques, adherence to rituals), although even in these terms it shows considerably more strength than the Russian Orthodox Church. What really matters is the whole range of social attitudes dominated by Islam *and* the reality of national–religious symbiosis.

Among the characteristic social attitudes, inspired by the religion, are rarity of intermarriage with members of another faith (especially between Muslim girls and Christian men, an alliance prohibited by the Shari'a), limited social intercourse with Russians outside of workplaces, universal circumcision, rejection of pork, observance of major Muslim religious holidays, etc. Again, statistical data are both spotty and unreliable. Soviet sources estimate percentages of believers from as high as 45 percent in the remote Kara-Kalpak ASSR to as low as 20 percent (with another 20 percent listed as 'in-between', that is, mildly religious) in more modernized areas of Uzbekistan. These figures compare with only 10 percent believers and 20 percent 'in-between' reported for such traditional Russian Orthodox areas of Russia proper as Penza and Voronezh. Among educated classes the gap is said to be even larger: between 1 percent and 1·5 percent believers among the Russians along the Volga river as against 10–15 percent in Muslim areas.[13] However, it must be borne in mind that Soviet sociologists list among the 'non-believers' those who only 'perform Muslim rites' and those who 'perform Muslim rites under the influence of their relatives', an approach aimed at overestimating the number of atheists.[14] On the other hand, circumcision, abstention from pork and observance of principal holidays are reported by recent Jewish emigrants from the area as practically universal.

The rarity of marriages between Muslims and non-Muslims and especially between Muslim women and non-Muslim men is not only reported by emigrants, but also confirmed by a number of Soviet sources.[15] Soviet surveys admit also the persistence of local traditions. Thus, among Uzbeks, Soviet surveys report an 87 percent preference for their own national cuisine, an 80 percent preference for traditional (i.e. religious) marriage, an 88 percent (city) and 92 percent (village) insistence on parental consent for marriage, etc.[16] All indices point to the continuous existence of ethnic exclusiveness in which Islamic consciousness plays a dominant role. Thus, while an educated Uzbek may fail to observe most of his religious rituals, it is still his religion that makes him an Uzbek: a Christian or a Jewish Uzbek is a totally unthinkable combination.

Thus, ethnic identity exists exclusively within the Muslim *umma* (community) context. When added to the youth and vitality of the group, this national–religious symbiosis creates serious obstacles to outside claims for allegiance.

Identity and Allegiance

Crucial problems of national, ethnic or religious identity and consequent political allegiance among the members of non-ruling groups in the states in which competing groups hold the upper hand are both very simple and very complex. Simple is the clear feeling of *my i oni* ('we and they') or, as the Soviet ethno-geographer Lev Gumilev puts it, 'we are such and the others are different'.[17] This is a common feeling among the Catholics in Northern Ireland, the Muslims on Israel's West Bank or in Soviet Central Asia, the Blacks in the United States, the Jews in the USSR, etc. But anything further becomes very complex, especially the variety of identities a group or an individual may assume according to circumstances, the connection between such identities and political allegiance, and finally conflicting allegiances which may result from variable identities. The case of Soviet Central Asia is further complicated by the absence of statistical indicators one finds in Western situations (voting preferences, political public-opinion polls, etc.) which usually provide the numerical data for further discussion, even if such data are only partially valid.

Nevertheless, Western scholars have been able to come forward with models of Central Asian Muslim identities and allegiances. Among them the best known is Alexandre Bennigsen's classification of three allegiances:

(1) subnational (or tribal), the oldest of the three, directed toward the extended family, the tribe or the territory;
(2) national, directed toward the union republics as they were created out of the 1924 delimitation in the territories of old Turkestan and of the former khanates (later People's Republics) of Khiva and Bukhara;
(3) supranational, a feeling of being a part of the Islamic community (*Dar ul Islam*), or at least of Central Asian Islam as a whole, in opposition to the alien world of the rest of the Soviet Union.[18]

All schematization being by definition imperfect, this model misses the fourth possible allegiance, the one directed toward the Soviet Union as a federal state. Even if one argues that Muslims of Soviet Central Asia rarely share such allegiance, it is still the one most actively promoted by Moscow, along with the national allegiance, with both directed against the subnational and supranational ones. Furthermore, the national and the federal allegiances conflict with each other, creating a strange competition between two officially promoted goals.

Moreover, conflicting allegiances can coexist not only within the same ethnic groups, but also within the same person. An Uzbek may feel Uzbek, Muslim, Soviet, or just part of his extended family, depending on the situation, the identity of the interlocutor, or just his own mood of the moment. Facing a Kazakh he feels Uzbek, facing a Tatar he feels Turkestani, while confronting a Christian or a Jew he feels Muslim. A Russian makes him feel all three (Uzbek, Turkestani, Muslim) and awakens the latent resentment of a native against a settler. These multiple identities, all opposed to the Russian, significantly increase the distance between these two groups. But the same Uzbek on a mission abroad may introduce himself as a Soviet in the United States or as a Muslim in Afghanistan (or maybe as an Uzbek when dealing with a Pushtu), or again as a Soviet if circumstances warrant.[19] Certainly, the more educated and 'cosmopolitan' the man, the larger is his choice of identities, but not lesser his feeling of being different from a Russian.

Hélène Carrère d'Encausse discusses these feelings of identity but refrains from classifying allegiances. She opposes the continuously unassimilable *Homo islamicus* to the dominant *Homo sovieticus*,[20] following the basic 'we' versus 'them' pattern.

A completely opposite position is taken by the former Soviet and now Israeli orientalist Michael Zand, who analyzes cultures rather than feelings of identity or allegiance, obviously considering the latter as mere by-products of the cultural process. According to Zand, the present-day cultures (in the plural) of the peoples of Soviet Central Asia are local subtypes of the general Soviet subculture, which emerged after the October Revolution on the ruins of the Russian version of Christian civilization. Zand sees local Muslim variants of this subculture as its Tadzhikized, Uzbekized images, akin to the Soviet whole despite religious and ethnic differences, which amount to not much more than 'local color'. Nevertheless, Zand concedes the reality of the 'we' *and* 'they' feelings (rather than 'we' *versus* 'they'), but discounts their ultimate political significance.[21]

A different path is taken by Lev Gumilev, whom we have quoted above, whose attempts to define the meaning of *ethnos* are pertinent to this discussion. Gumilev sees *ethnos* as a kind of 'inner drive' acquired from early childhood and bound to last as long as the custom or tradition of the 'ethnos' survives.[22] Until exhausted, this drive, habit or tradition will overcome all possible obstacles, even the loss of mother tongue, of motherland and of own culture.[23] (We may add that such was the case with many apparently assimilated Jews throughout the ages.)

In brief, Gumilev seems to visualize only two possibilities for ethnic assimilation: (1) biological absorption through intermarriage, or (2) loss of inner drive after a very long process of acculturation, spread over an entire 'historical period'.

When applied to the Muslims of Soviet Central Asia, Gumilev's yardstick of inner drive, habit or tradition cannot appear otherwise than Islamic in nature. But distinction is again to be made between Islam as a religion and a feeling of Islamic identity to which even an agnostic can adhere, a feeling of belonging to a group distinguishable from the others by what Gumilev calls a 'particular rhythm'. This rhythm is felt in the religion, the way of life, the moral values, habits, traditions and so on, which for the Uzbeks or the Tadzhiks we classify as Islamic for lack of a better common denominator.

Another key point is the difference between identity and allegiance. Can a person possibly identify himself with one group but feel allegiance to another? Or can an ethnic entity such as the Tadzhiks, for example, identify itself with Central Asian Muslims, but bear allegiance to the Russians rather than to its Muslim neighbors? Western experts on Soviet Central Asia seem to discard such a possibility, although there are precedents of this kind. Thus, in pre-Revolutionary Transcaucasia, the relations between the Georgians and the Armenians, both subjected to Tsarist rule, were worse than their separate relations with the Russians. Volga and Crimean Tatars often felt closer to the Russians than to − in their eyes − less advanced Central Asian coreligionists. Michael Zand does not seem to think that Tadzhiks identify themselves with the Uzbeks to the extent of feeling a common supranational Islamic allegiance, as in Bennigsen's classification.

In addition, both Zand and the American political scientist Gregory Massell believe in the high level of successful co-optation of Muslim elites into the russified all-Soviet 'new class', thus presuming that, if not the identity, at least the allegiance of such Muslim *apparatchiki* will go to their Russian class colleagues rather than to members of their own ethnic groups, if only for purely opportunistic motives.[24] Against such a proposition, there are two valid counter-arguments.

First, the modern history of nationalism, whether in the Soviet Union or elsewhere, teaches us that, contrary to Marxist predictions, ethnic or national solidarity (whether 'sub', 'national' or 'supra') emerges more strongly than the class one. Secondly, the undeniable opportunism of Muslim communist elites makes a fragile allegiance, which could melt away in the heat of changing circumstances and is, therefore, a highly unreliable insurance against nationalism.

In order to neutralize nationalism, elite co-optation must go as far as to give the co-opted elite not only the same privileges, but also the same powers enjoyed by the ruling elite. This was the case of the Jews in Lenin's time or of Georgians and Armenians in Stalin's. It is still the case of Ukrainians and Belorussians. The elites of other national groups, with few exceptions, are for all practical purposes confined to their own national areas (while the Jews who lack such an area are, by the same logic, no longer eligible for elite status).

Uzbek elites share power in Tashkent, but not in Moscow, nor in such fields of activity in Tashkent which are of primary concern for Moscow's security, and this is the basic rule for all Soviet Muslim elites. Thus, Muslim elite co-optation must be viewed as a kind of halfway acceptance, with previously described local 'affirmative action' compensating for lack of access to the centers of real power at all-Union level.

Welfare Colonialism

Tolerance of Muslim nepotism, graft or overstretched private initiative, educational and hiring priorities given to less qualified Muslim candidates, or even indifference to minor nationalist incidents sweetens the reality of continued Russian control. They are not unrelated occurrences, but parts of a specific policy aimed at counteracting the effects of growing Muslim vitality without making far-reaching political concessions.

In addition to tolerances and priorities, Moscow has also been granting direct subsidies to local economies, such as the restitution of turnover taxes collected in Muslim republics (an almost 100-percent return as against about a third for the RSFSR or Ukraine).[25] As a result, in a republic such as Uzbekistan, turnover tax accounted during the 1970s for between 41·8 and 49·2 percent of total revenues,[26] as compared to 29·5 to 34·6 percent for the USSR as a whole.[27] This provides a compensation for lower per-capita (but not per-family) investments in Central Asian economies. But even that is no longer viewed by leading Western economists as a desire to exploit the non-Russian republics but, rather, as an objective policy aimed at practical, often short-term, results.[28]

French sovietologists are aptly calling the Soviet Union 'a state unlike other states' (Besançon, Carrère d'Encausse). Similarly, 'Soviet colonialism', if one prefers to use this term, is different from the traditional colonialisms we have known before. It is indeed a welfare colonialism: it is a politico-ideological, not a socio-economic one. It is willing to go as far as to subsidize its dependencies instead of exploiting them. It is willing to offer the inhabitants of these dependencies the equality of personal opportunities with the Russians, curtailing them only when state security is in question. Ideologically inspired, it is willing to strive for economic, social and educational equalization between the ruling and the ruled ethnic groups. It seeks no personal advantages for the individual members of the former group, and it is genuinely surprised to see the ungrateful 'privileged' natives failing to appreciate all the benefits arising from the status of junior partners guided by the Russian 'elder brothers' along the path devised by the latter.

Central Asian Muslims are no longer what they were at the time of the Revolution. With Moscow's assistance and under Moscow's guidance, they evolved into a group of quasi-modern sister nations, socio-economically not much behind all-Union levels. But this nation-building process did not proceed as planned. Instead of becoming 'national in form and socialist in content', the five sister republics of Soviet Central Asia emerged 'socialist in form and national in content', physically part of Moscow's universe, but spiritually alienated from the latter, and this despite all the undeniable material, social and educational progress accomplished during the six decades of the Soviet regime.

Notes: Chapter 1

1 V. Perevedentsev, 'Narodonaselenie i demograficheskaia politika partii', *Politicheskoe samoobrazovanie*, no. 8 (1981), p. 50.
2 *Vestnik statistiki*, no. 12 (1981), p. 57.
3 *Skol'ko budet detei v sovetskoi sem'e?* (Moscow: Statistika, 1977), p. 23.
4 G. A. Bondarskaia, *Rozhdaemost' v SSSR* (Moscow: Statistika, 1977), p. 96.
5 ibid., p. 101.
6 S. M. Mirkhasimov, 'Sotsial'no-kul'turnye izmeneniia i otrazhenie ikh v sovremennoi sem'e sel'skogo naseleniia Uzbekistana', *Sovetskaia etnografiia*, no. 3 (1979), p. 9.
7 *Narodnoe khoziaistvo SSR v 1979g. Statisticheskii ezhegodnik* (Moscow: Statistika, 1980), pp. 411, 419.
8 *Narodnoe khoziaistvo SSSR v 1978g. Statisticheskii ezhegodnik* (Moscow: Statistika, 1980/1) and *Narodnoe khoziaistvo Uzbekskoi SSR v 1978g. Statisticheskii ezhegodnik* (Tashkent: Uzbekistan, 1979).
9 cf. K. Bedrintsev, 'Sotsial'no-ekonomicheskie problemy razvitiia proizvoditel'nykh sil Uzbekistana', *Kommunist Uzbekistana*, no. 12 (1978), p. 17; Alastair McAuley's calculations of 'private receipts' in Uzbek personal income (1975), in this volume, Table A3, p. 112; and interviews with émigrés.
10 Steven L. Burg, 'Russians, natives and Jews in the Soviet scientific elite: cadres composition in Central Asia', *Cahiers du monde russe et soviétique*, vol. 20, no. 1 (January–March 1979), p. 51.
11 ibid., p. 54.
12 *Natsional'nye otnosheniia v SSSR na sovremennon etape. Na materialakh respublik Srednei Azii i Kazakhstana* (Moscow: Nauka, 1979), p. 150.

13 T. S. Saidbaev, *Islam i obshchestvo. Opyt istoriko-sotsiologicheskogo issledovaniia* (Moscow: Nauka, 1978), pp. 180–1.
14 Alexandre Bennigsen and Chantal Lemercier-Quelquejay, 'Muslim religious dissent in the USSR', *Religion in Communist Lands*, vol. 6, no. 3 (August 1978), p. 158.
15 Saidbaev, *Islam i obshchestvo*, p. 194; Iu. V. Bromley (ed.), *Sovremennye etnicheskie protsessy v SSSR* (Moscow: Nauka, 1975), pp. 473 ff.
16 I. V. Arutiunian and S. M. Mirkhasimov, 'Etnosotsiologicheskie issledovaniia kul'tury i byta v Uzbekistane', *Obshchestvennye nauki v Uzbekistane*, no. 1 (1979), pp. 40–1.
17 Lev Gumilev, 'O termine etnos', *Doklady geograficheskogo obshchestva SSSR*, no. 3 (Leningrad, 1967), p. 5.
18 Alexandre Bennigsen, 'Several nations or one people? Ethnic consciousness among Soviet Central Asian Muslims', *Survey*, vol. 24, no. 3 (108) (London, Summer 1979), p. 51.
19 Lecture by Michael Zand at the Tel Aviv University Symposium on The Soviet Union and the Muslim World, entitled 'A Muslim literature sovietized: Tadzhik literature in the first three decades of Soviet rule'. (For reasons of ill health Professor Zand was unable to prepare his paper for publication in this volume.)
20 Hélène Carrère d'Encausse, *L'Empire éclate: la révolte des nations en URSS* (Paris: Flammarion, 1978), pp. 255 ff.
21 Zand, 'A Muslim literature sovietized'.
22 Lev Gumilev, 'Landscape and ethnos. Part XII: The nature of ethnic wholeness', *Soviet Geography: Review of Translations* (September 1973), p. 472; translated from *Vestnik Leningradskogo universiteta*, no. 24 (1971), pp. 97–106.
23 Gumilev, 'O termine etnos', p. 16.
24 Lecture by Gregory Massell at the Tel Aviv University Symposium on The Soviet Union and the Muslim World, entitled 'The collective identity of the Soviet Central Asians: patterns, potentialities and limits'. (For reasons beyond his control Professor Massell was unable to prepare his paper for publication in this volume.)
25 *Natsional'nye otnosheniia v SSSR*, p. 102.
26 *Narodnoe khoziaistvo Uzbekskoi SSR v 1978g. Statisticheskii ezhegodnik*, p. 317.
27 *Narodnoe khoziaistvo SSSR v 1979g. Statisticheskii ezhegodnik*, p. 554.
28 Alec Nove, 'The economics of nationality policy', paper presented at the 22nd National Convention of the American Association for the Advancement of Slavic Studies (AAASS), Philadelphia, Pa, 5–8 November 1980.

2
The Central Government and Peripheral Opposition in Khiva, 1910–24

DOV. B. YAROSHEVSKI

In seeking the roots of the early Soviet involvement with the Muslim world, Soviet historians point to the ethnic strife which plagued the native population of the former states of Bukhara, Khiva and Turkestan prior to the ethnic and territorial delimitation and the formation of the Soviet Central Asian republics in 1924–5.[1] This malady of suspicion and hatred, they assert, reached dimensions of ethnic self-destruction, especially among Uzbeks and Turkmens, and particularly in Khiva.[2]

This judgment stems from the stereotypes which were created by the Soviet proponents of the delimitation of Khiva, Bukhara and Turkestan in the early 1920s. Nobody has tried to question this view of the ethnic conflicts in these regions, but such a scrutiny appears warranted. Did 'Uzbek great chauvinism' in Bukhara and Khiva become as pervasive as Stalin painted it in 1923?[3] Did the Uzbek–Turkmen relationship deteriorate so badly that 'to butcher each other till the third generation' became the only mutually satisfactory solution, as the official propagandists portrayed it?[4] Did the water and land disputes between the Uzbek majority and Turkmen minority in Bukhara and Khiva become so dangerous and explosive that the only alternative to bloodshed turned out to be segregation along ethnic lines?[5]

This view of Uzbek chauvinism and ethnic conflicts over economic resources in Central Asia as the breeding-ground for the ethnic segregation which followed turns out to be exaggerated and poorly documented. Indeed, many contemporary observers of ethnic developments in the 1920s, particularly in Khiva, noted, rather, the Islamic solidarity of different ethnic groups in their

1916 revolt against Khan Isfendiyar, the ruler of the country, and later in the 1920 and 1924 uprisings against the Soviet authorities.[6] Others agreed that the disputes over water allocation had nothing to do with the real political balance of power among the various ethnic communities.[7]

Nevertheless, the Turkmen–Uzbek relationship presented an acute problem in this period. The ethnic aspects of the conflict disguised a political conflict over the scope and limits of the self-rule of the peripheral groups (Turkmens, Karakalpaks and Kirgiz),[8] over the vigorous and continuous efforts of the central government to reduce this autonomy, to replace it by ever more pervasive governmental controls, and finally to nullify it.

The discussion of these problems provides the context for our examination of the case of the khanate of Khiva, which had become a Russian protectorate in 1873, reestablished its independence in 1918, was transformed in 1920, after its conquest by Soviet troops, into the Khorezm People's Soviet Republic and finally in 1924 was dissolved and absorbed within the framework of the general delimitation of the region as a whole into the Turkmen, Uzbek and Kirgiz Soviet Socialist Republics.

In the traditional Muslim khanate of Khiva, the central government was identified with the person of the ruler, the khan, who concentrated in his hands the legislative, executive and judicial power. Being a member of the Uzbek dynasty of Qungrat, the khan together with his officials at the court and in the provinces articulated the interests, beliefs and attitudes of the sedentary (Uzbek) population of the Khivan oasis. These were later inherited in 1920–4 by the (mostly Uzbek) government of the Khorezm People's Soviet Republic. In contrast, the elders of the Turkmen tribes (the *kedhuda*) habitually served as speakers and articulators of peripheral interests.

To be sure, the Turkmene opposition was not the sole peripheral opposition in the khanate of Khiva. At various points of time the role of opposition was played by Uzbek tribal aristocrats, elders of other nomadic tribes, such as the Kirgiz and Karakalpaks, or even the leaders and members of the religious, Sufi, orders. The central government fought these peripheral oppositions vehemently and, whenever it could, crushed them indiscriminately, but sometimes was forced to learn to live with them and to allow the periphery meaningful autonomy in administrative, legal and economic affairs. In this chapter, based on Imperial Russian, Soviet and German sources,[9] I shall examine three stages in the relationship between the central government and peripheral opposition: the maturing of the peripheral opposition in Khiva up to 1916; its transfer to the political center in 1918–19; and the center–periphery checks and balances created by Soviet interference in 1920–4.

The basic fact crucial to understanding the pattern of relationship between the central government and the Turkmen periphery in Khiva is that the Khivan khans themselves promoted the immigration of the Turkmen tribes into the khanate at the beginning of the nineteenth century.[10] From the seventeenth century the Turkmens had taken part in Khivan political and military affairs, acting usually as mercenaries, but it was only from the early nineteenth century that they integrated into the Khivan social fabric as a permanent component. At this stage, the Turkmen tribes were in some cases actually compelled by the Khivan central authorities to immigrate into Khiva from their earlier habitats. In return for their services as a military resource they received land allotments, financial help (mostly for the tribal leadership), transport facilities (camel caravans) and tax exemptions.

The Khivan khans courted in particular the tribal elders, the *kedhuda*. The most loyal of them were awarded the titles of Khivan officials, *muhirdars*, literally 'those who have the seal'. They were authorized to recruit military detachments and collect taxes, two major duties of government officials. Their privileged social standing in Khivan society became visible through the many favors the rulers bestowed on them: titles, money awards, land, wheat and cloth allocations. Being the leadership of a privileged military estate, many of the Turkmen elders had access to the khan's court and felt themselves part and parcel of the Khivan political elite.

The favorable attitude of the Khivan rulers toward the new immigrants in the first decades of the nineteenth century did not last long. A student of the first hundred years of Turkmen absorption into Khivan society (approximately 1810–1910) would discover a first quarter of initial symmetry in central government–periphery relations and three subsequent quarters of asymmetry as a result of the growing power of the central authorities, especially after the Russian conquest, that led to the deterioration of the alliance and the growth of mutual hostilities and conflicts.

Expediency was the governing principle for the Khivan khans in shaping the relationship with the immigrant Turkmens. They capitalized heavily on the services of the immigrant warriors in order to institutionalize their Qungrat dynasty, to suppress the opposition within their own Uzbek tribes, and to impose their sway upon the other nomadic tribes (Kirgiz and Karakalpaks). The decline in demand for Turkmen support, due to the strengthening of the central power and increasing opportunities to mobilize alternative recruits (for instance, the Karakalpaks), diminished the value of the Turkmen military in the eyes of the Khivan khans. In the second quarter, approximately after 1835, the central authorities began to tighten controls with an eye to curbing the autonomy of the Turkmen tribes; they also pressed them to raise large sums of taxes for the khans' wars. This provoked a prolonged and violent revolt of the Turkmen tribes which lasted from 1855 to 1867 and was followed by a temporary endorsement of the original equilibrium of forces between the central power and the Turkmen periphery.

Six years after the termination of the revolt Khiva was conquered by the Russians and the very foundations of the Turkmens' existence, their occupation as a military estate, were liquidated. Logically, perhaps, this dramatic change should have ruined the Turkmens and led them to surrender to the Khivan khan. However, their situation did not deteriorate so drastically. The Turkmen tribes succeeded in maintaining their autonomy *vis-à-vis* the Khivan government: economically, they established themselves as cattlemen and peasants, and so were able to pay the specific tax, *salgut-kesme*, introduced by the authorities for those who had earlier enjoyed tax exemption as military men. Administratively, the Turkmen elders, although deprived of their military assignments, enjoyed vast power within their tribes, equal to that granted to provincial government officials among the native population, and they retained responsibility for taxation and internal order. Politically, the Russian patrons were interested neither in strengthening the Khivan khan against the Turkmen periphery nor in jeopardizing the rulers of the khanate by support of the periphery (see below).

None the less, psychologically this turnabout, from a privileged to a subordinate status, had a traumatic effect upon this section of the Khivan population. They felt humiliated and discriminated against and became embittered not only by the real loss of income and of the opportunity to become wealthy through military campaigns, but also by their sudden superfluity in a state which earlier had courted them. Nor did their resentment fade with the passing years of the Russian protectorate. Some of the Turkmen elders publicly renounced their Khivan nationality and asked to become Russian nationals.[11] Moreover, *alaman* ('brigandage') against the settled Uzbek population came to be perceived as a struggle for national dignity. Finally, the sense of being discriminated against was strengthened by many acts and decrees of the Uzbek establishment such as closing the water supply to the fields of Turkmen peasants. Nor did the common labelling of Turkmens by officials as *haiwan*[12] ('brutes') help to heal their wounded national pride. In the eyes of the Turkmens, the whole situation cried out for retribution.

After the Russian conquest of 1873, social change in Khiva came about gradually without revolutionizing the age-old traditional way of life. Russian rule did not affect the patriarchal order of this Islamic state and traditional forms of religious education were kept intact. No improvements were introduced into Khivan administration, and the ruler's authority in domestic affairs was in no way limited. Instituting social change was anathema to the Khivan ruler, Khan Muhammed Rahim II (1865–1910), and he vigorously opposed attempts on the part of the Russian colonial administrators in Turkestan to introduce even minor innovations in Khiva, such as a bank or telegraph lines or navigation along the Khivan canals.[13]

By contrast, the enthronement of his son Khan Isfendiyar in August 1910 was accompanied by an edict that proclaimed the onset of modernization and social reforms. Isfendiyar and his close associate, and later prime minister, Islam Khoja,[14] had grown up under the Russian colonial regime and become acquainted with Russia by visits to St Petersburg and Moscow. Relatively young men when they came to power, they were intent upon promoting reform in Khivan government. The edict called for salary allowances for civil servants, a division between the budgets of the state and the ruler, and investments in communications, roads, education and health services. As a basic source for financing all these changes, another fundamental reform in the land-tax system was devised.[15]

Although the land-tax reform was expected to triple treasury revenues, it would also clearly harm the economic status of the Turkmen minority. Instead of an advantageous *salgut-kesme* tax, the projected reform would impose upon the Turkmen farmers the tax applied usually to *wilayat*, the settled Uzbek population. The nomadic Turkmens who combined agriculture with cattle-grazing and who previously had paid no permanent taxes, now had to be prepared to pay the so-called tent tax. Furthermore, this second class of Turkmens, who were in the process of becoming settled, would also become liable to *wilayat* taxation.[16] As elsewhere in *wilayat* lands, the introduction of the new taxation scheme in the Turkmen lands was to be preceded by land surveys while the final decisions concerning the size of the taxes would be made by committees composed of officials, *kazis* (Muslim judges) and representatives of the local population.

In February 1911, on the occasion of the arrival of a Russian delegation, sent to investigate the content of Isfendiyar's reforms, the Khivan authorities stressed that they would have to be imposed gradually and cautiously in the Turkmen areas.[17] However, less than a year later, at the beginning of 1912, the Turkmen *muhirdars* were summoned to the khan of Khiva. (In the intervening period Isfendiyar had begun implementing his reforms by inaugurating telegraph and postal facilities and constructing a modern hospital.) The *muhirdars* were now peremptorily told: that the sum of the land tax imposed upon the Turkmens had been doubled from 32,000 tillas to 64,000 yearly (the tilla was equivalent to 1·8 roubles); that they were obliged also to pay tax in kind, namely in wheat; and that the Turkmens from now on would lose their exemption from dredging irrigation canals, obligatory for the entire settled population.[18] Notwithstanding the khan's understanding of the need for caution, the decision was made without the necessary preparatory work. It clearly upset the already precarious *status quo* between the central government and the Turkmen political leadership. The third point was especially disagreeable to the Turkmen *muhirdars*. Embittered and crying 'Dirty yourselves with the mud of the canals', the *muhirdars* walked out of the ruler's palace in protest.[19] This rebuff signaled an open challenge to the khan's decision.

Isfendiyar was now faced with a major dilemma. Without the Turkmens' contribution, the entire reform would be grounded for lack of funds, but he was unable to make the Turkmens pay the taxes. The chieftains' refusal to obey his injunctions was binding upon the entire Turkmen masses and only a purge of the entire social stratum of the chieftains could stop the rebellion. However, this would be tantamount to declaring war on the whole Turkmen minority, which the khan could not do, both because of the small size of his army[20] and, more important, because of the Russians' well-known opposition to such an action.

Intent on carrying through his reform, for which the suppression of Turkmen opposition seemed imperative, Isfendiyar saw his opportunity in the visit to the area in the spring of 1912 of the Russian Minister of War, V. A. Sukhomlinov, who was also responsible for the government of the Turkestan *krai* and the two protectorates of Bukhara and Khiva. Since Sukhomlinov could not reach the Khivan capital – the nearest railway station was in the town of Chardzhui (now Chardzhou), a distance of about 250 miles – the khan of Khiva decided to send his prime minister, Islam Khoja, to Chardzhui to welcome the minister. Islam Khoja, circumventing his immediate superiors (the commandant of the Amu-Dar'ia *otdel*[21] and the governor-general of the Turkestan *krai*), informed Sukhomlinov directly of the blocking of the reform by the Turkmen opposition and asked for Russian help to expel 2,000 Turkmen chieftains from Khiva.[22] The aims of the khan and Islam Khoja were obvious: to obtain Russian aid to strengthen the central government in Khiva and to eliminate peripheral opposition in the khanate.

The Russian minister, perceiving the aims behind the Khivan initiative, rejected the request.[23] This reaction was merely a logical continuation of the Russians' ambivalent policy towards the central government and the peripheral Turkmen opposition in Khiva. Following the conquest of Khiva in 1873, the Russians had twice sent punitive forces against Turkmens (1874 and 1880), but they had not let the central government suppress the peripheral opposition altogether. The Turkmens had therefore felt confident of their strength *vis-à-vis* the central Khivan government. Now in 1912, besides their traditional political balancing act, the Russians also had a military response to the probable Turkmen uprising: in 1911 the Turkestan military district headquarters had completed a secret plan for a possible campaign in Khiva based on the assumption that merely showing a Russian military presence in Khiva would suffice to frustrate a Turkmen uprising.[24] To ensure the rapid dispatch of troops to this theater of war, across the Kara-Kum desert, Sukhomlinov applied for funds from the Ministry of Finance for the construction of a railway to Khiva.[25]

It is doubtful whether the Turkmen leadership had knowledge of the contents of the Sukhomlinov–Islam Khoja negotiations. However, knowing Russian policy, they had reason to believe Russian support would not be forthcoming for an expansion of the central government's authority at the expense of Turkmen self-rule. Thus, the resistance to the central government persisted in 1912–15, taking on different forms characteristic of Khiva: banditry, robbery, warfare against the punitive troops sent against them by the khan, and even an attack on the Khivan capital in March 1915 for the first time since the Russian conquest. This open breach of the political balance in the khanate of Khiva ultimately caused the Russian authorities to intervene and to move Russian troops into the khanate (June 1915), and a general peace agreement between the rebels and the central government was imposed.[26]

But perhaps the most important outcome of the unrest was not the settlement but, rather, the rise from oblivion of a 50-year-old Turkmen called Qurban Mamed, later known as Junayd Khan.[27] A man of wealth, a judge and water-allocation official in his village, he was chosen in 1914 by Khan Ishan, the Sufi leader most popular among the Turkmens, to lead military operations against the khan of Khiva.[28] The choice proved to be a fit one. Qurban Mamed showed himself an effective administrator who achieved what had seemed impossible: to settle at least temporarily the permanent strife among the Turkmen tribes and to unite them within a very short period of time against the khan of Khiva. In doing so, he made a breakthrough and pacified 1,500 blood-feuding people. His military and political achievements were widely appreciated both among his own people and in the capital: the Junayd tribe awarded him the honorary title of Junayd Khan, and the khan of Khiva, in an attempt to win his loyalty, presented him with the honorary title of *serdar*, 'the commander'.[29]

Although the title of *serdar* was borne by many Turkmen tribal elders, the khan's award of the title to Junayd Khan was distinctive: it heralded a radical change in the relationship between the government and the Turkmen periphery and signaled the self-rule of the periphery. It acknowledged also the co-optation of the most distinguished Turkmen leader into the Khivan Establishment. As follows from the correspondence between the Prime Minister, Mad Wafa Baqqalov,[30] and Junayd Khan of approximately November 1915, Junayd Khan perceived himself, and was accepted in the capital, as a kind of High Commissioner for Turkmen affairs, with a position that seemed equal to that of minister.[31] In this correspondence Junayd displayed a public-minded statesmanship, even if we take into account the rhetoric of public correspondence. He asked, for example, that the Prime Minister discharge one of the Uzbek provincial governors, who, he alleged, had taken part in a secret anti-governmental meeting.[32] In another case, he advised the Prime Minister to suggest to the Russian commandant of the Amu-Dar'ia *otdel* that he expel from Khiva a certain official who was charged with crimes against the regime.[33]

The vigorous improvement in the position of the Turkmens and the extension of their self-rule led two other peripheral groups in Khiva to imitate them: the Uzbek provincial bureaucracy and the Sufi leadership (the *ishans*). Both tried to exploit the Turkmen achievements to press their own claims upon the khan of Khiva.

The Uzbek provincial bureaucracy originated from the central provinces of the khanate, north of the line of the towns

Tashauz–Shavat–Gurlen. It represented the formerly nomadic Uzbeks, who had preserved their tribal organization into the twentieth century, and from whose ranks the regime of the Khivan khans had drawn recruits for the civil and military service. This social stratum felt itself the backbone of the regime and regarded the officials from the population of the southern part of the country, the Sarts, as a threat to their status and profession.[34] Friction between the Uzbek provincial and Sart officials was traditional. However, at this time the Uzbeks were especially disappointed by the growing influence of the Sarts who, under Prime Minister Mad Wafa, monopolized the crucial positions in the central government.

The second focus for the peripheral political ferment was the group of Sufi *ishans* who commanded thousands of followers in Khiva.[35] The central figure in this loose group was Muhammed Yusufjan. In the spring of 1914, he returned home from Mecca where he had been building a *tekke* (guesthouse) for Khivan hajjis. The funds for the construction were donated by Khivan dignitaries, including the khan himself. Yusufjan was an influential person in Khiva,[36] and was called by the natives Hazrat, 'the holy one', a term used also for the khan of Khiva. The second most important figure among the *ishans* seems to have been Khan Ishan, who became the personal advisor of Junayd Khan throughout the years of the latter's campaigns against Khan Isfendiyar and later against the Soviet Khivan authorities in 1920–4. This group of religious leaders felt frustrated by the reforming policies of Isfendiyar, which they considered a violation of Islamic Shari'a law. In their view, the khan, by his corrupt administrative practices, personal immoral behavior (he had introduced into the palace such things as cinema, electricity and telephones, previously unknown in Khiva) and puppet services for the Russian colonial authorities, was bringing about the decay of Khivan society.

These two groups, the Uzbek provincial bureaucracy and the Sufi *ishans*, entered into a coalition in the second half of December 1915.[37] The notables and Sufi leaders from seven Uzbek provinces (there were twenty-two provinces altogether, of which seventeen were Uzbek and five Turkmen) in the central part of the country agreed at a special meeting on the nature of their demands to the khan of Khiva. Six other provinces promised their support to the opposition.[38] Only later did a delegation of Uzbek notables and *ishans* visit Junayd Khan in his home on their way to the khan of Khiva and ask him to support them in their condemnation of the khan's regime. Junayd Khan agreed and dispatched with the Uzbek delegation his favorite commander, Charrik Bey, and two sons of his chief political advisor, Khan Ishan. In fact, however, the Turkmen leader vacillated between loyal support for the khan and support for the opposition. Indeed, he told the members of the delegation that he was not competent to judge the faults of the Khivan government and that he would follow the instructions of the khan. It would seem that Junayd Khan's speedy political rise had made him cautious and that his close associates among the Turkmens were satisfied with the recovery of Turkmen autonomy and with Junayd's position as *de facto* minister for Turkmen affairs.

However, the situation changed at the beginning of January 1916. When the Uzbek–Turkmen delegation of the khan's adversaries was arrested by Russian soldiers stationed in the capital of Khiva, Junayd Khan urged Prime Minister Mad Wafa to effect the release of the delegates. The response of the Khivan authorities or, to be more precise, of the Russian administration in Khiva was negative.[39] Thus, the central Khivan government, in alliance with the Russians, contested the united peripheral Uzbek–Turkmen opposition. Such a situation, according to Islamic medieval political thought, imposed upon each faithful Muslim the duty of disobedience to the ruler and even legitimized his overthrow.[40] Under these circumstances a group of the most influential Khivan *ishans* decided to transfer power in the khanate to Junayd, by now the most influential leader within the opposition. Following this decision, the central provinces in Khiva switched their allegiance to the new ruler and began to address their everyday requests to the Turkmen elders.[41] This was a turning-point in the constitutional development of the Khivan khanate and could be seen as a voluntary (albeit with the sanction of religious intermediaries) act of sanctioning a new ruler by the local population, something resembling a referendum. And so it was understood by the ruler sitting in the capital, Isfendiyar. Embarrassed and angered, he proclaimed an edict which under threat of punishment forbade the Uzbek population of the khanate to apply to the Turkmen administration of Junayd for the settlement of their daily matters and called them to denounce those Uzbek officials who cooperated with the Turkmen administration.[42]

The Turkmen detachments of Junayd responded by opening war on the regime. After occupying the central provinces of the khanate at the beginning of February 1916, they attacked the capital. Despite the resistance of the small Russian military force which defended the Russian residents of the capital as well as the palace of the khan, the Turkmens reached the palace. They executed the Prime Minister, dragged out the khan, took from him a ransom for not entering his harem, spared his life and abandoned the capital.

The scope of the revolt and the humiliation of the ruler enthroned by the Russian imperial power was perceived by the Russian authorities in Petrograd and Tashkent not as a reversal in the balance of forces between the center and periphery in Khiva but, rather, as a challenge to Russian imperial domination in the region. This time, therefore, the Russians, abandoning their traditional ambivalent position of supporting both sides, one against the other, chose the side of the ruler and decided to punish the rebels, Uzbeks and Turkmens alike. A punitive force was sent to crush the revolt, and once again the political balance in Khiva changed: the Russian authorities and the central government dominated, and the peripheral opposition was eliminated, Junayd Khan fleeing to Iran.

In a paradoxical way, the break-up of the periphery in 1916 contributed to the meteoric rise of the Turkmens and increased their access to positions of central power in Khiva. This transformation was accomplished in approximately one and a half years from spring 1916 till winter 1918 owing to important political developments both in Khiva and beyond its frontiers. First, the establishment of the provisional regime in Russia in February 1917 and the Bolshevik takeover in October 1917 led to the decline of Russian influence in Khiva and then, in January 1918, to the withdrawal of Russia from this Muslim protectorate. And, secondly, this period evidenced the gradual paralysis of the Khivan central government. In the aftermath of the 1916 revolt the Russian imperial authorities decided to install a Russian military commissar in Khiva whose duties were to control the khan's government.[43] Had this commissar been installed, the khan would have been reduced to a mere puppet. However, before the tsar could sanction this decision, he was deposed, and the new provisional government did not sanction the change. Although saved from this particular threat, new trouble awaited Khan Isfendiyar: in April 1917 an amorphous and marginal group of Khivan Muslim modernists known as 'Young Khivans' won the support of the Russian soldiers stationed at the Khivan capital and forced the khan to proclaim a constitutional monarchy and the formation of a *mejlis* (parliament).[44] The convocation of the *mejlis* and formation of the Young Khivan government restricted for the first time in Khivan history the vast authority of the khan in the legislative, executive and judicial fields. However, the khan was saved once more. Within a month the situation changed, and under the pressure of the conservative forces, especially of the religious establishment, the Young Khivans were purged from the government and *mejlis*. Yet even now the khan remained a powerless figure dependent upon Russian support. He continued to rule solely with the help of the Russian garrison force.[45] Meanwhile, during the course of 1917 the Turkmen military detachments mushroomed in opposition, threatening the khan's regime, internal order and economic development. Taking advantage of the weakening of the Russian military command in the khanate, they raided Uzbek settlements. In the second half of 1917, Junayd Khan returned to Khiva from exile in Iran and resumed the hard business of integrating under his command the continuously squabbling Turkmen detachments.

Then, in January 1918, the Russian troops left Khiva, upsetting the established relationship of the central government *vis-à-vis* the Turkmen periphery. The Turkmen tribal leadership, as before the Russian conquest of 1873, challenged the power of the central government, demanded self-rule for the Turkmen territories and a return to the traditional social standing of Turkmens in Khivan society as a military estate. Since Khan Isfendiyar lacked any meaningful army he was compelled to come to an agreement with his foremost enemy, Junayd Khan, and to co-opt him into the Khivan leadership. The latter was invited to serve as the chief commander of the Khivan army, with the honorary title *serdar karim*, 'noble commander' – in other words, to take into his hands military power while Isfendiyar retained full authority in the civilian sphere. Junayd Khan accepted.

But for both sides it was clear that this agreement represented only an interim sharing of power. Both were aware that each would seek complete power in the near future. Both were haunted by the memory of 1916: Isfendiyar of the terrible humiliation he had suffered at the hands of Junayd's Turkmens, and Junayd of horrible frustration upon being deprived of victory and the Khivan throne. At this stage, Isfendiyar considered three options: to have Junayd assassinated by his own men, or through Soviet or German help. The first, unsuccessful attempt to murder Junayd by a court official has been reported by Soviet historians.[46] The second is depicted in a novel by a well-informed Soviet writer.[47] And the third, seemingly the most fantastic and mysterious, is described in German diplomatic papers preserved in the Political Archives of the German Foreign Office in Bonn.[48] According to this source, an unofficial envoy of the Khivan khan, a certain

German officer (probably from among the German prisoners of war located in Russian Central Asia), came to the German embassy in Moscow in July 1918. Twice in July 1918 the German chargé d'affaires in Moscow, Kurt Riezler, cabled to Berlin about the Khivan appeal for German assistance against both the Bolsheviks and gangs which were ruining the country. But nobody in the embassy gave the envoy any answer.[49] It is doubtful, however, whether even a positive German response would have been of benefit to Isfendiyar. The political reality of Khiva had passed a death sentence on him. By the end of the summer of 1918, Junayd had succeeded in reconsolidating under his sway the constantly contesting Turkmen tribes of Khiva. He now turned to deal with his chief enemy. In September 1918 a group of Turkmens led by Junayd's son murdered the khan of Khiva.[50]

The Turkmens, the formerly privileged and later humiliated and marginal ethnic group, now became the dominant one in the Khivan political and economic arena. The retaliation which the Turkmens took against the Uzbek majority seemed to be the natural outlet for their feelings of inferiority and wounded pride. This retaliation took the form of raids on the settled Uzbek population, on the one hand, and the heavy taxes imposed on the Uzbek population by Junayd, formally for military expenditures, on the other, which were a kind of massive state plundering directed against the bulk of the population. At the same time the Turkmen leaders were aware of the outstanding importance of maintaining normal relations with the Uzbek majority. Already during the 1916 revolt, the problem presented by a reversal in the relationship between minority and majority in Khiva had occupied some of the *ishans*, Junayd's religious allies and ideologues. One of them, the venerable Idris Mahdum, advised Junayd that in order to secure the state's existence in the long run, given Khiva's very unstable environment (an obvious allusion to Russian expansionist policies), Junayd, in his role of national leader, must not rule the majority of the Khivan population, the Uzbeks, arbitrarily. The relevant Islamic directive for treating the Uzbeks prescribed that they be regarded as 'liberated from the rule of the enemies of God' rather than as a conquered population (since the latter would be conducive to the collapse of the state).[51]

On acceding to power in 1918, Junayd Khan adopted such a course. First, he did not proclaim himself khan of Khiva, preferring to keep in power the existing Uzbek dynasty of Qungrat, as a facade for his regime, in this way maintaining the basic symbol of the country.[52] Although most decisions were taken at his residence near the town of Takhta, they were sanctioned officially by the Uzbek khan in the capital. Secondly, Junayd did not abolish the Uzbek provincial administration but, rather, established alongside it a parallel one, of Turkmen military supervisors, who shared their authority. Thirdly, his coalition with the leaders of the Sufi orders who had thousands of followers, along with his clear emphasis upon fundamentalist Islamic values, secured him a footing in a most important grouping in Khivan society, which encompassed all the ethnic groups in the country. And, fourthly, Junayd in a sense bought the support of a large part of the Khivan population by his aggressive policy against the adjacent Russian territories, the Turkestan Soviet Republic. This policy was conceived by the Khivans as a retribution for the suppression of the Uzbek–Turkmen revolt of 1916, as an excellent opportunity for gaining booty, and as an expression of Khivan independence.

This last factor, which meant a drastic change in Khiva's political status, led the Russians, both Whites and Reds, to take Khiva seriously. The leader of the White Russian government in Siberia, Admiral A. V. Kolchak, sent Junayd Khan a letter, naming him the ruler of Khiva and bestowing upon him the title of Major-General of the Orenburg Cossacks.[53] Simultaneously, representatives of the Turkestan Republic of the Russian Soviet Federation approached Junayd with many requests to open talks. Eventually he agreed to negotiate a peace treaty with them. The treaty, signed at the residence of Junayd, became known as the Takhta Peace (although ratified by the khan in the capital).[54] The symbolic meaning of this title was transparent: the agreement that sealed the conquest of Khiva by Imperial Russia had been signed in 1873 in the khan's palace in a suburb of the capital, which gave it its name — the Gendemin peace treaty; now the agreement that ratified Khivan independence and its recognition by Soviet Turkestan was signed in the palace of the Turkmen dictator near the town of Takhta.

However, this new pinnacle of revenge, the recognition of Junayd Khan's fundamentalist Khivan regime by Soviet Turkestan, was soon to be followed by the downfall of this Muslim country. It was caused by an issue which could perhaps be called the 'lend-lease' of Turkmen horsemen.

Just as in the nineteenth century the khans of Khiva had brought the Turkmen to Khiva because they needed their military services, in 1919 these mercenary horsemen became an article in great demand in the political game between Soviet Turkestan, Bukhara and Khiva. In May 1919 the Soviets asked Junayd to lend them 700 Turkmen horsemen for military operations in the Transcaspian area. Junayd Khan demanded for this prospective *alaman* an exorbitant sum for each horseman: 599 cartridges, pay of a hundred roubles daily for forty days in advance, as well as four machine guns and two mountain cannon. The horsemen were to be empowered to plunder and take booty but not to be used to fight against Muslims.[55] The Soviets refused.

A month later Bukhara asked Junayd for 2,000 horsemen for use against the common Russian enemy. The deal seemed to be advantageous for both sides; Bukhara was ready to supply weapons and economic aid to Khiva.[56]

This emerging alliance of Bukhara and Khiva greatly worried the Soviet authorities in Tashkent, who had planned to use the Turkmen horsemen in a future assault upon Bukhara, despite the high cost of this military force. Seeing in the Bukharan–Khivan alliance a threat to Soviet tactics in Central Asia, the People's Commissar for Foreign Affairs of Soviet Turkestan, Sagdulla Tursun Khodzhaev, thought it an opportune time (memorandum dated 17 November 1919) to destroy Junayd's regime. Even if this action would complicate future Soviet operations against Bukhara, it was seen as preferable to a strengthening of the Bukharan–Khivan coalition.[57] The proposal was accepted by the Soviet 'proconsuls', who had just arrived in Turkestan,[58] but with one essential amendment: they planned not only the destruction of Junayd and the conquest of Bukhara, but also the subsequent use of Turkmen horsemen against British dominion in India.[59]

The decision to intervene in Khiva was taken in November 1919. By the end of December, Soviet troops had crossed the Khivan border and after bitter resistance by Turkmen detachments[60] they occupied the country. Junayd and his followers fled to the desert. The Soviet commanders tried to broaden native support for their new regime which was primarily confined to small groups of Young Khivans. In particular they welcomed among their supporters three Turkmen leaders, former auxiliaries of Junayd who decided to desert to the Soviets (all the Young Khivans were Uzbeks). The Soviet commanders presented these men as great Turkmen leaders and included them in the newly established government of the Khorezm People's Soviet Republic: Qosh Mamed Khan as deputy prime minister and the two others, Ghulyam Ali and Shah Murad Bakhshi, as ministers for health and welfare respectively.

Yet for these ministers their primary interest was not participating in the government's sessions, but their influence in the Turkmen areas. The 'triumvirate' preferred to rule there without the intervention of the central government, thus transforming the Turkmen region into a state within the state. The deputy prime minister, Qosh Mamed Khan, told the government directly not to send Bolshevik agitators to the Turkmen territories since they 'corrupt the people'.[61] When the chieftain of one of the Turkmen tribes was arrested by the Soviet Red Army authorities and the Soviets tried to appoint a body of chosen representatives to govern his tribe, Qosh Mamed Khan prevented them from exerting authority and sent one of his followers to act as a new chieftain.[62] The central government had to comply. Qosh Mamed Khan taxed the population heavily for his own purposes, and the Soviet central government could not hinder him.

This instance of having created by their own hands a kind of separate self-governing polity which did not accept the power of the central government embarrassed the Soviet military and political envoys in Khiva. The solution worked out by them in cooperation with the Uzbek Young Khivan group included the suggestion proposed earlier by the Imperial Russian officials in Turkestan: to disarm the Turkmens, i.e. to purge their leadership. However, while the Russian Imperial authorities in St Petersburg had always resisted these proposals, preferring soft measures and palliatives, this time, owing to lack of any effective central control over the activities of the Soviet envoys in Khiva, the purge was sanctioned on the spot.

On 3 September 1920 the Soviet military and political envoys in Khiva (Valentin Dubianskii and Rizauddin Shakirov) and the Uzbek members of the Khorezm Council of People's Nazirs (commissars) agreed that Turkmen self-rule had exceeded all tolerable bounds, and decided to summon the three Turkmen ministers and their military detachments to Khiva and to disarm them.[63] In the third week of September two of the three responded to the summons and on arriving in Khiva were duly captured and executed with many of their followers.[64] The Soviet representatives and their Uzbek Young Khivan supporters attempted to use the liquidation of their former Turkmen allies to bring about a social revolution within the Turkmen segment of the population. The aim was to subordinate the Turkmen periphery to the central government, depriving it of the self-rule which it had enjoyed under the triumvirate. A week after the murder of the Turkmen ministers the Soviet political representative in Khiva and the government of the Khorezm People's Soviet Republic called on the Turkmens to disarm their leaders and the military detachments, to expel the tribal elders and to elect new ones. Aware of the importance of compensating psychologically for this political takeover, the authors of the appeal emphasized that 'we consider you equal to Uzbeks'.[65] This declaration, however, was meaningless for the Turkmen masses and their leaders, who saw in the murder of their kinsmen another link in the long chain of humiliations and injustices to which they had been subjected. In defiance of the appeal for social revolution in the interests of the central government, the Turkmen tribes revolted against that government and were even joined in this rebellion by other ethnic groups, including Uzbeks, Kirgiz and Karakalpaks.[66] The rebellion was led once more by Junayd Khan, who emerged from his refuge in the desert.

As in previous cases, the main difficulty for the Soviets in Khiva was not the military suppression of the rebels (this had been accomplished by December 1920) but the imposition of central authority in the Turkmen districts. As the Soviet representative in Khorezm, Shakirov, wrote: 'it will be necessary to establish some kind of power' in the Turkmen districts.[67] Since the Soviets had rejected the old forms of self-rule, the path chosen was decentralization of the central government in this area, i.e. empowering native (Turkmen) soviets to perform governmental functions under close supervision by the capital. Such decentralization was made possible by the removal from power of the Young Khivans in March 1921. This government of Uzbek modernists, which had been at odds with the Turkmen leadership since 1917, was dispersed by the Political Command of the Khivan Red Army, who were mostly Tatars and who wanted to speed up the revolution in Khorezm. However, an extraordinary mission from Moscow sent by Narkomindel (the People's Commissariat for Foreign Affairs) decided to act with greater caution.[68] This mission established a new government in Khorezm and organized a new Uzbek-Turkmen dialogue.

The Second *Qurultai* (congress of people's representatives) held in May 1921 was chosen as the venue for this dialogue. After proclaiming peace between the Turkmens and Uzbeks, the Turkmen delegates elected their representatives to a special Turkmen department (seven officials) within the Khorezm Executive Committee (the highest legislative body in the periods between the sessions of the *Qurultai*). This department was intended to articulate the interests of the Turkmen population, to keep watch upon the government's activities and – presumably the most important function for the initiators of this institution – to convey to the Turkmens in both the countryside and the towns the instructions and orders of the central government.[69] But, although this Turkmen department was created, the hopes placed in it as a sort of 'transmission belt' turned out to be exaggerated. First, the Turkmens, as a result of past experience, did not trust initiatives of the central government. For instance, at the Second *Qurultai* the Turkmen delegates rejected a proposal for conducting a statistical census in the Turkmen districts, recalling the efforts of the Khivan khan and Russian authorities in 1912–14 to carry out a similar survey in order to implement the land tax reform.[70] Secondly, the Turkmen department had to reckon with the actual structure of the leadership in the Turkmen districts, which wielded considerable military, economic and judicial power: it had no leverage even with those tribal leaders who supported the Soviet regime, let alone with those who, with their detachments, attacked Soviet institutions and Red Army troops from their bases in the desert and whose influence upon the native population was decisive.

This apparent stalemate was broken during the winter of 1923–4 when, in accordance with the decisions of the Fourth *Qurultai* (October 1923), the country was proclaimed a socialist republic and the *waqf*, or religious property, one of the fundamentals of the Islamic religious establishment, was declared confiscated.[71] Once more, the leading Uzbek *ishans* called the population to disobedience, again, as in 1916, asking Junayd Khan for help. As in the past, Junayd Khan and his detachments left the desert and within a short period the major part of Khorezm had been captured by the rebels. On 19 January 1924 they besieged the capital. Only the concerted action of a cavalry regiment and the airforce of the Red Army saved the Soviet regime in the country.[72]

Despite this military victory, the troublesome problem of creating a balance of power between Uzbeks and Turkmens in the Khorezm periphery remained. Another purge of the Turkmen leadership, suggested by the commanders of the Soviet troops in Khiva under the usual guise of 'disarming the Turkmens', was rejected by the delegation of the Central Committee of the Russian Communist Party (of Bolsheviks) which had hastened to Khiva from Moscow.[73] The Soviets had no alternative but to give in to the political aspirations of the Turkmens. In March 1924 the Central Committee of the Khorezm Communist Party passed a decision to establish a Turkmen *oblast'*, which in May 1924 was ratified by the Khorezm Executive Committee.[74]

Just possibly this legislative fiat could have signaled a breakthrough for Turkmen self-rule, paving the way for a federal arrangement in the Khivan multinational state. Such a possibility was, however, very slight. As the sources inform us, the decision was intended to be merely an administrative expediency, a device for effective government in the Turkmen ethnic milieu.[75] Simultaneously, in May, the Central Asian Bureau of the Russian Communist Party (of Bolsheviks) decided that the newly created Turkmen *oblast'* of the Khorezm republic should be integrated into the planned Turkmen Soviet Socialist Republic.[76]

The final dissolution of the Khorezm Republic in November 1924 and its integration into the Turkmen, Uzbek and Kirgiz republics according to the decision of the highest party bodies of the USSR, has been well chronicled and documented.[77] The lot of the Khivan Turkmen elders who were integrated into the Turkmen Soviet Socialist Republic is less well known. This entire social layer was eliminated in the newly proclaimed Turkmen Republic, mostly by Turkmen hands, in 1925.[78] For the first time the elders were treated not as political adversaries, a peripheral opposition, as they had been in Khorezm, but as criminals. The only one who was awarded an honorable pardon was Junayd Khan: he himself had asked the new republic for an amnesty, which was granted him in his capacity of 'Turkmen national hero'.[79]

For fourteen years, from 1910 till 1924, the internal and international politics of Khiva were dominated by the Turkmen question. The central government (the khan and then the Soviet government) tried to subdue the Turkmen periphery; the latter resisted vehemently and counter-attacked. In this contest the Turkmens mostly had the upper hand, and an outstanding victory was achieved. The opposition was transformed from a marginal into a dominant group in 1918–19. These two years could be considered as the pinnacle of Turkmen absorption into the Khivan Establishment.

During these fourteen years the central government, sometimes with and at other times without Russian/Soviet support, undertook many efforts to undermine the standing of the peripheral opposition and to eliminate the Turkmen leadership. These attacks by the central government caused many of the conflicts of the period. Even when the center won, it could not consolidate its achievements. Soviet arms were of no use. It was only a political decision, namely the integration of the Khivan Turkmens into the newly established Turkmen Soviet Socialist Republic, that succeeded in liquidating the Turkmen tribal leadership, who so stubbornly opposed Soviet rule.

For over a hundred years the Turkmen immigrants and the Khivan/Khorezm state had tried to find mutually acceptable forms of coexistence: quarreling with each other, exploiting each other, and learning from one another. It seemed in the first half of the second decade of the twentieth century that through their trials and errors they had approached a closer understanding. But what appeared to be the apex of the *rapprochement* of the two communities in their achievement of a working arrangement based on Muslim values, the Soviet politicians in Central Asia perceived as further testimony of an innate ethnic malady among the natives. Consequently they advocated the expulsion of the Khivan Turkmens from the Khivan state and the dismantling of the latter as a non-viable polity. The Soviet view of Khiva, molded by Bolshevik ideology, left no room for inter-ethnic cooperation between Uzbeks and Turkmens based upon fundamentalist Islamic values. While some contemporaries conceived the 1917 Revolution as assisting Khiva to revive,[80] in fact the Soviet position on the inter-ethnic conflict in that country led inevitably to the dismantling of Khiva as a Muslim state.

Notes: Chapter 2

I have benefited from the comments of Dr Yaacov Ro'i and Professor Murray Baumgarten of the University of California, Santa Cruz. I appreciate the copy-editing of the earlier draft by Ester Zeitlin, and acknowledge thankfully the help of Professor Yuri Bregel for his reading of an Uzbek document.

1. See review article by S. A. Radzhabov, 'Istoricheskoe znachenie natsional'-no-gosudarstvennogo razmezhevaniia Srednei Azii', in *Sovetskoe gosudarstvo i pravo*, no. 10 (1974), pp. 14–22. On the Western approach to the subject, see Edward Allworth (ed.), *The Nationality Question in Soviet Central Asia* (New York: Praeger, 1973).
2. G. P. Vasil'eva, *Preobrazovanie byta i etnicheskie protsessy v Severnom Turkmenistane* (Moscow: Nauka, 1969).
3. I. V. Stalin, *Sochineniia*, Vol. 5 (Moscow: Gospolitizdat, 1947), pp. 189, 250.
4. M. Nemchenko, *Natsional'noe razmezhevanie Srednei Azii* (Moscow: Izd. Litizdata *NKID* (Narodnyi Komissariat Inostrannykh Del), 1925), p. 10.
5. ibid. The economic causes of these disputes (the Khivan economy being dependent on water allocation and canal maintenance) were emphasized by Imperial Russian and later Soviet analysts. See *Turkestanskie vedomosti*, 9 (22) March 1916; G. B. Skalov, 'Khivinskaia revoliutsiia 1920 goda', *Novyi Vostok*, vol. 3 (1922), p. 246; P. Alekseenkov, *Khivinskoe vosstanie 1916 goda* (Tashkent: Uzbekskoe gosudarstvennoe izdatel'stvo, 1920), p. 52.

6. Dubianskii Papers, 'Doklad o razoruzhenii iomudskikh khanov', September 1921, fo. 11. (The Dubianskii Papers are a collection of the documents of Valentin Dubianskii, the former Soviet military commander in Khiva in 1920. These papers are in my possession.)
7. 'Zametka diplomaticheskogo chinovnika pri Turkestanskom general-gubernatore Minorskogo o polozhenii v Khive', 14 January 1906, in N. N. Kanoda (ed.), *Revoliutsionnoe dvizhenie v Turkmenistane v 1905–1917 godakh (Sbornik arkhivnykh dokumentov)* (Ashkhabad: Ylym, 1970), p. 245.
8. In Russian and Soviet parlance until the late 1920s the Kazakhs were included in the general nomenclature 'Kirgiz'. Thus, although I shall use throughout the term 'Kirgiz', I am in fact referring to Kazakhs. (The Kirgiz inhabited the more eastern Semirechensk *oblast'*.)
9. TsGVIA (Central State Archives for Military History), Moscow, *fond* 400, *Aziatskaia chast'* (hereafter *Az. ch.*) (Asian Department of the War Ministry); TsGAOR (Central State Archives of the October Revolution), Moscow, *fond* 1318 (People's Commissariat for Nationalities Affairs); Dubianskii Papers; Politisches Archiv des Auswaertigen Amtes, Bonn, Russland 97 b, Russisch Zentralasien, Bd 1–10.
10. See the classic monograph on the subject by Iu. E. Bregel, *Khorezmskie turkmeny v XIX veke* (Moscow: Izdatel'stvo vostochnoi literatury, 1961). The two best source collections are *Materialy po istorii turkmen i Turkmenii*, Vol. 1 (Moscow: Izdatel'stvo Akademii Nauk SSR, 1938), and P. P. Ivanov, *Arkhiv khivinskikh khanov XIX v.* (Leningrad: Izdatel'stvo gosudarstvennoi publichnoi biblioteki, 1940).
11. 'Zametka diplomaticheskogo chinovnika', p. 244.
12. 'Raport nachal'nika Amu-Dar'inskogo otdela Turkestanskomu general-gubernatoru', 10 February 1913, TsGVIA, *fond* 400, *Az. ch., opis'* (hereafter *op.*) 262/912–15, *ed. khr.* 178, p. 24 (obverse). (The Russian/Soviet archival material which has been used in this volume, specifically in this chapter and in that of M. Volodarsky, will be denoted using Russian archival terminology. Roughly speaking, *fond* is 'collection', *opis'* is 'inventory' and *ed. khr. (edinitsa khraneniia)* is 'file'.)
13. The Russian diplomatic official V. F. Minorskii vividly portrayed Muhammed Rahim as having been an Islamic ruler of medieval posture: unruffled, calm, sagacious and kind, yet strong – a man of gigantic physical stature who sat at court personally, was deeply religious and shared much of his time with Muslim scholars (Minorskii, 'Otchet o komandirovke v Khivu 15 sentiabria–17 oktiabria 1909g.', TsGVIA, *fond* 400, *Az. ch., op.* 262/912–15, *ed. khr.* 130, ch. 1).
14. Islam Khoja (1871–1913), well acquainted with the idea of reform as propagated by Tatar Muslim reformers in Russia, was murdered on 9 August 1913 by unidentified persons.
15. 'Obrashchenie Khana Khivinskogo k svoemu narodu', 15 September 1910, TsGVIA, *fond* 400, *Az. ch., op.* 262/912–15, *ed. khr.* 62.
16. 'Voennyi gubernator Samarkandskoi oblasti Turkestanskomu general-gubernatoru', 5 February 1911, TsGVIA, *fond* 400, *Az. ch., op.* 262/912–15, *ed. khr.* 62, p. 124.
17. ibid.
18. G. I. Karpov and D. M. Battser, *Khivinskie Turkmeny i konets Kungradskoi dinastii* (Ashkhabad: Turkmenskoe gosudarstvennoe izdatel'stvo, 1930), p. 48.

19 ibid.
20 There were some 2,000 troops in Khiva, badly trained and poorly armed.
21 After the conquest of Khiva in 1873 the Russians annexed to the Turkestan government-general the part of the khanate on the right bank of the River Amu-Dar'ia and formed the Amu-Dar'ia *otdel* (district). The Russian troops which were stationed on the territory of the *otdel* were ready to move into Khiva whenever the need might arise.
22 Karpov and Battser, *Khivinskie turkmeny*, p. 49.
23 ibid.
24 V. Lobachevskii, *Voenno-statisticheskoe opisanie Turkestanskogo okruga. Khivinskii Raion* (Tashkent: Izdanie Shtaba Turkestanskogo voennogo okruga, 1912), p. 111.
25 'O sooruzhenii Khivinskikh zheleznykh dorog dlia soedineniia Khivy s sushchestvuiushchei rel'sovoi set'iu', 31 December 1913, TsGVIA, *fond* 400, *Az. ch., op.* 262/912–15, *ed. khr.* 203, pp. 6–7.
26 For an account of events in 1912–15, see Karpov and Battser, *Khivinskie turkmeny*, and Seymour Becker, *Russia's Protectorates in Central Asia: Bukhara and Khiva, 1865–1924* (Cambridge, Mass.: Harvard University Press, 1968).
27 Junayd Khan (Qurban Mamed serdar) (1862–1938), Turkmen tribal leader and Khivan statesman; died in exile in Afghanistan.
28 In 1914 the khan of Khiva had arrested the Turkmen elder Shah Murad Bakhshi for brigandage. As ransom the khivan authorities asked for the enormous sum of 611 thousand *tillas*. It was this case that provoked Khan Ishan to appeal to the Turkmens to revolt against the Khan and propose to Qurban Mamed to lead the Turkmen detachments against the government.
29 The Russian commandant of the Amu-Dar'ia *otdel* thought of Junayd as 'being one of the few persons who could pacify the native population and install order in Khiva': 'Raport nachal'nika Amu-Dar'inskogo otdela Turkestanskomu general-gubernatoru', 10 December 1915, TsGVIA, *fond* 400, *Az. ch., op.* 262/912–15, *ed. khr.* 36 (1) p. 194.
30 Mad Wafa Baqqalov, merchant and banker, became prime minister in 1914 after the death of Islam Khoja; murdered by Turkmens in 1916.
31 'Raport nachal'nika', 11. 195–7.
32 ibid., 1. 196.
33 Yu. Bregel, 'The Sarts in the Khanate of Khiva', *Journal of Asian History*, vol. 12, no. 2 (1978), p. 144.
34 ibid.
35 At the beginning of the twentieth century a network of Sufi brotherhoods *(Naqshbandiya* and *Kubrawiya)* covered the entire area of the khanate. See V. A. Gordlevskii, 'Bahauddin Nakshbend Bukharskii', in his *Izbrannye sochineniia*, Vol. 3 (Moscow: Izdatel'stvo vostochnoi literatury, 1962), and G. P. Snesarev, *Pod nebom Khorezma* (Moscow: Myse' 1973), pp. 78–97.
36 'Raport nachal'nika Amu-Dar'inskogo otdela Turkestanskomu general-gubernatoru', 29 July 1914, TsGVIA, *fond* 400, *Az. ch., op.* 262/912–15, *ed. khr.* 178, p. 83 (obverse).
37 Soviet writings give conventionally a ridiculous reason for the revolt: the abduction of young girls for the khan's harem. See G. Nepesov *et al., Velikii Oktiabr' i pobeda narodnoi revoliutsii v Khorezme* (Tashkent: Izdatel'stvo 'Uzbekistan', 1971), p. 27.

38 Alekseenkov, *Khivinskoe vosstanie 1916 goda*, pp. 21–3.
39 The commandant of the Amu-Dar'ia *otdel*, Colonel V. P. Kolosovskii, had moved into Khiva from Petro-Aleksandrovsk in 1915, and he remained there until the spring of 1916.
40 Medieval Islam never elaborated the legal procedure for enforcing the duty of disobedience against the ruler. The decision was left to informal consensus by the religious elite. See Bernard Lewis, 'Islamic concepts of revolution', in P. J. Vatikiotis (ed.), *Revolution in the Middle East* (London: Allen & Unwin, 1972).
41 Karpov and Battser, *Khivinskie turkmeny*, p. 109.
42 ibid., pp. 106–7.
43 'Zhurnal soveshchaniia po khivinskim delam', 8 July 1916, TsGVIA, *fond* 400, *Az. ch., op.* 262/912–15, *ed. khr.* 36 (1), p. 210.
44 *Turkestanskie vedomosti*, 8 April 1917, 28 April 1917. On the Young Khivan *coup d'état* see I. V. Pogorel'skii, *Ocherki ekonomicheskoi i politicheskoi istorii Khivinskogo khanstva kontsa XIX i nachala XX vv. (1873–1917gg.)* (Leningrad: Izdatel'stvo Leningradskogo universiteta, 1968), pp. 120–7.
45 The Turkmen leadership was also hostile to the Young Khivans since the *mejlis* proposed to disarm the Turkmens, and decided to make them pay the indemnity imposed on them by the Russian punitive force in the aftermath of the 1916 revolt. Thus, there was continuity between the khan's traditional opposition to Turkmen autonomy and the policy followed by the Young Khivans.
46 Karpov and Battser, *Khivinskie turkmeny*, p. 162.
47 Boris Cheprunov, *Junayd Khan* (Tashkent: Gosudarstvennoe izdatel'stvo UzSSSR, 1936), p. 40.
48 'Riezler an das Auswaertige Amt', Moscow, 13, 19 and 25 July 1918, Politisches Archiv, Russland 97 b, Bd. 9, A 29936, A 3075, A 31463. See also documents in the same volume, A 33634.
49 For Kurt Riezler, German chargé d'affaires in Moscow, and his attitude to the Russian Civil War, see Karl Dietrich Erdmann (ed.), *Kurt Riezler, Tagebuecher, Aufsaetze, Dokumente* (Göttingen: Vandenhöck & Ruprecht, 1972).
50 There is no agreement on the exact date of Isfendiyar's death. Nepesov, *Velikii Oktiabr'*, gives 30 October 1918 (p. 67); Pogorel'skii, *Ocherki*, gives 1 October 1918 (p. 142). I prefer another source, the unpublished manuscript of the history of the German Mennonite community in Khiva, which gives 17 September 1918: Gustav Toews, 'Jubilaeumsgedicht', Aq Mechet, Khiva, 4 May 1934 (manuscript in the possession of Marie Toews, Lagelippe, FRG), fo. 25.
51 'Khiva i Rossiia (k istorii vosstaniia khivinskikh turkmen v 1916 godu)', *Turkmenovedenie* (June-July 1929), p. 43.
52 Seyid Abdulla Khan, brother of Isfendiyar, was proclaimed khan of Khiva; he was deposed after the Soviet conquest in February 1920.
53 E. L. Shteinberg, *Ocherki istorii Turkmenii* (Moscow: Sotzekgiz, 1934), pp. 76–7.
54 I. Fed'ko, 'Mirnye peregovory', in *Oktiabr'skaia sotsialisticheskaia revoliutsiia i grazhdanskaia voina v Turkestane* (Tashkent: Gosudarstvennoe izd. Uzbekskoi SSR, 1957), pp. 478–82.
55 Nepesov, *Velikii Oktiabr'*, p. 82.
56 B. I. Iskandarov, *Bukhara (1918–1920gg.)* (Dushanbe: Donish, 1970), pp.

85–6; Nepesov, *Velikii Oktiabr'*, p. 81.
57 *Inostrannaia voennaia interventsiia i grazhdanskaia voina v Srednei Azii i Kazakhstane*, Vol. 2 (Alma-Ata: Nauka, 1964), pp. 487–8.
58 The reference is to the Turkkomissiia, the Committee for Turkestan Affairs. Established in 1919, it was the highest-level body in Central Asia in the years 1919–21.
59 Dubianskii Papers: 'Doklad o razoruzhenii iomudskikh khanov', Moscow, September 1921, fo. 8.
60 ibid., fo. 5.
61 ibid., fo. 7.
62 Dubianskii Papers: 'Raz''iasnenie k osobomu mneniiu tov. Malysheva otnositel'no instruktsii, dannoi kombrigu 2' (probably written by R. Shakirov), September 1920.
63 Dubianskii Papers: 'Doklad o razoruzhenii', fo. 8.
64 ibid., fo. 9.
65 Dubianskii Papers: 'Obrashchenie k turkmenam', 29 September 1920.
66 The Soviet commander who led the suppression of this rebellion wrote that 'the movement did not bear traits of a struggle between two tribes, the Uzbeks and Yomuts (Turkmens): rather, it was a definite international (within a Muslim context) counter-revolutionary uprising of the khans, the mullahs, and the beys against the Republic and the revolutionary government' (Dubianskii Papers: 'Doklad o razoruzhenii', fo. 11).
67 Dubianskii Papers: 'Komandiru 2–oi strelkovoi brigady tov. Dubianskomu', September 1920.
68 D. Gopner, 'Otchet o komandirovke v Khorezm (avgust-oktiabr' 1922 goda)', 20 December 1922, TsGAOR, *fond* 1318, *op.* 1, *ed. khr.* 670, pt 2, p. 96.
69 'Doklad vremennogo revoliutsionnogo komiteta KhNSR II Vsekhorezmskomu kurultaiu o politicheskom polozhenii', 19 May 1921, in *Istoriia Khorezmskoi narodnoi sovetskoi respubliki (1920–1924gg.)* (Tashkent: Fan, 1976), p. 91.
70 'Turkmeniia i polozhenie turkmen v Khorezme (Khive)', *Zhizn' natsional'nostei*, 6 March 1922, p. 5.
71 *Istoriia kommunisticheskikh organizatsii Srednei Azii* (Tashkent: Izdatel'stvo 'Uzbekistan', 1967), p. 654.
72 I. Kutiakov, *Krasnaia konnitsa i vozdushnyi flot v pustyniakh* (Moscow: Gosudarstvennoe izdatel'stvo, 1930).
73 ibid., p. 177.
74 Nepesov, *Velikii Oktiabr'*, p. 207.
75 'Protokol zasedaniia Ispolbiuro TsK KhKP ob obrazovanii Turkmenskoi oblasti KhSSR', 26 March 1924, in *Istoriia Khorezmskoi narodnoi sovetskoi respubliki*, pp. 312–13.
76 R. Vaidyanath, *The Formation of the Soviet Central Asian Republics* (New Delhi: People's Publishing House, 1967), pp. 170–1.
77 e.g. ibid., pp. 151–202.
78 Turkmenskaia Sovetskaia Sotsialisticheskaia Respublika, *1–2 sessii. Tsentral'nyi Ispolnitel'nyi Komitet. Stenograficheskii Otchet* (Poltoratsk, 1925), p. 11.
79 ibid.
80 Iu. I. Poslavskii and G. N. Cherdantsev (eds), *Sredne-Aziatskii ekonomicheskii raion* (Tashkent: Izd. TES, 1922), p. 119.

3
Central Asian Political Participation and Soviet Political Development

STEVEN L. BURG

Increasing rates of participation by Central Asian nationalities in the modern sectors of Soviet society have had unanticipated consequences both for the Soviet leaders who have sponsored these increases and for the Central Asians who have experienced them. The mobilization of Central Asian nationalities into the Soviet polity has not resulted in the creation of a new homogeneous Soviet people, nor even in a reduction in the level of tensions. On the contrary, increased contact between Central Asians and Europeans under conditions of social, economic and political competition has resulted in many cases in an intensification of ethnic self-consciousness and self-assertiveness in precisely those segments of society on which the Soviet leadership had thought it could rely. Despite these problems, however, the Soviet leadership is none the less likely in Central Asia to persist in its longstanding cadres policy in the belief that the further nativization of Central Asian social and political institutions and organizations will provide key sectors of native society with important stakes in the established political order, while attenuating feelings of collective political deprivation among the masses and strengthening symbolic identification with the regime.

In this chapter I point out some of the inherent problems of such a strategy, and some of its potential consequences for the development of the Soviet political system. I examine these processes in most detail for the Uzbek republic. I have chosen Uzbekistan for three reasons: first, a greater amount of data is available for Uzbekistan than for the other Central Asian republics; secondly, the larger size of the social elite in this republic means that changes there are both practically and statistically more significant; and, thirdly, the Uzbeks traditionally have exercised a leadership role throughout Central Asia. But there is sufficient evidence to allow confidence that these processes are taking place in the other republics of Central Asia and Kazakhstan as well.

The Development of a Central Asian Native Elite

Until recently, Central Asian participation in modern sectors was limited by cultural and historical conditions. These included: first, a tradition of looking to other Turkic peoples – primarily Tatars – for cultural leadership; secondly, a Muslim cultural heritage which inclined Central Asian intellectuals toward humanistic careers rather than scientific and technical ones, and which severely restricted the participation of women in public and social life; thirdly, an instinctive racism of the Europeans – primarily Russians – who dominated the political system, and especially of those Europeans settled in Central Asia itself; and, fourthly, the generally low levels of education and training among Central Asian nationalities. It was the magnitude and intractability of these obstacles more than a lack of official commitment or a covert official racism that made nativization a relatively slow process in the first decades of Soviet power.

Since 1917, Soviet policy has been to modernize the occupational structure of Central Asian society and to promote the participation of Central Asians in Soviet organizations. While the regime has been unable to eliminate either the racism of European settlers or the legacy of Islamic culture, it has acted to control the public expression of racism in that region and to promote native cadres into responsible positions in the state and party apparatuses. Among the measures by which the regime sought to accelerate this process were the creation and rapid expansion of a system of native language schools and a network of adult education institutions, the introduction of preferential quotas for Central Asian students at higher educational institutions in that region, the relaxation of class criteria in the selection and promotion of native cadres, and the preferential appointment and advancement of native cadres.

By the middle 1930s the Soviet leadership was less willing to sacrifice efficiency to ethnicity in making key appointments. Nevertheless, sizable numbers of young Central Asians acquired some training and entered the modern sector of Central Asian society during this period, bringing them into direct contact with skilled European cadres for the first time. However, many of these new native cadres – like the earlier native political elite – were later accused of bourgeois nationalism and fell victim to the purges of the late 1930s. The Europeanization of the Central Asian elite that resulted from these purges was reinforced during World War II, when many European cadres were uprooted from the Western territories and the center of the Soviet Union and shifted to Central Asia.

The war also had the effect of reducing the total number of skilled cadres available to the regime. After the war, this cadre deficit and the increased priority placed on Central Asian development impelled the Soviet leadership to increase investment in the educational infrastructure of Central Asia and once again to adopt a program of affirmative action, in order to ensure increased native participation. This, in turn, permitted the recruitment of more natives to the industrial workforce and to the upper levels of the state and party bureaucracies. In numerical terms, the regime has been extraordinarily successful in its efforts to increase rates of native participation. However, the meaning of this success for both the Soviet leadership and the Central Asians themselves is somewhat ambiguous. As Western studies of cultural diversity in European states and Soviet studies by Iu. V. Arutiunian and other scholars suggest, increased rates of participation do not necessarily promote social and political integration.

Evidence concerning the extent of native participation in the state and party apparats *as such* is limited. However, the more abundant data on the national composition of Soviet scientific and technical cadres enable us to draw a number of pertinent inferences. The Soviet definition of 'scientific worker' is sufficiently broad to encompass many members of the state and party apparatus, including those at the middle and upper levels. According to the authoritative definition of the Soviet Central Statistical Administration, this category includes:

> ... academicians, full and corresponding members of academies of science; all persons having the academic degree of doctor of science, candidate of science or the academic rank of professor, docent, senior scientific co-worker, junior scientific co-worker, assistant, *independently of the place and character of their work*; persons conducting scientific research work in scientific institutions and scientific pedagogical work in higher educational institutions *independently of whether they have an academic degree or academic rank,* and also specialists who *do not have either an academic degree or academic rank* but systematically carry out scientific work in industrial enterprises.[1] (My italics).

Over time, the proportion of individuals in this Soviet category whom we in the West would call 'scientists', in the strict meaning of the word, has declined. In Soviet usage, a large segment of the social elite qualifies as 'scientists', and the same is also true of many political cadres.[2]

At the end of World War II, the number of 'scientific workers' in Soviet Central Asia was relatively small and predominantly European. Since that time, the scientific and technical infrastructure of Central Asia has expanded dramatically and the number of Central Asians acquiring the qualifications for inclusion in the category 'scientific workers' has increased even more rapidly. The increasing production of qualified native candidates for membership in the social elite is likely to continue in the future. This is because of the large numbers of Central Asian youth now attending, or soon to enter, higher educational institutions and because of the increasing proportion of these students who are choosing to pursue careers long dominated by Europeans.

The number and proportion of Uzbeks in the social elite of the Uzbek republic has increased dramatically since World War II. In 1947 there were only 568 Uzbek 'scientific workers' and they comprised 3·9 percent of the total. By 1960 these figures had risen to 3552 and 34·4 percent, respectively. By 1975 the number of Uzbek 'scientific workers' had grown to 14,821, comprising 48·1 percent of this social elite.[3] Even more dramatic changes can be seen when we compare the numbers and proportions of all Central Asians with those of all Europeans in the social elite of Uzbekistan. This dynamic is yet stronger at the upper levels of this elite, as can be seen in Table 3.1, below. This trend toward 'nativization' of the social elite is evident in every one of the Central Asian republics and Kazakhstan.[4]

These developments were facilitated by the relatively rapid economic development of the region. This meant that Central Asians could be absorbed into the social elite without displacing the Russians and other Europeans already there. In recent years, rates of economic expansion have slowed down; and the finding of places in the elite for ever-increasing numbers of Uzbeks and members of other Central Asian nationalities may be becoming ever more difficult. Indeed, in 1976 two Soviet sociologists – both of them apparently Slavs – concluded from a lengthy review of the 'sociodemographic characteristics of science personnel' that:

The high rates of increase in numbers of researchers and scholars during the past decade have essentially met the quantitative needs of the scientific and higher educational institutions of the country for research and teaching personnel. This will permit some reduction in the annual rate of increase in total numbers of researchers and scholars . . . This is a result of the purposeful policy of the CPSU and the Soviet government, which have taken a number of measures to create the required conditions for training scholarly personnel in formerly backward areas of the country.[5]

Thus, despite the continuing need for skilled native workers at lower levels of the Central Asian economy – and especially in industrial enterprises, where they are in short supply[6] – the continuing unimpeded entry of Central Asians into the social elite appears to depend on a continuing expansion of the more advanced sectors of the Central Asian economy. And in the event that new positions cannot be created for them their entry would require a concomitant exit of the Europeans already there. The rapid upward mobility of Central Asians into the social elite since the war has generated a revolution in raising expectations among those already in the elite. The increasing experience of these Uzbek and other Central Asian cadres will no doubt lead them to contest with Europeans for advancement and preferment. In the short term, the regime has been able to alleviate such competition in Central Asia by granting the requests of Jewish personnel to emigrate and replacing them with native cadres.[7] However, the supply of such Jews is limited. And, more important, the revolution of rising expectations has undoubtedly affected the children of native cadres as well. Thus, present conflicts are likely to intensify in the future and to be invested with ever greater ethnic meaning.

Ethnic tensions within the Central Asian social elite are already apparent. Mark Popovskii, a recent émigré from the Soviet Union who has written extensively on Soviet science, has reported that by the mid-1970s native functionaries were already using their authority to prevent the upward mobility of European cadres and to replace Russians and other Europeans (primarily Jews) with natives.[8] The conflicts that resulted from such actions had not yet led to bloodshed; but, he reports, they had come very close.[9]

Additional evidence on the responses of native cadres to competition for advancement within the social elite of their own republics has been supplied by Soviet 'concrete sociological research'. Soviet investigators confirm that one consequence of the competition for positions is the appearance of inter-ethnic tensions within this highly educated and modernized stratum of

Soviet society. Arutiunian, in his 1969 study of ethnic relations in the Tatar ASSR, reported that 'professionals . . . do not have a higher level of positive attitudes in cross-national relationships than do other sections of the population, *but rather the opposite*' (my italics). He conceded that 'a narrow ethnic orientation' may result from 'cultural isolation and backwardness and the retention of obsolete forms of a traditional culture', but noted that 'professionals have the greatest success both in education and in overcoming the vestiges of the traditional culture'. He concluded, therefore, that 'the narrow ethnic orientation found among professionals and para-professionals is . . . primarily related to a set of socio-economic causes — the supply and demand relationship for skilled employees, the opportunities for social advancement and so forth'.[10]

'The very possession of higher education', Arutiunian suggested, 'presumes broader "expectations".' However, accelerated real mobility is not associated with 'either a positive or negative manner in attitudes'. Rather, he found that it is 'when social "expectations" are not wholly realized, [that] a dissatisfaction appears that is projected upon inter-ethnic attitudes'. Arutiunian's colleague, L. M. Drobizheva, developed this argument further in a later article using the same data set to examine the 'sociocultural features of the personality and ethnic attitudes'. She concluded that negative attitudes toward inter-ethnic contact arise out of 'higher "social expectations" ' that 'are by no means always entirely realizable'. And 'where factors of competition on the social scale are present (for example, in admission to higher educational institutions or assignments to jobs), some [professionals] show an inclination to introduce an ethnic factor into their explanations of the successes or failings of a given individual'.[11]

These findings confirm that rapid mobilization and development have given rise to a 'revolution of rising expectations' among the native populations of formerly underdeveloped areas of the Soviet Union. Arutiunian concludes, therefore, that 'the more favorable the conditions for the mobility of non-Russian personnel, the more successfully possible tension in ethnic relationship is eliminated'.[12] And this conclusion is supported by Drobizheva and others. At the same time, however, the converse would also appear to be true: the unwillingness or inability of the regime to provide levels of mobility commensurate with the expectations of native cadres would engender feelings of relative deprivation likely to find expression in inter-ethnic hostility.

It is not only competition between nationalities which generates inter-ethnic hostility, however. Supervision by persons of a different nationality, Arutiunian reported in another study, also tends to generate such hostilities.[13] As a result, the increasing expectations of upward mobility among native elites and elites-in-training present the regime with a double-edged problem. For their advancement into positions of authority over European cadres would be likely to engender a 'backlash' among the latter. Indeed, the Soviet sociologist A. A. Susokolov reported in 1976 that in recent years there had been 'some activation of national life, an increase in national consciousness, national feelings' among the nationalities. 'Growth of the ethnic intelligentsia under conditions in which contact between the nationalities is stable or even rising,' he noted, 'produces in it a more pronounced tendency to preserve what is distinctive to that nation.' And he warned that it 'is dangerous . . . to let these processes occur spontaneously, to leave them without conscious regulation' because this would 'permit hostile, nationalist elements to influence the rise of national consciousness'.[14]

Cadres Competition in the State and Party Apparats

As I noted above, evidence concerning these two institutions is relatively scarce, especially for the critical middle levels. The one level for which we have relatively complete information is that of mass party membership in the Central Asian republics. These data are shown in Table 3.2. Native participation at this level is relatively high and has been so during most of the Soviet period. These figures are indicative of the extent to which native cadres dominate the party at the lower levels. Parallel to this is the dominance of natives in local state institutions – especially rural soviets. But these figures tell us little about relations between national groups within the elite. More indicative of the latter are data concerning the participation of these nationalities at the higher and middle levels of the *apparat*.

For the Uzbek republic, we can identify the cadres who have occupied leading positions in the republican Central Committee *apparat* and in the Council of Ministers. We have only fragmentary evidence about the participation of natives in *oblast'*, *raion* and city party committees and among secretaries of primary party organizations. And we have even less concerning the middle levels of the state *apparat*. It is precisely here that we would need more detailed cross-time data to be sure that our findings concerning the social elite as a whole apply with equal force to these two important bureaucracies. Nevertheless, the evidence we do possess makes it reasonable to conclude that inter-ethnic relations within these *apparats* look very much like those within the social elite as a whole.

During the 1920s native participation at the upper levels of the state as well as the party in Central Asia was largely symbolic. People of local nationalities were installed in highly visible positions, but ones which had little actual power.[15] They served primarily to attract support from among their co-nationals. The formal requirements for these positions were limited to nationality, loyalty and pliability. The possession of specific skills was relatively unimportant. Since that time, however, the nature of both the state and society has changed, and consequently the nature of the requirements for positions in the state and the party has changed as well.

The upper- and middle-level positions in the party and state bureaucracies now require more skilled cadres whose educational background and work experience frequently make them members of the Soviet category 'scientific workers'. This overlap has increased over time because of the tendency of cadres at the higher levels of the state and party apparatus to acquire academic degrees.[16] Thus, while it would be wrong to apply what we know about 'scientific workers' to the state and party *apparatchiki* of earlier periods, it is now becoming increasingly appropriate to do so.

Since World War II, Uzbek cadres have risen to positions of authority in the middle and upper levels of both the party and state bureaucracies of the Uzbek republic. They now occupy most positions at the highest levels of the republican party apparatus and in the Council of Ministers.[17] In each of these bureaucracies, however, there is one position which no native has occupied in the contemporary era: the organizational secretaryship of the republican central committee and the chairmanship of the KGB.[18] The organizational secretary controls the republican *nomenklatura* and so is in a position to determine which native cadres will be assigned there. The chairman of the KGB controls the secret police, which is charged with the supervision and control of cadres in both the party and state *apparats*. In the Uzbek republic both positions have been occupied exclusively by Russians. The Russian organizational secretaries tend to be appointed directly out of the upper-middle ranks of the central committee *apparat* in Moscow or to be shifted from the first or second secretaryship of a different non-Russian union or autonomous republic. For these cadres, these appointments constitute a 'tour of duty' and frequently are followed by promotion to all-union responsibilities or reassignment to a comparable position in either the all-union central committee in Moscow or in another nationality area.[19] Clearly, the Russians who occupy these positions are closely tied to the central party apparatus in Moscow and use their positions in the non-Russian areas to implement central policies. This pattern is strongest in Uzbekistan and Kazakhstan, but somewhat weaker elsewhere in Central Asia. No less could be expected from the Russian incumbents of the republican KGB chairmanships. These positions have been held *exclusively* by non-native cadres in Uzbekistan, Tadzhikistan and Turkmenistan, and only a small proportion of incumbents in Kazakhstan and Kirgizia have been natives. Thus, the Russian organizational secretaries have been charged with carrying out the regime's policy of promoting Central Asians into responsible positions at the upper and middle levels of the state and party bureaucracies; and the Russian chairmen of the KGB have been charged with supervising, controlling and, in some cases, removing native cadres so promoted.[20]

Uzbeks have been moving into positions at lower levels of the party *apparat* as well. As can be seen from Table 3.3, increasing numbers of native cadres have become secretaries of primary party organizations not only in areas of traditional native dominance but also, to a lesser extent, in industrial and urban party organizations. This pattern is also evident in data available for the Kirgiz republic, although 'nativization' of that party organization does not appear to have proceeded as rapidly as in Uzbekistan.[21]

As Jeremy Azrael has pointed out, this represents the reproduction of a pattern already established in Georgia, Armenia and Azerbaidzhan. In the latter republic, over 72 percent of the secretaries of primary party organizations and over 76 percent of the *oblast'*, city and *raion* committee secretaries in 1970 were Azeris.[22] There is every reason to believe, as Azrael has suggested, that 'as the demographic facts – meaning not only population growth, but also rising education levels and increased levels of urbanization, and so on – have their impact, there is a good chance we will see the same thing in Central Asia that we have already seen in the Caucasus'.[23]

Although the entry of increasing numbers of Muslim cadres into positions of responsibility in the party and state *apparats* of Central Asia has been sponsored by the Soviet leadership, it has not occurred without instances of intense friction between natives and Russians. Native functionaries in positions of authority have sometimes executed this policy in ways which the central leadership must find unacceptable. Indeed, in a leading article in *Pravda*, the Brezhnev leadership made it clear when it took over the reins of power that it would not tolerate 'any manifestations of national setting-apart . . . in the training and employment of personnel of various nationalities in the Soviet republics' because 'the growing scale of Communist construction requires a constant exchange of cadres among the people'.[24] Yet Popovskii reports, for example, the case of a Minister of Health of the Kazakh republic, a native Kazakh, who removed five doctors of science from positions in Karaganda simply because they were not Kazakhs. 'We have our own Kazakh doctors of science,' the Minister explained, 'and they must head the institutes and laboratories of Kazakhstan.'[25] Such exclusionary practices appear to be the subject of Brezhnev's cautionary remarks to the twenty-sixth CPSU Congress concerning the rights of each nation to 'proper representation in their party and government agencies' and the necessity for republican provincial party leaderships to consider the 'language, culture and everyday life' needs of 'citizens of non-indigenous nationality'.[26]

Ethnic significance may also become attached to processes at lower levels of the party and state bureaucracies. At these levels – especially in rural soviets and primary party organizations – positions increasingly are being filled by native cadres. Indeed, as early as 1961 – the most recent year for which election results in the republics were broken down by nationality – Muslims already constituted 81·9 percent of the deputies in the *raion-* and *oblast'*-level soviets of Uzbekistan, over 84 percent of the deputies at the village and 'urban village' level, and even 45·8 percent of the deputies at the city or urban level. A similar pattern is evident in the data for the other Central Asian republics as well.[27] Leadership positions in these institutions are such that on day-to-day issues functionaries in them increasingly act as representatives of their constituents against cadres at upper levels of the party and state *apparats*. Despite the steady process of nativization noted above, many of the cadres at these levels are not of the same nationality; and, as a consequence, conflicts over the local implementation of policies and the allocation of sometimes scarce resources are easily invested with ethnic meaning.

While active participation in Soviet institutions and successful upward mobility in the Soviet hierarchy necessarily involve a certain degree of acculturation to the predominantly Russian character of the regime, they do not necessarily entail the divorce of native cadres from their native roots, or even their assimilation. Even at the highest political levels, where pressure to assimilate to 'Soviet' culture must be greatest, native cadres may retain much of their native culture. The Harvard anthropologist, Marjorie Mandelstam Balzer, recently reported, for example, the following story of cultural persistence in Kazakhstan:

> The tale begins with some Russian friends of mine who were travelling on a train, on a five-day trip to Kazakhstan. Much to their amazement, they found themselves in a compartment with the Kazakh Minister of Culture and his wife. The Kazakh minister invited the two Russians to come to his home. The home was a large, beautiful traditional house with a typical Central Asian floorplan, where many rooms are built around a central courtyard. The Russians were led inside by the Minister of Culture who was wearing a long caftan. He seated them on sumptuous oriental rugs in front of a large low table, laden with traditional food — a *plov* with lots of grain, lamb and greens. After a while the Russians could no longer hold back. They asked, 'Where is your wife?' because she in fact had been absent since they had arrived. And the minister answered, 'Oh, she's in the kitchen. She couldn't possibly be eating with us. In my own home I do things in the traditional way.'[28]

Indeed, there is a built-in incentive at this level of the elite *not* to assimilate, to guard against deracination or even the perception of such deracination. For it is the very 'nativeness' of the Central Asian political leadership that strengthens mass identification with the Soviet regime. As Azrael has argued,

> The symbolic identification with the ruling elite that can occur as the result of extensive ethnic representation within it is likely to be strongest where the representatives are perceived to be authentic members of the community that they purportedly represent, where they are perceived by the community to share important traits and norms and values with the bulk of the community's members.

Consequently,

> At least some native informants tend to stress that [Uzbek First Secretary] Sharaf Rashidov can recite Persian poetry, is steeped in the culture of the area, is 'our' great writer, etc. These informants would quickly concede that Rashidov is also a protagonist of Russification, that he cooked data, that he did all the things that party secretaries after all, in that kind of situation, are supposed to do. Nonetheless, in conversations which I have had of Rashidov,

I've been struck by the degree to which folks have identified with him as an articulate spokesman for Uzbek culture, as somebody with a feel for it, and very much have talked about him as a leader.
... Similarly, people who have spent time with [Kazakh First Secretary] Dinmukhamed Kunaev tend to mention his observance of native traditions. They invariably describe what apparently was a very famous wedding in which he married off his daughter in a traditional festivity, in which he had native policemen screening off the area.[29]

There are, however, important limits to the extent to which any leader of a non-Russian party organization can allow himself to become identified with his nationality and still hold on to his position.

At lower levels of the social elite, Soviet sociologists provide overwhelming evidence that upward mobility, the use of Russian language on the job, high levels of contact with Russians or other nationalities, and high levels of education do not deter non-Russians from preserving at least some elements of their native culture. Thus, contrary to the assumptions of both some Western social scientists and the Soviet leaders themselves, increased mass participation by natives, increased entry of native cadres into the social and political elites of Soviet Central Asia, and concomitantly increasing levels of internationality contact have not resulted in extensive assimilation of modernized Central Asian elites or their transformation into 'new Soviet men'. Rather, these phenomena appear to have resulted in the creation of a large and ever-increasing pool of cadres seemingly competent to take over the reins of real power in Central Asia, likely to press to do so, and possessed of the powerful legitimizing – and potentially mobilizing – force of nationalism behind them. It is particularly noteworthy that, for the first time since the 1920s, incidents of internationality violence at the mass level are once again being reported. The present situation in the Soviet Union thus appears to hold much in common with the pre-crisis periods of other multicultural and multinational states long dominated by a single group or set of groups that later experienced intense domestic political conflict and crisis, which led to significant and even transformative changes in the distribution of power in the domestic political order.

Implications for Soviet Political Development

This situation would seem to require some sort of response from the regime. There are several options available to the Soviet leadership, including: repression of native cadres, political socialization of native cadres, general economic expansion in the region, reduction in the rate of production of new native cadres, or withdrawal of European cadres from Central Asia. Given its own experiences, the present Soviet leadership will probably be unwilling both to employ the degree of coercion necessary to repress this problem completely and to incur the costs associated with a reduced rate of production of native cadres; and it probably will not be successful if it intensifies political socialization efforts among native cadres in Central Asia. Barring outside help or the transfer of substantial resources from other regions of the USSR, the central Soviet leadership will probably be unable to expand the economy in Central Asia to provide a sufficient number of positions to satisfy the increasing number of upwardly mobile native cadres. And it is unlikely to be willing to withdraw Russian and other European cadres, lest its control in the region be called into question. It is probably unwilling or unable to do any of these things not only because of the costs involved, but also because of the risks inherent in such 'solutions': each of these responses carries the potential not only for solving the problem of increasing inter-ethnic hostility in Central Asia, but also for intensifying it. To devise specific policies which will achieve these goals without making the problem worse is likely to be an extremely difficult task for the Soviet leadership. This may explain why, despite the potentially explosive nature of this problem, the central leadership seems to do nothing at all.

As Jeremy Azrael has emphasized,[30] the Muslim masses in Central Asia have been extraordinarily quiescent since the armed resistance of the 1920s and have shown only a limited inclination to engage in the kinds of protest that have occurred in the Caucasus, the Ukraine and the Baltic republics over the past two decades. Moreover, there is no evidence as yet of the rise of an organized dissident movement among native intellectuals. However, given the conditions outlined above, the political turmoil in the Muslim world abroad — much of it in areas contiguous to the Muslim areas of the Soviet Union — and the clear interest of Muslim political leaders abroad in the fate of their brethren in Central Asia, it is not hard to imagine the rise of a politically active native Muslim intelligentsia and a restive native political elite.[31]

We must not forget, however, that the Soviet regime — like every well-established modern state — has an enormous capacity to absorb and repress internal tensions, conflict and even violence. Indeed, the soviet regime may have a greater capacity than most.

Consequently, we must resist the temptation to interpret the rise of inter-ethnic tensions in Central Asia as a harbinger of the end of Soviet power there. We must also resist the temptation to interpret incidents of inter-ethnic conflict within the elite as necessarily being indicators of the alienation of native cadres from the Soviet system. Such behavior may, in fact, reflect an attempt by these cadres to gain more complete enfranchisement in it. Indeed, the extension by the regime of further local decision-making authority and central participation to Central Asian cadres may represent a potentially effective means of averting disintegrative conflict.

Such local authority and movement by regional cadres into positions of importance in the central party and state *apparats* are not without precedent. Ukrainians, after all, have not only enjoyed extensive control over their own republic for decades, but have also staffed key positions at the center in relatively large numbers. Georgians, Azeris and Belorussians have achieved positions of some prominence in the Politburo and central party and state *apparats*. However, while there are now three Muslim members of the Politburo — Kazakh First Secretary Kunaev and Azerbaidzhan First Secretary Geidar Aliev (full members) and Uzbek First Secretary Rashidov (who has been a candidate member since 1961 and seems unlikely to be promoted) — there appears to have been no concomitant movement of Muslim cadres into the central apparatus, and no extension of increased local authority to the native leaders of the Central Asian republics. Cadres policy — and therefore elite mobility — in their republics remains under the control of central officials, and large sectors of the Central Asian economies remain under the control of ministries responsible directly to the center. Moreover, those Muslim party leaders who have achieved Politburo membership appear to have done so chiefly as clients of one of the Russians already there, or seem to occupy a largely symbolic position, or both. This makes it unlikely that any of them will be able to achieve even the limited power and authority of the most powerful of the regional leaders, the Ukrainian first secretary. For, under the conditions of collective leadership characteristic of the last decade or two, this would give that leader enormous leverage over central policy. And the potential economic and political costs of allowing the emergence of a genuine representative of Central Asian interests in the Politburo, capable of achieving decisions of the leadership more responsive to the demands of Central Asian development, are enormous — indeed, far greater than the present leadership appears to be willing, or able, to bear. Indeed, not even Geidar Aliev, the ethnic Muslim former Azerbaidzhan party and KGB chief recently promoted to full Politburo membership and the post of First Deputy Prime Minister, appears to behave as a 'representative' of Muslim economic interests. On the contrary, his rise to a position of seemingly 'real' power appears to be contingent on his remaining a spokesman for central interests, a role he played even in his native Azerbaidzhan.

Consequently, it would seem that at least for the short-term Azrael is correct in arguing that 'the main political function of the increasingly nativized local establishment' – and I would add here the Central Asian members of the Politburo as well – 'may be to provide the center with credible scapegoats for failures'.[32] The economic policies of the present leadership appear destined to increase inter-regional competition for capital resources – a competition that Central Asia appears destined to lose – and thereby increase cadres competition and perhaps even mass discontent in Central Asia. Rather than confronting the hard policy choices posed by such developments, the present leadership is likely to find it easier simply to replace Central Asian political leaders, blame them for local difficulties, and purge the native cadres of the region, as it has done in the past in the Ukraine, Georgia and Azerbaidzhan.

In the longer run, however, the presence of Central Asian leaders in the Politburo and the ongoing 'nativization' of regional institutions may take on increased importance. For, under the conditions of a succession struggle, heretofore symbolic participation may present Central Asian leaders with an opportunity to trade political support for enhanced political autonomy, *if* the Central Asians actually participate in that struggle and *if* it is played out under conditions of continued emphasis on collective rule – two conditions for which there are at present no guarantees.

Enhanced political autonomy for Central Asian and, therefore, other regional leaders certainly would transform the character of the central policy-making process in the Soviet Union. However, there is no reason why a succession struggle need result in such enhanced autonomy. In fact, there is good reason to believe that exactly the opposite might take place. Central Asian leaders, intent on achieving the transfer of greater resources from other regions to Central Asia, might throw their support behind the restoration of a more authoritarian arrangement for the post-Brezhnev period. They might be very willing to act as intensely loyal agents of central power if such loyalty is rewarded by the kind of economic benefits only a powerfully coercive central leader could be expected to deliver.

Table 3.1 *National Composition of Scientific Workers in Uzbekistan (1960–75)*

	1960 No.	%	1966 No.	%	1970 No.	%	1975 No.	%
Doctors of Science								
Uzbeks	78	35·1	155	44·7	258	52·2	446	59·9
Russians	80	36·0	98	28·2	121	24·5	141	18·9
Central Asians[1]	86	38·7	172	49·6	296	59·9	503	67·5
Europeans[2]	127	57·2	161	46·4	187	39·9	220	29·5
Others[3]	9	4·1	14	4·0	11	2·2	22	3·0
Total	222	100·0	347	100·0	494	100·0	745	100·0
Candidates of Science								
Uzbeks	821	33·6	2,010	45·9	3,636	52·6	5,919	56·3
Russians	915	37·5	1,203	27·5	1,624	23·5	2,193	20·9
Central Asians	1,014	41·5	2,417	55·2	4,268	61·8	6,890	65·6
Europeans	1,317	53·9	1,728	39·5	2,385	34·5	3,212	30·6
Others	111	4·5	231	5·3	254	3·7	403	3·8
Total	2,442	100·0	4,376	100·0	6,907	100·0	10,505	100·0
Other elites								
Uzbeks	2,653	34·6	5,114	38·8	7,364	41·3	8,456	43·2
Russians	2,976	38·8	4,635	35·2	5,847	33·3	6,289	32·1
Central Asians	3,410	44·5	6,441	48·9	9,180	51·4	10,356	52·9
Europeans	3,912	51·0	6,280	47·6	7,874	44·1	8,362	42·7
Others	343	4·5	459	3·5	789	4·4	867	4·4
Total	7,665	100·0	13,180	100·0	17,843	100·0	19,585	100·0
Total								
Uzbeks	3,552	34·4	7,279	40·7	11,258	44·6	14,821	48·1
Russians	3,971	38·5	5,936	33·2	7,692	30·5	8,623	28·0
Central Asians	4,510	43·7	9,030	50·4	13,744	54·4	17,749	57·6
Europeans	5,356	51·9	8,069	45·1	10,446	41·4	11,794	38·2
Others	463	4·5	804	4·5	1,054	4·2	1,292	4·2
Total	10,329	100·0	17,903	100·0	25,244	100·0	30,835	100·0

Notes
1 'Central Asians' includes Uzbeks, Tatars, Kazakhs, Karakalpaks and Tadzhiks.
2 'Europeans' includes Russians, Jews, Ukrainians and Armenians.
3 'Others' corresponds to the category 'other nationalities', which may include any nationality not specified above.

Sources: Narodnoe khoziaistvo Uzbeksoi SSR v 1967g. (Tashkent: Uzbekistan, 1968), p. 277; *Narodnoe khoziaistvo Uzbeksoi SSR za 50 let (1967)* (Tashkent: Uzbekistan, 1968), p. 225; *Narodnoe khoziaistvo Uzbeksoi SSR v 1975g.* (Tashkent: Uzbekistan, 1976), p. 41.

Table 3.2 *National Composition of the Kazakh and Central Asian Republic Party Organizations*

	1945		1950		1955		1960		1965		1970	
	No.	%	No.	%	No.	%	No.	%	No.	%	No.	%
Kazakh organization												
Kazakhs	49,255	43·1	91,600	40·6	93,363	39·9	115,357	36·2	148,755	33·0	190,892	34·3
Russians	39,685	34·7	91,656	40·6	97,028	41·4	138,147	43·4	201,918	44·8	242,991	43·7
Central Asians	53,176	46·5	99,821	44·3	101,905	43·5	126,163	39·6	164,393	36·5	210,671	37·9
Europeans	51,563	45·1	115,304	51·1	123,022	52·5	176,769	55·0	259,621	57·6	310,202	55·7
Others	9,522	8·3	10,431	4·6	9,161	3·9	15,570	4·9	26,472	5·9	35,715	6·4
Total	114,261	100·0	225,556	100·0	234,193	100·0	318,502	100·0	450,486	100·0	556,508	100·0
Uzbek organisation												
Uzbeks	35,205	42·7	57,901	43·8	67,679	47·0	102,663	50·6	163,982	52·2	226,357	54·9
Russians	19,088	23·1	35,811	27·1	36,073	25·1	46,514	22·9	70,248	22·4	84,849	20·6
Central Asians	47,305	57·3	79,549	60·1	90,264	62·7	134,280	66·2	212,718	67·7	289,784	70·3
Europeans	30,434	36·9	45,580	34·4	46,147	32·1	58,850	29·0	87,159	27·7	104,241	25·3
Others	4,766	5·8	7,207	5·4	7,467	5·2	9,735	4·8	14,402	4·6	18,296	4·4
Total	82,505	100·0	132,336	100·0	143,878	100·0	202,865	100·0	314,279	100·0	412,321	100·0
Turkmen organization												
Turkmen	7,655	39·7	14,865	44·4	17,211	47·2	22,918	50·8	29,755	52·0	37,515	55·3
Russians	6,298	32·7	10,270	30·7	10,519	28·9	11,906	26·4	14,542	25·4	14,761	23·2
Central Asians	10,108	52·4	19,417	58·0	21,982	60·3	28,532	63·2	36,585	64·3	46,163	68·0
Europeans	8,513	44·1	13,145	39·3	13,453	36·9	15,537	34·4	18,942	33·1	19,842	29·2
Others	663	3·4	901	2·7	1,019	2·8	1,083	2·4	1,679	2·9	1,887	2·8
Total	19,284	100·0	33,463	100·0	36,454	100·0	45,152	100·0	57,206	100·0	67,892	100·0

Tadzhik organization										
Tadzhiks	7,104	42·1	12,401	39·7	14,491	43·8	21,579	45·0	30,915	45·7	40,345	47·9
Uzbeks	2,423	14·3	4,658	14·9	5,247	15·9	7,560	15·8	11,077	16·4	14,430	17·1
Russians	4,121	24·4	9,173	24·4	8,431	25·5	11,927	24·9	16,245	24·0	18,593	22·1
Others	3,242	19·2	5,002	16·0	4,913	14·9	6,854	14·3	9,387	13·9	10,868	12·9
Total	16,890	100·0	31,234	100·0	33,082	100·0	47,920	100·0	67,624	100·0	84,236	100·0
Kirgiz organization										
Kirgiz	8,842	37·6	14,567	32·5	16,301	35·4	22,159	35·9	30,959	36·5	38,881	37·7
Russians	6,911	29·4	17,369	38·8	17,002	37·0	23,306	37·8	32,403	38·2	38,847	37·7
Central Asians	10,486	44·6	17,387	38·8	19,505	42·4	26,379	42·8	36,547	43·1	46,048	44·7
Europeans	9,603	40·9	22,831	51·0	22,167	48·2	29,980	48·6	40,111	48·1	47,852	46·4
Others	3,400	14·5	4,572	10·2	4,329	9·4	5,287	8·6	7,397	8·7	9,128	8·9
Total	23,489	100·0	44,790	100·0	46,001	100·0	61,646	100·0	84,055	100·0	103,028	100·0

Sources: Institut Istorii Partii, *Kompartiia Kazakhstana za 50 let* (Alma-Ata: Kazakhstan, 1972), pp. 172, 200, 241, 280, 324; Institut Istorii Partii, *Kommunisticheskaia partiia Uzbekistana v tsifrakh* (Tashkent: Uzbekistan, 1964), pp. 94, 117, 143, 168; Institut Istorii Partii, *Kommunisticheskaia partiia Turkestana i Uzbekistana v tsifrakh* (Tashkent: Uzbekistan, 1968), p. 187; Institut Istorii Partii, *Kommunisticheskaia partiia Turkmenistana v tsifrakh (1924–1974) (1925–1966)* (Ashkhabad: Turkmenistan, 1967), pp. 115, 140, 165, 188; Institut Istorii Partii, *Kommunisticheskaia partiia Turkmenistana v tsifrakh (1924–1974)* (Ashkhabad: Turkmenistan, 1975), p. 210; Institut Istorii Partii, *Kommunisticheskaia partiia Tadkhikistana v dokumentakh i tsifrakh (1924–1963gg.)* (Dushanbe: Irfon, 1965), pp. 121, 157, 215; Institut Istorii Partii, *Kommunisticheskaia partiia Tadzhikistana v tsifrakh za 50 let (1924–1974gg.)* (Dushanbe: Irfon, 1977), p. 77; Institut Istorii Partii, *Rost i regulirovanie sostava kommunisticheskoi partii Kirgizii (1918–1962gg.)* (Frunze: Kirgizskoe gosudarstvennoe izdatel'stvo, 1963), pp. 180, 212, 243, 268; Institut Istorii Partii, *Kommunisticheskaia partiia Kirgizii (1918–1973)* (Frunze: Kirgizskoe gosudarstvennoe izdatel'stvo, 1973), p. 216; Institut Istorii Partii, *Kommunisticheskaia partiia Uzbekistana v tsifrakh* (Tashkent: Uzbekistan, 1979), p. 279.

Table 3.3 *Native Secretaries of Primary Party Organizations in Uzbekistan, 1958–67*

Type of party organization	1958 Total number	1958 Number native	1958 Percent native	1961 Total number	1961 Number native	1961 Percent native	1965 Total number	1965 Number native	1965 Percent native	1967 Total number	1967 Number native	1967 Percent native
Industrial	1,446	343	23·7	1,642	489	29·8	1,833	549	30·0	2,254	726	32·2
Sovkhoz	174	111	63·8	198	139	70·2	303	210	69·3	340	238	70·0
Kolkhoz	1,277	1,215	88·1	912	796	87·3	997	880	88·3	1,015	897	88·4
Other	4,523	2,120	46·9	4,554	2,292	50·4	6,133	3,305	53·9	7,249	4,064	56·1
All secretaries	7,420	3,699	49·9	7,306	3,719	50·9	9,266	4,944	53·4	10,858	5,025	54·6

Source: Institut Istorii Partii, *Kommunisticheskaia partiia Turkestana i Uzbekistana v tsifrakh* (Tashkent: Uzbekistan, 1968), pp. 176, 184, 191, 205.

Notes: Chapter 3

This paper reflects collaborative work Jeremy R. Azrael and I carried out while we were both at the University of Chicago, and continuing discussions in the years since. Azrael reported on this theme to the Conference on The Soviet Union and the Muslim World, held by the Russian and East European Research Center, Tel Aviv University, 28–30 December 1980, and his presentation influenced the later preparation of this paper. All responsibility for the shortcomings of this paper, however, is my own.

1. Tsentral'noe Statisticheskoe Upravlenie (henceforth TsSU), *Narodnoe obrazovanie, nauka i kul'tura v SSSR* (Moscow: Statistika, 1977), p. 438. This category encompasses workers in fields of natural science and the social sciences and professions. It also includes workers in other unspecified fields. See the listing in *Narodnoe khoziaistvo Uzbeksoi SSR v 1975g* (Tashkent: Uzbekistan 1976), p. 40.
2. For the declining proportions of actual 'scientists' within this category, see the breakdown of this category shown in *Narodnoe obrazovanie, nauka i kul'tura v SSSR*, p. 301. On the increasing tendency of political elites in the USSR to acquire the formal qualifications for inclusion in this category, see A. Pravdin, 'Inside the CPSU Central Committee' (interview by Mervyn Matthews), *Survey*, vol. 20, no. 4 (Autumn 1974), pp. 94–104, but esp. p. 102.
3. TsSU, *Vysshee obrazovanie v SSSR* (Moscow: Statistika, 1961), p. 215, and *Narodnoe khoziaistvo Uzbeksoi SSR v 1975g*, p. 41.
4. Data on 'nativization' of the Central Asian scientific elite are presented in Steven L. Burg, 'Russians, natives, and Jews in the Soviet scientific elite: cadres competition in Central Asia', *Cahiers du monde russe et soviétique*, vol. 20, no. 1 (January–March 1979), pp. 43–59.
5. I. S. Puchkov and G. A. Popov, 'Sociodemographic characteristics of science personnel: part 2', *Soviet Sociology*, vol. 16, no. 4 (Spring 1978), p. 71.
6. M. Orazgel'dyev, 'Training cadres from the local population in the Central Asian Republics', *Problems of Economics*, vol. 22, no. 5 (September 1979), pp. 22–35.
7. See Burg, 'Russians, natives, and Jews'.
8. Mark Popovskii, 'Moral' sovetskogo uchenogo', *Novoe russkoe slovo* (New York), 11 June 1978.
9. Popovskii (ibid.) reports the following events as having taken place in the Institute of Zoology in Samarkand:

> The Director, an Uzbek, decided not to allow one of his Russian subordinates to defend a doctoral dissertation. The Director was outraged that he, an Uzbek, a native resident of his own republic, was still only a candidate of science and that this Russian was somehow going to become a Doctor of Science. In order not to allow this to happen, the Director ordered two of his Uzbek co-workers to steal the collection of animals which was the basis of the Russian's research and on which he was preparing his presentation for the academic council. Having found out about the planned theft, the Russian zoologists armed themselves with hunting guns and organized a round-the-clock guard at the laboratory.

This guard lasted for two months right up to the time when the academic council of the Institute would hear candidates for the doctor's degree. This case did not end in bloodletting, but it certainly could have.

10 Iu. V. Arutiunian, 'A concrete sociological study of ethnic relations', *The Soviet Review*, vol. 14, no. 2 (Summer 1973), pp. 14–15.
11 ibid., p. 16; and L. M. Drobizheva, 'Sociocultural features of the personality and ethnic attitudes (from data of a study in the Tatar ASSR)', *Soviet Sociology*, vol. 13, no. 1–2 (Summer-Fall 1974), p. 90.
12 Arutiunian, 'Concrete sociological study', p. 17.
13 ibid., p. 19; and the same author's 'A preliminary socio-ethnic study (based on data from the Tatar ASSR)', *Soviet Sociology*, vol. 11, no. 3 (Winter 1970–1), pp. 413, 416–17.
14 A. A. Susokolov, 'The influence on interethnic relations of differences in the educational levels and the number of ethnic groups in contact (based on data of the 1959 and 1970 censuses of the USSR', *The Soviet Review*, vol. 18, no. 1 (Spring 1977), pp. 31, 40, 41.
15 On participation of native cadres in the 1920s, see TsSU, *Gosudarstvennyi Apparat SSSR* (Moscow: Statizdat, 1929), pp. 54–9, but esp. table 44 (p. 59).
16 Pravdin, 'Inside the CPSU Central Committee', p. 102; and Popovskii, 'Moral' '.
17 The nativization of the republican Central Committee since the end of World War II is noted in James Critchlow, 'Nationalism in Uzbekistan in the Brezhnev era', in George W. Simmonds (ed.), *Nationalism in the USSR and Eastern Europe* (Detroit, Mich.: University of Detroit Press, 1977), p. 310. Occupants of the party secretaryships and upper-level positions in the Council of Ministers and state *apparat* since 1955 are listed in Grey Hodnett and Val Ogareff, *Leaders of the Soviet Republics, 1955–1972* (Canberra: Australian National University, 1973), pp. 381–407. See also Grey Hodnett, *Leadership in the Soviet National Republics: A Quantitative Study of Recruitment Policy* (Oakville, Ont.: Mosaic Press, 1978), pp. 101–3 (table 2.12: 'Native occupancy of leading positions by national republics, 1955–72').
18 This according to Hodnett and Ogareff, *Leaders of the Soviet Republics*; the directories of Soviet officials published by the Central Intelligence Agency since 1972; and Hodnett, *Leadership in the Soviet National Republics*, pp. 101–3.
19 John H. Miller, 'Cadres policy in nationality areas', *Soviet Studies*, vol. 29, no. 1 (January 1977), pp. 3–36.
20 See the discussion of career patterns in Hodnett, *Leadership in the Soviet National Republics*, pp. 263 ff.
21 Institut Istorii Partii, *Kommunisticheskaia partiia Kirgizii (1918–1973)* (Frunze: Kirgizskoe gosudarstvennoe izdatel'stvo, 1973), pp. 192, 234–5, 262, and *Kommunisticheskaia partiia Kirgizii v tsifrakh* (Frunze: Kirgizskoe gosudarstvennoe izdatel'stvo, 1976), p. 45.
22 Institut Istorii Partii, *Kommunisticheskaia partiia Azerbaidzhana v tsifrakh* (Baku: Azerbaidzhanskoe gosudarstvennoe izdatel'stvo, 1970), pp. 139–42, 148–51.
23 Jeremy R. Azrael, 'Prospects for political participation by Soviet Muslims in the 1980s', paper presented to the Conference on the Soviet Union and the Muslim World, held by the Russian and East European Research Center, Tel Aviv University, 28–30 December 1980.
24 *Pravda*, 5 September 1965, as translated in *Current Digest of the*

Soviet Press, vol. 17, no. 34 (15 November 1965), p. 4.
25. Popovskii, 'Moral' '.
26. 'Brezhnev's report to the Congress − II', *Current Digest of the Soviet Press*, vol. 33, no. 9 (1 April 1981), p. 6.
27. *Itogi vyborov i sostav deputatov mestnykh sovetov deputatov trudiashchikhsia 1961g*. (Moscow: Statistika, 1961), pp. 77–9, 85, 86, 88.
28. Marjorie Mandelstam Balzer, *Sovietization or Cultural Persistence?* (Cambridge, Mass.: Russian Research Center, Harvard University, January 1980), p. 12.
29. Azrael, 'Prospects', fos 3–4.
30. ibid., fo. 1.
31. See Yaacov Ro'i, 'The impact of the Islamic fundamentalist revival of the late 1970s on the Soviet view of Islam', below, pp. 149–80.
32. Azrael, 'Prospects', fo. 8.

4 Trends in the Soviet Muslim Population: Demographic Aspects

MURRAY FESHBACH

This chapter provides a statistical and analytical presentation of the trends in the population of Muslim origin of the Soviet Union (sometimes called 'Muslims' alone, without claim for their degree of religious belief), with some predictions of their number and demographic characteristics by the end of the century. The underlying data come from the three postwar censuses, current statistical publications, secondary Soviet sources, and some of my previous writings.

Not very many years ago, most estimates of the population of Muslim origin in the USSR projected a figure of about 50 million at the time of the 1979 census of population and 70–5 million by the end of the century. On the basis of the 1979 census results, it is clear that these figures are too high. None the less, despite the recent slowdown, the rise in number of Muslims during the first intercensal period of 1959–70 was more than 2·4 times the national growth rate of 1·34 percent per year, and it climbed to 2·74 times the national growth rate of 0·90 per cent per year during 1970–9. In large part, this was due to the drop in the growth rate in the number of Russians from 1·04 to 0·62 percent per year in the two periods respectively. What underlies the incredible growth differentials between the population of Muslim origin and the remainder of the Soviet population? This issue is analyzed through the discussion of nineteen tables included at the end of this chapter. Some aspects of the political policy implications are analysed by Professor Burg in this book (pages 40–62), the economic I have analysed elsewhere, and the social, which certainly is related to all of these issues, will be left for another volume.

Before commencing the detailed discussion it is important to note a data issue. The basic problem is that much of the data are available to us only for republics, and not by nationality. In some cases, therefore, the discussion will relate only to republic data because of the lack of corresponding nationality materials. Despite the fact that the republics have titular nationality titles, they contain a wide variety of nationalities, and the shares vary markedly. This chapter attempts to designate clearly the scope and coverage of each figure under discussion.

The first table, which is a ranking of thirty-eight listed nationalities in the Soviet censuses of population of 1939, 1959, 1970 and 1979, is arranged according to the Bennigsen model which he presented in 1971.[1] The prime purpose of this model was to distribute the Muslims of the USSR by language group. The basic pattern is followed with an internal ranking by size of population within each language group in 1979.

The total number of all Muslims grew between 1970 and 1979, but at a smaller rate than during the previous intercensal period, dropping to 2·47 percent per year in 1970 to 1979 compared with 3·25 percent per year in the period 1959 to 1970. Nonetheless, this rate of growth (2·47 percent) is more than four times the rate of the Russians alone, who grew by only six-tenths of a percentage point per year; and that may even be exaggerated if one is permitted to question the figures from the census. Doubts arise, in particular, from the unexpectedly low figure for the Ukrainians in the 1979 census results based on the crude birth rates for the titular republic, and the number of Jews seems too low given our information on emigration, general fertility characteristics, and expected mortality rates. Perhaps many of both groups were designated as or chose to opt for 'Russian' as documentation is not required for the census.

As expected, Table 4.1 shows that the Uzbeks are the largest single group among all Muslims and now comprise almost 30 percent of the current total number of persons of Muslim origin. Moreover, their share is growing as time passes, from 24·3 percent in 1959 to 26·2 in 1970 and to 28·5 percent in 1979. Their ranking also reinforces their standing as the leading group among all Muslims of the USSR. Although their fertility is declining, it still is not declining as fast as some of the other Muslim groups, particularly the Azeris (or Azerbaidzhanis), the Tatars and the Kazakhs.

Among the Azeris, the Tatars and the Kazakhs, there are cogent reasons for some of their decline in fertility. The Tatars are traditionally more assimilated and take on the lower fertility pattern of the surrounding Russians. The Azeris are different from the other Muslims in several ways. They are Shiite rather than Sunni, they tend to be more urban, with lower fertility, a higher educational level and more advanced general stage of development (probably because of the influence of the many Russian settlers who came to Baku in 1870 when oil was discovered). Indeed, about 25–30 percent of the total population of the republic lives in Baku, while in all the Central Asian republics the capital-city populations represent approximately only between 5 and 10 percent of the population of each republic. Thus, in Azerbaidzhan there is a different population concentration, and a different ambience of community relationships and ethnic contacts. As to the Kazakhs, the large-scale contact with Slavs in Kazakhstan very likely did have a demographic impact on them.

The second table shows the crude birth rates by republic which are projected up to the year 2000. (A report being prepared by the Foreign Demographic Analysis Division of the US Bureau of the Census will be making detailed estimates of birth rates by nationality.) We already know that in some cases this projection, made in 1977 for 1980, is too high, and there is the possibility that all the figures are too high: this situation is especially true for the Slavic republics for 1980 and beyond, the current national figure being 18·3 rather than the 19·2 as projected and shown in the table. At any event, the disparity between the figures for the Slavic republics – around 16 – and those for the Central Asian and Kazakh republics – 30 to 35 – is enormous, and this disparity will ripple throughout this chapter.

Table 4.3 is particularly interesting; it is a unique table that not only gives us data for Uzbekistan as a whole, which we normally have available to us, but it also gives us nationality data within the republic for 1959 and 1970, ranging from a low crude birth rate among Russians of 19·3 in 1970 to the high of Uzbeks of 39·2 in that year. This table is provided by O. B. Ata-Mirzaev, head of the Population Laboratory at Tashkent State University, who writes some of the best work on and analyses of the demographic situation in Central Asia, particularly Uzbekistan. Table 4.3 shows a drop in the period 1959 to 1970 in the Uzbek republic crude birth rate from 37·0 to 33·5 per 1000 population, or a 9 percentage point drop, but the Uzbek nationality rate declined by only 6 percentage points, while the Russian rate declined by 19 percentage points. Because most of the other rates dropped faster the proportion of children born to Uzbeks increased between 1959 and 1970. Since the republic-wide crude birth rate has continued to increase since 1970 (from 33·5 to 33·9 in 1978 and 34·4 in 1979), it seems likely that the birth rate among Uzbeks has *not* declined by much, if at all. Ata-Mirzaev believes that the rate will stabilize in the future and not decline as predicted by many others. He notes that only among the highly educated, highly urbanized groups is it going down even slightly; this point, I believe, will be demonstrated by some of the other material in this chapter.

Table 4.4 contains the only systematic series of nationality-related crude birth rates found in Soviet publications. The table was originally prepared by the late Dr B. Ts. Urlanis, one of the leading demographers of the Soviet Union. These data point very clearly to the differentials during the 1960s. The birth rate among the Muslim nationalities shown here is forty and over for this entire period, while the national rates were distinctly lower, and certainly the Russian, Ukrainian and Belorussian rates, let alone the Estonian and Latvian, are again lower. Undoubtedly, the Muslim rates have declined (with the possible, even probable, exception of the Tadzhiks), but the gap remains at three, four and five times depending on the measure used.

One vital question relates to the impact of all of these figures on the size of the population, which then leads to the question of demand for housing investment policies, labor supplies, educational facilities, regional differentials, and so forth. In part the changing structure and dynamics of the population are shown in Table 4.5, which demonstrates the consequence of these regional differentials. The table provides estimates and projections of the population aged 0 to 9 by the end of the century by republic groupings. The year 1970 is used as a reference point, and then two different projections are provided for the year 2000. Thus, if the rates prevailing in the period 1975–7 were to remain constant throughout the remaining years of the century, then the six Muslim republics of Central Asia, Kazakhstan and Azerbaidzhan would have a population 0 to 9 years of age, about 50 percent greater than the number in the RSFSR in the year 2000 (assuming no large-scale migration in the interval). But we know that the rates will not remain constant because of declines in age-specific fertility rates since 1975. The projection is given here only as a basis for comparison. The medium series shows a drop to 16,539,000, or 85 percent of the 19,641,000 projected for the RSFSR. (The latter figure for the RSFSR also may not hold given recent crude-birth-rate information in comparison with that available at the time of the projection: March 1977.) However, a figure of at least 85 percent is a remarkable increase from 52 percent in 1970 (11,105,000 divided by 21,297,000); the population of 0–9-year-olds by the year 2000 will be the labor force, armed forces and parents, etc., of twenty or so years later.

Table 4.6 provides data on the age distribution of the Soviet population. These data are given by nationality rather than by republic. Unfortunately, these data are available only for 1970, never having been published for the 1959 census date. As yet (1 April 1982), not a single age datum has been published from the 1979 census. If we take the publication patterns of the 1959 and 1970 censuses, at least a minimal set of age data for the population as a whole should have been published by this time; it is hoped that this pattern does not portend the non-publication of all age data, especially age by nationality. According to Table 4.6, the very young population group of 0 to 10 years of age represented 37 to 40 percent of the population of Central Asian and Kazakh nationalities in 1970, whereas among the Slavic populations it was less than 20 percent in every case. Thus, even in 1970, the number of children 0 to 10 among the Muslim nationality groups was more than twice as much as among the Slavs. Knowing the differential birth rates, we can expect that this gap has grown even more, again reinforcing the differentials for the future. Among all the Central Asian nationalities, young persons under 16 years of age comprised around 50 percent of their respective populations, while among the Slavic nationalities the 50-percent margin was not reached until the 30–39-year-old group for the three nationalities.

Table 4.7 contains information on the other side of the demographic balance, the death rates. Again, we lack data on nationality-related measures. Nonetheless, the crude death rates in part must reflect the differential age structures of populations in the republics which in turn reflect the underlying nationality fertility patterns. The difference between the northern tier and the southern tier of the Soviet Union is also demonstrated in the data of this table. Other issues such as male mortality rates due to alcoholism, especially in the Slavic and Baltic republics, may also underlie the higher crude death rates in these republics, and infant mortality rates, especially in the Central Asian republics, may have contributed to the increase in overall death rates.

It should also be noted that the 1980 figures shown in the table are based on a projection made in 1977 and are already somewhat out of date. The rate of 9.8 for the country as a whole in 1980 is too low given the figure of 10.3 per 1000 population officially reported for 1980 in the latest Soviet statistical yearbook.[2] However, since the later years are also the product of the 1977 projection, the figures have been left unchanged. None the less, according to the table, the northern republics of the RSFSR, Ukraine and Belorussia will show an increase in crude death rates from an average of 8·40 per 1000 in 1970 to 11·43 in 2000, while the crude death rates of the southern republics of the Transcaucasus, Kazakhstan and Central Asia will increase only slightly from 6·38 in 1970 to 6·80 in the year 2000. Thus, the differential in the death rates will increase by more than two times from 2·02 in 1970 to 4·63 in the year 2000 (8·40–6·38 and 11·43–6·80, respectively), and will add to the disparity in net growth rates.

The next two Tables (4.8 and 4.9) on infant mortality rates are interrelated and must be discussed simultaneously. Unfortunately, the Soviets have decided that the figures are not to be published for any year after 1974. In 1950, the infant mortality rates were 81 per 1000 live births, and declined remarkably to one-quarter of that level, to 22·9 deaths per 1000 live births by 1971. However, in 1972, 1973 and 1974 the figures increased remarkably by about 20 percent. Then, as noted above, publication of these figures ceased. According to the estimates prepared by Dr Christopher Davis and myself in a report issued by the US Bureau of the Census (*Rising Infant Mortality in the USSR in the 1970s*, Washington, DC, June 1980), it was determined that the current mortality rate is about 35 or 36, according to Soviet criteria. The Soviet definition omits children of less than twenty-eight weeks' gestation, less than 1000 grams in weight and less than thirty-five centimeters in length who die in their first week of life. Based on our calculations, the adjusted figure for the USSR should be 39–40 (US definition), or more than three times the infant mortality rate of the United States in 1979. With infant mortality being stated universally as being a prime indicator of the quality of health delivery in a country, the Soviet situation needs much more examination and analysis.

As I have noted earlier, the crude death rates in the southern tier are much lower than those of the Slavic republics. However, when we look at one major component of the deaths in a given year, that of children aged 0–1 per 1000 live births, the inverse is true. Thus, as far as we can tell, the Muslim republics have infant mortality rates which are much higher than those of the Slavic republics. As I have also stated earlier, the Soviet Central Statistical Administration has failed to publish estimates on these rates for any year since 1974. For some republics, especially those in which the rates are undoubtedly higher than the national average (see Table 4.8), figures have not been published for any year since 1967, while for Turkmenistan and Moldavia no figures have been published at all in the postwar period. However, from data on the capital cities of the republics (Table 4.9) we can see that the disparities are enormous and the situation very worrisome for the public health authorities. Thus, in 1974, when the national infant mortality rate was 27·9, Dushanbe, the capital of Tadzhikistan, demonstrated the highest rate of all, a rate of 51·8 per 1000, and Minsk, the capital of Belorussia, the lowest at 15·8, less than one-third the rate recorded for Dushanbe. If the capital city of one of these Central Asian republics has such an alarming rate, what could it be in the rural areas where the rates must be distinctly higher? That all of these rates are higher now than in 1974 is predicated in part on the trend in the national crude death rates overall.

Table 4.10 provides a summary format of the balance of birth rates minus death rates for all the republics. The major differences in births result in significant gaps in net increases in the natural increase rates of each republic (the differences in infant mortality rates do not affect the total sufficiently to change the patterns in natural increase, emanating from the overall birth and death rates; nor does the emigration level of Jews, Germans, Armenians, and other scattered peoples). Thus, the natural increase rate for Uzbekistan of 21·1 per 1000 population in the year 2000 is over fourteen times as large as the 1·5 per 1000 projected for the RSFSR in the same year. While the base populations to which these rates apply are very different in size, the implications for the future beyond the year 2000 are fascinating to contemplate, especially the growth in the number of children below the age of 10 in the Muslim republics referred to earlier.

Assuming that the crude birth rate of the population of Muslim origin in Uzbekistan will decline more than estimated here, and that the crude birth rate will increase in the RSFSR, then the differential in natural increase might be reduced to only ten times – still a very large difference. However, the current base populations of 15 and 140 millions in Uzbekistan and the RSFSR, respectively, are very different also and it will take many years for the number to draw very close. However, as will be described below, many Muslims reside in the RSFSR, and this is a fact which was not appreciated earlier.

Table 4.11 gives additional information on the fertility issue by use of data on average family size from the three postwar censuses. The averages shown here for total populations and the urban and rural populations are a measure of fertility trends throughout the period. While average family size may also reflect traditional differences regarding nuclear and extended families, the trends and gaps in size also must be based on differential fertility patterns. The salient features of Table 4.11 are the steady reduction of the average family size in the Slavic republics and the continual increase in three of the four Central Asian republics, and no reduction in the fourth (Kirgizia) after an increase in Kirgizia between 1959 and 1970. Thus, the difference between north and south becomes eminently clear, with the three Slavic republics declining in average family size from 3·6 in 1959 to 3·5 in 1970 and to 3·3 in 1979; in contrast, in Uzbekistan, the average moves from 4·6 to 5·3 to 5·5, and continues to increase.

Table 4.12 provides further details on family size by concentrating on the share of large families by republic and by nationality. The latter nationality data come from both 1959 and 1970 censuses, but the data from 1959 are suspect because they are inconsistent with other information on fertility or with the 1970 results, especially for four republics (Azerbaidzhan, Kazakhstan, Kirgizia and Tadzhikistan). Again as in Table 4.11, there has been the expected decline in the Slavic republics, and a surprisingly large increase in the four Central Asian republics. Moreover, when we utilize the data for nationalities in 1970 and 1979, the proportion of families with seven or more members turns out to be much smaller for Russians alone than for the RSFSR as a whole, whereas the proportion of such families in the Central Asian republics — and Kazakhstan — is at least 50 percent larger for the titular nationality than for each republic as a whole. How much the republic and nationality shares represent traditional extended families as opposed to fertility alone is not clear, but the upward trends in these republics undoubtedly must be based on underlying fertility patterns which are remarkable for their persistence.

If the data in the preceding table give the case for the past, what of the future? Table 4.13 largely demonstrates expected differences by providing data on individual nationality expectations of fertility. These data came from a national survey of 347,314 women aged 18 to 59 conducted by the Central Statistical Administration of the USSR in 1972. It shows that Slavic women expect to bear about one-third the number of children that the Central Asian women gave in their response. Expectations of giving birth to six or more children demonstrate the disparity even more, that is, 1 percent of Slavic women as contrasted to over 50 percent of the Central Asian women (excluding Kazakhs). Not all the infants born to these women will survive, owing to the infant mortality phenomenon, and this may be a contributor to the natural compensation for the wastage based on high child mortality in these regions.

One technique the Soviet central authorities have applied in their attempt to resolve the demographic problem of differential growth rates, in addition to relieving labor-deficit regions of their persistent shortages, is to encourage Muslim migration to other regions of the country. If they were to move, these Muslims might adopt local customs, intermarry, and therefore have a different – i.e. lower – fertility behavior. In other words, before they become 'sovietized' they must move out of the south. However, as Table 4.14 shows, they are just not moving at all out of the region. In 1979, out of the national total of 12,456,000 Uzbeks, there were only 91,000 residing outside Central Asia and Kazakhstan; this small number represents only seven-tenths of 1 percent of the total number of Uzbeks in the country. Over the entire two decades, 1959 to 1979, there were only 49,000 more Uzbeks outside the region than at the beginning of the period. Let us assume for the moment, as unrealistic as is the proposition, that none of this increment of 49,000 was due to births among those living outside the area during the entire twenty years, in other words, that all of this increment related only to outmigrants from the south. Even then the resulting average of 2,450 Uzbek migrants per year is minuscule in the extreme especially when considering that the entire Uzbek population grew by over 320,000 per year over the same period.

The table also shows that for four of the five nationalities the proportion resident in their native region either remained at the same level or grew. As to the Kirgiz, their residency ratio dropped by only 0·4 percentage point of the 99·4 percent resident in 1959 over the entire period 1959 to 1979.

A large number of Kazakhs reside outside the boundaries of the five republics, but the impact of this seemingly large number is much reduced if we include the population residing in the five *oblasts* of the RSFSR contiguous to Kazakhstan – the Astrakhan, Omsk, Orenburg, Saratov, and Volgograd *oblasts* – part of the traditional Kazakh pasturelands of the Southern Steppe. In 1970, 69·4 percent of the 477,800 Kazakhs in the RSFSR lived in these five *oblasts*, and in 1979 the share was 70·4 percent of the 518,060. If we add these areas to Central Asia and Kazakhstan, the proportion of Soviet Muslims in the region rises to 98·5 percent in 1970 (compared with 97·3 percent). These data confirm the reluctance of Soviet Muslims to move away from their traditional homelands, despite the fact that the government and party have tried to encourage laborers to leave the region.

The small changes in the rural populations in each of the republics according to the 1959 and 1970 censuses also show the reluctance of Soviet Muslims of Central Asia and Kazakhstan to move to cities (Table 4.15). This reluctance is partly due to the predominance of Russians in many cities as well as to the Muslims' large family size which retards movement to crowded cities in their own area, let alone to those in cold northern areas. Economic problems such as lack of housing and consumer goods also deter these Muslims from moving to labor-deficit areas in Siberia and the Far East.

The rural share of the titular nationalities within their own republics dropped very little between 1959 and 1970; that of the Kazakhs and Uzbeks dropped by less than 3 percentage points, of the Kirgiz by 3·5 points, and of the Tadzhiks and Turkmens by 5–6 points. Given indications of little migration to cities in the intercensal period between 1970 and 1979 and the number of births in rural areas according to the early 1979 census results, I do not expect a large change in this picture between 1970 and 1979 when the 1979 census data are released in fuller form.

Information on the share of the urban population by republic given in Table 4.16 shows a similar north–south dichotomy. In contrast to the increase of 14–17 percentage points in the urban shares of the USSR and RSFSR populations, respectively, the average increase among the Central Asian republics and Kazakhstan was 5·4 percentage points over the same twenty-year period. In Tadzhikistan the urban share of the population actually *decreased* during the last intercensal period owing to the continuation of high fertility and little migration to the cities.

From a projection prepared in the spring of 1977 (Table 4.17), it is apparent that a relative shift of the population will occur toward the south of the USSR – again assuming no massive shifts of the population through voluntary migration. Thus, the Slavic republics are expected to decline from 82 percent of the total population of the USSR in 1950 to 69 percent at the end of the century. Simultaneously, the southern republics of the Transcaucasus, Kazakhstan and Central Asia are expected to increase from 14 percent to 27 percent in 1950 and 2000, respectively.

Table 4.18 projects the population of Muslim origin until the year 2000. It provides ample evidence of their rapid growth. The table is based on a detailed tabulation of all Muslim nationalities residing in each of the designated regions or republics. Thus, while the 10 million or so persons of Muslim origin in the RSFSR represent a declining share of all Muslims owing to the continuing drop in fertility among the Tatars, the RSFSR in 1979 represents (an astonishing) one-quarter of the total number of all Muslims in the USSR.

In order to project the Muslim population until the year 2000, two separate projections were made, the first based on the rate of increase, the second on the absolute increase during the last intercensal period of 1970 to 1979. The entire period of 1959 to 1979 was not used because there has been a distinct slowdown in the overall rate of increase as well as in the relative increments for individual nationalities comprising the separate regions and republics. Thus, based on projection A, the result in the year 2000 would be an undoubtedly too high figure of 75 million persons, or one out of every four Soviet citizens. While many in the West, including myself, had projected such a high figure in the past based on the 1959–70 trend, based on present evidence this number undoubtedly will not be reached. Moreover, the figure of 75, and others up to 100, million were based on higher projections of the total population. For example, until quite recently even the Central Statistical Administration of the USSR was projecting a figure of 340–50 million for the year 2000. Projections by the Foreign Demographic Analysis Division of the US Census Bureau made subsequent to the data on which the Soviet figure was based were of 312 and 309 million, depending on the date of the projection, both of which figures are higher than the current expectation of 300–302 million persons for the entire Soviet Union.

On the basis of the alternative projection which uses the annual average absolute increase in each administrative unit, the total number of people of Muslim origin by the end of the century is a seemingly more reasonable figure of 64 million persons. The regional distribution of Muslims themselves changes slightly with somewhat less emphasis accorded to the Muslims residing in Central Asia and Kazakhstan, and more to those in the RSFSR. Regardless of the precise distribution within the total, the total number of all persons of Muslim origin represents somewhat over one of every five Soviet citizens projected for the end of the century. This figure for the year 2000 is a significant increase from one of every seven in 1970 and underlies much of the political, migration, investment, language and other issues being addressed in the USSR and discussed in the West.

Table 4.19 consolidates the calculations of the growth of Muslims with those for the total USSR, total Slavic (Russians, Ukrainians and Belorussians) and Russian populations. The figures for 1970 and 1979 are reported, or are based on reported figures, whereas those for the total population, the Slavs, and the figure for Russians in the year 2000 are based on the information furnished by the first Soviet scholar to publish absolute estimates for the Soviet population by nationality at the end of the century.[3] The Russian figure in Table 4.19 is derived from a percent relationship with the total population. The figures for the Muslims are from Table 4.18.

We can readily see the slowdown in the total population, as well as the Slavic and Russian growth in absolute and in relative terms, the Russian population growing according to this information by only one-tenth of 1 percent per year in the period 1979–2000! In contrast, the Muslim population will grow by 2·57 percent or 1·80 percent per year depending on the assumption adopted – a growth of 3 million Russians and 31 or 20 million Muslims, in absolute terms. In the former case, it is striking that the estimate shown in Table 4.18 for Central Asia and Kazakhstan using the annual average *rate* of increase is equal to that projected by M. B. Tatimov, the Kazakh demographer who published the nationality figures cited above (see source, Table 4.19). Even if we were to assume the lower figures, resulting from the use of an absolute average number of additions per year (as shown to be preferable earlier), the rates of increase are still many, many times higher than that for the Slavs or Russians alone.

The implications of all of the above for the Soviet central authorities relate to changing shares, the reduction in the number of young children, labor-force distribution, and so forth. Thus, it is no wonder that Brezhnev referred to the need for an 'effective demographic policy' which he did not spell out at the time of the 1976 Twenty-Fifth Party Congress. Undoubtedly, it related to increasing the birth rate among the Slavs, reducing mortality, encouraging migration, enhancing the prestige of the family, improving the Russian-language ability of the Muslim population in order to make it more mobile, and so forth.

The 'Basic Directions' of the Eleventh Five-Year Plan, released in December 1980, confirmed that such concern was growing among the leadership. To wit, they specified that the population policy of the Soviet government included issues related to family formation, maternity and labor-force participation of women, child care and invalid maintenance, life expectancy, and health status of the population.[4] However, how to carry out these policies, and whether to administer them uniformly or on a regional basis remained open to dispute in the Soviet Union. How to encourage fertility in the Slavic republics without simultaneously expanding the fertility of Muslim women was but one issue in this dispute between Urlanis and G. I. Litvinova, on the one hand, and E. L. Manevich and Tatimov, on the other.[5] Tatimov has written that any differentiated policy would in fact be a 'discriminatory policy' and that the Muslims would therefore be treated as less than equal. It remains to be seen how this and other matters which are viewed by the Russian leadership as a demographic threat from within will be treated. A decision seems to have been made since December 1980. A report on the Twenty-Sixth Party Congress, held in February–March 1981, revealed that the leadership had indeed opted to differentiate between republics and regions. Some of the details of its definition of a demographic policy were elaborated at the Congress itself and in the implementing legislation thereafter. The legislation, in particular, confirmed the leadership's concern about the population problem and especially its regional dimensions.

Table 4.1 *The Muslim Population of the Soviet Union by Nationality and Language Group: 1939, 1959, 1970 and 1979 (Ranked by Size in 1979 within Each Language Group)*

Language group and nationality	Absolute numbers				Percentages				
	1939 (1)	1959 (2)	1970 (3)	1979 (4)	Annual rate of change between 1959 and 1979 (5)	Annual rate of change between 1970 and 1979 (6)	Of all Muslims		
							1959 (7)	1970 (8)	1979 (9)
TOTAL	20,669,000	24,738,462	35,158,288	43,772,000	3·25	2·47	100·0	100·0	100·0
Turkic	17,601,400	21,104,170	29,922,808	37,203,000	3·23	2·45	85·3	85·1	85·0
Uzbek	4,844,000	6,015,416	9,195,093	12,456,000	3·93	3·43	24·3	26·2	28·5
Kazakh	3,099,000	3,621,610	5,298,818	6,556,000	3·52	2·39	14·6	15·1	15·0
Tatar	4,300,000	4,967,701	5,930,670	6,317,000	1·62	0·70	20·1	16·9	14·4
Azeri	2,275,000	2,939,728	4,369,917	5,477,000	3·69	2·52	11·9	12·5	13·5
Turkmen	812,000	1,001,585	1,525,284	2,028,000	3·90	3·22	4·0	4·3	4·6
Kirgiz	884,000	968,659	1,452,292	1,906,000	3·75	3·07	3·9	4·1	4·4
Bashkir	843,000	989,040	1,239,081	1,371,000	2·08	1·13	4·0	3·5	3·1
Karakalpak	184,000	172,556	236,009	303,000	2·89	2·82	0·7	0·7	0·7
Kumyk	95,000	134,967	188,792	228,000	3·10	2·12	0·5	0·5	0·5
Uigur	109,000	95,208	173,276	211,000	5·60	2·21	0·4	0·5	0·5
Karachai	76,000	81,403	112,741	131,000	3·01	1·68	0·3	0·3	0·3
Turks	(NA)	35,304	79,000	93,000	7·60	1·83	0·1	0·2	0·2
Balkat	42,600	42,408	59,501	66,000	3·13	1·16	0·2	0·2	0·2
Nogai	36,000	38,583	51,784	60,000	2·71	1·65	0·2	0·1	0·1
Iranian	1,697,000	1,910,256	2,774,228	3,609,000	3·45	2·97	7·7	7·9	8·3
Tadzhik	1,229,000	1,396,939	2,135,883	2,898,000	3·94	3·45	5·6	6·1	6·6
Osset	354,000	412,592	488,039	542,000	1·54	1·17	1·7	1·4	1·2
Kurds	46,000	58,799	88,980	116,000	3·83	3·00	0·2	0·3	0·3
Iranian (Persian)	39,000	20,766	27,501	31,000	2·59	1·34	0·1	0·1	0·1
Tat	29,000	11,463	17,109	22,000	3·71	2·88	(−)	(−)	0·1

Table 4.1 (continued) *The Muslim Population of the Soviet Union by Nationality and Language Group: 1939, 1959, 1970 and 1979 (Ranked by Size in 1979 within Each Language Group)*

Language group and nationality	Absolute numbers				Percentages		Of all Muslims		
	1939 (1)	1959 (2)	1970 (3)	1979 (4)	Annual rate of change between 1959 and 1979 (5)	Annual rate of change between 1970 and 1979 (6)	1959 (7)	1970 (8)	1979 (9)
Baluchi	(NA)	7,842	12,582	(NA)	4·39	(X)	(—)	(—)	(NA)
Afghan	(NA)	1,855	4,184	(NA)	7·68	(X)	(—)	(—)	(NA)
Caucasian	1,343,800	1,694,121	2,422,608	2,908,000	3·31	2·05	6·8	6·9	6·6
Chechen	408,000	418,756	612,674	756,000	3·52	2·36	1·7	1·7	1·7
Avar (D)	167,000[1]	270,394	396,297	483,000	3·54	2·22	1·1	1·1	1·1
Lezgin (D)	134,000[1]	223,129	323,829	383,000	3·44	1·86	0·9	0·9	0·9
Kabardian	164,000	203,620	279,928	322,000	2·94	1·57	0·8	0·8	0·7
Dargin (D)	126,000	158,149	230,000	287,000	3·50	2·45	0·6	0·7	0·7
Ingush	92,000	105,980	157,605	186,000	3·67	1·86	0·4	0·4	0·4
Adygian	88,000	79,631	99,855	109,000	2·08	0·98	0·3	0·3	0·2
Lak (D)	40,000	63,529	85,822	100,000	2·77	1·71	0·3	0·2	0·2
Abkhazian	59,000	65,480	83,240	91,000	2·21	1·00	0·3	0·2	0·2
Tabasaran (D)	28,000[2]	34,700	55,183	75,000	4·31	3·47	0·1	0·2	0·2
Circassian		30,453	39,745	46,000	2·46	1·63	0·1	0·1	0·1
Abazinian	14,000	19,591	25,448	29,000	2·41	1·46	0·1	0·1	(—)
Rutul (D)	13,000	6,732	12,071	15,000	5·45	2·44	(—)	(—)	(—)
Tsakhar (D)	3,300	7,321	11,103	14,000	3·86	2·61	(—)	(—)	(—)
Agul (D)	7,500	6,706	8,831	12,000	2·53	3·47	(—)	(—)	(—)
Sino-Tibetan	4,600	21,928	38,644	52,000	5·29	3·35	0·1	0·1	0·1
Dungan	4,600	21,928	38,644	52,000	5·29	3·35	0·1	0·1	0·1
Semitic	22,000	7,987	(NA)	(NA)	(NA)	(NA)	(NA)	(NA)	(NA)
Arab	22,000	7,987	(NA)	(NA)	(NA)	(NA)	(NA)	(NA)	(NA)

Notes to Table 4.1

(NA) = Not available   (X) = Not applicable   (–) = Negligible

Notes

All Ossetians and Abkhazians are included with the Muslim population, although some are Orthodox. Chuvash and gypsies, on the other hand, are excluded, although some are Muslims. The eight Caucasian nationalities marked with a (D) are the Peoples of Dagestan sometimes shown as a special sub-group.

1 1926.
2 Included in Adygian.

Sources

1939 Murray Feshbach, 'Prospects for outmigration from Central Asia and Kazakhstan in the next decade', in United States Congress, Joint Economic Committee, *Soviet Economy in a Time of Change* (Washington, DC: United States Government Printing Office, 1979), p. 693.

1959–79 Stephen Rapawy, 'Census data on nationality composition and language characteristics of the Soviet population: 1959, 1970 and 1979', unpublished paper of the Foreign Demographic Analysis Division, United States Bureau of the Census, May 1980, Table 1.

Table 4.2 *Estimated and Projected Crude Birth Rates, USSR and by Republic: 1950–2000 (Rates per 1,000 Population)*

	1950	1960	1970	1980	1990	2000
USSR	26·7	24·9	17·4	19·2	17·3	16·1
RSFSR	26·1	23·2	14·6	16·6	14·1	13·8
Ukraine	22·8	20·5	15·2	15·6	14·0	13·6
Belorussia	25·5	24·4	16·2	17·3	15·4	13·7
Moldavia	38·9	29·3	19·4	21·3	17·9	16·0
Estonia	18·4	16·6	15·8	14·6	13·7	13·7
Latvia	17·0	16·7	14·5	13·9	13·3	13·3
Lithuania	23·6	22·5	17·6	16·1	15·5	14·0
Armenia	32·1	40·1	22·1	24·4	19·9	16·3
Azerbaidzhan	31·2	42·6	29·2	27·6	26·6	19·8
Georgia	23·5	24·7	19·2	19·2	17·3	15·3
Kazakhstan	37·6	37·2	23·4	24·8	21·5	17·6
Kirgizia	32·4	36·9	30·5	31·5	28·1	23·2
Tadzhikistan	30·4	33·5	34·8	36·9	33·1	26·6
Turkmenistan	38·2	42·4	35·2	35·0	32·1	26·2
Uzbekistan	30·8	39·8	33·6	35·6	32·2	26·6

Source: Godfrey S. Baldwin, *Population Projections by Age and Sex: For the Republics and Major Economic Regions of the USSR, 1970 to 2000,* Series P-91, no. 26 (Washington, DC: United States Government Printing Office, September 1979), pp. 13–14, 25–7.

Table 4.3 *Number, Crude Birth Rate, and Share of Children Born in Uzbekistan, by Nationality: 1959–70*

Nationality	Number (percent) 1959	Number (percent) 1970	Crude birth rate (per 1,000 population) 1959	Crude birth rate (per 1,000 population) 1970	Share of children born (percent) 1959	Share of children born (percent) 1970
TOTAL	100·0	100·0	37·0	33·5	100·0	100·0
Uzbeks	62·1	68·5	41·7	39·2	68·9	74·4
Kazakhs	4·2	4·0	34·3	36·9	3·9	4·3
Tadzhiks	3·8	3·8	38·2	34·3	3·9	3·8
Karakalpaks	2·1	2·0	39·1	33·5	2·2	1·9
Kirgiz	1·1	0·9	24·4	31·6	0·6	0·9
Turkmen	0·7	0·6	32·1	32·8	0·6	0·6
Russians	13·5	12·5	23·7	19·3	8·3	7·0
Ukrainians	1·1	0·9	26·0	23·0	0·7	0·6
Belorussians	0·1	0·15	34·4	25·1	0·1	0·1
Others	11·3	9·65	36·0	22·8	10·8	6·4

Source: O. Ata-Mirzaev and B. Gol'dfarb, 'Perspektivy vosproizvodstva naseleniia Srednei Azii', in D. I. Valentei (ed.), *Nashe budushchee glazami demografa* (Moscow: Statistika, no. 26, 1979), p. 117.

Table 4.4 *Average Crude Birth Rate (CBR), by Nationality: 1959–69 (per 1,000 Population)*

Nationality	CBR	Nationality	CBR
Slavic nationalities		*Transcaucasian nationalities*	
Russians	19·0	Armenians	28·4
Ukrainians	15·8	Azeris	43·7
Belorussians	19·2	Georgians	24·0
Moldavian nationality			
Moldavians	24·8		
Baltic nationalities		*Central Asian nationalities and Kazakhs*	
Estonians	12·3	Kazakhs	41·2
Latvians	12·3	Kirgiz	44·0
Lithuanians	20·6	Tadzhiks	45·2
		Turkmen	45·6
		Uzbeks	45·2

Source: B. Ts. Urlanis, *Problemy dinamiki naseleniia SSSR* (Moscow: Nauka, 1974), p. 132.

Table 4.5 Estimates and Projection of the Population Aged 0–9, USSR and by Republic, 1970 and 2000

USSR and republic	1970 Number	1970 Percent distribution	2000 Medium series Number	2000 Medium series Percent distribution	2000 Constant series Number	2000 Constant series Percent distribution
USSR	45,021	100.0	48,037	100.0	50,348	100.0
RSFSR	21,297	47.3	19,461	40.5	17,462	34.7
Central Asia, Kazakhstan and Azerbaidzhan	11,105	24.7	16,539	34.4	25,836	51.3
Central Asia and Kazakhstan	9,549	21.2	14,654	30.5	23,476	46.6
Kazakhstan	3,288	7.3	3,678	7.7	4,470	8.9
Kirgizia	844	1.9	1,284	2.7	1,654	3.3
Tadzhikistan	973	2.2	1,698	3.5	2,373	4.7
Turkmenistan	689	1.5	1,195	2.5	1,595	3.2
Uzbekistan	3,755	8.3	6,799	14.2	8,914	1.8
Transcaucasus	3,146	7.0	3,515	7.3	4,109	8.2
Of which: Azerbaidzhan	1,556	3.5	1,885	3.9	2,360	4.7

Note: The medium series implies a modest 6 percent decline in fertility over the projection period, which is reasonable considering the trend in recent years. The constant series for the country as a whole assumes that fertility will remain at the level estimated for 1975 throughout the projection period. Only one assumption was made about the future course of mortality, namely that it will decrease at a modest rate throughout the projection period. It was arbitrarily assumed that the decline in mortality would be equivalent to an increase of 2·5 years in life expectancy at birth between 1975 and 2000.

Source: Based on Godfrey S. Baldwin, *Population Projections by Age and Sex: For the Republics and Major Economic Regions of the USSR, 1970 to 2000*, Series P-91, no. 26 (Washington, DC: United States Government Printing Office, September 1979), pp. 91–2, 112, 114, and 117–21.

Table 4.6 Age Distribution, by Nationality, 15 January 1970

Nationality	Total	0–10	11–15	16–19	20–9	30–9	40–9	50–9	60 and over	Not distributed by age
Russians	129,015,140	23,429,675	12,962,024	9,659,595	17,079,960	20,892,773	17,827,807	12,086,310	14,964,868	—
Ukrainians	40,753,246	7,066,001	3,425,130	2,562,407	5,365,872	6,510,874	5,832,705	4,143,772	5,794,802	—
Belorussians	9,051,755	1,738,773	873,827	575,955	1,166,065	1,595,896	1,204,831	727,520	1,165,193	—
Moldavians	2,697,994	617,864	297,277	194,510	316,655	357,552	298,910	204,981	247,722	162,523
Estonians	1,007,356	147,974	65,920	48,043	124,304	134,265	119,501	102,296	197,604	68,079
Latvians	1,429,844	215,689	94,056	64,234	179,944	202,149	170,654	133,817	295,966	73,335
Lithuanians	2,664,944	533,641	225,718	147,856	361,241	390,666	323,564	204,964	396,445	80,849
Armenians	3,559,151	895,936	418,308	251,545	383,917	522,356	382,454	197,892	325,484	181,259
Azeris	4,379,937	1,614,294	580,751	295,277	418,593	601,031	322,288	174,170	292,354	81,179
Georgians	3,245,300	695,604	307,697	206,645	394,323	503,117	392,484	248,548	382,265	114,617
Kazakhs	5,298,818	1,939,130	661,823	379,460	609,154	528,458	378,680	250,391	477,447	74,275
Kirgiz	1,452,222	565,707	186,140	97,668	131,426	159,028	110,053	51,631	123,118	27,451
Tadzhiks	2,135,883	852,301	264,021	140,830	212,368	241,345	155,220	85,463	156,794	27,541
Turkmen	1,525,284	585,914	192,930	102,094	147,103	164,295	114,046	71,046	101,051	46,805
Uzbeks	9,195,093	3,553,570	1,183,250	643,961	903,717	995,826	661,752	377,047	756,269	119,711

Percentage distribution									
Russians	100·00	18·16	10·05	7·49	13·24	16·19	13·82	9·37	11·60	—
Ukrainians	100·00	17·34	8·40	6·29	13·17	15·98	14·31	10·17	14·22	—
Belorussians	100·00	19·21	9·65	6·36	12·88	17·63	13·31	8·04	12·87	—
Moldavians	100·00	22·90	11·02	7·21	11·74	13·25	11·08	7·60	9·18	6·02
Estonians	100·00	14·69	6·54	4·77	12·34	13·33	11·86	10·15	19·62	6·76
Latvians	100·00	15·08	6·58	4·49	12·58	14·14	11·94	9·36	20·70	5·13
Lithuanians	100·00	20·02	8·47	5·55	13·56	14·66	12·14	7·69	14·88	3·03
Armenians	100·00	25·17	11·75	7·07	10·79	14·68	10·75	5·56	9·14	5·09
Azeris	100·00	36·86	13·26	6·74	9·56	13·72	7·36	3·98	6·67	1·85
Georgians	100·00	21·43	9·48	6·37	12·15	15·50	12·09	7·66	11·78	3·53
Kazakhs	100·00	36·60	12·49	7·16	11·50	9·97	7·15	4·73	9·00	1·40
Kirgiz	100·00	38·95	12·82	6·73	9·05	10·95	7·58	3·56	8·48	1·89
Tadzhiks	100·00	39·90	12·36	6·59	9·94	11·30	7·27	4·00	7·34	1·29
Turkmen	100·00	38·41	12·65	6·69	9·64	10·77	7·48	4·66	6·63	3·07
Uzbeks	100·00	38·65	12·87	7·00	9·83	10·83	7·20	4·10	8·22	1·30

Note: The distribution by age for Russians, Ukrainians and Belorussians includes all persons of these nationalities in all republics of the USSR. All other nationality data by age are shown only for residents of the titular republics and 'other territories of principal residence'. In all, these data cover 100 percent of the three Slavic nationalities and 93–9 percent of the remaining twelve nationalities. Approximately 10 percent of the total Soviet population belonging to the remaining hundred-odd nationalities are not given here.

Source: TsSU SSSR (Central Statistical Administration of the USSR), *Itogi Vsesoiuznoi perepisi naseleniia 1970 goda*, Vol. IV (Moscow: Statistika, 1973), pp. 360–4.

Table 4.7 *Estimated and Projected Crude Death Rates, USSR and by Republic, 1950–2000 (Rates per 1,000 Population)*

USSR and republic	1950	1960	1970	1980	1990	2000
USSR	9·7	7·1	8·2	9·8	10·2	10·6
RSFSR	10·1	7·4	8·7	10·5	11·4	12·3
Ukraine	8·5	6·9	8·9	10·6	11·5	12·1
Belorussia	8·0	6·6	7·6	8·9	9·2	9·9
Moldavia	11·2	6·4	7·4	9·6	10·0	10·5
Estonia	14·4	10·5	11·1	11·9	12·2	12·7
Latvia	12·4	10·0	11·2	12·5	12·8	13·4
Lithuania	12·0	7·8	8·9	9·8	9·7	10·3
Armenia	8·5	6·8	5·1	5·6	5·5	6·2
Azerbaidzhan	9·6	6·7	6·7	6·9	6·6	6·5
Georgia	7·6	6·5	7·3	8·2	8·4	8·9
Kazakhstan	11·7	6·6	6·0	7·2	7·3	7·6
Kirgizia	8·5	6·1	7·4	7·8	7·1	6·9
Tadzhikistan	8·2	5·1	6·4	7·7	6·9	6·4
Turkmenistan	10·2	6·5	6·6	7·6	7·0	6·5
Uzbekistan	8·7	6·0	5·5	6·9	5·9	5·4

Source: Godfrey S. Baldwin, *Population Projections by Age and Sex: For the Republics and Major Economic Regions of the USSR, 1970 to 2000,* Series P-91, no. 26 (Washington DC: United States Government Printing Office, September 1979), pp. 13–14, 25–57.

Table 4.8 *Infant Mortality Rates, USSR and by Republic, 1958–74 (Number of Deaths per 1,000 Live Births)*

USSR and republic	1958	1960	1965	1970	1974
USSR	40·6	35·3	27·2	24·7	27·9
Slavic republics					
RSFSR	41·0	37·0	27·0	23·0	23·0
Ukraine	38·0	30·0	20·5	17·3	(NA)
Belorussia	(NA)	34·9[1]	23·1[1]	19·0	17·0
Baltic republics					
Estonia	39·9	31·2	20·2	17·8	17·6
Latvia	30·0	27·0	19·0	18·0	19·0
Lithuania	(NA)	38·0	24·7	19·3	19·4
Transcaucasian republics					
Armenia	71·0	50·0	38·0	(NA)	(NA)
Azerbaidzhan	54·0	43·0	49·0	(NA)	(NA)
Georgia	(NA)	36·8	33·9	(NA)	(NA)
Central Asian republics and Kazakhstan					
Kazakhstan	(NA)	36·8	26·9	(NA)	(NA)
Kirgizia	28·0[2]	30·0	35·0	(NA)	(NA)
Tadzhikistan	35·0	30·0	(NA)	(NA)	(NA)
Uzbekistan	(NA)	28·0	30·0	(NA)	(NA)
Non-reported republics					
Turkmenistan	(NA)	(NA)	(NA)	(NA)	(NA)
Moldavia	(NA)	32·8[3]	(NA)	(NA)	(NA)

(NA) = Not available

Notes

1. TsSU Belorusskoi SSR, *Belorusskaia SSR v tsifrakhv 1965g., kratkii statisticheskii sbornik* (Minsk: Statistika, Belorusskoe otdelenie, 1966), p. 9.
2. TsSU Kirgizskoi SSR, *Sovetskii Kirgizstan za 40 let (1926–1966), statisticheskii sbornik* (Frunze: Kirgizstan, 1966), p. 18.
3. Infant mortality rates for Turkmenistan and Moldavia have never been published. Rates for all other thirteen republics are available for only two years during the period 1958–74. For these two years, 1960 and 1967, an estimate for the two republics, in combined form, was made by a residual method. Thus, infant mortality rates for all other republics were multiplied by the number of births in the given year to obtain a figure of all infant deaths in the thirteen republics for which rates are known. The sum of these infant deaths was then subtracted from the reported number of infant deaths for the country as a whole and the resultant residual number of deaths was divided by the number of births in the two republics to obtain a combined rate per 1,000 births.

Sources: Except where noted, all statistics are official Soviet figures as reported in John Dutton, Jr, 'Changes in Soviet mortality patterns, 1959–77', *Population and Development Review*, vol. 5 (June 1979), and Christopher Davis and Murray Feshbach, *Rising Infant Mortality in the USSR in the 1970s*, Series P-95, no. 74 (Washington, DC: United States Bureau of the Census, September 1980), p. 3.

Table 4.9 *Infant Mortality Rates for Twenty-One Soviet Cities, 1970, 1972 and 1974 (Deaths per 1,000 Live Births)*

City	1970	All infants 1972	1974
	(1)	(2)	(3)
All USSR	24·4	25·7	27·9
RSFSR, Ukraine, Belorussia, Moldavia			
Gor'kii	21·7	18·4	16·9
Kharkov	19·3	23·8	20·6
Kiev	17·4	16·8	19·6
Kishinez	16·8	17·4	24·4
Kuibyshev	26·6	28·9	29·6
Leningrad	19·8	18·0	17·8
Minsk	18·4	16·6	15·7
Moscow	20·4	21·2	22·9
Novosibirsk	25·2	23·9	22·0
Sverdlovsk	22·2	21·9	23·7
Baltic region			
Riga	15·3	15·5	22·2
Tallin	18·2	14·9	19·5
Vilnuis	14·4	13·6	17·0
Transcaucasian region			
Baku	24·1	23·4	20·7
Tbilisi	21·3	26·3	33·9
Erevan	26·8	28·4	21·4
Central Asian region			
Alma-Ata	26·7	30·9	29·2
Ashkhabad	32·4	36·4	46·4
Dushanbe	46·7	47·7	51·8
Frunze	25·3	21·6	24·1
Tashkent	40·4	40·8	45·5

Note: These rates were calculated by dividing the number of deaths at ages 'younger than one year' by the number of births during the year.
Sources
Column 1: *Vestnik statistiki,* no. 11 (November 1971), p. 89.
Column 2: M. S. Bednyi, 'Current tendencies in the health status of the population', *Zdorovokhranenie Rossiiskoi Federatsii,* no. 8 (August 1976), p. 13.
Column 3: *Vestnik statistiki,* no. 11 (November 1975), p. 80.

Table 4.10 *Estimated and Projected Natural Increase, USSR and by Republic, 1950–2000 (Rates per 1,000 Population)*

USSR and republic	1950	1960	1970	1980	1990	2000
USSR	17·0	17·8	9·2	9·4	7·1	5·5
RSFSR	16·8	15·8	5·9	6·1	2·7	1·5
Ukraine	14·3	13·9	6·3	4·9	2·6	1·5
Belorussia	17·5	17·8	8·6	8·4	6·3	3·8
Moldavia	27·7	22·9	12·0	11·7	7·9	5·4
Estonia	4·0	6·1	4·7	2·6	1·4	0·9
Latvia	4·6	6·7	3·3	1·4	0·5	−0·1
Lithuania	11·6	14·7	8·7	6·3	5·8	3·7
Armenia	23·6	33·3	17·0	18·8	14·3	10·2
Azerbaidzhan	21·6	35·9	22·5	20·6	20·0	13·3
Georgia	15·9	18·2	11·9	11·0	8·9	6·3
Kazakhstan	25·9	30·6	17·4	17·6	14·2	10·0
Kirgizia	23·9	30·8	23·1	23·6	21·0	16·3
Tadzhikistan	22·2	28·4	28·4	29·2	26·2	20·2
Turkmenistan	28·0	35·9	28·6	27·3	25·1	19·6
Uzbekistan	22·1	33·8	28·1	28·7	26·3	21·1

Source: Godfrey S. Baldwin, *Population Projections by Age and Sex: For the Republics and Major Economic Regions of the USSR, 1970 to 2000*, Series P-91, no. 26 (Washington, DC: United States Government Printing Office, September 1979), pp. 13–14, 25–57.

Table 4.11 *Average Size of Families, USSR and by Republic, 1959, 1970 and 1979*

USSR and republic	1959 Total	1959 Urban	1959 Rural	1970 Total	1970 Urban	1970 Rural	1979 Total	1979 Urban	1979 Rural
USSR	3·7	3·5	3·9	3·7	3·5	4·0	3·5	3·3	3·8
RSFSR	3·6	3·5	3·8	3·5	3·4	3·8	3·3	3·2	3·4
Ukraine	3·5	3·4	3·7	3·4	3·3	3·6	3·3	3·2	3·3
Belorussia	3·7	3·5	3·8	3·6	3·5	3·7	3·3	(NA)	(NA)
Moldavia	3·8	3·5	3·9	3·8	3·4	3·9	3·4	3·2	3·6
Estonia	3·1	3·1	3·1	3·1	3·2	3·1	3·1	(3·1)	(3·1)
Latvia	3·2	3·1	3·2	3·2	3·2	3·2	3·10	3·08	3·13
Lithuania	3·6	3·4	3·7	3·4	3·4	3·5	3·3	3·3	3·3
Armenia	4·8	4·5	5·1	5·0	4·7	5·5	4·7	4·5	5·2
Azerbaidzhan	4·5	4·1	4·9	5·1	4·5	5·7	5·1	4·5	5·8
Georgia	4·0	3·7	4·2	4·1	3·8	4·3	4·0	3·9	4·2
Kazakhstan	4·1	3·9	4·3	4·3	3·9	4·8	4·1	(NA)	(NA)
Kirgizia	4·2	3·9	4·4	4·6	4·0	5·1	4·6	3·8	5·3
Tadzhikistan	4·7	4·1	5·1	5·4	4·5	6·0	5·7	(NA)	(NA)
Turkmenistan	4·5	4·0	5·0	5·2	4·6	6·0	5·5	(NA)	(NA)
Uzbekistan	4·6	4·1	4·8	5·3	4·5	5·8	5·5	4·6	6·2

(NA) = Not available.

Source: As reported in 1959, 1970 and 1979 census volumes, newspaper reports and *Vestnik statistiki*.

Table 4.12 *Percentage of Families with Seven or More Members Jointly Residing Together, USSR and by Republic, 1959, 1970 and 1979*

USSR and republic	By republic			By titular nationality		
	1959	1970	1979	1959	1970	1979
USSR	5·7	5·8	4·9	5·7	5·8	4·9
RSFSR	5·0	3·6	1·9	4·2	2·2	1·0
Ukraine	3·3	2·1	1·6	3·6	2·3	1·7
Belorussia	4·5	3·0	1·5	4·6	3·2	1·6
Moldavia	7·6	7·5	3·7	10·1	9·5	4·8
Estonia	1·4	1·0	0·8	1·5	0·9	0·9
Latvia	1·8	1·2	0·9	1·8	1·0	0·9
Lithuania	4·3	2·5	1·6	4·5	2·6	1·6
Armenia	19·4	19·7	15·1	17·5	15·6	11·9
Azerbaidzhan	16·1	26·3	25·0	20·3	34·6	31·1
Georgia	8·4	7·6	7·6	8·5	6·4	6·7
Kazakhstan	9·9	13·4	11·7	15·8	33·5	22·3
Kirgizia	10·6	19·4	20·2	14·9	33·8	35·7
Tadzhikistan	18·4	32·0	35·5	24·0	42·2	47·4
Turkmenistan	15·6	20·9	32·4	45·5	41·9	44·9
Uzbekistan	16·1	29·7	32·2	40·0	40·6	43·3

Sources

1959 and 1970: TsSU SSSR. *Itogi Vsesoiuznoi perepisi naseleniia 1970 goda*, Vol. 7 (Moscow: Statistika, 1974), pp. 234–7 and 272–3. The 1959 figures are based on a 5-percent sample, and are questionable in four republics: Azerbaidzhan, Kazakhstan, Kirgizia and Tadzhikistan – because they were so low in 1959.

1979: TsSU SSSR, *Naselenie SSSR. Po dannym Vsesoiuznoi perepisi naseleniia 1979 goda* (Moscow: Poltizdat, 1980), p. 17, and *Vestnik statistiki*, vol. 12 (December 1981), p. 57.

Table 4.13 *Expected Number of Children, Percentage Distribution and Average Number by Nationality and by Share of Married Women, 1972*

Nationality	All women	\multicolumn{7}{c}{Share of married women, in percent Number of children}	Average expected number
		0	1	2	3	4	5	6 or more	
Russians	100·0	2·9	24·9	52·0	14·2	3·5	1·5	1·0	2·00
Ukrainians	100·0	2·8	18·4	56·0	16·8	3·9	1·3	0·8	2·08
Belorussians	100·0	2·0	14·0	51·8	21·2	6·9	2·9	1·2	2·31
Moldavians	100·0	3·2	14·6	42·4	19·5	9·6	5·3	5·4	2·62
Estonians	100·0	2·6	18·3	51·5	18·8	5·3	2·5	1·0	2·18
Latvians	100·0	2·3	26·3	51·1	14·9	2·8	1·6	1·0	1·99
Lithuanians	100·0	2·1	20·1	48·7	18·3	6·5	2·5	1·8	2·23
Armenians	100·0	0·6	4·2	24·0	28·3	24·8	10·2	7·9	3·42
Azeris	100·0	0·7	3·3	12·2	15·0	18·3	14·5	36·0	4·89
Georgians	100·0	1·4	5·0	36·7	33·9	15·6	5·1	2·3	2·83
Kazakhs	100·0	1·4	2·9	13·3	14·9	14·3	15·6	37·6	5·01
Kirgiz	100·0	0·4	1·1	5·4	9·6	14·2	17·0	52·3	6·04
Tadzhiks	100·0	1·5	1·1	6·3	8·0	14·4	15·3	53·4	5·97
Turkmen	100·0	2·3	3·3	5·1	8·1	11·5	15·7	54·0	5·93
Uzbeks	100·0	1·2	1·5	5·4	7·1	13·0	13·0	58·8	6·26

Note: Based on a survey of 347,314 women, aged 18–59 years.
Source: V. A. Belova *et al., Skol'ko detei budet v sovetskoi sem'e* (Moscow: Statistika, (1977), p. 26.

Table 4.14 *Number and Distribution of the Central Asians and Kazakhs in Their Titular Republics, by Nationality and Republic, 1959, 1970 and 1979 (in Thousands)*

Nationality / republic	1959 Kazakhs	1959 Kirgiz	1959 Tadzhiks	1959 Turkmen	1959 Uzbeks	1959 Kazakhs	1970 Kirgiz	1970 Tadzhiks	1970 Turkmen	1970 Uzbeks	1970 Kazakhs	1979 Kirgiz	1979 Tadzhiks	1979 Turkmen	1979 Uzbeks
Total in USSR	3,622	969	1,397	1,002	6,015	5,299	1,452	2,136	1,525	9,195	6,556	1,906	2,898	2,028	12,456
Number outside Central Asia and Kazakhstan[1]	389	1	6	12	42	490	11	18	23	76	530	20	23	27	91
Total in five republics	3,233	963	1,385	986	5,973	4,809	1,441	2,118	1,502	9,119	6,026	1,886	2,875	2,001	12,365
Kazakhstan	2,787	7	8	(−)	137	4,234	10	16	3	216	5,289	9	19	2	263
Kirgizia	20	924	15	(−)	219	22	1,285	22	(−)	333	27	1,687	23	1	426
Tadzhikistan	13	26	1,051	7	454	8	35	1,630	11	666	10	48	2,237	14	873
Turkmenistan	70	(−)	(−)	924	125	69	(−)	1	1,417	179	80	(−)	1	1,892	234
Uzbekistan	343	93	311	55	5,038	476	111	449	71	7,725	620	142	595	92	10,569
Percentage of USSR total	89·3	99·4	99·1	98·4	99·3	90·7	99·2	99·2	98·5	99·2	91·9	99·0	99·2	98·7	99·3

(−) = Not reported or less than 500.
Note: 1 See text regarding Kazakhs in RSFSR.
Source: Published census results.

Table 4.15 *Rural Population as a Percentage of Total Population and Total Nationality by Republic and by Nationality, 1959 and 1970*

Republic	Total population 1959 (1)	Total population 1970 (2)	Nationality population 1959 (3)	Nationality population 1970 (4)	Nationality within titular republic 1959 (5)	Nationality within titular republic 1970 (6)	Nationality
USSR	52·1	43·7	52·1	43·7	(X)	(X)	
RSFSR	47·6	37·7	42·3	32·0	45·1	34·4	Russians
Ukraine	54·3	45·5	60·8	51·5	63·4	54·2	Ukrainians
Belorussia	69·2	56·6	67·6	56·3	74·5	62·9	Belorussians
Moldavia	77·7	68·3	87·1	79·6	90·4	82·8	Moldavians
Baltic republics	51·7	42·6	58·7	49·9	59·7	50·8	Baltic nationalities
Estonia	43·5	35·0	52·9	44·9	53·1	45·3	Estonians
Latvia	43·9	37·5	52·5	47·3	53·3	48·3	Latvians
Lithuania	61·4	49·8	64·9	53·3	66·4	54·1	Lithuanians
Transcaucasian republics	54·1	48·9	57·6	51·1	60·5	53·0	Transcaucasians
Armenia	50·0	40·5	43·4	35·2	47·8	37·7	Armenians
Azerbaidzhan	52·2	49·9	65·2	60·3	63·7	58·7	Azeris
Georgia	57·6	52·2	63·9	56·0	65·1	57·2	Georgians
Kazakhstan	56·2	49·7	75·9	73·3	75·7	73·7	Kazakhs
Central Asia	65·1	61·9	79·1	75·3	80·2	76·5	Central Asians
Kirgizia	66·3	62·6	89·2	85·4	89·0	85·5	Kirgiz
Tadzhikistan	67·4	62·9	79·4	74·0	80·4	74·5	Tadzhiks
Turkmenia	53·8	52·1	74·6	69·0	73·7	68·3	Turkmen
Uzbekistan	66·4	63·4	78·2	75·1	79·8	77·0	Uzbeks

(X) = Not applicable.
Source: Murray Feshbach and Stephen Rapawy, 'Soviet population and manpower trends and policies', in United States Congress, Joint Economic Committee, *Soviet Economy in Perspective* (Washington, DC: United States Government Printing Office, 1976), p. 127.

Table 4.16 *Share of Urban Population, USSR and by Selected Republic, 1959, 1970 and 1979*

USSR and selected republics	1959	1970	1979
USSR	48	56	62
RSFSR	52	62	69
Kazakhstan	44	51	54
Kirgizia	34	37	39
Tadzhikistan	33	37	35
Turkmenistan	46	48	48
Uzbekistan	33	36	41

Source: Published census results.

Table 4.17 *Estimated and Projected Percentage Distribution of the Soviet Population by Region, 1950–2000*

Regions and republics	1950	1960	1970	1980	1990	2000
USSR	100·0	100·0	100·0	100·0	100·0	100·0
Slavic	81·6	79·9	77·0	74·8	71·7	68·9
RSFSR	56·8	56·1	53·8	52·3	50·1	48·0
Ukraine	20·5	20·0	19·5	18·9	18·0	19·3
Belorussia	4·3	3·8	3·7	3·6	3·6	3·6
Moldavia	1·3	1·4	1·5	1·5	1·5	1·6
Baltic	3·1	2·9	2·9	2·8	2·6	2·5
Transcaucasus	4·3	4·6	5·1	5·4	5·9	6·3
Central Asia and						
Kazakhstan	9·6	11·3	13·6	15·5	18·2	20·8
Kazakhstan	3·7	4·6	5·4	5·6	6·3	6·7
Central Asia	5·9	6·7	8·2	9·9	11·9	14·1

Sources: Godfrey S. Baldwin, *Population Projections by Age and Sex: For the Republics and Major Economic Regions of the USSR, 1970 to 2000*, Series P-91, no. 26 (Washington, DC: United States Government Printing Office, September 1979), p. 11; except for 1980, which is from TsSU SSSR, *SSSR v tsifrakh v 1979 godu, Kratkii statisticheskii sbornik* (Moscow: Statistika, 1980), pp. 10–11.

Table 4.18 *Population of Muslim Origin, USSR and by Republic, 1959, 1970, 1979 and 2000*

USSR and republic	1959		1970		1979		2000 A		2000 B	
	Number	Percent	Number	Percent	Number	Percent	Number	Percent	Number	Percent
USSR	24,738,462	100·0	35,158,288	100·0	43,772,000	100·0	74,562,000	100.00	63,880,000	100·0
Central Asia and Kazakhstan	13,768,661	55·7	20,737,635	59·0	27,156,000	62·0	51,203,000	68·7	42,232,000	66·1
Kazakhstan	3,261,379	13·2	5,005,391	14·2	6,196,000	14·2	10,194,000	13·7	8,974,000	14·0
Kirgizia	1,189,676	4·8	1,802,827	5·1	2,270,000	5·2	3,886,000	5·2	3,360,000	5·3
Tadzhikistan	1,616,177	6·5	2,432,677	6·9	3,279,000	7·5	6,581,000	8·9	5,254,000	8·2
Turkmenistan	1,173,758	4·7	1,752,969	5·0	2,300,000	5·3	4,335,000	5·8	3,676,000	5·8
Uzbekistan	6,527,671	26·4	9,743,771	27·7	13,111,000	30·0	26,107,000	35·1	20,968,000	32·8
Azerbaidzhan	2,654,863	10·7	4,004,146	11·4	4,968,000	11·3	8,218,000	11·0	7,217,000	11·3
RSFSR	7,258,085	29·3	9,395,609	26·7	10,438,000	23·8	13,342,000	17·9	12,870,000	20·1
Other republics	1,056,853	4·3	1,020,898	2·9	1,210,000	2·8	1,799,000	2·4	1,671,000	2·6

Sources

1959, 1970 and 1979: Published census results by republic and by nationality within each republic.
2000: A. Extrapolated on the basis of 1970–9 trends of annual average rate of increase.
   B. Extrapolated on the basis of 1970–9 trends of annual average absolute increase.

Table 4.19 *Number and Growth of Total, Slavic, Russian and Muslim Populations of the USSR, 1970–2000 (in Millions and in Percentages)*

Population group	1970	Year 1979	2000	Absolute growth 1970–2000	1979–2000	Average annual rate of increase 1970–2000	1979–2000
Total population of which:	242	262	300	58	38	0·72	0·65
Slavic of which:	179	189	195	16	6	0·29	0·15
Russians	129	137	140	11	3	0·27	0·10
Muslims	35	44	A. 75	40	31	2·57	2·57
			B. 64	29	20	2·03	1·80

Sources
1970 and 1979: Based on published census results and Table 4.18.
2000: Based on M. B. Tatimov, *Razvitie narodonaseleniia i demograficheskaia politika* (Alma-Ata: Nauka Kazakhskoi SSR, 1978), pp. 120–1, and Table 4.18.

Notes: Chapter 4

1. Alexandre Bennigsen, 'Islamic or local consciousness among Soviet nationalities', in Edward Allworth (ed.), *Soviet Nationality Problems* (New York/London: Columbia University Press, 1971), pp. 170–3.
2. Tsentral'noe Statisticheskoe Upravlenie (TsSU), *Narodnoe khoziaistvo SSSR v 1980 godu, statisticheskii ezhegodnik* (Moscow: Statistika, 1981), p. 33.
3. G. A. Bondarskaia, *Rozhdaemost' v SSSR (etnodemograficheskii ocherk)* (Moscow: Statistika, 1979), pp. 101–12. The author's graphic presentation in this book was useful as indicating Soviet interest in this issue, but explicitly incorporated some unrealistic assumptions.
4. *Trud*, 2 December 1980, p. 2.
5. B. Ts. Urlanis, 'Demograficheskaia nauka i demograficheskaia politika', *Vestnik Akademii nauk SSSR* (January 1980), pp. 41–9; G. I. Litvinova, 'Vozdeistvie gosudarstvo i prava na demograficheskie protsessy', *Sovetskoe gosudarstvo i pravo*, no. 1 (January 1978), pp. 132–6; E. L. Manevich, 'Vosproizvodstvo naselenia i isopol'zovanie trudovykh resursov', *Voprosy ekonomiki*, no. 8 (August 1978), pp. 34–8; M. B. Tatimov, *Razvitie narodonaseleniia i demograficheskaia politika* (Alma-Ata: Nauka Kazakhskoi SSR, 1978), p. 74.

5

The Soviet Muslim Population: Trends in Living Standards, 1960–75

ALASTAIR McAULEY

Over the past four or five years I have been engaged upon a study of economic welfare and inequality in the USSR in the post-Stalin period.[1] In this paper I attempt to marshal evidence from this broader study that will cast light on the question of the standard of living of the Muslim population of the Soviet Union. This topic, once formulated, immediately raises two methodological issues: how should one measure living standards and whom does one include in the Soviet Muslim population? These questions are addressed briefly before I turn to a review of the empirical evidence.

Economists have traditionally used either real wages or per capita national income as the most appropriate summary measures of the standard of living of particular populations. However, for the task in hand neither of these indicators is wholly appropriate. Indices of real wages are normally derived by deflating a nominal earnings series with a cost-of-living index. Such indices will not, therefore include non-employment incomes; they will also be insensitive to changes (differences) in participation rates. Hence they will understate absolute living standards whenever non-wage components form a significant fraction of family income and will lead to bias in inter-group comparisons where dependency ratios are widely different. In the USSR in general both of these conditions hold, and so real-wage comparisons may be extremely misleading indicators of relative living standards.

Per capita national income avoids both of the problems mentioned above; but it, too, suffers from certain weaknesses as an index of material welfare. National income can be thought of as the sum of factor incomes accruing to the residents of a particular territory in a given time-period. If the factors are hired on competitive markets to produce goods and services that are subsequently sold under competitive conditions, national income will also represent the value of goods and services made available within the same time-period. But, if some of the output is produced in response to the instructions of the authorities rather than the preferences of individuals, this equivalence may break down. For example, if educational services are made available free of charge by the government (but in quantities determined by it), one cannot be sure that the value of the earnings of teachers, etc., will correspond to the value placed upon education by the population at large. In such circumstances increases in measured national income per capita will not correspond to increases in perceived living standards by the population in question.

For these reasons I do not use either an index of real wages or per capita national income as my primary measure of the standard of living of particular groups within the USSR. Rather, I make use of various concepts of family income. As these have been described in detail elsewhere[2] I will give only brief definitions here. The basic indicator of well-being is what I term *personal income*. This consists of money receipts and the value of goods that pass through the budgets of households (families) within a given period of time. *Money income* is defined to exclude the value of receipts in kind. In this paper, however, I make no use of measures of money income. There are two reasons for this. First, as a result of the way in which the authorities publish the statistics, it is easier to calculate personal income than money income at both the national and republican levels. Thus, estimates of personal income are likely to be more accurate than those of money income. Secondly, the most important categories of *in natura* income in the USSR are (or have been) payments in kind for labor services by the collective farm and the value of the output of the private plot that is consumed by the producing household. The importance of these components in average household income is likely to vary with the degree of urbanization. Thus, comparisons of the money incomes of groups which differ in the extent to which they live in rural areas (and derive a livelihood from agriculture) are likely to yield a distorted impression of relative levels of material welfare.

Both money and personal income, as defined here, exclude the value of services provided for households by the state. But access to education, for example, or to medical care certainly adds to the living standards of individual families (even if not to the extent indicated by the cost of providing such services) and, again, if expenditure on such services differs by region, indicators of welfare that exclude these components will give a biased idea of relative living standards. *Total income* is defined as personal income plus an allowance for the value of free and subsidized services made available by the state. It is the main indicator of living standards used in this paper (and it corresponds more or less to the Soviet concept of *sovokupnyi dokhod sem'i*).

In principle, the welfare indices introduced above can be computed for any population group in the USSR. They could, therefore, be calculated for Soviet Muslims – once one had agreed on whom to include in this population category. Unfortunately, limitations on the form in which the statistics are published may make such calculations impossible in practice. Average values of total and personal income can be derived, if at all, only for geographically or socially defined subdivisions of the USSR. One must rest content with various approximations to the per capita income of Soviet Muslims, etc. The approximation that one chooses will depend upon one's definition of this latter group – and, to some extent, one's operational definition of the group may well be influenced by the possibility of saying something about its standard of living.

There are no reliable published statistics on the religious affiliations of the Soviet population. But I doubt whether strictly religious (as opposed to more general cultural) identification lies behind most people's use of the term 'Soviet Muslim'. In this more general sense 'Muslim' is used to refer to the local populations of those areas that at some time in the past adhered to Islam. It is in this sense that it is used here. 'Muslim', then, corresponds to a very large extent with the Turkish and Iranian language communities, with the various ethnic groups associated with these and, finally, with the administrative subdivisions based on the Soviet nationalities. That is, in defining the 'Muslim' population of the USSR one might enumerate those ethnic groups that speak either Turkish or Iranian languages (together with some Caucasian dialects) or one might list the territories (republics, *oblasti*, etc.) associated with such groups. Both approaches are followed here. But, rather than attempt to assess the living standards of the full range of territories or peoples that result from such an enumeration (for which the relevant statistics do not exist), I shall limit my attention to those groups which are associated with union republics. That is, for the purposes of this paper I define the *Muslim population of the USSR* to consist of

Kazakhs, Azeris, Uzbeks, Kirgiz, Tadzhiks and Turkmens; I define the *Muslim territories of the USSR* to comprise the four republics of Central Asia, Azerbaidzhan and Kazakhstan.

Such an approach results in bias of two kinds. First, numerous groups which are Muslim in terms of my general cultural definition are excluded from my operational definition of 'Muslim'. The most important of these are the Tatars and Bashkirs, but many smaller groups are in the same position. Secondly, a significant fraction of the population living in the 'Muslim territories' is non-Muslim in cultural orientation. If the average incomes of 'Muslims' and non-Muslims in these areas differ, territorially defined living standards will not correspond to culturally defined ones. In what follows, some attempt is made to allow for the second problem. The first is completely ignored.

Living Standards in the 'Muslim Territories', 1960–75

In this section I present evidence about the living standards attained in the 'Muslim territories' of the USSR as compared with the rest of the country. The indicator used to measure material well-being is total per capita income as defined in the previous section. Values of per capita total income were calculated for the six 'Muslim' republics and for the rest of the USSR for a number of years since 1960. They were then deflated by a cost-of-living index and expressed in terms of the per capita total income of the USSR as a whole in 1970 (928 roubles per year).[3] The results are given in Table 5.1.

Before discussing the figures themselves, two comments are in order. First, in so far as direct taxes are used to finance the goods and services provided by the state, total income as defined above will overstate absolute living standards since it includes both. But Soviet tax rates are low and Soviet tax schedules are almost proportional, so the failure to allow for direct taxes does not result in substantial bias in inter-group comparisons, although it will result in some overstatement of absolute living standards. (When the entries for 1975 in Table 5.1 were recalculated in terms of disposable income – and expressed in terms of disposable per capita total income in 1970 – the figure for the Muslim territories as a whole was raised from 88 to 89 and that for the rest of the country was lowered from 120 to 119. Similarly, the entry for Kazakhstan was reduced by one point, those for other republics were raised by the same amount.) Secondly, in spite of plausible evidence of open as well as repressed inflation, official Soviet price indices show almost no change in the price level since 1955. The authorities do not publish a cost-of-living index nor an implicit deflator for the consumption components of GNP. In the figures given below I have therefore had to rely upon the unofficial cost-of-living index published by the CIA. Since this is designed to measure the upward bias only in personal consumption components, the deflated series will overstate growth in material well-being if cost increases in the services comprising the social wage have been more rapid than those in other consumption components. (This has been the case in Western Europe.) Also, the CIA index refers to the USSR as a whole; if the cost of living has evolved differently in the different republics, the use of a single deflator will introduce additional bias. Finally, in so far as the price level (or, possibly, the real cost of maintaining a particular standard of living) differs between different parts of the USSR, the use of unadjusted rouble incomes will distort relative living standards. It is claimed that prices are somewhat lower in Central Asia but no attempt is made to allow for this in the figures given here.

Table 5.1 *Real Per Capita Total Income: Muslim Republics, 1960–75 (USSR (1970) = 100)*

	1960	1965	1970	1975
Kazakhstan	60	70	91	104
Azerbaidzhan	47	53	68	75
Uzbekistan	49	56	76	82
Kirgizia	46	61	75	83
Tadzhikistan	43	57	66	76
Turkmenistan	51	63	81	87
All Muslim Republics	52	62	79	88
Rest of USSR	64	79	104	120

Sources: Per capita total income calculated from Alastair McAuley, *Economic Welfare in the Soviet Union* (Madison, Wis./London: Wisconsin University Press/Allen & Unwin, 1979), app. B, and converted to 1970 prices by the cost-of-living index given in M. Elizabeth Denton, 'Soviet consumer policy', in Joint Economic Committee, *Soviet Economy in a Time of Change* (Washington, DC: United States Government Printing Office, 1979), p. 766.

Turning now to the figures in Table 5.1: these suggest that living standards in each of the 'Muslim territories' have grown rapidly in the past fifteen or twenty years, but that standards are still substantially lower here than in the remainder of the country. Indeed, the gap appears to have widened since 1960. More precisely, over the fifteen-year period covered by the table, real per capita total income in the 'Muslim territories' increased at an annual average rate of 3·6 percent per annum; in the rest of the country, income grew at an annual rate of 4·3 percent over the same period. As a result, whereas in 1960 living standards in the 'Muslim territories' were approximately four-fifths of those in the rest of the country, by 1975 they had fallen to less than three-quarters. This increase in the disparity between the standard of living in the 'Muslim territories' and the rest of the USSR has occurred during a period of generally increasing regional inequality in the USSR. At least, the coefficient of variation in republican total incomes increased from 10·5 percent in 1960 to 14·0 percent in 1975. Most of this increase in inequality occurred in the Brezhnev period, indeed, the bulk of it in 1970–5. At the same time, casual inspection of the figures for individual republics in Table 5.1 suggests that, while inequality within the 'Muslim territories' (except for Kazakhstan) may have increased between 1960 and 1970, differentials narrowed in the next five years.

The figures in Table 5.1 also show that in the 'Muslim territories', as in the rest of the USSR, growth in per capita income, after speeding up in the first quinquennium of the Brezhnev period, was slower in 1970–5 than it had been in 1960–5. Although I do not yet have explicit figures for the post-1975 period for individual republics, what information there is does not suggest that the experience of the tenth five-year plan has been radically different from that of the ninth.

As pointed out above, in the USSR as a whole in 1970 total per capita income was 928 roubles per year. The figures in Table 5.1 imply, therefore, that in the 'Muslim territories' in that year per capita total income was only 733 roubles, or 61·09 roubles per month. In 1960 it had been as low as 40·20 roubles per month. It is perhaps difficult even for specialists to appreciate what sort of living standards such figures imply and both rouble inconvertibility and the inflationary experience of the past decade make the official exchange rate a dubious guide.[4] But the following argument suggests that levels of material welfare in these areas have been – and remain – modest.

In the mid-1960s Soviet economists published estimates of the cost of attaining a minimum of material well-being (a poverty level) which they set at 50 roubles per month per capita.[5] This was subsequently ratified by the Soviet authorities, if only implicitly, when a money income of 50 roubles a month per capita was specified as the eligibility limit for the family income supplement introduced in 1974. But money income must necessarily be less than total income; in 1965, for the USSR as a whole, total income exceeded money income by 30 percent. If the same relationship were to hold at the poverty level, this would imply a minimum total income of sixty-five roubles per month per capita as a poverty level. Allowing for changes in the cost of living, this standard translates into the following series in terms of the scaling used in Table 5.1:

	1960	1965	1970	1975
Notional Poverty Standard	77	84	88	96

Two things about this series stand out. First, it is based on a relatively ambitious definition of poverty. In 1965 the per capita income of the rest of the USSR as shown in Table 5.1 was barely above the poverty line, and the average for the country as a whole was below it. It is only since 1970 that average incomes in the rest of the USSR have clearly exceeded the notional poverty level. Secondly, among the 'Muslim territories', it is only in Kazakhstan that average incomes have been above the poverty line since 1970. Elsewhere in the region incomes remain below – and sometimes substantially below – what Soviet analysts regard as the minimum required to maintain an adequate standard of consumption.

Finally, the standard on which all of these calculations are based was laid down in 1965. One may legitimately ask whether what could be purchased for fifty roubles a month per capita in 1965 (and, according to the cost-of-living index, could be purchased for fifty-seven roubles in 1975) still represents an adequate minimum in the opinion of society at large. My belief is that from the perspective of Moscow, at least, such a standard would now appear somewhat niggardly.

Table 5.2 provides information about differences in the composition of personal and total income between the 'Muslim territories' and the rest of the USSR in 1975. For example, the table shows that, on average, the population in the six 'Muslim' republics received 460 roubles per year from state employment while in the rest of the country almost 700 roubles a head were earned from this source. I should point out that such a difference need not (and in this instance does not) imply that average earnings per employee are substantially lower in the 'Muslim territories' than elsewhere. It can also be a reflection of differences in participation rates and dependency ratios; it is affected by the relative importance of the state and collective-farm sectors as employers of labor, too. These factors should be borne in mind when the table is being interpreted.

Taking the figures in Table 5.2 at face value, however, they suggest that, both absolutely and relative to total income, earnings from state employment are larger in the rest of the USSR than they are in the 'Muslim territories'. Receipts from social consumption funds (transfer payments and the social wage) are smaller in absolute terms in the 'Muslim territories', but relative to total income are much the same in both parts of the country. Earnings from the kolkhoz are the same in absolute terms – and are thus relatively more important in the 'Muslim' part of the country. Finally, receipts from private (agricultural) activity are absolutely and *a fortiori* relatively larger in the 'Muslim territories'.

What has been said here about the 'Muslim territories' as a whole applies to each individually – with the exception of Kazakhstan. Structurally, this last region is more similar to the rest of the country than it is to other 'Muslim' republics. But the five other republics exhibit greater dependence upon collective-farm and private activities; they derive a smaller proportion of income from the state than do the so-called Slav homelands.

Table 5.2 *The Composition of Total Income: Muslim Republics, 1975 (Roubles Per Capita Per Year)*

	Earnings from State	Earnings from Kolkhoz	Private Receipts	Transfers	Other receipts	Personal Income	Social Wages[1]
Kazakh SSR	626	26	58	160	10	880	174
Azerbaidzhan SSR	375	36	84	132	6	633	127
Uzbek SSR	373	88	104	130	5	700	134
Kirgiz SSR	428	65	64	140	7	705	135
Tadzhik SSR	334	85	88	121	5	633	133
Turkmen SSR	413	154	59	125	7	758	125
All Muslim	461	63	79	140	7	750	146
Rest of USSR	697	67	69	202	16	1051	168

Note: 1 Per capita expenditure on education (net of stipends), health and housing subsidies. Total income is defined as the sum of personal income and the social wage.
Source: Appendix, Table A.3.

The figures in the table also suggest that differences between the 'Muslim republics' and the rest of the country are particularly marked in respect of transfer payments (that is, pensions, allowances and stipends). In 1975 transfers in the 'Muslim republics' amounted to 140 roubles per capita per year, little more than two-thirds of what was received in the rest of the country and less than a fifth of personal income. Now, differences in family size, in the number of dependants supported by one economically active member of the population, are arguably the feature that differentiates most clearly between the 'Muslim' republics and the rest of the country; if the state's welfare programs were designed to alleviate regional inequalities one would expect to observe a positive correlation between transfers per capita and the ratio of dependants to the economically active part of the population. Such was not the case in 1975 as the following regression results show:

$$t_i = 227\cdot 1747 - 62\cdot 6404 \quad (d/w)_i \qquad R^2: 0\cdot 7120$$
$$(3\cdot 66) \quad(1\cdot 69)$$

In this equation t_i is per capita transfer payments in the ith republic, $(d/w)_i$ is the ratio of the dependent to the active population in the ith republic and the figures in parentheses are t-statistics. It was fitted to data on all fifteen republics in the USSR and not only to the 'Muslim territories'. Although the coefficient on the dependency ratio is not particularly well determined, the proportion of the variance in transfers explained is reasonable; the equation suggests that, on average, the more dependants one has the less, both absolutely and per capita, one's family receives by way of transfer payments.

One can classify the personal income of Soviet families into two components: transfers and rewards to economic activity (that is, what I have elsewhere called primary income). There is a high correlation between transfers per capita and average primary income in a republic as the following equation (for 1975) shows:

$$t_i = -0\cdot 4510 + 0\cdot 2329 y^*_i \qquad R^2: 0\cdot 9345$$
$$(0\cdot 04) \quad(13\cdot 6)$$

In this equation y^*_i is the sum of per capita earnings from the state and collective-farm sectors and receipts from private activity in the ith republic, and the other symbols have the same significance as in the previous equation. The coefficient on primary income is well determined, and the amount of variance explained is impressive for what is essentially a crude cross-sectional equation. But the interpretation is not altogether clear. If transfers were financed out of tax revenues generated within the republic, then since with given tax-schedules revenue would increase with primary income the equation may cast light on a constraint facing republican governments in the USSR. But it is more plausible to interpret it as a reflection of the proposition that the so-called socialist principle of distribution has been applied to social security as well to other forms of income.

Table 5.3 reports on another dimension of inequality, both

within the 'Muslim territories' themselves and between them and the rest of the country. It shows the ratio of personal per capita income for *kolkhozniki* and state employees for the three years 1960, 1970 and 1974. (This last was chosen in preference to 1975 for two reasons: first, at the time of writing I only have preliminary estimates for the latter year available; secondly, 1975 was not a good year for Soviet agriculture, and this may have had an adverse effect on *kolkhoznik* incomes. Use of 1975 figures might give a misleading impression of trends.)

Table 5.3 *Ratio of Per Capita Personal Incomes of Kolkhozniki and State Employees: Six Muslim Republics, 1960–74*

	1960	1970	1974
Kazakhstan	71·3%	88·6%	78·4%
Azerbaidzhan	56·7	74·6	63·9
Uzbekistan	91·1	76·3	72·7
Kirgizia	70·0	76·0	78·0
Tadzhikistan	44·1	66·3	76·8
Turkmenistan	55·2	104·4	86·0
Six Muslim republics	68·2	75·5	69·6[1]
Rest of USSR	66·1	81·2	74·4

Sources: Calculated from McAuley, *Economic Welfare in the Soviet Union*, apps. C and D, and the same author's 'Personal income in the USSR: republican variations in 1974', in NATO, *Regional Development in the USSR: Trends and Prospects* (Newtonville, Mass.: Oriental Research Partners, 1979), pp. 53–5.

Note: 1 The entries in the seventh and eighth lines are calculated as follows: in 1974, for example, total personal income accruing to state employees and their dependants in the six 'Muslim' republics amounted to 24·705 billion roubles; at that date there were 32·086 million state employees (and dependants) in these republics. (Both figures from McAuley, 'Personal income in the USSR', pp. 54–5.) Thus, on average, state employee personal income was 769·96 roubles per year per capita. In the same year the figures for *kolkhozniki* and their dependants in the six republics were 5·401 billion roubles and 10·072 million persons respectively (ibid., pp. 53, 55). These figures imply a personal per capita income of 536·24 roubles per year for *kolkhozniki* in the six 'Muslim' republics. The two per capita income figures calculated above together yield a ratio of 69·6 percent, as recorded in Table 5.3. The other figures were calculated in the same manner.

The figures in Table 5.3 suggest that the relative living standards of these two basic social groups in the USSR were more variable in 1960 than they were in 1970 or 1974. That is, over the decade of the 1960s, the impact of income growth and social change in the USSR and in the 'Muslim' territories separately was to produce a situation where the incomes of *kolkhozniki* amount to some 75–80 percent of those of state employees. This appears still to be the position at the end of the 1970s. But the position in 1960 was different. On the whole, at that date *kolkhozniki* were better off relative to state employees in the 'Muslim territories' than *kolkhozniki* were in the rest of the country. But it is important to realize that at this date, as later, in absolute terms *kolkhozniki* in the 'Muslim territories' were worse off than those in the rest of the country. This is not to say that the 'millionaire *kolkhozy*' beloved of Soviet propaganda do not exist; but they are not sufficiently common to offset the grinding poverty encountered elsewhere.

Turning to individual entries: *kolkhozniki* in Azerbaidzhan and Tadzhikistan were particularly badly off in 1960 because rates of pay in these two republics were so low. On the other hand, *kolkhozniki* in Uzbekistan appeared well off in the same year to a considerable extent because earnings in the state sector were so low. That is, oversimplifying somewhat, the ratio given in Table 5.3 is high not because Uzbek *kolkhozniki* enjoyed a high standard of living, but because Uzbek state employees were so badly paid.

Although I report figures for *kolkhozniki* in Kazakhstan in 1970 and 1974, they are somewhat misleading as by this time the collective-farm sector had almost disappeared in this republic. In 1974 *kolkhozniki* and their dependants accounted for no more than 6·6 percent of the population. Also, not too much reliance should be placed on the apparently erratic evolution of the incomes of *kolkhozniki* and state employees in Turkmenistan. This is the second smallest republic in the USSR and it publishes very few statistics. Consequently, one is forced to estimate rather more here than in other places. One's estimates may be affected by errors which, though small on the scale of the USSR as a whole, can have a substantial impact on the results for Turkmenistan. The changes recorded in the table could reflect no more than the accumulated errors of the estimation process.

Finally, it appears that both in the 'Muslim territories' and in the rest of the USSR the incomes of *kolkhozniki* grew less rapidly in 1970–4 than did those of state employees. And in 1974 as in 1970 'Muslim' *kolkhozniki* were worse off *vis-à-vis* their state-employee compatriots than was the case in other parts of the country. In the USSR as a whole the relative decline in collective-farm incomes in the period 1970–6 was made up in the two years 1976–8. I have found nothing to suggest that the experience of *kolkhozniki* in the 'Muslim territories' differed in this respect from that of their fellow-*kolkhozniki* in the rest of the country.

Thus, one may conclude that the standard of living in the 'Muslim territories' of the USSR is lower than that in the rest of the country and that, although incomes have grown rapidly in the past two decades, the gap has not been narrowed. In 1975 the standard of living in this part of the country was perhaps three-quarters of that attained elsewhere. Secondly, the inhabitants of the 'Muslim territories' derive a higher proportion of their income from the kolkhoz sector and private activity than those who live in the rest of the country; they derive fewer benefits from the Soviet welfare state. Indeed, the evidence suggests that Soviet social welfare programs do not alleviate (even if they do not accentuate) regional inequalities in primary income. Finally, in all the 'Muslim territories' and in all years (with the exception of Turkmenistan in 1970) the incomes of *kolkhozniki* have fallen short of those of the rest of the population. Since the titular (and hence Muslim) population of each of these republics resides disproportionately in rural areas, this last conclusion provides *prima-facie* grounds for believing that the results given so far will understate differences in the living standards of 'Slavs' and 'Muslims'. What the available evidence has to say about this last question is taken up in the next section.

Living Standards of the 'Muslim Population' of the USSR, 1970

I must emphasize at the outset of this section that there are no published Soviet statistics which refer to the incomes of particular ethnic groups in the USSR and, to the best of my knowledge, there are no official unpublished statistics on the subject, either. The figures given here result from making various more or less plausible assumptions about the distribution of ethnic groups among known income classes.

Two approaches to the question are explored here. First, since the proportion of 'Muslims' and 'non-Muslims' living in urban and rural areas differs, the standard of living of the two groups will also differ even if it is assumed that incomes within each residence class are identical. These calculations can set a plausible lower bound on the scale of inter-ethnic differentiation. Secondly, an alternative estimate of the scale of differentiation (but not, I fear, an upper bound) can be derived from differences in the geographical distribution of 'Muslims' and 'non-Muslims' together with assumptions about their incomes in different parts of the country.

First, then, let us consider the implications of differences in the degree of urbanization for the standard of living of 'Muslims' and 'non-Muslims'. In actual fact, the Soviet authorities do not publish income statistics in such a way as to permit one to calculate the living standards of the rural and urban populations separately. The figures in Table 5.3 are the closest that one can come to measuring this differential directly. Now, it is possible to classify the population of any area in the USSR into three categories: the collective-farm population, the rural non-collective-farm population and the urban population. These three categories are mutually exclusive apart from that small proportion of *kolkhozniki* who reside in urban areas. Further, again with the same exception, the income of the state-employed population is the average of the incomes of the second two categories listed above, while the income of the rural population is the average of the first two. Finally, if one assumes that the income of the rural non-collective-farm population will lie between that of the other two groups, one can compute limits to the scale of urban–rural differentials by assuming that the incomes of this group are successively equal to those of *kolkhozniki* (Assumption A) and those of urban state employees (Assumption B). Since a major portion of this group will consist of state-farm workers and their dependants and of rural intelligentsia, this seems a plausible assumption to make.

Given the proportions of the population that fall into each of these three groups in the six 'Muslim republics' and in the rest of the USSR one obtains the following estimates of rural per capita personal income in 1970 as a percentage of that received in urban areas:

	Assumption A	Assumption B
Six Muslim republics	65	88
Rest of the USSR	76	92

Thus, it is possible that the rural population in the 'Muslim republics' is relatively better off than that in the rest of the country and it is possible that urban–rural differentials are modest; but I regard both of these possibilities as somewhat remote. In any case, these figures imply that rural incomes in the six 'Muslim republics' are not more than a half to two-thirds of urban incomes in the rest of the country (i.e. 500–580 roubles per year as compared to 860–930 roubles per capita).

Finally, if one assumes that 'Muslims' and 'non-Muslims' in each residence class received the same average income, one can calculate the following estimates for the personal per capita income of 'Muslims' in 1970 as a percentage of that for 'non-Muslims':[6]

	Assumption A	Assumption B
Six Muslim republics	89	95
USSR as a whole	71	75

Since it is plausible to assume that the per capita incomes of 'non-Muslims' living in urban areas will exceed those of 'Muslims' –

and I see no reason why the reverse should be true in the countryside — these figures give an upper bound to the relative incomes of the 'Muslim' population of the USSR. That is, it appears plausible to claim that 'Muslims' in the six republics in 1970 received no more than 570–600 roubles per person per year; in the USSR as a whole the upper bound was slightly greater — 580–610 roubles personal income per capita per year.

The arguments of the preceding paragraphs have set an upper bound on the average income received by 'Muslims' in 1970. Ideally, one would also like to be able to suggest a lower bound on their incomes — and thus an upper bound on the scale of differentials. This has not proved possible.

A Tentative Comparison with the World Outside

So far in this paper I have concentrated on comparisons between the Soviet Muslim territories and the rest of the USSR since this has been the focus of my own research. But this is only half the picture. One would also like to determine how well off the USSR's Muslims are when compared to those living beyond its borders — and particularly to the populations of various Middle Eastern countries with whom so much of their cultural heritage is shared.

There are very many conceptual and empirical problems that must be resolved if one is to make scientifically valid international comparisons of living standards. No attempt has been made to overcome most of these here; consequently, the figures given below should be thought of as suggestive rather than demonstrative. But the differences that they reveal are sufficiently great — to me, at least — for it to be unlikely that the rank-ordering would be reversed if such a methodologically acceptable comparison were made.

Two issues, however, must be resolved for any international comparison to be made: the selection of an indicator of material well-being and of a common set of units in which to measure it. Because I have made no special study of the economies of the USSR's southern neighbors, one is limited to indicators that have been published by others. In practice, I have chosen to rely upon national accounts data made available by the United Nations Organization. For all its limitations this has the advantage that it is readily available; also, some attempt has been made to ensure cross-country comparability of components. Hence, all that I had to do was to select from among the aggregates published by the UN that which comes closest to the indicators that I have used in this paper for the USSR. And I have chosen to use per capita disposable national income. Since this is broader than total or personal income as defined above, comparisons will understate Soviet living standards relative to those in other countries.

Again, since the UN publishes its national accounts statistics in local currencies and in US dollars, the second problem mentioned above was reduced to one of selecting an appropriate rouble–dollar exchange rate. In Table 5.4, I use the 1970 official rate of exchange. This might be thought surprising, but the official exchange rate is lower than any of the implicit purchasing-power parity rates derivable from recent American studies of Soviet national income.[7] Thus, the figures in the table will, if anything, be biased against the USSR.

Table 5.4 *Soviet Muslim Living Standards: International Comparisons (US Dollars of 1970)*

	1970	1975
Soviet 'Muslim' Territories		
Real total per capita income	821	915
Soviet 'Muslim' population		
Real personal per capita income	661	NA
Turkey		
Real per capita disposable national income	352	NA
Iraq		
Per capita disposable national income	300	796
Saudi Arabia		
Per capita disposable national income	474	2,894

Notes and Sources: Line 1 rouble values of R733 for 1970 and R817 were derived from Table 5.1 above and converted at the official rate of exchange (R1 = $1·12). In line 2 the mid-point of the range for 'Muslims' in the USSR as a whole (R590) was converted at the official rate of exchange. If I had used the PPP (purchasing-power parity) rates mentioned above on p. 100, rather than the official rate of exchange, lines 1 and 2 would read:

	1970	1975
Soviet 'Muslim' territories	1,059–1,700	1,152–1,953
Soviet 'Muslim' population	852–1,387	NA

Turning now to the figures themselves: they suggest that in 1970 living standards in the Soviet 'Muslim' territories were between two and three times as high as elsewhere in the Middle East. The living standards of Soviet Muslims themselves were, perhaps, twice those of Muslims elsewhere in the region. Of these propositions, the second is the less securely based, since biases run in both directions and I have no way of assessing their relative magnitudes.

The figures for disposable income in Iraq and Saudi Arabia in 1975 reveal the impact of the OPEC-organized price rises of 1973. They also demonstrate the limitations of disposable national income per capita as an indicator of perceived changes in living standards in the short run. It is surely not the case that the average Saudi citizen felt himself to be six times better off in 1975 than he was in 1970. But that is what the figures show. In the longer term, the greatly increased oil revenues may be transformed into higher consumption, etc., but it is doubtful how far such a process had gone by 1975. I therefore believe that the 1970 figures give a better impression of relative standards of living as perceived by the man in the street.

In their study of Soviet Central Asia, published in 1967, Alec Nove and J. A. Newth pointed out how much these regions of the USSR had benefited from incorporation into a modern industrial state.[8] This is still true today. Because they are a part of an essentially European state, the Muslim territories of the USSR (and especially their rural hinterlands) are equipped with an educational system, a network of medical facilities, a public health organization and so on that are far more extensive than anything to be found in the countries to the south of the USSR. These facilities affect vital statistics, and they affect living conditions in ways that may be only imperfectly captured by data on per capita incomes.

The evidence from this paper, then, is mixed. First, it appears that the standard of living in what I have referred to as the 'Muslim' territories of the USSR is significantly lower than in the rest of the country. Also, there is reason to suggest that the gap has widened since 1960. This can be attributed, in part at least, to the failure of the Soviet social welfare system to make proper allowance for the demographic explosion that has occurred in these areas in the postwar period.

Secondly, I have suggested that the incomes of the 'Muslim' population of the USSR are lower than those of the rest of the population. Again, in part this can be attributed to large families and so on. But it is also a consequence of the fact that Soviet 'Muslims' are disproportionately rural in their residence and remain heavily concentrated in the 'Muslim' territories.

On the other hand, I have suggested that Soviet 'Muslims' are better off than are the populations of such countries as Turkey, Iraq or, possibly, Saudi Arabia. Since there is no reason to suppose that living standards in Soviet Central Asia were higher than those elsewhere in the region in 1928, this must be counted as a successful consequence of the Soviet development model.

Appendix

Total Income in the USSR, 1975

Table A1   *Total, Personal and Money Income: USSR, 1975 (Million Roubles)*

	Total	Money	In kind	Services
Earnings from state employment	166,480	166,480	–	–
Earnings from *kolkhoz* employment	16,700	15,865	835	–
Private (agricultural) receipts	17,950	10,158	7,792	–
Social consumption	90,100	48,159	–	41,941
Other receipts	3,710	3,710	–	–
Total receipts	294,940	244,372	8,627	41,941

Sources: Earnings from the state calculated as the product of average annual employment and average annual earnings less an allowance for holiday pay: *Narodnoe khoziaistvo SSSR* (henceforth *NK SSSR*), *1975*, pp. 535, 545; *earnings from kolkhozy:* ibid., p. 414 (proportion paid in cash assumed equal to 95 percent); *private receipts:* Table A2; *social consumption: NK SSSR, 1975*, p. 568 (money payments assumed equal to stipends, pensions, allowances and holiday pay); *other receipts* equal to the sum of interest (at 2 percent on savings bank deposits (*NK SSSR, 1975*, p. 597), net loans to housing cooperatives (ibid., p. 750) and an arbitrary 1·05 percent of the state wage bill.

Table A2   *Receipts from Private (Agricultural) Activity, 1975 (Million Roubles)*

Source	Calculation	
NK SSSR, 1975, p. 414	Earnings from *kolkhozy*	16,700
NK SSSR, 1975, p. 491	Earnings from *kolkhozy* account for 44 percent of the total income of *kolkhoz* families Hence total income	37,944
NK SSSR, 1975, p. 491	Private receipts amount to 25·4 percent of the income of *kolkhoz* households	9,640
NK SSSR, 1975, p. 344	*Kolkhozniki* occupy 53·7 percent of privately farmed land. Hence equal yields imply total private receipts	17,950

Note: The cash receipts of private households were calculated as the sum of the value of collective-farm market-sales (*NK SSSR, 1975*, p. 611) and the population's share of sales to the state (ibid., pp. 326–7).

Table A3 Total Income: USSR and Republics, 1975 (Million Roubles)

	Earnings from state	Earnings from kolkhoz	Private receipts	Social consumption	Other receipts	Total income
USSR	166,480	16,700	17,950	90,100	3,710	294,940
RSFSR	103,861	6,600	6,849	52,641	2,191	172,142
Ukrainian SSR	27,386	4,824	4,175	16,112	759	53,256
Belorussian SSR	5,016	1,023	1,212	3,017	137	10,405
Uzbek SSR	5,103	1,211	1,419	3,613	74	11,420
Kazakh SSR	8,866	369	822	4,732	149	14,938
Georgian SSR	2,295	311	695	1,421	73	4,795
Azerbaidzhan SSR	2,104	203	469	1,454	36	4,266
Lithuanian SSR	2,103	356	584	1,166	75	4,284
Moldavian SSR	1,636	518	517	1,096	32	3,799
Latvian SSR	1,814	184	265	1,001	45	3,309
Kirgiz SSR	1,412	216	212	908	24	2,772
Tadzhik SSR	1,134	289	297	862	18	2,600
Armenian SSR	1,534	99	172	797	47	2,658
Turkmen SSR	1,036	387	148	627	17	2,215
Estonian SSR	1,171	109	114	654	31	2,079

Sources: Earnings from state calculated as the product of average annual employment (*NK SSSR, 1978*, p. 368) and average annual earnings (Table A4) less an allowance of 6·8 percent for holiday pay; *earnings from kolkhoz:* Table A5; *private receipts:* total receipts for *kolkhozniki* in 1975 were allocated between republics in the proportions of 1970, adjusted for changes in the distribution of *kolkhoznik* households (data from McAuley, *Economic Welfare in the Soviet Union*, p. 340 and *NK SSSR, 1975*, p. 418); total receipts for each republic derived from the ratio of *kolkhoznik* and total privately farmed land: *NK SSSR, 1975*, p. 344; *social consumption:* Table A6; *other receipts:* total for the USSR distributed in proportion to savings-bank deposits, *NK SSSR, 1975*, p. 599.

Table A4 Average Monthly Money Earnings: State Employees, 1975 (Roubles)

USSR	145·8	Lithuania	142·0
RSFSR	153·2	Moldavia	117·0
Ukraine	133·5	Latvia	144·0
Belorussia	125·5	Kirgizia	135·0
Uzbekistan	136·6	Tadzhikistan	136·2
Kazakhstan	147·6	Armenia	139·3
Georgia	118·5	Turkmenistan	161·5
Azerbaidzhan	125·0	Estonia	159·0

Sources: USSR: *NK SSSR, 1975*, p. 546; RSFSR: *NK RSFSR, 1977*, p. 192; Ukraine: *NK UkSSR, 1978*, p. 217; Belorussia: *NK BSSR, 1979*, p. 155; Uzbekistan: *NK UzSSR, 1978*, p. 205; Kazakhstan: *NK KaSSR, 1978*, p. 136; Moldavia: *Sovetskaia Moldaviia k 60-letiiu Velikogo oktiabria* (1977), p. 125; Tadzhikistan: *NK TaSSSR, 1976*, p. 134; all other republics: *Bol'shaia sovetskaia entsiklopediia – ezhegodnik* (1976), passim.

Table A5 Earnings from Kolkhoz Employment: USSR and Republics, 1975 (Million Roubles)

USSR	16,700	Lithuania	356
RSFSR	6,600	Moldavia	518
Ukraine	4,824	Latvia	(184)
Belorussia	(1,023)	Kirgizia	(216)
Uzbekistan	1,211	Tadzhikistan	(289)
Kazakhstan	(369)	Armenia	(99)
Georgia	311	Turkmenistan	(387)
Azerbaidzhan	(203)	Estonia	109

Sources: USSR: *NK SSSR, 1975*, p. 414; RSFSR: *NK RSFSR, 1977*, p. 135; Ukraine: *NK UkSSR, 1978*, pp. 161, 217; Uzbekistan: *NK UzSSR, 1978*, p. 135; Moldavia: *Sovetskaia Moldaviia k 60-letiiu Velikogo oktiabriia* (1977), p. 81; Georgia, Lithuania, Estonia: *Bol'shaia sovetskaia entsiklopediia – ezhegodnik* (1976); other republics: balance distributed in the same proportions as in 1974, McAuley, 'Personal income in the USSR', p. 50.

Table A6 Social Consumption Expenditures: USSR and Republics, 1975 (Million Roubles)

USSR	90,100	Lithuania	1,166
RSFSR	52,641	Moldavia	1,096
Ukraine	16,112	Latvia	1,001
Belorussia	3,017	Kirgizia	908
Uzbekistan	3,613	Tadzhikistan	862
Kazakhstan	4,732	Armenia	797
Georgia	1,421	Turkmenistan	627
Azerbaidzhan	1,454	Estonia	654

Sources: USSR: *NK SSSR, 1975*, p. 568; RSFSR: *NK RSFSR, 1977*, p. 206; Ukraine: *NK UkSSR, 1978*, p. 216; Belorussia: *NK BSSR, 1979*, p. 164; Uzbekistan: *NK UzSSR, 1978*, p. 215; Kazakhstan: *NK KaSSR, 1978*, p. 145; Moldavia: *Sovetskaia Moldaviia k 60-letiiu velikogo oktiabria* (1977), p. 131; Tadzhikistan: *NK TaSSR, 1976*, p. 133; other republics: *Bol'shaia sovetskaia entsiklopediia – ezhegodnik* (1976), passim; entries from all these sources were adjusted to sum to the total for the USSR as a whole.

Notes: Chapter 5

1. Alastair McAuley, *Economic Welfare in the Soviet Union* (Madison, Wis./London: Wisconsin University Press/Allen & Unwin, 1979); 'Personal income in the USSR: republican variations in 1974', in NATO, *Regional Development in the USSR: Trends and Prospects* (Newtonville, Mass.: Oriental Research Partners, 1979); and *Women's Work and Wages in the Soviet Union* (London/Boston, Mass.: Allen & Unwin, 1981).
2. McAuley, *Economic Welfare*, pp. 8–16.
3. Allowing for direct taxes, *per capita* total disposable income in 1970 was 874 roubles.
4. Recently published figures suggest that the purchasing-power parity equivalent of a rouble spent on consumption in 1965 was $2·39 using Soviet weights and $1·41 using US weights. In 1975 the equivalents were $2·25 and $1·48 respectively. Imogene Edwards, Margaret Hughes and James Noren, 'US and USSR: comparisons of GNP', Joint Economic Committee, *Soviet Economy in a Time of Change* (Washington, DC: United States Government Printing Office, 1979), p. 393. In the early 1970s the official exchange rate was $1·12 to the rouble.
5. G. S. Sarkisian and N. P. Kuznetsova, *Potrebnosti i dokhod sem'i* (Moscow: Nauka, 1967).
6. The 1970 census gives the following ethnic composition for the population of the six 'Muslim' republics:

	Rural	*Urban*
Muslim	0·73	0·27
Non-Muslim	0·32	0·68

The calculations underlying Table 5.3 imply a state-employee personal income of 657 roubles per year in the six republics in 1970; similarly, *kolkhoznik* personal income was 496 roubles. Thus, assumption A implies:

Muslims: $0·73 \times 496 + 0·27 \times 657 = 541$
Non-Muslims: $0·32 \times 496 + 0·68 \times 657 = 606$

Also in 1970 there were 10·1 million *kolkhozniki* and 21·3 rural inhabitants in the six republics; this implies that rural state employees and their dependants totaled 11·2 million. Using these population shares as weights, the figures from Table 5.3 cited above yield a rural *per capita* income of 580 roubles per year on assumption B. Thus, one may calculate:

Muslims: $0·73 \times 580 + 0·27 \times 657 = 602$
Non-Muslims: $0·32 \times 580 + 0·68 \times 657 = 633$

It is the ratios of these income figures that are reported in the text. (Figures for the USSR as a whole are calculated analogously – using income estimates from the six republics for the Muslim population but estimates for the country as a whole for non-Muslims.)

7. See, for example, Edwards, Hughes and Noren, 'US and USSR', pp. 369–401.
8. Alec Nove and J. A. Newth, *The Soviet Middle East* (London: Allen & Unwin, 1967), pp. 105–13.

PART TWO

The Soviet Domestic Context:
Cultural and Ideological Aspects

6

The Significance of Increasing Bilingualism among Soviet Muslims

PAUL B. HENZE

Most states foster use of a dominant language. Some pursue active programs encouraging the national language among citizens whose command of it is inadequate. Even without governmental encouragement, economic growth and social development encourage linguistic assimilation and uniformity. Among large states, the United States and the USSR have taken almost totally contrasting approaches – theoretically – to language policy.

A nation of immigrants but predominantly Anglo-Saxon in political and cultural traditions, the US has operated on the melting-pot principle: everyone learns English and all groups tend to fuse into a common society. This principle is balanced by strong recognition of the value of pluralism and aversion to social and cultural coercion. All groups have the right, and most find the opportunity, to preserve those parts of their own traditions and individual heritage – including their language – which they value. In American society, the approach to all these issues is further tempered by pragmatism and a disinclination to tolerate a high or sustained level of governmental interference in social and cultural affairs. When theorists and special advocates become too insistent about bending society to their desires, contrary reactions develop rapidly. We see this process operating now in the widespread antagonism to recent liberal–idealist schemes for bilingual education in English and Spanish.

Both the theory and the practice have been very different in the USSR and imperial Russia before, though in some instances there are similarities in the results. In theory the Soviet Union is the most rigidly multilingual state in the world. Each nationality has the right to its own language and the resources of the state are used to foster all languages. There are times when this has led to highly uneconomic diversion of funds and personnel. History left the theorists of Soviet communism with a complex legacy. Until the end of the eighteenth century, the position of the Russian language itself was challenged by German in the Baltic provinces and by French among the educated elite of the Russian Empire. Russian was never adopted as the language of a major proportion of the population of any of the territories conquered in the nineteenth century in the Caucasus and Central Asia, though efforts to impose it upon some of them were made. War, revolution and the strains of the early Soviet period probably resulted in a net decline in knowledgeability of Russian among the Muslim peoples of the Caucasus and Central Asia. In practice Russian remained the language of Soviet administration in all these areas, but in theory – and to some degree in fact – prime emphasis during the early Soviet period was on development of the local languages. The Muslim peoples of the USSR underwent a confused period of language engineering and alphabet changes during the first thirty years of the Soviet era.[1]

Language development has continued to be a major preoccupation of Soviet leadership and society up to the present. The problem has many aspects: political, economic, cultural and psychological. As Soviet society has modernized, many of these issues have become more difficult for the always dogmatically inclined Soviet leadership and party apparatus to handle. Language gets mixed up with many other things. Debate about language – because it is a permissible field for discussion – becomes a camouflage for more sensitive political issues which could be dealt with more openly in a less regimented society. Thus, just as the Soviet leadership is forced to face the contradictions of operating an overly centralized economy, maintain an elaborate educational and mass-communications system and support a larger military and security establishment than any other country in the world, it has also to deal with language problems of increasing complexity. There have been several good studies of many facets of this problem in recent years.[2] In this brief discussion I will not attempt to summarize most of this fascinating material but only to review evidence of increasing bilingualism in the USSR and assess its political significance.

From Soviet census data two basic facts about language use in the USSR emerge:

(i) gradual, though slow, expansion of Russian as a primary language, and
(ii) accelerated acquisition of Russian by non-Russians as a second language.

The following table sums up the basic data for the principal Muslim nationalities:

Table 6.1 *Soviet Muslims: Native and Second Language*[3]

Nationality	Native language			Russian as second language	
	1959	1970	1979	1970	1979
Uzbeks	98·4	98·6	98·5	14·5	49·3[4]
Kazakhs	98·4	98·0	97·5	41·8	52·3
Tadzhiks	98·1	98·5	97·8	15·4	29·6
Turkmen	98·7	98·8	97·9	19·1	29·4
Azerbaidzhanis	97·6	98·2	97·9	16·6	29·5
Tatars	92·1	89·2	85·9	62·5	68·9
Dagestanis	96·2	96·5	95·9	41·7	60·3
Bashkirs	61·9	66·2	67·0	53·3	64·9
Chechens	98·8	98·7	98·6	66·7	76·0
Karakalpaks	95·0	96·6	95·9	10·4	45·1[4]

The 1979 census demonstrates continuation, with some degree of acceleration, of established trends, but the census data and an increasingly large body of auxiliary information also reveal that these general propositions encompass a far more complex, and in some respects even contradictory, reality. They do not justify the facile conclusion that some observers derive from these trends: that russification in a political, social and cultural sense is advancing steadily and inexorably in the Soviet Union.[5]

The entire Soviet population is becoming better educated and more mobile. Soviet Muslims have had greater opportunities to educate and modernize themselves than Muslims in most of the countries south of the USSR and have been less inhibited about taking advantage of their opportunities. Military service for men, work experience for women, media exposure at all levels of society, the dying off of an older generation — all these factors result in an increase in the proportion of Muslims who have some command of Russian. It would be surprising, considering the sustained efforts Soviet authorities have made to teach Russian, if the statistics did not reveal an increase in command of the language, however it is measured. Common sense even leads to the conclusion that in the Soviet Union by 1990 or 2000 a significantly higher proportion of the population than at present will be using Russian as a primary or secondary language.

It may be premature to leap to this conclusion, however. The non-Russian and non-Slavic portion of the population is increasing at a far more rapid rate than the Slavs. While the rate of increase has slowed slightly and may continue to decelerate, the predominance of a young, rural population among Muslim peoples ensures that relatively high rates of increase will continue well beyond the end of the present century.[6]

Moreover, the general tendency for Muslim and some other non-Slavic nationalities to concentrate in their own republics seems likely to continue.[7] This tendency strongly encourages maintenance of native languages and discourages use of Russian, even when a high level of proficiency in the language is acquired, for any other than public and official use where contact with Russians or other non-native-language speakers is routine. In addition, the Russian and Slavic proportion of the population of these republics is declining. This contributes to a problem that is already apparent in the educational systems of the Muslim republics: a severe shortage of teachers of Russian and reluctance on the part of those who are available to serve in schools in rural areas where few Slavs reside.

What are the most likely trends over the next two decades? Muslim population growth is likely to continue high, but can the decline in Slavic birth rates be reversed? Prospects appear poor. Infant mortality rates have been increasing over the past decade and the effects of rising alcoholism appear to be evident in both birth and death rates among Slavs – much less so among Muslims.[8] There are increasing indications that the Soviet leadership may be considering measures for encouraging Slavic population growth. The implications of such measures for communist theory are formidable in a system where no principle is more fundamental than the basic equality of all nationalities. The political consequences among Muslims abroad of discrimination against Muslims at home could undermine Soviet efforts to influence the former. Measures encouraging Slavs to reproduce do not necessarily imply efforts to discourage Muslim population growth, but it is difficult to maintain the illusion of evenhandedness if such measures are taken. A recently proposed formula may provide a convenient political dodge: to consider population policy a matter for republican and regional development and application rather than something which should be applied uniformly throughout the whole USSR. This creates the illusion of greater autonomy – but gives the central government the opportunity to tailor its objectives behind the scenes. There is some evidence that a differentiated approach is already being applied in some areas. Families in the RSFSR may be receiving monetary incentives to have more children — while Uzbeks in Uzbekistan are not eligible for such payments. In an area as large as the RSFSR there are major differences, however. Are Tatars receiving the same subsidies as Slavs? What about North Caucasian Muslims who form part of the RSFSR but who have birth rates as high as any in the USSR? Do Russians and other Slavs living in Central Asia receive bonuses? There is too little information available to permit conclusions as to how these policies may be working and they are probably regarded as experimental. It is quite conceivable that such policies could heighten Slav–Muslim tensions and sense of separateness without actually rectifying the sharp disparities in birth rates to any significant degree. Experience elsewhere in the world does not offer strong justification that bonuses for more children actually produce significantly higher birth rates over an extended period of time.[9] It is an awkward dilemma for the Soviet leadership, and one which probably will not be faced directly. When confronted by difficult choices, the Soviet leadership has usually opted to postpone decisive action.

The possibility that a sizable proportion of the Muslim population could be dispersed throughout the USSR, or at least persuaded to migrate temporarily to satisfy labor shortages in the European USSR, has been examined by several analysts. Migration on a large scale is judged impractical and does not seem to be envisioned by Soviet planners themselves.[10] This leads to the conclusion that the firm pattern demonstrated in the last three census returns will probably persist: there is likely to be almost no shift to Russian as a *primary* language among Soviet Muslims. Adherence to the national language is almost 100 percent among all major Muslim nationalities. This is the best evidence we have that russification in the political and cultural sense is not occurring.[11]

On the other hand, knowledge of Russian as a *secondary* language is likely to continue to expand, though use of it may not increase to the same degree. This will be the natural result of the continuing modernization of the Soviet economy and society, more efficient educational performance and, to some degree, the effect of mass media. The trend is not simply a unitary movement in a single direction — there are cross-currents and reverse currents. The increasing concentration of nationalities in their core republics and an even more decisive phenomenon, the well-attested trend toward concentration of republican and local affairs in the hands of republican nationalities, not only reinforce the trend toward increased use of the primary republican language but also reduce the frequency of contact with Russian-speakers. Secondary education and even higher education in Muslim areas require less than complete mastery of Russian. Publication in these republics in native languages continues to expand, with regard both to the numbers of books and the scope of their subject-matter. Nevertheless, for Soviet Muslims who seek the benefits and rewards of modern education, who embark on careers in industry and public administration and who aim to be active in public life — these include an increasing proportion of women — acquisition of a reasonable command of Russian is a necessity. It is a natural aspiration and one that should be easier to fulfill — in terms of access to courses and teaching materials — than it has been in the past. This is very different from russification, however — almost the opposite of it.

A large amount of information has recently become available on the ethnic factor in the Soviet armed forces. Russian is the exclusive official language of the Soviet military, and substantial encouragement and pressure are exerted to bring non-Russian recruits to a workable level of understanding Russian. A Muslim who wishes to have a career in the Soviet armed forces must, of course, acquire fluent Russian; but very few do. Though the armed forces are not in principle organized on ethnic or territorial lines, well-established patterns of discrimination and segregation (largely having to do with perceptions of political reliability, but also in part 'traditional', i.e. a thinly veiled survival of colonial practice)[12] result in situations where many service and support units consist overwhelmingly of men of Muslim, Turkic origin. Many of these learn only enough Russian to understand commands. Among themselves they use their own language(s). The Soviet armed forces do not appear to function as a 'melting pot' for Soviet nationalities. Though Muslim recruits — especially those of rural origin — usually emerge from service knowing more Russian than when they entered, they also come out with their own Muslim national identity strengthened because most of them will have experienced active and passive forms of discrimination to a much greater degree during military service than in their native republics. As Muslim consciousness grows in the USSR, and as the Soviet leadership becomes more concerned about the reliability of the steadily growing contingents of Muslim recruits on whom it must rely to meet its military manpower needs, these trends seem likely not only to persist but perhaps also to intensify.[13]

Another aspect of the second-language question is worth noting: the well-attested trend toward acquisition of a non-

Russian second language. There can be no question that this trend demonstrates a movement contrary to russification. It shows an orientation toward Muslim culture and Muslim values. In Central Asia, Uzbek continues to expand as a *lingua franca* among Turkic and Tadzhik speakers. Turko-Persian (i.e. Uzbek–Tadzhik) bilingualism has been common in Central Asian cities since medieval times and has apparently persisted to a greater degree than many observers realized. Data from the 1979 census reveal that more and more Central Asian minorities in the Uzbek republic are acquiring Uzbek as a second language. This is a striking trend among the Karakalpaks, who are more closely related to the Kazakhs linguistically though they form part of the Uzbek Republic. Information on practices in the Soviet armed forces indicates that Uzbek sometimes functions as a *lingua franca* among Central Asians, including Tadzhiks. As the natural heir of the most developed traditional form of Central Asian Turkic, Chagatay–Uzbek is the most prestigious as well as the most widely spoken modern Central Asian Turkic language.[14]

In Dagestan and other parts of the North Caucasus, there is evidence that Azeri Turkish, which is very close to Anatolian Turkish and to most of what in tsarist times were called 'Tatar' dialects in the Caucasus, may be expanding in somewhat the same way,[15] but in Dagestan itself Arabic also seems to have remained alive, primarily because of its religious prestige. The expansion of regional second languages occurs primarily for practical reasons, but there are good grounds for assuming that religious, cultural and political attitudes – some of them still largely subconscious or traditional – are also involved. Pragmatic considerations are probably predominant; i.e. except in rare instances and among intellectuals, Russian as a second language and Uzbek or Azeri as a second language are not perceived as competitive, for they are used in quite different spheres of life. What emerges from consideration of the information we possess is that no simplistic conclusions can be drawn about nationalism or political attitudes from language data alone, and least of all from census data where there is always some reason to question the reliability of the statistics[16] and a great deal of room to debate the use of terms such as 'native language', 'fluency' and other concepts which entail a wide range of subjectivity by all parties involved in compiling the statistics.

Communists and apologists for communist systems have encouraged the notion that socio-cultural processes in the Soviet Union and their political implications are so unique that comparison with historical experience in other parts of the world is inappropriate. There is no validity to this contention. Societies under communism do not operate according to a set of 'laws' that are intrinsically different from those that apply in societies elsewhere in the world. Developments relating to nationalism and religion in the USSR have to be studied and judged according to the same criteria that are applied to study of such phenomena in other parts of the world. Trends among Muslim peoples in the USSR have parallels among the dominant Russians. National consciousness among Russians, sometimes in very conservative form, and interest in religion as an aspect of national identification, have been growing for a long time. These developments have taken directions quite different from those predicted by the 'science' of Marxism–Leninism. Advance of education and modernization of economic conditions were supposed to cause religion to wither away. Instead it seems to have acquired new meaning. Contrary to the situation among Muslim peoples in the USSR, language *per se* does not play an important role in generation of Russian nationalist attitudes or feelings. This is because the status of the Russian language is not at issue. Nor has it been subjected to severe pressures for 'reform' and restructuring. It has been free of the politically oriented pressures that have impacted on languages such as Uzbek, Kazakh and Azeri from the 1920s onward. Russian nationalists do not have to struggle to maintain the status of their language. Language becomes of primary interest when we evaluate russification processes among former Orthodox and non-Muslim minority peoples such as those who live in the Urals and along the Volga. Among these peoples Russian has been making rapid progress, both as a primary and as a secondary language. But do Mordvins and Udmurts feel more like Russians when they adopt Russian at home and begin to make less use of their own native languages? Perhaps, indeed, they do. This does not necessarily follow, however, for the world offers many examples of peoples who have lost their native languages but retained their nationalist feelings intact – e.g. the Irish or the Jews. We have to keep in mind, however, the fact that russification in the Volga–Ural region has been taking place over a long period of time. There is good reason to believe, in fact, that a sizable proportion of the people who today are unequivocally regarded as Russians derive from Finno-Ugric, Baltic, Turkic and Caucasian peoples who were assimilated over centuries. What is now going on among Volga–Ural nationalities may be nothing more than a continuation – and perhaps an acceleration – of this trend. These peoples include one interesting example of a Turkic nationality — the Chuvash — who were never Islamized. They were, in fact, largely converted to Orthodoxy by the eighteenth century. Can it be that Turkic peoples, without Islam, are more vulnerable to assimilation? Tatars and Bashkirs, however, Volga–Ural peoples of Turkic origin but Islamic from the fourteenth or fifteenth century, also show some indications of russification. These indications may, however, relate primarily to representatives of these nationalities who are resident outside their native republics — a situation particularly common among Tatars.[17]

Among Muslims, it has been possible to observe similar processes of accelerated assimilation in recent decades in Turkey, where the descendants of large numbers of nineteenth-century Circassian and other North Caucasian immigrants have been absorbed as Turks. When Muslims are absorbed into a Muslim society, as in Turkey, the issue of religious identity does not arise. The context in which national self-assertion has been occurring among Muslims in the USSR in recent decades is very different. Religion is an essential feature of their culture and may now be more important culturally than as a matter of ritual or belief. In Muslim areas of the Soviet Union, Russian culture in its Soviet form is perceived as antithetical to Islam. The boundaries between Muslim nationalities in Central Asia are still vague and there is evidence of some degree of supranational Islamic consciousness — and a Turko-Iranian consciousness as well — which appears to be growing. The languages of Central Asia have all been deeply influenced by Islam. It is unclear how strong national feeling may be in the confines of the divisions which have been imposed on Central Asia during the Soviet period. Language is an important measure of this feeling, but not necessarily the only one.[18]

Dialect differences within major European languages, e.g. French, Italian or German, are very wide and have maintained themselves for hundreds of years in face of widespread official use of a standardized version of the national language. Turkic languages tend toward greater grammatical and lexical uniformity than Indo-European ones. There is probably a broader basis for mutual intelligibility between, let us say, Kazakh and Turkmen than exists even today between North German *Platt* and *Oberbayrisch* or between Provençal and the French of Normandy. A more natural — i.e. less politically manipulated — development of Turkic languages in Central Asia might well have led to consolidation of a common Turkic idiom that could have formed the basis for communication and administration among most, if not all, the peoples of the present five republics, except for

Iranian-speakers. The basis for this kind of evolution, much more difficult today than it would have been a half a century ago, may still exist.

The present Soviet leadership has been extremely conservative about experimentation with new policies in any field. What would be the effect of differentiated policies encouraging Slavs to reproduce while promoting population control among Muslim peoples? What would be the effect of a spectrum of measures, ranging from moderate to extreme, to discourage use of native languages for higher education or to restrict publication and media use of them? Could such policies be implemented and, if implemented, be expected to be effective? Or would they prove counterproductive, even in mild form? My expectation is that only rather subtle and sophisticated pressures and forms of discouragement of native languages and encouragement of Russian would be feasible in the USSR (this is essentially what is happening now) and even these may not succeed. The development of ethnic consciousness and of institutions through which it is expressed has gone too far to be easily reversed. Draconian measures to deprive the principal Muslim nationalities of their cultural autonomy would be likely to generate strong resistance. The resistance would take many forms. Nothing the Soviet leadership attempts to do in respect to its Muslim citizens can be done without taking into account the ferment which has welled up in the Muslim lands immediately to the south of the Soviet borders, and especially Afghanistan, where the Soviets are part of the problem and have demonstrated only a limited capacity to turn it their way.[19]

Let us assume for a moment that it would be possible to create a homogenized population in the Soviet Union, all speaking perfect Russian and with only dim memories of Tatar and Azeri and Uzbek. Would Muslim/Turkic and other forms of national consciousness have disappeared? If such a development were possible, or is likely to occur sometime in the twenty-first century, then a new breed of Soviet man will certainly have been created and will have to be a very different kind of human being from the Irish, for example, who lost their language but became more intensely nationalistic as the process advanced; or from the Algerian leaders, who fought successfully to free themselves from being part of France and had to begin learning Arabic after they won; or from the Indians, who have not been able to dispense with English as a functional national language and appear to have given up trying; or from the Israelis, who revived a language which for most practical purposes was long dead. One could cite examples and variations *ad infinitum*. It leads me to the conclusion that increasing bilingualism among Soviet Muslims has very little to do with increasing russification. It may, in fact, eventually put Soviet Muslims in a much stronger position to assert their prerogative to manage their own fate as full-fledged nations. Mastering the language of the imperial power did not inhibit all the members of the United Nations who once formed part of the Spanish, French and British empires from becoming independent nations and asserting their own national identity.

Notes: Chapter 6

1. For a summary of much of this experience in Central Asia, see my 'Politics and alphabets in inner Asia', in Joshua A. Fishman (ed.), *The Creation and Revision of Writing Systems* (The Hague: Mouton, 1976), pp. 371–420.
2. Two of the best and most recent are: J. R. Azrael (ed.), *Soviet Nationality Policies and Practices* (New York: Praeger, 1978); and W. O. McCagg and B. D. Silver (eds), *Soviet Asian Ethnic Frontiers* (New York: Pergamon, 1979).
3. Census data have been drawn primarily from the Radio Free Europe (Radio Liberty) (RFE/RL) *Research Bulletin*: 'The All-Union Census of 1979 in the USSR' (September 1980). The approach to language questions has varied from one census to another. For a discussion of the subjective factors, both on the part of the census-takers and of the respondents, which affect this data, see Rasma Karklins, 'A note on "nationality" and "native tongue" as census categories in 1979', in *Soviet Studies*, vol. 32, no. 3 (July 1980), pp. 415–22.
4. While all other figures in this table are within the range of the credible, the enormous increase of Russian as a second language among Uzbeks between 1970 and 1979 not only 'strains credulity, but it hardly accords with the picture presented in the Soviet media of serious shortcomings in the teaching of Russian in Uzbekistan' (Ann Sheehy, in 'Language affiliation data from the census of 1979', in RL/130/80 in the RFE/RL *Research Bulletin* cited in n. 3 above). Either lax criteria for judging mastery of Russian were used by census-takers or the aggregate figures were deliberately adjusted upward at the republican level.
5. A good example of fresh research which reveals the persistence of strong national consciousness and increasing awareness of opportunities for expressing it is Rasma Karklins, *Nationality Power in Soviet Republics* (Cambridge, Mass.: National Council for Soviet and East European Research, 1980).
6. These increases have been commented upon by many analysts. The most comprehensive analysis is Murray Feshbach, 'Prospects for outmigration from Central Asia and Kazakhstan in the next decade', in US Congress Joint Economic Committee, *The Soviet Economy in a Time of Change* (Washington, DC: United States Government Printing Office, 1979), pp. 656–709. Statistics relevant to this analysis were updated by Dr Feshbach in his 'Trends in the Soviet Muslim population: demographic aspects', in this volume.

7. See, among others, Brian D. Silver, *Population distribution and the ethnic balance in Transcaucasia*, Kennan Institute of Advanced Russian Studies Occasional Paper No. 102, Washington, 1980; and Ann Sheehy, 'Demographic trends moving in Uzbeks' favor', RL/442/80 (20 November 1980).
8. See C. Davis and Murray Feshbach, *Rising Infant Mortality in the USSR in the 1970s* (Washington, DC: US Bureau of the Census, 1980).
9. A document approved by the 26th Party Congress envisions possible measures to encourage reversal of the decline in the Slavic birth rate; see Sergei Veronitsyn, 'The XXVI Congress of the CPSU – the beginning of a differentiated demographic policy?', RL/91/81 (2 March 1981).
10. cf. Michael Rywkin, 'Central Asia and Soviet manpower', *Problems of Communism* (January–February 1979), pp. 1–13.
11. A decline among the Tatars in use of their own language may reflect the situation primarily among Tatars resident outside their own republic. It is offset by an increase of almost the same proportion among their close kindred, the Bashkirs; cf. Ann Sheehy, 'Tatars lose some ground in population in the Tatar ASSR', RL/378/80 (15 October 1980). The number of Bashkirs claiming Russian as their first language increased only from 2·6 percent to 4·5 percent during the period 1970–9, while the number of Bashkirs claiming Bashkir as their first language increased from 61·9 percent to 66·2 percent during the same period. Tatar used to hold a higher status among Bashkirs as a literary language than their own. Some older Bashkirs who would earlier have claimed Tatar as their first language are now dying off. See Ann Sheehy, RL/247/80 (15 July 1980).
12. The traditional practice, as with many colonial military formations, was in large part a convenience, especially where recruits were drawn from varied linguistic and tribal backgrounds. There are many parallel examples in French, Belgian, Portuguese or British experience in various parts of Africa. The use of language need have no relationship to questions of political reliability.
13. S. Enders Wimbush and Alex Alexiev, *The Ethnic Factor in the Soviet Armed Forces* (Santa Monica, Calif.: Rand, 1980).
14. Edward Allworth, *Uzbek Literary Politics* (The Hague: Mouton, 1964), is the classic work on the evolution of modern Uzbek. See also James Critchlow, 'Nationalism in Uzbekistan in the Brezhnev era', in G. W. Simmonds (ed.), *Nationalism in the USSR and Eastern Europe* (Detroit, Mich.: University of Detroit Press, 1977); and, for the most recent data, Sheehy, 'Demographic trends moving in Uzbeks' favor'.
15. S. Enders Wimbush, 'Divided Azerbaijan . . .', in McCagg and Silver, *Soviet Asian Ethnic Frontiers*, pp. 72–3.
16. For example, as far as is known, a census respondent cannot state two second languages even though he may be equally fluent in Russian and a second local language.
17. See note 11 above.
18. See Alexandre Bennigsen, 'Several nations or one people? – ethnic consciousness among Soviet Central Asian Muslims', *Survey*, vol. 24, no. 3 (1979), pp. 51–64; and Kemal Karpat, 'The Turkish nationalities . . .', in McCagg and Silver, *Soviet Asian Ethnic Frontiers*, pp. 117–44.
19. The dilemmas and frustrations which the Soviets face in trying to manipulate ethnic and linguistic factors in Afghanistan are discussed in starkly realistic fashion and with much specific detail by Eden Naby in 'The ethnic factor in Soviet–Afghan relations', *Asian Survey* (March 1980), pp. 237–56.

7

The Effect of the USSR's Language Policy on the National Languages of Its Turkic Population

MICHAEL BRUCHIS

The Bolshevik position on the languages of the numerous nations and nationalities of pre-revolutionary Russia was reflected in Lenin's statement that the 'workers support the equality of nations and languages', and that 'full equality includes the negation of any privileges for one of the languages'.[1] In mid-1914 the Bolsheviks prepared to introduce in the State Duma a bill on the 'equality of nations and the defense of the rights of national minorities', which contained a special point on the unconstitutionality of any privileges for any nation or language. The bill stated that while, in the multinational Russian state, the language 'in which the affairs of all state and social establishments' of respective locales or regions would be conducted would have to be determined by local institutions and autonomous parliaments 'any national minority had the right to insist upon the unconditional rights of its language'.[2]

In pre-revolutionary Russia the Bolsheviks considered enforced ties between nations as perpetuating special privileges for the Russian language at the expense of the languages of the non-Russian peoples and nationalities. The call for the equality of languages formed an integral part of the Bolsheviks' demands for the equality of nations.[3] Long before the October Revolution, the Bolsheviks repeatedly clarified and elaborated the program they adopted in 1903 at the Second Congress of the Russian Social-Democratic Workers' Party (RSDWP) regarding the right of nations to self-determination and the equality of languages. For example, in the second half of 1913, Lenin wrote in his theses on the nationalities question that the political meaning of paragraph 9 of the 1903 program ('The right to self-determination of all nations in the state') was, on the one hand, that the Bolsheviks unconditionally recognized the right of each nation to self-determination, including secession from Russia and forming an independent state, and, on the other hand, that they had to evaluate the expediency of secession in each specific concrete instance, considering 'first of all' the interests of the 'class struggle of the proletariat for socialism'.[4] After the overthrow of tsarism, the Seventh (April 1917) Conference of Bolsheviks noted (in the resolution that Lenin had written on the nationalities question) that to negate the right 'of free secession and the forming of an independent state . . . amounted to supporting a policy of seizure or annexation' and would lead to 'a direct continuation of tsarist policy'.[5] However, Lenin again stressed that the question of free secession should not be confused with 'the question of the expediency of the secession of this or that nation at a particular moment', which should be decided 'from the viewpoint . . . of the interests of the class struggle of the proletariat for socialism'.[6]

While the political significance of the 1903 program's affirmation of the right of nations to self-determination was repeatedly explained in the pre-October period, the program's position on the equality of languages underwent a complete transformation. Paragraph 8 of the 1903 program demanded the 'introduction of the native language *equal to the state language in all local, social, and state institutions*'[7] (my italics). Later, however, although the program remained unchanged, Lenin repeatedly wrote that he opposed a state language in Russia,[8] that the Bolsheviks insisted on 'the full freedom and equality of languages',[9] that they demanded abolition of a 'required state language',[10] and that a required state language meant that 'in practical terms the language of the Great Russians . . . would be imposed on all the rest of the population'.[11]

The disharmony of the 1903 program with later official documents of the RSDWP on the question of a required state language was one of a complex of reasons that led the April 1917 Conference of Bolsheviks to examine the question of 'revising the Party program'.[12] But the new program was eventually adopted after the Bolsheviks had seized power, when the issues of the right of nations to self-determination and the status of the languages of non-Russian peoples and nationalities of the country had to be converted from demands aimed at the tsarist government into policies declared by the Soviet leadership. It is significant that when the Bolsheviks became the ruling party they no longer considered it necessary to elaborate in their party program either paragraph 8 or paragraph 9 of the 1903 program.

The program adopted by the March 1919 Eighth Congress of the Russian Communist Party (Bolsheviks-RCP(b)) was dedicated to examining 'concrete tasks of proletarian dictatorship as adapted to Russia'.[13] As to the relations between nationalities, the compilers of the program and the congress that confirmed it considered neither the rights of the non-Russian peoples and nationalities of Russia to self-determination nor the equality of languages. Indeed, the introduction to Paragraph 9 of the 1919 program, devoted to the question of national relations, indicated that it was not designed for Russia, but for the non-socialist world.

Having thus converted the question on the right of nations to self-determination from a domestic Russian question to a foreign-policy slogan, the Bolsheviks sought to protect themselves from a possible demand for self-determination by the non-Russian Soviet republics that might arise after the October Revolution on the territory of the former Russian Empire. The resolutions adopted at the Eighth Congress on the 'organizational question', especially in point 5 (in which the rights of national communist organizations of non-Russian Soviet republics were defined) established the absolute subordination of the national party organizations of the non-Russian Soviet republics to the RCP(b) and its ruling institutions and of the Soviets to those of the party and thus effectively excluded any possibility of secession by a non-Russian republic.[14] The right granted to each Soviet republic to 'free secession from the Union', which was included in the texts of the Declaration and Treaty on the Formation of the USSR (30 December 1922) and repeated with no changes in subsequent USSR constitutions (1924, 1936 and 1977) was, therefore, from the outset deprived of all domestic-policy content.

In reality not only can no union republic *freely secede*, but also no socialist nation can freely secede from the Soviet bloc. The program adopted in 1961 at the Twenty-Second CPSU Congress states that 'a course to the building of socialism that is exclusive or isolated from the community of socialist nations is bankrupt in theory . . . harmful in economics . . . and reactionary and dangerous in politics'.[15] The program asserts that 'the combined forces of the socialist camp hopefully protect each socialist country from the encroachment of imperialist reaction'.[16] Such formulations justify a variety of measures, including the armed suppression of supposedly anti-Russian actions in Soviet national republics or anti-Soviet actions in the countries of the socialist camp, by labeling these actions not only harmful and dangerous to socialism but also inspired by imperialist reaction.

As we have seen, after the Bolshevik seizure of power, the

demand for the self-determination of nations was turned into a propaganda slogan for external consumption, while inside the Soviet Union the fate of the vast majority of non-Russian peoples and nationalities was decided not by their own representatives, but from above, i.e. by Moscow.

In the first postwar revolutionary years, the Bolsheviks actually moved from supporting the right of the non-Russian peoples and nationalities to self-determination to a position of defending, by all available means, 'a single, indivisible Russia'.

By contrast, the post-revolutionary language policy was in harmony with the slogan in pre-revolutionary party documents on the equality of all nations and languages (cited above) as well as with Lenin's 'Critical notes on the nationalities question', which asserted that not only a community of 500,000 persons, but even one of 50,000, had the right to create its own autonomous national region.[17]

Based on these principles, the Soviet authorities' 'language construction' embraced the languages of over one hundred nationalities in the country. The vast majority of these had until then lacked not only a literature but even a written form. Language construction therefore included creating alphabets for languages that lacked them, modernizing old scripts and creating literary forms for new-written languages. From the outset language construction was designed to create the conditions for achieving the Bolsheviks' overall goal in the sphere of nationalities policy: 'purging national differences, especially language differences'.[18] This was shown by their language policy, and the language construction that was based on it, on the territories of Turkic-speaking Soviet poeples.

The program, which the Bolsheviks had adopted in March 1919, had considered language policy only regarding tasks in the area of national enlightenment. Moreover, while the pre-revolutionary (1903) program demanded the introduction of the 'native language . . . in all local organizations and government institutions', the post-revolutionary program did not. Indeed, instances of Great Russian Imperial chauvinism, including continued Russian efforts in the Soviet period to force the Russian language upon all local public and government institutions, led to an open anti-Russian reaction and nationalist tendencies. In order to deal with this problem, the Tenth RCP(b) Congress in March 1921 added to the resolution on the immediate tasks on the nationalities question a point on the need 'to help . . . the toiling masses of the non-Russian peoples

(a) to develop and fortify Soviet state forms that correspond to the ways of these peoples;
(b) to develop and fortify, in the native languages, courts, administration, organs of economy and authority, composed of local people who know the local ways and psychology of the local population;
(c) to develop the press, schools, theater, clubs and general cultural-enlightenment institutions in the native languages . . .'[19]

These goals, however, proved difficult to realize. For example, regarding the second of these subpoints (the main one from the viewpoint of CPSU language policy), the languages of the non-Russian peoples were used neither in the administrative work of Soviet organs of the non-Russian population nor in the political organizational activity of party organs simply because Russian and Russian-speaking representatives of other nationalities – chiefly Ukrainians and Jews – occupied the key positions in these organs. As one Soviet author admitted, in national regions of the North Caucasus, out of 1,310 officials in regional institutions in the second half of the 1930s (i.e. after two full decades of Soviet rule) there were only seventeen representatives of the local nationality.[20] In such a situation, the resolutions encouraging the use of the native languages remained on paper, and the non-Russian languages seemed doomed to be ousted by the dominant language, Russian.

By contrast, the central Soviet authorities took measures to carry out the third of the above-mentioned subpoints. The first decades after the October Revolution saw the founding of many primary and secondary schools with instruction in the local languages and the publication of educational material in these languages (as a rule translated from Russian), as well as newspapers and magazines, and *belles lettres*.

The question of perfecting existing alphabets and creating new ones was given high priority and frequently had political significance. The question of perfecting the alphabets of the Turkic languages, the number of whose speakers was second only to that of the Slavic languages, was raised in Azerbaidzhan soon after the overthrow of the Musavatist (Azerbaidzhani nationalist) government in April 1920. The Musavatists, according to Soviet sources, had been 'the enemies of the brotherly unity of the Azerbaidzhani and great Russian nations' who 'disseminate pan-Turkic propaganda'.[21] Nor was the deviation 'from Communism toward bourgeois-democratic nationalism, which sometimes took the form of pan-Islamism or pan-Turkism (in the East)' (as the resolution of the Tenth RCP(b) Congress put it),[22] limited to

Azerbaidzhan. The end of 1921 saw a revival of the anti-Russian movement in Central Asia which aimed at creating a Muslim state in Turkestan, Afghanistan, Sinkiang and Iran and was aided by 'pan-Turkist and pan-Islamist nationalists in Turkestan and in ruling circles of the Bukharan Peoples' Soviet Republic'.[23] One of the weapons used to counteract these broadly based movements and in particular to separate the Turkic-speaking population of Azerbaidzhan from the Muslim world outside Russia, was alphabet reform. The Russian authorities decided to abolish the Arabic script altogether, instead of perfecting the Arabic alphabet to suit the Azerbaidzhani language (though they had been content in December 1917 merely to reform the Russian alphabet for themselves). However, in the historical circumstances of the early 1920s, they did not dare to make an immediate switch to the Russian alphabet as any attempt to impose the Russian alphabet on non-Russian languages would have to be seen as a return to the Tsarist policy of russification. This is why the transfer from an Arabic to a Latin script that began in 1922 in Azerbaidzhan was fully supported by Moscow, even though it did not correspond to the officially declared long-range goal of 'purging language differences'. This transfer was accompanied by the removal of Arabic and Iranian words and constructions from the Turkic languages of the USSR, the subordination of these Turkic languages to the influence of Russian, and the preparation of the ground for the eventual achievement of the main CPSU language goal.

Latinization ran into resistance not only from Russian chauvinists but also from nationalists in outlying Turkic-speaking areas, who, aided by the Muslim clergy, openly supported the retention of the Arabic alphabet. But, despite this resistance, the Latinization policy promoted by Moscow soon embraced the Central Asian Turkic and non-Turkic-speaking republics and other national areas. Four years after a committee was organized in Azerbaidzhan in 1922 to prepare for the transition to the new alphabet, a Central Committee on the New Turkic Alphabet was created in February 1926 in Baku at the First All-Union Turkological Congress on the Latinization of the Alphabets of Turkic-Speaking-Peoples. On 15 August 1930, since the process of Latinization had gone far beyond the borders of Azerbaidzhan, the Presidium of the Soviet of Nationalities of the All-Union Central Executive Committee (VTsIK) resolved to transfer the Central Committee on the New Turkic Alphabet from Baku to Moscow and to reorganize it into the All-Union Central Committee on the New Alphabet of the CEC USSR.[24]

By 1935 the languages of seventy nationalities with a total population of 36,000,000 had been transferred to the Latin script.[25] But the process of Latinizing the Turkic alphabets was not accompanied by their unification. Although on the surface the coalescence of many Turkic languages into a single Turkic language would have corresponded to the CPSU program position on 'purging language differences', it would have contradicted the Bolsheviks' real aim, that is, to 'purge language differences' in such a way that the Russian language would eventually supersede all other languages. Consequently, even though the common origin and the great similarity of the grammar, vocabulary and phonetics of the vast majority of the Turkic languages allowed 'almost all speakers of the Turkic languages to understand each other on their territories, from East Europe and the Caucasus to Central Asia and Siberia',[26] effective measures were not taken in the period of Latinization to unify the Turkic alphabets. 'As a result,' noted one well-known Soviet Turkologist, N. A. Baskakov, 'there was no language unification.'[27]

The Latinization of the script of the Turkish languages was ideologically justified in various ways by the central authorities in Moscow. Lenin himself stated that the transfer to the Latin alphabet was 'a revolution in the East',[28] while a resolution of the Presidium of the CEC USSR on the special cultural and economic significance of the Latin alphabet, adopted on 7 August 1929, said that this was the 'will of the workers and toiling peasants of the Soviet peoples who used the Arabic alphabet'.[29] The All-Union Committee for the New Alphabet argued that with the future victory of world revolution the Latin alphabet would be used by all nations.[30] Given this situation, it is not surprising that the adoption of the Latin alphabet tended, on the one hand, to protect the Turkic languages from penetration by Russian words and international words that came via Russian and, on the other hand, to borrow Europeanized forms, e.g. *sotsialistik* (socialist) and *populiar* (popular) in Tatar and other languages.[31]

In the second half of the 1930s, at the onset of the massive repression, among others, of 'national deviationism', the language situation in the republics where the Latin script had been adopted turned out to be intolerable from Moscow's viewpoint. Beginning in 1936, the Latin alphabets, viewed as interfering with the ultimate aim of russifying non-Russian languages, were replaced by Cyrillic (Soviet authors write in this regard that 'the Latin alphabet interfered with the learning of Russian'.)[32] This decision was made by the Central Committee of the All-Union CP(b) itself: Soviet author S. Kalmykova, noting that a list of orthographic rules of the Nogai literary language was compiled in 1936 on the basis of the Latin alphabet, writes that this list 'was not implemented because soon after came the decision of the CC All-Union CP(b) on the transfer of alphabets to Russian'.[33] This policy of russification was also reflected at the 1937 party congresses of Uzbekistan and Kirgizia, among others, which resolved not to rest content with merely introducing Russian into the national schools (as previously required by Moscow) but to ensure that students gained a complete mastery of the language.[34]

The russification of alphabets began in various republics in similar fashion. For example, only a month after the final bill on the Latin-based Bashkir alphabet and orthography was confirmed by the Presidium of the Supreme Soviet of the Bashkir ASSR on 3 March 1939, and then published in a special brochure, the Bureau of the Bashkir Obkom of the All-Union CP(b) 'raised the question of transferring to the Cyrillic alphabet'.[35] In Kirgizia we find a similar pattern: in late 1938 a 'New Orthography for the Kirgiz Language', based on the Latin alphabet, was published. Within a few months, in early 1939, 'the question of the alphabet was raised again', and in 1940 the Republic's Supreme Soviet approved a bill on a new, Russian-based alphabet.[36] Likewise in Uzbekistan: a group of Uzbek scholars (F. Kamalov, A. Usmanov and others) led by the Russian Turkologist, Prof. A. Borovkov, created a new orthography, based on the Latin alphabet, for Uzbek and submitted it for consideration. But within a few months, in 1939, the same people, led by the same Russian professor, were given the task of creating a new alphabet, this time based on the Russian one. A Soviet Uzbek author, one of the scholars who participated in the creation of the Russian-based alphabet in 1939, admitted in 1972 that its adoption had been 'somewhat hasty and insufficiently tested'.[37] This understatement to which the Soviet author understandably resorted could not hide the fact that the transition from the Latin to the Russian alphabet did not correspond to the natural, gradual evolution of Uzbek according to the recommendations of specialists on Turkic languages. The transition corresponded, rather, to Moscow's one-sided decision, to which, in the terror of 1937–8, the linguists had to submit unquestioningly.

The change from the Latin to the Russian alphabet was indeed 'hasty', accomplished in only two or three years. This haste, caused by political pressure, led to serious deficiencies from the linguistic point of view. Thus, while the combined Latinized alphabet for all Turkic languages was composed of thirty-nine letters, which, as Baskakov notes, 'fully reflected the phonetic structure of all Turkic languages',[38] the combined Cyrillic-based alphabet for all these languages which replaced it consisted of seventy-four signs, although 'the composition of sounds that require separate signs in the Turkic languages did not change and remains at 39 units'.[39] Furthermore, in the Russian-based Turkic alphabets 'the length of vowels, one of the chief phonetic features of Turkoman, was not reflected'.[40] The Russian-based Uzbek alphabet had several superfluous signs, while lacking 'letters for specific Uzbek sounds'.[41] Certain letters (e.g. 'o') signified two sounds. As a result, words with different meaning and pronunciation were written in exactly the same way. In the Russian-based Kirgiz alphabet use of certain letters led to other difficulties. (For example, 'k' and 'g' signified two phonemes with three hard and soft variants.[42]) Soviet scholars have noted that the Russian-based alphabets of the various Turkic languages often use different signs to signify the same sound. This 'not only separates closely related Turkic languages', observes Baskakov, 'but is a serious fault in the alphabet, which often fails to correspond to the phonetic structure of the given language'.[43]

Following the decision to change from the Latin system, the All-Union Committee on the New Alphabet was liquidated and replaced by the Scientific Research Institute of the Languages and Alphabets of the Soviet Peoples. This institute, whose task was to russify alphabets, was concerned even less than its predecessor with unifying the alphabets of the Turkic languages – specialists on Turkic languages have repeatedly noted the great lack of coordination of the Turkic alphabets.[44] The party's aim in introducing Russian-based alphabets was not to unify the alphabets of Turkic languages but quite the opposite – to divorce each of them from its Arab-Iranian roots and to facilitate a broad penetration into these languages of a stream of Russian words and syntactic models. The Russian-Kirgiz dictionary, compiled by Prof. K. Iudakhin, which appeared in 1944, a few years after the confirmation, in September 1941, of the Cyrillic-based orthographic code,[45] provides numerous examples of this massive flow of Russian words into Kirgiz. Frequently we find that the Kirgiz equivalent is merely the same Russian word with or without modified spelling: *absoliutnyi* (absolute) = *absoliuttyn; avtobaza* (motor depot) = *avtobaza; aviabomba* = *aviabomba; aviazavod* = *aviazavod; aviasemka* = *aviasemka; aviarazvedka* = *aviarazvedka; agitpunkt* = *agitpunkt; vegetarianets* = *vegetarianets; vezdekhod* = *vezdekhod; velikoderzhavnyi* = *velikoderzhavnyi; klichka* = *klichka; lozhnoklassitsism* =

lozhnoklassitism; monter = monter; oboima = oboima; oboishchik = oboishchik; povest = povest; povestka = povestka; polka = polka; samolet = samolet.[46] The Russian-Uzbek dictionary also offers many examples of this process of russification: *abzats = absats; abiturient = abiturient; aviamodelist = aviamodelchi; aviamodel = aviamodel; avianosets = avianostsa or avianos; avtobiograficheskaia povest = avtobiografik povest; avtozavod = avtozavod or avtomobil zavoda; zastava = zastava; komandnyi sostav = komanda sostavi; porshen = porshen; reaktivnyi samolet = reaktiv-samolet; shatun = shatun;* etc.[47] This process, in which the Turkic languages were subjected to Russian phonological, morphological, syntactic and lexical semantic influences, led on the one hand to the undermining of their structures and systems and, on the other, narrowed their social functions, creating the necessary preconditions for the dominant language eventually to supersede them. The transfer of the Turkic alphabets to Cyrillic was the beginning of the implementation of the CPSU language policy, which aimed at russifying all non-Russian languages, regardless of genealogical classification.

After the change from the Latin alphabet, not only Turkic but many other national languages were submitted to intensified russification. A necessary preliminary step in the process was the elimination as far as the Turkic languages were concerned of numerous Arabic and Iranian words and constructions. One Soviet linguist writes, for example, that in Tatar 'in 1927 fifteen thousand words were introduced, mostly as substitutes for Arabic words' and that this process continued in 'the late 1930s',[48] i.e. right up to the introduction of the Russian-based alphabet. In the period of Latinization, Arabic and Iranian words were replaced by literal translations of international terms,[49] while limiting the penetration of *transliterated* Russian words into the non-Russian languages.[50] With the introduction of Russian-based alphabets, however, the accelerated pace of this russification of languages began to disturb the Soviet authorities. Moscow was concerned that the national intelligentsias might become isolated from the masses and would then cease being able to transmit to these masses Soviet values and ideas.[51] Thus, the authors of the chief paper at an All-Union Conference on Terminology, held in Moscow in May 1959, had to admit that, for example, in the Komi Autonomous Republic 'local workers who had played a leading role in language construction in the 1940s began to replace even common words from the literary language with Russian words'.[52] They noted that this attitude toward the literary language especially affected school textbooks, leading to the introduction of unnecessary Russian vocabulary. They added that many delegates to the First Congress of Komi Writers in 1958 had reported that 'to understand the language of various writers, one first had to translate their writing into Russian'.[53] A scholar from the Kabardino-Balkar Autonomous Republic told the same conference that 'during the creation of socio-political terminology in the post-war years, Kabardian vocabulary was completely rejected'.[54] He cited the *Russian–Kabardian Dictionary of Political Terminology* published in Nal'chik in 1951 and stressed, disapprovingly, that it contained 'a vast majority of untranslated Russian terms, including *krepostnoe pravo* (serfdom), *pisatel'* (writer), and many others . . . that represent concepts known to the Kabardian people and having national forms'.[55]

The All-Union Conference on Terminology was convened in response to the growing dissatisfaction with this situation on the part of the national intelligentsia in the various non-Russian republics. The Moscow initiators of the conference tried, therefore, to reassure these people who frequently and openly expressed indignation at the work of the linguists who, in obedience to Moscow played a leading role in the language construction, which they saw as hastening the demise of the non-Russian languages. These 'overzealous linguists' were duly criticized by the conference — but this was criticism by the General Staff of those detachments who, carried away by the ardor of battle, threw themselves forward and thus endangered the overall attack. That the overall strategy had remained unchanged was indicated by V. Vinogradov, director of the Institute of Linguistics of the Soviet Academy of Sciences, who raised the question of regulating and unifying terminology on the basis of the 'principle of minimal differences among various Soviet literary languages'.[56] The authors of the chief paper, led by Iu. Desheriev, explained that this principle, on the one hand, was directed against tendencies to eliminate from all Soviet languages terms borrowed from all other languages[57] and on the other hand would lead 'to the unification of terminology on the basis . . . of a single source', which, 'for many Soviet peoples, is Russian'.[58] In addition to this principle of minimal differences, these authors put forward two no less significant theses. One held that 'the further development of social processes connected with the building of Communism in the USSR would lead not to an increased number of existing languages but to their gradual reduction and to the successive replacement of some by others'.[59] The second thesis held that 'the role of Russian in the life of Soviet peoples is increasing daily' and that 'it is becoming the second native language of hundreds of thousands and millions of speakers of various languages [of the USSR]'.[60]

Such statements showed that those in charge of the CPSU language policy had by no means abandoned the further russification of the non-Russian languages of the USSR. Rather, the authors of the chief paper were attempting to devise a theory that would justify eliminating the non-Russian languages altogether. Indeed, several of the conference participants who did research on the non-Russian national languages criticized the principle of minimal differences at the conference itself. N. Andreev, a linguist from the Chuvash Autonomous Republic, declared that 'it is totally impossible to justify the unnecessary replacement of Chuvash terms by Russian ones', that 'in cultural construction it is impermissible to ignore the wealth of the native language', and that 'the whole history of the development of borrowing into Chuvash shows that this language cannot borrow words without making certain changes in them'.[61]

Attempting to deflect this criticism, one of the authors of the chief paper, M. Isaev, explained in the debate that the principle of minimal differences should be understood merely in the sense that 'of all the possible variants, the one chosen will be the closest to Russian'.[62] None the less, he insisted, as in the paper, that in the North Ossetian Autonomous Republic and in 'most autonomous republics and regions . . . the activity of government institutions, conferences, meetings, documentation, etc., correspondence in organizations, government institutions, and business on the republican, district, and even village levels will be in Russian'.[63] But such statements only reinforced the concern over the future of non-Russian languages that was expressed during the conference.

This concern was expressed by a number of other representatives of national republics (e.g. by the Kazakh scholar M. Balakaev).[64] B. Borkovskii, a corresponding member of the USSR Academy of Sciences, attempted to calm these fears in his concluding remarks to the conference. He noted that 'certain comrades' understood the principle of minimal differences 'broadly, supposing that the [chief] paper advanced the slogan "minimal language differences", as a call to the creation of a regional language'. He argued that the principle referred to 'mimimal differences only in *terminology* and only in borrowed terminology', that 'the enactment of the principle did not have to destroy the norms of the national language or historical traditions', and that 'to enact it did not require the full coalescence (in alphabet, orthoepy, etc.) of terms in every Soviet language'.[65]

Borkovskii's assurances, however, corresponded neither to the situation of the non-Russian languages in the USSR nor to the real intentions of the organizers of the 1959 All-Union conference. Within a few years, in November 1962, the chief paper at an All-Union conference on the development of Soviet literary languages, held in the capital of Kazakhstan, expressed dissatisfaction with the fact that, according to the new Yakut orthography, 'schoolchildren had to write (in their native language) forms like *diriektor, ogurunyom, sonotuorui,* and *internneet*' although 'Uzbeks, Kazakhs, Kirgiz, Turkmens, and other Central Asians write and pronounce these words as *direktor, agronom, sanatorii,* and *internat*'[66] – i.e. as in Russian. In this case pressure from above had its effect. A collection published in 1969 revealed that the Russian influence on non-Russian languages was one-sided and that, in Yakut, for example, 'words borrowed from or through Russian are written with Russian stems and pronounced as in Russian or as close as possible to the Russian original'.[67] The one-sided influence of Russian on other languages had reached the point where, 'in the Turkic languages of Central Asia, new types of syllabification had appeared', and 'the stress' and 'syntactical constructions had changed'.[68] The result was the restructuring of the 'phonetics of Soviet languages', including Turkic ones,[69] and the overwhelming adoption of Russian terminology by most Soviet languages. Thus, for example, although Bashkiria is one of the major Soviet chemical industry centers, Bashkir terminology (according to 1959 statistics) includes '1948 chemical terms, of which only 148 come from the native language and all the rest, i.e., 1800, come, to one degree or another, from Russian and international terminology'[70] (borrowed through Russian). Thus, the one-way influence of Russian leads to the destruction of the systems and structures of non-Russian Soviet languages. But the main path to their extinction (what the authors of the chief paper at the 1959 conference called the 'gradual and successive replacement of some languages by others') is the rapid taking over of their major social functions by Russian.

Those responsible for the CPSU language policy took pains to provide a theoretical basis for this interpretation. The leading role of Russian over the other Soviet languages was justified in a thesis advanced by Iu. Desheriev, one of the most active proponents of the official language policy. Desheriev asserted with characteristic ambiguity that each people has the *'sovereign right* to use its language *within the bounds* of its vital interests'[71] (my italics). Similarly, another writer argued, 'Soviet reality shows that languages can have equal rights but not always equal value'.[72] Another thesis held that, in the conditions of bilingualism, a 'division of labor' among languages could be observed.[73] One proponent of this thesis, M. Isaev, cites the Tatar writer, R. Mustafin, as saying that 'in the process of life itself, Russian and the national languages charted their spheres of use. In science, technology, and industry, Russian reigns alone. In customs and national culture, Tatar reigns, and will for a long time.'[74] But, as Isaev admitted, 'Ossetians willingly read [novels] in Russian rather than in Ossetian translation'[75] and Tatars (10·8 percent of whom, according to the 1970 census, no longer consider Tatar their native language and 62·5 percent of whom speak Russian fluently)[76] also have no need for translations of Russian artistic literature. Consequently, even in the sphere of 'national culture', their languages have ceased to predominate and have begun to be replaced by Russian.

Indeed, it is argued that Russian 'has become the second native language of the intelligentsia of all Soviet peoples'.[77] This thesis, advanced at the end of the 1950s, was immediately adopted by the linguists in charge of language construction and interpreted in the widest sense. In the new, 'more exact', formulation at the beginning of the 1960s, Russian changed from being 'the second native language of the non-Russian intelligentsia' to being 'the second native language of all Soviet people'.[78] Such statements blatantly contradicted the actual situation of languages in the USSR. For example, toward the end of the 1960s, those in charge of language policy and concerned with strengthening the position of Russian in the national republics, pointed out that, for example, in the Turkmen SSR, national–Russian bilingualism was at an early stage of development and that the 'mass of Turkomans . . . still did not know Russian to the degree needed for reading and studying political and artistic literature'.[79]

If Russian really succeeded in becoming a *second* native language for Soviet Central Asians, the definition of its status among the other languages of the USSR would have to be reformulated, in accordance with the party's assertion that a new historical community – 'the Soviet people' – is being formed and with the tasks of language construction implied by this assertion. The formulation 'a second native language' implies a *non-native language (Russian) has achieved equality with native (non-Russian) languages*. The actual situation would require a formulation closer to the party's final goals in language construction, one that would reflect not equality with non-Russian languages but the progressive ousting of their major social functions by Russian.

Instead of disappearing from works of the late 1960s and early 1970s, the outdated formulation of a second (*vtoroi*) native language was circulated as implying a secondary (*vtorichnyi*) native language: 'a secondary native language is one that is overlaid on the mother tongue'.[80] Such an 'overlaying' means in practice that an ever-increasing number of non-Russians not only violate the norms of their native language in their dialect but also completely cease using it. As a result, as one Soviet author admits, 'some linguists suppose that bilingualists must degrade one of the languages or assimilate one of them (usually the primary one)'.[81] 'Some linguists' means non-Russian linguists. They are the ones with reason to fear, for they see the efforts made by proponents of the CPSU language policy to veil Moscow's goal of Russian superseding all other Soviet languages with declarations about their equality and flowering, while establishing a theoretical basis for that final goal.

This process in which non-Russian languages are gradually being ousted by Russian is reflected in the ever-increasing number of non-Russians who call Russian their native language. During the thirty-three years between the 1926 census and that of 1959, this figure averaged 103,000 people per year. In the eleven-year period between the census of 1959 and that of 1970, the number of non-Russians whose national language ceased being their native language reached an average of 254,000 per year.[82] During the nine years between the census of 1970 and that of 1979, the annual average came to 373,000.[83] But non-Russians who see this officially encouraged process as a threat to the existence of their respective nations are in no position to do anything about it.

The Soviet Turkic and Iranian peoples in particular have often attempted to oppose the destruction of their linguistic systems and structures. Thus, two full decades after the introduction of a Russian-based alphabet (when non-Russian languages received a 'deluge of words borrowed from Russian'[84]), Tadzhik linguists who were compliant with the official language policy complained that 'in the republican press, several previously accepted terms were being replaced by others' and that 'on a level with the word for university (*universitet*) one finds *donishgah*; along with *student* – *donishjuii;* for *korrektor*, (proof-reader) – *musakhkhekh;* for *tirazh* (edition) – *addadi nashr,* etc.'[85]

There was a similar tendency to return to the terms which

Russian had replaced in the same period in the Tatar Autonomous Republic. In the press and on the radio, instead of words like *vodoprovod* (water supply), *premiia* (prize), *politika* (policy), *kultura*, etc., adopted from Russian there was a reversion to the Tatar terms *su-uktergech, bulek, paiasat, medeniiat*, etc.[86] Young Tatar writers also began to turn to the original archaic layers of Tatar vocabulary.[87] The same tendency was observed in Uzbekistan in these years. An Uzbek author who was a proponent of the language policy complained, for example, that the writer Aibek's translation of *Eugene Onegin* used 'many Arab-Iranian words'.[88] By the end of the decade, in 1969, the Soviet Turkologist Baskakov pointed out that 'contemporary Uzbek poetry . . . is dotted . . . with words having their roots in Arabic and Persian'.[89]

The recurring attempts to oppose the ever-increasing russification of national languages demonstrate that within the intelligentsia of Soviet peoples and nationalities are not only those who accept the official language policy, but those who reject it and try, as much as possible, to struggle against its consequences.

This chapter has dealt with the ultimate aim pursued by the CPSU in its language policy and the influence of this policy on the evolution of the languages of the Soviet Union at the present stage. To a greater or lesser extent these tendencies are characteristic for all non-Russian languages of the country.

The transformation of the Russian language into a 'Superlanguage' of the USSR thus means that the non-Russian languages are yielding their position as the main means of communication in the national republics and regions of the USSR. Over 80 percent of new terms enter the non-Russian languages from or through Russian, frequently replacing the traditional terms, deeply rooted in those languages. Consequently, the massive penetration of alien elements into the national languages of the USSR gradually destroys their systems and structures, and, instead of enriching them, leads to their decline. As we have seen, this process accords with the thesis put forward by proponents of the official language policy that languages 'may possess equal rights but may not always be of equal value'.

However, along with this open admission of the true situation in language construction, we find numerous claims that give a quite different picture, such as the claim concerning the interaction and mutual enrichment of languages in the conditions of Soviet reality and the accompanying claim that in this process the active role is played not by the language from which the lexical, morphological, syntactic, stylistic, etc., elements and models are borrowed, but by the language which adopts them. This argument is based on a phenomenon often encountered in the development of languages: the borrowing by one language from others of certain means of expression which the latter acquired in the course of their evolution and which, for some reason, became indispensable for the receiving language. This explains the circumstances that many languages in the world have borrowed terminology in specific spheres of human activity from those nations which first or most actively developed it. Such a result of the necessity to *broaden the social functions* of the language usually not only enrich the receiving language but strengthen its position as the main means of communication of the national community which speaks it.

Yet the flooding of the non-Russian languages — encouraged by the Soviet authorities — by socio-political, scientific, administrative, business, technical, etc., terminology borrowed from the dominant Russian language is explained by reasons completely different from the objective necessity to widen the social functions of those languages. On the one hand the party (mainly guided by exterior political considerations) aims to create the appearance of a blossoming of national languages during the years of Soviet rule, as this paper has shown, while on the other hand pursuing the ultimate goal of establishing Russian as the sole language in the USSR.

The decline of the non-Russian languages of the USSR is seen not only in the increasing number of borrowings from the Russian language which we find there and which lead to a *narrowing*, and not widening, of their most important social functions. It is also seen in the fact that in the USSR we witness instead of a narrowing of the differences between the written and spoken language speech which is taking place in Russian and other developed languages of the world, an increasing rift between these two forms. This decline has reached such proportions that the great majority of the non-Russian languages have already ceased to be the main means of communication between the corresponding national communities as their possibilities to express human thought are most limited. As a result, they can no longer be called *languages in the full meaning of the word* and should more appropriately be termed 'idioms'.

This does not mean that the possibility of a future rebirth of these 'idioms' and their retransformation into languages of standard value, in the sense of a natural broadening of their social functions, can be excluded. History has known similar cases. The first years of Soviet rule, for example, saw the beginning of a rebirth of many national languages which had been in decline during the hundreds of years of russification conducted by Tsarism. For this to happen, however, a qualitative leap (as at the time of the overthrow of the Tsarist autocracy) would be necessary, which would alter the essence of the regime. Failing this, the languages of the non-Russian peoples of the USSR seem doomed to eventual extinction.

Notes: Chapter 7

1. V. I. Lenin, *Sochineniia*, 4th edn (Moscow: Politizdat, 1948), Vol. 20, p. 267.
2. ibid., Vol. 20, p. 267.
3. ibid., Vol. 19, pp. 12, 25, 54–6, 204, 368 and passim.
4. ibid., Vol. 19, p. 214.
5. *KPSS v rezoliutsiiakh i resheniiakh s"ezdov, konferentsii i plenumov TsK*, 8th edn. (Moscow: Politizdat, 1970), Vol. 1, p. 448.
6. Lenin, *Sochineniia*, Vol. 19, p. 386.
7. *KPSS v rezoliutsiiakh*, Vol. 1, p. 63.
8. Lenin, *Sochineniia*, Vol. 19, p. 452.
9. ibid., Vol. 19, p. 499.
10. *KPSS v rezoliutsiiakh*, Vol. 1, p. 448.
11. Lenin, *Sochineniia*, Vol. 20, p. 54.
12. *KPSS v rezoliutsiiakh*, Vol. 1, pp. 455–6.
13. ibid., Vol. 2, p. 41.
14. See, e.g., ibid., Vol. 2, pp. 73–4 and 76–7.
15. *Programma kommunisticheskoi partii Sovetskogo Soiuza* (Moscow: Politizdat, 1973), p. 21.
16. ibid., p. 20.
17. Lenin, *Sochineniia*, Vol. 20, pp. 32–3.
18. *Programma kommunisticheskoi partii*, p. 113.
19. *KPSS v rezoliutsiiakh*, Vol. 2, p. 252.
20. I. Groshev, *Bor'ba partii protiv natsionalizma* (Moscow: Politizdat, 1974), p. 103.
21. *Bol'shaia sovetskaia entsiklopediia*, 2nd edn, Vol. 8, pp. 579–80.
22. *KPSS v rezoliutsiiakh*, Vol. 2, p. 255.
23. *Bol'shaia sovetskaia entsiklopediia*, Vol. 2, p. 287.
24. A. Baziev and M. Isaev, *Iazyk i natsiia* (Moscow: Nauka, 1973), pp. 115–16 (hereafter cited as *Iazyk i natsiia*).
25. ibid., p. 116.
26. N. Baskakov, *Vvedenie v izuchenie tiurkskikh iazykov* (Moscow: Vysshaia shkola, 1969), p. 84 (hereafter cited as *Vvedenie*).
27. *Voprosy sovershenstvovaniia alfavitov tiurkskikh iazykov SSSR* (Moscow: Nauka, 1972), p. 230.
28. I. Khansuvarov, *Latinizatsiia – orudie leninskoi natsional'noi politiki* (Moscow: OGIZ, 1932), p. 21. Khansuvarov recorded that S. Agamaly-ogly, President of the Azerbaidzhan SSR Central Executive Committee recalled Lenin's exact words to him: 'The Latin alphabet is the first step

on your path to a cultural revolution among the Turkic people.'
29 *Bratskoe sodruzhestvo narodov SSSR (1922-1936)* (Moscow: Politizdat, 1964), p. 384.
30 Khansuvarov, *Latinizatsiia*, p. 21.
31 *Vvedenie*, p. 203.
32 *Sovetskoe iazykoznanie za 50 let* (Moscow: Nauka, 1967), p. 268.
33 S. Kalmykova, 'Alfavit nogaiskogo iazyka', in *Voprosy sovershenstvovaniia alfavitov* p. 121.
34 *Iazyk i natsiia*, pp. 129-30.
35 A. Biishev, 'O bashkirskom alfavite', in *Voprosy sovershenstvovaniia*, p. 53.
36 S. Kudaibergenov, 'Sovershenstvovanie i unifikatsiia alfavita kirgizskogoiazyka', in ibid., p. 94.
37 S. Ibragimov, 'Uzbekskii alfavit i voprosy ego sovershenstvovaniia', in ibid., p. 165.
38 N. Baskakov, 'O sovremennom sostoianii i dal'neishem sovershenstvovanii alfavitov tiurkskikh iazykov narodov SSSR', in ibid., p. 16.
39 ibid., p. 7.
40 B. Charyiarov, 'Iz istorii turkmenskogo alfavita', in ibid., p. 154.
41 Ibragimov, 'Uzbekskii alfavit', in ibid., p. 169.
42 Kudaibergenov, 'Sovershenstvovanie', in ibid., p. 95.
43 Baskakov, 'O sovremennom sostoianii, in ibid., p. 7.
44 In ibid., p. 9.
45 Kudaibergenov, 'Sovershenstvovanie', in ibid., p. 94.
46 *Russko-kirgizskii slovar'* (Moscow: Izd. inostrannykh i natsional'nykh slovarei, 1944).
47 *Russko-uzbekskii slovar'* (Moscow: Izd. inostrannykh i natsional'nykh slovarei'', 1954): *Russko-uzbekskii slovar'* (Tashkent: 'Ukutuvchi', 1972).
48 *Voprosy terminologii (Materialy Vsesoiuznogo terminologicheskogo soveshchaniia)* (Moscow: Izd. AN SSR, 1961), p. 218.
49 A. Abdrakhmanov, 'O printsipakh sostavleniia russko-kazakhskikh otraslevykh terminologicheskikh slovarei', in ibid., p. 195.
50 *Vvedenie*, p. 203.
51 Iu. Desheriev and I. Protchenko, 'Osnovnye aspekty issledovaniia dvuiazychiia i mnogoiazychiia', in *Problemy dvuiazychiia i mnogoiazychiia* (Moscow: Nauka, 1972), p. 41.
52 *Voprosy terminologii*, p. 21.
53 ibid.
54 B. Balkarov, 'O rabote po sozdaniiu obshchestvenno-politicheskoi terminologii kabardinskogo iazyka', in ibid., p. 147.
55 ibid., p. 145.
56 V. Vinogradov, 'Vstupitel'noe slovo', in ibid., pp. 9-10.
57 T. Bertagaev, Iu. Desheriev, M. Isaev *et al.*, 'Rol' russkogo iazyka v razvitii slovarnogo sostava iazykov narodov SSSR', in ibid., p. 42.
58 ibid., p. 43.
59 ibid., p. 40.
60 ibid., p. 43.
61 N. Andreev, 'Rabota nad uporiadochneiem chuvashskoi terminologii', in ibid., pp. 142-3.
62 ibid., p. 150.
63 ibid., pp. 30, 150.
64 ibid., p. 183.

65 V. Borkovskii, 'Itogovoe vystuplenie na zakliuchitel'nom zasedanii plenuma', in ibid., pp. 221–2.
66 V. Vinogradov et al., 'Osnovnye itogi i zadachi razrabotki voprosov pis'mennosti i razvitiia literaturnykh iazykov narodov SSSR', in *Voprosy razvitiia literaturnykh iazykov narodov SSSR* (Alma-Ata: Izd. AN Kaz. SSR, 1964), p. 13.
67 N. Petrov, 'Problema vzaimodeistviia iazykov i vopros o sovershenstvovanii iakutskoi orfografii, in *Vzaimodeistvie i vzaimoobogashchenie iazykov narodov SSSR* (Moscow: Nauka, 1969), pp. 223, 225.
68 See *Voprosy razvitiia*, p. 20.
69 E. Akhunzianov et al., 'Russkii iazyk – odin iz osnovnykh istochnikov razvitiia i obogashcheniia iazykov narodov SSSR', in *Vzaimodeistvie i vzaimoobogashchenie*, p. 78.
70 Iu. Desheriev, *Zakonomernosti razvitiia i vzaimodeistviia iazykov v sovetskom obshchestve* (Moscow: Nauka, 1966), p. 38.
71 Ibid., pp. 369–70.
72 K. Khanazarov, 'Kriterii dvuiazychiia i ego prichiny', in *Problemy dvuiazychiia i mnogoiazychiia*, p. 123.
73 *Literatura i zhizn'*, 17 December 1961.
74 M. Isayev, *National Languages in the USSR: Problems and Solutions* (Moscow: Progress Publishers, 1977), p. 202.
75 *Voprosy terminologii*, p. 150.
76 *Izvestiia*, 16 April 1971.
77 *Voprosy terminologii*, p. 39.
78 I. Beloded et al., 'Russkii iazyk – iazyk mezhnatsional'nogo obshcheniia narodov SSSR', in *Voprosy razvitiia*, p. 36 and passim.
79 P. Azimov, 'O turkmensko-russkom dvuiazychii', in *Problemy dvuiazychiia i mnogoiazychiia*, p. 45.
80 T. Bertagaev, 'Bilingvizm i ego raznovidnosti v sisteme upotrebleniia', in ibid., p. 83.
81 ibid., p. 86.
82 S. Bruk and M. Guboglo, 'Dvuiazychie i sblizhenie natsii v SSSR (po materialam perepisi naseleniia 1970g.)', *Sovetskaia etnografiia*, no. 4 (1975), p. 21.
83 *SSSR v tsifrakh v 1979* (Moscow: Statistika, 1970), p. 16.
84 N. Petrov, 'Alfavit iakutskogo iazyka', in *Voprosy sovershenstvovaniia alfavitov*, p. 210.
85 *Voprosy terminologii*, p. 140.
86 ibid., p. 157.
87 ibid., p. 158.
88 Dzh. Sharipov, 'Nekotorye problemy khudozhestvennogo perevoda', in *Materialy regional'nogo soveshchaniia po perevodu literatury s russkogo na iazyki narodov Srednei Azii, Kazakhstana i Azerbaidzhana* (Alma-Ata: Kaz. Gos. Izd., 1960), p. 213.
89 *Vvedenie*, p. 189.

8

The Impact of the Islamic Fundamentalist Revival of the Late 1970s on the Soviet View of Islam

YAACOV RO'I

The purpose of this chapter is to survey the Soviet attitude to Islam in the light of the resurgence of fundamentalist Islam as a potential political force in a number of Muslim countries, first and foremost in neighboring Iran. Given the traditional Soviet attitude to religion as a whole and Islam in particular, the USSR could have been expected to condemn the Iranian revolution and the ideology that has come to be known as Khomeinism. Yet this has not happened. On the contrary, Moscow has gone out of its way to condone the revolution in Iran and the Islamic Republic which it engendered, despite Khomeini's pan-Islamic aspirations that have included calls for greater freedom of religion for the Soviet Union's own Muslims.

This chapter, then, will consider the Soviet attitude to the Islamic aspects of the revolutions in Iran and Afghanistan, where the April 1978 coup established a Marxist–Leninist regime in another Muslim country bordering on the USSR. It will examine the influence of these two revolutions on the Kremlin's view of Islam and its role both abroad and within Soviet society, where it has become impossible to ignore the implications of these developments for the increasingly self-conscious and rapidly growing Soviet Muslim population.

In the post-Stalin period the Soviet attitude to Islam changed from one of unreserved censure to one of ambivalence. In the first years after World War II, Islam had been described as reactionary, an instrument 'for the spiritual oppression of the workers and . . . the enslavement of the peoples of the East'.[1]

Yet in the 1960s it was conceded that in certain Middle Eastern countries, for example, Islam served the 'progressive bourgeois-nationalist leaders . . . in their struggle for the liquidation of the colonial system of imperialism and the achievement of national independence'.[2] By the early 1970s, it was actually admitted that 'the social principles of Islam' had been 'significantly revised' and that Islam was essentially not only compatible with communism but even – in certain circumstances – a stimulus to social progress.[3] True, the Soviet Establishment took care not to apply this reassessment to the domestic arena,[4] where different criteria were employed in evaluating Islam.

This different evaluation of the role of Islam at home and abroad has emanated from the different needs of Soviet domestic and foreign policy. In the domestic arena, the prevalent trend was a traditional basic apprehension of the strength of Islam that might conceivably – if controls were loosened – undermine the values of communism, and eventually even the Soviet regime's authority, in its Muslim territories. In the foreign arena, on the other hand, the chief desire was to close the gap that separated the Muslim countries from the USSR, for which essential differences of outlook and conception were considered to be largely responsible; this clearly necessitated a more conciliatory attitude and greater flexibility than were possible at home.

None the less, the Kremlin's hope of allaying the fears of the communist threat entertained by foreign Muslim states and populations was not sufficiently powerful to bring about any far-reaching changes in the basic Soviet stand. By the mid-1970s, Islam was once again being presented in a totally negative light, even with regard to its role in foreign countries. In a paper I wrote in 1973 I suggested that the reasons for this reversion to type may have been Soviet Muslim resentment of the preferential treatment given to Islam in the USSR's international relations and the difficulties created by the contradiction between the official evaluation of Islam at home and abroad. Alternatively, the hardened Soviet attitude may have been caused by apprehensions in Moscow that, if a genuinely socialist Muslim society came into being outside the USSR, it might appear unduly attractive to the Soviet Muslim population.[5]

Officially, Moscow's principal concern in the context of the Islamic revival of the late 1970s has been to counter the use by the West of the Islamic 'card', the attempt to 'turn the Moslem religious and political movement which emerged on an anti-imperialist basis against the progressive states and liberation forces of the Middle East and against the Soviet Union', and to frighten the masses in the Muslim countries with 'the bogey of a nonexistent "Soviet threat to the traditional values of Islam" '.[6] The content of the Soviet counterattack and the plethora of material published in the USSR on Islam, as well as the careful differentiation between materials intended for audiences at home and abroad, indicate that the Kremlin is not only anxious about the influence of Muslim revivalism on its foreign policy but perhaps even more concerned by its effects within the USSR's own confines. Once again it is impossible for Moscow to ignore the interaction between the foreign and domestic settings.

The vigorous denials by both the Soviet media and foreign propaganda mouthpieces that the Kremlin's concern is justified only reflect its apprehensions. 'Western propaganda', one typical article notes, 'betrays its secret hopes for the beginning of something like "a political Islamic opposition" to the Soviet regime,' while reactionaries in the Muslim countries talk 'bluntly of the need to create such an opposition, "to build strong bridges" to the Muslims of the Soviet Union. They believe that their co-religionists in the USSR "experience a most acute need of support and assistance" and that it is necessary that the Soviet Muslims "together with their brothers activate an Islamic movement" . . . According to the logic which Muslim reaction wishes to impose on believers, fidelity to Islam obligates Muslims to be anticommunists. It stems from this logic that Muslims in the socialist countries are automatically in political opposition.' Yet, as the chairman of the Muslim Religious Board for Central Asia and Kazakhstan, Mufti Ziautdin Ibn Ishan Babakhan, pointed out, he was a Soviet patriot.[7]

The Kremlin has traditionally sought to demonstrate the material achievements of its own Muslims, comparing them with those of foreign Muslim societies in order to prove the advantages of the Soviet way of life. The implication is that the Soviet Muslims have adopted the materialistic belief system of Soviet society as a whole without sacrificing their freedom of religious worship. This contention is invariably put forward when Soviet Muslims make the Hajj (the pilgrimage to Mecca), when Soviet religious functionaries travel abroad, and when their foreign counterparts visit the USSR. However, the vast literature devoted to descriptions of, and an onslaught upon, vestiges of traditional Islamic customs belies both contentions: of free religious worship and increasing acculturation on the part of the great mass of the Soviet Muslim population.

The contradictions between the official position and reality become blatant when we compare, on the one hand, statements made at international Islamic forums,[8] in the Soviet Muslim publication *Muslims of the Soviet East* or in Soviet broadcasts to foreign Muslim countries and, on the other hand, writings on Islam in Soviet publications intended primarily for a Soviet readership. *Muslims of the Soviet East*, which appeared at first (as of 1968) in Uzbek and Arabic, later also in English and French, and (as of 1980) in Persian as well, is put out officially as the journal of the Muslim Religious Board for Central Asia and Kazakhstan and is presumably intended primarily for export. (Significantly, the size of the *tirazh*, that is, the number of copies published, is not indicated, which is extremely unusual in the USSR.) It strives to give the impression of a thriving Muslim community which upholds the traditional Islamic way of life,[9] maintains regular relations with fraternal communities in other countries,[10] is proud of Muslim thinkers and theologians born in previous centuries in what has since become Soviet Central Asia,[11] finds Islamic beliefs and customs compatible with Soviet ideology and practice,[12] and boasts its own autonomous Establishment, with regular meetings and activities as well as houses of worship and religious functionaries.[13]

Mufti Ziautdin Babakhan was reported by Radio Moscow in Arabic as having told Soviet journalists that Soviet Muslims 'have relations with Muslims in over 70 countries . . . have exchange visits with other Muslims . . . take part in Islamic conferences and periodically hold conferences in the USSR'. Moreover, 'Soviet Muslims, who have been brought up on the principles of the pure, holy faith and humanitarian spirit, stand firmly by the peoples struggling in the cause of their national and social liberation and by whomever is subjected to imperialism, aggression and suppression', as had been shown in 1956, 1967 and 1973. Finally, according to Babakhan, Soviet Muslims 'unanimously welcomed the victory of the revolutions in Iran and Afghanistan. Together with other prominent Muslim figures in 25 countries they recorded at the September 1979 Dushanbe conference . . . their profound solidarity with the peoples of Iran and Afghanistan who are struggling in the cause of building the just society. They also strongly condemned the intrigues of imperialism and its supporters, those intrigues that aim to deprive those two peoples of their gains and restore the former inhuman regimes to their countries.'[14]

The impression created by all these foreign-language publications that relate to the position of Islam and Muslims in the USSR is (*a*) that the Soviet Union considers as Muslims all its citizens belonging to ethnic groupings that were traditionally

Muslim and (*b*) that Islam, admittedly of a modernist, non-traditional character, flourishes in the USSR with the blessing of the Kremlin.[15] The first impression is further borne out by occasional references to Soviet Muslims as numbering so and so many tens of millions and by statements such as that of Imam Mahmud Validov, who in a broadcast to Iran talked of 'the Muslims [in the USSR], that is the Tadzhiks, Uzbeks, Turkomens and Kazakhs, together with representatives of other republics, including believers and non-believers'.[16] However, Soviet publications intended for a domestic audience or directed at a foreign audience but designed to refute statements and insinuations concerning the possible threat to the Soviet regime of the rapidly growing Muslim population, give a totally different impression. While there can be little doubt that unofficially the Soviet Europeans (including the Establishment) look upon the Muslim peoples as different from themselves and refer to them collectively as Muslims, in the media a careful distinction is drawn between Muslim believers and members of nationalities that previously professed Islam. Radio Moscow in an English-language broadcast, for example, pointed out that it was no more relevant to talk of the Soviet Muslim population than it would be to talk of France having a 53-million-strong Christian population, that country having many non-Christians and non-believers among its inhabitants. 'The word Muslim', Radio Moscow commented, 'relates to a certain religious belief . . . Over the 60-plus years of Soviet Government, religion has declined sharply in this country, and although we have no figures . . . it would be hard to imagine more than 10 per cent of the once Moslem population actually being religious today.'[17] Interestingly enough, a Russian-language journal that in 1980 made a similar distinction, between 'the adherents of Islam, those who profess the Muslim religion' and 'all the representatives of peoples, among which according to tradition Islam was propagated', put the figure of believers a great deal higher, at 30 per cent – presumably it was impossible to contend to a domestic audience that only 10 per cent of the Muslim population was religious. The higher figure was apparently the more accurate, and indeed was said to be based on 'the results of sociological research carried out in different regions of the USSR'. It, too, however, was probably an underestimate since the Soviets were obviously interested in inflating the category of 'non-believers'.[18] Be this as it may, the results of the research were that 'up to 70 per cent of the representatives of these peoples do not abide today by the requirements of Islam and are not believers, i.e. cannot be called

Muslims'. If, the journal went on, one wished 'unfoundedly to reckon them among the Muslims', the total number according to the 1970 census would reach at most 35 million.[19] (The journal did not mention that this figure was close to 45 million by the time of the 1979 census.)

The second impression, that Islam flourishes freely in the USSR, is also gainsaid by the Soviet media: they depict Islam as fighting a tough rearguard action in order to forestall what Marxist-Leninist ideology still officially considers the inevitability of its demise, in the face of heavy and incessant attack and encroachments. This is true not only of *Nauka i religiia (Science and Religion)*, the manual or catechism of the ever-increasing host of propagandists of atheism in which Islam has become a – if not *the* – major single object of onslaught. It is true even of the daily press, particularly in the Muslim republics. In December 1979, for example, *Pravda Vostoka*, the Uzbek SSR daily organ, published a long article on the struggle against Islam in Uzbekistan, which only highlighted religion's strength in the republic. Although in Uzbekistan there had been 'tremendous successes in overcoming the vestiges of religion,' the rite of circumcision as well as religious weddings and burial services still prevailed. 'One encounters also worship in holy places and appeals to tabibs [faith-healers] and mullahs to cure illnesses and ailments.' A study conducted in Uzbekistan had shown that 36 percent of those who observed religious rites did so under the influence of 'parents, relatives or milieu', 35 percent out of habit, 19 percent 'for lack of a suitable alternative, that is of new rites', and only 10 percent 'out of religious motives'. Thus, although religious tuition had ceased with the establishment of the Soviet regime and currently 'a considerable majority of believing Muslims are totally unfamiliar with either the Qur'an or the requirements of the Shari'a', the change in the emphasis and content of religiosity had not led to a meaningful decline in religious practice and affiliation.

Two phenomena in particular aroused the concern of *Pravda Vostoka*. One was 'the prevalent tendency among a certain part of the intelligentsia to underestimate the reactionary role of Islam in the way of life, conduct and consciousness of Soviet people', as a result of which they became reconciled to religious survivals and 'the observance of the old harmful traditions, rites and customs'. These intellectuals not only failed to see the socio-ideological harm caused by religious survivals but also frequently identified the national with the religious. The danger inherent in this last point was stressed by other Central Asian newspapers as well. According to *Sovetskaia Kirgiziia*, 'some people suggest that a person who preserves Islamic rites demonstrates thereby a greater "respect" for his nation, and in deviating from them insults it. This profound fallacy', this source insisted, 'comprises a viewpoint that is foreign to us' (i.e. to the Central Asian republican-level Establishment).[20] The second focus of concern consisted of 'those people who for one reason or another are not occupied in the sphere of material production, are cut off from socio-productive collectives and active social life and shut themselves up in the small world of their homes'. The paper went on: 'It must be remembered that a certain part of this category of people is connected with the education of children: being religious, they wish to inculcate religiosity in their children, and we are often considering the way of life of large Uzbek families.'

Pravda Vostoka insisted that, in the long run, raising the cultural level of the population and improving its material circumstances would bring about its final liberation from the shackles of religion — a contention that rings somewhat hollow given the authorities' manifest disconcertment (as expressed in the press of all the Central Asian republics) at the local intelligentsia's favorable attitude toward, and even practice of, Islam. In the meantime, the challenge of overcoming religious survivals 'is a broad complex problem, the solution of which depends on an aggregate of socio-economic, national, moral, family–domestic and other everyday problems'. The paper was categorical in denying the compatibility of Islam and Marxism–Leninism. Religion undisputedly obstructed participation in 'communist construction' and there could be no coexistence in the ideological sphere despite the Muslim clergy's 'modernist tendencies' and insistence on the identity of the principles of communist morality and those of Islam and on Islam's 'lofty mission ... in confirming our moral ideals'. All aspects of religion, *Pravda Vostoka* concluded, whether pertaining to dogma or popular tradition, were unacceptable in citizens of a socialist society.[21]

An even more frankly concerned article under the significant title 'It will not wither away by itself' appeared in *Kommunist Tadzhikistana* (the Tadzhik SSR Russian-language daily) written by Head of the Scientific Atheism Department of the Institute of Philosophy of the Tadzhik SSR's Academy of Sciences, S. Dadabaeva. The author stressed that atheist education and anti-religious propaganda were often ineffective because they limited themselves to criticizing and exposing religious ideology and attempting to influence the believer's reason. Insufficient account was taken of 'the nature of the manifestation of religion, the composition of the worshippers, the reasons for religiosity in a given locality, and other factors'. Interestingly, this writer (in contrast to the rosy picture portrayed in material intended for foreign audiences) pointed to inadequate health and other social services in Central Asia as the reason why belief in ' "holy" places, *mazars*, still prevails and why individual believers, particularly women, turn for assistance to mullahs and ishans'. Indeed, she, too, emphasized that many women in Tadzhikistan, like in Uzbekistan, were housewives and therefore played a greater role in the upbringing of their children than did their European counterparts and 'there are indeed more believers among them'.

Dadabaeva made three particularly salient points: first, that 'religion does not amount just to views and convictions, but profoundly permeates a person's frame of mind, feelings and emotions'. Ministers of religion played actively on the feelings of every person they wished to attract to religion and 'addressed those aspects of his life which are associated with profound psychological experiences'; secondly, that although representatives of the intelligentsia who were guided in their everyday lives by their 'stock of knowledge' could be expected to become nonbelievers this was not the case, particularly in the countryside. Thus, they sometimes developed 'a split personality, as it were, with knowledge ensconced on one side and convictions on the other'; thirdly, that the disinclination to abandon religious rites and customs (the article was particularly concerned at the continued prevalence of bride money) was so widespread because some people were 'inclined to consider a departure from religious rites a departure from national traditions'.[22]

There is, then, no evidence in these and innumerable other articles that the Soviet Establishment considers Islam a positive factor in reality, or even in potentiality, within the Soviet Union itself, even if it is careful not to present its true views in its foreign-language publications. In the Middle Eastern context, however, Moscow takes pains to refute allegations of hostility to Islamic values.[23] One Arabic broadcast even insisted that respect for Islam as a religion and assistance to Muslim peoples in the defence of their spiritual and cultural values were 'foundation stones' of Lenin's policy.[24] This statement was based on a rather blatant exercise in sophistry that endeavored to blur the difference between Islam and 'the Muslim nations' or peoples, and which has become a common feature in Soviet writings and broadcasts.[25] There were, however, some signs of a more sophisticated approach to the problem, including an admission that religion could conceivably play a positive role. One Russian-language broadcast sought to explain to the audience at home the *volte-face* in the Soviet attitude to Islam as a result of the events of the late 1970s. Pan-Islamism, it argued, was a reactionary, religious-political current that had originally been used by ruling exploiter classes to foment national and religious discord and stifle the revolutionary movement in the countries of the East. Yet the victory of the anti-monarchist revolution in Iran and the isolation of Cairo after it concluded a separate peace treaty with Israel, 'revealed some tendencies and potentialities of the Islamic movement in a new way'. A process in which the Islamic countries were increasingly being consolidated on an anti-imperialist basis was taking place, and progressive tendencies had started to assert themselves. Religion, like nationalism, had two sides, one reactionary and one progressive, each of which manifested itself 'at various stages of local development, depending on where and when religious slogans are put forward, whose interests they reflect and which aims they pursue.'[26]

This 'dialectical' view of religion is propounded specifically with regard to the countries of Asia and Africa. A 'roundtable' discussion on 'Religion in the countries of Asia and Africa' conducted early in 1980 by the orientalist journal *Narody Azii i Afriki* explained that because of the influence retained by religion in these countries and the relatively backward stage of their socio-economic development, which enhanced religion's potential as a revolutionary, anti-Western force, religion was a factor which the USSR and the 'forces of progress' could, and indeed must, use. Religion, as one member of the USSR Academy of Sciences Institute of Oriental Studies pointed out, was 'the symbol of a bygone, pre-colonial independence' and a means for mobilizing the masses for the struggle for national liberation. Another Orientalist, from the same institute, said that on the whole the influence of religion was dwindling and the secularist world-view was expanding[27] – religion in a number of states was making room for such new ideologies as nationalism and 'national socialism'. Nevertheless, he pointed out, the new trends paid lip service to religion and refrained from any open split with it. Indeed, political parties still often used religion to appeal to different groups among the population. In particular, religion was influential in the spheres of ideology and morals: religious motifs were emphasized both in education and in the official ideologies of a number of states. It was very often the integrating component of nationalism – of nationalist conceptions and politico-ideological trends – also taking on the ideological form of mass anti-imperialist and anti-colonialist movements.

The basic trends in contemporary religious life – according to a third view – were the traditional, the modern and the revivalist. Of these, the strongest was the revivalist which contained elements of both traditionalism and modernism. Its adherents called for a return to the original precepts of Islam (or Buddhism or Hinduism) which they considered the just foundations of society. This trend suited the mood among the masses and had become 'an influential political and ideological force, uniting with the nationalist and popular radical movements for "a just reconstruction of society" '. Revivalism was usually particularly forceful after attempts at partial modernization had failed. It had asserted itself as the heir to popular heresies and sectarian rebellion, absorbing in the process the traditions of messianic and eschatological, millennistic movements and demanding a return to religious 'purity' and the elimination of the defects of this world. The credo of revivalism was 'the omnipotence of God, democracy and justice'.[28]

Discussing the two trends in Islam, the 'anti-imperialist' and the 'counter-revolutionary', a senior political commentator on Near Eastern affairs, Leonid Medvedko, drew a parallel between them and the historical split and strife between Islam's two main factions, the Sunnis and the Shiites (without attributing positive or negative traits to either). While Muslim theologians ascribed the rift and contradictions to different interpretations of the Qur'an and the Shari'a, he said, the real reasons were national and, more often, social contradictions. Today, 'an anti-imperialist revolution under the banner of Islam has been carried out in Iran – its economy and politics are being cleansed of the roots of American neo-colonialism and a number of progressive reforms are underway. At the same time, under what purports to be the same banner, imperialist agents and counter-revolutionaries are at work in neighboring Afghanistan. Cooperating closely with the Peking hegemonists and the Moslem reactionaries, they would like to start a "holy war" against what all honest Moslems hold sacred.

'Revolutionary democrats in South Yemen, Syria, Libya and Afghanistan, where large sections of the population are still deeply religious', Medvedko went on, 'invoke Islam to explain to the people progressive social reforms . . . Such a course meets with the understanding and support of the working masses and of many religious leaders who help to popularize and carry out the policy of socialist orientation.' Medvedko quoted Algerian president Benjedid Chadli as saying that Islam ' "is essentially a progressive religion based on social justice" '. Indeed,

Medvedko wrote, Marxist–Leninists 'speak of solidarity and militant alliance with the Moslem working masses'.[29]

As to 'the present-day "regeneration of Islam" ', on the one hand, it found expression 'in the Moslem peoples' anti-imperialist solidarity in the struggle for national liberation and social justice', a process that reflected the growth of positive tendencies in the Islamic movement. On the other hand, 'attempts are made to use that movement as an instrument of neo-colonialism and hegemonism, confine it within nationalistic and religious bounds, and contrapose it to the progressive and democratic forces'. In a very interesting example of the 'mirror theory' (according to which Soviet commentators reflect Moscow's own intentions or deeds in their description of those of their adversaries), Medvedko said that 'the neo-colonialists have begun building bridges between different faiths and seek to promote mutual understanding allegedly to "defend them from the godless". If the worst comes to the worst, they are prepared to ignore the anti-imperialism of the religious slogans, provided it is "balanced" by anti-communism and anti-sovietism . . . The allegations made by some religious and political leaders that the "communism of the East" poses as much danger to the Moslem countries as to the "capitalism of the West" play into the hands of the neo-colonialists and direct Islam into the channel of reaction and counter-revolution. The plans of contemporary imperialism aim precisely at alienating the Moslem states from the socialist world.' Islam 'with its pervading fatalism', according to Medvedko, 'suited the colonialists so long as it permitted them to conquer Moslem nations and hold them in subjection'. But this attitude had changed. When Islam turned against them and 'Islamic slogans' were 'raised by anti-imperialist and anti-Zionist movements, as was the case in Libya and later in Iran, the imperialists see a mortal danger to Western civilization and launch a crusade against Islam'. The Americans had not a good word to say about Babrak Karmal, although he 'not only rectified past mistakes and improved relations with the clergy, but has shown real respect for Islam . . .

'What distinguishes the present stage of the national liberation movement which often raises the banner of Islam, is that this movement is not spearheaded only against imperialism, but gradually turns against the very foundations of capitalism. The conflict between the capitalist West and the Moslem East . . . is a vivid reflection of the ideological crisis of neo-colonialism, for it is in effect evidence of loss of faith in capitalism, which not so long ago regarded Islam as its ally. This evidently explains the West's fear of the process sometimes called the "regeneration of Islam".'[30]

The apparent discrepancy between the reactionary role traditionally attributed by Moscow to Islam (and, indeed, to all religion) and the major role played by Islam and the clergy in the Iranian revolution — of which the Soviets approved — bred a very extensive literature that was intended to explain how in fact Islam came to play a revolutionary role in Iran.[31] In the first place, Shiism was said to be particularly conducive to a popular revolt against tyranny. This explained how in Shiite Iran the clergy had become the focus of the opposition to the Shah. For Iran's 'broad, popular masses . . . Islam is not only a religion — it is a way of life that prescribed their socio-political and economic existence, a codex of morals and mores, and popular aspirations concerning social justice and equality which were embodied with special vividness in early Islam'. Khomeini used 'the dogma and traditions' of Shiite Islam as an offensive weapon against 'the Shah-tyrant and "Westernization" and in defence of "Muslim spiritual values" ', both tyranny and Western imperialism long having been objects of attack by the Shiite clergy which saw them as a threat to Islam as a whole and themselves in particular. While orthodox (Sunni) Islam allowed the election of a ruler (a khalif) and recognized the sovereignty of the secular authority, the Shiite clergy was uncompromising in its insistence on the sole legitimacy of the descendants of Muhammad as rulers. The historical opposition of the Shiite clergy to the oppression practiced by secular rule had led the masses to identify the Shiite leadership with their own interests. Secondly, that is in addition to the ideological and traditional suitability of the Shiite clergy to an oppositional role, circumstances had polarized the positions of the Shah and the clergy. Under the last Shah, 'who was an obedient tool of American imperialism', the restrictions imposed on the clergy and their activities in the realms of education, land ownership and the legislature led to the peak of oppositional activity of the late 1970s when the clergy charged the Shah's regime with ignoring the need to improve the living conditions of the people and increasing foreign influence in Iran, and called for the abolition of all innovations that ran counter to Islam and the Shari'a.[32]

Another commentator, specialist on Middle Eastern affairs Pavel Demchenko, took up this point in greater detail. In addition to 'the traditional adherence of the Iranian middle classes and the urban and rural poor to Shiism,' he pointed out that the clergy had benefited from the dissatisfaction of 'the numerous petty and middle bourgeoisie' with 'the influx of Western commodities and the cosmopolitanism of Iran's big bourgeoisie, the provocative luxury of the Shah's court and the sway of American standards in culture.' These had 'conflicted overtly with the material and moral values of the "traditional" bourgeoisie, artisans, [and] residents of poverty-ridden outskirts, yesterday's peasants who had migrated to the cities and populated slum areas.' These people had found in the Muslim priests 'the champions of their interests,' who advocated 'a return to strict observance of Islamic standards' in order to 'save society "from evil" and bring the people their former well-being back'.

It was not, however, only the coincidence of interests between the clergy and the petty and middle bourgeoisie that drew the attention of the Soviets. Demchenko also noted the methods which the clerical opposition had used to bring a simmering discontent to crisis proportions. It had taken advantage of the previous regime's 'dual attitude' to religion, which side by side with the repression of popular Muslim preachers had allowed the mosque to remain 'the meeting place of believers, where they could converse freely with the mullah'. At no stage had the police or military been 'allowed to bring arms into mosques or make arrests there. These circumstances were used by the opposition . . . Khomeini's sermons advocating the overthrow of the Shah, the banishment of US advisers and the army's transition to the side of the people, were taped in France and then brought in hundreds and thousands of copies to Iran, where they were played to millions of people during evening prayers.'[33]

The approval of the Iranian revolution as a whole and Khomeini in particular seemed to be general. The accession to power in Iran of the Shiite priesthood led by Khomeini, with its program for setting up an Islamic state in which Islam not only would be proclaimed as the state ideology, but was also to provide a basis for economic regulation and for reforming the whole structure of political power, was explained by the well-known orientalist G. Kim as a reaction to the former regime's attempts to ignore tradition. 'At the same time the ideological principles advocated by Khomeyni and his associates say that traditions should not be seen as a totally autonomous, independent force in the ideology and politics of newly free states. Religion and religious feelings, tradition and traditional customs are just forms that can be filled with different socio-class content . . . Thus, Khomeyni does not merely call for a struggle against all that is Western and assert the primacy of Islam . . . he has attempted to formulate a programme for an Islamic revolution in contrast to the reactionary bourgeois model of the "white revolution".' While it was still too early to foretell the final form Khomeini's model would take, it promised to free Iranian society from economic exploitation by 'a handful of property-owners . . . Khomeyni and his followers . . . are not simply trying to revive traditional religious institutions, but are evidently looking for ways to ensure a comprehensive solution to both social and national problems.'[34] This does not mean that there have not been some sceptics among Soviet commentators who have noted, side by side with the Islamic revolution's 'positive' features, the contradictions and frictions between the government and 'the revolutionary Islamic committees' which the former tried 'to bring under its authority', between the religious and the secular, including the competition between Qum and Tehran over the administration of everyday government offices, and between the government's avowed 'policy of "modernisation and revolutionary realism" ' and the reactivation of traditional Muslim rites.[35]

The position in Afghanistan was more complex than that in Iran. On the one hand, Moscow endeavored to show that the April 1978 revolution that had introduced a Marxist regime was not anti-Islam; on the other hand, the existence of a religious opposition was undeniable. Nor, indeed, could Moscow consent to religion being the dominant force in the Afghan revolution. Even though Khomeinism could be condoned in Iran where it had replaced the pro-American Shah, it clearly could not be accepted as an alternative to, or a predominant partner in, a Marxist regime. One of the senior commentators of *New Times* wrote deprecatingly of those in Afghanistan's neighboring countries who maintained that 'the "Islamic liberation movement" should be extended also to Afghanistan'. None the less, the same writer insisted that those who sought to 'play on the religious sentiments of Moslem believers to try to make it appear as if the new government had no roots in the national psychology or history and hence was inimical to Islam' were ignoring the realities of the situation. The leaders of the revolution 'consistently underscore their respect for Islamic values and deny that there is "any struggle between Moslems and infidels" '. It was 'the policy of the state', Prime Minister Hafizullah Amin was quoted as saying in June 1979, 'to give effect to revolutionary changes while fully respecting Islam'.[36]

The Soviets' sensitivity to this issue grew after their December 1979 invasion of Afghanistan. Afghanistan was not only the first Muslim country outside the USSR to undergo an avowedly

Marxist–Leninist revolution – and a Muslim country where religion played a major role in everyday life – but it was also a country that bordered on the USSR's own Muslim republics and was now overrun by Soviet troops. From the point of view of the Soviet Union's own domestic requirements, religion in Afghanistan had to be given similar treatment to that meted out to the Muslim areas of the USSR.

Agitator, the CPSU Central Committee's organ for party propagandists, indicated the line Moscow adopted regarding the problem of Islam in Afghanistan, in an article published just over a month after the Soviet invasion and significantly entitled 'The difficult path of the Afghan revolution'. It argued that while the April revolution had been 'the point of departure . . . for the downfall of the absolute rule of the tribal aristocracy and the Islamic religious elite', the difficulties in implementing 'progressive reforms' continued to be 'aggravated by the existence in the Democratic Republic of Afghanistan of deeply-rooted religious survivals and manifestations of tribal discord'.[37]

Religion, another article on Afghanistan asserted, was unquestionably being used by counter-revolution. Explaining how this had come about, the author wrote that the late President Hafizullah Amin's 'fits of anti-religious fanaticism' (Amin had deposed, murdered and replaced Taraki in September 1979 only to meet a similar fate at the hands of the Soviets in December) had driven 'ordinary Moslems, who only sought to defend their faith, under the wing of avowedly fascist groups of "the devil's brothers" ', as the Muslim Brotherhood was called. From the beginning 'the feudal landowners' had leaned on the support of 'the most reactionary part of the Moslem clergy', telling the people that if the state gave them land they would not be able to pray on it: ' "God will not hear your prayers". '[38]

Afghan counter-revolutionaries working as Western agents, according to one Soviet source, were 'inciting the local population against the new regime [of Babrak Karmal], saying that the government in Kabul was composed of atheists (*bezbozhniki*). In particular, they try to provoke hostility toward the Soviets, saying that they violate the mosques and abduct women and girls, and that tens of thousands of Afghans have been sent to Siberia.'[39] The multiplicity of the 'hostile actions against the country under cover of the banner of Islam' compelled the Afghan regime to pay 'special attention' to the religious question. 'The new Afghan government expends considerable effort not only to correct the mistakes of the past and to mend relations with the religious functionaries but also to demonstrate the Islamic character of its republic. The day begins and ends in Kabul, as in other cities, with the mullahs' calls to the faithful . . . On the Prophet Muhammad's birthday all the leaders of the Republic visited the mosque, and the session of the Council of Ulemas dedicated to the occasion was televised.'[40]

The paper most widely read by the Soviet intelligentsia, *Literaturnaia gazeta*, published an interview given to a Spanish newspaper by Molavi Abdul Aziz Sadeq, chairman of Afghanistan's Council (Soviet) of Ulemas. (The Council, which had existed since the April 1978 revolution, the paper pointed out, was composed of thirteen ulemas and 'represents the interests of Islam *vis-à-vis* the government'.) Sadeq claimed that 90 percent of the country's population professed Islam, 95 percent of these being Sunnis and 5 percent Shiites. He differentiated between 'two forms of Muslim dogma': the Muslim opponents of the regime had emigrated and were, according to Sadeq, ' "English Muslims" who march hand in hand with American imperialism and Pakistani reaction', whereas the Afghans who had remained in Afghanistan were 'advocates of the transformations taking place in the country and of the new political line of the present government'. Sadeq admitted that there had been arrests, some of them 'mistakes', and the Soviet of Ulemas had 'fought for the release of some people, not always successfully'. Yet when asked whether he was 'prepared to become the Afghan Khomeini', should the present political situation not stabilize and power pass into the hands of a religious leader, Sadeq replied that for the moment the regime was consolidating its position and the question could only be posed if the contrary should happen and the regime became weaker. 'As the representative of believing Muslims and a patriot,' Sadeq concluded, 'I want the present regime to become stronger.'[41]

In contrast to the anti-imperialist position Islam adopted in Iran and its ambivalence in Afghanistan, Moscow argued that in some of the 'progressive' Muslim countries of the Third World Islam was playing its traditional anti-revolutionary role. In particular the Soviets were perturbed by the resurgence of the Muslim Brotherhood, the traditional embodiment of Muslim fundamentalism. In Syria, for example, the Brotherhood, 'a reactionary organization operating with religious slogans', was the 'chief organizer' of 'subversive acts aimed at undermining national unity, sowing doubt among certain sections of the population, and provoking religious strife'.[42] 'The intrigues of the Muslim Brotherhood gang', according to one Soviet source, began simultaneously with Syria's opposition to the American–

Israeli–Egyptian agreements concerning the Sinai. Quoting the Syrian *al-Ba'th*, this source sought to show how this 'armed gang', arming itself with religious slogans in order to deceive the popular masses, put itself at the disposal of the enemies of the people. Yet the Syrian people knew how to tear off the masks and reveal the agents of imperialism 'who have not the slightest relation to religion and patriotism'.[43] The implication of the writer, that religion as partner to patriotism was basically a positive component in the Third World was perhaps lost on the Soviet reader. Certainly, the role of Islam in the Arab countries and the frequent need to portray Islam's positive contribution to the 'national liberation movement' in these countries has given rise to not a few awkward, obviously embarrassed articles.[44]

It seems, indeed, that even such sophisticated readers as the Soviet orientalist community, whether scholars or journalists, have had difficulty in mastering the intricacies involved in Soviet dualism regarding the nature and role of religion in the Muslim world. It is, therefore, perhaps not surprising that Soviet specialists have preferred wherever possible to evade discussion of the issue of Islam and its role in the Third World. This position, however, has become increasingly difficult to maintain. In what was obviously a reprimand, the journal *Aziia i Afrika segodnia* noted that at 'the conference of Soviet Arabists' that took place in May 1979 in Erevan (Armenia) 'unfortunately, for different reasons, scientific communications on such topics as . . . the place of Islam in the contemporary life' of the Arab countries 'could not be made'.[45] This glaring omission at a serious, scientific symposium on the Arab world just a few months after the Iranian revolution seems to have provoked the Establishment's displeasure. Presumably as a result of consequent pressure, a later report on the very same symposium stated, in contradiction to the earlier report, that 'the significant role of Islam in the Arab world, especially after the Iranian revolution, drew the attention of the conference participants'. However, even this report gave as sole examples discussion of the co-optation of Islam in Algeria – where the leadership of the Front de Libération Nationale was said to have striven to combine the principles of Islam 'with the development of the country on the path of socialist orientation' – and in Iraq, despite the generally negative attitude of the Iraqi Muslim clergy to the reforms introduced in that country after the 1958 revolution.[46] Not only did these instances concern events well before the Iranian revolution – indeed, hardly 'contemporary' – but they were also clearly not central in illuminating Islam's 'significant role in the Arab world'.

The disparate attitudes to Islam in different situations, specifically in post-revolutionary Iran and Afghanistan, can be summarized in the words of the head of the Institute of Oriental Studies, Academician Evgenyi Primakov. According to Primakov, 'the Islamic movement as a whole clearly cannot be seen as a single entity. It comprises several trends. There is a radical trend which is strongly charged with anti-imperialism. And there is, as it were, a bourgeois-landowner trend which is loaded with a large charge of anti-communism and anti-Sovietism.'

Primakov dwelt at length on the Iranian example. In Iran, he wrote, 'the revolutionary process is largely tainted with a religious color and assumes in a number of cases a religious form that at times gives it a complex character. At the same time the active participation in the revolutionary events in Iran of certain groups of the Muslim clergy led to the previously unanticipated politicization of the most backward part of the population. In the specific conditions [of Iran] this enabled the bourgeoisie to be ousted from the leadership of the mass movement, which had a positive significance.'

The USA, according to Primakov, fears the strengthening of the anti-imperialist direction of Islam and tries to speculate on its conservative aspect by strengthening the anti-Soviet and anti-communist element. To quote Primakov: 'At present the USA is indeed particularly interested in this deformation of the Islamic movement . . . first . . . to try to direct political activity in Iran against the Soviet Union, and second . . . to use the green flag of Islam to set up a front of struggle against the Afghan revolution.'[47]

The different criteria applied by Moscow to different countries and different situations[48] thus enable it to support Khomeinism and the Iranian Islamic Republic as being first and foremost anti-American in their international orientation and as being Shiite in essence and origin. Neither reason for supporting Khomeini applies to Afghanistan, where the Soviet Union, viz. the Babrak Karmal regime, deprives the official Afghan Muslim Establishment of any political significance or influence. Nor has support for Khomeini lessened disquiet at the growing influence of Islam, and especially of Islamic revivalism or fundamentalism, which threatens to become the major ideological and socio-political influence in the Muslim countries of Asia and Africa. Although the Soviet Union has been amazingly reticent – at least in its public utterances – about Khomeini's pan-Islamic aspirations, including his occasional references to the lot of its own Muslim population, it did not conceal its severely adverse reaction to Khomeini's attempts at military intervention in Afghanistan in the spring of 1979.[49]

But, even more than it fears losing Afghanistan, the Soviet Union seems concerned with the long-term implications of revivalist Islam for its own Muslims, taking great pains to attribute the Islamic revival to conditions that are specific of the non-Soviet Third World. A number of journals seem to have been given the assignment of explaining the reasons, in the words of one of them, 'for the upswing of religious sentiments, obvious enhancement of political movements having a religious tinge in the Moslem countries, and for the sharp "politicization" of Islam in the present-day world'. The reasons given were clearly irrelevant to Soviet conditions and were perhaps designed to prevent any illusions in the minds of Soviet Muslims that these trends might be applicable in their areas. These sources dwelt upon the prevalence of the 'pre-capitalist mode of life' in these countries, the illiteracy of the majority of their populations and the fact that 'Islamic traditions, customs, institutions and beliefs are part of their everyday life, and are often the only familiar forms of social being and consciousness'. As a result of these circumstances it was 'natural for them . . . to express their socio-political aspirations and protest against colonial and imperialist oppression in religious form'.[50]

However, the danger of Islamic revivalism spreading to the USSR cannot be dismissed so easily, as is revealed by Moscow's closest associates in the Soviet Muslim regions.

Thus, at a meeting in December 1980 to celebrate the sixtieth anniversary of the establishment of the Azerbaidzhan SSR's Cheka, first Secretary of the Azerbaidzhan SSR Communist Party, Politburo candidate member Geidar Aliev, and head of the Azerbaidzhan KGB, Zia Iusif-zade, called for more effective security measures in that republic. Aliev explained obliquely that this was necessary in view of 'the increasingly complex international situation, especially in the region of the Near East in states immediately adjacent to the southern borders of our country'.[51] In an earlier article in the Azerbaidzhan party organ Iusif-zade was more specific, openly voicing the fears regarding Islam. 'In connection with the situation in Iran and Afghanistan,' he wrote, 'the US special services are trying to use the Islamic religion as one of the factors in influencing the political position in our country, especially in places with a Muslim population.' The ideological diversions which were being subjected to 'chekist' suppression in Azerbaidzhan, Iusif-zade went on, were, in addition to 'nationalism and chauvinism, national narrow-mindedness and local patriotism', the 'anti-social activities of the sectarian underground and the reactionary Muslim clergy'.[52]

The Central Asian press was also worried about 'Western attempts' to infect the Soviet Muslim population with the ideas of Muslim revivalism. Bourgeois propaganda, the Kirgiz SSR Russian-language daily asserted toward the end of 1981, was trying 'to inspire Soviet peoples with views and ideas which contradict the Marxist–Leninist world view'. In particular, 'imperialism and foreign Muslim reaction are making great efforts to introduce "the flame of the Islamic rebirth" into the Soviet Union in order to destabilize the position in the republics of Central Asia, Kazakhstan, Azerbaidzhan and the Caucasus, to inflame nationalistic prejudices in these regions and arouse among believers dissatisfaction with the policy of the Communist Party and the Soviet State'.[53]

The fact that the republican party press has spelt out its anxieties so plainly clearly demonstrates a serious problem. That the central, all-Soviet media have not yet addressed themselves directly to this question, and even deny the existence of any Muslim problem within the USSR, can hardly convince the analyst either of its non-existence or of official Soviet indifference to it.[54] Surely, for example, the fact that the Soviets dwelt on the role of the mosques and the Muslim clergy as sources of trouble in Iran (see above) is evidence that Moscow has earmarked these as potential sources of danger to itself and has no intention of letting either the official mosques and Establishment Muslim functionaries or the less easily controllable unofficial clergy, officiating at rites at Muslim shrines and holy places, incite believers against the regime.

In Azerbaidzhan – and the Northern Caucasus – the main internal threat appears to be 'the sectarian underground'; namely the Sufi brotherhoods and the 'parallel', non-Establishment (and thus 'reactionary') clergy.[55] In Central Asia, on the other hand, although these phenomena prevail there as well (see below), it is the native intelligentsia and the coincidence of nationalist and religious identification that seem to cause the main concern. As we have seen, the numerous articles in the local republican press on the need for more 'atheist' and 'internationalist' education indicate that at least the more ethnically or nationally conscious groupings among the major Central Asian peoples actively identify their national aspirations with their Islamic heritage. An explicit warning against both the non-Establishment clergy and 'national narrowmindedness' was sounded by the Turkmen SSR First Party Secretary, M. G. Gapurov, in a concluding speech to a republican 'scientific–practical conference on "The Basic Questions of the International and Patriotic Education of the Workers..."'. He explained that, as there were many believers in the Turkmen SSR it was 'necessary to bear in mind' the 'special stress' laid on propagating Islam by 'our ideological foes'. These foes sought to make use of 'patriarchal–feudal customs as a means of fanning national animosities and undermining the political and ideological unity of Soviet peoples. Their aim is to engender religious feelings on an anti-Soviet basis and to sow anti-sovietism in the soil of Islam.' Moreover, Gapurov went on, 'Muslim charlatan-priests, the bearers of old reactionary principles and rites, functioning without warrant at the so-called "holy places", try to kindle religious fanaticism and to evoke sentiments of national narrow-mindedness and to propagate harmful feudal–tribal survivals and rituals in family relationships'.[56]

The Central Asians may not be orthodox Muslims in the traditional sense but they are conscious and proud of being Muslims and practice many of Islam's central rites. (Interestingly, Western sources have attested that the Tadzhik nationalist intelligentsia, for example, talk with sympathy about the religious aspect of the struggle against Babrak Karmal and his associates and mock at Karmal's attempts to prove his loyalty to the Islamic religion.[57]) The result has been a seemingly curious and contradictory policy toward Islam on the home front: on the one hand there is a greater tolerance of Islamic practice in fact (if not in theory) – an official Muslim Establishment has been set up and new limits have been defined for Soviet Muslim activity and practice of religious rituals, which, it is hoped, will satisfy the Soviet Muslims.[58] On the other hand, we witness an ever-increasing ideological onslaught on the vestiges of Islam, its tenets and customs, evidently motivated by the fear that Islam's new form and growing attraction for intellectuals among the Soviet Muslim peoples, along with the tenacity with which the large rural population and especially the womenfolk hold on to their traditions, will make it a force that cannot possibly coexist with the Soviet way of life.[59]

An *Izvestiia* article entitled 'Islam's Peking "Friends"' provides an interesting Aesopian reflection of the various aspects of the Soviet dilemma as well as giving us an unusual insight into Soviet thinking on the wide implications of the upsurge of Islam. The Chinese People's Republic's 'intent interest' in its 13 million Muslim citizens, *Izvestiia* wrote, 'is by no means fortuitous. It is dictated by the leadership's pragmatic approach to the fluctuations in the politics, economics and socio-religious movements in the world.' The paper explained that Islam had emerged upon the international arena as an 'active socio-political force' because of 'the objective increase in the clout in world affairs of the Near and Middle Eastern countries which are taking an increasingly active part in the nonaligned movement, coming out for political and economic independence from imperialism, and also in connection with the aggravation of problems of capitalism's energy raw material resources'. *Izvestiia* described the lack of political and social homogeneity of 'the multimillion masses abroad who practice Islam'. In addition to 'the conservative section of the Muslim clergy', were 'the progressive figures of the Muslim movement' who saw 'in the new upsurge an opportunity to alter the prevailing structure of their countries' ties with imperialism, to strengthen national independence, and create conditions for the solution of urgent domestic economic, political and social problems'.

The Chinese leadership, *Izvestiia* argued, was considerably worried about the future direction of the activity of the Muslim masses and how 'to make the [new] powerful popular demonstrations serve their own selfish considerations'. As a result, the Chinese were seeking 'with the aid of a powerful propaganda machine' to create in 'the consciousness of believers' belief in the CPR's 'constant and "paternal" concern for Muslims within the country'. *Izvestiia* noted that 'the Peking rulers' had been compelled to make 'certain indulgences with regard to religion', realizing that 'under the conditions of the sharp aggravation of the domestic political situation in the country and the masses' distrust of government programs, it is better to allow a certain expansion of religious freedoms (under state control, of course) than to allow political dissatisfaction with the ruling circles' course to build up'.

'No less important' than domestic considerations, *Izvestiia* went on, were those of foreign policy, namely 'the attempt to win trust in the Muslim world abroad . . . One of the Chinese Muslims' most important tasks is the consolidation of "friendly" relations with their fellow believers in other countries. However, the Chinese leadership's foreign-policy practice forces the Islamic world to follow Peking's latest maneuvers with caution.'[60]

For the student of Soviet policy the substitution of Peking and Chinese with Moscow and Soviet comes easily. It is not only that the Soviets attribute to the Chinese (possibly with good reason) their own motives, but their description of Chinese policy clearly reflects their own thinking as well as practice.

The dichotomy in the official Soviet attitude, as well as policy, toward Islam both at home and abroad indicates the dilemma which the rising force of Islam creates for Moscow in both arenas. The dilemma itself is twofold: in the first place it implies that, while the Soviet Union is aware that the Marxist–Leninist doctrine of the inevitable withering away of religion is irrelevant in the current situation, it has not yet found a formula that will allow it to coexist with the growing Islamic revivalism in the Muslim world outside, and particularly on its own borders, let alone within its frontiers. The sense of frustration and ineffectiveness in the face of this challenge is exacerbated by the fact that fundamentalist Islam (abroad) tends to adopt political radicalism, while the 'new' (Soviet) Islam has manifested a theological reformism that has enhanced its appeal to the Soviet Muslim intelligentsia. Yet attacks on the new Islam are more likely to reinforce than to weaken the influence of religion. In the second place the dilemma emanates from a consciousness of Islam's strength in the international arena and of Moscow's inability to channel this major political force into Soviet-initiated activity (as at the abortive Tashkent conference of September 1979); and also from the awareness of Islam's resilience inside the USSR where one trend (the Sufi brotherhoods) has emphasized its age-old practices, while the other (the 'new' Islam) has demonstrated an amazing adaptability to Soviet conditions, and both have achieved popularity and success. While Soviet spokesmen describe Islam as a 'social' religion, implying that it is a positive, constructive force,[61] the Soviet authorities cannot allow themselves to extend this definition and its implications to the domestic arena. Indeed, it is interesting that Soviet reports stress the Shiite nature of the positive elements in the Iranian revolution, whereas only a very small percentage of the Soviet Muslim population is Shiite. One article devoted to contemporary Shiism even insisted that the differences that existed between Shiites and Sunnis in other countries had been minimized, if not totally invalidated, by Soviet 'socio-political' circumstances.[62] Another article entitled 'Sectarianism as a form of social protest' showed how, in the conditions of Southeast Asia, Muslim sectarian activity had definitely positive features.[63] It is obvious that the Soviet Establishment did not attribute these constructive features to Soviet Muslim sectarianism.

There can indeed be little doubt that the Kremlin is concerned by Islamic revivalism, whatever form it may adopt, among its own Muslims. With the foreign Muslim countries there is always the possibility of finding a community of interests (under the umbrella formula of anti-Americanism or anti-imperialism) that will offset the inconvenience of having a common platform with an ideological opponent or the embarrassment of demands by foreign Muslim leaders on behalf of their Soviet co-religionists. With large sections of the Soviet Muslim population, the only conceivable future is one of conflict, given the totally contradictory worldview and the continuing mutual suspicions, compounded by the political implications of the Soviet Muslim population's adherence to its Muslim identity. Until now the Islamic fundamentalist revival seems to have had no direct contact with or influence upon Muslims within the USSR, although they are clearly aware of its existence and strength;[64] their own growing religiosity seems to be primarily the result of an augmented Muslim national consciousness and a disillusionment with the Marxist–Leninist alternative to Islam and its socio-political implications. The question that clearly troubles the Soviet central Establishment is what will happen if and when the barrier between these two forces – at home and abroad – is breached.[65]

Notes: Chapter 8

1. *Bol'shaia sovetskaia entsiklopediia*, 2nd edn (1953), Vol. 28, pp. 516–19.
2. N. Ashirov, 'Evoliutsiia islama v SSSR', *Nauka i religiia*, nos 3, 4, 6, 7, 9 (1971).
3. ibid.
4. Nedir Kuliev, *Antinauchnaia sushchnost' islama i zadachi ateisticheskogo vospitaniia triudiashchikhsia v usloviiakh sovetskogo Turkmenistana* (Ashkhabad: Akademiia Nauk Turkmenskoi SSR; 1960), pp. 156–9.
5. Yaacov Ro'i, 'The role of Islam and Soviet Muslims in Soviet Arab policy', *Asian and African Studies*, vol. 10, no. 2 (1974), pp. 157–81, and no. 3 (1975), pp. 259–80.
6. Dmitry Volsky, ' "Islam card" bluff', *New Times*, no. 5 (February 1980), pp. 6–7.
7. Hasan Ismailov, 'Reply to the soothsayers', *Nauka i religiia*, no. 1 (1980), pp. 40–3.
8. Soviet Muslim functionaries both attended Muslim conferences abroad and held Muslim conferences in the USSR. Tashkent, for example, hosted an international conference dedicated to the tenth anniversary of the journal *Muslims of the Soviet East*, 3–4 July 1979, and a second such conference, 9–11 September 1980, to celebrate the inception of the fifteenth century of the Hijra.
9. See, e.g., 'International problems of Muslims in the light of Quran teachings and Fatwas', 'Explanations on the question of the mourning over a dead person', *Muslims of the Soviet East*, no. 3 (1978), pp. 1–3 and 19–20 respectively. Also 'Moslems in the Soviet Union', *Asia and Africa Today*, no. 5 (September–October 1980), pp. 36–9.
10. ibid., and 'A trip of the Soviet Muslim delegation to Saudi Arabia (Mecca)', *Muslims of the Soviet East*, no. 3 (1978), pp. 3–5.

11 'Imam al-Sarahsi about work of man', *Muslims of the Soviet East*, no. 3 (1978), pp. 6–8.
12 'Truth about Soviet reality', *Muslims of the Soviet East*, No. 3 (1978), pp. 8–11.
13 'Muslims of Bashkiria, inauguration of new cathedral mosques' and 'VII Congress of Muslims of Transcaucasus', *Muslims of the Soviet East*, no. 3 (1978) pp. 12–15, 15–17 and 17–18.
14 Radio Moscow in Arabic, 14 January 1980/Foreign Broadcast Information Service, Daily Report, Vol. III (Soviet Union) (*FBIS III*), 15 January 1980. In 1980, Babakhan was reported to have published a book entitled *Islam and Muslims in the Land of the Soviets*. See Abdulla Vahabov, 'Moslems in the Soviet Union', *Asia and Africa Today*, no. 5 (September–October 1980), pp. 36–9.
15 Vahabov (ibid.) quotes the Jordanian minister of Waqfs, Kamil Sharif, who visited the USSR in 1977, as saying: " 'In the USSR one can see everywhere positive changes in the life of the Moslems . . . In the course of 60 years they have overcome stagnation and economic backwardness." ' The author goes on to comment: 'In fact, the socialist system has for the first time ever ensured Moslems unprecedentedly broad rights in all areas of political, economic and cultural life.'
16 Radio Moscow in Persian to Iran, 15 February 1980/British Broadcasting Corporation, Summary of World Broadcasts, Pt I (Soviet Union) (*SWB I*), 4 March 1980.
17 Radio Moscow in English for North America, 30 March 1979/*SWB I*, 2 April 1979.
18 Yet more research on the state of religion and the effectiveness of atheist measures in Tadzhikistan revealed that no less than 46 percent of those questioned openly admitted to participating in religious festivals only (*Kommunist Tadzhikistana*, 31 October 1980); that is, they refused to participate in the secular festivals and ceremonies that the state was seeking to introduce throughout the country to replace religious rites. For these secular holidays and ceremonies, see David E. Powell, 'Rearing the new Soviet man', in Bohdan R. Bociurkiw and John W. Strong (eds), *Religion and Atheism in the USSR and Eastern Europe* (London: Macmillan, 1975), pp. 151–70, esp. pp. 157–65; for the Soviet use of indices of religiosity, see Ethel Dunn and Stephen P. Dunn, 'Religious behaviour and sociocultural change in the Soviet Union', in ibid., pp. 123–50, esp. pp. 131–4. For estimates of the proportion of believers among the Muslim population of the Caucasus (based on Soviet figures), see Alexandre Bennigsen and Chantal Lemercier-Quelquejay, 'Muslim religious conservatism and dissent in the USSR', *Religion in Communist Lands*, vol. 6, no. 3 (Autumn 1978), pp. 153–61.
19 Ismailov, 'Reply to the soothsayers'. In conversations with Westerners, natives of Central Asia described themselves first and foremost as Muslims – specifying nationality only later. While they did not practice their religion in their everyday lives, many, for example, had Qurans and tried to read and learn from them (*Washington Post*, 31 December 1978).
20 *Sovetskaia Kirgiziia*, 16 September 1980.
21 *Pravda Vostoka*, 20 December 1979.
22 *Kommunist Tadzhikistana*, 31 October 1980.
23 *New Times*, no. 8 (February 1980), pp. 6–7.
24 Radio Peace and Progress in Arabic, 1 February 1980/*SWB I*, 4 February 1980.

25 Radio Moscow in Persian for Iran, 22 January 1980/*SWB I*, 25 January 1980, stated: 'The great Lenin stressed that the Soviet communists never regarded it as their duty to wage war against religion. From the first days of its existence the Soviet government has respected nations that adhere to the dogmas of Islam and has expressed its support for their struggle for national rights and freedom.' The broadcast demonstrated its contention by referring to 'the message to all the Muslim workers of Russia and the East . . . one of the fundamental documents of the Soviet Union'. (For this document, issued on 20 November/3 December 1917, see Jane Degras (ed.), *Soviet Documents on Foreign Policy*, Vol. 1, *1917–1924* (London: Oxford University Press, 1951), pp. 15–17.)

26 Radio Moscow, 28 March 1980/*SWB I*, 31 March 1980.

27 This part presumably was the homage paid by scholars in any discussion to the Marxist-Leninist ideology they were officially representing. Their actual views, as expressed subsequently, did not reflect this position. This discussion was a follow-up to a working conference on 'The place of religion in the ideological and political struggle of the developing countries' held on 25–6 December 1978 with the participation of scholars from a broad spectrum of academic institutes: *Narody Azii i Afriki*, no. 3 (March 1979), pp. 165–6; *Aziia i Afrika segodnia*, no. 11 (November 1979), pp. 35–6.

28 'Religion in the countries of Asia and Africa', *Narody Azii i Afriki*, no. 1 (January–February 1980), pp. 40–54.

29 In South Yemen, for example, it was admitted that both 'during the armed struggle for independence and after the attainment of independence, Islam as the ideology of the masses assisted in consolidating their struggle against English imperialism'. The leadership of the South Yemen National Front had assumed that 'Muslim ideas can play a positive role both in the struggle for national liberation and in the struggle for social progress. The ideology of the front was characterized on the whole by attempts at a radical interpretation of Muslim dogmas': A. S. Gus'kov, 'The process of establishing an avant-garde party in the People's Democratic Republic of Yemen', *Rabochii klass i sovremennyi mir*, no. 1 (January–February 1979), pp. 91–102.

30 Leonid Medvedko, 'Islam: two trends', *New Times*, no. 13 (March 1980), pp. 23–5. Radio Moscow's 'International observers at the round table' (27 January 1980/*SWB I*, 30 January 1980) sought likewise to highlight the basic incongruity of any alliance between the West and the Islamic revival. Washington, one of the commentators participating in the program pointed out, 'has decided . . . to attempt to turn against the Soviet Union and local left-wing forces the complex and contradictory religious-political processes which the West calls the "Muslim revival" . . . to give the impression that the Soviet Union and communism threaten the traditions of the Muslim peoples, their distinctive traits and independence. Under this false pretext they try to contrast the Afghan revolution with the Iranian one which they see as a real Muslim revolution.' Yet, as a second commentator stressed, 'The anti-imperialist tendency which has appeared in the Muslim movement over the past few years' reflected, rather, 'the incompatibility of the fundamental interests of the Muslim peoples with the new form of Western imperialist neo-colonialist aspirations'.

31 e.g. Dmitri Kasatkin and Vyacheslav Ushakov, 'Iran and aspects of the revolutionary movement', *Asia and Africa Today*, no. 3 (May–June 1979), pp. 10–13; and N. Kianuri (First Secretary of the Communist People's Party of Iran), 'The popular revolution in Iran', *Kommunist*, no. 5 (March 1980), pp. 79–89.

32. E. Doroshenko, 'Iran: Muslim (Shiite) traditions and the present day', *Aziia i Afrika segodnia*, no. 8 (August 1980), pp. 59–61.
33. P. Demchenko, 'Iran takes a new road', *International Affairs* (Moscow), no. 10 (October 1979), pp. 80–6.
34. G. Kim, 'Social development and ideological struggle in the developing countries', *International Affairs* (Moscow), no. 4 (April 1980), pp. 65–75.
35. Demchenko, 'Iran takes a new road'. For one important exception to the general approval of Khomeini's Iran, a major article by *Izvestiia* political correspondent Aleksandr Bovin, see: M. Volodarsky and Y. Ro'i, 'Soviet–Iranian relations during two revolutions', *Slavic and Soviet Series*, vol. 4, no. 1–2 (1979), p. 49.
36. D. Volsky, 'The target: Afghanistan's revolution', *New Times*, no. 24 (June 1979), pp. 12–13.
37. A. Kniazev, 'The difficult path of the Afghan revolution', *Agitator*, no. 3 (February 1980), pp. 46–8.
38. Martine Monod, 'Afghanistan: hopes and difficulties', *New Times*, no. 5 (February 1980), pp. 20–31. (Monod was correspondent in Kabul of the French communist paper *L'Humanité*.)
39. Aleksandr Prokhanov, 'What are the bandits doing?', *Literaturnaia gazeta*, no 9 (27 February 1980), p. 9.
40. Pavel Demchenko and Leonid Mironov, 'The Republic's business-like rhythm', *Za rubezhom*, no. 7 (February 1980), p. 7. Another source (Radio Moscow in English, 2 February 1980/*SWB I*, 4 February 1980) gave a more detailed picture of religious life under Babrak Karmal: 'Each day in the Afghan capital and other towns and villages starts with calls by the Muezzin for the morning prayer, and every Muslim performs the prayer. All the mosques and religious schools are open. Religious holidays are observed. Take January 21, the birthday of the Prophet Muhammad, which is observed in Afghanistan just as in other Muslim countries as a holiday when all work stops. Islam is taught at schools. A Department of Theology operates in Kabul University. The Government led by Babrak Karmal has repeatedly declared it respects religion and the clergy . . . Communists being atheists does not mean there are bans on, and persecution of, religion. Communists have always recognized and still recognize freedom of conscience and religion.'
41. Molavi Sadeq, 'The rights of believers', *Literaturnaia gazeta*, no. 8 (20 February 1980), p. 9.
42. Yuri Tyunkov, 'From El Quneitra to al-Thawrah', *New Times*, no. 42 (October 1979), pp. 8–9.
43. *Za rubezhom*, no. 42 (October 1979), pp. 14–15.
44. See, for example, A. Ignatenko, 'To see the social essence of the phenomenon', *Nauka i religiia*, no. 11 (November 1981), pp. 60–1.
45. Iu. Andreev, 'Conference of Soviet Arabists', *Afrika i Aziia segodnia*, no. 8 (August 1979), pp. 56–7. This was the first time that such a forum, a conference of Soviet Arabists, was ever convened. The occasion reflected the Soviet reappraisal of the Arab world and its own policy toward it, in the light of the difficulties Moscow encountered there in the latter half of the 1970s.
46. S. Grishin, 'Erevan forum of Arabists', *Narody Azii i Afriki*, no. 1 (January–February 1980), pp. 147–57.
47. 'When black is passed off as white', *Literaturnaia gazeta*, no. 11 (12 March 1980), p. 14.

48 Aware of its own double standards concerning religion abroad, Moscow explains them by internal contradictions within the various religions and religious organizations – in our case, Islam. Its adherents, for example, while seemingly 'guided by the same religious dogmas and values, are very often to be found on opposite sides of the class barricades: in one set of cases, they take an anti-imperialist stand and take part in the overthrow of obsolete regimes, while in others they collaborate with the neo-colonialists and pursue a policy opposed to the people. Thus, the revolution in Iran began and was carried out under the slogans of Islam, yet among the believers and the Muslim clergy of that country, representing various class forces, there are appreciable differences of opinion regarding the further development of events. The enemies of the people's power and of the revolutionary achievements in Afghanistan (such as the notorious "Muslim Brotherhood", agents of international imperialism and other reactionary forces) are trying to exploit the slogans of Islam, although the majority of the believers – the masses of the working people – support the policy of the revolutionary leaders' (*Pravda*, 16 November 1979). Primakov, too, had noted the lack of homogeneity in Islam's influence on 'the processes of social development'.

49 See, for example, *Pravda*, 19 March 1979.

50 A. Vasileyev, 'Islam in the present day world', *International Affairs* (Moscow), no. 11 (November 1981), pp. 52–9. For another article with a similar message, see S. Aliev, 'Islam and politics', *Aziia i Afrika segodnia*, no. 12 (December 1981), pp. 5–9.

51 *Bakinskii rabochii*, 25 December 1980.

52 ibid., 19 December 1980.

53 *Sovetskaia Kirgiziia*, 27 December 1981.

54 As one of the doyens of Soviet orientalist journalism, Igor' Beliaev, wrote: 'Sometimes one comes across, in the pages of the Western press, fantastic nonsense that an "Islamic explosion" is as it were on the point of taking place in . . . the Soviet Union, in those republics where Soviet Muslims live. The purpose of these falsehoods of Western "specialists on Islam" is quite clear. The issue, of course, is not the Soviet Muslims. We have no problems on this count' (*Literaturnaia gazeta*, no. 3, 16 January 1980).

55 Alexandre Bennigsen has written extensively on the Sufi brotherhoods and the unofficial unauthorized Muslim religious functionaries. See, for example, his chapter, 'Muslim conservative opposition to the Soviet regime: the Sufi brotherhoods in the North Caucasus', in Jeremy R. Azrael (ed.), *Soviet Nationality Policies and Practices* (New York: Praeger, 1978), pp. 334–48.

56 *Turkmenskaia iskra*, 15 June 1980.

57 Radio Hamburg, 16 June 1980 (quoting Der Spiegel)/*FBIS III*, 20 June 1980.

58 See, for example, Hélène Carrère d'Encausse, *Decline of an Empire* (New York: Newsweek Books, 1979), pp. 232–5. Professor d'Encausse shows how in the USSR the five daily prayers have been officially reduced to one, which can be recited whenever convenient to the believer; how workers have been exempted from fasting, a 'special effort' in their spiritual life or even at work being recognized as a substitute; and how a donation to the mosque of the value of an animal has come to replace sacrifices on the *Kurban Bairam* (Festival of Sacrifices). See also Rasma Karklins, 'Islam: how strong is it in the Soviet Union?', *Cahiers du monde russe et soviétique*, vol. 21, no. 1 (January–March 1980), pp. 65–81; also Vl. Rosen, 'The

church and the state', *New Times*, no. 8 (February 1979), pp. 24–6. The latter article quotes the chairman of Moscow's Muslim community, Zinatullah Iakubov, as pointing out: 'In the Arab countries women are not allowed in the mosques. We allow women in our mosque. In some countries women still wear the veil . . . We have forbidden the observance of this custom as an infringement of women's equality.'

59 For a description of the new latent force of Islam in the USSR, the political implications of Moscow's policy of seeking ways to accomodate itself to a minimal framework of Islamic practice, and growing Soviet awareness of the problem, see Carrère d'Encausse, *Decline*, ch. 7.

60 *Izvestiia*, 19 June 1980. An article for propagandists in the Muslim sector, clearly intended to show Soviet Muslims that the lot of their co-religionists in the CPR was not to be envied, further illuminates the Soviets' thinking and practice *vis-à-vis* their own Muslims: G. Saltykov, 'The Muslims in China', *Nauka i religiia*, no. 9 (September 1981), pp. 59–63.

61 Vadim Zagliadin, Deputy Head of the CPSU Central Committee International Department, said in Paris: 'We do not think the roots of the resurgence of Islam are purely religious. They have more of a social character. Islam is probably the most social of religions. The present Muslim resurgence is the expression of a desire to change the situation. In Iran especially the Muslims were the main force in the struggle against the Shah's regime for economic and social change' (*Le Monde*, 4 December 1980). Soviet journals even publish articles under such titles as 'Muslim movements of social protest', *Aziia i Afrika segodnia*, no. 10 (October 1980), pp. 36–9.

62 Similarly, Soviet explanations of the evolution of Shiism's positive features were careful to attribute it to conditions prevalent in other countries, specifically Iran, excluding any hopes that Soviet Shiism might be regarded favorably. See, for example, I. Vasil'ev, 'Islam: trends, currents, sects', *Aziia i Afrika segodnia*, no. 2 (February 1980), pp. 54–7.

63 A. Ionova, 'Sectarianism as a form of social protest', *Aziia i Afrika segodnia*, no. 2 (February 1981), pp. 57–60.

64 One N. Bairamsakhatov, said to be responsible for *agitprop* in Turkmenistan, reportedly revealed in a brochure published in 1979 that some of the Turkmen population had been listening regularly to religious broadcasts from Iran. Cassette tape recordings of these broadcasts had even been made, according to this same source, by mullahs and played before groups of believers throughout the republic: Bohdan Nahaylo, 'The Islamic time bomb', *The Spectator*, 21 February 1981.

Apart from broadcasts from Iran the Soviet Muslim population receives daily information – in seven languages – from Radio Liberty in Munich (a station that broadcasts to the USSR under the supervision of the Board for International Broadcasting). A computer projection developed by the station estimated apparently at the turn of the decade that 2·5 percent of the adults among the Soviet Muslim population heard Radio Liberty: *The New York Times*, 10 January 1980.

65 It is otherwise impossible to explain such statements as the *Sovetskaia Kirgiziia* reference to attempts to make use of Islamic revivalism outside the USSR to destabilize the Soviet Muslim areas. *Turkmenskaia iskra*, June 15 1980, virtually admitted that Turkmens heard foreign broadcasts. *Newsweek*'s Moscow bureau chief was told in Baku: ' "Our hope is in Afghanistan . . . If the Muslim rebels there succeed in throwing out the Communist government, Moscow must think again' (*Newsweek*, 2 April 1979).

PART THREE

Foreign Policy Aspects

9

Soviet Central Asia: A Model of Non-Capitalist Development for the Third World

TERESA RAKOWSKA-HARMSTONE

The Soviet Muslim republics are an important asset in the promotion of Soviet foreign-policy objectives in the Third World, because they serve as an example of how backward societies can successfully build socialism while by-passing the capitalist stage of development. The four union republics of Central Asia (Uzbekistan, Tadzhikistan, Kirgizia and Turkmenia), and those of Kazakhstan and Azerbaidzhan, were created after the 1917 Revolution in the former Russian colonial areas; these were non-European, economically backward and socially and politically traditional – 'feudal' in communist parlance – characteristics which were shared at independence by a great many Asian and African states. Under the impact of Moscow-directed policies the traditional Muslim society of these areas has been transformed into a Soviet-style socialist society – a transformation that is acclaimed as a model for all other developing countries wishing to avoid capitalism and imperialist exploitation, and as a panacea for all the problems of development. The relevance to post-colonial societies of the Soviet Muslim experience has always been implicit in the Soviet message to the Third World. But its explicit value as a model to be imitated came to the fore in the 1970s, in response to the perceived shift in the 'correlation of forces' in favor of the socialist camp, and to the growing realization in the Kremlin that an element of direct control is indispensable for the consolidation of Soviet gains in the Third World. The history of Soviet Central Asia and other Soviet Muslim areas (and of Mongolia, the first Third World country to avail itself of the Soviet model) provides an example of how such control can be established, maintained and perpetuated in the name of the 'friendship of the peoples', 'proletarian internationalism' and 'socialist construction'. The theme of a 'Central Asian model' in Soviet foreign policy has made its appearance recurrently in Soviet writings and reemerged strongly as the 1980s approached.

Background

Soviet interest in the colonial countries and the so-called semi-colonial states dates to the early days of the October Revolution. Lenin was keenly aware of the revolutionary potential of national self-assertion movements in the Russian Empire as well as in contiguous Asia – an awareness that was reflected in his analysis of imperialism as capitalism's last stage, and its economic dependence on colonial exploitation. The importance Lenin attached to the question in the international arena and the fascination with the numbers that could be drawn into the revolutionary struggle emerge in his early polemics with Rosa Luxemburg:

> National wars waged by colonies and semi-colonies in the imperialist era are not only probable but *inevitable*. Some 1,000 million people, or *more than half* of the world's population, live in the colonies and semi-colonies (China, Turkey, Persia). Here, national-liberation movements are either already very powerful or are growing and maturing. Every war is the continuation of politics by other means. The continuation of the policy of national-liberation by the colonies will *inevitably* lead them to wage national wars *against* imperialism.[1]

Considerable attention was paid to the national and colonial question in the early days of Soviet power, in the efforts to use Russia's Muslims to extend the Revolution across the border, and to mobilize national revolutions in Western colonies under the aegis of the Comintern.[2] Although the failure of these endeavors and Stalin's preoccupation with 'socialism in one country' caused the colonial question to be downgraded – the interest in it was to be revived again only in the 1950s – major themes raised in the early debates have shown remarkable continuity and endurance and are still relevant today. One of them has been the Bolshevik conviction that world revolution is inevitable, and that the extension of revolutionary forces and their final victory are synonymous with the extension of power and influence by the Soviet state. The first part of this proposition has been shared by most non-Russian communists, but not the second. In consequence, the hegemonial pretensions of the Soviet party conveyed by the slogan 'proletarian internationalism',[3] and its insistence on centralism, have engendered a conflict with nationalism from the very beginning. This conflict has been a permanent feature of Soviet domestic politics, and has dominated relations between the Communist Party of the Soviet Union (CPSU) and foreign parties, and between the USSR and other socialist and 'socialist oriented' states as well.

Early debates over strategy and tactics also have contemporary significance, their perpetuation highlighting both diversity of conviction and the fact that no policy has proved effective in securing for Moscow unassailable control of Third World revolutionary movements despite Moscow's agility in implementing tactical shifts in pursuit of opportunity. The quarrel between the European and Asian communists over whether a revolution in industrialized Europe or in peasant Asia should take priority in order to achieve the final goal of world revolution has finally erupted in the Sino-Soviet quarrel; now each side has a competitive model for the Third World to emulate. Early disagreements over tactics in colonial and semi-colonial countries have recurred in alternating emphases in matters such as city- versus village-based revolutions and parties, the pursuit of revolutionary class-struggle as against national-front tactics, or the role assigned to communist parties in national/anti-colonial struggles: whether the former should lead, infiltrate, or subordinate themselves to, national–bourgeois revolutionary elements. Last but not least, early debates also featured an assertion, still valid today, that backward countries may move directly from precapitalist to socialist formation, providing that they do so in alliance with and under the guidance of the first victorious communist state, the USSR. It is in the latter context that the experience of the Soviet Union's southern and eastern republics has been of lasting relevance. Their level of development serves to convince sceptics that the assertion is valid; and their location and ethno-cultural characteristics facilitate contacts across the border and with related societies.

None of Lenin's contemporaries or successors could match his instinctive grasp of political realities or his doctrinal flexibility in accommodating to changing circumstances. Thus, Lenin's perceptions of the national and colonial questions still provide guidelines for Soviet policy, the more so because the older the party becomes the less capable it is of leaving the security of its legitimizing myths. There is substantial flexibility in the framework, perpetuated by selective interpretations. But the maintenance of the ideological parameters of Leninist thought has imposed an increasingly restrictive influence on seeking viable policy alternatives over half a century after Lenin's death. It was Lenin who liberated his vanguard-party concept from its dependence on a class base (thus giving it validity in pre-industrial societies), and it was Lenin who saw expediency in a temporary alliance with the national bourgeoisie and national revolutionary leaders. But, despite the recognition of the East's revolutionary potential, Lenin never budged from a Europocentrist position in debates with Asian communists. In foreign policy this strengthened the perception that the interests of the world revolution and of the Soviet state were synonymous and, in dealing with colonial matters, that revolutionary movements in the Third World could not be consolidated without Soviet assistance and direction. Both theses are still articles of faith in Soviet foreign policy.

In domestic affairs the Europe-first position served to emphasize the leadership of the 'more advanced' European proletariat, giving the Russian cadres practical preeminence in Asian areas. Muslim communists who resented the 'colonial mentality' of Russian revolutionaries and inclined toward an Asia-first emphasis (with Sultan Galiev, the leading Tatar communist and Stalin's deputy at the *Narkomnats* as their major spokesman), were all eventually branded 'bourgeois nationalists' and removed in the successive purges which denuded the Soviet Muslim republics of indigenous cadres.[4] In consequence, the 'socialist transformation' of these republics was carried out from above and from outside, using the instrumentality of European cadres, a point which is of major importance — if not always explicitly acknowledged — in the current campaign to sell the Central Asian model to the developing countries, as shall be seen below. Lenin's major failing was to underestimate the survival value and the growth potential of nationalism, especially as it has preempted the hoped-for emergence of class-based loyalties. The failure to understand the nature of nationalism and to take into account the strength and affective qualities of national self-assertion — a shortcoming that has been perpetuated by Lenin's successors — has been a source of problems in both Soviet domestic politics and in foreign policy, not least in relations with the Third World.

The revaluation of the USSR's Third World policies conducted by the Soviet Establishment in the latter half of the 1960s had been necessitated by the complex conditions created, on the one hand, by the instability of the new 'progressive' regimes and, on the other hand, by the assertion of national interests within the communist movement and the consequent polycentrism highlighted by the Sino-Soviet conflict and Romania's revolt against Soviet hegemony within the Warsaw Pact. This revaluation was based on two fundamental premisses: the inadequacy of simplistic assumptions regarding the 'natural' or 'lasting' alliance of the Third World 'peace zone' with the socialist camp, which the above-mentioned developments had rendered virtually meaningless from the practical point of view; and Moscow's improved intervention capabilities that gave new momentum to its identification with the goals of world revolution.[5]

Not unnaturally, the revaluation dwelt among others upon the value of the reliance on physical strength and direct controls as demonstrated in the consolidation of power in the Soviet borderlands in the twenties and, more recently, in the construction of the 'socialist camp' in contiguous Eastern Europe. In conditions of expanded capabilities and outreach, this experience obviously had acquired new relevance. In the Third World the example of formerly backward Soviet Asian frontiers came to be seen as particularly valid for the countries equally backward and beset by similar social and economic problems and political conflict and instability. Thus, in the seventies, the Soviet Asians once again became important in foreign policy, as they had been in the twenties. In the Soviet quest for influence the 'Central Asian model' combines ideological with practical appeal, and features the control mechanics indispensable, in Moscow's view, for the achievement by the USSR of the desired hegemonial goals. Third World leaders, for their part, strongly respond to the magic of the word 'socialism' and to negative images of 'imperialism' and 'neo-colonialism', and are impressed by the visible achievements of the Soviet Muslim republics while remaining largely ignorant of hidden costs. The model has primary relevance in relations with the states 'of socialist orientation' (a new label for 'progressive revolutionary democracies'), as the Soviet Union presses for advantage in strategic areas of the Third World. There, while continuing a general multidimensional effort to squeeze out Western influence throughout, a new initiative emerged in the seventies: an attempt to establish direct influence via the formation of regional sub-systems centered on a pivotal client state, either socialist or of socialist orientation. It is in the context of relations between Moscow and the new clients that the experience of Soviet Central Asia is presented as a paradigm to be imitated.

Central Asian Model

Early hopes of the Revolution spilling over from Soviet Asia into contiguous semi-colonial areas were not fulfilled in the interwar period. Despite their diminishing chances, however, these aspirations surfaced occasionally. When Russian Turkestan and other non-European areas were remodeled into constituent and autonomous republics in 1924 under the first Soviet federal constitution, the purpose, *inter alia*, was said to be to 'evoke a great echo beyond our frontiers'.[6] As the Tadzhik republic, for example, advanced from autonomous to union republic status in 1929 it was greeted by Stalin as the future 'model republic of the Eastern countries',[7] and a Tadzhik official history referred to the promotion, in retrospect, as an event of 'great international importance', because Tadzhikistan thus 'became a model of how . . . [to resolve] the national problem . . . [and] demonstrated the great care which the Communist Party and the Soviet Government took in the creation and development of the national statehood of a previously oppressed backward colonial people'.[8]

Domestic legitimation requirements were undoubtedly a factor in the maintenance of the myth of the republics' 'international importance'; but their foreign-policy potential came to be realized with World War II. The 1945 Soviet claims to Turkish Kars and Ardahan, for instance, were made in the name of Soviet Georgia and Armenia.[9] Similar claims may well be revived on behalf of Soviet Azeris, Turkmens or other border-straddling minorities, should conditions in Iran favor such claims.

The fifties brought the perception that the Third World was to be the Soviet Union's major partner in the global arena, thus upgrading the foreign-policy relevance of the Soviet Asian borderlands. The Soviet Muslim republics – Uzbekistan in particular – became a showcase for visiting Afro-Asian dignitaries whom Moscow sought to convince of the success of Soviet development policies. The 'official' Muslim clergy have developed lively contacts with co-religionists abroad,[10] and vigorous cultural, scientific and educational exchanges were initiated with the new states by the Soviet Muslim republics, which also provide training facilities of all kinds, military included, for Third World students. In relations with China the republics, Kazakhstan especially, began to be built up as the focus of attraction for border-divided minorities.[11] A sample of the resulting war of words is a US-published pamphlet by Victor

Louis, which envisages the eventual incorporation of Chinese Turkestan by Soviet Central Asia.[12]

The practical value of Soviet Asia as a model of development emerged in the early seventies owing to the new foreign-policy perceptions noted above: a shift in the global power-balance and an opportunity to expand, combined with a growing desire to control Third World allies. The practical advantages of the Central Asian model here were obvious. It was seen to be attractive because of its claim to have resolved the two crucial problems faced by the new states: economic development and ethnic (communal/tribal) conflict. And it featured control mechanisms within a political infrastructure which allowed for the extension of control lines to Moscow. Such mechanisms have already proved functional in an international setting in Eastern Europe.

The two attractive features have been played up in the campaign to convince potential customers, while control mechanisms have been minimized and portrayed in a beneficial light as prerequisites and accelerators of success. Thus, advocates of the model stressed the potential of each backward country developing economically to bypass capitalism and to proceed directly to socialism, and to achieve in the process an ethnic peace and harmony unobtainable under capitalism. These claims have been supported by evidence available to visitors in Soviet Central Asia, where the living standards and important economic and social indicators top most comparative statistics in developing areas, and the mixed ethnic character of urban and industrial centers and the Asians' visibility in the political structure create an impression of equality and good relations between Soviet nations and nationalities. But, in order to duplicate the Soviet Central Asian achievement, two absolutely indispensable conditions are said to be required: the adoption by the leaders of Marxist–Leninist 'scientific socialism', and outside assistance by 'more advanced' countries. Translated into a Third World context these conditions mean the adoption of a Soviet-style political system, and an alliance with the Soviet bloc led by the Soviet Union.

Theoretical Perspectives

Not surprisingly, the ideological pedigree of the relevance of Soviet Central Asia to the contemporary Third World begins with the Great October Revolution and encompasses the historical progression from colonialism to liberation and toward socialism, entering the seventies with high expectations. As formulated by the late Mikhail Suslov, the Politburo's foremost theoretician:

> The Great October opened before the oppressed peoples of the colonies real prospects for a national liberation struggle. The defeat of German fascism and Japanese militarism and the emergence and growth of the world socialist system, facilitated the powerful upheaval of the movement for national independence which . . . led to the break-up of the colonial system of imperialism and the emergence of new states many of which selected the path of socialist orientation.[13]

But, although a period of high promise, the seventies also marked a major challenge. National liberation having been achieved in most cases, the struggle for 'social liberation', for the choice of the 'road of further development', began and 'is being waged in conditions of acute class conflict'.

According to Boris Ponomarev, the Central Committee Secretariat's top specialist in non-ruling communist parties and 'progressive' movements, the crucial question now was no longer whether or not the imperialists could restore old forms of colonial oppression, but 'which path of development' would be chosen by the new nations. Would they follow a path of continuing struggle with imperialism, 'which inevitably arouses the question of a non-capitalist way of development', or would the attraction of the capitalist model 'gain an upper hand'? The latter would equally inevitably result in the strengthening of exploitation, even if in a different form.[14] As the class struggle continues, collaboration with socialist states is the only way developing countries can avoid a renewed subjection to neo-colonialism. It is obvious, Ponomarev tells us, that the real successes of the developing countries are 'tied with a billion threads to the role socialism plays in the international arena', because of the power of example and the assistance rendered by the Soviet bloc. Thus, 'close and sincere' collaboration between communist and revolutionary–democratic parties is *the* precondition of successful development.[15]

What all this means in practice is that, having largely missed the national liberation express, Soviet leaders are now climbing on the bandwagon of economic and social development and the political aspirations of the new states, to make up for lost time in furthering their long-term policy objectives. Because the situation is delicate and conditions are complex and vary from case to case, the need for a flexible approach is in the forefront of Soviet perceptions. Ponomarev recalls the lessons of the

Seventh Congress of the Comintern (which adopted 'popular front' tactics), and cautions against simplistic stereotypes in the adjustment of practical policies to the concrete historical experience of the states that liberate themselves from the colonial and neo-colonial yoke.[16] None the less, as Soviet spokesmen and selected socialist orientation leaders further point out, the historical experience of Soviet Central Asia and Azerbaidzhan (and Mongolia) carries important lessons for the new states as they begin the struggle for 'social liberation'. The vast colonial periphery of the Russian Empire was as backward as much of the Third World is now, and Soviet leaders there were faced with, and successfully solved, the same kind of problems which are now confronting Afro-Asian leaders.[17]

The Soviet regime's key to success in its own outlying areas was contained in Lenin's assessment of what can and should be done: 'with the help of the proletariat of the more advanced countries, backward countries may be able to by-pass the capitalist stage of development and to move directly into socialism'.[18] This proposition is held to be as relevant now for the developing world as it was then for Central Asia, *provided* that the key features of the latter's experience are in their main outline duplicated. Here, then, are the main theoretical ingredients of the Central Asian prescription for the Third World: a path to socialism is assured, if inexperienced colonials entrust their fate with enthusiasm and without reservation to the more advanced socialist countries where experience will assure the best application of past lessons in each case. Thus, submission to the Soviet leadership in all matters is the precondition of the successful transition from backwardness to socialism bypassing the capitalist stage, the key point to which we shall shortly return.

Validity of the Model

The meaning and current 'international significance' of the various stages in Soviet Central Asia's transition to socialism have been vigorously debated by Soviet scholars and propagandists, with much of the debate centered in the region itself. The main lines of the argument are that socialism was introduced there via two different routes: directly, in the case of Russian Turkestan, where revolutionary power was established from the outset, and indirectly, in the khanates of Khiva and Bukhara, where national people's republics were established first, introducing a bourgeois–democratic stage. It was only in 1924, at the time of the region's national delimitation, that Turkestan and the Bukharan and Khivan (now Khorezm) People's Republics were treated uniformly. From the point of view of the class character of the transformation in Central Asia as a whole, socialist and revolutionary–democratic elements existed side by side and collaborated broadly until the late twenties, when the process of direct transition to socialism was accelerated.

The national people's republic period in Khiva and Bukhara is of special interest because the conditions which existed there are directly comparable to those which obtain at present in many countries of socialist orientation. The significance of the similarities is well summarized by an Indian scholar educated in Tashkent, whose views closely parallel those expressed in Soviet sources:

> The historical significance of the People's Republics of Bokhara and Khiva as transitional forms of socialism lies in the fact that they were the first to give an example of a resolute and uncompromising anti-feudal and anti-imperialist struggle without which the people's way to socialism cannot be successful. The governments . . . under the leadership of the Communist Party began a series of democratic transformations . . . democratic state administration, transfer to the peasants of land . . . the reduction of taxes . . . a state sector in the economy . . . schools . . . cultural and medical facilities . . . All . . . in conditions of bitter struggle against . . . the feudals . . . aided by their foreign patrons.[19]

The supposed 'foreign patrons' of the period were the British. It may be noted that no direct reference is made in the above description to Islam as the main enemy in the 'class struggle'. This omission has been characteristic of much of the discussion earmarked for non-Soviet consumption.

The validity of the Central Asian model for all developing countries is generally accepted. As Aleksei Kosygin, the then Chairman of the USSR Council of Ministers, phrased it in 1974 in a speech he gave in Kirgizia: 'The experience of socialist construction in regions formerly underdeveloped and the experience of having solved the national problem accumulated by Kirgizia and other republics . . . opened up a revolutionary perspective for the majority of mankind: the nations of Asia, Africa, and Latin America.'[20] Yet there have been disagreements among the Soviet interpreters of Central Asia's socialist transformation over some of the specifics of the post-1924 period of transition. Were the reforms of 1925–9 (nationalization of land and water) 'socialist' or merely 'revolutionary–democratic'? Some feel that they were socialist because they were carried out by the government of the dictatorship of the proletariat; others consider them revolutionary–democratic because they allowed for the retention of property rights in the countryside, and for the survival of some traditional social structures.[21] What the argument is all about is whether the character of reforms is determined by the form of political power of the implementing authority or by their substance, and its resolution is important because of the label it attaches to similar reforms elsewhere, e.g. whether or not they imply the 'socialist orientation' or merely the 'revolutionary–democratic character' of a given state. The differentiation is subtle; and the label, when attached, suits a particular political expediency.

The overall value of the discussion has been to bring out similarities in the conditions prevalent in historical Central Asia and present-day tradition-bound countries, in order to facilitate the transformation of the latter into new members of the socialist commonwealth. Some points receive particular attention. One is the long timetable allowed for the transformation, a quarter of a century, as pointed out by Uzbek Party First Secretary Sharaf Rashidov.[22] Others include the gradual effect of the reforms on the traditional institutions (which they undercut), and the impact of immigrant Russian proletarian cadres (indispensable for the leadership). It was precisely the presence of the Russian workers which made it possible, according to Soviet spokesmen, to accelerate the timetable of the transformation and eventually to 'telescope' the revolutionary–democratic and socialist stages, so that Central Asia could enter socialism directly.[23] The process of acceleration and telescoping is seen as particularly instructive for countries of socialist orientation. They can do it, too, but only under a government of the dictatorship of the proletariat (i.e. a vanguard party), and with the assistance of the 'more advanced' countries.[24]

This brief review of the Soviet analysis of the Central Asian model indicates that it has specificities in the sequence of events and in characteristics of the process which constitute essential preconditions of success. The process's relevance to the Third World is made explicit. As Rashidov put it: the historical experience of 'our nation' cannot be overemphasized in its importance for the new nations of Asia and Africa.[25]

Attributes of the Model

The main characteristics of the model and its programmatic

importance for Soviet foreign policy were summarized by Boris Ponomarev in an important 1980 article in the CPSU's leading theoretical journal *Kommunist*.[26] Ponomarev begins the discussion by emphasizing the importance to the Soviet Union of the states of socialist orientation. Good relations with these states are essential, he says, in conditions of the 'struggle' with imperialism and with 'renegade' China and because of the need to support their 'socialist ideas', the general acceptance of which is by no means automatic. Ponomarev's concern over the adherence to 'true' socialism on the part of Third World states echoes growing criticism elsewhere in Soviet sources of the many so-called 'socialisms' of the Asians and Africans, none of which approximates the real thing. That the states of socialist orientation are currently considered vital to bloc interests is emphasized again at the end of the article, when Ponomarev concludes that 'all measures [undertaken] to strengthen the states of socialist orientation are of major international importance'.[27]

The article's main argument concerns the benefits to be derived from the Soviet Union's own historical experience by all those who wish to proceed directly from a traditional to a socialist society. One by one Ponomarev ticks off the attributes which should be developed by the states of socialist orientation if they want to safeguard their 'progressive positions'. These are: a revolutionary vanguard party which provides political leadership, acting from positions of 'scientific socialism'; organs of 'democratic power' (i.e. state structure), established after colonial rule is liquidated, operating on the basis of power flowing from the top downward (*sverkhu do nizu*) (i.e. applying the principle of democratic centralism); trained party and state indigenous cadres; national military forces; a network of ties between party and state organs and the masses (i.e. a broad application of communist techniques of social mobilization); and economic and social reforms. A prerequisite for the implementation of this program is a close link with the socialist countries, 'the most faithful and reliable friends of independent, freedom-loving states'.[28]

The sequence in which the attributes are discussed and the relative emphases are indicative of the thrust of Soviet policy and its primary concerns. First and foremost it spells the requirements of control, namely the *forms of political power* which have to be established to direct the transformation of society into a new system, and later on to sustain it in its new role. The points of substance, i.e. the type and nature of reforms, receive a distinctly secondary billing. Thus, the leading and primary condition is the establishment of a vanguard party, regardless of whether or not a proletarian base for it exists. The structural–operational attributes that follow are essential for the implementation of controls and for the introduction of reforms. And the ability to put in place, to maintain and to develop the six attributes is predicated on the Soviet alliance.

The vital importance of leadership by a vanguard party is underscored by all participants in the discussion.[29] The gist of this importance is succinctly stated by Ponomarev, who says that 'ideological and political leadership by a revolutionary vanguard party is a necessity', regardless of the level of development of the particular country, because the party is essential for the destruction of socially hostile elements of the old regime and for the resolution of national/ethnic and religious problems, as well as for attracting the youth and the conduct of political work in the armed forces intended, among others, to ensure their reliability.[30] To be successful a vanguard party has to operate on the principles of scientific socialism, which means that it plays the leading role based on a monopoly of political power. The key role assigned to such a party in a society still bound by traditional structures is illustrated by Rashidov's description of the Soviet party's tactics in Central Asia: an alliance between communists and national–revolutionary forces and a graduated timetable of reforms, which nevertheless relentlessly proceed to intensify the class struggle and to destroy traditional patterns of privilege and exploitation.[31] This description illustrates an important point – reiterated many times elsewhere – that the party's policies need to adjust in each case to particular conditions, but always have to be based on an alliance with local 'progressive' forces and to aim, in the long run, at a total destruction of the old regime.

The second crucial variable is a centralized state structure (the establishment of which may predate an emergence of the vanguard party), which provides an operational framework for policy implementation. Here again, the Central Asian experience offers valuable lessons. The first lesson is on the subject of how to solve the national problem by way of a new type of statehood ('national in form and socialist in content'), which combines outward autonomy with centralized control by the party and is claimed to guarantee equality to all national (ethnic/tribal/communal) groups. The second is how to establish and use foreign-controlled and largely foreign-staffed security police and armed forces for the purpose of the consolidation of power. Lesson number two is rarely discussed except in the most general terms. But it is applied in practice by Soviet and East European advisers in client states. Security services in all of them are assumed to be run by the KGB, at least on the evidence of defectors. In the case of national armies, the Central Asian experience cannot on the surface serve for comparison because no national armies were established there; only national units within a consolidated command structure. But the Red Army's experience in Central Asia in the early period and the views and policies of Mikhail Frunze, the first Soviet commander there, are of relevance to an Angolan or an Ethiopian army where command structures are penetrated by Soviet and East European officers, and sizable military contingents are composed of Cubans. In his Twenty-Sixth Congress report Secretary Brezhnev discussed Soviet military assistance to these two countries, assuring his listeners that in both cases the Soviet Union responded to urgent requests because both countries were 'faced with counterrevolution and internal threat'.[32] The military 'assistance' to Afghanistan, namely the full-scale Soviet invasion of that country, also has direct historical parallels in Central Asia where an invasion by the Red Army allied with some local units evoked the famous and protracted Basmachi resistance.

The lessons are valuable also for the development of other desirable attributes. In the education, placement and promotion of indigenous cadres Central Asia has had rich experience. The result is the modern elites, of whom Uzbek First Secretary Rashidov and other Central Asians in prominent positions are representative.[33] Social mobilization techniques used for socialist construction have been discussed at length by Central Asian spokesmen: the establishment and growth of the public sector, industrialization and the emergence of an indigenous working class; collectivization (the negative aspects of which, such as the heavy human losses entailed in nomadic areas in particular, are omitted), and the parallel destruction of 'traditional exploiters' and 'patriarchal feudal-bey structures'; and the cultural revolution, the landmarks of which were the mass extension of literacy, formation of the new intelligentsia and the emancipation of women. The discussion of economic and social reforms is usually accompanied by statistics. Impressive in themselves, they gain in comparison with indicators elsewhere in the developing world.[34]

As noted here more than once, the assistance by 'more advanced' elements is seen as absolutely crucial for 'socialist transformation'. In Central Asia, the leading role played by the Russian 'Big Brother' in just about everything has long been an article of faith. A representative sample comes from an Uzbek article written just prior to a conference in Tashkent dealing with the international relevance of the Central Asian experience, and shaped to reflect the focus of the conference:

> Having merged with the revolutionary struggle of the Russian proletariat led by the party, the liberation movement of the toilers of Central Asia brought about the victory of the socialist revolution in the former borderlands, which comprised the decisive political condition for a non-capitalist path of development.[35]

But, apart from ascribing to themselves lofty and altruistic motives and highest marks for experience, Soviet sources are not quite clear in their explanation of precisely why Soviet assistance is the precondition of success, and why countries of socialist orientation are incapable of 'building socialism' by themselves. Fortunately, we have an explicit treatment of the issue in Polish sources. In a book entitled *Ways of Escaping from Backwardness*, economist Jerzy Kleer analyzes the Central Asian case as an example of a model of 'interconnected development'. The characteristic of this model is that a more advanced country directs the transformation of the less advanced one. According to Kleer, the model's greatest asset is that it facilitates the destruction of the old system in the fastest, most efficient and most logical way. Several reasons are given why this is so. One is that the more advanced country has accumulated extensive experience which helps the less advanced one in avoiding its own past mistakes. But, says Kleer, there is another reason, which is often overlooked and/or unappreciated:

> ... this is the existence of traditions, attachment to the historical specificity of the country, its complex past, the shape of its value system, and lastly specific national characteristics, cultural traditions, etc. The native creative forces shaping up the new social, economic, and political system *are unable to break away* completely from all these conditions and accompanying variables. Even if the impetus of the initial destruction is sufficiently strong, once the most hated institutions, forms of action and models of behavior are swept away, the struggle with the remaining relics of old structures, old traditions and old institutions proceeds very stubbornly. But within the framework of the interconnected development model, the social forces which influence [the backward society] and the directing center from outside, *are free from all these impediments*. This [freedom] constitutes the particularly important advantage, albeit one that is difficult to measure, which a backward country derives from proceeding

toward development in tandem with a more developed economic center, rather than alone.[36]

This was precisely the type of advantage which benefited the Central Asians, says Kleer:

> The process of social change [in the Central Asian republics] was initiated not only from the top, an unavoidable condition of backwardness, but was also carried out *by the directing apparat which was composed in large measure of people who did not belong to the local population*. Thus we can say that in this context the process of the destruction of old structures was *an externally-directed process*. Cadres, capital and inspiration came from the more developed republics, mostly Soviet Russia. Then, a most interesting process commenced from the point of view of developing societies: local directing groups . . . began to emerge out of the debris of the old traditional structures . . . This took time, however, and it was not possible to wait with the implementation of introductory changes until [local] social forces were formed.[37]

Kleer's conclusions, which, not surprisingly, support the overall thrust of Soviet policy, are that the experience of the Soviet Asians clearly indicates the relevance of European models even in societies which have never had any historical or cultural preconditions for the adoption of European-type organizational, technical or economic solutions: 'the experience of the Asian republics of the USSR validates in practice [the assumption of] the universal character of the socialist social system born in Europe'.[38]

Kleer's analysis, which does not beat about the bush, contains the Soviet argument in a nutshell. But it is debatable whether the specific 'advantage' of the interconnected development model singled out by Kleer is, or can be, perceived as an advantage in the here and now, by even the most 'progressive' Third World leader struggling to modernize his country.

A couple of additional points still need to be discussed. As noted above, the subject of Islam is treated gingerly. In the discussion of the model for foreign audiences it is rare for Islam to be explicitly credited with resistance to socialism, or to be explicitly identified with 'traditional structures' and 'traditional exploiters' (no such restraint applies in internal debates). Citations above illustrate the point. Why this is so is perhaps explained by a comment made by two Soviet specialists on the Third World:

> . . . in specific conditions of developing countries, proclamation

of a struggle against a religious world view would inevitably doom to defeat any political force which seeks to win the confidence of the middle strata, the urban dwellers and the peasant masses. In countries where the population is almost one hundred percent religious and seventy-five to ninety percent illiterate, an appeal to the masses from atheistic positions . . . can only play into the hands of the enemy . . . Therefore . . . [there is] no other choice except to utilize on the basis of a positive social policy, the motives of social equality and struggle against foreign oppression contained in the religious world view . . . that is, to lead the masses gradually to the understanding and implementation of the Soviet [sic!] political and socio-economic program.[39]

This perception may well be based on Central Asian experience also, although it is not acknowledged, the extraordinary tenacity of Islam there being well documented.[40] In foreign contacts the Soviet Union has supported religious leaders if they are in command and can be, even minimally, regarded as 'progressive'. Iran's Ayatollah Khomeini fits the bill here. A recent source, for example, makes a distinction between the 'modernized/bourgeois' and the 'traditional' (egalitarian) stream in contemporary Islam, with Khomeini included in the second category.[41] Members of the official Soviet Islamic establishment are busy, in the meantime, trying to convince their co-religionists abroad that communism and Islam are fully compatible, and that a perfect symbiosis has been achieved between the two in the Soviet Muslim republics.[42] But even temporary accommodations with religion carry their own limitations. It is therefore noted that, although 'tribal institutions and traditions and religious structures . . . can be used more or less effectively for the development of initial socialist tendencies', social struggle cannot be won except through 'decisive interference' by 'progressive forces' from 'outside the traditional structures';[43] Kleer's point, but much less explicit. The bitter war in Afghanistan where Islam-inspired resistance denies to the Soviets and their Afghan allies any area except major urban centers and connecting key routes, occasioned an angry comment by Soviet-supported Babrak Karmal that 'the imperialists [there] are playing on the profound national and religious emotions of our people, covering themselves with the mantle of Islam'.[44] (This comment is fairly typical in blaming the resistance to Soviet interference on foreign intervention.)

Judging by the prominence the discussion of the Central Asian model receives in Central Asian sources, the issue seems as important in the domestic context as it is in foreign policy. The reasons for this are a matter for speculation. One may be to counteract the already noted revival of Islam and its ties with the new nationalism of the modern Central Asian elites. Another may be the need to convince the Central Asians themselves that the Central Asian experiment has indeed been a great success or even, perhaps, to use this perception as a leverage in pressing for greater autonomy from Moscow. It may also be helpful in bolstering the Central Asians' role as they participate in Soviet foreign 'outreach' activities not only as propagandists but also as advisers, particularly in other Muslim areas.[45] But their share among 'advisers' is significantly lower than their numbers or special position – as the 'living proof' of the model's success – would warrant. In Third World client states (except Afghanistan) they play a distinctly secondary role to the Russians or the East Germans.[46] Perhaps this is because the Central Asians, who are still at the bottom of the development scale in the Soviet Union, are neither as skilled nor as reliable as the effort requires.

Significance and Effectiveness

The Central Asian model with all of its implications obviously represents a paradigm, which has its propaganda as well as its practical aspects. In a major propaganda effort a chorus of obligatory accolades comes from the Central Asians, led by the much-cited Rashidov, as well as from the Third World leaders of 'socialist orientation'.[47] At the Twenty-Sixth Congress of the CPSU in February 1981 the standardized Soviet formula was presented by Geidar Aliev, first secretary of the Azerbaidzhan republic:

> We should note that the experience . . . in our country has been of tremendous international importance. Now when the national liberation movements are powerfully developed . . . our experience in overcoming centuries-old backwardness . . . in the shortest historical period acquires still greater validity for the young national governments, especially those which have chosen the socialist orientation. As Comrade L. I. Brezhnev just emphasized, we do not push anyone onto our path of socialist construction, but we would not change it for any other. It has been proven right, it has been validated by our whole history.[48]

Foreign praise at the Congress came selectively from representatives of socialist and socialist-orientated countries. Significantly, perhaps, the leaders of neither Cuba nor Vietnam contributed anything on the subject of either the model or Soviet assistance. Mongolia's Yumzhagii Tsedenbal dutifully acknowledged that for the new countries success was possible only through adherence to Marxism–Leninism and the ideas of proletarian internationalism.[49] Ethiopia's Mengistu Haile Mariam was explicit in citing Leninism as 'our compass in charting out the correct road of development in our country'. He further acknowledged that

> the Ethiopian revolutionaries and working people are walking the path of Lenin and of the Great October side by side with the CPSU, and consider themselves to be a component of the world socialist system. They realize that the more than half a century of experience the USSR has had in the task of building socialism is for them a model and a hope that guarantees a shining tomorrow.[50]

Babrak Karmal's contribution was extensive, explicit and, being so much at variance with conditions in Afghanistan, hardly calculated to inspire the confidence of an observer in either the model or its sponsors:

> The outstanding achievements of the Soviet Union and the rich experience of the CPSU have historical importance not only for the world socialist system and the international communist and workers' movement. They inspire . . . the struggle for national liberation and social movements, and the young governments which, having consolidated victory over internal reaction and having liquidated exploitation by foreign monopolies, have now entered upon the path of basic social, political, economic and cultural transformation . . . This has particular meaning now . . . From this high rostrum I turn my voice to the people of the world . . . had it not been for the help shown by the great Soviet Union to heroic Afghanistan, we would not have a revolutionary, free, independent, and non-aligned Afghanistan today.[51]

Propaganda efforts notwithstanding, the Soviets' practical approach to the implementation of the model has tended to be soft (except in Afghanistan). It is said repeatedly that, although the model's benefits are self-evident, each country has to seek out its own adaptation, and that the Soviet Union is not forcing anyone to do anything. Obviously, as past and current experience indicates, the issue has been extremely sensitive while direct enforcement capabilities have been tenuous and likely to remain so. Moreover, even the leaders of client states tend to resist dictation and the penetration of their infrastructures by Soviet 'advisers', as illustrated in Egypt and Somalia and some less publicized cases.[52]

The reception of the Soviet model of non-capitalist development in the Third World has been mixed and not uncritical, even by parties with strong pro-Soviet leanings. Evidence of social and economic progress has been accepted positively, and assistance has been welcomed, but not the strings attached. Some of the costs involved (the evidence of which is available even in official Soviet histories) have been perceived, and the benefits of collaboration have been, in most cases, far less than their advertised value, particularly in economic relations. *Caveats* have been sounded even by ideologically 'sound' spokesmen. Devendra Kaushik, for example, whose analysis of Central Asian history follows the Soviet party line and who finds the process of socialist transformation there both benign and praiseworthy, and its speed and results admirable, notes explicitly that the model is not applicable to developing countries:

> ... it would be wrong to overstress the importance of the Central Asian model of non-capitalist development ... The experience of Soviet Central Asia was of a different nature than the adoption of the non-capitalist path of development by several Afro-Asian states ... which is an altogether new phenomenon. In Central Asia the transition to socialism took place in close connection with the revolutionary process in Russia and under the direct guidance of the Russian proletariat.[53]

The Soviets' own assessment of the practical value of the model seems also to recognise its limitations. Soviet specialists admit that the overall conditions of backwardness which existed in the Russian borderlands at the outbreak of the Revolution are approximated most closely in Africa, but only partly in Asia and rarely in Latin America, because many countries there have already opted for capitalism. Therefore, the non-capitalist approach does not denote a direct path to socialism *à la* Central Asia, but a 'national–democratic, anti-imperialist, anti-feudal, anti-monopoly' policy in preparation for the emergence of conditions when the 'democratic stage' may evolve into the 'socialist stage'.[54] In other words, the concept can be used 'as a political platform for uniting all the progressive forces',[55] an approach which offers rich possibilities to Soviet diplomacy, but precludes direct 'outreach'. The latter has been reserved for the states of socialist orientation, which are targeted for the actual introduction of the model.[56]

The roster of countries considered by Moscow to fit the socialist-orientation category has varied somewhat over the seventies. Some of them, notably Cuba and Vietnam, have become full-fledged members of the socialist commonwealth. Both of these, as well as Angola, Ethiopia, Afghanistan and, perhaps, Mozambique, have been seen as anchor states within the potential pro-Soviet regional subsystems, the nuclei of the future worldwide extension of the 'world socialist system'. Others, such as the PDRY, have an auxiliary role. Some of the less advanced may play supporting roles or eventually join the new nuclei, depending on their strategic importance. The two obvious targets which at present are not of socialist orientation but are classified as 'progressive' are India and Iran. India in particular has been ardently wooed with encouraging but not entirely satisfactory results from the Soviet viewpoint. The volatile politics of Iran, on the other hand, pretty much imposes a 'wait and see' attitude.

The choice of regional anchors seems to have been dictated by opportunity and strategic considerations. The most responsive targets have been the countries in need of political, economic and military assistance because of domestic instability and/or foreign threat, which are, however, unwilling or unable to get such assistance from the West. So far the pattern of the evolution of Soviet–client ties has been characterized by two principal stages. First, after an initial period of growing friendly relations comes the establishment of a relationship of dependence of the prospective client upon the Soviet Union, in the form of bilateral political, economic and military agreements, culminating in a treaty of friendship and cooperation.[57]

But a pattern of economic dependence and a need for political support do not assure reliability when interests diverge and alternative arrangements become available, as the cases of Egypt and Somalia demonstrate. Thus, to secure its influence, the Soviet Union seeks to promote the extension of a network of direct controls. Once this starts, a second stage in the relationship begins, the stage at which the relevance of the Central Asian model comes into play.

The insistence on ideological trappings and the constant invocation of Lenin's writings must not obscure the intensely practical nature of the endeavor, as it is being pushed by Moscow on its Third World protégés. If and when properly in place, the model's trio of 'indispensables' – the vanguard party *cum* centralized governmental, police, and military structures, *cum* 'fraternal assistance' – plus the extensive economic ties, go a long way to secure Moscow's control over its strategically located allies, the primary goal of Soviet Third World policy in the seventies and early eighties. But so far the paradigm has been approximated only imperfectly. As noted in the introduction, the

Leninist framework carries with it the seeds of dysfunctionality, particularly in its over-reliance on the mechanics of power and its Europocentrism (read: Soviet hegemony). By the late seventies Cuba, perhaps, came closest to the ideal in the wake of internal changes, and by virtue of its foreign role as Soviet surrogate and of the depth of Soviet penetration. But a major condition of Cuba's conformity has been the massive Soviet economic subsidy, indicating that there, as elsewhere, economic dependence on the bloc has been of much greater import in securing strong Soviet influence than allowed by the theoretical model. Indeed, the secondary role assigned to economics in a model which claims to take off from Marx would be surprising, but for the primacy of politics which is the hallmark of all Leninist systems.

It also appears that the very leaders of socialist orientation who dutifully mouth the appropriate slogans tend to resist as much as possible the implementation of the control mechanisms. If the East European experience is of any value, the control pattern does not guarantee a total long-term subservience even if securely in place as was the case in Eastern Europe in the 1948–53 period. Moreover, the model's effectiveness owes much to the client's proximity to the Soviet Union, a condition which does not exist in the case of most Soviet Third World clients and, even when it does (viz. Afghanistan), is not always decisive.

In the final analysis, even if the Soviet Union succeeds in setting up a network of regional subsystems based on the Central Asian model – an ambition that at present is in the realm of wishful thinking – the control aspects are not likely to work in the long run because of the inevitable polycentrism. Nevertheless, Moscow has had not inconsiderable successes in securing the dependence of a number of strategically located Third World countries. In the short run, even a partial emplacement of the model has been useful for the extension of Soviet influence, has undercut and/or denied Western access, influence and interest, and has preempted the option of genuine choice to many of the new countries.

Notes: Chapter 9

1 Quoted in Hélène Carrère d'Encausse and Stuart R. Schram, *Marxism and Asia: An Introduction with Readings*, trans. from the French (London: Allen Lane, 1969) (hereafter cited as *Marxism and Asia*), p. 145 (Lenin's italics).
2 For a detailed analysis, see ibid., ch. 2 and the relevant texts.
3 'Proletarian internationalism' assumes that class loyalty overrides any particular national loyalty, because it is historically more progressive. The

parameters of proletarian internationalism *are always defined by the CPSU*, which assumes that the Soviet Union is at all times the beneficiary of class loyalty. Both Lenin and Stalin are on record defining relative priorities: 'The interests of socialism are higher than the interests of the right of nations to self-determination' (V. I. Lenin, *Collected Works* Vol. 26 (Moscow: Progress Publishers, 1964) p. 449); 'There are occasions when the right to self-determination conflicts with . . . the higher right — the right of a working class . . . to consolidate its power. In such cases . . . the former must give way to the latter' (J. V. Stalin, *Marxism and the National Question* (New York: International, 1942), p. 158). The so-called Brezhnev Doctrine of 1968 explicitly invoked the same principle. In relations between communist states 'proletarian internationalism' becomes 'socialist internationalism', an advancement in historical progression.

4 *Marxism and Asia*, pp. 23 and 38 and relevant texts.
5 'Now, no serious world problem and no crucial contemporary question is resolved, or can be resolved, without the participation of the communist movement and without the participation, in the first place, of the movement's most powerful component, the ruling parties of the socialist commonwealth': B. Ponomarev, 'Neodolimost' osvoboditel'nogo dvizheniia', *Kommunist*, no. 1 (January 1980), p. 12.
6 Vernon V. Aspaturian, *Process and Power in Soviet Foreign Policy* (Boston, Mass.: Little, Brown, 1971), p. 481.
7 Quoted in *Kommunist Tadzhikistana*, 13 December 1946, and numerous other Soviet sources.
8 AN Tadzhikskoi SSR, *Istoriia*, vol. 3, bk 1 (Dushanbe: AN TaSSR, 1964), p. 218.
9 Aspaturian, *Process and Power*, pp. 468–72.
10 See Yaacov Ro'i, 'The role of Islam and the Soviet Muslims in Soviet Arab policy', *Asian and African Studies*, vol. 10, no. 2 (1974), pp. 157–89, and no. 3 (1975), pp. 259–80.
11 See Rasma Silde-Karklins, 'The Uighurs between China and the USSR', *Canadian Slavonic Papers*, vol. 17, nos 2–3 (Summer–Fall 1975), pp. 341–65.
12 Victor Louis, *The Coming Decline of the Chinese Empire* (New York: Times Books, 1979).
13 'Vstupitel'noe slovo M. A. Suslova' at an international scientific-theoretical conference on the theme 'The Great October and the contemporary epoch', Moscow, 10–12 November 1977: *Kommunist*, no. 17 (November 1977), p. 19.
14 B. Ponomarev, 'Kommunisty v bor'be protiv fashizma i voiny, za mir, demokratiiu i sotsializm', a speech at a conference on the anniversary of the 7th Congress of the Comintern, Moscow, July 1975: *Kommunist*, no. 11 (July 1975), p. 22.
15 ibid., p. 22 (my italics).
16 ibid., pp. 22–8.
17 G. Aliev, 'Oktiabr'skaia revoliutsiia i natsional'no-osvoboditel'noe dvizhenie', *Kommunist*, no. 9 (June 1977), pp. 24–38. Based on a speech delivered at an international conference on the same theme held in Baku, 26–8 May 1977.
18 Iumzhagiin Tsedenbal, 'Lenin v istoricheskikh sud'bakh narodov Vostoka', *Kommunist*, no. 8 (May 1980), pp. 17–32.
19 Devendra Kaushik, *Socialism in Central Asia: A Study in the Transformation of Socio-Ethnic Relations in Soviet Central Asia* (Bombay/Calcutta: Allied Publishers, 1976), p. 46.

20 *Pravda*, 3 November 1974.
21 AN Turkmenskoi SSR, Inst. Istorii im. Batyrova, *Velikii Oktiabr' i sotsial'no-ekonomicheskii progress v Turkmenistane* (Ashkhabad: Ylym, 1977) (hereafter cited as *Velikii Oktiabr'*), pp. 85–8.
22 Sh. R. Rashidov, 'Leninizm – znamia osvobozhdeniia i progressa narodov', a speech at the International Scientific Conference 'Experience of socialist transformation in the USSR and its international significance', held in Tashkent and dedicated to the fiftieth anniversary of the formation of the USSR: *Pravda Vostoka*, 17 October 1972.
23 *Velikii Oktiabr'*.
24 ibid.
25 Rashidov, 'Leninizm'.
26 B. Ponomarev, 'Sovmestnaia bor'ba rabochego i natsional'no-osvoboditel'nogo dvizheniia protiv imperializma, za sotsial'nyi progress', *Kommunist*, no. 16 (November 1980), pp. 30–44.
27 ibid., p. 44.
28 ibid., pp. 41–2.
29 See, for example, *Istoricheskii opyt Velikogo Oktiabria i ego mezhdunarodnoe znachenie* (Tbilisi: Izd. 'Metsniereba', 1977); and *Voprosy natsional'no-gosudarstvennogo stroitel'stva v Srednei Azii i Kazakhstane* (Alma-Ata: Izd. 'Nauka', 1977); *Velikii Oktiabr'*; Rashidov, 'Leninizm'.
30 Ponomarev, 'Sovmestnaia bor'ba', pp. 42–3.
31 Rashidov, 'Leninizm'.
32 L. I. Brezhnev, 'Report of the Central Committee to the 26th Congress of the CPSU', 23 February 1981: *Partiinaia zhizn'*, no. 5 (March 1981), p. 10.
33 For a discussion of this issue, see Steven L. Burg, 'Central Asian political participation and Soviet political development', in this volume, passim.
34 Brezhnev, 'Report', and most other sources.
35 O. Dzhamalov, 'Torzhestvo leninskogo predvideniia', at the Tashkent Conference (see n. 22): *Pravda Vostoka*, 14 October 1972.
36 Jerzy Kleer, *Drogi Wyjscia z Zacofania* (Warsaw: Panstwowy Instytut Wydawniczy, 1974), p. 169 (my italics).
37 ibid., pp. 170–1 (my italics).
38 ibid., p. 184.
39 R. Ulyanovsky and V. Pavlov, *Asian Dilemma*, 2nd edn (Moscow: Progress, 1975), pp. 232–3 (hereafter cited as *Asian Dilemma*)
40 See Alexandre Bennigsen and Chantal Lemercier-Quelquejay, *Islam in the Soviet Union* (New York: Praeger, 1967); T. S. Saidbaev, *Islam i obshchestvo, Opyt istorichesko-sotsiologicheskogo issledovaniia* (Moscow: Nauka, 1978); and B. R. Bociurkiw, 'Changing Soviet image of Islam', *Journal of the Institute of Muslim Minority Affairs*, vol. 2, no. 2, and vol. 3, no. 1 (Winter 1980–Spring 1981), pp. 9–25 and others.
41 N. Ivanov, 'Sotsial'nye aspekty traditsionnogo islama', *Aziia i Afrika segodnia*, no. 3 (1982), quoted in *The Central Asian Newsletter*, vol. 1, no. 4 (May 1982), pp. 2–3. Traditional Islam is seen as fundamentally opposed to capitalism, placing community over individual, and embracing progressive economic policies and egalitarian philosophy.
42 See *Moslems of the Soviet East*, a quarterly journal of the Muslim Religious Board for Central Asia and Kazakhstan in Tashkent, passim.
43 *Asian Dilemma*, p. 219.
44 *Pravda*, 26 February 1981. For further discussion of the Islamic issue and

the different criteria for treatment of Islam within the USSR and beyond its confines, see Yaacov Ro'i, 'The impact of the Islamic fundamentalist revival of the late 1970s on the Soviet view of Islam', in this volume, passim.

45 Central Asians serve as diplomats, specialists and technicians in the Third World as a whole and in Muslim countries in particular. In Afghanistan, for example, they have participated in significant numbers in the Soviet 'assistance' effort in the running of the Afghan political and educational infrastructure. See Eden Naby, 'The ethnic factor in Soviet–Afghan relations', *Asian Survey*, vol. 20, no. 3 (March 1980), pp. 237–56.

46 For the East German involvement, see Anita Dasbach Mallinckrodt, 'International political communication, the DDR's vital foreign policy instrument' (Washington, DC: The George Washington University, n.d.), reprinted from *Deutschland Archiv Sonderheft*, November 1971; and Michael J. Sodaro, 'The GDR and the Third World: supplicant and surrogate', in M. Radu (ed.), *Eastern Europe and the Third World: East vs. South* (New York: Praeger, 1981).

47 See, for example, articles in *Kommunist* by: Denis Sassu-Ngesso (Congo Republic), no. 3 (1980); Aziz Muhammad (First Secretary of Iraqi Communist Party) and Abdus Salam (General Secretary of Bangladesh Communist Party), no. 18 (1972); and Ton-Dyk Thang (President, Democratic Republic of Vietnam), no. 17 (1977).

48 *Pravda*, 25 February 1981.

49 ibid., 26 February 1981.

50 ibid.

51 ibid.

52 Apparently, for instance, Colonel Mengistu was very reluctant to allow the entry of Cuban troops into Ethiopia, but was forced to accept Cuban military help after Somali troops almost overran the Ogaden in the fall of 1977. This in turn was made possible because of the continuation of Soviet military help to Somalia while Moscow was negotiating with Mengistu: press reports and oral communications from visitors in Ethiopia; see also Jiri Valenta, 'Soviet–Cuban intervention in the Horn of Africa: impact and lessons', *Journal of International Affairs*, vol. 34, no. 2 (Fall–Winter 1980–1), pp. 353–67.

53 Kaushik, *Socialism in Central Asia*, p. 159. Another book by Kaushik, *Central Asia in Modern Times*, was published by Progress Publishers in Moscow (1970).

54 *Asian Dilemma*, p. 217.

55 Kaushik, *Socialism in Central Asia*, p. 47.

56 For the roster of countries varyingly considered by Moscow at different periods in the past decade to fit the socialist orientation category, see *Voprosy natsional'no-gosudarstvennogo stroitel'stva*, p. 123; M. B. Baratov, 'Oktiabr' i natsional'no-osvoboditel'noe dvizhenie narodov zarubezhnogo Vostoka', *Obshchestvennye nauki v Uzbekistane*, no. 11 (177), pp. 86–91; E. Primakov, 'Nekotorye problemy razvivaiushchikhsia stran', *Kommunist*, no. 11 (July 1978), pp. 81–91; Ponomarev, 'Neodolimost'', p. 12.

57 At the 26th CPSU Congress, Brezhnev enumerated the countries with which the USSR had such treaties: Brezhnev, 'Report', p. 10.

10

Soviet Experience of Muslim Guerrilla Warfare and the War in Afghanistan

CHANTAL LEMERCIER-QUELQUEJAY and *ALEXANDRE BENNIGSEN*

The Soviets did not launch into the Afghan adventure as guileless neophytes. As heirs of the Russian empire they had the benefit of two centuries of experience in guerrilla warfare in a Muslim milieu during which they learned how to crush revolts and to cope with political agitation. This experience was rich and diversified: Russian and Soviet rulers had to deal with advanced modern Tatar communities as well as with sophisticated feudal nomadic societies (Kazakhs, Turkmens) and with pre-feudal clanic communities in North Caucasus. During these two centuries they had come up against various challenges:

The conservative challenge of the 'parallel' (unofficial) popular Islam represented in Central Asia, the Caucasus and the Volga region by the Sufi *tariqats* (brotherhoods) – in particular the Naqshbandiya and Qadiriya – that had inspired the anti-Russian *jihad* of Shamil and his *murids* in the Caucasus, the Andizhan uprising of 1898, the Dagestani–Chechen uprising of 1920–1, various Chechen revolts (1928–36) and had actively participated in the Basmachi movement which led popular uprisings in most of Central Asia in the first two decades of Soviet rule.

The reformist–modernist challenge (Jadidism, after the *jadids*, the late-nineteenth-century intellectuals who opposed obscurantism and fanaticism in certain quarters of the Islamic community). Jadidism had more or less inspired various nationalist pan-Islamic and pan-Turkic movements and influenced, in part, the Chechen revolt of 1942–3 and the Basmachi movement.

The national-communism challenge of Sultan Galiev and of

Turar Ryskulov, the last avatar of the nationalist pan-Turkic movement.

Soviet policy-makers drew from this experience several lessons which, taken together, form if not a doctrine or a corpus of theories, at least a practical knowhow which has enabled them to preserve their colonial Muslim Empire.

This experience in dealing with pre-modern, not consolidated nations, may be summarized as follows:

(1) *Utilization of ethnic, religious and tribal rivalries* – a strategy successfully used during the Caucasian wars (Ossetians versus Chechens; Lezgins versus Avars, etc.), in 1918 in the Volga region (Bashkirs versus Tatars), in Kazakhstan (the Qypchaq tribe versus the other Kazakh tribes), etc.

(2) *Opposing cities to the countryside* – practiced with success in the Fergana valley during the Basmachi uprising.

(3) *Co-optation (temporary or permanent) of national elites (traditional or modern)* – a most successful strategy employed in the Caucasus during the nineteenth century (co-optation of the Kabardian and Dagestani nobility), in the Volga region (co-optation of Tatar *jadid* leaders), in Kazakhstan (admission of tribal leaders into the Communist Party), etc.

(4) *A 'dialectical' attitude toward the Muslim religious establishment:*

   (a) *Elimination of the 'parallel' (Sufi) Islam* – the brotherhoods' cooperation with the Soviets being utterly impossible.

   (b) *Cautious cooperation with the leaders of 'official' Islam* (since 1943 when the four Muslim Spiritual Boards were used both abroad as 'ambassadors', and within the USSR, as 'moderators' guaranteeing the loyalty of the believers).

(5) *Deep mistrust of 'fellow-travellers' and native communists* (when such communists had not been trained in Moscow).

(6) *Equal mistrust of the native armed forces* – (one of the main points of Sultan Galiev's nationalism was the creation of a 'Muslim Red Army' commanded by Muslim officers). But at the same time both the fellow-travellers and the native armed forces were cautiously utilized with the object of achieving a smooth transition from the prerevolutionary feudal or tribal society to socialism.

(7) *Alternate use of terror (the destruction of Kokand in February 1918) and of comparative liberalism* (support of the Young Bukharans, who, after the Red Army occupied Tashkent in May 1920, formed the first government of the People's Republic of Bukhara) — used with success in Central Asia.

The application of these lessons in Afghanistan is the subject of this chapter.

In the light of this past experience in the Caucasus, the Volga region and Central Asia, Afghanistan seemed to present the most favorable conditions. Theoretically, its occupation and even its transformation into a Soviet Socialist Republic appeared easy and destined to be rapid. But from the start everything seemed to go wrong. At the time of writing, the end of the second year, the Soviet Army is hopelessly bogged down in a guerrilla war which obviously will be a lasting one. The efficiency of the Afghan resistance has increased and the communist government of Kabul manages to survive only because of the protection of Soviet tanks.

What happened? Why have the sophisticated tactics which finally proved successful in Central Asia, in an environment not basically different from that of Afghanistan, failed here? This chapter does not claim to answer this question but, rather, to provide some basis for its discussion.

We suggest that an important reason for the situation lies in the lack of good Soviet specialists on Afghanistan. Since the death of the orientalist historian Petr Mikhailovich Reisner in 1958 (pioneer of Indian and Afghan studies in the USSR), there is no competent Afghanologist in the USSR, and this can explain Soviet ignorance about the real conditions in that country, especially the underestimation of its will and capacity to resist.

Consequently, although Soviet leaders did apply in Afghanistan the seven lessons acquired in the century-long relationship of Russians with Muslims, they did so in a clumsy, counterproductive manner.

(1) Ethnic–Religious Rivalries

Theoretically, Afghanistan presented an ideal territory for applying the strategy of opposing one or several nations to others. It was possible either to support the 'oppressed' nations (Hazaras, Uzbeks, Baluchis, Turkmens), or the 'oppressed' religions (Izmailis, Shiites) in their struggle against the Pushtun *Herrenvolk,* or, on the contrary, to play the card of Pushtun supremacy. Yet the Soviets never succeeded in making a final choice between the two policies. The three communist governments of Kabul constantly switched from one option to another, finally antagonizing everybody. At present, every national and religious group in Afghanistan, from the Shiite Hazaras, the 'underdogs' of the country, to the ruling Pushtuns is participating in the *jihad* against the regime. There are but few exceptions: for instance, certain Pushtun tribes, such as the Mangals, who fought on the Soviet side in the Panjshir battle in September 1980.

(2) Opposition between Cities and Countryside

The Basmachis were finally defeated because they never went beyond the stage of the purely peasant or nomad uprising: the cities of the Fergana valley remained in the hands of the Soviets. In Afghanistan the Soviets are up against both the urban guerrillas (in Herat, Kunduz, Kandahar and even Kabul) and a rural maquis-type warfare.

(3) Co-optation of the Elites

The successful policy of co-optation of tribal feudal leaders in Central Asia was one of the main factors in the Soviet victory in Central Asia and Kazakhstan during the Revolution and the Civil War. When a leader such as the Kazakh Ali Khan Bukeykhanov joined the Communist Party, he was followed by the whole of the Bukey Horde. This same policy failed in Afghanistan because the Pushtun tribes were more 'democratic': important decisions are taken by the tribal *jirga* (assemblies) and the personal prestige of a tribal chieftain cannot be compared with the absolute authority of a Bukeykhanov, a Kazakh khan, descended from Genghis Khan himself. Moreover, after the slaughter of the tribal aristocracy by the President of the Afghanistan Revolutionary Council, Hafizullah Amin, in 1979, his Soviet-supported successor Babrak Karmal could not possibly hope to win over the survivors.

The massive adhesion of modern elites (the Tatar and Azeri *jadids*, the Young Bukharans) to the Bolshevik regime was another major Soviet success during the Revolution and the Civil War. It was due mainly to the fact that the native young intellectuals were faced with a dramatic choice between the White

Generals and the Bolsheviks and the latter appeared as a 'lesser evil'. In Afghanistan, only a minority of modernist intellectuals agreed to serve the communist regime. The majority was submitted to such harsh treatment both by Hafizullah Amin and his predecessor Nur Mohammad Taraki that at present it is either engaged more or less actively in the resistance, or remains at least passively hostile. Moreover, the majority of Afghan intellectuals, who are still deeply religious, could hardly be attracted by the Soviet brand of Marxism–Leninism, especially as presented in the crudest possible form by the Afghan communists.

Anyway, the few fellow-travellers and the even fewer Afghan Marxists are rapidly decreasing in number between the two factions of the Afghan Marxist party, the Khalq and the Parcham. They are also being systematically eliminated by the *mujahidin*. In a year or two hence, the Afghan left will probably disappear completely as an independent political force. (See also below.)

(4) The New Regime and Islam

The courtship of the progressive Tatar clerics and their utilization against the conservative clerical class and the Sufi orders constituted another success of the Bolsheviks during the Revolution and the Civil War period, except in the Caucasus. The same strategy failed in Afghanistan, mainly for the following reasons:

(*a*) The 'progressive' Muslim clerics were not as numerous in Afghanistan as in Russia in 1917, and those who agreed to join the communist regime of Kabul have been – or are being – physically liquidated by the *mujahidin*.

(*b*) Unlike Russia in 1917, Afghanistan has no real ecclesiastical establishment. An Afghan *mullah* does not possess the same authority as the Soviet mufti and his political options obligate only himself and not the believers.

(*c*) In Afghanistan, religious authority belonged not to the mullahs but to certain families, some of them descending from the Prophet, for instance the Mojedidi family. Soviet authorities were not aware of this special aspect and the religious families were treated as 'feudal' tyrants and slaughtered as such by Taraki and Amin.

(*d*) Before 1978, Sufi brotherhoods played no political part in Afghanistan, which was a purely Muslim territory, where Islam was not threatened by any hostile force. The Soviet authorities who had learned to fear and respect the *tariqats* in the USSR and to despise the too submissive official authorities were logically enough inclined to minimize the importance of the religious opposition.

(e) From the beginning (1978), a *jihad* against the bad Muslims (*bi-din*) and the Russian *Kafirs* became the main slogan of the resistance. Religion has thus been monopolized by the resistance and it is now extremely difficult to change the position of Islam in favor of the communist regime.

(5) The Afghan Left

In this field the Soviet failure has been especially spectacular. First, the Soviets did not have enough time to train and educate 'reliable' Afghan communists in the USSR, and the locally trained Marxists are unruly and unreliable, as demonstrated by the useless (from the Soviet point of view) bloody feud between the Parcham and the Khalq. Moreover, both factions are equally untrustworthy: at present there are both Khalqi and Parchami militants with strong anti-Soviet feelings who are ready to betray their protectors.

Secondly, the traditional Soviet distrust of fellow-travelers and the indiscriminate slaughter of the Afghan intelligentsia by Taraki and Amin eliminated all moderate liberal elements that could have ensured a smooth transition from the clanic monarchy of Zaher Shah to Soviet-style socialism. The survivors have either emigrated or enrolled in the resistance. Consequently, there is now no organized political group to the right of the Parcham, able to cooperate with the Soviets, nobody to rely on should there occur – and this is highly improbable – a political compromise in Afghanistan. The Soviets are thus forced to rely more and more on Babrak Karmal's government, whose authority is shrinking, on a huge but inefficient secret police, and *on themselves*.

There is no Afghan equivalent of the Young Bukharans or of the Tatar *jadids*, who in the 1920s took over authority in Central Asia and facilitated its pacification.

(6) The Soviets and the Afghan Army

By the end of the Civil War in 1920 there were thousands of Muslim soldiers and officers (Tatars, Bashkirs, Kazakhs, etc.) fighting on the Bolshevik side against the White Armies. Muslim troops represented almost one-third of the Sixth Red Army led by Marshal Frunze, which conquered Central Asia. Red Muslim units represented, therefore, a capital asset for the Bolsheviks in the Civil War, although a dangerous one because these same troops could (and did) easily become hotbeds of various nationalist trends (as mentioned above, Sultan Galiev was deeply interested in the creation of an autonomous Red Army).

In view of the precedent and the inherent changes, the Soviet treatment of the Afghan army was ambitious and in the final analysis counter-productive, even though the army apparently constituted a major pro-Soviet element in the country. Indeed, the building up of a pro-Soviet, ideologically secure Afghan army had begun in 1954, when Mohammad Daoud was Prime Minister. The first Afghan officers were then sent to Soviet military academies. Between 1954 and 1978 some 700 young Afghan officers were trained in the USSR, where they were submitted to intensive political brainwashing. At the same time, the Afghan army was modernized and received Soviet arms and numerous Soviet advisers.

When Taraki overthrew President Daoud, in April 1978, the Afghan army, 85,000 men strong, was an efficient instrument, loyal to the new regime. In 1978–9 it crushed several uprisings and in December 1979, though weakened by two years of hard fighting and by desertions, it still represented a serious military force. One wonders whether it was really in order to avoid its collapse that Soviet troops invaded Afghanistan.

In January 1980, the Afghan army was practically disarmed by the Soviets themselves. Today, reduced to about 30,000 soldiers, it is used mainly as an auxiliary force for protecting the roads. We do not know exactly what happened and why the Soviet High Command decided to destroy an organization which it had been building for twenty-five years and whose cadres were apparently loyal to the communist regime. As a result, the Afghan army – in spite of some recent attempts to reinforce it by means of general mobilization – has proved unable to act as a *revolutionary spearhead* replacing the non-existent native proletariat (which is what the Red Tatar units did in 1919–20).

At present, the Soviet Union is in the uncomfortable position of fighting a colonial war in Afghanistan not only without the help of a strong Afghan army, but also with Soviet troops consisting of European (Russian, Ukrainian, Balt, etc.) soldiers alone. In December 1979 the Soviet units invading Afghanistan were made up of around 40 percent Central Asian (Muslim) soldiers. Only six weeks after the invasion, however, these units were pulled out and replaced by purely European ones. Again, we do not know what happened exactly. Apparently the Soviet High Command did not want to use Muslim soldiers to fight the *mujahidin*, and there have been reports that the Central Asian soldiers proved unreliable in this task. Whatever the reasons, the Soviets have failed to apply in Afghanistan their experience in Central Asia (in the struggle against the Basmachis) or even in Dagestan in 1920, when native revolutionaries were extensively used against the conservative resistance.

(7) Terror Alternating with Liberalism

The policy consisting of alternating terror with liberalism also failed in Afghanistan. At the beginning of communist rule in Afghanistan, it is possible that the Khalq was assigned by the Soviets to personify terror and the Parcham liberalism but, after the Soviet invasion, very rapidly the Parcham government also began to use terror (not that terror is an entirely successful weapon against the Afghan; war is part of his 'way of life' and death in a Holy War is deemed an honor). However, in the eyes of the population, the main responsibility for the Afghan genocide is that of the Soviets and not that of the Khalq or the Parcham.

And Now?

Two years after the Soviet invasion, by a strange paradox, most Western observers, instead of trying to analyze the miracle of the Afghan resistance, credit the *mujahidin* with but little chance of success. They consider that the game is not worth the candle in view of the desperate circumstances. It is lost in advance: the Soviets had always wanted expansion in this direction, and this was their chance. Unable either to unify their military efforts or to formulate their war aims, or indeed any clear political program, and divided by their ideologies, the Afghan resistance is considered as a gallant but anachronistic phenomenon. The *mujahidin* are viewed as medieval warriors attacking the most powerful military machine in the world. Sooner or later, it is argued, the Soviets will double or treble the strength of their army in Afghanistan and crush the resistance. The Afghan *mujahidin* will join the long list of brave but unfortunate adversaries of Russia and the Soviet Union, from the eighteenth-century religious leader Imam Mansur to the Basmachis.

Against this pessimistic approach we can advance five arguments:

(i) The absence of unity among the guerrilla fighters is not necessarily proof of weakness. Indeed, after four years of fighting against the communist regime and the Soviet army, the resistance appears stronger, better armed and in control of greater territory. For the first time, in September 1980, during the battle of the Panjshir, groups of *mujahidin* from other areas – some of them very far away, Pakhtia, for instance – rushed to the aid of the Panjshiri.

(ii) The absence of a 'political program' or of 'clearly stated war aims' need not be considered a weakness. The *jihad* for the expulsion of infidels is a large enough 'political program'. Shamil himself had no other.

(iii) In the 1920s in Central Asia, the Bolsheviks, while fighting the Basmachis, were at the same time busy organizing the economic, cultural and political life of the country. Repression was only one side – a negative one – of the general policy. Many reforms, some of them welcomed by the population, were introduced and they represented the positive side. In Afghanistan no positive reform can counterbalance the repression, because the authority of Karmal's regime is limited to the city of Kabul.

(iv) Shamil in the nineteenth century, the Dagestanis and the Basmachis in the 1920s, and the Chechens in 1940–3 were fighting alone and never received any outside assistance. The Afghan resistance is beginning to receive limited help from abroad, in money, in publicity and even in arms.

(v) In the 1920s the Bolsheviks who were fighting the Muslim guerrillas in Central Asia or Dagestan had, besides the political genius of Lenin and Stalin, a victorious army led by one of their most prestigious commanders, Marshal Frunze, and inspired by the conquering revolutionary enthusiasm. This was a very different picture from the current incoherent strategy of the Soviet High Command in Afghanistan, which is obviously at a loss and unable to command the initiative, leading an overarmed but unwieldy and inefficient military machine, with soldiers who do not seem eager to die for Babrak Karmal.

11

First Steps in Soviet Diplomacy towards Afghanistan, 1917–21

MICHAEL VOLODARSKY

The first foreign-policy steps taken by the Bolsheviks in Afghanistan were made easier by the generally favorable climate for Russia that developed in Asia as a whole following the February Revolution. The overthrow of tsarism, which in Afghanistan had always been viewed as a power that threatened the country's independence no less than Great Britain, aroused the sympathy of Afghanistan toward the Russian people.[1] When, in May 1918, Persian translations of the first Soviet decrees and appeals reached Afghanistan, they were received with enthusiasm as evidence of the political course of the new Russia that had arisen in February 1917.[2] Equally positive was the reception of the news that the Brest-Litovsk peace treaty, signed on 3 March 1918, required both signatories 'to respect the political and economic independence and territorial integrity of Persia and Afghanistan'.[3]

The actions of Great Britain in the Middle East and Central Asia, by contrast, were viewed with great suspicion by the Muslim nations of those regions. The British occupation of all of Persia and the entry of British troops into Russian Central Asia after the departure from Persia of Russia's expeditionary force in March 1918, according to the instructions of the Bolshevik government, were seen in Kabul as steps which would lead to the complete surrounding of Afghanistan by British possessions and the inevitable liquidation of the Afghan state. In this context Afghan patriots saw the new Russia as the only power on which they could rely in the fight for preserving their independence. Thus, with no particular effort, the Bolsheviks acquired in Afghanistan considerable moral and political capital, all the more so since their main antagonist – Great Britain – made no effort to counter the myth of the anti-imperialist and anti-colonialist nature of the Soviet regime. On the contrary, Britain's actions in the region confirmed the basic postulates of Soviet propaganda.

During the two decades, before the Russian Revolution, dissatisfaction with Afghanistan's domestic and international position had been growing inside the country and was expressed in the opposition of a group of Young Afghans who had the sympathy of the Crown Prince Amanullah and who openly criticized the capitulatory policy of Emir Khabibullah. News of the events of 1917 in Russia reached Kabul, Herat and other Afghan cities in a largely distorted and exaggerated form and, against the background of British activities, inflamed this dissatisfaction even more. Tension in the country rose to crisis point and led to the murder of Emir Khabibullah on 21 February 1919. Within a week, on 28 February 1919, the new emir, Amanullah, announced that 'Afghanistan would henceforth be a free and independent state, which recognizes no foreign domination over it'.[4]

The time had come for a serious decision in London. Indeed, some voices in British government circles had been calling for a review of Britain's Middle East policy, but as they were not part of the narrow circle of those who actually formulated policy their influence on policy had been minimal. Among these was, first of all, the Viceroy of India, Lord Chelmsford, who had been continually urging a change in the very essence of British policy in the Middle East ever since the Bolsheviks came to power.[5] Given Amanullah's posture, the British government was faced with the choice of either persisting in its compromised course or of making a sharp turn and boldly challenging Moscow. Not long before, Lord Chelmsford had defined such a turn: to show support everywhere in Asia for the spirit of nationalism, which was objectively opposed to the Bolshevik dogmatists and not to democracy.[6] On 3 March 1919, Emir Amanullah proposed in a letter to Chelmsford the establishment of fundamentally new relations, based on the equality of all sides. Chelmsford requested the opinion of the British government, adding his own opinion on the need to review Anglo-Afghan relations. London's answer was totally negative.[7]

Meanwhile in Kabul rumors were spreading that Moscow had announced recognition of the full sovereignty and independence of the Afghan state (27 March 1919). Indeed, the RSFSR government sent participants of the Paris Peace Conference a document containing the conditions for concluding peace with Soviet Russia, of which the first was the mutual obligation of all states not to use force to subvert the legal government of

Afghanistan.[8] As a result, Moscow and Kabul began their diplomatic correspondence on the highest level.

On 7 April 1919, Amanullah sent a personal message to Lenin, stressing that Afghanistan, throughout its modern history, 'had been deprived of the possibility of maintaining ties and relations with other governments and states' and that Lenin and his comrades, whom the emir called 'friends of humanity', had created a new reality, in that they 'voiced the principle of the freedom and equality of nations and peoples of the whole world', and instilled in the Afghan people confidence that it would win its fight for independence. At the same time, the Afghan Minister of Foreign Affairs, Mahmud Tarzi, sent a letter to G. V. Chicherin, his counterpart in Moscow, expressing a desire to develop and strengthen friendly relations between Russia and Afghanistan.[9] Both letters were handed to their addressees on 21 May 1919.

On 21 April 1919, Amanullah had sent Lenin a second message, advising him that he was sending a delegation headed by General Muhammed Vali Khan, who 'was empowered to conduct personal talks and to prepare the ground for establishing the necessary friendship between the two governments and the satisfaction of mutual interests'.[10]

On 27 May 1919, Lenin wrote to Amanullah: 'An attempt by Afghanistan to follow the Russian example would be the best guarantee of the strength and independence of the Afghan state.' Lenin proposed to the emir the establishment of permanent diplomatic relations, which 'would open the possibility of mutual assistance against any encroachment by any foreign adventurers on the freedom and property of anyone else'.[11]

Being in the midst of the Third Anglo-Afghan War, which Britain had launched on 3 May, Kabul reacted positively to Lenin's proposal. Afghanistan was not accustomed to receiving such treatment from a great power. Amanullah also could not help feeling that he was indebted to the Soviets for his victory over the British – the war terminated on 3 June with the total collapse of the British campaign – as it was the Soviets who, in the spring of 1919, had turned back an attack in Turkestan and forced the British command to abandon a plan to open a new front against Afghanistan from the north.[12]

Just over two months after the Third Anglo-Afghan war ended, on 8 August, a preliminary treaty was signed between the two countries in Rawalpindi. One of its points was official British recognition of Afghanistan's independence in both its domestic affairs and foreign relations. By this time, Soviet troops had taken control of all the territory of Russian Central Asia and reached the Afghan border, thus enabling practical cooperation between the two sides. On 4 June 1919 the first official Afghan mission arrived in Tashkent on its way to Moscow. On 23 June the RSFSR government appointed Ia. Z. Surits 'extraordinary and plenipotentiary representative of the RSFSR in Central Asia with his residence in Kabul' – a somewhat enigmatic title. Surits was given general control of diplomatic relations with the countries of Central Asia, but his precise function has not been explained in Soviet historiography. However, if we recall that in Russian terminology 'Central Asia' refers to countries to the east of Afghanistan, not to Russian Central Asia[13] (as it was officially called in those years in Soviet documents), it is clear that Surits's duties included northern India, which bordered on Afghanistan and the Russian Pamirs, and the western provinces of China (Kashgar, the Gobi Desert and bordering regions of Mongolia). This meant that Surits was in charge of directing subversive activity against Britain and China.

In early October 1919, the Afghan embassy staff arrived in Moscow. On 14 October the head of the embassy, General Muhammed Vali Khan, met with Lenin for the first time, and they met again six weeks later. During his conversations with the Afghan ambassador, Lenin stressed that, in so far as Afghanistan was the only independent Muslim state in the world, the 'great historical task befell it of unifying around itself all the enslaved Muslim nations and of leading them on the path of freedom and independence'.[14] Lenin was clearly playing upon pan-Islamic feelings, trying to draw the emir into Soviet actions directed at subverting the British position in the Islamic world.[15]

Although the Afghan ambassador declined further discussion of this question, Amanullah, unlike his grandfather, Emir Abdurrahman (1880–1901), and his father, was a pan-Islamist and took Lenin's words as encouragement for his own views. As a result of the Afghan delegation's activity in Moscow, a permanent Afghan embassy was opened there and, on 14 December 1919, Surits, the first Soviet ambassador, arrived in Kabul. There the Soviet embassy began intense activity, as writer Maksim Gorkii indicated in an article entitled 'V. I. Lenin': 'From the distant villages of India, Hindus, oppressed by the age-old yoke of British civil servants, secretly traverse hundreds of miles on mountain and forest paths, risking their lives to sneak into the Russian mission in Kabul'.[16]

The British representatives in Kabul not only failed to draw the necessary conclusions from what was happening before their eyes, but by their actions they also pushed Amanullah further into the arms of the Bolsheviks. There was not one attempt by the British to enter into serious dialogue with Amanullah and the ideologist of the Young Afghans, Foreign Minister Mahmud Tarzi, on the question of their relationship with the Bolsheviks and possible inherent dangers for Kabul. On the contrary, in stereotyped fashion, the British representatives continued to support conservative opposition to the Amanullah regime, which was virtually ineffective, the British mission in Kabul and the British press both taking a sharply negative position toward the emir himself. This was expressed in the closing of the mountain passes leading to India, which was tantamount to a declaration of an economic blockade.

True, there remained important differences of outlook between Amanullah and Moscow: the former's open sympathy for the resistance movement in Central Asia, which sought to withstand that region's subjugation to Soviet rule; the desire to correct his country's northern border; his pan-Islamic sentiments and dreams of a Central Asian federation under the aegis of Afghanistan, etc. None the less, in view of the British failure to take advantage of these differences and the potential threat to the emir's regime of the Soviet connection, on 8 May 1920 Amanullah requested general assistance from Moscow, as well as a commercial and military treaty. The talks, conducted by Foreign Minister Tarzi and Surits, progressed quickly and on 13 September 1920 the two sides initialed the first text of the treaty.

The Soviet–Afghan talks caused great anxiety in New Delhi. Lord Chelmsford, who was deeply concerned by the deficiencies and failures of British policy in Afghanistan, began pleading again for a basic change in the approach toward Kabul. On 31 May 1920 he proposed to London 'obtaining our own agreement before the Soviets and Afghans reach theirs'.[17] The viceroy no doubt had in mind an agreement that would paralyze the Soviet–Afghan friendship. The British government, however, had no intention of making major changes in its approach to the Afghan problem. As early as the first conversation with Tarzi of the 'extraordinary plenipotentiary ambassador of Great Britain', Sir Henry Dobbs, it became clear that London 'forgot nothing and learned nothing'. Dobbs suggested that Afghanistan reject the ratification of the treaty with Moscow and that the Soviet embassy be withdrawn from Kabul. In exchange, he offered military and financial assistance and the renewal of personal subsidies to the emir; further, Afghanistan would receive the right of duty-free transit of goods through India. But Kabul would have to agree to conduct talks with other states only through the British government. These proposals were regarded as insulting for Afghanistan and angered the emir and the ruling circles of Kabul. Indeed, to a certain extent the British proposals influenced their decision to sign the Soviet–Afghan agreement on 28 February 1921, even though by that time serious differences of opinion had arisen between Kabul and Moscow on two cardinal issues.

In the first place Kabul did not conceal its dissatisfaction with what amounted to the Bolshevik annexation of Khiva and Bukhara, brought about under the guise of 'popular' revolutions which, as it were, ripened naturally and took place without external interference. In fact the 'popular' revolutions in Khiva (February 1920) and Bukhara (September 1920) were the result of subversive activities directed by Bolshevik agents in Tashkent. (This matter is dealt with openly in Soviet works devoted to the establishment of Soviet rule in Uzbekistan.[18]) The Bolsheviks' activities contradicted the spirit of paragraphs 7 and 8 of the Soviet–Afghan agreement which had already been initialled by the time of the 'popular revolution' in Bukhara. These paragraphs state:

> The High Contracting Parties agree to the Freedom of the Nations of the East on the basis of independence and in accordance with the mutual desire of each of its [the Eastern] Nations. In confirmation of paragraph 7 of the current agreement the High Contracting Parties agree to the effective Independence and Freedom of Bukhara and Khiva, whatever form of government may exist there, conformably to the desire of their Nations.[19]

Confronted with the open export of revolution and the breach of faith on the Soviet side, Amanullah considered himself entitled to accord the emir of Bukhara all possible assistance. When the emir was compelled to leave the boundaries of Bukhara in March 1921, the Afghan authorities welcomed him as a guest of honor, disregarding the protests of the 'government' of the Bukhara People's Soviet Republic.[20]

Another point of conflict between Amanullah and Moscow was caused by evidence that the Bolsheviks were involved in the creation and activities of organizations and groups in Central Asia whose goal was to overthrow the Afghan monarchy and replace it by a pro-Soviet regime. One party, which was formed in Bukhara toward the end of 1920, called 'The Central Committee of the Young Afghan Revolutionaries', declared in its program that:

The goal of the Committee is to overthrow the existing capitalist regime, to establish a Republican government in accordance with the People's will and thus to liberate the Afghan Nation from the despotism of the Emir and Beys and also to pave free roads for science and industry . . . All Afghans who [are in] favor [of] a revolution in Afghanistan can be members of the Committee, whether they originate from Afghanistan or are inhabitants of Bukhara, Turkestan or Russia.[21]

The activity of this and other Afghan antimonarchic organizations had the full support of the soviet and party organs in Turkestan and was coordinated by Moscow through the channels of the Turkestan Bureau of the Central Committee of the Russian Communist Party (Bolshevik).[22] The Soviet historian A. N. Kheifets considers that there are sufficient grounds to argue that the aims of this and other Afghan 'radical political groups were close to the ideas of Marxism–Leninism'.[23]

Indeed, the Bolshevik aim of sovietizing Afghanistan was welcomed quite openly at the very time when the warm exchange of messages between Lenin and Amanullah was taking place. Toward the end of 1919 the journal of the Stalin-headed People's Commissariat of Nationalities (*Narkomnats*) suggested the following program of activities: 'The Sovietization of the Muslims of Central Asia and with their help, the sovietization of their brothers in Iran, Afghanistan and India.'[24] A year and a half later, when the Bolsheviks' hopes for a prompt world revolution began to crumble, the same idea, in a more moderate form, was set forth in an instruction handed by Foreign Minister G. V. Chicherin to the newly nominated ambassador in Kabul, F. F. Raskol'nikov: 'We are telling the Afghan government that we have one social structure, you – another. We have certain ideals, you have others. Not for a minute do we think of imposing on your nation a program which is foreign to it at the current stage of development.'[25] This meant that Moscow was willing to give Afghanistan a certain respite, the length of which would be determined by Moscow itself. This respite in fact lasted fifty-seven years (1921–78). Meanwhile Moscow had to content itself with Afghanistan's commitment, written into the agreement, not to participate in international alliances hostile to Moscow and not to assist forces struggling against the sovietization of Central Asia.

These factors caused Tarzi drastically to change his views on Soviet–Afghan and Anglo–Soviet relations immediately after the signing of the agreement, which was foreign to the Afghan nation at that stage of its development. Tarzi concluded that the obvious shift toward Moscow in Afghan policy could be detrimental to

Afghanistan and in the long run would not correspond to its interests. The Minister of Foreign Affairs began to plead for a more balanced policy and advised against haste in ratifying the Soviet–Afghan agreement until a corresponding Anglo–Afghan agreement was signed. Moreover after the *de facto* annexation of Bukhara and Khiva by the Bolsheviks and after Soviet troops invaded Persia in May 1920 and continued to occupy part of that country's territory, the principles of equality proclaimed in the treaty lost much of their luster in the eyes of the Afghans. Finally, Moscow's desire to open consulates not only in Herat, Mazari-Sherif, and Maimen, but also in Kandahar and Gazni, namely near the Afghan–Indian border, as stipulated in Article 5 of the draft treaty,[26] surprised and disturbed everyone. Wits at the Kabul bazaar asked why, for the sake of parity, Afghanistan did not demand the right to open consulates in Chita and Vladivostok.

Tarzi had to admit that British anxiety over the situation was well founded. He informed Surits that the opening of consulates near the Afghan–Indian border, where Soviet Russia had no real interests, would be resisted by members of the Afghan government and could serve as a pretext for a deterioration of relations with Great Britain, which Kabul was trying to avoid. Surits had to retreat. On 28 June 1921 he informed Tarzi that he was ready, 'immediately after ratification of our treaty', to inform his government 'about all difficulties connected with the opening of consulates in Kandahar and Gazni and he expressed his confidence at the same time that the Soviet government would in the meantime not open these consulates'.[27]

But Surits's assurances had no effect on Tarzi. On 18 July 1921 the new Soviet ambassador, Raskol'nikov, in conversation with Tarzi, again brought up the question of the ratification of the Soviet–Afghan treaty. He expressed a desire for the question to be resolved within a week. Tarzi's reaction was the same as it had been earlier. Raskol'nikov's letters of 24 and 30 July, in which Surits's assurances were confirmed, did not change Tarzi's position. Only a second letter of 30 July, which hinted at the possibility of a worsening of Soviet–Afghan relations and of a change in Moscow's position in the Anglo–Afghan conflict, produced an effect. On 7 August a meeting of high state officials and nobles was called. After four days of sessions, it recommended that the emir ratify the treaty.[28]

On 13 August 1921 the Soviet–Afghan agreement was ratified, conditional upon Moscow's refraining from opening consulates in the cities indicated. As a result of the conditions regarding the consulates, Raskol'nikov's presentation of credentials was delayed by the Afghans until Moscow gave official notification that it conceded the point. Moscow, for its part, did not hasten this matter, somehow hoping to succeed in establishing observation points right on the border with British India. But the Afghan government remained firm on this point. In mid-November 1921, Raskol'nikov received Moscow's official reply that the consulates in Gazni and Kandahar would not be opened, and on 17 November 1921 he finally presented his credentials to the emir. On 21 November, Raskol'nikov wrote a letter to Tarzi, informing him that the government of the RSFSR confirmed Surits's letter of 29 June 1921 and Raskol'nikov's letters of 24 and 30 July 1921, 'and, because of difficulties experienced by the friendly government of Afghanistan, the consulates in Kandahar and Gazni would not be opened'.[29] This proviso opened the way to the signing of the Anglo-Afghan agreement on 22 November 1921. The following day saw the publication in New Delhi of an official announcement that the agreement with Afghanistan had been signed 'after receiving satisfactory assurances from the Afghan government that Russian consulates would not be allowed in the regions of Jalalabad, Gazni, and Kandahar'.[30]

A protest registered on 5 December 1921 by the Soviet embassy in Kabul in connection with this announcement showed that Moscow did not in principle relinquish the right to open these consulates and that Kabul's assurances to London had the same force as the annulment of Article 5 of the Soviet–Afghan agreement.[31] The Afghan government declined to answer the Soviet ambassador's protest. The incident remained unsettled, but the consulates in the cities of southeast Afghanistan were not opened.

Despite numerous gains, Soviet diplomacy did not succeed in achieving its immediate goals in Afghanistan. Afghanistan did not become a 'Suez Canal' of revolution. Indeed, for over a decade its territory remained a base and a refuge for forces of resistance to the Soviets in Central Asia. Nor did Kabul become, right up to World War II, despite the agreement of 1921 (and the later agreement of 1926), neutral or friendly to Moscow.

Nevertheless, it was precisely in these early years that Moscow acquired certain positions in Afghanistan, which it fortified, in readiness for the time when conditions in the country would be appropriate to proceed with the sovietization of Afghanistan.

Notes: Chapter 11

1. V. S. Vasiukov, *Vneshniaia politika Vremennogo Pravitel'stva* (Moscow: Mysl', 1966).
2. N. Khalfin, *Proval britanskoi agressii na Srednem Vostoke (XIXv.-nachalo XXv.)* (Moscow: Nauka, 1959), p. 175.
3. *Dokumenty vneshnei politiki SSSR* (Moscow: Gospolitizdat, 1957–) (hereafter cited as *DVP SSSR*), Vol. 1, doc. 40, p. 72.
4. *Papers Regarding Hostilities with Afghanistan, 1919* (London, 1919), pp. 4–5.
5. On 26 December 1917, Lord Chelmsford wrote to his government that a widening of British military intervention in the Persian affair would be taken in India and in the entire Muslim world 'as further and unprovoked aggression against a Muslim state, with all the consequences that implied' (Arkhiv Instituta Vostokovedeniia Akademii Nauk SSSR, National Archive of India (hereafter cited as AIVAN SSSR, NAI), Persia Series, pt 16, notes, doc 68, p. 42.

    This meant not occupying Persia, not imposing an unfair treaty upon it, not orienting Britain toward conservative elements in Persia and Afghanistan, and changing Britain's attitude toward the liberal national forces in those countries. Lord Chelmsford considered it possible that with such an approach those regional elements who intuitively mistrusted the Bolsheviks, seeing that their actions differed from their slogans, might convince the peoples of their countries of the danger of trusting their Bolshevik friends. In the event, however, this viewpoint did not prevail and, as Chelmsford had warned, Britain became in the eyes of the entire Muslim world the embodiment of those forces that were destructive to Islam. The continued British 'presence', he wrote, whether military or economic, blinds nationalistic leaders and prevents them from seeing that the real danger is Moscow, not London (*Documents on British Foreign Policy, 1919–1939* (London: Her Majesty's Stationery Office, 1963) (hereafter cited as *DBFP*), 1st series, Vol. 13, p. 706).
6. ibid.
7. AIVAN SSSR, NAI, Persian Series, pt 16, doc. 71, p. 54.
8. *DVP SSSR*, vol. 2, p. 92.
9. ibid., p. 175.
10. *Materialy po natsional'no-kolonial'nym problemam* (Moscow, 1934) (hereafter cited as *MNKP*), no. 7 (22), pp. 72–3.
11. *DVP SSSR*, vol. 2, p. 174. The Afghan-Soviet dialogue developed against the background of a rapid deterioration in relations between Kabul and London. The British government had categorically refused to recognize Afghanistan's independence, and on 3 May 1919 launched a war against Afghanistan – the third within eighty years (the first Anglo-Afghan war had been in 1838–42, the second in 1878–80). See *The Third Afghan War, 1919: Official Account* (Calcutta, 1921).
12. L. I. Miroshnikov, *Angliiskaia ekspansiia v Irane (1914–1920gg.)* (Moscow: Nauka, 1961); W. E. R. Dixon, *East Persia: A Backwater of the Great War* (London, 1924).
13. Relations with Bukhara and Khiva were conducted by Tashkent when the Turkkomissiia VtsIK and SNK RSFSR (the Commission for Turkestan of the All-Union Central Executive Committee and the Council of

People's Commissars of the RSFSR) with its Department of Foreign Affairs was located there.
14 *MNKP*, no. 7 (22), p. 72.
15 A. N. Kheifets, *Sovetskaia diplomatiia i narody Vostoka (1921–1927gg.)* (Moscow: Nauka, 1969), p. 79.
16 *Kommunisticheskii Internatsional*, no. 12 (1920), p. 1933.
17 AIVAN SSSR, NAI, Frontier, A, December 1920, doc. 16, p. 7.
18 See, for example, the monograph by Corresponding Member of the Uzbekistan SSR Academy of Sciences A. Imanov, *Rol' Kompartii i Sovetskogo Pravitel'stva v sozdanii natsional'noi gosudarstvennosti uzbekskogo naroda* (Tashkent: Uzbekistan, 1978).
19 *DVP SSSR*, vol. 3, p. 552.
20 ibid., vol. 4, p. 720.
21 A. Kheifets, 'Uzy dobrososedstva i bratstva nerastorzhimy', *Aziia i Afrika segodnia*, no. 2 (1981), pp. 17–18.
22 See *Istoriia kommunisticheskikh organizatsii Srednei Azii* (Tashkent: Fan, 1967).
23 Kheifets, 'Uzy dobrososedstva', p. 18. It is interesting to note that the document quoted above is safeguarded in the Central Party Archive of the CPSU Marxism–Leninism Institute (*fond 61, op. 1, ed. khr. 28, p. 24*) and was published for the first time in 1981 by Professor Kheifets. Evidently, the publication of such facts before the April 1978 revolution could have provoked an undesirable reaction in Afghanistan. After the establishment of a pro-Soviet regime in Afghanistan such revelations could no longer change anything. In this article Kheifets also publishes another, no less curious, document for the first time: Svodka sobytii za 7–14 noiabria 1920g.', which was sent to Moscow by the RSFSR plenipotentiary in Bukhara, V. V. Kuibyshev, and from which we learn that the Afghan revolutionary organization aimed to infiltrate the ranks of the Afghan army and overthrow the emir with its help: Tsentral'nyi partiinyi arkhiv Instituta Marksizma-Leninizma pri TsK KPSS (hereafter cited as TsPA IML TsK KPSS), *fond 122, op. 1, ed. khr. 11*, pp. 83–9.
24 *Zhizn' natsional'nostei*, no. 36 (44) (1919), p. 1; quoted in Ivor Spector, *The Soviet Union and the Muslim World, 1917–1958* (Seattle, Wash.: University of Washington Press, 1959), p. 92.
25 Arkhiv Ministerstva inostrannykh del SSSR (hereafter cited as AMID SSSR), *fond* 04, *op.* 6, *papka* 43, *delo* 592, p. 4. (*Papka*, hereafter *p.*, means 'file' or 'box'; and *delo*, hereafter *d.*, means 'subject'.).
26 See text in *DVP SSSR*, Vol. 3, p. 551.
27 AMID SSSR, *fond* 2, *op*, 4, *p*. 1, *d*. 8 p. 6.
28 Kheifets, *Sovetskaia dipolomatiia*, pp. 76–7.
29 ibid., pp. 78–9.
30 ibid., p. 79.
31 *An Assessment of the Afghanistan Sanctions: Implications for Trade and Diplomacy in the 1980s* (Washington, DC: United States Government Printing Office, 1981): report prepared for the subcommittee on Europe and the Middle East of the Committee on Foreign Affairs, US House of Representatives, by the Office of the Senior Specialist, Congressional Research Service, Library of Congress, April 1981.

12

Soviet Policy and the Constraints of Nationalism in Iran and Afghanistan

MARVIN G. WEINBAUM

Soviet policies in the Islamic Middle East, particularly since Iran's revolution and the decision to intervene militarily in Afghanistan, are regularly scrutinized for their strategic implications for the region's northern tier and beyond. In a continuing debate over Soviet motives and goals, one view asserts that policy-makers in Moscow have engineered a carefully drafted set of policies, moving to a conscious timetable in the drive toward the Persian Gulf and Indian Ocean. Another essentially polar view insists that the Soviet Union remains reactive in its foreign policies. Not unlike the United States, the Soviets are conceived as being forced to adjust to events and clients in a fashion not usually of their own making and frequently not to their liking. From one perspective, Soviet leadership is creative and aggressive, whether out of a sense of superiority or of inferiority; from the other, it is adaptive and conservative, either by inclination or by calculation.[1] In practice, of course, the two interpretations are not necessarily mutually exclusive, nor the policies they imply always incompatible. More reflective observers appreciate the possibility of discerning clear goals and synoptic planning by the Soviets and also of finding them acting pragmatically and *ad hoc*. Small gains made under unfavorable conditions can be every bit as creative as major thrusts and often suffice in an anticipation of more propitious times. Low-risk strategies may be jettisoned in the face of a high level of external threat and a cautious approach superseded by a decision to project their power forcefully. In all probability, policy emerges from a combination of desired long-term outcomes and perceived short-term opportunities, and from both offensive and defensive motives.

On one issue there is little debate: geographically proximate Iran and Afghanistan command a regular place on the Soviet policy agenda. Moscow has not traditionally reconciled itself to these two countries falling into the sphere of influence of other powers. Over the last thirty-five years, a steady and often intensive flow of diplomatic, political and economic interactions has taken place with regimes in Tehran and Kabul. Soviet goals and decision styles are valuable in appreciating the direction and pace of these activities, but they are likely to be incomplete in explaining the successes and setbacks in foreign policies. For this the analyst must also consider Soviet capabilities, measured in terms of both the available resources and the major obstacles to policy, especially those posed by domestic constraints in Iran and Afghanistan. This essay argues that in Iran and Afghanistan Soviet actions in these two countries must be understood in the context of several strains of nationalist ideology and doctrine in the two countries. Soviet capacity for awareness, accommodations, and manipulation of nationalism in Iran and Afghanistan figures significantly both in limiting and in furthering Moscow's aims. From the way Soviet strategists have fashioned policies to deal with various ethnic groups, popular leaders and mass sentiments in Iran and Afghanistan during the post-World War II period, we have a clearer picture of their problems and progress. As these discussions show, the Soviets have exhibited sensitivity as well as callousness, prudence as well as impatience. Policies have been neither always consistent toward these two countries, nor applied simultaneously to both.

Forms of Nationalism

In encounters with nationalism in Iran and Afghanistan, Soviet policy-makers have had to deal with at least six distinct though sometimes overlapping and reinforcing strains. Each presents constraints on Soviet actions, but also offers the basis for Soviet penetration and alliances. The first of these forms is an *ethnosectarian-regional* nationalism. It asserts the existence of a people with shared language, origin and territory, to some extent separate in their interests and aspirations. Typically, these nationalists or, more accurately, subnationalists comprise a minority group in the country, politically if not numerically. In belief and behavior, they stress their differences with other national groups and often find themselves in opposition to ruling elites at the center. The aims of these nationalists may include the quest for increased respectability and identity, better recognition in the allocation of national resources and a measure of political autonomy, even total separation. The region's Kurds, Baluchis, Azeri Turks, Arabs and Turkomans are only the better known of these populations, each with varying degrees of political consciousness and sense of nationhood.

A national vision of another kind is also rooted in a distant history and involves a distinct people. But this nationalism of *race and land* is that of a numerically dominant population whose aspirations are frequently irridentist and whose aims, deliberately or not, override the identities and interests of minorities. Movements of this type have appeared in Iran in the form of authoritarian groups determined to strengthen the Farsi-speaking character of the country and incorporate historically Iranian populations in the Gulf and elsewhere. As a political and ideological force, Afghanistan's Pushtun nationalism has more contemporary relevance. Its most obvious manifestation is the struggle to detach Pakistan's Northwest Frontier Province to form a new ethnic state. But Pushtun nationalism is also commonly viewed by minorities in Afghanistan as synonymous with economic privilege and cultural imperialism.

A third, highly visible form in the two countries derives its appeal from an opposition to perceived threats to the independence and integrity of the state. It portrays the country as laboring under foreign exploitation and denied self-determination. It rallies citizens to the liberation of the nation by excluding foreign economic domination and political interference. In what can be termed *autarchic* nationalism, an anti-imperialist rhetoric rejects concessions to foreign powers and questions the desirability of foreign credits and loans. Xenophobic, anti-Western popular attitudes in present-day Iran, and the major thrust of Afghan insurgency against a Soviet influence and presence exhibit many of these qualities. But the 'negative equilibrium', as defined by Mohammad Mossadeq and his National Front in Iran during the late 1940s and early 1950s, provides no doubt the clearest illustration of autarchic sentiments as the basis for creating a national unity.

A fourth form, a *modernizing* nationalism, focuses on directing national and human resources of the state to economic and social development. This national consciousness is largely secular and integrative. Primordial distinctions are minimized and people exhorted to give their energies to a state committed to increased economic growth and to modifying, if not rejecting, traditional social practices and values. These changes are expected to enhance the country's respect regionally and internationally. Modernizing nationalism is sometimes referred to as 'positive' to distinguish it from the negativism of the autarchic form. It is compatible with conservative, *laissez-faire* regimes as well as with socialist ones, and finds natural and common adversaries among feudals and the religious establishment. The last Iranian monarch and Afghanistan's Prime Minister (later President) Mohammad Daoud conspicuously adopted modern nationalism as a principal legitimizing ideology.

Liberal nationalism in the two countries encompasses many of the same qualities of modern and even autarchic forms in striving for self-realization through independent national development. By contrast to the modernists, liberals are unwilling to ignore political reforms in their advocacy of social and economic change. They are most identified with free elections, active parliaments, and other political and civil rights, both for themselves and as means to other ends. In Iran and Afghanistan, liberal nationalism has its origins and continues to be nourished by constitutionalism. It was a constituent element in Iran's 1905–6 movement, had a following among the National Front, and was well represented in the moderate secular and religious opposition to the regime of Mohammad Reza Shah. Liberal nationalists made their first appearance in Afghanistan during the late 1920s aligned with modern constitutionalists, surfaced briefly in a period of political relaxation twenty years later, and seemingly realized most of their aims in the country's 1964 Constitution. Concentrated among professionals and intellectuals, the liberal nationalists are far more visible and influential than their numbers alone would suggest. Yet without links to the masses, urban or rural, they are often forced into uncomfortable alliances in order to bid seriously for power or to govern effectively.

Traditional Islamic assertiveness fuses with national feelings of pride and awareness to form a sixth type. *Islamic-state* nationalism is, of course, theologically a contradiction for a religion built on principles of universalism. In fact, though, Iran's Jafari Shiism has been the state religion in Iran for nearly five centuries, and many of its key doctrinal beliefs are forged in the experience of Iranian political self-determination. Khomeini's Islamic republic is only the most contemporary manifestation of a continuing religious-secular struggle for supreme authority over the state. Though neither shaped by nor contributing historically to a modern Afghan state, a Sunni Muslim leadership, fearing extinction in the radical changes of the late 1970s, became critical to national cohesion and the survival of an independent

Afghanistan. Under more normal circumstances, Islamic-state nationalists in both countries are likely to be pitted against secular liberal and modernizing nationalists.

These strands of nationalism offer potentially constraining factors in Soviet efforts to formulate effective policies. There are inherent difficulties in fashioning consistent policies when the several forms of nationalism in Iran and Afghanistan are often competitive and may be mutually exclusive. Unavoidably, often out of expediency, the Soviets have alienated some nationalists in currying favor with others. Particularly complicating is the fact that the species of nationalism in the two countries do not coincide with a left-right spectrum. Each may have its Marxists and *laissez-faire* capitalists, its communists and democratic socialists. These intersections give the Soviets possible entry into any national group including, as the recent Iranian situation reveals, militant Islamic circles. It can also divide, however, the Soviet's natural allies and friends and show how, when nationalists are forced to choose, older allegiances take precedence over ideological ones.

Whenever possible, the Soviets have sought to align themselves with what they perceived to be the ascendant national force and to exploit the most pervasive sentiments. Moscow has normally endorsed territorial integrity and the preservation of Afghan and Iranian historical traditions, and echoed calls for resistance to imperialism. Even so, policymakers have not always gauged correctly the changing balance of popular feelings, or entirely appreciated the degree of convergence, even if temporary, of nationalist interests and adherents. In their desire to take advantage of antagonisms, the Soviets have repeatedly underestimated the cohesiveness that binds a country's nationalists.

At the level of ideology, nationalism finds its champions among the urban, educated middle classes, where attachments to a larger geographic entity have usually supplemented other allegiances. Nationalism becomes a vehicle for realizing economic, social and political goals, as well as a basis for individual self-identification. But under conditions of incomplete political integration in the two countries, especially Afghanistan, nationalism as a doctrine does not normally reach and mobilize large majorities. Appeals to race and land have been the most persuasive, capable of becoming the basis for collective attitudes and actions. Autarchic feelings are likely to be powerful as popular doctrine where mass deprivations are linked in the popular mind with distinctly alien, external forces. Pervasive Islamic-state nationalism requires a strong sense of threat to the belief system and the perception of national leaders as its principal defenders. Ethnosectarian-regional nationalism involves considerable extension of attitudes on language and culture to a more inclusive group, likely only in face of strong repressive measures by an ethnic majority. The other forms have far less penetration, seldom touching the consciousness of the urban working class and the peasantry. The largely abstract goals and typically imported principles of liberal and modern nationalism are found irrelevant and may even fail to compete with newly formed class attachments. Still, while the principal bearers of nationalist ideas occupy positions of central authority or lead counter-elites, the formulation of effective foreign policies toward Iran and Afghanistan requires strategies to deal with the values and aspirations associated with nationalism.

Doctrinal considerations of another kind constitute potentially limiting factors for the Soviets. If Marxist–Leninist theory conceives of nationalism as an ephemeral phenomenon, then there is understandably a tendency to minimize this sentiment, or at least to consider it solely for its instrumental value. Accordingly, it is unnecessary to fashion long-term policies to deal with extra-class attachments. Of course, since the mid-1950s, the Soviets have made often finely tuned adjustments and sustained commitments in support of opposition national movements in the Third World. They have not as a rule posed strict ideological tests as conditions of assistance. Yet there is also evidence that doctrinal factors at times constrain policies in Iran and Afghanistan. The Soviets in their continuing attachments to urban, middle-class communists have shunned mass mobilization of urban workers but especially rural populations. In consequence, they have often discounted the widening appeal and deepening roots of nationalist feelings in Iran and, more lately, Afghanistan. The stance of the communist Tudeh party in Iran during the Mosaddeq period and Moscow's support for the Shah over much of the following quarter-century are good cases in point. In general, the Soviets have tended to neglect or even stifle those progressive national movements they were unable to control directly, and to develop working relations with conservative or centrist regimes that conceded Moscow other economic and foreign-policy objectives.

Soviet experiences with their own nationalities also condition policies toward neighboring Islamic countries. It is commonly agreed that the Soviet leadership feels deeply concerned about a heightened social and political consciousness in its Central Asian republics, and fears a contagion from the religious and ethnic feelings that propel contemporary Iranian and Afghan nationalists. Though probably no immediate threat to the communist order, underground religious movements are increasingly active and influential. The Soviets are as a result alert to events and precedents affecting contiguous populations abroad that could serve as models or sources of inspiration for their own citizens and, for that matter, those in satellite countries. Moscow has until very recently managed to separate endorsement of ethnic self-determination and identity in Iran and Afghanistan from what it has been willing to tolerate within its borders. Official policies that restrict and harass Islam for its supposed reactionary role in Soviet life have never been made an example for Muslim countries seeking Moscow's aid. Just the same, the general patterns of cooptation and intimidation applied to Soviet nationalities have frequently guided or, more typically, misguided policy in Iran and Afghanistan. Heavy-handed postwar policies in Iran's Azerbaijan, the flawed decision to place Soviet (Central Asian) nationals in the Afghan bureaucracy, and poor assessments of the influence of the *ulema* in both countries, described below, illustrate perceptions formed from Moscow's successes in controlling their own minorities.

Much as Soviet domestic constraints and, to some extent, the general state of East–West relations help to determine Moscow's risk-taking, political and social forces within Iran and Afghanistan are still more critical to understanding Soviet policies. In this essay particular attention is devoted to those individuals and groups that serve as the principal advocates and disseminators of nationalist ideology. The intelligentsia, Islamic clergy, military, and the national left, including local communists, furnish much of this cast. Soviet aims, whether short- or long-term, derive significance from the nationalism which shapes the politics of the two countries.

Iran

The active, competing nationalist forces of Iran have posed a formidable and continuing challenge for Soviet policymakers. Iran's post-World War II history is marked by examples of serious Soviet miscalculations and errors, but also evidence of an accumulated sagacity in coping with Iranian nationalism in its several forms. Any discussion of Soviet strategies in Iran over this period must begin with events in Iran's Azerbaijan and Kurdish regions between 1944 and 1946. These events reveal the full strength of ethnosectarian nationalism as well as the costs to the Soviets of pursuing inconsistent, blatantly opportunistic policies.

The Soviet Occupation

The distinctive ethnic and linguistic character of Iran's northwestern province of Azerbaijan has long formed the basis for resentment against the political and cultural domination of central authority. Under the Reza Shah dictatorship beginning in 1921, any meaningful autonomy was impossible. The monarch had largely succeeded in suppressing regional and tribal influences in a political integration designed to further plans for modernization and a consolidation of power. The forced abdication of Reza Shah in August 1941 followed his refusal to bow to Allied demands that he end German activities in the country, and ushered in an occupation by Soviet and British forces. The northern provinces of Iran fell within the sector administered by Soviet authorities.

The occupying Soviets readily capitalized on Azerbaijan's ethnic nationalist tendencies, strengthened, it is argued, by a psychological alienation created by Reza Shah's aggressive modernizing policies.[2] Avoiding the potentially wider geographic and political implications of appeals based on race and the Turkishness of the province's majority, the Soviet-backed communist party, the Tudeh (Masses) party, instead stressed the accumulated social and economic grievances against the central authorities. The Tudeh everywhere acknowledged brotherly ties with the Soviet Union and took its cues from Moscow; but only in Azerbaijan was the party firmly in the hands of Soviet agents. In Tabriz, Azerbaijan's major city, Ja'far Pishevari, a trusted Moscow-trained communist, headed the Tudeh. Together with the leftist leadership of the nationalist Kumelah movement in the Kurdish-speaking areas of western Azerbaijan, the Pishevari communists were provided with arms, cash and Soviet advisors.[3] It was under Soviet guidance that the Tudeh party in Azerbaijan, in a new guise of a popular-front Democratic Party, declared an Autonomous Republic of Azerbaijan in December 1945. The nominal provincial governor appointed by Tehran was removed, and Soviet armed forces prevented central-government troops from advancing on Tabriz. In Kurdish Mahabad, Kumelah forces, similarly at Soviet urging, adopted the façade of a Democratic Party, and established a Kurdish People's Republic.

Aside from a puppet state in Azerbaijan, the Soviets set their sights on an oil concession covering the northern part of the country. But when this concession was first proposed in 1944 the Iranian parliament (Majlis), led by veteran deputy Mohammad Mosaddeq, declared that no concessions would be granted until a postwar elected Majlis could approve them. Despite this clear assertion of autarchic nationalism, the Soviets were confident that they had sufficient leverage to force an agreement on the Iranians when the time came.

Subsequent events demonstrated a gross underestimation of the broad domestic support for Iran's national integrity. The Soviets exhibited, moreover, a ready willingness to abandon minority liberation movements, even those ideologically compatible, when they stood in the way of strategic interests and possible economic gain. Against the backdrop of Iranian complaints at the United Nations, and unexpectedly strong warnings from the USA, the Soviets concluded an agreement with Iranian Prime Minister Qavam es-Saltaneh in April 1946, to withdraw their forces from Iran in exchange for promised Majlis approval of long-term oil rights and the inclusion of Tudeh ministers in the Qavam cabinet.[4] After months of fruitless negotiations with the secessionists, Iranian troops entered Azerbaijan and the Kurdish areas, and the republics quickly collapsed. Not only had the Soviet Union failed to equip its regional nationalist allies to resist the central government, but also its policies throughout the occupation, described below, particularly in the Azeri-speaking areas, had severely undermined the emergence of an independent, popular government, able at least to force concessions by Tehran to regional nationalism.

The erosion of local support for the Pishevari government no doubt helped to convince the Soviets to settle for the economic gains of an oil concession. Yet Moscow bears much of the responsibility for the Democratic Party's difficulties in failing to hold popular confidence. The Soviets had, in effect, smothered the regional nationalists by demands for full control; they made little effort to disguise the local leaderships' dependence on them for political strategies and survival. Whatever the injustices dealt the province during Reza Shah's reign, a majority in Azerbaijan retained supra-regional nationalist sentiments that could not be overlooked. Those with some familiarity with Soviet Azerbaidzhan had good reason, moreover, to be suspicious of the Soviet nationalities' policy. These feelings were strengthened by the Pishevari government's increasing resort to police-state methods as opposition to it grew.

For a while the Soviets had moved cautiously in advising secession in Azerbaijan and had denied that a rebellion existed against the central authorities. In finally imposing the Republic, they deviated from their own, at the time more rigid doctrine about the necessary conditions for a revolutionary socialist state. Initially strong support from workers and peasants was largely dissipated by the inability of the Democratic Party to effect redistributions of wealth or land.[5]

The Kumelah party had deeper popular roots and offered a more genuine national liberation movement. The close cooperation of its leftist leaders with the Soviets had not destroyed their credibility as Kurdish patriots, and Moscow's agents, in any case, were unable to infiltrate so successfully into the tribal areas. The easy fall of the Kurdish People's Republic and the execution of its leaders by the Tehran government revealed, however, a fatal schism in the secessionist movement. The resentment by tribal chiefs of the more urbanized, ideological leadership of the Kumelah probably helps to account for the failure of the usually martial tribes to put up stiff resistance against central government forces.[6]

Many autarchic-minded nationalists had welcomed a wartime Soviet role in anticipation that it would furnish a useful counterweight to British influence in Iran. But, whatever the credibility of the Soviets in seeking to focus nationalist, xenophobic feelings against the British, it suffered as their own, older image as economic and territorial imperialists was revived. Richard Cottam, the foremost student of Iranian nationalism in this period, writes that efforts to convince Iranians that the Soviet Union was different from tsarist Russia were undermined by the Azerbaijan affair.[7] Tudeh party leaders in Tehran argued that a joint Soviet–Iranian oil company to explore in the north would be in Iran's long-term interests; but domestic opinion viewed the concession as still another attempt to whittle away national sovereignty. Within the Tudeh party itself, many liberals concluded that, after all, the aims of international communism and those of nationalists in Iran were inherently incompatible.[8] The Soviet army did nothing to allay fears that Iran was slated to become a sphere of Soviet influence by its delay in abiding by the terms of withdrawal in the 1942 Tripartite Treaty. When finally, in October 1947, a new Majlis rejected the Quavam-negotiated oil agreements, it was with the kind of unanimity and resolve rarely displayed in the normally faction-ridden assembly. Yet, despite this setback, Soviet policy over the next several years suggests that Moscow's theoreticians and strategists had not learned some obvious lessons from the events of the mid-1940s.

The National Front

Following their rebuff over oil rights, Soviet relations with Iran entered a tense period that served both as cause and effect in the drift of Iranian policy toward closer ties with the USA. But, while Moscow frequently resorted to intimidation to try to halt pro-Western policies, the Soviet-oriented Tudeh party and other front organizations in Iran were actively working to calm popular fears of Soviet intentions. Local communists tried to put the best face on the Azerbaijan affair, and in their propaganda organs stressed the Soviet Union's sympathy with Iran's national aspirations. The party portrayed itself as the best alternative to Iran's squabbling, opportunistic politicians and feudally dominated politics. But, for a larger number of nationalists, doubts lingered that Iranian communists would, if forced to choose, put Iranian interests ahead of Soviet ones. A preferred vehicle of parliamentary opposition appeared in the form of the National Front, a broad coalition of parties, led by Mosaddeq, whose extreme autarchic nationalism allowed for a balanced suspicion of both Western and Soviet imperialism.

The National Front coalesced national parties, religious fundamentalists, and most of the liberal left, all united by the cause of oil nationalization. Each constituent in the Front envisioned its own nationalist aims as furthered in the negation of foreign control over Iran's oil resources. The issue was also ostensibly tailor-made for the Soviet Union, since nationalization would come directly at the expense of British interests. The Soviets backed the Front's demands and supported Iran's arguments in international forums. Still, Moscow tempered its enthusiasm for nationalization and had not instigated the crisis, for a victory for economic self-determination would also foreclose the possibility of concessions to the Soviet Union. Moreover, such a victory would enhance the reputation of Mosaddeq – whom the Shah had been obliged to name as Prime Minister in April 1951 – who, whatever his antipathy toward the Americans, was the scion of an aristocratic, landholding family and, by his own admission, anti-communist.[9] Mosaddeq's role in the Majlis in 1944 and 1947 had proved to the Soviets that he was no friend. Hence, while the nationalists were praised in Moscow for their anti-imperialism, the Tudeh party attacked Mosaddeq personally and heaped criticism on defectors from the communist ranks in the National Front leadership. However impelling the logic of collaboration between the Tudeh and the Front — together they could form the dominant political force in the country — it was clear that much of the time the Tudeh party preferred to compete with a movement beyond its ability to control. Marxist doctrine notwithstanding, Moscow was unprepared to foster as a dialectical stage what it conceived as bourgeois–nationalist rule in Iran. For the Soviets and the Tudeh, the opportunity for communist rule in Iran seemed much closer at hand.

A February 1949 attempt on the Shah's life, allegedly linked to a communist plot against the regime, had been used to justify outlawing the Tudeh party. Numerous new communist front organizations appeared, however. While going underground slowed recruitment of members, the Tudeh tightened itself organizationally and ideologically. Behind other labels it contested for Majlis seats and, though winning none, was able to demonstrate its continued large urban following. The Soviet Union was meanwhile able to divorce its diplomatic relations from internal developments when the occasion dictated. Government repression of the Tudeh did not deter Moscow from offering aid in 1950 to Tehran authorities disappointed by the low level of American economic assistance. The Soviets could also return quickly to a policy of overt hostility, as in April 1952 when Mosaddeq sought to renew agreements with the USA.

Over the period of Mosaddeq's rule, the Tudeh party surfaced with increased frequency and boldness. It had a hand in the strikes that erupted in Azerbaijan and Khuzistan during 1951 and 1952. In political rallies and demonstrations beginning May 1951, the party pictured the National Front's policies and Mosaddeq in particular as selling out to American imperialists, even while resisting the British.[10] But as Iranian–American relations cooled again after mid-1952 this line fell flat and probably damaged the party's credibility among nationalists.[11] Before the end of the year, the communists were calling for a partnership against the Shah and the country's conservative elites. Opponents of the Tudeh within the National Front blocked a formal alliance, but a willingness to tolerate the Tudeh increased as Mosaddeq's popularity faded in economic adversities created in the cutoff of oil income. By early 1953, the National Front's middle-class support was much diminished, and key leaders in the parliamentary coalition deserted in disgust over the Prime Minister's increasingly dictatorial behavior. In need of allies to counter the growing threat from the Shah and the political right, Mosaddeq drew closer to the communists. Convinced that the

Tudeh could inherit the nationalist mantle from a government on its way out, the party made a bold bid in mid-August 1953 for leadership of progressive forces opposed to the monarchy and reactionary clergy. But communist-led street riots, instead of mobilizing Mosaddeq's former broad constituency, frightened these same elements, giving credence to arguments by the right that a communist takeover was imminent. Moreover, Mossaddeq struck back hard at the communists, his police forcing them from the streets, when he realized that his authority had been challenged in the disorders. Thus, when the troops loyal to the Shah made their move for power the next day, the Tudeh was badly dispersed and, surprisingly, without instructions to resist the army.

The British, in their callousness toward nationalist feelings in Iran, had no doubt helped to radicalize anti-imperialist sentiment. In the end, they had no choice but to relinquish their monopoly over Iran's oil resources. American policymakers were confounded by Mosaddeq as a national leader and, particularly after the Eisenhower Administration took office, were unable to distinguish Iranian desires for self-determination from procommunist sympathies. While the US emerged from the military coup of 19–20 August 1953 with a client state in Iran, it had forfeited its once charmed role as a disinterested friend of Iranian nationalism. The USA became linked with a regime forever tainted in the eyes of liberals, religious and autarchic nationalists, as a tool or outpost of Western imperialism. But it was the Soviet Union which at least over the next two decades paid most dearly for its mistakes in the early 1950s. In allowing Iran's communists to undermine the National Front, and in trying to undercut its popular leader, the Soviets traded a probable neutralist regime on its border for a pro-Western one. Moscow left exposed the Middle East's largest communist party and committed many of its activists to exile or execution. The Tudeh has still to recover from the popular belief that it had contributed to the downfall of the National Front. Moscow suffered, then, for policies that at the time insisted that progressive national movements, in order to be genuine and worthy of consistent support, had to be communist-led.

The Shah's Rule

Soviet setbacks in Iran were less important than the wider decolonization process under way in the postwar period in leading Moscow's theoreticians to reassess their 'two camp' doctrine.

It had become unrealistic and counterproductive to impose a class analysis on the Third World countries allowing no middle ground between socialist and capitalist forces, and to have this conception serve as the basis for picking allies and adversaries.[12] By the mid-1950s, the Soviets were assisting liberation movements that, while ideologically unacceptable to them, could demonstrate popular strength and were likely to free a country from traditional pro-Western attachments. Avowedly non-communist nationalists were often, in fact, preferable, as their assumption of power could allay fears in the West about fundamental political change and hence avoid counter-measures. Ironically, although Soviet policy shortcomings in Iran may have contributed to shaping new strategies in the Third World, Iran was not itself a suitable setting in which to apply the revised approach. The 1953 coup left all political opposition to the regime fragmented and demoralized. Not for many years would there be a significant liberation movement for the Soviets to consider adopting in Iran.

Over the next twenty-five years Moscow was content in its policies toward Iran to contain Western influence. While the Soviets periodically attacked the Shah's foreign policies and often gave aid and comfort to Iran's enemies in the Arab world, the monarchy was accepted along with a modern bourgeoisie which the Shah helped bring into existence.[13] Soviet policy fitted well with the brand of nationalism the Shah was seeking to have replace the 'negative equilibrium' espoused by Mosaddeq. The Shah's 'positive nationalism' advocated a foreign policy of forming ties with countries willing to help Iran preserve its independence and assist in its economic development and defense capabilities.[14] Indeed, Soviet cooperation could go far in helping the Shah to realize his ambition to lead a modern Iran.

Meanwhile, the Soviets kept up financial support for Tudeh party propagandists abroad through communist-bloc allies. Within Iran, however, Moscow's normalization of relations with the Shah's government furthered dissension and defections in the already skeletal communist party. The Soviet policy reversal, endorsing the Shah's White Revolution as progressive and democratic, weakened the National Front's argument that the reforms were counterfeit, and antagonized liberal nationalists who believed that the success of any programs would give the dictatorship a new lease of life. While some Tudeh members loyally followed the new Moscow line, dissenting factions formed and militant leftists generally resigned themselves to a struggle against the Shah without Soviet aid. By its actions in the early 1960s, then, the Soviet Union ensured that the revolutionary movement that took root in the 1970s would be fragmented on the left and would draw inspiration and support more from the radicalism of the PLO and Libya than from orthodox communism.

The Shah, for his part, was careful to distinguish between subversive communist forces in Iran and policies of the Soviet government. It was only as agitation against the regime rose in 1978 and Soviet gains were registered in Afghanistan and the Horn of Africa that the government-controlled press in Tehran raised the specter of a Soviet threat to Iran and its oil and publicly charged Soviet espionage in Iran. Moscow remained restrained, however, in its own propaganda. The Kremlin leadership refused to believe that the Shah's troubles would lead to a revolution in the near future. The spreading opposition to the regime was at first blamed on a reactionary clergy and the machinations by the USA to gain control over Iran's oil wealth. Not until September 1978 did the Shah and his government become targets of Soviet criticism. By that time, the Shah's brand of positive nationalism had been badly enough discredited by bureaucratic corruption and inequitable distribution of development benefits to lose the support of even the modern, technocratic middle class.

The Revolution and Beyond

Even with the revolution in full stride, the Soviets hedged their bets on the outcome. Moscow was reluctant to relinquish its marriage of economic convenience for the uncertainties of a government inspired if not dominated by Islamic and autarchic nationalists. When the break with the Shah became irrevocable the Soviets echoed a call first raised by the Tudeh in September 1978 for the unity of all opposition forces, regardless of ideology and class. The Soviet press and broadcasts to Iran stressed American complicity with the discredited Pahlavi regime and accused the US of plotting to thwart the popular will. By contrast, Moscow Radio sought to portray the Soviet treaties of the 1920s with Iran as pacts between equals, and to hail the economic accords reached with the Shah since the 1960s as exemplary, nonexploitative agreements.[15]

If the Soviets made little progress in selling the notion that they were a constant friend of Iran's national interests, they also failed to help erase the poor image of the Tudeh party. In fact, the revolutionary and non-revolutionary periods only reaffirmed the role of the local communists as apologists and obedient servants of Kremlin policy makers. The Tudeh, now joined by several communist-front organizations, were repeatedly asked to test the waters, to adopt those policies which Moscow was not yet prepared to commit itself to publicly. Members who differed with the Moscow line quit the party. At no time was there reason to suppose that, in a Eurocommunist tradition, the Tudeh leaders would be allowed to use their own judgments on the best application of Marxist–Leninist doctrine to domestic conditions.[16]

In another sense, the Iranian revolution brought about a clear departure for the Soviets from past policies. Until mid-1978, the Tudeh spokesmen had claimed that a well-organized communist party, leading a politically conscious urban proletariat, was a precondition for a successful revolution in Iran. Urban guerrilla attacks against the Shah's regime, in progress since the early 1970s, were labeled as *petit-bourgeois* adventurism. But, even as the Tudeh party backed away from its doctrinal opposition to an armed struggle, it retained ideological blinders. Burned by the tactical errors committed in the early 1950s, the party leaders contended that following the Shah's fall a political struggle with a national democratic government must precede a people's democratic regime.[17] The survivors of Mosaddeq's National Front were expected, at least over the short run, to establish a liberal, non-aligned government, possibly even a constitutional monarchy. The aging leadership of the National Front was identified as the driving force behind the mass movement, this despite the ample evidence to the contrary. Soviet views about the course of change in Iran left little room for an understanding of the appeal to intellectuals, students and the educated underemployed of the writings of Dr Ali Shariati and Ayatollah Taleqani, both of whom envisioned radical economic and social reform within the Shiite religious tradition. But the most striking miscalculation was the Soviets' failure to appreciate the commanding role being assumed by the fundamentalist Muslim opposition to the Shah. Moscow had revised its attitude toward the Shiite clergy it had attacked for years as anti-democratic and unprogressive.[18] Beginning in November 1978, the fundamentalists and Ayatollah Khomeini in particular were cautiously praised for their now correct, anti-imperialist, revolutionary attitudes. Yet it remained difficult for the Soviet Union to assign a leading role to Shiite Islam while continuing to view it as a backward-looking and utopian substitute for secularized modernism, let alone scientific socialism.[19]

The post-revolutionary governments posed a new set of

problems for the Soviets. In an early exercise of national interest, Iran's leaders halted the flow of natural gas to the Soviet Union, demanding a far better deal for the resource. The strongly religious complexion of the new constitution, as well as government policies toward ethnic minorities, students and women, were criticized by the communists. The Tudeh party suffered along with the rest of the left from attacks by mobs of Islamic militants and the raids by Revolutionary Guards. Though Khomeini was personally spared direct criticism, his public speeches left no doubt that he saw the Soviet Union and its Iranian communist sympathizers as a threat to the republic. In turn, the Tudeh and the various Marxist factions conceived of the uneasy coalition of fundamentalists with religious-oriented modernists and liberals that characterized the governments of provisional Prime Minister Medhi Bazargan and President Bani-Sadr as non-revolutionary, petty bourgeois and, deep down, pro-Western.[20]

Until November 1979, the Soviets had watched anxiously as the possibilities improved for a post-revolutionary reconciliation between the United States and Iran. Moscow welcomed and then tried to instigate a prolongation of the US embassy hostage crisis that kept anti-Americanism at a fever pitch and that also, after the invasion of Afghanistan, deflected attention from the Soviets. In the continuing struggle between the pragmatists associated with President Bani-Sadr (those anxious to end the hostage affair so that Iran could address its serious economic problems) and the leaders of the Islamic Republic party who used the crisis to undermine public confidence in their domestic rivals, the Soviets sided with the religious fundamentalists whose anti-Americanism could be counted on. Attacks by militants on local communists and, more seriously, against the Soviet embassy, were dismissed by Moscow as the work of religious fanatics in the employ of counter-revolutionaries.[21] When the mullahs won effective control over the government apparatus in late 1980 the Tudeh moved toward an awkward, informal partnership.

By embracing the fundamentalists, the Tudeh severed what remained of its ties with the fractured revolutionary movements on the left. Relations between the Tudeh and the militant Marxist groups had never been close or trusting. The *mujahidin* and *fedayin* – one trying to fuse Islamic thought with Marxism, the other secular Marxist–Leninist – had carried on the fight at home against the Shah's regime while Tudeh leaders were in safe exile in Eastern Europe. Over the long struggle it was these 'ultra-leftists' who succeeded in capturing most of the symbols of autarchic, revolutionary nationalism for an urban mass convinced of the West's responsibility for an overheated economy and a debased culture. The Tudeh's efforts to form a grand alliance of opposition groups were viewed as a transparent attempt by Moscow's communists to lay claim to an unearned share of power. Early post-revolutionary cooperation grew more out of common enemies than common purposes. And even then the Tudeh failed to go along with most of the left in boycotting the referendum on the Islamic constitution. Later, when the militant Marxist factions were driven underground and outright warfare erupted between the Islamic Republican party and its most formidable antagonist, the *mujahidin*, Tudeh members were spared the bloody retributions taken against the left. Indeed, Moscow and the Tudeh appeared pleased with the attacks on their Marxist rivals, hoping, no doubt, that pro-Soviet elements would survive as the only alternative on the left. By late 1981 the Tudeh party was openly condoning the execution of anti-regime terrorists. Rumors of a pending treaty of friendship and mutual assistance with Moscow and KGB involvement in Iran's security and intelligence networks attested to an expanding Soviet presence.[22]

Adoption of the new Islamic government entailed a shift in Soviet policy toward Iran's minorities. Initially, Moscow returned to a familiar tactic of encouraging the separatists in Kurdistan and elsewhere. Not alone, the Soviets expected an early withering away, if not collapse, of central government authority. But as the Soviet stake in the Tehran regime grew, particularly with the American hostage crisis, their backing for regional autonomy wavered and was then withdrawn. The regime's enhanced nationalist credentials through the very creditable performance of government forces in the war with Iraq further strengthened Moscow's resolve to support Tehran's use of force in rebellious areas.

The Soviets have found, then, far more to be gained by endorsing (and infiltrating) the Islamic Republic party and government administration than by standing outside in opposition. With the deaths of so many ranking members of the regime, anti-Western clerics, some with known pro-Soviet sympathies, have, it is believed, risen in importance within the ruling party. Yet communism remains anathema to the circle of religious leaders around Khomeini, and any overt bid for real power by local communists would be brutally put down. Significantly, the Tudeh does not appear to have gained members, while the militant left is being suppressed. Any attempt through direct Soviet involvement to create a people's democracy would, of course, have to contemplate provoking a full East–West confrontation. A premature coup led by the militant, autarchic left would not necessarily be to Moscow's liking. For the time being, the Soviets seem willing to settle for Iran's expanding dependence on economic and technical assistance, and even to be used opportunistically and cynically by the Ayatollah. A post-Khomeini leadership, still challenged by regional minorities and the militant left, and beset by a disunified religious party, is expected to turn more to the Soviets to ensure political survival. Soviet support, whether direct or indirect, is also expected to figure in any plans to try to implant a Shiite regime in Iraq or to export an Islamic revolution to the conservative Gulf states.

The Islamic regime enables the Soviet Union to realize its principal long-term objective in the country – to deny the West its strategic foothold in Iran. The post-revolutionary leadership took Iran out of CENTO and is willing to use its oil politically. In withdrawing troops from Oman, Iran signaled that it would no longer police the Gulf against leftist rebellions. The regime has also taken its place within the Middle East's radical camp, a grouping increasingly tied to Soviet arms supplies. Whatever else the Islamic regime may stand for, it is stridently anti-Western and has a continuing special contempt for the United States. Iran's diplomatic and economic difficulties strengthened the Soviets' hand in convincing the Tehran government to temper during 1981 its support for the insurgents in Afghanistan, and to soften criticism of the occupation by Soviet troops. In calling for neighborly ties and in characterizing the government by mullahs as progressive, the Soviets have sought as well to demonstrate that, no matter what they do in Afghanistan, they are prepared to work cooperatively with nationalists of a fundamentalist Muslim state. Unavoidably, in the process, the Soviet Union has again drawn the enmity of the wide spectrum of nationalist forces in Iran.

Afghanistan

Similar nationalist strains, blended differently in Afghanistan, have presented Soviet policymakers with less room for maneuver but, over time, more predictable and usually satisfying returns. At least until April 1978, the overreaching strategies and miscalculations of popular national feeling we have seen in Soviet relations with Iran were absent from Soviet–Afghan relations. By comparison, Soviet policies toward their neighbor across the Amu Darya were consistent and sensitive. Those less ambitious and more realistic policies could be explained mainly by the fact that in Afghanistan the Soviet Union had attained most of what it sought in Iran – a country without pro-Western military ties and economically inclined toward the communist bloc. Afghan political independence and non-alignment were, in fact, highly compatible with Soviet regional objectives, perhaps more so than if the country had been a typical client state.[23]

Over most of the postwar period, leftist movements in Afghanistan were sufficiently unimportant so as not to complicate Moscow's relations with the Kabul government, either by requiring regular Soviet protection or by drawing Moscow into premature actions. Indeed, the socio-economic backwardness of the country made any thought of applying revolutionary Marxist–Leninist theory seem as foolhardy as it was unorthodox. Despite the country's many separate ethnic identities, Soviet policy managed to support the dominant Pushtuns in their territorial ambitions for a separate state to be carved out of northwest Pakistan without alienating other important but less politically mobilized ethnic groups. The clergy, though influential in rural areas, contrasted with their counterparts in Iran by their lack of formal hierarchy, organization, or historic identification with an Afghan state. Liberal nationalists were limited largely to a small urban elite that cut its teeth politically in a brief respite from government authoritarian rule during the 1949–52 period. Modern nationalism had made a slow recovery from the too ambitious social and economic reforms pressed by King Amanullah, ousted in 1929 by an uprising of conservative tribal and religious elements. In its brief ascendance under Amanullah, however, modern nationalism had accepted that a special relationship with the Soviet Union providing for economic assistance was a necessary ingredient to any substantial progress.

A historically strong autarchic nationalism posed the most obvious constraint on Soviet influence. It had sustained Afghan independence through the Great Game played by the Russians and British for south central Asia in the nineteenth century and, while a poor basis for political integration, its call to arms could unite elements, otherwise antagonistic, against foreign penetration. Autarchic nationalism was revived in the wake of the overthrow of Amanullah and the assumption of the throne in 1929 by the royal family of Nadir Shah. Through the next fifteen years, neutrality and diversified economic relations were the hallmarks of a cautious domestic and foreign policy. Even after the Soviets gained an imposing presence in Afghan economic life during the 1950s and 1960s, they never questioned the need to respect Afghan sovereignty. Why, then, did the Soviet Union in the late 1970s break so sharply from past practices? Had Moscow's objectives in the country and the region changed, or had developments internal to Afghanistan forced revisions? Certainly there is a need to comprehend how the Soviets could find themselves by December 1979 in armed combat with a broad nationalist insurgency.

'Bi-Tarafi'

Commerce between the Soviet Union and Afghanistan expanded very slowly in the late 1940s and early 1950s, and the Kabul government resisted overtures for closer political ties. Particularly after Iran's Azerbaijan affair, the royal family was reluctant to give the Soviets any pretext for extending their influence over Afghanistan. With the British departure from the subcontinent in August 1947, however, the time-honored formula for balancing Russian ambitions in the region had been removed. Fearful of Soviet intentions, the Afghan rulers deviated from traditional adherence to non-alignment and followed the course taken by Iran and Pakistan – seeking the US as an absentee substitute for the British presence. Yet, despite Washington's pursuit of a global policy of containment of the Soviets, the US declined to offer a defense arrangement or to satisfy Afghan requests through the mid-1950s for arms.[24]

A new era in Afghan-Soviet cooperation was inaugurated with the premiership of Mohammad Daoud (1953–63). A modernizing nationalist, Daoud was convinced of the need for large-scale foreign assistance in order for his country to shed its underdevelopment. The Soviet Union figured centrally in these plans by virtue of its own impressive achievements and its willingness to help. No less important was the indispensability of northern transit routes to replace those through Pakistan periodically blocked in retaliation for Daoud's championing of Pushtunistan. The Prime Minister ignored the warnings of autarchic-minded nationalists who feared that Soviet aid would in time become a smothering embrace. Daoud's insurance against this outcome was founded on a policy known as *bi-tarafi* (literally, 'to be neutral'). In effect, it invited the USA and other Western countries to compete with the Soviets in Afghanistan's development, thereby assuring the country's political non-alignment.[25]

Afghan evenhandedness extended to the drafting of a new

constitution in 1964, when neither Soviet nor American experts were consulted. The Soviets tolerated, moreover, the more liberal political climate created by the constitution. Despite the removal of Prime Minister Daoud by his cousin, the more Western-oriented King Zahir Shah, the Soviets found their economic ties with Afghanistan unaffected and no attempts made to end Moscow's near-monopoly over the supplying and training of the Afghan military. The democratic experiment that allowed many conservative, provincial, influentials to assert influence on the central government also permitted pro-Moscow groups to take a more active role in Afghan domestic politics.[26]

The Left and Two Revolutions

Hard evidence is lacking that the Soviets used the climate of cooperation late in the Amanullah reign to cultivate local communists. Soviets employed by the Afghan government were in any event dismissed after the king's fall, and through the next two decades domestic Marxism remained alive only in the confines of intellectual circles. To maintain its network of agents in the country, the Soviets turned to foreign nationals, principally Indian communists. Not until 1948 were indigenous communists recruited. The first contacts occurred in Bombay, and among the earliest to join was Nur Mohammad Taraki. Even then, Afghan communists were largely isolated until Daoud's opening to the Soviet Union in the mid-1950s brought in advisors who gave encouragement to local communists and helped them facilitate contacts with communist parties elsewhere, especially with Iran's exiled Tudeh party.

The formal inauguration of a communist party in 1965 coincided with the implementation of the new Constitution. The People's Democratic Party (or Khalq), as it became known in 1967, made inroads at Kabul University and attracted recruits among young, educated employees in the government bureaucracy. By the end of the decade, Khalq had also established cells in the military. Running as individuals, several communists won seats in the parliamentary contests held in 1965 and 1969. By the second election, however, factions had formed within the party, the most important of which, Parcham (flag), was formed by Babrak Karmal. Of the two major factions, the Parchamis were considered Moscow loyalists, while the Khalqis gained a reputation as more independent communists. Parcham supposedly stood for a broad national-democratic front during an initial stage of an Afghan revolution, against the insistence of Khalq on the need for a working-class party subject to a Leninist discipline.[27] In reality, the differences between the two major factions were more personal than doctrinaire. In both, there was probably a majority of members whose autarchic, even liberal and modern, nationalism was stronger than their internationalist Marxism. Even among those with clear pro-Moscow sympathies, ethnic attachments and resentments often remained prominent. The several thousand local communists were united, just the same, in opposition to the monarchy and the prevailing social class structure.

As successive centrist governments were unable to form a national consensus on public policy, the various nationalists lost faith in the political formulas created by the 1964 Constitution. The Afghan nationalist Millat (Nation) party, with its own program of social change, was resentful of its exclusion from power and a *de facto* deemphasis of Pushtun expansionism by a government favoring economic cooperation with Pakistan. Modernists were no less disillusioned as scandals evoked doubts about the political acumen of Zahir Shah. With the king's appointment of Mussa Shafiq as Prime Minister in 1971, liberal nationalists were given a supposedly last chance to make the proto-democratic institutions work. But Shafiq, one of the architects of the Constitution, proved unable to end the economic paralysis or provide inspiring leadership. Much of his political currency was spent in trying to win approval for a negotiated agreement with Iran over the long-disputed division of the Helmand River waters in the southwest. Shafiq's enemies used the accord to play on autarchic feelings, accusing the Prime Minister of selling out to the Iranian Shah. Khalq and Parcham led the opposition to Shafiq that sought by discrediting him to make certain that no centrist government remained a viable option.

The Soviet Union took no direct hand in efforts to undermine the Shafiq government or the monarchy. Despite the growing popular discontent in Afghanistan, the Soviets doubted that either of the communist parties was organizationally prepared to seize and hold power. Neither, for example, had experienced much success in recruiting outside the urban areas; Parcham in particular had much to do to overcome its image as a band of young, non-Pushtun, Kabuli atheists. Local communists complained about inadequate financial support from Moscow and its too cautious policies. But the signs of an imminent palace-promoted coup from the right prompted Soviet-trained military officers, some with Parcham connections, to act on their own. Former Prime Minister Daoud's identification with the coup was considered indispensable for Pushtun tribal elements as well as many modernists to accept the political changes that included an end to the monarchy. Zahir Shah was deposed with surprising ease, and Moscow signaled its quick approval of the new regime by endorsing Parcham's participation. The Khalq group balked, however, at joining a non-communist government headed by a man who by instinct and origins was considered incapable of transforming the country's prevailing economic and social structures. The Soviets felt more confident in view of the leftist orientation of those who brought Daoud to power and the recollection that it was under Daoud that the current cooperation with the Soviet Union had first taken form.

Khalq's judgment proved largely correct. Over the next several years, President Daoud gradually reduced the influence of the Parchamis, many of whom had been assigned posts in the provincial government in order to reduce their influence in Kabul. The generally hostile reception given the communists in the provinces dispirited their rank and file, while association with the increasingly conservative republican regime discredited them in the cities.[28] By 1975, most of the military men instrumental in his coming to power had also been removed from public life. In time, President Daoud managed to alienate virtually every important national group. He initially stirred fears among the ethnic minorities with his revival of the Pushtunistan issue and possible preoccupation with this irredentist cause. Tribal leaders and other rural influentials objected to what they perceived to be the central government's intrusion into traditional areas of provincial authority. The liberals were naturally resentful of Daoud's imperious, dictatorial rule and his broken pledges to institute early constitutional government. An official government party created in 1975 excluded other organized political activity. Even the modernists found scant praise for Daoud, who displayed little of his former effectiveness and had scared off much private economic investment. Most critical, as one observer notes, an important symbol of legitimacy had been destroyed with the dynasty's overthrow. Whatever the failings of the king, the monarchy had served to unify Afghanistan's multi-ethnic, divided society.[29]

The Soviets watched anxiously as Daoud pursued a series of moves that could gradually lead to a substantial decrease in their leverage over the republican regime. The Afghan president went ahead with the Helmand water agreement with Iran and welcomed offers of oil sales and expanded development assistance from the Shah's government that culminated in 1975 in a promise of up to $2 billion over ten years for a number of projects. He also reached an understanding with Pakistan's President Z. A. Bhutto in 1976 and renewed with his successor, General Zia ul-Haq, that went far toward resolving border differences. With the Pushtunistan dispute defused, most of the traditional rationale for a Soviet economic option and military assistance would disappear. None the less, Daoud was careful not to break any military agreements with the Soviets or to suggest a downgrading of their economic role, although he withstood Soviet attempts to gain increased control over the country's media and cultural programs.

The steady drift in policy led the Soviets to begin looking for a more reliable alternative Afghan regime. While in opposition to the Daoud government, Khalq had expanded organizationally and, under its aggressive *de facto* leader, Hafizullah Amin, a loyal following was recruited in the military. In the Soviets' reassessment of the Afghan communists' potential, they directed Babrak's Parchamis to arrange a reconciliation with the Khalqis in July 1977. The Soviets themselves remained in the background, avoiding an open break with Daoud, at least in part because they still had doubts – wisely, as it turned out – about the left's ability to succeed without a broader front of nationalists. When finally the President tried to deal sternly with the mounting threat from the communists, his security apparatus proved inept. The coup that ended his rule and life on 27 April 1978 was carried out by Afghan officers responding to a call from Amin. On this occasion, Soviet advisors were widely believed to have been kept fully informed and may have participated in the planning. Whatever their degree of involvement, power had passed to their clients, ready or not.

In the Socialist Camp

In the months following the coup, government leaders repeatedly denied that a communist revolution had taken place. While they conceded that the Soviet Union would provide inspiration and assistance, the new Democratic Republic would not be obliged to sacrifice Afghan sovereignty. They insisted that their regime was akin to socialist governments that had emerged throughout the Arab world. They argued, furthermore, that their doctrines were compatible with Islam. By staying officially non-aligned, the

Khalq leadership in the government hoped to retain Western development aid, and conceivably the modest leverage it offered in dealing with Moscow. The Soviets had no objection to the soft-peddling of ideology. For Moscow remained concerned about the regime's limited popular base. The Soviets were satisfied to tighten their grip through a series of economic agreements, some in fact already negotiated (but delayed) under Daoud, that insured fuller integration of the country's trade with the Soviet Union and Eastern-bloc countries.

At first, the government met with little resistance from liberals and modern nationalists. Despite past experiences with the communists, many centrists collaborated with the regime because they approved of the proposed reforms and expected to be called on for their expertise. Perhaps the largest numbers simply hoped to advance in the bureaucracy. Initially at least, the autarchic-minded were willing to accept the government at its word that it would not automatically follow the Soviet line. Delighted to be rid of Daoud, most ethnic elements were also ready to give the new regime the benefit of the doubt. The first signs of dissension came from within the ruling coalition as the Khalqis and Parchamis again fell on one another. As before, the differences were over tactics and the competing ambitions of leaders and not yet, in 1978, over proper fealty to the Soviet Union. Vice-President Babrak Karmal lost out in the power struggle to President Taraki and Foreign Minister Amin when the Soviets pragmatically backed the larger faction. Moscow's embassy did, however, throw its protective cloak over Babrak and several Parcham leaders and helped to facilitate their diplomatic exile in June 1978 to embassies in Eastern Europe. Other Parchamis were purged from positions in the bureaucracy. Another challenge to the leadership was raised by several military officers and civilians who, either because they were simply anti-Khalq or sincerely feared a headlong rush into the Soviets' embrace, plotted to overthrow the government. Led by air force Major-General Abdul Qadar, a leading figure in both the 1973 and 1978 coups, the group sounded out Western envoys in Kabul for their support for a more independent regime but were arrested in August 1978 before they could act.

The honeymoon did not last long with most nationalists, either. Ignoring Soviet advice against 'infantile left-wing programs', the Khalqis pushed ahead quickly on radical agrarian reforms. Amin was anxious to break the hold of conservative forces in the countryside and to win adherents among the rural poor to his still largely urban-based party. But the actions of Khalq agents in the provinces were frequently crude, and the policies they tried to implement showed little regard for the traditional norms and economic relationships that bound peasant farmers to landlords and local influentials. Some government edicts, such as releasing the rural poor from all loans and mortgages, were generally well received. But most changes were unenforceable and offended the provincial mullahs. The introduction of a new national flag, almost indistinguishable in design from those in Eastern Europe, and lacking the Islamic green, seemed to confirm charges that a godless group ruled in Kabul.

The recent politicization of Afghanistan's *ulema* dates from spring 1970. Mullahs from the provinces — some say at the instigation of rightists in the royal court — descended on Kabul to demonstrate in favor of enforcement of religious prohibitions and new laws. The government authorities eventually forced the mullahs to return home, but not before they had served the purpose of reminding the left of the still conservative temper of the countryside and had learned the value of collective action. Sporadic violence continued for a time in the provinces, and during the Daoud republican years local religious leaders occasionally clashed with the left. The Marxist regime and its alleged challenge to Islam revived a broader militancy which coincided with the opposition of Pushtun tribes, Shiite Hazaras in central Afghanistan, and other disgruntled ethnic groups. The full emergence of an Islamic-state nationalism in Afghanistan required, however, the finding of common ground between anti-communist and anti-Soviet nationalists, and the popularization of their cause by insurgent groups based in Pakistan.

Clearly fearing for its security, the Taraki–Amin regime turned ever more heavily to the Soviets for assistance. In December 1978, the Kabul government entered into a defense pact with the Soviet Union. The number of Soviet advisors increased sharply in the military and the ministries during 1979, in large measure to compensate for army desertions and the growing flight to Pakistan of middle-class professionals and government officials. The placement of Soviet personnel in the government bureaucracy, giving orders to high Afghan officials, was evidence enough for most liberals, modernists and Pushtun nationalists that the regime had thoroughly compromised its independence. It made no difference from the point of view of the Afghans that many of these personnel were Central Asians, although these had been especially chosen by Moscow in order to soften the impression of Soviet domination. Though the Khalq leadership continued to distinguish itself from the sycophantic Parchamis, members of the party's dominant faction headed by Amin were generally viewed as pro-Soviet opportunists.[30] They accepted an expanding Soviet role as necessary to protect the revolution and to allow the party to implement its ideas for changing Afghan society. To carry out his aims, Amin also stepped up his repression of dissent from whatever quarter.

The Soviets understood Khalq's need to broaden its rule, but otherwise underestimated the nature and scope of nationalist opposition. In their view, Amin's hard line and ruthless policies had unnecessarily antagonized citizens to the regime, and he personally had become the major obstacle to pacifying the country. The Soviets agreed, then, to assist Amin's enemies in demoting or ousting the foreign minister (also vice-premier), leaving President Taraki in command of the party. But since Taraki was never more than a propagandist and was presumed to be incapable of furnishing day-to-day government leadership, a reconciliation with Babrak is believed to have been arranged by the Soviets during a brief visit of the President to Moscow. The scheme backfired when Taraki was himself captured on 14 September 1979 and soon after killed by Amin's followers. The Soviets were left with having to support Amin and were forced in effect to admit their complicity in his attempted ouster by agreeing to replace their ambassador in Kabul.

The ineffectiveness of the Afghan military troubled the Soviets, as did the prospect of a Marxist government succumbing to a geographically contiguous regime dominated by Islamic nationalists. Yet an insurgent victory, which would, among other things, expel the Soviets, was not imminent, and government army units had, in fact, made some progress in late 1979 in containing the rebel opposition in several provinces. What prompted the Soviets to move against Amin was the belief that the Afghan leader, for all his past reliance on the Soviet Union and ideological purity, could no longer be trusted. The Soviets had begun to take more seriously Parcham charges that the American-educated Amin had too easy relations with Western diplomats in Kabul and would strike his own deal.[31] Indeed, after the September shootout, Amin no doubt realized that sooner or later the Soviets would again find him expendable and, during the fall of 1979, he actively explored other political options – pro-Western and Muslim – for himself and his government. Arguing that the Afghan people would not tolerate it, Amin also resisted Soviet attempts to assume control of an air base near the Iranian border.[32] But Amin's outside contacts proved unproductive, and, by the year's end, he agreed to the Soviets' demand that they be permitted to begin stationing combat forces in the country. This rapid military buildup, of course, set the stage for the deposing of Amin and his replacement by the Parchamis.[33]

A Soviet Afghanistan

Moscow had few illusions about the size of Babrak's following or his organizational talents, at least compared to those of Amin. Still, Soviet experts believed that the possibilities for creating a national front of progressives would improve with the Parchamis in power. The new regime reflected the more pragmatic approach toward change favored by the Soviets, and its exiled leaders could not be held responsible for the mistakes of the Khalq government. Amin had already put the brakes on the regime's more radical social programs and had sought to make amends with religious opinion through exhibitions of personal piety and concessions to the ulema. The Parchamis would go further, allowing some land in effect to revert to the original owners and seeking more seriously a basis for a *rapprochement* with the regime's enemies. The ousting of Khalq's urban Pushtun-dominated leadership was expected to please the ethnic minorities. But, with all of Babrak's overtures, he made little headway in winning popular approval. His own largely Persian-speaking faction naturally drew the resentment of urban and tribal Pushtuns. Religious-minded people were unconvinced that Babrak would tolerate religion for any more than tactical reasons. Most serious, however, was Babrak's total lack of credibility as a nationalist – a handicap emphasized by his being lifted into office on the back of a Soviet invasion.

The presence in the country of more than 80,000 Soviet military personnel succeeded as nothing had before in galvanizing the opposition and stimulating the resistance movement. Nationalists could agree, whatever their orientations, that the early eviction of the Soviets should carry the highest priority. This convergent interest on one basic issue could not ensure regular cooperation among opposition elements, but it did mean that the Soviets and their Afghan loyalists would find no friendly quarter. Soviet efforts to employ the time-honored policy of playing off tribe against tribe, ethnic group against ethnic group, failed to buy reliable allies. If autarchic nationalism gave the opposition direction and historical justification, it was Islamic nationalism that motivated the largest number of people and was best able to cement over the traditional differences. The actual fighting was mainly in the hands of small tribal units operating locally, but the several Peshawar-based insurgent groups, varying in their fundamentalism, turned the insurgency into an Islamic cause. The Islamic motif earned them the support of Pakistan's own religious parties and at least the sympathy of Iran's new government. But, unlike Iran, the rebellion's strong anti-Sovietism invited financial support from conservative Middle East states, the Chinese, and the US.

The intervention in December 1979 represented a watershed in Afghan–Soviet relations, ending three generations of recognition and often careful cultivation of Afghan national feelings. It was not that nationalism had ceased to be a determining factor in Soviet policy calculations. But once the country was in effect mortgaged by Afghan communists to the Soviet Union it became much like any other satellite, a country where primordial allegiances were to be subordinated to socialist solidarity. To allow Afghanistan an exemption from this rule would be to create an unfortunate precedent which could be tolerated only when the political costs, in terms of Western reaction, were considered too high. With Afghanistan's neighboring governments in political disarray and the USA preoccupied with its hostages in Tehran, the constraints on a Soviet invasion were few. The opposition in Afghanistan had thrown down the gauntlet to the Soviets. No Marxist government in the foreseeable future could be accepted as legitimately nationalist and hope to survive the withdrawal of Soviet forces. A political compromise that might have restored the *status quo ante*, a non-aligned but Soviet-tilting government, was unlikely after April 1978 and was certainly passed by 1982. Whatever the supposedly enhanced geo-strategic position gained by the Soviets through their invasion, they could hardly be pleased with their protracted military involvement in the country. Yet a political solution compatible with Afghan nationalism eluded them.

Conclusion

Nationalism as a hurdle, if not always a barrier, for Soviet political and economic penetration is hardly peculiar to Iran and Afghanistan, or to the Middle East. Particularistic attachments to culture, history and religion, and fears of relinquishing national destinies to Soviet designs have ordinarily proven stronger than prospects of material assistance and the appeals of class and anti-imperialist theory. As this essay describes, Moscow's policies toward neighboring Iran and Afghanistan unavoidably stimulated nationalist feelings which it sought to exploit as well as to combat. If the task was until recently less formidable in Afghanistan, it was because Soviet strategic aims more often coincided with the interests of Afghan nationalists. The contradictions within Iranian nationalism were, by comparison, always sharper and more confounding.

Soviet defense concerns along its southern tier stand as a constant in fashioning strategies toward the two countries. Yet Moscow's policies were otherwise largely opportunistic. The Soviets were willing to compromise (though never entirely desert) ideological allies for economic gains when the dividends from the latter seemed more promising. And economic returns were sacrificed to political advantage when the likely benefits of the latter seemed greater. Through its surrogates, Moscow frequently tried and repeatedly failed to broaden its nationalist alliances. For all of their success in the Middle East in remaining on good terms with antagonist states, the Soviets showed far less adeptness in serving as a power broker between opposing domestic factions in Iran and Afghanistan. As elsewhere, the Soviets were less dogmatic with elements at the center and on the right, whose positions of power Moscow would ordinarily concede, than with schismatic and revisionist Marxist groups (often with nationalist tendencies) with whom the competition was political.

Moscow's policy objectives, as described above, may be both incompatible and in harmony with nationalist aspirations. Over time, the Soviets have cooperated most easily with the modernists and ethnosectarian-regional nationalists in the two countries. The aims of the modernists were served by Soviet trade and aid that ordinarily came on better terms than could be obtained in the West. The Soviets offered, moreover, a model of development that, regardless of ideological differences with recipients, gave guidance to regimes committed to a large public sector and centrally planned change. Soviet assistance was acceptable to the modernists so long as it was not seen as an attempt to dictate development or foreclose other policy options. There was, perhaps for this reason, a hesitancy on both sides, and a sense that a coincidence of interest was likely to be temporary.

To ethnosectarian nationalists, the Soviet Union offered a valued source of moral and material support. Backing for regional autonomy could in turn clear the way for Soviet ideological and even military penetration, or be used as a lever in relations with incumbent governments. If these alliances often found common cause in testing central authority, they were also likely to be discarded when Moscow saw opportunities to exercise influence directly on regimes in Tehran and Kabul.

Liberals often found themselves on the same side as the Soviets in the advocacy of social and economic reforms. In opposition to the regime, particularly in Iran, liberals were subject to the same repressive measures dealt to the militant left. Although Moscow criticized liberal nationalists for bourgeois tendencies, it tolerated them for the part they were expected to play in the evolution toward a socialist society. But cooperation between the two foundered in the Soviets' reach for expedient agreements with those in power, or dissolved in contacts with conspiratorial, doctrinaire local communists.

Autarchic-minded nationalists in Iran and Afghanistan have normally viewed the Soviets as no more to be trusted than the West. But, while the latter is often perceived as the more insidious, common borders make the Soviets a more tangible threat to national independence. Moscow is able to use autarchic nationalists to neutralize Western influence even when it fails to gain their full confidence. In turn, these nationalists have found the Soviets convenient counterweights to Western pressures, economic and political. But accusations of Soviet interference and subversion are inevitable as Moscow becomes drawn into factional politics in the two countries. Moreover, the more generous the programs of Soviet assistance, the more likely they are to arouse suspicions.

Islamic-state nationalists stressed an inherent conflict with communism and, in particular, the dangers for Muslims of a secular state on the Soviet model. Events demonstrate, however, Moscow's flexibility and deferential policies where it seeks to mitigate Islamic antipathy in Iran and Afghanistan or tries to convince Muslim regimes in the region of its benign intent toward religion. Local communists quickly adopt, when required, all the outward signs of religious piety. For their part, Islamic leaders forced to manage an economy and defend a regime, as in Iran, have a way of divorcing day-to-day policies from their deep biases against communist ideology. Finally, the Kremlin's own large Muslim population has also given Soviet policy-makers considerable experience in accommodating (as well as suppressing) Islamic national feelings.[34]

On balance, the Soviets have dealt more successfully with Iranian and Afghan nationalism in its several forms when these incorporated a wide spectrum of ideologies and interests. The more narrow the base, almost regardless of complexion, the more difficult it has been for the Soviets to influence and manipulate.

At the same time, to the extent that nationalist doctrines have generated popular movements, the Soviets have found these difficult to predict and control. Paradoxically, it was the failure to mobilize large numbers of people that repeatedly doomed most efforts of the left to prevail. In general, nationalists of whatever stripe resist an association which leaves their goals subordinated to Soviet ones, and the Soviets try to avoid being locked into supporting causes that deny them flexibility in adapting to new requirements and optimizing their choices. Moscow, on this account, has failed badly in recent years in both countries.

Whatever the contrasts in Soviet policy and nationalist behavior in Iran and Afghanistan during the three and a half decades examined here, there were notable similarities in 1982. The Soviet Union was backing regimes which were under heavy pressure from within and without and was linked to unpopular communist parties. Though in one case they had massively intervened to prop up a government of their choosing, and in the other an uncertain alliance had evolved, the ruling elite in both had come to depend on a growing Soviet rule. The fall of either regime, the Afghan or the Iranian, seemed almost certain to bring to power bitterly anti-Soviet groups, a consequence in both countries of Moscow's alienation of virtually every shade of nationalist feeling.

Notes: Chapter 12

1 Among the varied assessments see: Galia Golan, 'Soviet power and policies in the Third World: the Middle East', *Adelphi Paper 152: Prospects of Soviet Power in the 1980s*, pt 2 (London: International Institute of Strategic Studies, 1979), pp. 47–52; Vernon V. Aspaturian, 'Moscow's Afghan gamble', *New Leader*, 28 January 1980, pp. 7–13; Edward N. Luttwak, 'After Afghanistan, what?', *Commentary* (April 1980), pp. 40–9; Jiri Valenta, 'From Prague to Kabul: the Soviet style invasion', *International Security* (Fall 1980), pp. 114–41; and the debate between Richard Pipes and George Kennan, 'How real is the Soviet threat?', *US News and World Report*, 10 March 1980, p. 33.
2 Rouhollah K. Ramazani, *Iran's Foreign Policy, 1941–1973* (Charlottesville, Va: University Press of Virginia, 1975), pp. 112–13.
3 See William Eagleton, Jr, *The Kurdish Republic of 1946* (London: Oxford University Press, 1963), pp. 43–5, 74–5.
4 George Lenczowski, *The Middle East in World Affairs*, 4th edn (Ithaca, NY: Cornell University Press, 1980), pp. 180–4.
5 B. Jazani, *An Introduction to the Contemporary History of Iran* (Tehran: Iran Committee, 1979), pp. 47–8.
6 Richard W. Cottam, *Nationalism in Iran* (Pittsburgh, Pa: University of Pittsburgh Press, 1964), p. 72.
7 ibid., pp. 198–9.

8. ibid.
9. Peter Avery, *Modern Iran* (New York: Praeger, 1965), pp. 425–6.
10. Lenczowski, *Middle East*, pp. 193–4.
11. Cottam, *Nationalism in Iran*, p. 222.
12. See 'Soviet policy in the Middle East', MERIP (Middle East Research and Information Project) Report no. 39 (July 1975), pp. 9–10.
13. Walter Laqueur, *The Struggle for the Middle East: The Soviet Union and the Middle East, 1958–68* (Baltimore, Md: Penguin, 1972), p. 50. For Soviet relations with the Shah's Iran, see Mikhail Volodarsky and Yaacov Ro'i, 'Soviet-Iranian relations during two "revolutions" ', *Slavic and Soviet Series* (Tel Aviv), vol. 4 no. 1–2 (1979), pp. 33–58.
14. Mohammad Reza Shah Pahlavi, *Mission for My Country* (New York: McGraw-Hill, 1960), pp. 125, 297.
15. Muriel Atkins, 'The Kremlin and Khomeini', *Washington Quarterly* (Spring 1981), p. 58.
16. See interview by Fred Halliday with an unnamed Tudeh leader in MERIP Report no. 86 (March–April 1980), pp. 17, 20–1, for a party view that argues otherwise.
17. Ervand Abrahamian, 'The guerrilla movement in Iran', in ibid., pp. 7–8.
18. Sepehr Zabih, *Iran's Revolutionary Upheaval* (San Francisco, Calif.: Alchemy Books, 1979), pp. 43–4.
19. Atkins, 'Kremlin and Khomeini', p. 60.
20. Abrahamian, 'Guerrilla movement', pp. 13–14.
21. Robert O. Freedman, 'Soviet policy towards the Middle East since the invasion of Afghanistan', *Journal of International Affairs*, vol. 34, no. 2 (Fall–Winter 1980–1), pp. 283–310.
22. *The International Herald Tribune*, 21 January 1982.
23. Rouhollah K. Ramazani, 'Afghanistan and the USSR', *Middle East Journal*, vol. 12, no. 2 (Spring 1958), pp. 144–52.
24. Zalmay Khalilzad, *The Return of the Great Game: Superpower Rivalry and Domestic Turmoil in Afghanistan, Iran, Pakistan and Turkey* (Santa Monica, Cal.: California Seminar, September 1980), pp. 15–16.
25. For Soviet economic aid to and trade with Afghanistan during this period, see Louis Dupree, 'Afghanistan's big gamble. Part II: The economic and strategic aspects of Soviet aid', *American Universities Field Staff Reports*, vol. 4, no. 4, South Asia Series (2 May 1960), p. 3, and 'Afghanistan's big gamble. Part III: Economic competition in Afghanistan', *American Universities Field Staff Reports*, vol. 4, no. 5, South Asia Series (9 May 1960), pp. 3, 7.
26. See M. G. Weinbaum, 'Afghanistan: nonparty parliamentary democracy', *Journal of Developing Areas*, vol. 7, no. 1 (October 1972), pp. 57–74, for a study of style of politics in the constitutional period. Also the same author's 'The legislator as intermediary: integration of the center and periphery in Afghanistan', in Albert F. Eldridge (ed.), *Legislatures in Plural Societies* (Durham, NC: Duke University Press, 1977), pp. 95–121.
27. Fred Halliday, 'Revolution in Afghanistan', *New Left Review* (December 1978), p. 25.
28. Louis Dupree, 'Afghanistan: 1980', *American Universities Field Staff Reports*, no. 37, Asia Series (June 1980), pp. 1–2.
29. Leon B. Poullada, review of Louis Dupree, *Afghanistan* (1980 edn) in Asia Society, *Afghanistan Council Newsletter*, vol. 8, no. 4 (October 1980), p. 28.
30. Louis Dupree, 'The Democratic Republic of Afghanistan, 1979', *American Universities Field Staff Reports*, no. 32, Asia Series (September 1979), p. 7.

31 Selig S. Harrison, 'Dateline Afghanistan: exit through Finland', *Foreign Policy*, no. 41 (Winter 1980–1), pp. 170–1.
32 Dupree, 'Afghanistan: 1980', p. 2; also *The Sunday Times* (London), 28 December 1980.
33 See Valenta, 'From Prague to Kabul', for a discussion of the preparation and decision to intervene.
34 This topic is beyond the scope of this chapter, but different aspects of it are discussed in several other chapters of this book.

# 13

Saudi Arabia's Attitude toward the USSR, 1977–80: Between Saudi Pragmatism and Islamic Conservatism

JACOB GOLDBERG

Saudi Arabia's attitude toward the Soviet Union – indeed, toward the international system as a whole – has traditionally been determined by three factors: its strong desire to perpetuate a highly conservative, traditional system of government and society; its firm interest in maintaining the political *status quo* in general and in the Middle East in particular in the face of radical forces bent on disrupting order and stability; its self-image as guardian of the Islamic spirit and community against hostile political, social and economic forces.

It is against the background of these three factors that one must judge the Saudi perception of the Soviet Union: first, as a force striving to overthrow conservative regimes of the Saudi kind and revolutionize their social system; secondly, as a superpower interested in altering the *status quo* and actively supporting local radical forces instigating upheavals and tensions throughout the region; thirdly, as a power representing an alien, hostile, atheist ideology, communism, that constitutes a real threat to the traditional world of Islam, its values, beliefs and norms.

It seems that the Saudis, whose worldview is molded by an uncompromising religious ideology, cannot see the conflict with communism in any other terms than those of good and evil. They, to be sure, do not have much liking for Western materialistic civilization. The 'East', however, represents communism, atheism, radicalism and social upheaval and is regarded, therefore, as a far more dangerous enemy than the forces and ideas of the West. Thus, the elimination – or at least the containment — of Soviet influence has become a cornerstone of the Saudis' peninsular and regional policy.

The Saudi perception of the Soviet Union has been widely expressed in the Saudi media. The themes emphasized by the media, the terminology used and the genuine sense of danger conveyed are exemplified by the following editorial which appeared in the Saudi paper *'Ukaz* in early January 1979:

> The Soviet Union is persistent in creating tension, generating class struggle and sowing sedition in all areas in order to achieve its expansionist and aggressive ambitions. International communism is pursuing its basic objectives aimed at assailing the unity of the peoples, destroying their economic resources, spreading moral decay and combating heavenly ideologies in order to ensure the realization of their ulterior motives of domination and rule. Communism is against peaceful instincts and against all religions and beliefs. And since communism poses a real danger to all mankind, confronting its conspiracies and exposing its false slogans and misleading allegations must be the duty of all those who believe in one God.
>
> All Communist moves reveal the truth about the Communist plan to incite disturbances and encourage rebellion and chaos, so that in such a state of confusion, the Communists can take over power. The Arab and Islamic nations must, therefore, be aware of the Communist plan to destroy the Muslim man and erase all human values.[1]

For the greater part of the period since the Soviet penetration of the Middle East in the mid-1950s, Saudi Arabia has not really had to confront the Soviets directly, as Moscow did not seem to pose an immediate and concrete danger to the stability and security of the House of Saud. This was because the USSR concentrated its efforts during most of the 1955–75 period in the so-called core countries of the Middle East, particularly Egypt, Syria and Iraq, rather than in the periphery of the region. Under such circumstances, the extreme anti-Soviet posture of the Saudis and their strong condemnation of Soviet ideology and strategy did not actually necessitate the adoption of active, conspicuous anti-Soviet policies.

The situation, however, changed radically in the second half of the 1970s when the USSR shifted its pressure to the Indian Ocean, the Horn of Africa and the Persian Gulf regions. With Soviet and Cuban forces already present within the Peninsula, in the People's Democratic Republic of Yemen, which is perceived by Riyadh as being the Saudi backyard, and with the ever-growing

Soviet naval presence in the Indian Ocean, the danger of a Soviet takeover in the Horn of Africa exacerbated Saudi anxieties and revived fears of Soviet penetration into the Red Sea as well. This was particularly true at the height of the Ethiopian–Somali military confrontation at the end of 1977. The Saudi state-controlled radio accused the Soviets at the time of 'open interference in the conflict on the basis of a long-term plan aimed at disrupting peace and security throughout Africa in general and the Horn in particular'. It warned that 'once it penetrates any country, communism leaves its evil imprint and spreads its subversive principles which destroy all values and civilizations'.[2] Allusion to a so-called long-term Soviet plan was to become a recurring motif in Saudi references to Soviet strategy and goals. Furthermore, the Soviet and Cuban presence on and around the fringes of the Arabian Peninsula raised the specter of Soviet-supported revolutionary elements attempting to attack the oilfields or the petroleum supply-routes. It was against such threats that Saudi Arabia strove, unsuccessfully, to establish a so-called 'security belt' intended to embrace itself, the Gulf states, Iran and eventually Iraq,[3] based on a 'strategy of containment of Soviet expansionism towards the oilfields'.[4]

This sense of encirclement was further compounded by the 1978 revolution in Afghanistan, an Islamic country, which brought a pro-Soviet regime to power in Kabul. In an interview with a prominent American journalist at the end of 1978, the Saudi Crown Prince and First Deputy Prime Minister, Fahd Ibn 'Abd al-'Aziz, offered some insight into the Saudi perception of the new political realities created in the region. Standing by a map, Crown Prince Fahd placed his right hand on Pakistan and solemnly swept it across Afghanistan and Iran to the Persian Gulf. His left hand traced a path through Ethiopia and across the Red Sea to South Yemen and the tip of Arabia. 'That is what we call the Soviet and Communist pincer movement,' he said; 'and if Iran goes, then God help us.'[5]

It was merely days later that Iran did indeed 'go'. Under the Shah's rule, there had been little love lost between the two monarchies, with the Saudis resenting the vastly superior strength of Iran and the Shah's large-scale military buildup and desire to become the so-called 'policeman of the Persian Gulf'. At the same time, Riyadh had regarded Iran as a pro-Western bulwark in the face of Moscow's persistent attempts to establish a foothold in the Persian Gulf region and, as such, as serving Saudi interests as well. On the whole, the common anti-Soviet posture of the two countries had tended to outweigh the competition and distrust between their respective leaderships. The upheavals in Iran constituted, in the Saudi view, 'a part of a grand Soviet-orchestrated strategy in the region'. Having already established footholds in the Horn of Africa, South Yemen and Afghanistan, the USSR and international communism were bound, according to this view, to exploit the crisis in Iran to further their designs on the Arabian Peninsula, i.e. to obtain control over the Saudi oilfields and the vital supply-routes to the West. The Saudi media accused the Soviets of devising and implementing 'horrible bloody strife not only in Iran but also in Turkey and Ethiopia, with the aim of destroying the state of Islam'.[6]

An immediate object of concern was Oman. With the Shah and his peace-keeping force no longer there, the re-eruption of the Dhufar rebellion by Soviet-backed forces fed Saudi anxieties over a communist military intervention in the Arabian Peninsula akin to the one in Ethiopia and the Horn of Africa. Consequently, in view of what Riyadh perceived as Soviet inroads around the Peninsula – i.e. Afghanistan and Iran to the east, the Indian Ocean and South Yemen to the south and Ethiopia to the west – and in view of the Saudi fears that Somalia and Sudan were in line as objects of Soviet subversion and takeover, the Saudis' sense of isolation and encirclement deepened.

The most ominous phenomenon in the new situation, from the Saudi viewpoint, was the apparent paralysis of the United States, reflected in its inability to check the Soviet encroachments throughout the region. The change of regime in Iran constituted merely an additional manifestation of US weakness and lack of purpose and determination in the face of Soviet gains and advances in various regions of the world, such as Vietnam, Angola, the Horn of Africa, Afghanistan, Taiwan and finally Iran. As the Iranian crisis heightened, in September 1978, the Saudis called on the USA to give 'moral and material support to the regional elements who endeavored to contain the destructive activities of the Soviets and prevent them from realizing their strategic goals'.[7] Yet the USA had remained, at least in the Saudi perception, dangerously passive.

The new geopolitical realities in the region, namely the fall of the Shah and his replacement by Khomeini's Islamic Republic, constituted a Soviet challenge which called for an appropriate Saudi response. It was one thing to condemn the USSR in sharply worded statements at a time when the Soviet menace was neither immediate nor real; it was another to rely on this method once the Soviet presence around the Arabian Peninsula became concretely threatening. Given the changed circumstances, the

Saudis felt that they had to devise a more sophisticated approach which would take into consideration both the recently established Soviet proximity and the dubious character of the US security umbrella on which they had relied exclusively in the past. The Saudi leadership also began to wonder whether it was not politically imprudent to put all its eggs in the American basket and whether it was not preferable to take out an additional insurance policy with the Soviet Union.

At the end of 1978, two cumulative developments took place which enabled the Saudis to modify their public attitude toward the USSR and to open some line of communication with Moscow. As the Israeli–Egyptian dialogue culminated in the conclusion of the Camp David accords, Saudi Arabia decided to participate in the Arab summit conference convened in Baghdad in November 1978 along with other Arab states which rejected and condemned the Egyptian move. The Saudis thus found themselves in one camp with those Arab states that were identified as pro-Soviet. The convergence in the positions of Saudi Arabia and the Soviet Union *vis-à-vis* the Camp David accords led to a second development, namely the first public Soviet overtures toward Saudi Arabia in January 1979. In December 1978 there had been reports of Soviet attempts to contact the Saudis through the good offices of PLO Chairman Yasir 'Arafat. According to these accounts, Leonid Brezhnev had conveyed a message to Crown Prince Fahd, expressing satisfaction at the establishment of contacts with Riyadh and hoping that they would continue, deepen and develop into full diplomatic relations. The Brezhnev message allegedly outlined the Soviet position on the Persian Gulf and the Horn of Africa, categorically denying any offensive designs against Saudi Arabia.[8] These reports were matched by other reports to the effect that Riyadh had decided 'in principle' to establish diplomatic relations with Moscow.[9] It was in reaction to the latter that Foreign Minister Sa'ud stated in January 1979 that Saudi Arabia was not contemplating relations with communist countries – a policy based on its strong hostility to communism.[10] Shortly afterwards the Soviets embarked on a public overture. On 30 January an article in *Literaturnaia gazeta* by Igor' Beliaev, one of the leading Soviet experts on the Middle East, pointed out that Saudi Arabia and the Soviet Union had never fought each other and had never had any insoluble conflict. True, they had different social systems, but could this be a basis for mutual hostility? Ignoring the previous Soviet labels of Saudi Arabia as 'reactionary', 'feudalist', 'the kingdom of darkness and obscurantism', the article now portrayed it in sympathetic terms, stressed common positions – such as rejection of the USA-sponsored Camp David accords – and was full of assertions of conciliation.

The Soviet approach apparently enabled the Saudis to translate their readiness to adopt a new attitude toward the Soviet Union into concrete lines. For within a few weeks Crown Prince Fahd made a statement, unprecedented in its accommodating and conciliatory nature toward the USSR. In an interview with *Newsweek*, Fahd stated: 'While we have ideological differences with the USSR, this does not mean we should ignore the importance of the Soviet role in global politics. The question of diplomatic relations is, however, premature.'[11] Not only was this the first positive Saudi reference to the Soviet Union, but this was also the first time that the Saudis had not rejected the idea of diplomatic relations altogether but, rather, made it a question of appropriate timing.

That this statement signified a change in the Saudi attitude became clear when the Saudi Foreign Minister, Sa'ud al-Faisal, not only repeated Fahd's formula of 'recognition of the important Soviet role in global politics', but also expressed gratitude for 'the positive Soviet stance towards Arab causes'. In an obvious attempt to put some distance between Saudi views and those of the United States, and thus stake out a line more favorable to the Soviet Union, Prince Sa'ud said: 'The USA feels that the Soviets try to exploit and deepen disputes and encourage violence. It considers this a grave danger which it cannot accept because it disrupts the international balance. We explained to the United States that we are not interested in international strategies.'[12] It is hard to ignore the cynicism with which this last statement is imbued, considering that the Saudis themselves had publicly condemned the USSR precisely for 'exploiting and deepening disputes and encouraging violence'. At any rate, the obvious objective of the new Saudi line toward the USSR was to dispel the widespread extreme anti-Soviet image of the Kingdom and its unconditional association and identification with the United States.

Nor was the new Saudi line confined to public statements. As of April 1979, the Soviet airline Aeroflot resumed direct flights from Moscow to San'a, the capital of North Yemen, flying over Saudi air space.[13] Moreover, the Soviet Narodny Bank sought to open a branch in Jedda and a Soviet trade mission was said to be about to visit the Kingdom for talks on mutual trade.[14] Contacts between the two countries were reported to have been maintained through a third party, the PLO,[15] and Crown Prince

Fahd was even said to have met Soviet officials while visiting Morocco in May 1979.[16] It thus became clear that the Saudis did not rule out improved relations with the Soviets in various fields, short of diplomatic relations.

The Saudi-Soviet *rapprochement* reached its peak in October 1979. In an interview with a Lebanese paper, the Saudi Defense Minister, Prince Sultan, made the following statement:

> We are aware of the Soviet attempts to improve relations with us. We have noted that the Soviet media do not attack Saudi Arabia as they used to do in the past. Though we do not have diplomatic relations with the Soviet Union, we have mutual relations in several other fields. We do not oppose the establishment of diplomatic relations provided the Soviets will understand that our position emanates from the principles and values of Islam. We do not wish to see foreigners (i.e. foreign diplomats) in our country who preach heresy. If and when the causes for our concern are removed, there will be no reason for the absence of diplomatic relations between us.[17]

This was undoubtedly the most far-reaching statement ever made by a Saudi leader regarding the Soviet Union. Not only could he foresee diplomatic relations with the USSR, but the conditions he puts forward were such that the Soviets could reasonably live with. Indeed, in an interview with the Lebanese weekly, *al-Hawadith*, Crown Prince Fahd revealed that contacts between Saudi Arabia and the USSR had gotten underway through a third party, which he did not identify.[18]

While still indicating that Islam and communism were irreconcilable Fahd asserted that the USSR could not be ignored as 'a world power'. Indeed, toward the end of December 1979 there were reports indicating that Saudi Arabia was about to establish diplomatic relations with the Soviet Union.

But, at this particular juncture, the Soviet Union invaded Afghanistan, throwing the Saudi leadership into disarray. Unlike in Iran, where the Soviets were perceived to have been acting by proxy, through pro-Soviet elements, their action in Afghanistan constituted a blatant, direct threat and challenge. With the invasion of Afghanistan, the Saudi attitude toward the USSR changed promptly and drastically, reversing the short-lived *rapprochement*. Sharp and repeated condemnation of the Soviet action abounded in the Saudi media, and Saudi Arabia was the first country to announce a boycott on the Moscow Olympics.[19] Most Saudi statements carried strong Islamic overtones, claiming that 'the hour of the confrontation between Islam and communism has begun violently' and that 'the atheist Soviet threat' had to be checked.[20] The Saudis played a leading role in convening the Islamic conference in Islamabad in late January 1980; in securing a sharp condemnation of the invasion; and in the decision to support the Afghan rebels fighting the Soviets.[21] In his speech at the conference, Foreign Minister Sa'ud al-Faisal described the Soviet action as 'a flagrant challenge to the Islamic nation; a gross disregard for Muslims and Islam; intervention in the domestic affairs of a sovereign state; and violation of all international ethics, laws and behavior'.[22]

In assessing the significance and potential impact of the Soviet invasion, Saudi leaders focused on its political and strategic aspects. They stated that the Soviets sought 'to spread instability and social, political and ideological disturbances in order to create opportunities to intervene and realize their expansionist goals since communism thrives in an environment of chaos and uncertainty'.[23] Saudi leaders expressed conviction that the invasion was part of a Soviet grand strategy to establish hegemony over, and eventually capture, the oil-rich Persian Gulf region, on which Western economies relied for their energy, and to turn the Gulf countries into satellites of the Soviet bloc.[24] Offering an economic explanation for the long-term Soviet objective, the Saudi Petroleum Minister, Ahmad Zaki al-Yamani, stated that it was motivated by declining Soviet oil production which would force the USSR to become an oil importer over the next few years.[25] What was most alarming from the Saudi viewpoint, *ex post facto*, was the fear that, if the Soviets were not opposed and punished, 'it will only whet Moscow's appetite for further action'.[26] Summing up the Saudi perception of the invasion, Crown Prince Fahd stated that, contrary to his hopes, the United States seemed incapable of 'taking urgent and bold action to stop the Communist thrust'. Saudi Arabia, he concluded sadly, had never dreamed that 'in the 20th century, such an invasion could take place with impunity'.[27]

In view of such an extreme hard-line anti-Soviet posture, one could have expected Saudi Arabia to cement its weakening alliance with the United States and offer tangible support to the Americans in their efforts to confront the USSR in the Persian Gulf region. Instead, the Saudi leadership reverted gradually, as of March 1980, to its pre-invasion policy, the central component of which was the desire to cultivate normal, if not friendly, relations with those forces which could potentially constitute a danger to the Kingdom, and first and foremost the Soviet Union.

In the absence of any force capable of standing up to the

Soviet challenge and with the consolidation of the Soviet presence in Afghanistan, the Saudis evidently realized that it was risky to antagonize Moscow. In the light of the American reaction to these events, the Saudis apparently concluded that no effective regional security, in which they could safely take part, was in the offing and decided to appease Moscow and remove their anti-Soviet label as the only means for minimizing the Soviet danger *vis-à-vis* the Kingdom. Consequently, they not only toned down their criticism of the Soviet Union and sought to avoid references to the invasion, but they also reverted to conciliatory statements showing Saudi goodwill toward the Soviets. Reflecting this Saudi approach, Foreign Minister Sa'ud stated that an end to the Soviet occupation of Afghanistan would remove 'any inhibition' Saudi Arabia might have 'about evolving and developing good relations with the Soviet Union'.[28]

In devising a new attitude toward the USSR, the Saudis were more keenly aware than ever of the fact that they were essentially trying to reconcile two mutually exclusive systems: communism and Islam. Hence they sought to provide their new policy with some ideological legitimacy. Whereas in the past they had constantly emphasized that communism and the USSR were inherently atheist and expansionist and, by definition, enemies of Islam and Saudi Arabia, Saudi leaders now started to differentiate between communism and the USSR, and consequently also between Saudi Arabia and Islam. While still maintaining that communism was totally irreconcilable with Islam, they proposed, however, that the USSR be regarded as a global power and, as such, be treated on the basis of pragmatic considerations.[29]

Certainly, the traditional Saudi outlook, according to which the USSR is wicked and hostile to religion, did not disappear. Yet it was replaced, for the time being, by considerations of expediency dictated by two main factors: the magnitude and proximity of the Soviet threat on the one hand, and the power and determination of the United States effectively to confront the Soviets on the other. Thus, the more concrete and close the Soviet menace became, and the more timid the US reaction seemed to have been, the more conciliatory and accommodating became Saudi Arabia's approach toward the USSR. While pursuing this somewhat sophisticated line, the Saudis none the less realized that it constituted no more than short-term crisis management, which could not serve as an appropriate long-term response to the Soviet challenge. In the absence, however, of any other real option, the Saudi leadership settled for such a line, presumably hoping that external circumstances, specifically a re-emergence of a determined and purposeful United States, would alleviate, if not solve, their problem.

The fluctuations in the Saudi attitude toward the USSR in the 1977–80 period tended to illustrate Saudi dilemmas in shaping a coherent foreign policy in rapidly changing circumstances in the region. For the first time in this century, the Saudis had to face, as of the second half of the 1970s, a concrete Soviet threat to the security of the Kingdom and the stability of the regime. Condemning the Soviet Union and communism on pure ideological grounds, as the Saudi leadership had done in the past, could not serve any more as a basis for Saudi attitudes toward the USSR. The Saudis were, thus, forced to decide whether to continue their public opposition and criticism of the Soviet Union or to adopt a new approach, which would not antagonize Moscow and would remove the extreme anti-Soviet label attached to Riyadh. It seemed that the Saudi perception of the USA as weak, impotent and lacking in determination in face of Soviet advances was the major factor in Riyadh's opting for the latter course of action. In their pursuit of a more accommodating line toward Moscow, however, communism did not seem to have posed an insuperable impediment for the Saudi leaders. Proceeding on the basis of pragmatic considerations, they managed to draw a line between communism as an ideology, totally rejected, and the USSR as a superpower, which must be reckoned with for the sake of Saudi security and interests. The distance between this pragmatic response to the Soviet threat and the establishment of diplomatic relations between Saudi Arabia and the USSR still seemed to be insurmountable.

Notes: Chapter 13

1 *'Ukaz* (Jeddah), 3 January 1979.
2 Radio Riyadh, 6 February 1978, monitored by Foreign Broadcast Information Service, Daily Report, Vol. V (The Middle East and North Africa) (hereafter cited as *FBIS V*), 8 February 1978.
3 *Al-Nahar al-'Arabi wal-Duwali* (Paris), 25 March 1978; *Defense and Foreign Affairs – Weekly Report on Strategic Middle-East Affairs* (Washington, DC), 26 April 1978.
4 *The Observer* (London), 17 September 1978.
5 *Newsweek* (New York), 15 January 1979.
6 *'Ukaz*, 21 February 1979; Radio Riyadh, 31 December 1978/*FBIS V*, 3 January 1979.
7 *Al-Riyadh*, 30 September 1978.
8 *Al-Nahar al-'Arabi wal-Duwali*, 1 January 1979; *Afro-Asian Affairs* (London), 20 December 1978.

9. *Al-Siyasa* (Kuwait), 8 January 1979.
10. ibid., 15 January 1979.
11. *Newsweek*, 26 March 1979.
12. Interview with *al-Hawadith* (London), 2 March 1979.
13. *The International Herald Tribune* (Paris), 1 June 1979; *Afro-Asian Affairs*, 20 May 1979.
14. *Shield* (London), 9 February 1979.
15. *Al-Dustur* (London), 19 May 1979.
16. *Al-Hadaf* (Kuwait), 24 May 1979.
17. *Al-Jumhur* (Beirut), 11 October 1979.
18. *Al-Hawadith*, 11 January 1980. The interview was held prior to the Soviet invasion of Afghanistan.
19. *Al-Riyadh*, 6 January 1980.
20. ibid.
21. *The Financial Times* (London), 28 January 1980. For the Islamabad Conferences of January and May 1980, see Mina Graur, 'The Soviet Union versus Muslim solidarity following the invasion of Afghanistan', *Slavic and Soviet Series* (Tel Aviv), vol. 4, no. 1–2 (1979), pp. 74–89.
22. Saudi News Agency, 27 January 1980/*FBIS V*, 29 January 1980.
23. Crown Prince Fahd's interviews with *al-Riyadh* and *Le Figaro* (Paris), 23 February 1980, and *Newsweek*, 3 March 1980.
24. Defense Minister Sultan's interview with *Nouvel Observateur* (Paris), 22 March 1980.
25. Yamani's lecture in Geneva, quoted by *The New York Times*, 8 February 1980; and his lecture in Jedda, quoted by *The Guardian* (London), 18 April 1980. The analysis offered by Yamani has since been countered by what seems to be now the prevailing opinion, i.e. that the USSR will not be in need of Gulf oil to satisfy its needs during the 1980s; see Marshall I. Goldman, *The Enigma of Soviet Petroleum* (London: Allen & Unwin, 1980).
26. Foreign Minister Sa'ud's interview with *Die Presse* (Vienna), 6 February 1980.
27. *The Sunday Times* (London), 3 February 1980; *Newsweek*, 3 March 1980.
28. Interview with *Monday Morning* (Beirut), 27 July 1980.
29. For instance, Fahd's interview with *Newsweek*, 26 March 1979; and *al-Hawadith*, 11 January 1980.

14

Dilemmas of Arab Communism: The Case of the Syrian Communist Party, 1969–73

DINA KEHAT

This chapter examines the nature and dynamics of some of the longstanding dilemmas of Arab communism as they emerged during the internal crisis which the Syrian Communist Party went through in the late 1960s and the early 1970s.

The conflict opened with the emergence, at the party's Third Congress in June 1969, of a faction which turned out to be opposed to the leadership of veteran Secretary-General Khalid Bakdash and at variance with some prominent aspects of the party's traditional political line. Between this faction and the supporters of Bakdash there developed an ideological debate and a power struggle which were to last for several years. During 1970 the opposition faction succeeded in pushing through a controversial political program which deviated considerably from the party's past policies, and within another year both the party's central bodies and its provincial branches divided along a two-faction line. The inter-factional conflict was exacerbated in the spring of 1972 when, faced with a growing oppositional challenge, Bakdash first brought it out into the open in an appeal to the party's rank and file to reject the 'subversion' carried out by the opposition. A number of Soviet-inspired initiatives to restore the unity of the party were at first to no avail. In December 1973, however, Bakdash – who apparently had the support of both Moscow and the Syrian regime – managed to win over some of the opposition leaders, while the rest of the opposition faction, led by Riyad al-Turk, seceded and established their own, clandestine communist party.[1]

The conflict served as a unique opportunity, equalled only by the major crises of the late 1940s and the late 1950s, in affording insights into the party's operation and inner debates. First, a series of circumstances which will be noted below brought to a head and put on the party's immediate agenda problems which had been latent for years. Secondly, from the moment it came into the open in the spring of 1972, the inter-factional conflict was marked by an unusual abundance of substantial information much of which was leaked from inside the party by the opposing factions. The single most revealing publication in this respect was *Qadaya al-khilaf fi al-hizb al-shuyu'i al-suri (The Issues of the Conflict in the Syrian Communist Party)*, a book published in Beirut in the summer of 1972, presumably by the opposition faction. It included what appeared to be the authentic versions of important party documents which had not initially been designed to become public knowledge, such as the controversial draft political program of 1970; a Soviet critique of the draft program which was itself turned into part and parcel of the party's internal debate; and the contents of the deliberations held at the November 1971 session of the party's National Council.

The inter-factional conflict hinged upon two different sets of issues, both having deep roots in the history of the party and both having acquired additional acuteness during the 1960s. The first had to do with the highly personalized and allegedly undemocratic style of leadership exercized by Bakdash for nearly four decades.[2] This had been a recurrent plea in all previous instances of the opposition's challenge in the party, whatever their specific context.[3] Criticism of Bakdash was given added impetus by his self-imposed exile in Eastern Europe (from 1958 to 1966) which generated a measure of antagonism and bitterness combined with a sense of greater independence among those who stayed behind in Syria.[4]

A second complex consisted of such questions as the nature of the party's relationship with the Syrian regime; its attitude toward, and the scope of its involvement in, Arab nationalist affairs; and the meaning of its allegiance to Moscow and to the Soviet Communist Party. These questions related to the very nature and role of communism in Arab society in that they touched upon the fundamental difficulties of reconciling belief in Marxist–Leninist doctrine and allegiance to Moscow with dependence upon the local authorities for freedom of action and for participation in national politics, and with susceptibility to the overwhelming appeal of Arab nationalist aspirations, concerns and slogans even among communism's own constituency. Inherent in Arab communism, these difficulties had assumed special saliency at a number of previous critical moments, notably in the wake of the 1947 UN resolution on the partition of Palestine and upon the establishment of the (Egyptian–Syrian) United Arab Republic in 1958. Under the impact of the 1967 war and its consequences they were to come to a head once more.

The Impact of the 1967 War and the Debate on the Palestinian Question

The war worked in a number of ways to call for a revaluation of the party's traditional policies, not only in the obvious realm of the Arab–Israeli conflict but in some other spheres, too.

First, having maintained some sort of cooperation (limited though it had been) with the Syrian Ba'th regime on the eve of the war, and because they were associated with Moscow's assistance to Egypt and Syria which the war had proved to be ineffective, the local communists came to be regarded as partners to the Arab defeat, in both its military and its broader political sense. Against this background, it was natural for the Communist Party to partake in the broader ferment generated by the war's consequences and in particular to be exposed to questions concerning its own public image and potential appeal, its relationship with Moscow and with the Ba'th regime and its role in Arab politics.

Secondly, the loss of Arab territories in the war, and later the growing prominence of the Palestinian organizations and the Palestinian problem in general, modified the context of the Arab–Israeli conflict in a way that required changes in policy. Under the new circumstances, the party's traditional policy, combining a perception of Israel as a forward imperialist base in the region with an acceptance of the 1947 UN resolution on the partition of Palestine, became inadequate. The reemergence of the controversy within the party as regards Soviet and local communist acceptance of the 1947 resolution was given specific impetus by the analogy between Moscow's position in 1947–8 and its current acceptance of Security Council resolution 242 as a basis for a political settlement of the Arab–Israeli conflict.

Thirdly, Moscow's approval of resolution 242 ranged the Soviets and their local allies against those in the Arab world, notably Syria and the PLO, who were opposed to any political settlement whatsoever. Moscow's cautious attitude toward the armed Palestinian organizations in the first years following the 1967 war posed another difficulty for the local communists, especially when compared with the support granted these organizations by Peking, and with the efforts of pro-Chinese communist splinter groups in the Arab world to become associated with them and to capitalize on their growing popularity.[5]

The Internal Debate: The Palestinian Question

The pressures stemming from these developments were common to most Arab communist parties. Some parties were quick to adopt new policies,[6] while others were thrown into internal discords.[7] Within the Syrian party, it was mainly the opposition faction which proved susceptible to the implications of the war and its aftermath. To begin with, in the most conspicuous realm, that of the Arab–Israeli conflict, the opposition advocated the formulation of a whole new set of policies, while Bakdash and his followers sought to maintain the party's traditional policy with as few modifications as possible. The differences of opinion between the two factions as regards the conflict may be summarized in the following way:

(a) In their general concept of *the nature of the conflict*, Bakdash and his followers held to the party's traditional line, laying greater emphasis on the anti-progressive character of Zionism and its being an extension of world imperialism in the region, than on its specific challenge to the Arab nation.[8] As one of their spokesmen put it bluntly, the Palestinian problem was not, in their view, 'one between Arabs and Jews'.[9] The opposition faction, for its part, while it continued paying tribute to the same concept, came to adopt the customary Arab nationalist argumentation, i.e. that the core of the problem was the 'usurpation of the homeland of the Palestinian people', and that Israel was 'an alien entity in the midst of the Arab homeland' and 'a perpetual source of danger' not only for the progressive regimes but also for 'the very national existence' of the Arabs.[10]

(b) *The Soviet and local communist acceptance of the 1947 resolution on the partition of Palestine* – at the time a cause of both internal dissent and outside pressures[11] – became the subject of a renewed debate between the two factions. The opposition demanded that the party openly declare its mistake in having accepted the resolution in 1947, in the face of demonstrations of public disapproval.[12] The followers of Bakdash admitted that the party's acceptance of the resolution had been a bid 'to defend Soviet policy'; yet they claimed that, under the circumstances prevailing at the time, Moscow's own acceptance of it had been both 'unavoidable' and beneficial to the Arabs.[13]

(c) In visualizing *the prospective solutions to the Arab–Israeli conflict*, Bakdash's faction laid the main emphasis on the 'liquidation of the traces of the 1967 aggression', as the broadly accepted but divergently interpreted slogan was formulated. In their view, as in the Soviet approach, this was to be achieved through a 'just political settlement based on Security Council resolution 242'. They agreed that, alongside this, the Palestinian people's 'right to return to their homeland' and right to self-determination should be put forward, albeit as a strategic goal and without defining, for the time being, in what way these rights were to be accomplished. They rejected the call for the liquidation of the State of Israel under whatever slogan, whether 'liberation of Palestine', 'liquidating the Zionist establishment', etc. This, they claimed, was an unrealistic and non-proletarian objective, in that it disregarded the established fact of the Jewish presence in Palestine, the potentially positive role of the Jewish masses and the danger of another Arab–Israeli war developing into an international conflagration.[14] By contrast, the opposition faction not only dismissed the possibility of a political settlement, but declared the whole slogan of 'liquidating the traces of aggression' to be inadequate. In their view, the struggle should aim at 'liquidating Zionism and its aggressive and expansionist institutions' and at realizing the Palestinian people's right to 'liberate their usurped homeland . . . return to it and establish their own state'. Even replacing the call for the liberation of Palestine by one for Palestinian self-determination, as suggested by Bakdash, could be taken to imply recognition of Israel, and was thus unacceptable.[15]

(d) A specific controversy revolved around *the role and activities of the armed Palestinian organizations*. In the opposition's view, their activities constituted a most important aspect of the conflict and required the participation of all Arab 'progressive forces'.[16] Bakdash and his followers agreed that it was necessary to 'support the Palestinian resistance movement' and to 'join its ranks', albeit in an effort to 'direct it in the right direction'. But they insisted that the party could not support 'indiscriminately' the methods employed by those organizations. And they felt, in general, that the opposition faction went much too far in its assessment of their role.[17]

Only in one specific area did these differences have a practical implication. In March 1970, in an attempt to capitalize on the increasing popularity of the Palestinian organizations and to influence them from within, the communist parties of Syria, Iraq, Lebanon and Jordan set up a *fida'i* organization of their own, *al-Ansar* (literally, 'the Partisans').[18] Spokesmen of the opposition within the Syrian party claimed later that it was their own faction which had initiated and facilitated the participation of the party in *al-Ansar*, while the supporters of Bakdash had tried to prevent its establishment from the outset and to obstruct its operation once it had been set up.[19] In fact, however, the whole incident of *al-Ansar* was short-lived and insignificant. Having been denied admission to the Unified Command of the Palestinian Resistance Movement (then the supreme military body of all the factions belonging to the PLO), the organisation was dissolved in 1972 with the consent of all four participating parties.[20]

The Question of Arab Unity

In a less direct manner, the nationalist ferment generated by the 1967 war also invigorated the longstanding debate on the party's traditional attitudes toward one of the most cherished of all Arab-nationalist aspirations, namely, the quest for Arab unity. As demonstrated most conspicuously under the United Arab Republic, the Syrian–Egyptian union of 1958–61, the policy of the party on this question had been at best unenthusiastic or ambivalent.[21] One source for this traditional reservation was the party's adherence to Soviet policy which, for its part, was apprehensive that Arab unity might hamper Soviet and communist infiltration into the Middle East. Another was the concern of the disproportionately high percentage of party members who came from non-Arab minority communities – particularly Kurds in the Syrian case – with the potentially negative implications of Arab unity for their own position. (Neither in the late 1960s nor in the past, though, were the advocates and the opponents of unity within the party divided along a clear communal, i.e. Arab–Kurdish, line,[22] even though the former, as we shall see, played up the Kurdish theme in interfactional disputes.)

Following in the footsteps of like-minded factions which had emerged within the party's ranks in the past, the opposition faction of the late 1960s took up this issue and gave it much emphasis. They accused the party of being 'afraid' of Arab unity and of having based its policy toward the United Arab Republic, in particular, on 'hate of unity' and on 'separatism and propagation of separatism'.[23] This harsh criticism derived in part from their own attraction to Arab nationalist aspirations and myths (which was manifested in their references to such themes as the artificial fragmentation of the Arab world or to the alleged quest for unity in nineteenth-century Egypt).[24] They also believed that Arab nationalist aspirations had deep roots among the party's potential constituency, as in Arab society in general, and that the party's popular appeal depended to a considerable extent on whether or not it cultivated these aspirations. In accordance with this logic, they seemed to be blaming the party's anti-unionist policies for its scanty success (in terms of membership, popular support and influence on national politics) and specifically for its deterioration from the real or perceived strength of 1956–7 to a role of insignificance under the United Arab Republic and thereafter. This line of thought was clearly implied by Wasil Faysal, one of the leaders of the opposition faction, at the party's National Council, which convened in November 1971. 'We live in this country, we are familiar with the feelings of this people and we know that the desire for unity is prevalent among the masses,' he declared. 'The party has failed to raise the slogan of unity and we have been criticized by the masses and have reaped the results of this failure. Are we now to go on adhering to this line?'[25]

The spokesmen of the opposition faction sought to link what they described as the party's anti-nationalist and anti-unionist posture to the high proportion of Kurds among its ranks and to Bakdash's own Kurdish origin in particular. They addressed themselves more than once to genuine or to deliberately incited fears of Arab unity among the country's 'national minorities', and on at least one occasion inferred that such incitement was attempted specifically by Kurdish elements within the party.[26] Such utterances went hand in hand with the opposition's claim that Bakdash personally was to blame for the party's anti-unionist policies.[27] As quoted by one of his confidants, they even argued that Bakdash had opposed the establishment of the United Arab Republic in 1958 'only because he was a Kurd'.[28]

The terms of reference employed by the opposition in debating the party's policy on Arab unity remained, however, well founded in Marxist–Leninist doctrine, just as were those put forward by Bakdash's faction. The main arguments of Bakdash and his followers were that as communists they should examine the question of unity, like any other question, from the perspective of its effects on the class struggle; that past experience had shown Arab unity to comprise various phenomena, not all of them progressive; that the implementation of socialism should precede that of unity; and that preliminary conditions should be set with regard to the democratic character of the future unitary state, its contribution to socialism and its readiness to allow for the singularities of each member state.[29] The opposition faction, for its part, claimed that in the current historical phase any Arab unionist move – and, according to a more moderate formulation, any such move between 'liberated' Arab states – was bound to be progressive; that in a dialectical way the quest for Arab unity and that for socialism were mutually sustaining; that disregard of nationalist questions was a cosmopolitan, not a proletarian, attitude; that the class struggle was bound to continue within the unitary state; and that it was not necessarily required for socialism to be implemented first, nor for unity to be made dependent upon prior conditions.[30]

These differences were given practical expression in the position of the two factions on the tripartite Egyptian–Syrian–Libyan federation established in April 1971. Initially, the party appeared to be united in its endorsement of the federation.[31] Yet, at its National Council, which met in November 1971, Bakdash and his followers were said to have withdrawn from their earlier position and to have demanded that the party's approval of the federation be made dependent on several specific conditions.[32] As in past instances, this may have reflected a similar reversal in Moscow's attitude. Indeed, following the ousting of the 'Ali Sabri group in Egypt in May 1971 and the abortive communist-supported *coup d'état* in Sudan in July of that year – two events which they regarded as symptoms of a newly developing anti-Soviet and anti-communist trend – the Soviets themselves were then engaged in re-evaluating their own policy toward the federation.[33]

It is noteworthy that, while the inter-factional conflict was so concerned with the party's Arab identity, the question of the role of communism in a *Muslim* society did not figure at all in the controversy. This was in keeping with the traditional attitude of Arab communist parties, which was always marked by inability and unwillingness to cope with the subject and with the incompatibilities involved in it.[34]

Cooperation with the Regime

Another set of dilemmas which had been on the party's agenda continuously since the mid-1960s revolved around the question of cooperation with the Ba'th regime. The question first emerged for the Syrian communists on the theoretical level when, as of 1963, the concept of 'revolutionary democracy' was being developed and pushed forward by Moscow. The gist of the concept was that, in ex-colonial countries which were taking the 'non-capitalist road of development', it was acceptable for *petit bourgeois* 'revolutionary democratic' forces, as they were called, to be in power during the phase of transition to socialism, without necessarily co-opting the local communist parties into national fronts. Its most notable manifestation was Moscow's recognition of the Algerian and Egyptian regimes as 'revolutionary democratic' and the subsequent self-dissolution of the Algerian and Egyptian communist parties in 1964 and 1965 respectively.[35] The question assumed a practical nature for the Syrian Communist Party after the February 1966 *coup d'état* and the advent to power of the radical Ba'th faction of Salah Jadid. The party was given the opportunity to cooperate in some measure with the new regime, while Bakdash and some of his associates were allowed to return from exile in Eastern Europe. Within the span of about two years, however, communist cooperation with the regime faced new problems, as the internal struggles within the Ba'th Party raged on and the apparently anti-communist and 'rightist' faction of Hafiz al-Asad appeared to be gaining the upper hand.[36] Eventually, once he seized power in November 1970, the policies initiated by Asad proved less clear-cut, from the point of view of the local communists, than had been expected. As they had suspected, Asad did liberalize some parts of his predecessor's socialist policy. On the other hand, he demonstrated greater openness toward a number of non-Ba'thi political groups including the Communist Party, and proposed to co-opt them into the regime — if only in a very limited manner — by making them partners to a Ba'thi-led National Progressive Front. Within this framework, they were to be granted official recognition and to become partners of the Ba'th Party in certain governmental functions but were required, at the same time, to accept a number of restrictions. Most notably, they were to undertake not to be active among members of the armed forces or among university students. (Traditionally the students had been the most important constituency for the communists.)[37]

Unlike other major issues on the party's agenda, the question of cooperation with the Ba'th regime was not debated between the contending factions in explicit terms before the public disclosure of the inter-factional conflict by Bakdash in April 1972. Only then it transpired that this was another point of controversy in the party's internal conflict. As Bakdash presented the situation, then, it was his own faction which had all along encouraged and worked for cooperation with the Asad regime, while the opposition faction had been against it. He accused his rivals specifically of having refused to join Asad's cabinet in November 1970, of having attempted to obstruct the emerging cooperation and having turned down Asad's proposed terms for a National Progressive Front.[38] In practical terms, the only real and open indication of refusal to cooperate with the Asad regime was the establishment of an oppositional clandestine communist party by the leader of the opposition faction, Riyad al-Turk, after his secession from the mother party in December 1973. Bakdash's accusations were, however, corroborated much earlier, if only by the partial and lukewarm nature of the oppositions's own denials.[39]

Unlike the controversies on the Palestinian question or on the quest for Arab unity, the divergence of opinions within the party on the question of cooperation with the regime was neither longstanding nor consistent. In the mid-1960s, it should be recalled, it was Bakdash, personally, who figured as the most prominent opponent of the concept of 'revolutionary democracy' (and hence of cooperation with the *petit bourgeois* regime in power). In a number of international communist forums in 1964 and 1965 he declared that the *petite bourgeoisie* was totally incapable of leading the transition to socialism, and came out forcefully against the dissolution of the local communist parties in countries ruled by so-called 'revolutionary democratic' regimes.[40] His would-be rivals were later to imply that they, by contrast, had accepted the Soviet concept from the beginning and had consequently played the major role in the day-to-day cooperation established between the party and the regime of Salah Jadid after 1966.[41] (This may be borne out by the fact that one of their leaders, Wasil Faysal, was the only communist in the Ba'thi government between 1968 and 1970.)

The members of both factions, then, reversed their attitudes within a number of years. Bakdash's gradual shift from rejecting the theory of 'revolutionary democracy' to cooperating with the Asad regime and accepting Asad's terms for a National Progressive Front evolved under Soviet persuasion and pressure. Admittedly, it was during the series of meetings which the leadership of the party held with a Soviet team to discuss its draft political program (apparently in early 1971) that he waived his objections to the concept of 'revolutionary democracy'.[42] As shown elsewhere, it was the Soviets who, for their own reasons, had been behind the party's shift from deep suspicion of Asad (as compared with Salah Jadid) in 1968 to a stance of neutrality in the interfactional struggle within the Ba'th Party since early 1969, and to an immediate acceptance of the Asad regime once he seized power in November 1970.[43] During 1971 it was again the Soviets who urged the local communists in Syria and elsewhere in the Arab world to cooperate with existing regimes and enter into national fronts.[44] From Bakdash's point of view, this was a significant change for the better from the earlier concept which envisioned the dissolution of the local communist parties.

It is interesting, in this connection, to trace the origin of two statements made by Bakdash at the party's National Council session of November 1971. In the first statement, he recognized the 'leading role' of the Ba'th Party in the state and the National Progressive Front, using the rationalization that in actual fact leadership was a matter of the 'capacity . . . to respond to the needs . . . of the masses' and could not be acquired by 'formal declarations'.[45] In the second statement, he proposed that even during the stage of the establishment of socialism, the Communist Party did not necessarily have to assume exclusive power.[46] In both cases he was reiterating exact formulations or arguments used shortly before by spokesmen of the Soviet Communist Party.[47]

As for the opposition leaders, there are a number of possible explanations for their presumed shift from acceptance of the concept of 'revolutionary democracy' and from closer association with the regime of Salah Jadid to a more reserved attitude toward Asad's regime and a rejection of its proposed terms for a National Progressive Front. First, there were indications that they were more disappointed than their rivals with the attempt to liberalize some of Salah Jadid's socialist policies, which was discernible during Asad's first year in power.[48] This might have been so precisely owing to their previous acceptance of the theory of 'revolutionary democracy', which involved pinning greater hopes on the so-called 'revolutionary democratic' regimes and their prospective development in a more 'progressive' direction.

Secondly, their reluctance to cooperate with the Asad regime appeared to be connected with their advocacy of the party's right to formulate domestic policies independent of the Soviet Communist Party. This being their position, they were less susceptible than Bakdash to pressures for closer cooperation with the regime originating in Moscow.

Relations with Moscow

The last issue in the party's internal debate was its relationship with the Soviet Union and, in particular, with its Soviet counterpart, the CPSU. The debate on this question revolved specifically around the validity of a Soviet document of May 1971 which criticized in detail the controversial draft political program of the party, initiated sometime during 1970. In a more general manner, the spokesmen of the opposition stood for the party's right to formulate and enact domestic policies independent of the Soviet Communist Party and to adopt stands which differed 'tactically' from those of Moscow. They asserted that otherwise there was no justification for the existence of separate communist parties. At the same time, however, they insisted that this was not a call for independence from Moscow.[49] Bakdash, for his part, emphasized the importance of coordinating policies with the Soviet Communist Party and warned that pleading for freedom to disagree with it on one particular question or another was bound to lead eventually to a quest for total independence.[50]

As shown above, it was Moscow's specific policies on such issues as the Arab-Israeli conflict, Arab unity or communist cooperation with the 'progressive' regimes in power, which aroused objections in the opposition faction. Apart from being opposed to specific Soviet policies, though, they also felt uneasy about the party's general image of absolute loyalty to Moscow – an image derived first and foremost from Bakdash's own international reputation as Moscow's most faithful and valuable ally in the Arab communist movement. Bakdash had acquired, or at least had strengthened, this reputation through his activities in the 1960s to consolidate the pro-Soviet orientation of the Arab communist movement in the face of the Sino-Soviet conflict and the first Chinese advances in the Middle East.[51]

It should therefore be emphasized that, these attitudes notwithstanding, the conflict within the party was never between a pro-Soviet faction and a pro-Chinese one. The opposition faction apparently had no connections with any of the Maoist splinter groups which had existed in Syria since the mid-1960s.[52] In December 1973, Riyad al-Turk and his hardcore followers within the opposition faction seceded and established their own separate communist party, which was henceforth boycotted by the Soviet Union and most East European countries (as well as by the Ba'th regime).[53] But even under these circumstances the seceding party never became associated with Peking.

The inter-factional conflict in the Syrian party served to expose and to articulate quandaries and disputes which were common to many other Arab communist parties. The question of cooperation with the 'progressive', non-communist ruling elites, for instance, posed before different parties basically similar dilemmas. It was believed by many to promise greater leverage to the local communists; it could be justified ideologically; and it was urged by the Soviets, who sought to develop closer relations with the established Arab regimes, even at the expense of the local communist parties. But, on the other hand, it was bound to impair the independence of the local parties, which still had its strong advocates in such leaders as Bakdash and the Secretary-General of the Sudanese Communist Party, 'Abd al-Khaliq Mahjub.

Different parties chose or were driven to cope with the same dilemma in different manners, in accordance with local conditions and with the changing attitudes of Moscow. In Algeria and Egypt (officially still the United Arab Republic), whose ruling elites were the first in the Arab world to be recognized by Moscow as 'revolutionary democratic', the local communist parties were voluntarily disbanded in 1964 and 1965 respectively so as to enable their members to integrate into the one-party regimes in power. The Sudanese Communist Party was, in 1969 and 1970, a partner of Ja'far al-Numayri's newly established regime, while at the same time refusing to dissolve itself and integrate into his administration. But once he liquidated his other rivals, and considering the position of the Communist Party a challenge to his power, Numayri set out to cut off its influence and thus drove it, in July 1971, to support an abortive coup attempted by pro-communist army officers. This was then followed by a massive crackdown, from which the party has been unable fully to recover ever since. Finally, the Iraqi party, like its Syrian counterpart, entered into a nominal National Progressive Front coalition with the ruling Ba'th party in 1973, under Soviet pressure. By joining the Front, it acquired a legal status, more freedom of action and perhaps an added prestige, but no effective political influence.

Nor was it relieved of instances of repression, particularly at times of tension in Soviet–Iraqi relations.

The dilemmas and controversies stemming from the traditional ambivalence of the Syrian party on the questions of Palestine and of Arab unity were paralleled by similar phenomena in the Jordanian, Lebanese, Egyptian and Sudanese parties. In the Egyptian party the disadvantages involved in the adherence to unpopular, Soviet-inspired positions on these questions were a thing of the past. In the Jordanian and Lebanese parties, however, as in the Syrian party, the matter reemerged forcefully in the wake of the 1967 war. In the Jordanian party, an initial reservation toward the Palestinian armed organizations gradually gave way to growing support, and some of the opponents of the new line were ousted at the beginning of 1971. Yet, the party did not waive its acceptance of the UN resolution on the partition of Palestine, or of Security Council resolution 242. In the Lebanese party there appeared a faction which was openly opposed to Moscow's traditional positions on the Arab–Israeli conflict and which called for communist participation in the activities of the Palestinian organizations. They were apparently responsible for the removal of a group of veteran party leaders in late 1967. In 1968, they initiated the convocation of the party's Second Congress, where they succeeded in pushing through their stands on the Palestinian question as well as their criticism of the anti-unionist posture of the (then united) Syrian–Lebanese Communist Party at the time of the Syrian–Egyptian union of 1958–61. In the Sudanese party, which had not been previously associated with any particular anti-unionist policies, a faction led by 'Abd al-Khaliq Mahjub was strongly opposed to the Federation of Arab Republics since it was first envisaged in 1970. Their position, which preceded and was more vehement than Bakdash's reported opposition to the Federation in late 1971, derived primarily from the same concern which had motivated Bakdash back in 1958, namely, that the party would be required to disband itself and integrate into a mass political organization of the Egyptian type.

The pro-Soviet orientation of the Syrian Communist Party has been common to all its Arab counterparts, while the pro-Chinese groups in the Arab world have all been insignificant splinter factions. Soviet ambivalence on a number of Arab nationalist causes and the customary Soviet preference for relations with established regimes over the interests of the local communists could be expected to arouse in the Arab communist parties doubts and disputes concerning the desirable nature of their relations with, and commitment to, Moscow and the CPSU. In fact, however, apart from the Syrian party, only the Lebanese party has been known to have gone through disputes of this kind in the late 1960s and the early 1970s.

Notes: Chapter 14

1. The above account is based primarily on the following sources: *Qadaya al-khilaf fi al-hizb al-shuyu'i al-suri* (Beirut: Dar Ibn Khaldun, 1972); *al-Nahar* (Beirut), 15 June 1969, 6 and 9 April, 5, 13 and 16 May 1972, 4 and 27 December 1973, 3 January 1974; *al-Nida'* (Beirut), 9 May, 26 November, 1 December 1971, 18 March, 27 July, 12 August 1972; *al-Hayat* (Beirut), 25 November 1971, 17 March, 2 December 1973; *Le Monde* (Paris), 12 April, 13–14 August 1972; Bakdash's statement in *al-Hadaf* (Beirut), 20, 25 May 1972; Politburo statement in *al-Muharrir* (Beirut), 9–12 July 1972.
2. For the opposition's claims concerning Bakdash's leadership, see *Qadaya al-khilaf*, pp. 381–3; *al-Sayyad* (Beirut), 22 June 1972; Politburo statement in *al-Muharrir*, 10, 12 July 1972.
3. For previous instances, see M. S. Agwani, *Communism in the Arab East* (Bombay: Asia Publishing House, 1969), p. 102; W. Z. Laqueur, *Communism and Nationalism in the Middle East* (London: Routledge & Kegan Paul, 1956), p. 156.
4. Such feelings were alluded to in *al-Hawadith* (Beirut), 8 February 1963, and in Politburo member Yusuf Faysal's interview in *al-Sayyad*, 15 June 1972.
5. For the attitude of Moscow, and for the Chinese efforts concerning the Palestinian organizations in those years, see Robert O. Freedman, *Soviet Policy toward the Middle East since 1970* (New York: Praeger, 1978), pp. 36–7, 67–8; Galia Golan, 'Soviet–PLO relations', *Jerusalem Quarterly* (Summer 1980), pp. 121–2; *al-Nahar Arab Report* (Beirut), 16 March 1970.
6. See Naji 'Allush, 'Al-ahzab al-shuyu'iyya al-'arabiyya wal-qadiyya al-filastiniyya ba'd 'udwan 1967', *Shu'un Filastiniyya* (September 1971), pp. 158–9; Usama al-Ghazzi, 'Azmat al-hizb al-shuyu'i al-suri wal-qadiyya al-filastiniyya; dirasa muqarina ma' ba'd al-ahzab al-shuyu'iyya al-'arabiyya', *Shuoun Filastiniyya* (August 1972), pp. 128–30.
7. For the developments in the Lebanese party, see Agwani, *Communism in the Arab East*, pp. 230–1; Richard V. Allen (ed.), *Yearbook on International Communist Affairs 1968* (Stanford, Calif.: Hoover Institution Press, 1969), pp. 373, 376; 'Allush, 'Al-ahzab', pp. 161–2; A. Flores, 'The Arab CPs and the Palestine problem', *Khamsin*, no. 7 (1980), pp. 29–34; Ghazzi, 'Azmat al-hizb', pp. 131–2; Richard F. Staar, (ed.), *Yearbook on International Communist Affairs 1969* (Stanford, Calif.: Hoover Institution Press, 1970), p. 558; *al-Jadid* (Beirut), 12 April 1972. For the Jordanian party, see *al-Hayat*, 7 January 1971; Jordanian Communist Party statement quoted in *al-Ittihad* (Haifa), 23 February 1971; *al-Akhbar* (Beirut), 16 May 1971.
8. See Bakdash's article in *al-Akhbar*, 3 September 1967, quoted in W. Z. Laqueur, *The Struggle for the Middle East* (London: Routledge & Kegan Paul, 1969), pp. 304–16.
9. *Qadaya al-Khilaf*, p. 262.

10 ibid., pp. 322–5.
11 See S. Ayyub, *Al-hizb al-shuyu'i fi surya wa-lubnan, 1922–1958* (Beirut, 1959), p. 168; J. R. Swanson, 'Soviet and local communist perception of Syrian and Lebanese politics, 1944–1964', unpublished PhD thesis, University of Wisconsin, 1970, fos 115–17.
12 *Qadaya al-khilaf*, pp. 272–3, 399.
13 ibid., p. 247.
14 ibid., pp. 200, 216–18, 242–3, 246.
15 ibid., pp. 82–4, 322–3, 325–8, 363–8, 387–8.
16 ibid., pp. 84–5, 328, 369, 388.
17 ibid., pp. 218, 263; Bakdash's statement in *al-Hadaf*, 20 May 1972.
18 Robert O. Freedman, 'The Soviet Union and the communist parties of the Arab world: an uncertain relationship', in Roger E. Kanet and Donna Bahry (eds), *Soviet Economic and Political Relations with the Developing World* (New York: Praeger, 1975), p. 108; *al-Nahar Arab Report*, 16 March 1970.
19 *Qadaya al-khilaf*, pp. 369–89; Politburo statement in *al-Muharrir*, 11 July 1972.
20 See Naim Ashhab, 'To overcome the crisis of the Palestine resistance movement', *World Marxist Review* (May 1972), p. 75; Golan, 'Soviet–PLO relations', p. 131; Riad el-Rayyes and Dunia Nahas, *Guerrillas for Palestine* (London: St Martin, 1976), p. 35; Richard F. Staar (ed.), *Yearbook on International Communist Affairs 1971* (Stanford, Calif.: Hoover Institution Press, 1971), pp. 298–9.
21 For the party's policy toward the United Arab Republic, see Agwani, *Communism in the Arab East*, pp. 96–105; Ayyub, *Al-hizb al-shuyu'i*, pp. 184–5; Ilyas Marqus, *Ta'rikh al-ahzab al-shuyu'iyya fi al-watan al-'arabi* (Beirut: Manshurat Dar al-Tali'a, 1964), pp. 99–106, 108, 115, 120–31; Qadri Qal'aji, *Tajribat 'arabi fi al-hizb al-shuyu'i* (Beirut, n.d.), p. 164; Swanson, 'Soviet and local communist perception', fos 229–44, 272–319.
22 Ibrahim Bakri, one of the leaders of the opposition faction, was a Kurd.
23 See, for instance, *Qadaya al-khilaf*, pp. 287–8, 399, 413.
24 ibid., pp. 64, 68, 277.
25 ibid., pp. 412–13. See Middle East News Agency, 28 November 1971, monitored by US Foreign Broadcast Information Service, Daily Report, Vol. V, The Middle East and North Africa (hereafter cited as *FBIS V*), 2 December 1971; Politburo statement in *al-Muharrir*, 11 July 1972.
26 *Qadaya al-khilaf*, pp. 288, 415; Politburo statement in *al-Muharrir*, 11 July 1972.
27 *Al-Sayyad*, 22 June 1972; Politburo statement in *al-Muharrir*, 12 July 1972. But other opposition leaders admitted that they, too, had been partners to the party's policy toward the United Arab Republic at the time. See, for instance, *Qadaya al-khilaf*, p. 287.
28 *Al-Sayyad*, 15 June 1972.
29 *Qadaya al-khilaf*, pp. 213–15, 239, 261–2; Bakdash's statement in *al-Hadaf*, 20 May 1972, and *al-Sayyad*, 15 June 1972.
30 *Qadaya al-khilaf*, pp. 74–8, 281–6, 314, 320–1, 357–8, 413; Politburo statement in *al-Muharrir*, 11 July 1972.
31 The party's endorsement was quoted in *al-Nida'*, 24 April 1971.
32 *Qadaya al-khilaf*, pp. 287–8; *al-Hayat*, 25 November 1971; Politburo statement in *al-Nida'*, 26 November 1971. At least one member of Bakdash's faction (quoted in *Qadaya al-khilaf*, pp. 261–2) revealed

his displeasure with the federation (without asking, however, to present preliminary conditions).
33 Freedman, *Soviet Policy*, pp. 50, 55, 56.
34 See Emanuel Sivan, 'Marxism in the Arab world', in Shlomo Avineri (ed.), *Varieties of Marxism* (The Hague: Nijhoff, 1977), pp. 279–82.
35 For the theory and its embodiment in practice, see Oded Eran, 'Soviet perception of Arab communism and its political role', in M. Confino and S. Shamir (eds), *The USSR and the Middle East* (Jerusalem: Israel Universities Press, 1973), pp. 109–16; Freedman, 'Soviet Union and the communist parties', p. 103; Philip Mosely, 'The Kremlin and the Third World', Ishwer C. Ojha, 'The Kremlin and Third World leadership: closing the circle?', and R. A. Yellon, 'Shifts in Soviet policies towards developing areas, 1964–1968', in W. Raymond Duncan (ed.), *Soviet Policy in Developing Countries* (Waltham, Mass.: Ginn Blaisdell, 1970), pp. 290–1, 17–19 and 284 respectively; Uri Ra'anan, 'Moscow and the Third World', *Problems of Communism* (January–February 1965), pp. 22–31.
36 For the relations between the Communist Party and the Ba'th regime since 1966, see Avigdor Levy, 'The Syrian communists and the Ba'th power struggle, 1966–1970', in Confino and Shamir, *The USSR and the Middle East*, pp. 315–417.
37 For the full text of the National Progressive Front Charter, see Radio Damascus, 7 March 1972/*FBIS V*, 8 March 1972.
38 Bakdash's statement in *al-Hadaf*, 27 May 1972.
39 See Politburo statements and messages quoted in *al-Nahar*, 9 April 1972, and *al-Muharrir*, 10 July 1972.
40 'Problems of the National Liberation Movement of the Arab peoples' (an abridged text of discussion among Marxist theoreticians from Arab countries held in Prague), *World Marxist Review* (September 1964), pp. 61–3; Khaled Bagdash, 'The National Liberation Movement and the communists', *World Marxist Review* (December 1965), pp. 16–19.
41 *Al-Sayyad*, 22 June 1972; Politburo's statement in *al-Muharrir*, 10 July 1972.
42 *Qadaya al-khilaf*, p. 206.
43 Levy, 'Syrian communists', pp. 409–14.
44 For a detailed analysis, see Freedman, 'Soviet Union and the communist parties', pp. 111–24.
45 *Qadaya al-khilaf*, p. 208.
46 ibid., pp. 208–9.
47 Soviet remarks on the party's draft political program quoted in ibid., p. 159; R. Ulyanovsky, 'Marxist and non-Marxist socialism', *World Marxist Review* (September 1971), p. 126.
48 See Wasil Faysal's speech quoted in *Qadaya al-khilaf*, pp. 416–18.
49 ibid., pp. 268–71, 274, 237, 406, 409.
50 ibid., pp. 195–203.
51 Milorad M. Drachkovitch (ed.), *Yearbook on International Communist Affairs 1966* (Stanford, Calif.: Hoover Institution Press, 1967), p. 290; William McLaughlin, 'Will success spoil Khalid Bakdash?', *Radio Free Europe Research*, 6 May 1966; *Le Monde*, 13 July 1966. For some of Bakdash's activities in face of the Chinese challenge, see *Foreign Report* (London), 10 December 1964, 14 January, 24 June, 23 September 1965; *al-Kifah* (Beirut), 5 May 1966.
52 For these groups, see Allen (ed.) *Yearbook on International Communist Affairs 1968*, p. 782; D. Dishon (ed.), *Middle East Record 1967*

(Jerusalem: Israel Universities Press, 1971), p. 497, and *Middle East Record 1968* (Jerusalem: Israel Universities Press, 1973), pp. 737–8.
53 The only known exceptions were a visit to Romania reported in *al-Hayat*, 17 March 1973, and the somewhat sympathetic position of the Yugoslav press toward the newly established party, reported in Richard F. Staar (ed.), *Yearbook on International Communist Affairs 1975* (Stanford, Calif.: Hoover Institution Press, 1975), p. 610.

Afterword

Although the papers in this book were prepared by fourteen different authors for an academic conference, with no prior collaboration, they tend to give us a largely complementary picture of the problem at large: the relationship between the Soviet Union and the Muslim world. The issues discussed are varied, but the theme of the papers and many of the conclusions are often supportive of each other. While none of these probably is of a revolutionary nature, they bring new evidence to strengthen the trend of previous scholarship in this field and perhaps it is worthwhile to try to sum up some of them very briefly.

(1) The Soviet central authorities have not in practice implemented what they preach. There is virtually no equality between the Russians or Europeans, as a whole, and the Muslim elements in the Soviet population, either on the group or on the individual level. The Muslims' culture and way of life are considered inferior and backward, and as an individual he has unquestionably less opportunity, a lower standard of living, and so on. (Rywkin, Burg, McAuley)

(2) A number of the demographic phenomena and their concomitant social trends to which the Soviet authorities have directed their attention in the last decade or so continue to demand urgent treatment, so far with few results. (Rywkin, Burg, Feshbach, Henze)

(3) While the Soviet leadership has given recognition to the nature of the dilemma and made some attempts to solve at least some of its aspects, it has, generally, preferred to opt out rather than take decisive action. (Burg, Henze)

(4) Some marked short-term successes have been achieved by the Soviets in their language policy – an important feature of Leninist nationalities policy – but these do not necessarily mean effective russification. (Henze, Bruchis)

(5) The Muslim population, certainly in Central Asia and Kazakhstan where the greater part of the papers have concentrated their focus, has retained many of its specific characteristics, such as large families, closely knit, clan-like units, as well as many of its traditional socio-cultural,

socio-political and socio-economic priorities. (Rywkin, Feshbach, McAuley, Henze)
(6) The tensions that persist between Russians and Muslims and the isolationism of both populations in the Muslim republics have augmented the group consciousness of both, and led the latter to accentuate their separate ways of life and cultural traditions. The latter are not exactly national – as the term is defined by the Soviets – but, rather, Islamic, although not in the more rigid, conservative use of this term. While religious practice has unquestionably declined, some of its basics have been persistently adhered to. (Rywkin, Henze, Ro'i)
(7) The Muslims are indicating an increasing tendency to identify their national consciousness with Islam, reflecting among others a disillusionment with Marxism–Leninism as irrelevant to them as an alternative, substitute belief system or conceptual framework and with the Soviet regime as an optimal or even desirable political system in their particular socio-political ecology. Soviet theory and practice, despite the considerable flexibility of both, have demonstrated serious shortcomings in evaluating the inherent force and resilience of both religion and nationalism in the Soviet Muslim areas. (Burg, Ro'i, Rakowska-Harmstone)
(8) The use of the Central Asian example in Soviet foreign policy, in the context of the Soviet attempt to construct a special relationship with Third World client states (Rakowska-Harmstone), has had some serious backlashes. Notable is the fear that the Central Asians will not only fail to have a positive influence on foreign Muslim populations, but, rather, will be actively influenced by these – despite the material advantages the Soviet regime has brought them (if not in comparison with the Soviet European population, at least in comparison with foreign Muslim populations). (Ro'i, Rakowska-Harmstone, Bennigsen–Lemercier-Quelquejay)
(9) The complexity of the relationship between Moscow and its own Muslim population is not only reflected in, and has its impact on, Soviet foreign policy, that is, on its relationship with Muslim states abroad. It also has some very interesting parallels in the relationship with the forces of nationalism and religion in these states, both in the countries that border on the USSR (Ro'i, Bennigsen–Lemercier-Quelquejay, Weinbaum) and in the Arab world (Goldberg, Kehat).

(10) Pro-Soviet groupings and trends in Muslim countries are seriously handicapped on the domestic scene by the Soviets' tendency to subordinate both their own ideologies and their own friends to Moscow's interests, whether of a permanent, strategic or a provisionary, tactical nature. (Weinbaum, Kehat)

(11) The Soviets have, perhaps, learned surprisingly little from their own historical experience in building up relationships with their own Muslims and Muslims abroad, and many of the undercurrents that characterized these relationships over half a century ago continue to haunt the Kremlin. (Bennigsen–Lemercier-Quelquejay, Yaroshevsky, Volodarsky)

(12) The importance of Soviet historiography in understanding present-day Soviet policy trends and orientations, as well as shortcomings, is amply illustrated in its treatment of developments in Soviet and even Imperial Russian Central Asia. (Yaroshevsky, Rakowska-Harmstone)

Index

Entries in italics refer to tables.

Afghanistan 126, 128n., 162, 194, 197, 199, 201, 206, 263, 364; Afghan–Soviet cooperation 246–7; agreements with Pakistan 250; approaches to U.S.A. 246; autarchic nationalism in 245–6; Babrak Karmal 159, 169, 175n., 197, 199, 209, 211, 214, 247, 251, 254; Babrak Karmal's lack of credibility as a nationalist 254; *bi-tarafi* policy 246–7; clergy in 245; Council of Ulemas 164, 252; counter-revolutionaries 163; coup (27.4.78) 250; Democratic Republic 250–1; development assistance from Iran 150; Hafizullah Amin 162; 163, 209, 211, 250, 251, 253; Helmand water agreement 248, 249–50; inauguration of a communist party 247; Islam and 162–3, 164; Kabul 214; Khalq (People's Democratic Party) 247–50, 251; Khalq agents offend mullahs 252; Khalq–Parcham feuds 211, 251; leftist movements in 211, 245; liberal nationalists in 229, 245; Marxist party in 210; marxist regime 162; military challenge to leadership 251; minority groups in 228; Mohammad Daoud 212; 229, 246, 249–50, 251; *mujahidans* in 210, 213; mullahs' protest 252; Muslim Brotherhood 163; Nur Muhammad Taraki 210, 211, 247, 251, 253; opposition to Soviet military presence 254–5; Parcham 247–50, 251; policies pursued by Soviet leaders 208–14; predictions for A. 213–14; Pushtuns 208–9, 228, 245, 248; religion in 210–11; revolution in 149, 152, 158; slaughter of tribal aristocracy 209; Soviet attitude to 162–3, 166–7, 227, 244–5; Soviet military presence 254–5; Soviets move against Amin 253–4; Soviet treatment of army 212–13; strains of nationalism in 252, 254, 255–8; Sunni Muslim leadership 229–30; Taraki-Amin regime turn to Soviets 252–3; terror and liberalism 213; unrest in 248; Zahir Shah 247, 249

Afghanistan 1917–21: Anglo-Afghan agreement 221–3; antimonarchic groups 220–1; Bolshevik aim of sovietizing A. 221; Brest-Litovsk peace treaty 215; British representatives in Kabul 218–19; differences between Amanullah and Moscow 219, 220; Emir Amanullah 216, 217, 218, 219; first Afghan mission to Moscow 218; first Soviet ambassador in Kabul 218; General Muhammed Vali Khan 217, 218; Great Britain recognizes independence 217; Lenin on 218; Mahmud Tarzi 219, 221–2; Moscow's desire to open consulates 222, 223; Moscow's support of A. independence 216–17; murder of Emir Khabibullah 216; Raskol'nikov, Soviet ambassador 221, 222–3; Soviet–Afghan agreement 221–3; Soviet–Afghan talks 219; Soviet troops reach border 218; Surits, representative of RSFSR 218, 222; suspicions of Great Britain 215–16; sympathetic to Bolsheviks, 215; Third Anglo–Afghan war 217, 224n.

Agitator 163
Algeria 280, 284
Aliev, Gaidor 54, 198
All-Union Central Committee on the new Alphabet of the CEC USSR 134, 135, 137
All-Union Conference on Terminology 139
All-Union CP(b) *see* CPSU
Amanullah, Emir of Afghanistan 216, 217, 218, 219
Amin, Hafizullah, prime minister of Afghanistan 162, 163, 209, 210, 211, 250, 251
Andizhan uprising 206
Angola 201
Arab comunist parties 272, 284–6
armed forces 122, 211–13
Armenia 48
Arutiunian, Iu. V. 42, 45, 46
Azerbaidzhan SSR./ Azeris 48, 53, 64, 66–7, 70, *76, 81, 88,* 98, 105, 133, 167, 168, 181
Azerbaijan (Iranian) 232–6
Aziia i Afrika Segodnia 165
Azrael, Jeremy 48, 50–1, 52

Babakhan, Mufti Ziautdin Ibn Ishan 151, 152
Bakdash, Khalid 272, 275, 276–7, 278, 280
Balzer, Marjorie Mandelstam 50
Bani-Sadr, Abolhassan, president of Iran 242

294 The USSR and the Muslim World

Bashkirs 128n.
Basmachi movement 206, 207, 209, 214
Ba'th party 280–3
Belorussian SSR 5, 53, 68, *84*
Bennigsen, Alexandre 10, 64, 176n.
Bolsheviks *see* RSDWP(pre-October 1917) and CPSU (post-October 1917)
Borkovskii, B. 140–1
Bovin, Aleksandr 175n
Brezhnev, Leonid 49, 53, 194, 198, 265
Bukeykhanov, Kazakh Ali Khan 209
Bukhara 16, 30, 189–90, 208, 220, 224–5n.

Camp David accords 365
Caucasian wars 207
Caucasus 206, 207, 208
Central Asian model 186–7, 291; attributes of model 191–8; significance and effectiveness of 198–202; theoretical perspectives 187–9; validity of m. 189–91
Charrik Bey 25
Chechen revolts 206
Chelmsford, Lord, Viceroy of India 216, 219, 224n.
Chinese people's republic 169–70, 184, 186
CPSU (Communist party of the Soviet Union) 182–3, 210, 214; adhesion of modern elites to 209–10; aims for 'single indivisible Russia' 132; aims of 132–3; All-Union CP(b) 135–6; Central Committee 40; conferences and congresses of 49, 129, 130, 131, 132, 198–9; language policy 129–31; 132; lower-level positions in 48; Muslim cadres in 48, 53; Muslims fighting for 211–12; native cadres in 49–50; organization 46, *57–8, 59*; organizational secretaries 47–8; Politburo 53–4; prevent secession of non-Russian republics 131; Syrian CP and 283–6; upper- and middle-level positions in 46–7
Cuba 198, 200, 202, 205n.

Dadabaeva, S. 155–6
Dagestani–Chechen uprising 206
Daoud, Mohammad 212, 229, 246, 249–50, 251
Demchenko, Pavel 160–1
demographic problems 3–4, 63, 65, 69, 71, 72–5, 119–21; *see also* language and Soviet Central Asia: population
Desheriev, Iu. 139, 141-2
Dobbs, Sir Henry 219–20
Drobizheva, L. M. 45

Egypt 157, 199, 201, 262, 280, 284, 285; *see also* United Arab Republic
Encausse, Hélène Carrière d' 11, 13, 176n.
Ethiopia 199, 201, 205n., 263

Fahd Ibn' Abd al-' Aziz 263

Galiev, Sultan 184, 207, 212
Georgian SSR 48, 53
Ghuyam Ali 30
Great Britain: Anglo-Afghan agreement 221–3; Anglo-Afghan relations 216; entry of troops into Russian Central Asia 215; Iran and 238; Lord Chelmsford 216, 219, 224n.; occupation of Persia 215; recognizes Afghan independence 217; representatives in Kabul 218–19; Sir Henry Dobbs 219–20; Third Anglo–Afghan war 217, 224n.
guerrilla warfare 206–14
Gumilev, Lev 9, 11

Hafiz al-Asad 280
Horn of Africa 262, 263, 264

ideology: Khomeinism 149, 162, 166; language and 118–19, 122; nationalism and 123–4, 127, 230–1, 257; Saudi Arabian i. 261–2, 265, 266, 267, 269–70; *see also* Central Asian Model, Islam and Marxism–Leninism
Idris, Mahdum 28
incomes (in USSR): average monthly earnings *112*; composition of total income *102*; i. from *kolkhoz* employment *114*; i. from private activity *111*; i. of *kolkhozniki* and state employees 104–5; money i. 96, *111*; per capita i. 95–6, 97, *113*n.; per capita i. im Muslim republics 98–101; personal i. 96, 101, 103, *111*; total i. 97, 10, *102, 111, 112*
Indian Ocean 262, 263
Iran 186, 263; Azerbaijan province 232–6; Communist party (Tudeh) 231, 233, 234, 235, 236–8, 240, 241, 242; complains to U.N. about USSR 234; Evgenyi Primakov on 166; Farsi-speakers 228; fundamentalists 241; 242; growing opposition to Shah 240; Islamic republican Party 243; Kurdish People's Republic (Mahabad) 232–5; minority groups in 228; Mohammad Mossadeq 228, 234; Mohammad Reza Shah 160, 229, 238–40; National Front in 228, 229, 236–8, 239; oil nationalization 236; oil question 234, 235; Persia 215; post-revolutionary I. 241–4; President Bani-Sadr 242; relations with USA 236, 237, 238, 242; relations with USSR 239–40, 244; revolution in 149, 152, 157, 158, 160, 240–1; Reza Shah 233; Shiism in 160, 229; Shiite clergy 160, 161; Soviet attitude to 149, 160, 161, 162, 166, 227; strains of nationalism in 227–32; US

hostages 242; *see also* Khomeini, Ayatollah
Iraq 109, 110, 165, 262, 277, 285
Isaev, M. 142
Isfendiyar, Khan of Khiva 20, 25, 38n.; abandons capital 26; alienates Turkmens 21; assassination of 28; Junayd Khan and 27; opposition to 24–6; reforms land-tax 20–1
Islam 8–9, 149–50, 196–7; 'anti-imperialist' trend 158; communism and I. 197; 'counter-revolutionary' 158; 'dialectical' view of religion 157; dichotomy of Soviet attitude to 171–2, 175–6n.; I. and Marxism–Leninism 155; Muslim Brotherhoods 164–5; Muslims of the Soviet East 152; press comments on 154–6; 'regeneration of I.' 159–60; Shiism 160, 161, 229; Soviet attitude to Islam at home 150, 151, 169; Soviet Muslims compared with foreign Muslims 151; Soviet fears of Islamic revival 167–8, 171–2; Western attitude to 150–1; *see also* Pan-Islam and Sufi Brotherhoods
Islam Khoja 20, 22, 36n.
Izvestiia 169–70, 177n.

Jadidism 206
Jews 64
Jordan 277, 285
Junayd Khan (Qurban Mamed) 23, 24–5, 34, 37n.; accedes to power 28; aggressive policy against Turkestan Soviet Republic 29; assassination attempts on 27–8; flees from Russians 30; flees to Iran 26; leads rebellions 32, 33; made chief commander 27; policy of 28–9; returns to Khiva 27

Karakalpaks 17, 19, 32, 123
Karmal, Babrak 159, 169, 175n., 197, 199, 209, 211, 214, 247, 254
Kaushik, Devendra 200
Kazakh SSR 41, 48, 49, 50, *57*, 64, 65, 66–7, 68, 70, 71, *76, 79, 81, 84, 88, 90,* 98, 10, 102, 181, 186, 207
KGB 47–9
Khan, General Muhammed Vali 217, 218
Khan Ishan 23, 24, 25, 37n.
Khiva 16, 17, 220, 224–5n.; alliance between Bukhara and K. 30; between 1916 and 1918 26; conquered by Russians (1873) 19, 20, 37n.; declared a socialist republic 33; dominance of Turkmens 28–9; downfall of 29–35; ethnic strife 16; Gendemin peace treaty 29; immigration of Turkmen tribes 18–19, 35; Islam Khoja 20; Khan Muhammed Rahim II 20; khans of 17, 18; land-tax reform 20–1; 'lendlease' of Turkmen horsemen 29–30; opposition to government 17–18, 22, 23–6; power sharing 27; purge of leadership 31, 33; reform in government 20; revolt against Khan Isfendiyar 17; risings against Soviet authorities 17; Russian intervention 30–4; Russian punitive force in 26; Russian troops leave 27; Russian troops move in 22; Takhta Peace 29; Turkmens in 19, 25–6; Turkmen *oblast'* established 33–4; Turkmen question 34–5; Turkmen Soviet Socialist Republic 33; Turkmen–Uzbek relationship 17–19, 20, 23–6, 28; water and land disputes 16, 17, 35n.; 'Young Khivans' 26–7, 30, 31, 32, 38n.; *see also* Isfendiyar, Khan of Khiva
Khodzhaev, Sagdulla Tursun 30
Khomeini, Ayatollah 149, 160, 161–2, 166–7, 229, 241
Khomeinism 149, 162, 166
Khorezm People's Soviet Republic 17, 30–4
Kim G. 161
Kirgiz SSR/Kirgiz 5, 17, 19, 32, 36n., 48, 70, *88*, 98, 136, 190
Kleer, Jerzy 195–6
kolkhoz 5, 102
Kommunist 192
Kommunist Tadzhikistana 155–6
Kosygin, Aleksei 190
Kumelah movement 233, 235
Kurdish People's Republic *see* Iran

language: acquisition of non-Russian second language 122–3; All-Union Committee on the New Alphabet 134, 135, 137; All-Union Conference on Terminology 139; Arabic 123; bilingualism 142; Bolsheviks' attitude to 129, 132–3; concern over non-Russian languages 140–1, 143–4; deficiencies in russification 136–7; elimination of Arabic words 138; equality of languages 129–30; lack of unification of Turkic alphabets 135, 137; 'language construction' 132; l. in the armed forces 122; l. policy of the USA 117; l. policy of the USSR 117–18; 126–7, 138, 140, 141, 144–6; Latinization policy 134–5; Muslim population and 118; native and second language *119*; perfecting alphabets 133; Russian l. 118, 119, 121–2, 123, 124, 127n., 142–3, 144; russification of alphabets 135–6; scientific Research Institute of the Languages and Alphabets of the Soviet Peoples 137; state l. 130; USSR Academy of Sciences, Institute of Linguistics 139–40
Lebanon 277, 285, 286

Lenin, Vladimir 129–30, 135, 182, 183, 189, 217, 218
Libya 158
Literaturnaia gazeta 164
Luxemburg, Rosa 182

Mad Wafa Baqqolov 23, 24, 25, 37n.
Mahabad *see* Iran
Marxism-Leninism 149, 155, 159, 163, 171, 174n., 187, 199, 241, 273
Massell, Gregory 12
Medvedko, Leonid 158–9
Mohammed, Reza, Shah of Iran *see* Iran
Mongolia 181, 199
Mossadeq, Mohammad 228, 236–8
Mozambique 201
Muhammed Rahim II, Khan of Khiva 20, 36n.
Muhammed Yusufjan 24
Muslim Brotherhood *see* Islam
Muslims Religious Board for Central Asia and Kazakhstan 151
Muslims (of Soviet Central Asia) 14, 153–4, 290–1; acquisition of non-Russian second language 122–3; in the ermed forces 122; attacks against the clergy 168–9; Chinese interest in 169–70; co-option of Muslim elites 12–13; definition of 'Muslim' population 97–8, 113n.; estimates of population of Muslim origin 63, 73, *94*; ethnic identity 9; family stability 4; identities and allegiances 10–13; importance of Muslim republics to Soviets 181, 183; language and 188, 119, 125–7; make the Hajj 151; managers 7; marriage 8, 9; members of the Politburo 53–4; migration of 121; Muslim cadres in party organizations 48, 53; native and second language *119*, 120, 121; nature of society 5; population growth 3–4; population of Muslim origin 72–3, *93*; quiescence of 52; radio broadcasts to 177n.; social mobility 6–8; Soviet fears of Islamic revival 167–8; Soviet Muslims as model for Third World 181–2, 185; vitality of 3–8
Muslims of the Soviet East 152'Muslim' Soviet Socialist Republics: composition of total income *102*; incomes for *kholkhozniki* 104–6, 114; incomes for state employees 104–5; living standard of 95, 98, 99–101, 105–6; living standard compared with other Muslim countries 108–10; living standard of rural and urban populations 106–8; per capita income 98–101; personal income 96, 101, 103, *111*; poverty level and 100; real wages 95; taxation in 98; total income 101–2, *111*, *112*; transfer payments 102–3

Naqshbandiya 206
Narody Azii i Afriki 157
nationalism 12–13, 227–32, 244, 254, 255–8
Nauka i religiia 154

October Revolution 182, 187
Oman 264

Pahlavi, Mohammad Reza, Shah of Iran *see* Iran
Pakistan 250, 252
Palestine: partition of 275–6
Palestinians and Palestinian organizations 274–5, 276–7
Pan–Islam 149, 150–1, 152–3, 156–7, 159–60, 167, 168, 169–72
Pan–Turkism 133
Persia *see* Iran
Persian Gulf 262
Politburo 53–4
Ponomarev, Boris 188–9, 192–3
Popovskii, Mark 44, 49, 60–1n.
Pravda 49
Pravda Vostoka 154, 155
Primakov, Evgenyi 166, 176n.

Qadiriya 206
Qosh Mamed Khan 30–1

Radio Moscow 153
Rashidov, Sharaf 190
Raskol'nikov, F. F. 221, 222–3
Reisner, Petr 208
religion 157, 158
Riyad al-Turk 272, 273
Romania 184–5
RSFSR 5, 66, 68
Russian Communist Party (Bolsheviks; ACP(b)) *see* CPSU
Russian Orthodox Church 8, 9
Russian Social Democratic Workers' Party (RSDWP) 129, 130
Ryskulov, Turar 207

Sadeq, Molavi Abdul Aziz 164
Sa'ud al Faisal, Prince 266, 268, 269
Saudia Arabia 109, 110; attends Arab summit conference 265; boycott of Moscow Olympics 267; Brezhnev message to 265; concern over Oman 264; dilemmas of Saudi attitude to USSR 269–70; factors determining international relationships 261; Fahd Ibn' Abd al-'Aziz 263, 266–7, 268; fear of antagonizing USSR 268–9; fears of communism 261; fears of Soviet encirclement 262–3, 264; improving relations with USSR 266–7; lack of USA support 264, 268, 269, 270; modifies

attitude towards USSR 265, 266; perception of the USSR 261, 269; relations with USSR after Afghanistan invasion 267–8; Sa'ud al Faisal 266, 268, 269; Saudi media on USSR 262, 263; view of Iranian revolution 263–4
Scientific Research Institute of the Languages and Alphabets of the Soviet Peoples 137
Shafiq, Mussa 248
Shah Murad Bakshi 30
Shamil, Imam 206, 214
Slavic Soviet Republics 65, *79*
Slavs 3
Somalia 199, 201, 263
South Yemen (PDRY) 158, 174n., 201, 262, 264
Sovetskaia Kirgiziia 155
Soviet Central Asia 3, 17, 29–35, 57–8, 98, 189, 198; age distribution 67, 82–3; agriculture 5; allegiances 9–13; anti-Russian movement 134; birth rate 65, 69, *79*; cadres 40, 41, 44–5; Central Asians in social elite 44; Central Asian press 168; central leadership and natives 49; death rates 67–8, *84*; development of native elite 41–6; economy of 13, 95; economic development in 43, 54–5; education 6–7, 41, 43, 133; estimates of population 66–7, 74, *81, 94*; frictions between natives and Russians 49; infant mortality rates 67–8, *85, 86*; inter-ethnic hostility 45–6; inter-ethnic tensions in 53; international relevance of 195; Jerzy Kleer on 195–6; Latinization policy 134–5; mass party membership 46; as model for Third World 181–2, 185, 291–2; nationalist and religious identification 168; native participation in 1920s 47; 'nativisation' 40, 41, 43, 48, 54; need for greater security 167; number and distribution of Central Asians 72, *90*; participation in modern Soviet society 40–2; private initiative in 4–6, 8; purges in 42; retention of native culture 50–1; role of S.C.As in Third World 205n.; 'scientific workers' in 43, 47; size of families 69–70, *87*; Soviet leadership and native cadres 52–5; Soviet policy in 41; transition to socialism 189–91; upward mobility 45, 51; vitality of 3–8; *see also* Central Asian Model; Muslims (of Soviet Central Asia); Tadzhik SSR; Turkmenian SSR; Uzbek SSSR
Soviet Central Asia: Population 3–4, 8, 72, 74–5, *92*, 120–1; age distribution 67, *82–3*; birth rate 65, *79*; birth rate in Uzbekistan by nation 65–6, *79*; birth rate by nationality 66, *80*; death rate 67–8, *84*; difference between Muslim and Russian growth rates 63, 64, 120; estimated and projected natural increase 69, *87*; individual nationality expectations of fertility 70, *89*; infant mortality rate 68–9, *85, 86*; Muslim population by nationality and language group 64–5, *76–8*; number and distribution of Central Asians and Kazakhs 72, *90*; number and growth of p. 73–4, *94*; p. of Muslim origin 72–3; *93*; rural p. 72, *91*; size of families 69–70, *87*; urban p. 72, *92*; use of data 64
Soviet constitution 131
Soviet foreign policy 201–2; Afghan–Soviet co-operation 246–7; Afghanistan and 220–1, 227, 244–5; attempts to contact the Saudis 265; Azerbaijan province 232–6, 246; change of policy 262; dissatisfaction with Daoud government 249–50; economic agreements with Afghanistan 251; encounters with nationalism 227–32, 244, 252, 254, 255–8; favours Pachamis 254; help to Parcham leaders 251; implementation of central Asian Model 199; interest in colonial countries 182, 186; Iran and 227, 232–3, 238–9; Iranian National Front and 236–8; Iranian revolution and 240–1; Kurdish region and 232–5; lack of political solution in Afghanistan 255; Lenin and 182, 183–4; long-term objectives in Iran 244; military presence in Afghanistan 254; Moscow and revolutionary movements 183; motives and goals in the Middle East 226–7; move against Amin 253–4; Muslim as a model for Third World 181–2, 185, 291–2; oil concessions in Iran 234; public overtures to Saudi Arabia 265–6; reception of Soviet model 200; relations with Khomeini's Iran 244; relations with Shah 239–40; respect for Afghan sovereignty 246; revaluation of Third World policies 184–5; Saudi reaction to invasion of Afghanistan 267–8; Sino–Soviet conflict 184; Soviet advisers in Egypt and Somalia 199; states of 'socialist orientation' 192, 200–2; Taraki–Amin regime turns to Soviets 252–3; *see also* Central Asian Model
Soviet policy: guerrilla warfare: cautious co-operation with official Islam 207, 210–11; cities against countryside 207, 209; co-option of national elites 207, 209–10; elimination of Sufi brotherhoods 207; mistrust of fellow-travellers 207, 211; mistrust of native armed forces 207; alternate use of terror and liberalism 208,

213; utilization of ethnic-religious rivalries 207, 208–9
sovkhoz 5
Sudan 284, 285
Sufi brotherhoods 24, 37n., 206, 207, 210 *see also* Naqshbandiya and Qadiriya
Sufi *ishans* 23–5, 29
Sukhomlinov, V. A., Minister of War 21–2
Surits, Ia Z. 218
Suslov, Mikhail 188
Susokolov, A. A. 46
Syria 158, 164, 262, 274
Syrian Communist Party: Bakdash emphasises co-ordination with CPSU 283; Bakdash on Arab unity 279; controversy over Arab–Israeli conflict 275–7; co-operation with Ba'th regime 280–3; differences over Palestinian question 275–7; factions' views on tripartite federation 279; impact of 1967 war upon 274–5; interfactional conflict within 272, 284–6; Khalid Bakdash 272, 273, 275, 276–7, 278, 280, 281–2, 284; Kurds as party members 277, 278; National Progressive Front 280, 282; nature of Arab communism 273–4; 'opposition' against co-operation with Asad regime 281; 'opposition' in favour of Arab unity 278; 'opposition' leaders 282–3; 'opposition' want independence from CPSU 283; Palestinian question and 274–5, 285; pro-Soviet orientation of 285–6; question of Arab unity 277–80, 285; relations with CPSU 283–6; Riyad al-Turk 272, 281, 284; Riyad al-Turk forms separate party 284; Soviet influence on 282; Third Congress of 272; Wasil Faysal 278, 281

Tadzhik SSR/Tadzhiks 3, 5, 48, 70, *88*, 98, 105, 186
Taraki, Nur Muhammad 210, 211, 247, 251
Tarzi, Mahmud 219, 221–2
Tatar ASSR 45, 64–5, *76*, 98
Third World 181–5
Transcaucasia 5, 68
Tudeh *see* Iran
Turkestan 16, 20, 21, 29, 30, 31

Turkey 110
Turkmenian SSR 98, 186, 189
Turkmens (and Khiva) 34–5; declare war on Isfendiyar Khan 25–6; dominance of 28–9; elders (Kedhuda) 17, 18, 19, 25, 34; immigration into Khiva 18–19; Junayd Khan and 23; land-tax reform and 20–1; 'lendlease' of Turkmen horsemen 29–30; *muhirdars* 18, 19; revolt of the Ts. 19; revolts against government 32; rise of the Turkmens 26; Russians and 31–2; T.-Uzbek dialogue 32–3; T.-Uzbek relationship 17, 19–20, 28; Turkmen *oblast'* established 33

Ukrainian SSR 5, 53, 64, 68, *84*
United Arab Republic 274, 277, 278, 284
USA 166, 167; lack of support for Saudi Arabia 264, 268, 269, 270; relations with Iran 236, 237, 238; U.S. embassy hostages 242
USSR Academy of Sciences: Institute of Linguistics 139–40; Institute of Oriental Studies 157
Uzbek SSR/Uzbeks 3, 5, 13, 40–1, *59*, 64, *76*, 98, 181; birth rate by nationality 65–6, *79*; cadres in party organization 46–7; conflicting allegiances 10–11; Islam and 154; Russians in 136; scientific workers in 43, *56*; showcase for Afro-Asian visitors 186; taxation in 13; Us. in lower levels of party *apparat* 48, 49; Us. in social elite 43
Uzbeks (and Khiva): ethnic self-destruction 16; provincial bureaucracy 23–4; U.-Turkmen dialogue 32–3; U.-Turkmen relationship 17, 19, 20, 28

Vietnam 198, 201
Vinogradov, V. 139
Volga region 207–8

welfare colonialism 13–14

Young Burharans 208, 209, 211
Young Khivans *see* Khiva

Zand, Mikhail 11, 12

CARLETON LIBRARY SERIES

The Carleton Library Series publishes books about Canadian economics, geography, history, politics, public policy, society and culture, and related topics, in the form of leading new scholarship and reprints of classics in these fields. The series is funded by Carleton University, published by McGill-Queen's University Press, and is under the guidance of the Carleton Library Series Editorial Board, which consists of faculty members of Carleton University. Suggestions and proposals for manuscripts and new editions of classic works are welcome and may be directed to the Carleton Library Series Editorial Board c/o the Library, Carleton University, Ottawa KIS 5B6, at cls@carleton.ca, or on the web at www.carleton.ca/cls.

CLS *board members*: John Clarke, Ross Eaman, Jennifer Henderson, Paul Litt, Laura Macdonald, Jody Mason, Stanley Winer, Barry Wright

236 *Trade, Industrial Policy, and International Competition*, Second Edition
Richard G. Harris
Introduction by David A. Wolfe

237 *An Undisciplined Economist*
Robert G. Evans on Health Economics, Health Care Policy, and Population Health
Edited by Morris L. Barer, Greg L. Stoddart, Kimberlyn M. McGrail, and Chris B. McLeod

238 *Wildlife, Land, and People*
A Century of Change in Prairie Canada
Donald G. Wetherell

239 *Filling the Ranks*
Manpower in the Canadian Expeditionary Force, 1914–1918
Richard Holt

240 *Tax, Order, and Good Government*
A New Political History of Canada, 1867–1917
E.A. Heaman

241 Catharine Parr Traill's *The Female Emigrant's Guide*
Cooking with a Canadian Classic
Edited by Nathalie Cooke and Fiona Lucas

242 *Tug of War*
Surveillance Capitalism, Military Contracting, and the Rise of the Security State
Jocelyn Wills

243 *The Hand of God*
Claude Ryan and the Fate of Canadian Liberalism, 1925–1971
Michael Gauvreau

244 *Report on Social Security for Canada* (New Edition)
Leonard Marsh

245 *Like Everyone Else but Different*
The Paradoxical Success of Canadian Jews, Second Edition
Morton Weinfeld with Randal F. Schnoor and Michelle Shames

246 *Beardmore*
The Viking Hoax That Rewrote History
Douglas Hunter

247 *Stanley's Dream*
The Medical Expedition to Easter Island
Jacalyn Duffin

248 *Change and Continuity*
Canadian Political Economy in the New Millennium
Edited by Mark P. Thomas, Leah F. Vosko, Carlo Fanelli, and Olena Lyubchenko

249 *Home Feelings*
Liberal Citizenship and the Canadian Reading Camp Movement
Jody Mason

250 *The Art of Sharing*
The Richer versus the Poorer Provinces since Confederation
Mary Janigan

THE ART OF SHARING

The Art of Sharing

The Richer versus the Poorer Provinces since Confederation

MARY JANIGAN

Carleton Library Series 250

McGill-Queen's University Press
Montreal & Kingston · London · Chicago

© Mary Janigan 2020

ISBN 978-0-2280-0130-0 (cloth)
ISBN 978-0-2280-0210-9 (paper)
ISBN 978-0-2280-0267-3 (ePDF)
ISBN 978-0-2280-0268-0 (ePUB)

Legal deposit third quarter 2020
Bibliothèque nationale du Québec

Printed in Canada on acid-free paper that is 100% ancient forest free (100% post-consumer recycled), processed chlorine free

Funded by the Government of Canada / Financé par le gouvernement du Canada

Canada Council for the Arts / Conseil des arts du Canada

We acknowledge the support of the Canada Council for the Arts.

Nous remercions le Conseil des arts du Canada de son soutien.

Library and Archives Canada Cataloguing in Publication

Title: The art of sharing : the richer versus the poorer provinces since confederation / Mary Janigan.
Names: Janigan, Mary, author.
Series: Carleton library series ; 250.
Description: Series statement: Carleton library series ; 250 | Includes bibliographical references and index.
Identifiers: Canadiana (print) 20200189956 | Canadiana (ebook) 20200190008 | ISBN 9780228002109 (paper) | ISBN 9780228001300 (cloth) | ISBN 9780228002673 (ePDF) | ISBN 9780228002680 (ePUB)
Subjects: LCSH: Transfer payments—Canada—History. | LCSH: Canada—Economic policy. | LCSH: Canada—Economic conditions.
Classification: LCC HJ795.A1 J36 2020 | DDC 336.1/850971—dc23

This book was typeset by True to Type in 10.5/13 Sabon

To Tom Kierans

Always

Contents

Acknowledgments ix
Introduction 3

1 Sharing in Australia and Depression-Era Canada, 1935–38   15
2 The Poorer Provinces Stake Their Claims, 1867–1919   39
3 The Maritime Provinces Lead the Way for Canada – *and* Australia, 1919–30   57
4 The Poorer Endanger the Richer, 1930–35   79
5 King Stalls as the Depression Continues, 1935–37   103
6 The Poorer versus the Richer at the Royal Commission, 1937–40   135
7 Inequality in Wartime, 1940–44   175
8 Mackenzie King's Last Showdowns, 1945–48   215
9 The Compromise, 1948–57   247

Conclusion   289
Notes   299
Bibliography   377
Index   399

Acknowledgments

In fairness, everyone warned me: a thesis is a long, tough journey. Without help along the way, it could even be impossible. I was foolhardy, but I was also fortunate. So many people across Canada and Australia were there as I plodded through the archival records. They were often baffled and bemused by the topic: "You want to write about fiscal arrangements?" But they abetted the quest. And I am so grateful. Many of those same people were also there when I wanted to turn the thesis into a readable book that could help everyone to see what I saw: equalization is hugely important.

First, there was the invaluable academic assistance. At York University, historian Jennifer Stephen patiently supervised the initial journey, pushing the boundaries of the analysis. I later benefited from the exceedingly helpful insights of York University historian Marcel Martel and political scientist Ann Porter. All three steered me in directions that deepened the breadth of the thesis. Historian Shirley Tillotson at Dalhousie University added final polish and clarity to the work.

When I first decided on the topic, Queen's University political economist Tom Courchene delivered a care-package of his books and articles on fiscal federalism. He and his spouse Margie were endlessly encouraging, especially in times of dejection. Queen's University social policy analyst Keith Banting provided the heartening confirmation that the topic would fill a gap in the literature. Carleton University historian Norman Hillmer found time to provide information about the Skelton family – and the Royal Commission on Dominion-Provincial Relations. Political scientist Stephen Azzi generously shared his startling files on the commission's secretary D.A. Skelton. Ryerson University political scientist Patrice Dutil added so many dimensions to my knowledge of Louis St-Laurent. At York University, Roberto Perin, Anne Rubenstein, William Westfall, Craig Heron, Carolyn Podruchny, and the late Myra Rutherdale were so thoughtful and astute. Ryerson University's Gene Allen taught a marvellous, eye-opening course on media history. And, what I shall never forget, health policy analyst Dr David Naylor encouraged me to leave my journalism job – and enrol in university.

The archivists were amazing. At Library and Archives Canada, Alex McEwen was so helpful from the start, and she performed a last-minute rescue at the finish. I am also grateful to Sophie Tellier (whom I nicknamed "Hercule Poirot"), Gilles Bertrand, Steve Irwin, Neale MacDonald, Suzanne Lemaire, Lucie Séguin, and Martin Bédard. At the Queen's University Archives, Heather Home and Susan Office were always there. Marta Dabros adroitly copied my selections from the John Dafoe Fonds at the University of Manitoba – and she even found an important reference to Australia. The librarian at the Douglas J. Sherbaniuk Research Centre at the Canadian Tax Foundation, Judy Singh, graciously provided documents that were no longer available online, as did Shirley Cardenas, the communications coordinator at the Institute for Research on Public Policy.

There were more rescuers. The library technician at the Canadian Tax Foundation, Theodora Todorova, obtained articles and books – and even helped to print one huge document. At the Bank of Canada, Katherine Macklem provided wisdom – and archivist Jane Boyko combed the files from the mid-1930s into the 1940s. She diligently uncovered key records from the desperate times in the Prairie provinces as well as the bank's crucial interactions with Australia. Barry Smith at the Public Archives of Nova Scotia cheerfully provided the report of the Royal Commission Provincial Economic Inquiry. And Jane Fry, the data services librarian at the MacOdrum Library at Carleton University, guided me through the records to gain access to past Gallup polls.

Through the recommendation of the National Archives of Australia, I found the remarkable researcher Glenda Lynch, who photographed lengthy Royal Commission reports and early Commonwealth Grants Commission reports that I could not secure online. When I went back to find more material, she copied books and additional Royal Commission reports. At the University of Saskatchewan Archives, thanks to the advice of archivist Cheryl Avery, Jasmine Liska copied the J.B. McGeachy Confederation Clinic columns. At the Scotia Bank Archives, Andrea McCutcheon supplied the *Bank of Nova Scotia Monthly Reviews* for 1937, 1938, and 1939. Sarah Ravanat at the Tasmanian Parliamentary Library was so gracious when I arrived unannounced at the Hobart Parliament House: she digitized all of the files on L.F. Giblin as well as those on his remarkable family, including his father William Giblin, the former Tasmanian premier. Patricia Finlay secured files at the Toronto Reference Library and York University's Scott Library; she also made an epic trip to Library and Archives Canada to secure additional Dafoe correspondence.

I also needed friends to pull me through. Some have even stayed friends. Former Massey College principal Hugh Segal and Donna Armstrong Segal have been amazing. I could not have lasted without the encouragement of Judi and Mickey Cohen, Sandra Martin and Dr Roger Hall, Heather and the Honourable Donald Johnston, Maria Helena Higino, Senator Donna Dasko, Marianne Miller, Helen Burstyn, Lorna Marsden and Edward Harvey, Joy and David Garrick, Kaye Fulton, Joyce and Darcy McKeough, Liz Herron, Ann Shortell and Herb Solway, public relations wizard Marcia McClung and Dr Franklyn Griffiths, Renata Kierans and Graham Lee, Maxine and Drew King, Diane and Peter Jermyn, Kathy Kilburn, Kathleen and Mohit Sahni, Robert Monzon, Anna Janigan, Michael Janigan and Patricia Finlay, Carol Goar, Dr Lloyd Brown-John, Patricia Treble, and the amazing Angela Ferrante and Michael Gerard. So many people have held my paw that I feel torn singling out a few.

I am so grateful to McGill-Queen's University Press executive director Philip Cercone, managing editor Kathleen Fraser, and the two peer reviewers who added so much. Copy editor K. Joanne Richardson was a meticulous lifesaver. My book agent John Pearce has been inspired and inspiring. (Thank you for being there, John!)

Most of all, I would like to thank my extraordinary husband, the polymath Tom Kierans, whose belief in me has never flagged – even as I lost faith in myself.

THE ART OF SHARING

Introduction

With his white shirt tugged open at the collar and an Alberta flag on the wall behind his head, Jason Kenney was preaching the gospel of grievance. The leader of the United Conservative Party was amiable, occasionally almost folksy. But his message was designed to arouse Albertans' ire. "Alberta only ever pays into the equalization system," Kenney declared, singling out the federal program that supports the poorer provincial governments. Alberta was contributing billions of dollars to the equalization plan, while Quebec pocketed roughly $12 billion in 2017 alone. "This just doesn't make sense," Kenney declared, looking straight at the camera, frowning, and briefly shaking his head. "We are in a recession and are sending money to a province that is in a period of growth."[1]

The veteran politician knew that his denunciation was not quite true. Alberta taxpayers – *not* the provincial government – send money for equalization to Ottawa, which distributes it to the poorer provincial governments. In fact, *all* taxpayers, including those from Quebec, send money to Ottawa to fund equalization: more than $20 billion in 2020–21, with more than 60 percent earmarked for Quebec. But the former federal cabinet minister, who once cordially welcomed new Canadians as minister of citizenship and immigration, has been leaner and edgier in his provincial role. His election victory in mid-April 2019 has not curbed his aggression towards Ottawa. The precise facts of equalization did not matter as much as the political message: Alberta's plight was unfair. Kenney demanded that Ottawa change the formula so that the payments to poorer provinces were less generous. Albertans did not begrudge assistance to other provinces in tough times, he added, but they wanted "a fair deal."[2] And they were not getting it.

It was an unsettling message. Equalization is the improbable glue that holds the nation together. It does not inspire fierce patriotism like a flag or a pledge of allegiance. It is not flashy. Money whisks between governments with a digital flicker. But those transfers create an east-west bond that is stronger than trade ties or cultural differences. Poorer governments know that when times are tough, Ottawa will contribute to their bottom lines. Wealthier provinces may resent the amount that their taxpayers send to Ottawa, but they know that federal funds will likely be available to them if their revenues drastically decline.

The problem in Alberta is that its troubled economy still has the capacity to generate more tax revenues per person than those of its poorer kin, including Quebec (the rather nightmarish formula calculates revenues in all provinces at hypothetical levels of taxation). Perhaps worse, in June 2018, Ottawa arbitrarily renewed the five-year formula for equalization without discussion, extending its arrangements to 2024. It was almost certainly a political ploy to avoid damaging discussions in an election year. It has created a phony fragile peace. Kenney's exasperated remarks, which he has repeated numerous times, indicate that the program could be headed for trouble, at least in the wealthier provinces. In late December 2019, Alberta treasurer Travis Toews took another approach: he demanded that Ottawa increase the pitifully low cap and qualifying thresholds on another transfer program that assists provinces in economic downturns if their non-resource revenues fall by more than 5 percent year-over-year and their resource revenues decline by 50 percent. Finance Minister Bill Morneau was receptive, noting that Saskatchewan, Newfoundland and Labrador, and Alberta were "going through difficult financial times."[3] But the tensions between the richer and the poorer provinces remain.

So far, even though most Canadians feel that their province or territory gets less respect and has less influence than it deserves, three-quarters of them support the federal equalization program. Fewer than one in five in this January 2019 poll oppose it. Environics Institute executive director Keith Neuman notes that support is weakest in Alberta, but that "even there, support outweighs opposition." The question was not asked in previous years so there is no direct comparison, "but in broader terms it would appear that support among

Canadians as a whole is probably comparable to what it was fifteen years ago."[4]

Now politicians such as Kenney are attacking equalization in inflammatory terms. Such continuing animosity in a so-called wealthy province could shift public opinion sharply. And that should be very worrisome for all Canadians.

Equalization is vital to the survival of the nation. But it can only continue if the poorer and the richer provinces deem the bargain to be fair. The grants ensure that the poorer provinces can provide vital services for their residents – such as education, health care, and road construction – without crushing levels of taxation. In effect, equalization tackles the economic disparities among the provinces – so that the provinces can ease the inequalities among their citizens. In theory, at least, that ensures that no poorer province loses taxpayers who have to move to richer provinces in search of better care. No richer province is inundated with people from poorer provinces in search of that better care. Workers move "for reasons which contribute to economic growth and development ... not for access to better public services."[5]

Ottawa sent the first equalization cheques to the poorer provinces on 1 April 1957. Such generosity represented a dazzling breakthrough in the almost century-old struggle to make Canada work. Finally, there was general agreement on the *principle* of sharing among governments. Few Canadians noticed. They were following dramatic events elsewhere: the difficult Suez Canal settlement, the right-wing riots in Paris over the ongoing civil war in Algeria, the turmoil in the Russian economy. In Toronto, Progressive Conservative leader John Diefenbaker was already campaigning energetically – even though a lamentably over-confident Prime Minister Louis St-Laurent had not yet called a federal election for 10 June.

So on that mild Ottawa Monday, no one marked the occasion with fireworks or flowery speeches. No one hailed the transfer program as the solution to decades of searching at home and abroad for a better way to remedy inequality in fiscal capacity among governments in a federation. Few remembered the generations of determined, often idealistic and occasionally eccentric Canadians who had fought for a fairer world since Confederation. Even fewer realized that Canada's close observation of Australia had provided the first crucial model for equalization, which the Canadian plan modified.

Equalization grants narrow the gap between the average per capita revenues that the poorer provinces could hypothetically collect and the comparable amount that the wealthier provinces could raise – that is, their so-called fiscal capacity. In 1957, they worked miracles. *Now* the richer provinces could expand their social programs for health care, post-secondary education, and welfare with the knowledge that the poorer provinces could also (just barely) afford them. *Now* Quebec could pocket unconditional federal funds that it could earmark for its own priorities (it had forfeited large amounts of money for its refusal to cooperate with Ottawa's postwar efforts to centralize revenues). *Now* Canadians could take a (very) temporary break from the struggle to preserve federal harmony. *Now* the provinces that resented Ottawa's intrusions into their bailiwicks could count on one reliable source of funding, which arrived without application forms or heavy-handed conditions and which was calculated using a neutral formula.

The effects were almost immediate. Equalization became the cornerstone of the expanding welfare state. In Europe, boisterous class politics had forced governments to create social programs to preserve the peace with the working class. In Canada, the welfare state "arose not so much as part of an inclusive national social contract among citizens but as a way of addressing interregional and interprovincial equity."[6] Inequality among governments effectively created as much pressure for the expansion of social security on Prime Minister Louis St-Laurent and his government as class conflict did in Europe.

The prime minister got little thanks and much trouble for his efforts. Although he viewed equalization as his proudest achievement in federal-provincial relations, politicians were reluctant to boast. The richer provincial governments, especially Ontario, resented the program: in late February 1957, Ontario, which was the only province that did *not* qualify for any equalization, complained that the upcoming transfers "will come to a large extent from Ontario taxpayers."[7] Many poorer provinces, such as the Maritimes, were reluctant to draw too much attention to their windfall – especially because some were unhappy with the size of their grants.

Indeed, few provinces, richer or poorer, were wholly satisfied when the enabling legislation passed on 31 July 1956. St-Laurent largely ignored those complaints, and he would eventually rue his decision bitterly. But no province refused to cash its cheque.

More than six decades later, in the confounding world of the early twenty-first century, equalization remains pivotal to the nation's survival. Most modern federations, with the unusual exception of the United States, use some form of equalization to create rough per capita equality in spending or revenues among their members. As political scientists Daniel Béland and André Lecours have argued, the United States has not embraced equalization because there has been no direct threat to its territorial integrity since 1865, and the idea of social citizenship is comparatively weak there. Instead, it uses targeted grants for specific purposes.[8] In contrast, Ottawa's program will distribute roughly $20.5 billion on a per capita basis to the poorer provinces in 2020–21. Although Quebec receives the largest proportion of the funds, "provinces such as New Brunswick, Manitoba, and Prince Edward Island rely more on equalization payments than Québec."[9] On a per capita basis, they get more funding. In New Brunswick alone, the grants represent roughly 20 percent of its revenues – which is a veritable bonanza.

But the crucial importance of equalization only becomes clear through an examination of the decades *prior* to its introduction. That past – from the battles over subsidies at Confederation to Louis St-Laurent's decision to resolve fiscal inequalities – adds relevance *and* urgency to today's debates. This history explains why the program was such an audacious breakthrough – and why complaints about unfairness, such as Jason Kenney's allegations, are so dangerous to national unity.

The history of equalization is the *real* story of Canada's coming-of-age as a nation in the twentieth century – and of its very survival. Then, as now, the operation of the federal form of government was a constant challenge. How could Ottawa and the provinces stay together amidst constant squabbling about which level of government collected the taxes and administered the programs? For decades, Ottawa insisted upon its right to collect the bulk of the tax revenues. The provinces took a dim view of that resolve, often equating federal control with a threat to their constitutional responsibilities and rights. They became more aggrieved across the decades as their taxes raised proportionately less money than did federal taxes.

The federation creaked along throughout the nineteenth century into the twentieth because provincial responsibilities were relatively limited – so their duties came closer to matching their revenues. The richer provinces would never have tolerated overtly unequal treatment of the poorer provinces when equality of the provinces was the generally accepted creed. The poorer provinces mostly scraped by – even into the 1920s – as their economies and societies changed. They could usually make ends meet through penny-pinching along with the federal subsidies that *implicitly* and, in rare instances, *explicitly* favoured them.

But the struggle for a fairer world intensified as provincial obligations escalated. By the middle decades of the twentieth century, Ottawa and the provinces could not escape their citizens' impatient, and often desperate, pleas for an expanded role for the state. Many Depression-era Canadians were desolate, stranded in bleak communities, often jobless and occasionally homeless, dependent on meagre relief payments to survive. Their churches were overwhelmed. Their extended families often lived far away. But which state should act – and what should it do? Which level of government should pocket the revenues – and which level of government should administer the programs? The very questions provoked deep divisions along linguistic, provincial, religious, ethnic, gender, and class lines. Governments fought vehemently over revenues and responsibilities. Citizens debated the rights that they could and should expect from those governments. Almost everyone had a view.

But few recognized the fundamental issue: the fiscal inequalities among the provinces meant that the poorer provinces could not afford the extra costs for social care. The richer provincial governments argued that they had barely enough money for their own programs. The poorer provinces blamed the very act of Confederation, coupled with Ottawa's ongoing policies, for their plight. Quebec viewed any federal spending on social programs as a threat to its distinct identity: the Roman Catholic Church provided many educational and social services (later, as the provincial government assumed oversight of those services, it prudently guarded its turf).

Ottawa did not accept that the huge cultural and social differences among the provinces precluded the imposition of strong central control over the collection of revenues or the administration of social programs. The federation skittered along with ad hoc loans and grants to the poorer provinces throughout the Depression – while Ottawa shuffled the examination of revenues and responsibilities to the Royal Commission on Dominion-Provincial Relations, which became unexpectedly influential in later years.

THE KEY MODELS AND METHODS FOR SHARING

Answers took decades to devise. In the beginning, there were few models that could provide guidance – because there were so few federations. The first modern federal constitution was adopted in the United States in 1789.[10] Switzerland transformed itself into a federation in 1848 after a short civil war, and it revised that pact in 1874. Canada was also an experiment: although it seems remarkable now when federations are more common, Canada became the third modern federation in 1867. In 1871, the North German Federation of 1867 swallowed the southern German states. During the late nineteenth century, several Latin American nations, including Argentina and Mexico, adopted unstable federal structures that imitated the American model.[11]

For Canadian politicians and officials, along with a handful of well-informed academics and journalists, one nation stood out: Australia. In 1893, Canada's first trade minister and future prime minister, Mackenzie Bowell, led a delegation to the Australian colonies to find new markets for Canadian exports.[12] The framers of the Commonwealth Constitution consulted the Canadian Constitution throughout the 1890s as the six self-governing colonies negotiated their uneasy union, which debuted on 1 January 1901.[13] The two dominions did not often see eye-to-eye on trade policy or on their relationship with the British Empire.[14] But they always watched the workings of each other's federation, how the courts interpreted their respective constitutions, and how they handled crises. Despite the distance, as historians Margaret MacMillan and Francine McKenzie observe, the two nations "are close in ways that are difficult to quantify ... They pay attention, as they have always done, to what the other is doing, whether it is to disapprove or to imitate."[15]

Australia furnished a key model for equalization. When disgruntled voters in the state of Western Australia voted to secede in 1933, the central government created the Commonwealth Grants Commission, which transferred non-conditional payments to the poorer states. Federal politicians and bureaucrats – along with a handful of their more policy-oriented provincial counterparts – avidly followed that effort. In turn, Canberra watched Ottawa's often ineffective efforts to tackle inequalities among its querulous provincial governments. The close consultations between the two nations, especially during the 1920s and 1930s, were astonishing, and they remain largely unrecognized. But the few federal politicians and bureaucrats who understood the issue of inequality could not bring themselves to adopt similar unconditional transfers. Ottawa wanted to control most tax revenues because it viewed such control as pivotal to the survival of the federation – and its role in the lives of its citizens.

In wartime, Ottawa adeptly dodged the central issue of inequality. Instead, in 1941, it exerted control over three key sources of provincial revenues through the threat of invoking the War Measures Act. In return, it offered compensatory grants that were carefully designed to look equal – but which tacitly favoured the poorer provinces to a small extent because the richer provinces pocketed more money for each percentage point of tax and there were minimum base grants to the poorer provinces.[16] Ottawa then attempted to maintain such control in peacetime through the renewal of those tax-collection deals.

It was a dangerous course. Quebec flatly refused to allow Ottawa to collect its taxes in return for compensatory grants (this federal approach is called "renting" a province's tax revenues). Other provinces also resisted, conducting hardball negotiations with Ottawa to extract higher grants. Such stalemates from the early postwar years into the mid-1950s meant that Ottawa only introduced programs that it could run: Unemployment Insurance in 1940, Family Allowances in 1944, and expanded Old-Age Security in 1951.

Meanwhile, groups such as trade unions and women's organizations demanded that Ottawa pay attention to their members' escalating needs. Their clout remained relatively limited. "In comparison with other Western nations, especially European ones, unionization is low, the labour movement is divided into several federations, and the system of collective bargaining is decentralized," observes social policy analyst Keith Banting.[17]

But politicians could no longer ignore those lobbyists – even though they did not adequately address, let alone suggest remedies for, the fiscal inequalities among the provinces. Those inequalities were simply not an issue outside government circles. Advocacy groups put growing pressure on Ottawa for the expansion of social security, but they often did not care what level of government provided the programs. Few understood that one of the primary barriers to programs such as hospital care was the inability of the poorer provinces to afford them. The notion of equalization amounted to an arcane art that was largely espoused by political initiates.

FEDERALISM AFTER THE SECOND WORLD WAR

After the Second World War, federalism became an increasingly popular method for governing states with a high degree of diversity. There was a "proliferation of federations," including Burma (now Myanmar) in 1948, Nigeria in 1954, Austria in 1945, and the restored federation of Germany in 1949.[18] The change has been astonishing: in the mid-nineteenth century, "two-thirds of the world's landmass was governed by imperial edict" while, in the early twenty-first century, "This same proportion of the world is governed by federal arrangement."[19]

The federal structure allows for endless flexibility. Smaller geographic units can govern key aspects of their residents' lives while remaining part of a larger whole. In each nation, the divisions of responsibilities and revenues among member governments remain delicate balancing acts: each finds workable adjustments or it fails. Since Confederation, Canada's federation has been especially challenged.

The Canadian Constitution was drafted in the mid-nineteenth century when the state's social obligations to its citizens were limited – and there was little thought of expanding those duties. Under the British North America Act, 1867, the provinces assumed responsibility for property and civil rights, public lands, education, and hospitals. They could raise funds through direct taxation "within the Province ... for Provincial Purposes."[20] In turn, Ottawa handled the regulation of trade and commerce, the military, foreign policy, the currency, and "Indians, and Lands reserved for the Indians."[21] The federal government could raise money "by any Mode or System of Taxation."[22] Almost from the start, of course, the categories have overlapped and occasionally conflicted.

But federalism was probably the only viable model of government for a nation that was not simply a pact among provinces but a union of two peoples: francophones largely in Quebec and anglophones largely in the Rest of Canada (Indigenous peoples were largely ignored then). Provincial rights were particularly important to Quebec: the Constitution guaranteed Quebec's control of its civil law system along with the use of French and English in its courts and legislature; it also protected the education rights of Roman Catholic and Protestant minorities. In effect, the province emerged from Confederation with authority over those matters deemed essential to the preservation of French Canadian culture.[23] Equality among the provinces "did not mean that fundamental differences were not recognised."[24] In a shameful afterthought, Indigenous rights were only belatedly incorporated in the 1980s.[25]

In the decade after the Second World War, the strains among member governments were evident. Canada lagged behind other developed nations, such as Great Britain, Australia, and, to a lesser extent, the United States, in the expansion of social security. Perhaps worse, the contrast between Canada and Britain, which was a unitary state, and with other federations, such as Australia, was particularly marked. In Britain, there was no need for messy negotiations with provinces to institute social programs. Before the First World War, British leaders had introduced workers' compensation, old-age pensions, health insurance, and, "most extraordinary of all," the world's first compulsory unemployment insurance program.[26]

In federations, progress was usually made when the central government was free to take action or when strong lobbies could combine their voices across classes.[27] In Australia, from the beginning, the Commonwealth had the constitutional right to legislate on behalf of the elderly and invalids. In June 1908, legislation was passed to implement that right: it provided for means-tested age and disability pensions at flat rates from general revenue.[28]

In the United States, the efforts of unified women's groups that crossed geographical and class boundaries ensured that the nation's first publicly funded social benefits – with the exception of military pensions and poor relief – were mothers' pensions. Forty states adopted such laws between 1911 and 1920 to enable communities to support newly widowed mothers.[29] But groups that could not muster the necessary resources were largely out of luck: unbelievably, in 1934, more than half of American elderly lacked enough money to be self-supporting. State pensions were rare before 1930, after which thirty states adopted some form of old-age pensions, but they were "generally inadequate and ineffective," and only roughly 3 percent of the elderly received them.[30] It was only with the passage of the Social Security Act, 1935, that many elderly were given pensions with a reliable floor.

Many Canadians were uneasily aware of these trends, but their governments did not accept the need for equalization until the postwar prosperity of the mid-1950s (even then, Ontario and Atlantic Canada extracted steep prices before they would come around). Meanwhile, federal politicians were trapped amid conflicting pressures either to create national social programs or to respect provinces' rights to create their own (when the poorer ones could not afford them). The federation was floundering. And, in the beginning, Ottawa did not handle these challenges well.

The solution had been apparent for decades – if governments had been willing to listen. In 1940, the Royal Commission on Dominion-Provincial Relations called for the equalization of key areas of provincial spending – and official Ottawa still remembered that proposal. That Royal Commission scrutinized the efforts in other federations to share money among their states, and it devoted considerable attention to Australia. Prime Minister Louis St-Laurent had been the francophone counsel for that Royal Commission. And the civil servant who worked most closely with St-Laurent on the design of equalization was John J. Deutsch, who had been the assistant research director and then research director for that Royal Commission. Indeed, the prime minister was much more involved in the issue than most of his senior bureaucrats have maintained.

The timing was right – if not long overdue. As historian P.E. Bryden notes, "a system of universal regional equalization grants arose not only because of the lessons of the Depression and the regional inequalities surfacing during the 1930s, but also as a by-product of the move to universal social security measures, such as family allowances and, later, health insurance."[31] In fact, it was more likely that the move towards shared-cost programs with the provinces, such as hospital insurance – as opposed to federal spending programs, such as family allowances – really pushed Ottawa to act.

Ottawa had sufficient funds for equalization as it "began to tap into Ontario's rich fiscal capacity, and Ontario agreed on a political level to this form of redistribution."[32] The federal government eased away from the concept of a federation with an exceedingly strong central government: instead, equalization transfers were unconditional. The grants were sufficiently restrained – so that the poorer provinces could not become dangerously dependent on them. But they were still sufficiently large to knit the wealthier and the poorer states into the expedient and yet uplifting act of sharing among federation kin. Ottawa did not amend the Constitution: it did *not* formally shuffle the division of revenues and responsibilities – although it eventually tucked the principle of equalization into the Constitution in 1982. Instead, it simply passed enabling legislation – and sent out the cheques.

Equalization is a legacy from the Canadians who came home from the Second World War to make a better world. It was the culmination of nearly a century of ruthless competition for funds among federal governments and richer and poorer provincial governments: finally, Canada decided to save itself. This history explains how governments reached that solution, and why they should address grievances such as those of Jason Kenney and Alberta – *where* they are justifiable – before they destroy this heritage. These are dangerous times.

1

Sharing in Australia and Depression-Era Canada, 1935–38

The members of the Royal Commission on Dominion-Provincial Relations knew that their Australian star witness was brilliant and eccentric. But the sight of Lyndhurst Falkiner Giblin on a warm August day in Ottawa in 1938 was still startling. In his homemade red flannel tie, blue shirt, and collarless suit, set off against his dubbin-smeared boots, Giblin stood out in the sultry committee room on Parliament Hill. He had dressed as he pleased since his student days in the 1890s. And he was already a legend. The commissioners knew most of his lifetime highlights: Cambridge University mathematician, gold prospector, northern British Columbia lumberman and hunter, daring rescuer of stranded gold miners in the freezing Canadian North, Solomon Islands explorer, expert seaman, rugby player, orchid cultivator, sheep farmer, martial arts instructor, fruit grower, Labour politician in the Tasmanian Assembly, decorated war hero (Military Cross and Distinguished Service Order), former Tasmanian statistician, and friend of John Maynard Keynes and the Bloomsbury Group.[1]

They also knew that this pioneering political economist was a member of the Commonwealth Bank of Australia Board – even though the bank's suspicious elevator operators would not let the peculiar stranger into the lift when he first appeared.[2] Most important, Giblin was one of the three founding members of the groundbreaking Australian Commonwealth Grants Commission (CGC), which sent money from the central government to the poorer Australian states. His testimony was avidly anticipated: more than a month before Giblin's arrival, Royal Commissioner John Dafoe wrote to the CGC's chairman about their good fortune in securing "the benefit" of Giblin's presence, adding that Australia "has figured largely in the [Royal Commission] discussions."[3]

The Canadians needed to know how Giblin had brought fairness to the nation that they regarded as their sister dominion. In May 1930, Perth accountant H.K. Watson had founded the scrappy Dominion League of Western Australia, which called for secession to protest the state's unequal position within the federation. League founders had marshalled the political clout of sheepherders and wheat farmers, who were fed up with their shoddy roads and ports. Those Western Australians – some of whom were the feisty descendants of convicts transported from Britain in the nineteenth century – also despised the punitive tariff walls around the nation that protected manufacturers in the richer eastern states from competition while driving up the cost of imported machinery and consumer goods.[4]

Western Australia had been dubious about federation in 1901, but the Great Depression had brought ruin and resentment. In June 1930, when the Commonwealth government refused to lower its tariffs on imported secondary goods "while declining to grant assistance to farmers for the production or export of wheat and wool," the movement grew rapidly.[5] Outraged members argued that the federation had treated them unfairly from the start. They "generated a nationalist culture of poetry, political rhetoric, and even produced a national anthem."[6] At meetings, they sang rousing songs such as "This Bit of the World Belongs to Us."[7]

League members wanted to form an independent dominion like New Zealand within the British Commonwealth. In response to this fierce lobbying, Western Australia premier Sir James Mitchell called a plebiscite on secession for the same day as the state election, 8 April 1933. Voting in the plebiscite was compulsory – although voting in the election was not. The result was a majority of two to one in favour of secession.[8] (Two years later, a British parliamentary committee flatly rejected the secession petition because it did not come from the Commonwealth government.)[9]

Although Giblin came from a leading family – his father had been the first native-born premier of Tasmania – his roustabout early life had aroused his compassion "for the under-paid and under-privileged."[10] He had sympathized with Western Australia's plight: his home state of Tasmania also resented the central government in Canberra and the wealthier states that always seemed to have more money for services, even in the depths of the Depression. In March 1935, Tasmanian premier Albert Ogilvie had supported the Western Australian petition for secession. In February 1934, South Australia premier Richard Layton Butler had threatened to call a vote for secession rather than face default.[11] Australia had seethed with grievances – and Giblin understood the threat to social peace.

The Western Australia vote forced the unnerved central government, known as the Commonwealth, to take action. In July 1933, after consultations between economist Giblin and Australian prime minister J.A. Lyons, the central government established the Commonwealth Grants Commission to compensate the poorer states for their fiscal inequalities.[12] In effect, Giblin became "the intellectual founding father of the Australian equalization system."[13] He devised the commission's so-called "fair" formula, which put more federal money into the coffers of the poorer state governments so that they could do more for their citizens. The Australian scheme worked because the formula was really dependent on Giblin's meticulous calculations of fiscal need – what the states required for spending – including "the degree of economy in administration, the scale of social services and the severity of taxation."[14] He had added suitable quirks: no poorer state could get more money per capita for spending than any richer state could raise, no matter what the so-called formula seemed to indicate.[15]

The CGC did not immediately pacify Western Australia, partly because its first report in July 1934 was viewed as "condescending in tone…[and] attributed some of the state's distress to its own mismanagement, and actually made deductions from the grant" for objectionable policies.[16] But Labor premier Philip Collier gradually steered public sentiment away from secession. The hard-liners gave up when the British Parliament formally rejected their petition in November 1935.

Meanwhile, the CGC grants gradually mollified all poorer states because they now had enough money to make a visible difference in their citizens' lives. The richer states were satisfied because the amounts were not high enough to foster suspicions of dependency and wasteful expenditures (otherwise, *their* citizens would object to the thought of *their* federal taxes subsidizing their kin in the poorer states). True, the CGC could chide states – indeed, penalize them – for "past culpability as reflected in losses on loan expenditure."[17] But Giblin's quirky formula and the apolitical commission were almost above dissent. The brawny Australian understood the inequalities of income and opportunity that beset societies in Great Britain and the dominion federations. He had figured out how to share among federation members.

In Ottawa, his fascinated listeners – the members of the Royal Commission that would later be known as the Rowell-Sirois Commission – could scarcely believe their good fortune. They needed to learn from Australia's nation-saver how this unique system of equalization worked. In the 1930s, Australia, like Canada, was one of the world's few federations. How had Australia handled the resentments among state governments and citizens? Did the Australians know something that the Canadians could use to save themselves?

Something had to be done or this endless Depression could tear Canada apart. Without a cradle-to-grave social safety net, Canadians were still struggling with hunger, poverty, and ill health. Theoretically, Ottawa had the money to expand basic social programs. Barely. But Ottawa did not want to act: Prime Minister Mackenzie King was pinching pennies, partly to preserve the federal credit rating. The provinces were divided. Many provinces did not want to lose their constitutional right to care for their citizens' basic social needs – even if they were hard-pressed to do so. Quebec viewed the mere prospect of such federal spending as a threat to its distinct identity.

But no government had the funds to do much anyway. Richer provinces such as Ontario could barely afford their share of the relief payments that municipalities doled out to needy families. They resented the very idea of increased federal spending on the poorer provinces. Those poorer provinces, such as Manitoba, were teetering on the brink of financial collapse. They blamed Ottawa's economic and fiscal policies for their plight. Across the nation, politicians reproached each other for their continuing predicament – and their citizens' despair. As Royal Commissioner Henry Angus from British Columbia later recalled: "Canada was a profoundly discontented country, every region of which was obsessed with a sense of injustice and a sense of self-pity."[18]

Perhaps Giblin's advice could guide them in their search for answers.

CANADA'S DEPRESSION-ERA WORLD

The Royal Commissioners had led fascinating lives, prowling the globe in war and peace, looking for ways to resolve the century's challenges. Their times had been far from bland. Their formal attire at the commission hearings belied their adventurous minds. But, collectively, the commissioners now faced the most daunting task of their careers. In February 1937, Prime Minister Mackenzie King had created the Royal Commission to redesign the federation of 1867 for the benefit of *all* Canadians in the stricken 1930s. How were the finances and the economies of the Confederation partners really working? Months later, King elaborated on that request: the commission was to undertake "a re-examination of the economic and financial basis of Confederation and of the distribution of legislative powers in the light of the economic and social developments of the last seventy years."[19]

Few disputed the need for change. Surely there was a better way to share the nation's diminished wealth? Surely the nation could do more for the jobless? The unemployment rate had reached a staggering high of more than 19 percent in 1933. Ottawa had closed its controversial work camps for single, unemployed vagrants in June 1936 – but unemployment now hovered around 11.5 percent.[20] The survival of the nation could hang on the commission's findings.

On 8 August 1938, as the commissioners faced Giblin, their dilemma could be seen on city street corners, where ragged men and women still begged after almost nine years of economic misery. Small children skipped school to run errands for pennies for anyone who would hire them. Boxcars chugging across the nation were still packed with men who were scavenging for temporary work, no matter how arduous. For most Canadians, luxuries were faded memories. The middle class now lived with the financial insecurity that had plagued the working class throughout the decade. Canadians had endured the horrors of the First World War and relished the brief joys of prosperity in the last half of the 1920s. But the Thirties had been grim.

Threats were seemingly everywhere. As staff members of the Royal Commission later recollected, they were becoming increasingly aware of the seeming incongruity of their mandate in an ever-more-dangerous world – although they did not doubt the importance of their mission.[21] Flickering newsreels of goose-stepping Nazis confirmed that the main foe of the Great War was back with ominous ambitions. In March, German troops had invaded and absorbed Austria with little resistance. Chancellor Adolf Hitler had then moved troops to the border of Czechoslovakia on the pretext of safeguarding Germans in the Sudetenland. Canadians who had survived the Great War no longer believed that they were immune to those once-faraway showdowns.

The headlines provoked shudders. The Japanese army, which had invaded China in July 1937, was still slaughtering civilians in a brutally stalemated war. In Spain, the Nationalist forces of General Francisco Franco were gaining ground against the democratically elected government: Franco's Nationalist aircraft had just sunk a British freighter in an eastern port. British politician Sir Winston Churchill would later title the first volume of his memoirs *The Gathering Storm*, catching the ominous sense that so much was amiss on so many fronts.

Canadians found fun where they could during that difficult summer, often through American movies and American entertainers. They protested against the very thought that Winnipeg-born actress Deanna Durbin would elope in her next Hollywood movie – because she was only in her mid-teens in real life.[22] They gasped at actress Joan Crawford's separation from her second husband after less than three years of marriage.[23] On the morning that the commissioners met Giblin, Canadian celebrities, the four-year-old Dionne quintuplets in Ontario, were making front-page headlines because of throat infections.[24] That very evening, Toronto residents could "swing" to "Artie Shaw, King of the Clarinet" and his CBS New York Orchestra. Shaw played four nights at a waterfront club; women paid seventy-five cents for entry while men paid $1.25.[25] If Torontonians could not afford to swing, Christian Science Reading Rooms offered free access to the Bible, promising that it contained "the answer to every human problem."[26]

But there were few answers anywhere to the problems that most Canadians confronted: How could they pull each other through these brutal years? How could they share, or allow their sparse tax dollars to be shared, and remain confident that the recipients would not be wastrels and their money would not be squandered?

The Depression had shaken them and their governments out of their complacency. Many families now lived among strangers, scattered across towns and cities, dependent on the husband's weekly wage packet for survival. The loss of a job, however temporary, or the desertion of the husband could mean catastrophe. The needy were mired in poverty, and they often contended with poor health due to meagre food and flimsy housing. Cities and towns doled out relief payments or vouchers to families and single women – but they often disqualified single men. The qualifications for relief – which could be coupled with inspections – were humiliating. Ontario's York Township, for one, demanded that deserted wives take out an arrest warrant against their husbands when they applied for funds.[27]

Churches assisted their parishioners and sometimes other impoverished families. Donors knew that their gifts usually stayed within the parish. They could often identify those who received their food hampers and old clothing. They could even watch the recipients for damaging signs of dependency. But the recipients saw themselves as the objects of charity. They were usually among the so-called "unemployed employables" who had lost their jobs in factories or stores or offices. They spent their days in the futile search for any work at any wage while their families barely survived on relief and parish care.

This help was not their social right as citizens of Canada. Not surprisingly, both the donors and the recipients often had ambivalent reactions to these exchanges. Municipal governments and churches simply could not cope with the huge numbers of people who were adrift in this urbanizing and industrializing society.

THE PLIGHT OF DEPRESSION-ERA GOVERNMENTS

There was a cascade of misery. Many poorer provinces could barely ensure that their poorer citizens were fed and clothed. Their citizens could not even hope for adequate provincial spending on their wretched hospitals. Their children's schools were inferior: school boards could scarcely afford to buy supplies and pay teachers' salaries. Governments could only respond on an ad hoc basis.

Belatedly, many Canadians realized that senior levels of government were the only institutions that could help so many people with so many social needs. But the provinces, which were constitutionally responsible for social programs, were struggling to cover the interest charges on their debts and their portion of municipal relief. The federal government had more money than the provinces, but, even if it had wanted to act, it was clear in 1938 that it did not have the constitutional power to create such social programs as unemployment insurance (both the Supreme Court of Canada in 1936 and the Judicial Committee of the British Privy Council in 1937 had ruled against the constitutionality of most of former Conservative prime minister R.B. Bennett's New Deal package, including unemployment insurance). It would now take a constitutional amendment to introduce unemployment insurance, which would require the consent of all provinces. Ottawa contributed to the relief that other governments distributed – but it dodged many provincial and municipal requests for help.

It was an ironic standoff at this worst of times: governments lacked either the power *or* the money *or* an imaginative overview of the economy to help the helpless. None of them could win. Some might even lose power when they lost the trust of their desperate voters. There were ongoing protests, including the birth of the social-democratic Co-Operative Commonwealth Federation, which farm and labour leaders along with academics had founded in 1932. But Ottawa could only keep doling out funds for relief or temporary public works jobs. On the eve of the Depression, Ottawa had transferred $16.5 million in statutory subsidies, grants, and conditional subsidies to the provinces. By 1934, that number was $55.9 million. A year later, it was $74 million. In 1938, Ottawa was sending $104.3 million.[28] But the provinces were still scrambling for funds. What had barely worked at the turn of the century was now an anachronistic approach to the needs of a modern federation – as Australia had learned.

Most Canadians had abandoned their sunny delusion that this downturn was merely cyclical. But Ottawa had not yet embraced the theories of John Maynard Keynes, who argued that governments should stimulate consumer demand in downturns by spending strategically and cutting taxes. The politicians and bureaucrats at the very top of the Ottawa pecking-order could not be tempted to try them – although some were familiar with his work.[29] The economic causes of the Great Depression eluded most politicians and bureaucrats.

Even in the 1930s, however, the link between funds for poorer governments and the provision of social services for poorer citizens was clear to top politicians and bureaucrats. Premiers from the poorer provinces complained to Ottawa that they could barely afford relief payments, let alone find money for proper schools and hospitals. They certainly had no notion of expanding social programs that they could not afford – although they feared protests from their voters. But they also wanted to be able to perform their *basic* government functions in unruly times. A few exceptional premiers, such as Nova Scotia's Angus L. Macdonald, were deeply worried about their citizens' well-being. They, too, watched Australia, where approaches to inequalities among federation members were far more advanced.

But those politicians and bureaucrats could not even conceive of an *unconditional* federal program that would allow all provinces to provide reasonably comparable levels of services for reasonably comparable levels of taxation. The mechanism of equalization to apportion federal funds among the poorer provinces was less than two decades in the future – but it might as well have been a lifetime away. Remedies simply appeared elusive – an indication of how much Canada would eventually change.

KING TAKES POWER

Prime Minister Mackenzie King regained power in the fall of 1935, having promised little and doing almost nothing. He fended off his petitioners for more than six months through an early but inconclusive Dominion-Provincial Conference, at which he responded frugally to the appeals for permanent increases in relief from desperate governments. Then the dominos started to topple. In April 1936, Alberta defaulted on its bonds. A month later, in response to unanimous demands at the December 1935 Dominion-Provincial Conference, King finally appointed the National Employment Commission, which "would have supervision of unemployment relief and whose duty it would be by co-operation with public bodies and in other ways to find work for the unemployed."[30] This was a predictable ploy: prime ministers often promised studies to defuse tense situations, to suggest solutions that would validate their schemes – or to postpone any action. The employment commission was a stalling tactic that would return to haunt King.

The situation became worse. In December 1936, Manitoba premier John Bracken told Finance Minister Charles Dunning in Ottawa that his province was in desperate financial straits. He asked for a review of the fiscal and economic basis of Confederation. King hesitated. In mid-February 1937, the governor of the Bank of Canada, Graham Towers, told the prime minister that both Manitoba and Saskatchewan were on the brink of bankruptcy.

That got King's attention: more provincial defaults would endanger Ottawa's prized credit rating. The prime minister blinked. He extended temporary aid to those two provinces – and promised to appoint a royal commission on dominion-provincial relations to figure out what should be done. Then he dawdled again. He did not formally spell out the Royal Commission's terms of reference or appoint its members until mid-August 1937. He clearly hoped that the economy would improve significantly before he had to act.

THE COMMISSIONERS

King did not pick superstars for the Royal Commission, but the five commissioners were prominent people who grasped the enormity of their challenge. They could emerge as the new Fathers of Confederation. Or they could fail utterly. They did neither. What they did not anticipate was that their report would trigger so many wartime fights and figure in so many postwar debates. Nor did they realize that one of their key ideas would eventually become another model for equalization. They were daring. The commission was "highly creative in its time," and "it remains a remarkable storehouse of ideas and proposals about the characteristics of the Canadian federal system."[31] Their pivotal breakthrough on how to share among governments would inspire postwar politicians and bureaucrats. By then, only two of the five commissioners would be alive.

Their lack of superstar status probably played against them. As Bank of England advisor Raymond Kershaw, who was an expert on Commonwealth countries, confided to his friend, Bank of Canada governor Graham Towers, in early September 1937: "The scope of the enquiry seems wide enough, but I cannot help wondering whether the Commission has enough width of experience and weight of authority to produce and put over a report that will do justice to such fundamental terms of reference."[32] Towers replied that he was "afraid that there may be some foundation for the doubt expressed in your letter ... If so, the moral is that the weight of the report itself will have to make up for the lack of a name for outstanding business and financial importance."[33]

In the beginning, their chairman was the eloquent former politician Newton Rowell. The sixty-nine-year-old Rowell had been born on an Ontario farm into a family "rooted in the moderate Reform movement of Robert Baldwin in Upper Canada and the social conservatism" of evangelical British Methodism.[34] True to his heritage, Rowell wrestled with the woes of a brutal industrializing world. He had worked with missions for the poor in downtown Toronto. He cared about the less fortunate. But he was often on the wrong side of time. He had opposed Sunday streetcars. He had resisted any easing of the Methodist opposition to dancing, cards, and theatre. He would never work on Sundays. He was a teetotaler who vehemently advocated temperance. He would never accept a drink, no matter how much trouble his hosts had gone through to provide it: he had refused to sample a very old brandy that his Irish hosts had offered as a special courtesy – and he would not taste a bottle of Scotch whisky that a South African farmer had ridden all night to procure for his Canadian guest.[35] He was kindly, but "not always gentle."[36]

By 1937, Rowell was an elder statesman and a respected jurist. Although he had become an active Liberal in the mid-1890s, he had somehow escaped his partisan roots. In 1917, as the leader of the Ontario Liberal Party, he had moved from Sir Wilfrid Laurier's Liberals to Sir Robert Borden's wartime Unionist government because he believed fervently in conscription. There, he had served as the high-profile Privy Council president during the conscription crisis that had threatened national unity. At the end of the First World War, to the dismay of his more conservative Unionist colleagues, he had called for subsidized housing along with health protection and improved education for the poor. In 1920, he had left the cabinet, weary of the fray and probably unwelcome as a candidate in the 1921 federal election. In peacetime, he had concentrated on his law practice and strongly promoted the League of Nations.

He was an estimable man, curious about the world and regarded as incorruptible in difficult times. He had travelled to Australia in the 1920s, and he had been involved in the Institute of Pacific Relations. His commission colleague, Winnipeg journalist John Dafoe, who had huge influence in Ottawa, had advocated his appointment in a letter to Resources Minister T.A. Crerar in April 1937: Rowell had "practical knowledge of the difficulties of government, and the administrative difficulties which arise from our federal form of government ... [he] would make an admirable chairman."[37] Dafoe was right. Most Canadians lauded the appointment. British Columbia commissioner Angus even claimed that the commission owed "its procedure, its research programme and its status" to him.[38] That was an exaggeration – because Rowell had enormous help from commission staff, especially from the remarkable (and very eccentric) research director and anglophone secretary Alex ("Sandy") Skelton. But Rowell did understand that federations were perilous creatures that required constant attention. He also had acute political antennae. When he suffered a crippling stroke and heart attack in May

1938, the commission lost his crucial insights into how the real world of federation politics worked.

The role of Quebec commissioner had been more difficult to fill. For three months, Supreme Court of Canada justice Thibaudeau Rinfret had represented his province. But, before the commission's hearings could begin in Winnipeg in late November, he had resigned because of ill health. To replace Rinfret, King's trusted Quebec lieutenant, Justice Minister Ernest Lapointe, had consulted the francophone counsel to the commission, Louis St-Laurent. The future prime minister – who would later play an enormous and often unrecognized role in the creation of the federal equalization program – recommended Quebec City notary and constitutional law professor Joseph Sirois. When Sirois demurred, St-Laurent leaned on their long friendship to convince Sirois that it was his duty to accept the offer, even though he had "no particular interest in the work of the commission at the outset."[39]

Although Sirois did not know his fellow commissioners when he joined, it was a coup to have him. Within Quebec, Sirois was hugely admired for his expertise in constitutional and administrative law – he was also a Laval University law professor – and for his presence on top-drawer business boards. He brought "the prestige of one of the oldest legal firms in Quebec City and ... the seal of approval of the Quebec élite."[40] Although he was known as a Liberal, he had avoided the pitfalls of an active political life – along with the tough positions on federalism that politics would have entailed. His fellow commissioners realized that his political aloofness could be a benefit: as Rowell concluded, their report "would carry more real weight among the people of Quebec" than one that Justice Rinfret would have signed.[41] When Rowell became incapacitated, Sirois replaced him as acting chairman and then as chairman.

The western commissioner was that fiercely proud Canadian journalist John Wesley Dafoe, who had known virtually everyone in public life for decades. Born in March 1866 in southeastern Ontario, he was a self-made man who became editor-in-chief of the *Manitoba Free Press* in 1901 – and he would continue in that role until his unexpected death in 1944. He cared deeply about western issues such as lower tariffs and freight rates – and he had worked closely with *Free Press* owner and Liberal politician Sir Clifford Sifton during Sifton's lifetime. His influence extended across the nation: although he had made enemies throughout his long career, friend and foe respected him enormously.

More remarkably, he did not restrict himself to domestic concerns. He wanted Canada to grasp a larger role on the world stage: he was the chairman of the Institute of Pacific Relations (IPR) and one of the founders of the Canadian Institute of International Affairs. He travelled widely, although his only trip to Australia and New Zealand was in July 1925. His subsequent articles from that journey were collected in the pamphlet *Under Southern Skies*, and they attracted widespread praise from Australians and New Zealanders. "None has touched our problems so profoundly as you have," wrote Edward Cunningham, the admiring editor of the *Angus* in Melbourne.[42] Dafoe had carefully nurtured his contacts: he had remained in close touch with Australians whom he had first met at the Imperial Press Conference in London in 1909, and he continued to add to those connections throughout his career, including at IPR meetings in different nations.[43] Rowell's illness was "a very serious matter" for Dafoe: to handle the commission workload, he stepped away from his IPR duties, including an upcoming IPR meeting in Sydney, Australia.[44] With Rowell gone, he became "in effect ... the senior commissioner."[45]

He did not view himself as a centralizer or as a provincial rights advocate. But, even before he took the job, he had concluded that the Constitution was not working for ordinary Canadians and destitute provinces during the Depression. He was seventy-one when he accepted King's offer to become the western representative on the Royal Commission – but his fellow commissioners marvelled at his energy and youthful appearance. The calculating King had thought ahead in his choice of Dafoe as commissioner. As historian Ramsay Cook notes, the prime minister was serving notice "on the extreme proponents of provincial rights that their submissions would be met by a convinced nationalist."[46] In the end, however, King would get more of a centralizer than he wanted. As Dafoe confessed in a startling letter in early January 1939 to Australian academic and writer Sir James Barrett: "There must be a considerable strengthening of federal powers in some respects in Canada."[47]

The British Columbia commissioner was Henry Forbes Angus. Born in Victoria in 1891, his education had spanned disciplines, which brought useful skills to the commission. He had obtained a bachelor of arts from McGill University and a bachelor of civil law from Oxford University, served in the First World War in India and Mesopotamia, and then gone back to Oxford to get his master of arts and to become a barrister of law at the Inner Temple. In 1919, as an economist *and* a lawyer, he was teaching economics at the University of British Columbia in the political science and sociology faculty. When the commission started its hearings in November 1937, he was forty-six, "quite overwhelmed by the importance of the assignment" and unable to figure out why he had been chosen. In the end, he concluded that his British Columbia roots – that is, his "geography" – cinched his role.[48] He was too modest.

The Maritime representative, R.A. "Bert" MacKay, had also served in the First World War – in the ranks of the Canadian Field Artillery. Then the Ontario-born MacKay continued his political science studies at the University of Toronto and Princeton University. In 1927, Dalhousie University lured him to Halifax from a teaching career in the United States. He was, Angus would later reflect, "a wonderfully good colleague."[49]

He was also a controversial colleague – and he had been so well before his appointment. In October 1931, when MacKay had been the prestigious Eric Dennis Memorial Professor of Political Science at Dalhousie University for four years, he had written an article for *Maclean's* magazine about the recent Beauharnois Light, Heat and Power Co. scandal. That firm – in return for permission to divert the St Lawrence River – had contributed to the Liberal Party's campaign funds prior to the 1930 election. MacKay had concluded that both parties had "become pensioners of selfish interests."[50]

Conservative prime minister R.B. Bennett was outraged – and he was a governor of Dalhousie University. He threatened to resign if MacKay was not fired. Another board member, prominent Halifax lawyer James McGregor Stewart, supported Bennett – and warned that the university would lose large donations if MacKay remained. The administration stood firm – and MacKay stayed in his post. But the hard feelings between Stewart and MacKay still lingered when Newton Rowell appointed Conservative Stewart as anglophone counsel for the commission. In fact, MacKay would not even mention Stewart when he reminisced about the commission in 1963 – eight years after Stewart's death.[51]

But the forty-three-year-old MacKay did have a powerful supporter in *his* corner: Prime Minister King loved the essay that MacKay had written on the political ideas of his rebel grandfather William Lyon Mackenzie. MacKay had presented his research to the Royal Society of Canada in May 1936 – and it had appeared in the *Canadian Journal of Economics and Political Science* in February 1937. He had concluded: "At heart Mackenzie always remained a Puritan with a mission."[52] By October 1937, King was referring to that essay in his diary. Fourteen months later, when the prime minister invited the commissioners to dine at Laurier House, he would virtually purr: "I was particularly pleased to have the talk I did with MacKay about my grandfather, whom we both greatly admire."[53]

THEIR WORK COMMENCES

Once appointed, the commissioners mustered their resources. Before they could gather for their first full meeting, Rowell and Dafoe held an informal gathering in Ottawa on 4 August 1937 with anglophone secretary Skelton, along with finance ministry and Bank of Canada officials. They set out a preliminary list of research studies and a proposed schedule of hearings.[54] Twenty-seven academics would eventually research the economy, and nine would look at legal and constitutional affairs. Their emphasis was on the workings of federalism during the first sixty years of Confederation – and the search for alternate ways to handle social and economic inequalities. The ensuing scholarship would emerge as "the greatest research effort undertaken by a Canadian royal commission up to that time."[55]

They also set out to examine how other federations, particularly Australia, tackled the problems with inequality among their member states. They drew up a list of formidable witnesses to the nation's ills. Their questions had huge implications. What level of government should collect the tax money? What level of government should distribute that money? Should every government get the same share of federal funds in the name of equality – or should poorer provinces get more money in the name of equity?

Their trips across the nation would become legendary. From 29 November 1937 to 1 December 1938, they were often on the road, trundling onto trains, for eighty-five days of public hearings.[56] They listened to witnesses in every provincial capital, including nine major groups in Quebec City. They recorded 10,702 pages of evidence and received 427 briefs.[57] The provincial briefs often offered extraordinarily bleak glimpses into daily life across the stricken land. The briefs from influential business and social organizations captured how their members saw the world – and how much change they could envision and tolerate. Many briefs made envious reference to Australia – and how it dealt with fiscal inequality among the states and state debts. In particular, the most thoughtful political witnesses, such as Manitoba premier John Bracken and Nova Scotia premier Angus L. Macdonald, along with wealthier groups such as the Canadian Chamber of Commerce, cited Australia often in their analyses and testimony.

The commissioners' search was exhaustive – and exhausting – and it played out against a background of rising impatience with unbridled capitalism. The social-democratic Co-operative Commonwealth Federation (CCF), which was founded in 1932, had captured seven seats in the 1935 federal election. Throughout the latter half of the decade, its appeal – and its demand for a more equitable world – was growing, especially across the west. The times demanded change. But the commissioners were wrestling with the structure of a federation in which the provincial demands for federal money for relief payments, debt charges, and the provision of basic social services were escalating – and clashing with strong provincial linguistic and cultural identities that would resist any surrender of fiscal control.

It was a seemingly impossible task. The commissioners did understand how much their society had changed. As their three-volume report would eventually outline, from 1874 to 1937, total per capita government expenditures had "increased by eleven times."[58] The cost of education and public welfare had gone from "the almost negligible figure of $4-million to $360-million."[59] Ottawa's share of the total cost of government had fallen from two-thirds to less than one-half – and that included federal contributions to the provinces for relief and old-age pensions.[60] The situation had placed a "heavy strain" on the constitutional division of powers – and forced provincial government to rely on taxes that "could hardly, if at all, have been envisaged at Confederation."[61]

Their investigative road show became a fixture of Canadian life during the last difficult years of the Depression. They had an avid national audience. *Winnipeg Free Press* editor Dafoe wanted to ensure that most Canadians – at least most anglophone Canadians – knew what the commissioners were doing – and what they heard. He assigned his newspaper's legislative correspondent J.B. "Hamish" McGeachy to follow them across Canada and file what would become a *syndicated* column, "Confederation Clinic," under the byline J.B.M. While other journalists, such as Carl Reinke of the *Canadian Press*, also trailed after the commission, McGeachy's reports managed to be both lively *and* accurate in terms of the operations of the federation. Skelton told Dafoe that, when he showed them to Australian federalism expert Giblin in August 1938, the Australian viewed them "as a really first-rate achievement, in journalism of the best kind – which is rare these days [*sic*]."[62]

The five commissioners bonded with each other readily – partly because of an accident. Three weeks before the first round of cross-Canada hearings in Winnipeg in late November 1937, anglophone counsel James McGregor Stewart slipped on a wax floor during a Halifax card party and fractured his leg. It was an oddly fortunate event for the commission's sense of fellowship because francophone counsel Louis St-Laurent had to take Stewart's place on this western circuit to Winnipeg and Regina. Sirois had been "a little diffident at first in what were to him totally new surroundings."[63] But, in the presence of his close friend St-Laurent, Sirois gradually relaxed amid the totally English-speaking atmosphere. That growing bond with St-Laurent would become evident when the commissioners came to write their report on their unequal world. And that report, in turn, would clearly affect St-Laurent when the time came to establish nonconditional equalization.

THE AUSTRALIANS WATCH AVIDLY

From the start, Australian diplomats avidly followed the Rowell-Sirois hearings – and kept Canberra up to date. The diplomats forwarded extracts from a talk about the history of Canadian constitutional reform that University of Manitoba historian R.O. MacFarlane delivered over the Canadian Broadcasting Corporation in October 1937:

"The desire for social and economic reform has been one of the most potent stimulants to constitutional change in Canada."[64] On 16 December 1937, the Australian external affairs secretary told the Australian trade commissioner in Canada that the treasury department was "very keenly interested" in the commission. The Australian minister requested copies of any progress reports as well as other reports that might be useful to the CGC.[65]

In response, the diplomats sent every major brief to Canberra until the central government finally told them to stop: they were apparently drowning in paper. In the future the Commonwealth government only wanted the provincial briefs: "We are concerned more particularly with the cases submitted to the Royal Commission by the various Canadian Provinces."[66] In turn, of course, the Royal Commission and its witnesses were even more interested in Australia's approach to inequality. The decades-long mutual fascination continued unabated.

GIBLIN'S REPUTATION

The 8 August 1938 meeting with their star Australian witness, L.F. Giblin, was a special day-long hearing – and the commissioners gathered in Ottawa for it. Giblin's presence was a stroke of luck. Under a high-level deal with Canada to exchange pertinent information, Australian prime minister J.A. Lyons had ensured that two copies of the four annual reports of the CGC were sent to the Royal Commission along with a letter to Canadian prime minister King in December 1937. Lyons noted that Professor Giblin, who had been a member of the grants commission for three years, was due to visit England in 1938: "Should you desire to get in touch with him, his address could be obtained from the High Commissioner for the Commonwealth of Australia in London."[67] Lyons followed up with King in February 1938: "[Giblin] is expected to be in England shortly, in case the Royal Commission should wish to have the opportunity of consulting him."[68]

In May 1938, commission secretary Alex Skelton wrote to A.H. Lewis, the London manager of the Commonwealth Bank of Australia. Skelton explained that the Royal Commissioners wanted to discuss with Giblin "the manner in which similar problems to those concerning us have been met in Australia."[69] Lewis replied that Giblin was at Cambridge, occupying the rooms of J.M. Keynes (he could not resist a snide reference to Keynes: "This signifies nothing, as long as he does not pick up a germ").[70] Giblin agreed to alter his plans for his return voyage to Australia in August after what would be his last visit to Great Britain, where he was made an honorary fellow of his alma mater, King's College at Cambridge. "For your sakes," Lewis added, "I hope he turns up. He is quite out of the ordinary. His dress is unconventional. I can just imagine how you and [Bank of Canada governor Graham] Towers would enjoy an evening with him."[71] Towers's biographer Douglas H. Fullerton hints at a "fun-loving Graham" in his private life, including "his fondness for mavericks and rebels" such as Alex Skelton.[72] Sadly, there is no record of any gathering of the three men.

Official Ottawa had known of Giblin's existence before Prime Minister Lyons's contact with Prime Minister King. Bank of Canada officials had first checked out Giblin when Deputy Finance Minister W.C. Clark had listed him as a possible royal commission member in a December 1936 memo: "Professor L. F. Giblin: a very able practical economist who was one of the six economists responsible for the 'Premier's Plan' adopted in Australia in 1931 and largely responsible for Australian recovery; also a member of the CGC and as such thoroughly familiar with the problems of relations between state and central governments in a federal country."[73] The Premiers' Plan, which the Australian state and Commonwealth governments endorsed in 1931, cut government spending, raised taxes, and reduced the interest rate on internal government loans.

On 17 April 1937, an unnamed bank official had sent a terse report after meeting with the Commonwealth Bank of Australia's Alfred Norman Armstrong, who was returning to Australia after a stint in London at the Commonwealth Bank of Australia offices and at the Bank of England offices. Armstrong "speaks very highly of Giblin ... Regards him as the real author of the Premier's plan [*sic*] ... He is a quiet, practical man, a fairly good speaker. Thinks there would be no difficulty in his leaving Australia as all Australians are anxious to take every opportunity to get outside experience."[74] He would be wrong about Giblin as a prospective member of the Royal Commission: Giblin had many opportunities to travel.

Two weeks later, Deputy Governor J.A.C. Osborne reported that he had spoken about Giblin with another Australian banker who was en route to London to take charge of the Commonwealth Bank's statistical department. "Giblin is now sixty-five [Not true: Giblin would only turn sixty-five in late November], but remains vigorous," Osborne wrote in a memorandum outlining their discussion. "He wears a sombrero, a coat without lapels, a red tie and hobnailed boots." That Australian banker, Roger Randerson, who would later become financial editor of the *Sydney Morning Herald*, told Osborne that the Commonwealth government had originally created the CGC as a temporary body. Randerson had speculated that the "wily" Giblin had prompted the Commonwealth government to ask the Grants Commission for a permanent formula to calculate each state's entitlements. This "enabled the Commission to say that no such formula could be devised, and thereby [would] help to prolong its existence."[75] As Giblin would testify, the CGC's calculations *were* quirky – but it was difficult to improve on them.

GIBLIN'S TESTIMONY

Giblin did exactly as he promised. On 5 August, he radioed his plans to Skelton from the Cunard White Star ship *Andania*: he would arrive on Sunday, 7 August, with his wife, the pioneering Australian feminist Eilean Giblin, who would stay overnight and then proceed to San Francisco.[76] The next day, on 8 August, Giblin, who was a political economist *and* an expert statistician, was in front of the Royal Commission.

For the four remaining commissioners and their staff, who were still struggling with Rowell's loss, it was a highlight. As Commissioner MacKay wrote to his wife Kathleen on 9 August, "the dean of Australian economists ... had a lot of interesting information and ideas."[77] Decades later, in writing a brief unpublished memoir about the commission, MacKay observed that the hearings had generated vast amounts of data. "But they [the hearings] were on the whole not very useful in suggesting remedies," he recalled. "One important exception was the evidence of Giblin, the Australian economist said to be the father of the Australian Grants Commission."[78] When MacKay sent his recollections to the commission's former legal secretary, Robert Fowler, he disputed MacKay's preemptory assessment of other witnesses. "The Communist Party was there merely to 'blow off steam,'"

Fowler declared, "but the provincial government[s] had real views to give."⁷⁹

Both men wrongly dismissed the value of too many witnesses – including the Communist Party. But Giblin was a guide to Canada's future. The commissioners knew that they were fortunate to intercept the creator of Australian equalization. In early 1938, their experts had gone to Australia to examine the CGC – but Giblin was away. As the respected economist J.A. Maxwell later explained, his greatest disappointment was that Professor Giblin had gone to Great Britain: "and it is my impression he is the best economist Australia has produced."⁸⁰

As Giblin settled into his chair, he peered curiously at the questioners who flanked him at wooden tables. No doubt, given the secessionist turmoil in Western Australia in the early 1930s, he smiled wryly as he delivered a brief opening address on the challenges that federal states faced. He was brutally frank about Canada's plight. The Australian states differed in political outlook and social standards and, especially, in economic strength. But they were not *that* different. It was possible, within the existing Australian Constitution, to make financial adjustments "without great difficulty which [would] enable the machinery of federated governments to work efficiently."⁸¹ That is, the central government could shuffle revenues among the states without huge opposition.

Canada was *very* dissimilar. There were significant differences "in political ideals and, what is more serious, in political responsibility" among the Maritimes, Quebec, Ontario, and the West (Giblin did not single out Quebec).⁸² Worse, some provinces spent almost twice as much per person on education as other provinces, whereas the comparable gap among the Australian states was less than 20 percent.⁸³ The per capita income in wealthy Ontario was roughly two and a half times the income in each of the four poorest provinces of Manitoba, Saskatchewan, New Brunswick, and Prince Edward Island. In contrast, per capita income in the richest Australian state of Victoria was only one-third higher than the per capita income in the poorest state of Tasmania.⁸⁴

The commissioners pounced. What did Giblin mean when he talked about political responsibility, asked Sirois? "What I mean is the attitude that is taken – 'this is our government and we have to make it work' ...

as opposed to the other feeling, 'damn the government; let it do what it likes. It has nothing to do with me.'"[85] The commissioners listened carefully. This could be promising – if only because many Canadians now accepted that they *had* to make governments work – because only governments could get them through their economic ordeal.

But Giblin's statistical observations were crushing. It was hopeless. How could any central government remedy such huge disparities? The differences among the provinces were simply too great. Richer provinces would never allow Ottawa to shuffle enormous amounts of money to the poorer provinces. Their taxpayers would not stand for it. "These transfers would be too large to be regarded as reasonable," Giblin argued, "and the conclusion would be, 'Why not be one country at once and have done with it?'"[86]

This was *not* what the commissioners wanted to hear. The option of converting Canada into a unitary state after more than sixty years of uneasy federation among peoples of different languages and cultures was *not* on their agenda. Quebec would walk out the door to protect its distinct society. Westerners would never trust far-off Ottawa to act fairly on their behalf. This was a non-starter.

But that did not mean that they could not learn from Giblin. The Australian spoke about everything from exchange rates to loan councils that could oversee state borrowing. But the pivotal moment for Canada's future actually came during the first few hours of his testimony when the commissioners compared the inequalities within the federations. First, Legal Secretary Robert Fowler noted that the Australian states had more responsibility for services than did the Canadian provinces – which might be one reason the CGC grants were comparatively large.

Also, the scale of the Canadian subsidies was currently "very much lower than the scale in Australia."[87] So there was "the possibility in Australia of taking up considerably more of the difference between the highest and the lowest [states]."[88] Ottawa had more responsibilities than Canberra – so its subsidies to the provinces were on a smaller scale than were Canberra's to its states. Giblin gravely agreed that there were "not such large activities [by state governments] to compensate [with grants]."[89] The implication was that Canadian grants did not have to be as proportionately large as the Australian ones to bring stability to the federation – because the provinces had fewer responsibilities.

Dafoe put their quandary bluntly. If he understood properly, Ottawa could vary the size of its subsidies to take account of provincial needs – there could be more federal money for the poorer provinces than the wealthier provinces – or it could take over more provincial responsibilities. Yes, said Giblin. Dafoe persisted. "You must take one road or the other," he observed.[90] Yes, said Giblin, but the subsidies would have to be much larger than they now were.

Giblin then discussed Australia's methods. It was impossible to set a "normal" standard for taxation and expenditure among the states. Commission members had tried everything from standards of wages to the standard of living of wage earners, but there were too few states and the variations among them were too great. So the commissioners made a "rather arbitrary decision" to select the state governments of Victoria ("rather economical") and Queensland ("rather expensive") as standards.[91] After four years, they had added New South Wales to the mix.

The standard was actually "quite unsatisfactory ... The thing is dressed up in arithmetical terms as much as possible, and that perhaps is politically useful."[92] But the commissioners actually used their "broad judgment ... as to what [was] a reasonable figure."[93] States accepted their decrees because "there [was] a widespread feeling that this method[,] not being political[,] [was] safer."[94] But, as Canadian tax expert Richard M. Bird later observed wryly, "the equalization process is inevitably *political*."[95] The extent to which decision-making politicians accepted the CGC's findings "depends on the political acceptability of the outcome."[96] Unfortunately, the creation of an ostensibly politically neutral commission to distribute federal funds to the poorer provinces was almost certainly a non-starter for the Canada of the 1930s.

The Australian did add a warning that was prescient. South Australia and Western Australia went back to the commissioners every year with further arguments that often led to modifications in their transfers. He did not believe that the two states were dissatisfied with the final results: "But you can go on almost indefinitely finding more and more difficult points in matters where the calculations are not quite convincing and where more elaborate ones are expected."[97] It was a warning that could apply to equalization in 1957 – *and* to today's federal-provincial bargaining over grants.

The commissioners learned from what Giblin said about federal transfers to the poorer provincial governments. They attempted to devise their own complicated formula for grants to those poorer provinces based on key areas of provincial spending. And they created huge problems for Mackenzie King, which he eventually dodged. There would be many more risky proposals before Ottawa implemented a program to assist the poorer provinces.

In fact, it would be nineteen tough years before equalization finally commenced.

2

The Poorer Provinces Stake Their Claims, 1867–1919

Nova Scotia was always wary of the idea of Confederation. There had to be winners and losers in this new-fangled form of government, where provinces and the central government divvied up their revenues and their responsibilities. And that fiery journalist and politician Joseph Howe, who was once forced to fight a duel because of his reformist inclinations, was convinced that Nova Scotia would be a loser. His province needed better communication links with its fellow British provinces in Central Canada, including an inter-colonial railway, before it could even contemplate union with such an alien entity. In 1866, he could see few ties that bound the disparate colonies together. He even wrote an intemperate pamphlet to warn the British about the perils of the union: the Maritimes were deeply devoted to the Mother Country and looked outward to the sea for their commerce and trade; the Province of Canada was divided by "the antagonism of races arbitrarily bound together, shaken by incompatibility of temper."[1] Who could predict what might happen to Maritimers' loyalty if their freedom to govern themselves was compromised? Why should they be bound into a union with unstable partners?

It would take more than a mere act of the British Parliament, the Halifax-born Howe argued, to unite the four provinces into a nation. Such hasty legislation was a disastrous approach to nation building, and it was doomed to fail. The former colonial premier was so opposed to the compromises and inequalities of federation that he campaigned against that legislation for ten months in Great Britain. His predictions in his thirty-seven-page pamphlet denouncing Confederation were dire. The Maritime provinces were free from the complicated system of dual leaderships and double majorities that plagued the central government of Ontario and Quebec. If Nova Scotia and New Brunswick were "arbitrarily annexed" to Canada through an act of Parliament, Maritimers would "go into mourning ... and wear their flags at half-mast on every sea as an expression of their sorrow and indignation."[2] They would be stranded in a nation where they were outnumbered. Their civil rights and their political rights could be endangered. The more populous provinces would always put aside their differences to combine so that "the centre of power and of influence will always be in [the Province of] Canada."[3]

Worse, federation would mean the ruin of the Maritime economy. Maritimers applied only light duties to British manufactured products – and they were anxious to foster trade relations within the Empire and with other foreign nations. In contrast, Canada imposed high duties on goods – and it would certainly expand those tariffs with Confederation. That would leave Maritimers in dire straits: their resource products, such as lumber and fish, could not reach the interior of Canada over frozen waterways for six months of the year.[4] And they would be forced to buy Central Canadian manufactured products.

As the London Conference on Confederation convened in December 1866, Howe skulked around the city as a lobbyist against union, his large eyes glittering under bushy eyebrows, his hair fluffed in an untidy corona around the back of his balding head. He was sixty-two years old and largely self-educated. To every British politician whom he could buttonhole between July 1866 and May 1867, he offered a terrible warning about fiscal inequality: "The wisdom of Solomon and the energy and strategy of Frederick the Great would seem to be required to preserve and strengthen such a people, if formed ... into 'a new Nationality.'"[5] Nova Scotia premier Charles Tupper found himself countering each submission that Howe made to the British Colonial Office, "and the two men conducted a debate through pamphlets and letters."[6] Confederation was never easy.

THE INEQUALITY AT THE HEART OF CONFEDERATION

Inequality was *always* a troublesome issue within the Canadian federation – as it would be in Australia. In the 1860s, as the creators of the world's third modern federation, the Confederation partners had to grope their way through the foreseen – and *unforeseen* – complaints about union. The future Maritime provinces fell back on the ploy of demanding more funds. Then, as now, money mattered. Indeed, financial concerns were one of the key factors behind Confederation. The notion of federation suited Central Canada. The Canadian Union was deadlocked, burdened with debts, and dangerously divided by cultural and linguistic differences. Confederation was a "thoroughly practical ... Canadian solution for Canadian problems."[7] The British agreed.

In contrast, many politicians from Atlantic Canada were concerned about their provincial governments' fiscal health in a federation that the Province of Canada would dominate. New Brunswick and especially Nova Scotia worried that union with the larger and more populous Province of Canada would upset their trade and shrink their revenues. They did not know how they could fulfill their responsibilities within a federation that would take over the collection of their vital customs duties (that concern about the loss of income from tariffs would later plague poorer Australian states). How could they cope if Ontario and Quebec burdened them with taxation to pay Canada's large debts for railways? From the start, fiscal inequality among the provinces became a theme of the federation. While the British pushed for Confederation, many Maritimers resisted it.

The beginning was not promising. In 1864, during rounds of hard bargaining over the federation's proposed revenues and responsibilities, Upper Canadian politicians urged Maritime finance ministers to reduce their bottom-line revenue needs to a bare minimum.[8] Those estimates took little account of any province's social responsibilities, especially towards its poorer citizens.[9] But the estimates became a rough basis for calculating the three principal subsidies at Confederation in 1867: the then substantial per capita grants, the subsidies to meet the cost of governance, and the debt allowances. The Fathers of Confederation made a trade-off: Ottawa would pay a fixed amount in per capita subsidies and collect all customs and excise duties, which would be the main source of federal funds.

At the time, it seemed like a fair deal – at least to the pro-Unionists in the Maritimes, whose newspapers chronicled "glittering predictions of state-driven wealth."[10] In contrast, the anti-Unionists viewed estimates of the money that would flow from the Maritime governments to Ottawa as "murkier ... [and] saw much evidence for quasi-imperial and predatory taxation."[11] They were correct: six decades after Confederation, economist J.A. Maxwell calculated that Nova Scotia lost 90 percent of its revenues with Confederation, "but only about 55 per cent of its spending responsibilities."[12]

Even at the time, the Maritime cheerleaders for Confederation at the Quebec Conference in October 1864 could glimpse the potential pitfalls. Weeks after those discussions, Nova Scotia premier Charles Tupper warned Canadian finance minister Alexander Galt that he had ably presented the goal of Confederation "altho' a little too much from the Canadian point of view."[13] A medical doctor and hospital surgeon, Tupper was an ardent advocate of union, convinced that it would strengthen Nova Scotia's commercial prospects and its influence within Canada and the British Empire. Throughout those crucial years of federation talks, Tupper argued fiercely with Howe. He finally secured the Nova Scotia legislature's approval for union in April 1866.[14]

Newfoundland Liberal Party leader Ambrose Shea, who was a strongly supportive delegate to the Quebec Conference, later told Galt: "Some of our mercantile men fear a large amount of increased taxation ... this is a point on which it is easy to alarm the masses everywhere."[15] Businessman Shea advocated Confederation to create colonial trade networks and to expand the transportation systems. That support hampered his political career – because many Newfoundlanders feared the colony's interests "would be compromised by a remote and indifferent government outside the colony."[16] Newfoundland would not join the federation until 1949.[17]

Prince Edward Island Liberal assemblyman and conference delegate Edward Whelan, who favoured union, was equally cautious with Galt: "You treat the question too much from a Canadian point of view ... and the asses of country people [in Prince Edward Island] .. .are afraid they are going to be tremendously taxed."[18] Journalist Whelan hoped that Confederation would deter the British Colonial Office from meddling in local affairs. But he was outnumbered: PEI resisted Confederation because it could not secure sufficient compensation for its lack of Crown resources. Whelan later complained that he "had never been subjected to so much abuse as over this issue" – and it cut short his political career.[19] But PEI could not hold out for long. In 1873, saddled with massive debts from railway construction, the government went back to Ottawa to make a better deal that included cash to buy out absentee landlords.

In New Brunswick, the newspapers accepted the need for a commercial connection with Canada, but some were dubious about a political and fiscal bond. As the *New Brunswick Courier* explained: "The financial part of the project has received the most attention."[20] In response, in speeches after the Quebec Conference, New Brunswick premier Samuel Leonard Tilley's "main purpose was to satisfy his audiences that Confederation would not increase their taxation."[21] It was a tough chore for the former pharmacist and temperance advocate, if only because he avoided populist oratory, mustering "cold logic and colder statistics."[22] But he prevailed.

Howe surely knew that Confederation was unstoppable when influential British railway financiers swung behind its promise of "the political stability and the economic security without which existing enterprises must remain in jeopardy and future developments [must] be limited and uncertain."[23] The odds were stacked against him. But many Maritime Canadians remained suspicious of a future when they would be pinned under Central Canada's weight, tugged into projects that would often benefit other regions.

THE "HAVES" AND THE "HAVE NOTS"

In contrast, the Central Canadian provinces were (temporarily) satisfied with their fiscal deal. Ontario Reformer Oliver Mowat, who was a Province of Canada cabinet minister, secured resource revenues – and the ability to levy direct taxes, which might then be applied to property. In 1872, when Mowat became premier, he was initially viewed as "no great threat" to Ottawa's centralizing instincts (a view that would turn out to be *very* wrong), but his fiscal cunning showed remarkable foresight.[24] Quebec, in turn, welcomed those resource revenues from lands, mines, and minerals. But its primary goals were linguistic and cultural preservation, which it secured through its control over education and civil and religious institutions. As historian A.I. Silver notes: "Quebec was to be the French-Canadian country, working together with the others on common projects, but always autonomous in the promotion and embodiment of the French-Canadian nationality."[25]

As those powerful Central Canadian politicians drove hard bargains, Atlantic Canadian politicians scrambled to ensure that their legislatures would have the funds to fulfill their basic responsibilities, such as hospital construction and transportation infrastructure. They had one advantage: federation negotiators were uneasily aware of the potency of Joseph Howe's financial warnings. In December 1866, in London, those negotiators offered extra compensation as an inducement to bring the nation into being. Nova Scotia premier Charles Tupper and former New Brunswick premier Samuel Leonard Tilley, who was now provincial secretary, obtained the promise of unusually large grants to meet government expenses, which were calculated "on no determinable basis, and [which] favored the Maritime provinces very considerably."[26] Tilley, whose pro-Confederation party had scored a tough victory in New Brunswick in June 1866, was pleased.[27] Howe remained in London, unappeased.

But the British government paid little attention to this prophet of doom. It could no longer defend Canada against possible American incursions, if only because the expense and the distance were prohibitive. It was dismantling its protectionist tariffs, easing away from its mercantilist ties with Canada. As well, in an industrializing era that required massive investments in infrastructure, the deadlock between anglophone Upper Canada and francophone Lower Canada "demonstrated the inadequacy of existing institutions and structures of government."[28] In unity, the colonies might find strength – and vaguely common cause to work towards prosperity. Howe could not fight the tide.

In May 1867, deeply disillusioned, the Nova Scotian returned to Canada. His faith in the wisdom of the Mother Country was shaken. But he had learned little. When the Dominion of Canada came into existence on 1 July, New Brunswick received a so-called "special grant" for which there was "no determinable basis ... except as the price to bring it into union."[29] There was no special grant for Nova Scotia. In September 1867, Howe won election as an anti-confederate MP to the House of Commons. After the first session of that first dominion Parliament, he rashly led a Nova Scotia delegation for repeal of Confederation back to Britain between February and July 1868. "He got only one concession," notes his biographer J.

Murray Beck: "The colonial secretary agreed to ask the dominion government to review the impact of its taxation, trade, and fishing policies on Nova Scotia with a view to their modification."[30] Back in Canada, Howe finally gave up hope in December 1868 when the new British government "confirmed that the union was to remain as it was."[31]

But federal politicians could not ignore the continued Maritime laments. Seven months after his return from Britain, after years of warnings and protests, Howe and his fellow Nova Scotia MP Archibald W. McLelan secured a financial agreement with Finance Minister John Rose that promised "better terms." Former Nova Scotia premier Charles Tupper – who now had a seat in the federal Parliament – helped to broker that deal.[32] The province received special grants of $83,000 per year for ten years – and Ottawa increased the per capita basis for the beleaguered province's "debt allowance," an arcane subsidy that initially rewarded more frugal provinces for lower debts.[33] In return, Howe had to "make the best of union."[34] But he had set a precedent. As political scientist Garth Stevenson observes, better terms ensured that "additional grants to any province may be made at the discretion of Parliament."[35]

Ottawa had handled inequality with subtlety, cunningly allotting unusually large grants for government operations to the poorer provinces. It was the start of covert solutions for inequality: federal subsidies still *appeared* relatively equal for all provinces. The fiction of equality among the provinces was maintained: the federal assistance was necessary. In Nova Scotia and New Brunswick, federal subsidies amounted to 80 to 90 percent of provincial budgets. In Ontario and Quebec, where natural resource revenues were significant, they accounted for 40 to 50 percent of revenues.[36] But such ingenious remedies could not last. Those deals with the Maritime provinces established precedents for special treatment of the poorer provinces that would preoccupy dominion governments into the 1950s. And beyond.

Howe had done his best – or, depending on the point of view – his worst. He had certainly demonstrated that the arcane business of federal subsidies to member states could evoke fierce emotions and endanger the political peace. But he could not do much to change Nova Scotia's destiny. He would turn out to be right, of course, but he did not live to see his prophecies come true. In January 1869, he took a federal cabinet post. Mollified, he used "his skills and connections, and a good deal of federal patronage, to make sure most other Nova Scotia MPs provided support to the government."[37] In 1873, in a somewhat ironic denouement, he accepted a federal appointment as lieutenant-governor of Nova Scotia. Less than three weeks later, on 1 June, he died at age sixty-eight at Government House in Halifax.

THE AUSTRALIAN COLONIES STAKE THEIR CLAIMS

For centuries, Australian settlers maintained that their continent was "terra nullius": that is, "a land that until its settlement in 1788 lacked human habitation, law, government or history."[38] They claimed that the estimated 750,000 Aborigines were "too primitive to be actual owners and sovereigns."[39] They ignored, and often attempted to erase, the intricate and rich cultures of Indigenous peoples who had arrived at least fifty thousand years before them. They damaged their "mode of life, health, welfare and very identity."[40] Remarkably, it was only in 1992 that the Australian High Court overturned the assertion that the land was without owners when Captain James Cook sailed the length of the east coast of Australia in 1770. The High Court did, however, recognize the British assertion of sovereignty in 1788 when officers, soldiers, civilians, and convicted felons came ashore in Sydney Harbour. Thereafter, the court decided, "there was only one sovereign power and one system of law."[41] Reconciliation would prove elusive and difficult.

The interlopers, who were often escaping poverty in the United Kingdom, were determined to control their vast world. By the early 1870s, despite ineffective Aborigine protests, and half a world away from Joseph Howe, colonists in the six Australian colonies – New South Wales, Victoria, Queensland, Tasmania, South Australia, and Western Australia – had staked out the continent. The separate colonies "gradually secured representative, and responsible, systems of administration" with "distinct and independent political factions and parties."[42] By 1859, five of the six had obtained full self-government (Western Australia would not attain this status until 1890).[43] Life was challenging but often satisfying.

It was a world on the cusp of change. In 1951, Sir Robert Garran set down his memories of his long life as a lawyer and public servant who was intimately involved in the drawn-out negotiations among the six colonies that led to federation in 1901. In the 1870s, when he was a boy in prosperous Sydney, the colonies were "a group of distant neighbours, with poor means of communication ... There was little Intercolonial travel – and that, mostly by sea ... Each colony set up custom-houses against the others."[44] Most Australians were not interested in federation, he added, even though the colonial premiers discussed the possibility at regular conferences to settle such issues as overseas mail contracts. Australians had spent so much time "trying to escape from the paternal attentions" of the British government that the Crown "was apt to be regarded rather as a common enemy than as a bond of union."[45] They were mostly content to enjoy the freedoms that they had attained and to avoid the gamble of uniting with their fellow colonists.[46]

THE SUBSIDY DILEMMA

The Confederation bargain provided "blunt evidence" of Ontario's and Quebec's primacy within the fledgling union. The Maritime provinces had come into the deal with substantial net assets while Quebec and Ontario had substantial liabilities. Ottawa absorbed "most of the assets and liabilities of the old provinces." It also assumed control of customs duties and tariffs, "though the sea-trading Maritimes needed low tariffs much more than the revenue-hungry Canadas did."[47] It was the start of the Maritimers' continuing sense of grievance.

Perhaps more important, as other territories and provinces joined Canada, they echoed the Maritime lament, elbowing each other aside with pleas of poverty and demands for financial remedies. As their populations grew, they could barely fulfill their existing social and economic responsibilities. Their politicians did not contemplate permanent formal solutions for inequality, nor did they dream of expanding beyond their current social duties, such as the construction of new schools. They simply wanted to meet basic needs – and keep their political jobs.

Their societies were changing dramatically, pushing aside so many people and bringing in so many others to face challenging lives. As the railway inched across Canada, reaching the Pacific Coast in 1885, Indigenous Canadians in Northern Ontario and the West were reluctantly signing the numbered treaties – and most were retreating onto reserves that were often isolated and clustered on poor lands. In the early decades after Confederation, settlers from the British Isles and Western Europe, along with some Americans, were streaming into Canada, and many were attracted by the promise of virtually free land in the Prairies. Towards the end of the century, those numbers were swollen with tens of thousands of immigrants from Southern and Central Europe.

Age-old prejudices were reawakening in New World ways. In Atlantic Canada, the federal fisheries department systematically excluded Indigenous peoples from the fishery, banning their modes of harvesting and instituting a strong enforcement regime.[48] In desperation, many band members became guides for wealthy white salmon fishers. In 1890, in Vancouver, the local Trades and Labour Council advocated whites-only hiring policies, the boycott of Chinese laundries, and the strict enforcement of Sunday-closing by-laws against Chinese businesses.[49] During the last decades of the nineteenth century, the railways turned to African Canadians as cooks, sleeping-car porters, and dining-car attendants, using cheap labour to thwart white unionization while creating a "viable career path" for those black men.[50] There were so many ways for those in power, usually white and male, to thwart the aspirations of other groups.

The economy was rapidly evolving. In Central Canada, factories were turning the nation's rich resources of lumber, grains, and animals into products for the growing number of consumers.[51] By the 1890s, high-voltage, alternating current transmission was bringing comfort to homes and greatly enhanced output to manufacturers.[52] Canadians were extracting vast mineral wealth from the Canadian Shield while the fledgling shipbuilding, steel, and pulp and paper industries were starting the development that would flourish during the First World War.[53]

The effect on governments was remarkable. In the mid-nineteenth century, states had relatively simple tasks. They kept the peace; they administered the courts and prisons; they established schools; they raised revenues from the sale or lease of lands and resources; and they imposed quarantines and oversaw basic health precautions. As the material world grew, as Canada industrialized and urbanized, as new immigrants streamed into the cities and countryside, the old methods of governance could not hold. The state had to establish new revenue streams and new institutions, expand its bureaucracy, stabilize measurements and update regulations, deal with unrest among the new working class, and provide moral regulation for the unruly. States struggled to provide infrastructure for this changing world, backing the bonds of firms that were building canals and railways, scrambling to meet their needs.

It was a daunting economic, political, and social task through time and space over the last half of the nineteenth century. The infrastructure needs were so great that the Province of Canada learned how to raise capital in the London markets. It was a time of unbridled capitalism, what has been christened "Monopoly's Moment."[54] And the state had evolved into a virtual accomplice in this capitalist enterprise.

Problems were almost predictable. The exact amounts of subsidy per person were spelled out in the Constitution, and Ottawa clung to the 1861 census for Ontario and Quebec to determine the number of residents. As new provinces such as Manitoba joined Canada, they had their per capita subsidies limited to population caps based upon more recent decennial census data, as did Nova Scotia and New Brunswick.[55] Fierce lobbying was the norm: by 1873, four of the now seven provinces were receiving special grants that were never enough.[56] The economy and the population were growing. Premiers in the later decades of the nineteenth century – along with their citizens – literally paid for their predecessors' controversial bargains.

The trouble was that the Constitution could not freeze time. In 1867, provincial subsidies consumed 20 percent of federal revenues. By 1887, as Ottawa's customs revenues grew, per capita provincial subsidies were only 13 percent of federal revenues.[57] The subsidies were theoretically set in constitutional stone. In the mid-twentieth century, a senior federal bureaucrat struggled to explain the late nineteenth-century subsidy hodge-podge to his baffled bosses: "Serious depression conditions which lasted for almost a quarter century following 1873" drove the provinces to lobby Ottawa continually for better deals; in response, Ottawa made many adjustments, even though the Constitution specifically stated that the subsidies were "to be in 'full and final settlement' of any claims" on the dominion.[58]

It became a game. As settlers trickled across the Prairies, as the Territorial government asserted its needs, Ottawa simply shuffled the inputs into its subsidy calculations: it increased the estimated number of people in a province to push up its per capita payments; it increased the amount of allowable debt. With new provinces, there were new arrangements. It was an untidy, slapdash system that created winners and losers among the provinces, endangering the political peace. As the Royal Commission on Dominion-Provincial Relations noted in 1940, the subsidy system was "chaotic and illogical."[59]

Provincial politicians leaned on federal politicians. Depending on the strength of their lobbying – and the dizzying proximity of an election – they could secure more funds. The federal government was perched amid this web, holding the disparate strings, as the key player in arrangements with the haves and the have-nots. All provincial governments competed for federal cash, emphasizing their needs and their political clout. There was no neutral commission to arbitrate between Ottawa and its petitioners. There was no set formula for aid. Few politicians cited the perils of provincial dependency or the moral value of inter-governmental sharing. Instead, the provision of extra funds was a tough, pragmatic political compromise. Ottawa made its decision after a province pleaded its case, which included citing everything from the unfairness of Confederation itself to immediate fiscal need.

But Ottawa would not, and probably could not, change the system during those first decades. The premiers realized that they had to take action. In October 1887, Quebec's Liberal premier Honoré Mercier invited the first ministers to a conference on provincial rights in Quebec City. No fool, Prime Minister Sir John A. Macdonald refused to attend. The premiers unanimously adopted twenty-two detailed resolutions, including demands for higher subsidies because the current payments "ha[d] proved totally inadequate," and sent them to Ottawa.[60] Significantly, the premiers demanded *equal* increases for each province, based solely on continuously *updated* census estimates. There was no provision for special treatment for the poorer provinces.[61] The premiers made an exception: they acknowledged that Manitoba and British Columbia were receiving subsidies based upon unrealistically high population estimates; those payments could continue until the population reached those levels and then increase with the census returns.[62] Sir John A. simply ignored them.

But that did not quell the unrest.

THE SIX AUSTRALIAN COLONIES
CONSULT CANADA'S METHODS

Observant Australians knew that the colonies could not continue forever on their happily isolated paths. In 1883, "amid rumours of intended annexations by Germany and France," Victoria premier James Service called for immediate federation.[63] He was too far ahead of public opinion and his fellow politicians. But he did manage to call a convention in Sydney, which created what Sir Robert Garran later dismissed as "a mouse": the Federal Council, "with scanty legislative powers, with no executive and no power to raise revenue."[64]

Around the same time, however, the influential New South Wales premier Sir Henry Parkes returned from Britain on a route through Canada and the United States, and Sir Robert had "no doubt that sight of the progress of those great federations" encouraged the premier to eventually swing behind full federal union.[65] Born in England, Parkes had arrived in Australia in 1839 as an impoverished immigrant with a wife and a young child. He first worked as a labourer on an estate; then he established businesses that eventually failed; and finally he found his niche as a journalist and politician. He opposed the colonial conservatives – and vehemently protested the transportation of convicts. He advocated equal educational opportunity and federation.

But in a new world with many unexpected challenges, the progress towards federation moved slowly. In 1890, as future Australian prime minister Alfred Deakin wrote, Sir Henry convened a meeting in Melbourne to discuss federation. That small gathering discussed a resolution "borrowed from the Canadian Conference," which specified that Australia's best interests could be served in a federal union under the British Crown, "provided such Union can be effected on principles just to the several colonies."[66]

Thereafter, almost every step of the way throughout the following decade, Australian politicians and bureaucrats looked to other federations, especially Canada and the United States, as their model for what they should do – and what they should avoid. As the Royal Commission on the Constitution observed in its 1929 report, the division of some powers, such as postal and telegraph services, was modelled on the Canadian and American constitutions.[67] Marriage and divorce laws followed Canada's procedures.[68] Witnesses carefully parsed Canada's "extremely complex" allotment of powers: how Canada provided residual powers to Ottawa but the judiciary had to untangle the overlaps with the provinces.[69]

The amending formula was a different story: "The framers of the Commonwealth Constitution had before them the Canadian Constitution, which does not provide the means for its own alteration." They wanted to avoid the Canadian trap with a formula that safeguarded their federation pact but that provided enough flexibility to change their rules.[70] The Royal Commission report even compared the powers of the Australian High Court with those of the Supreme Court of Canada, noting with satisfaction that, unlike Canada, the High Court from the start was the "sole interpreter" of the Constitution.[71]

Despite the careful study of other federations, however, the road to federation was rocky. In 1890, at a conference in Melbourne, the premiers agreed to work towards federal union. In 1891, at a convention in Sydney that Sir Henry Parkes chaired, representatives grappled with the drafting of an Australian constitution. Their initial bill died amid squabbling, colonial elections, and inertia. But, although Sir Henry's premiership ended that year, he remains "The Father of Federation."

In 1895, the premiers agreed to hold another convention: voters would directly choose the delegates. After meetings in Adelaide and Sydney in 1897 and Melbourne in 1898, a drafting committee produced constitutional legislation that passed in referenda in four colonies. With further changes, the Australian Constitution Bill passed in referenda in every colony except Western Australia, which did not share the enthusiasm for federation. The colony had only secured self-government in 1890 "in large part because of the small size of the European population concentrated in the south-west corner of a vast territory." As the other colonies attained self-government in the 1850s, Western Australia actually petitioned Britain to send convicts to hasten economic development. The practice of using convicts for labour continued into the late 1860s.[72]

But Western Australia had its own improbable secessionist movement: the influx of settlers from the eastern colonies during the 1890s after the discovery of the lucrative goldfields. Between 1890 and 1900, the colony's population had grown from 47,000 to 179,000. The Western Australian delegates to the constitutional conventions had largely reflected the "traditional elements ... [and] the isolationist sentiments" of the western part of the colony.[73] When the eastern newcomers realized that Western Australia might not join the federation, they formed their own secessionist movement to take the goldfields out of Western Australia and into the federation. Their protests were forceful. In response, the secretary of state for the colonies, Joseph Chamberlain, telegrammed the acting governor that it would be in the colony's "best interests" to join the federation. [74] The loss of the goldfields "would have been disastrous to Western Australia, both from an economic and a political viewpoint." The colony hastily agreed to a referendum.[75]

In 1900, delegates from the six colonies met with Chamberlain in London. After a "few slight amendments," the British Parliament passed the Constitution Bill. Queen Victoria gave Royal Assent in July 1900 – at the same time as Western Australia endorsed federation in a referendum. In September 1900, the Queen proclaimed that the six colonies would be united on 1 January 1901 under the name Commonwealth of Australia.[76] Finally, the dominion was a reality.

But there was a serpent in the new federation's garden. Approximately half of Western Australia's revenue in the 1890s came from the tariffs that it imposed on its fellow colonies. But the new federation prohibited inter-state tariffs. To mollify Western Australia, especially at a time of unprecedented prosperity from agriculture and mining, the Commonwealth allowed the state to maintain its tariff for five years, "in a formula which decreased the tariff by twenty percent each successive year."[77] The federation also promised to build a transcontinental railway that would link the state to its eastern kin. The decision on whether to impose national tariffs was left to the new Commonwealth government.

In 1901, the Commonwealth imposed a federal tariff on imported manufactured goods to protect existing manufacturers. That tariff effectively forced Western Australians to purchase goods from eastern states, "even though the imported goods, apart from the tariff, were less expensive than those made in Australia."[78] Western Australian industries could not compete against more established eastern ones. In 1906, as the state's tariff expired, a federal royal commission called for a tariff on agricultural machinery to protect against Canadian and American competition. The Western Australian Assembly promptly voted to call a referendum on the possibility of secession, but the premier did not support the demand. Still, resentment festered throughout the war and into the 1920s as other poor Australian states also voiced their discontent.

THE CANADIAN PREMIERS DO NOT GIVE UP

In 1902, the premiers at another interprovincial conference requested a subsidy increase. Prime Minister Sir Wilfrid Laurier deftly shelved that demand. In October 1906, when the premiers once again demanded more money, Laurier yielded – partly because the provinces genuinely needed more funds. The prime minister craved harmony. Higher subsidies would purportedly allow the premiers to tackle the wrenching problems of their industrializing age. Laurier also wanted an end to the persistent lobbying: the new subsidy levels constituted "a final and unalterable settlement."[79] But any changes to the basic subsidy required a constitutional amendment because the existing amounts were itemized in the Constitution. And Britain had to approve any amendments.

The Constitution Act, 1907, spelled out a new formula with higher specific numbers: the subsidy would increase as provincial populations grew; the maximum amount would take effect when the population in any province reached 1.5 million. Laurier also granted an extra $100,000 per year for ten years to British Columbia – partly because Conservative premier Richard McBride had demanded exceptional treatment. McBride was young, ambitious, mercurial, and impatient. He had been on the job since 1903 – after the lieutenant governor had dismissed his predecessor for glaring irregularities in the tendering of public contracts. He could be affable and charming, and he was a star on the social circuit. But he was also used to getting his way. The lawyer argued that the per capita cost of running *his* government was five times higher than the average costs in other provinces and that it had been that way for thirty years.[80] The premier disputed the very notion of provincial fiscal equality – and he won a *temporary* concession.

But – *and this is pivotal* – there was no thought of a permanent formal remedy for fiscal inequality. And no province spoke of new social programs: as their populations grew, they could barely handle their current responsibilities. It was folly to think that Laurier's new subsidies could last when provincial populations were growing and inflation was nibbling away at the value of the currency. Although such provinces as Manitoba would subsequently win extra cash through one-on-one negotiations, the provisions of the Constitution Act, 1907, would endure throughout the early twentieth-century boom and the horrors of the First World War.

Somehow, despite the wartime conflict between francophone and anglophone Canada over conscription, the federation endured. Somehow, despite the fury of the three Prairie provinces over their inability to secure the same constitutional control over their natural resources as the Rest of Canada possessed, the federation muddled through. But the federation partners were jealous and suspicious of each other – and that concoction was dangerous to federal harmony. In November 1918, as peace was finally declared in Europe, the Maritime premiers even disrupted a crucial dominion-provincial conference with their refusal to cede resource control to the West unless their special claims were *"adjusted at the same time"* as Ottawa dealt with the West.[81] They backed the other provinces' demand for a general subsidy increase. But they also wanted to revive their flagging influence, and they wanted special subsidies for their impoverished governments, partly as compensation for Ottawa's inability to increase their landmass through boundary extensions in 1912.[82] The battle for funds was never-ending.

CONCLUSION

In the years after the First World War, *all* provinces would demand larger subsidies from Ottawa to meet their growing social and economic responsibilities. And it was Howe's political heirs who provided much of the impetus for those Canadian campaigns. The Maritimers would demand more money for their governments, brandishing amorphous claims of fiscal need and the disabilities that the act of federation had created. Ottawa would often reject those claims but grant the money anyway. In turn, the Maritimers would come to view those subsidies as a moral right – and as virtually intrinsic to their identities. Ottawa would find that more funds could make the claimants go away, but only temporarily. The poorer provinces – just like the poorer Australian states – would seemingly always be with their federations.

Joseph Howe was not one of the Fathers of Confederation. But he was one of the founders of equalization. That is an accolade that he would likely view with very mixed sentiments – since he regarded

Nova Scotia as a proud trading colony as opposed to a Canadian province facing continuing fiscal adversity. By the early 1920s, the wisdom of Solomon along with the energy and strategy of Frederick the Great, which Joseph Howe had once deemed essential to the survival of the federation, would prove elusive.

3

The Maritime Provinces Lead the Way for Canada – *and* Australia, 1919–30

There were many heirs to Joseph Howe in the early decades of the twentieth century – and they came from every region of Canada. But the politician who best embodied Howe's concerns about fiscal inequality in the 1920s and 1930s was the remarkable Angus L. Macdonald. Born in 1890 on the eastern shores of the Northumberland Strait, the descendent of Scottish Highlanders and Acadians, Macdonald served as Nova Scotia's premier from 1933 to 1940 and again after the Second World War. Although his energy and aspirations waned after he spent almost five turbulent years in the federal wartime cabinet, he never lost his conviction that the state had an important role to play in the provision of basic services. He was a force for change. When the dignified Macdonald strode into dominion-provincial conferences, Prime Minister R.B. Bennett and after him Prime Minister Mackenzie King surely winced: the Nova Scotia premier constantly lobbied for more funds for his province's needs. He understood that the principle of equity among the provinces was more important than a rigid insistence on equality.

Nova Scotians were pleased. Their Maritime campaigns for more cash had become more vehement across the decades as the Canadian economy industrialized. More Canadians were taking manufacturing or industrial jobs within increasingly concentrated geographic areas, leaving many people on the sidelines, scrambling to stay afloat. Outdated plants were closing or moving or struggling to survive. During the more prosperous years of the 1920s, it was clear that citizens expected – and needed – far more from their governments than they could deliver. But governments could not cope with unequal economic development.

Mackenzie King temporarily appeased Maritimers during the mid-1920s. But in the depths of the Depression, as the economy faltered, Maritimers needed even more assistance. Municipalities begged provinces for more money. Provinces leaned on Ottawa. Maritime governments remained chronically short of cash: Nova Scotia's Conservative government resolutely refused to introduce the Old Age Pension during the late 1920s and early 1930s, partly because of the province's "relatively high average age," which would add to its costs.[1] In such desperate times, Premier Macdonald almost single-handedly revived the search for a coherent approach to the problems of the poorer provinces and their restless citizenry. Hailed as the new Joseph Howe from his first days in office, he became a powerful advocate for a revitalized federalism.

His life straddled decades of staggering change. Educated in the liberal arts at St Francis Xavier University in Antigonish, he became convinced of the need for "government social-insurance programs to protect the weak and improve the general welfare."[2] He enlisted in the militia in 1915, went overseas in October 1916 as an army officer – and was wounded while leading his men into battle in France on 7 November 1918, only four days before the Armistice. The bullet went through his neck, exiting between his spine and his right shoulder blade, miraculously missing major nerves and arteries.[3]

After eight months of convalescence in Europe, he returned to Nova Scotia, finding his way back into civilian life. He completed the two-year law program at Dalhousie University and was admitted to the Nova Scotia Bar in 1921. He served as the province's assistant deputy attorney general from 1921 to 1924. Then he taught at Dalhousie University while he took special studies in law at Columbia University. By 1928, he was doing postgraduate studies at Harvard Law School, where he received his doctorate in 1929. Along the way, between 1925 and 1936, he and his wife Agnes had four children.[4] His life was fulfilling – and it was already noteworthy.

But Macdonald had a yen for politics. In 1921, barely out of law school, he campaigned for the federal Liberal candidate in Inverness, which included his Cape Breton birthplace. By the mid-1920s, the Maritime Rights movement – "a spontaneous expression of the economic and social frustrations of the Maritime people ... that emerged before the end of 1919" – was gathering strength.[5] Many Maritimers turned against the provincial and federal Liberals, blaming them and

Confederation for their difficult economic prospects. Macdonald sympathized with the movement's goals – but he still worked for both wings of the Liberal Party throughout the decade. In October 1930, much to his surprise, he was nominated as Liberal Party leader – and won. Three years later, he sailed to victory in the Nova Scotia election after challenging the Conservative government's efforts to rig the voting list.

MARITIME TROUBLES IN AN UNEQUAL FEDERATION

The three Maritime provinces were in terrible shape. During the 1920s, nearly 150,000 people left the region in search of better lives. As the economy worsened in the 1930s, many of those Maritimers returned home in defeat, despairing and desolate.[6] Their lives were virtually unchanged. In 1918, Gwen Lefort was a sixteen-year-old English war bride who had married a French Canadian husband. She found herself in Cheticamp, Cape Breton, raising nine children, cooking meals, scouring floors, washing clothes on a scrubbing board, and hauling water from a well. As she ruefully reflected in 1984, "there was no indoor plumbing or anything," which was a basic comfort that she had enjoyed in England before the war. As Macdonald took office in August 1933, she and her family finally moved to the nearby town of New Waterford, where conditions were likely only marginally better.[7]

Perhaps the Liberal government could provide a better life. The new premier was charismatic, witty, warm, and intellectual. In photos, he appeared almost boyishly earnest – although his smile faltered in wartime Ottawa. He was also unusually well prepared for his job. From an early age, he had rejected the view that his society was starkly split between "the people" and the capitalists. Instead, Macdonald was convinced that all Canadians shared a common interest and that "the state could help elicit their mutual potential."[8] He aimed to heal the rifts that economic and fiscal inequality had fostered in his voters' lives.[9]

Angus L. – as Nova Scotians called him – was driven, poring over his files, always well informed – and a workaholic. He was also aware of the growing relationship between Canada and the Commonwealth of Australia: by the late 1920s, the fate of the Maritimes had become a key topic in that post–First World War bond. The two dominions were learning from each other's approach to everything from federal loan councils to ad hoc grants to the poorer states. And both nations relied heavily on each other's in-depth investigations into those issues.

AUSTRALIA PAYS ATTENTION

Australia was fascinated – because the two nations were so alike. "Of all other federations the one that most resembles Canada is Australia," Canadian taxation expert J. Harvey Perry observed in 1960. The two nations had adopted the basic British institutions of government, and their "geographic, economic, cultural and social characteristics" were roughly similar.[10] As Canada had already learned, Australia discovered after federation in 1901 that it was difficult to preserve the peace when its six states "differed widely in area, climate, topography, development and natural resources."[11] The three wealthier states in the east initially paid little attention to their two hardscrabble western kin or to the wild island of Tasmania to the south. But inequality proved to be a menace.

Unlike Canada, Australia had a nascent but explicit form of equalization from the start. To compensate for variations in wealth among the state governments, the Australian Constitution explicitly allowed the Commonwealth to provide assistance to any needy supplicant "on such terms and conditions as the Parliament thinks fit."[12] The new nation aspired to rough fiscal equality – because the poorer states were already worried about the consequences of federation. But there was no guarantee of generous assistance. There was no official formula for determining need. In Canada, *all* provinces asked for additional help within two decades of Confederation – even though they had no constitutional right to do so. In Australia, the poorer states could ask – but the central government would decide.

The absence of firm rules did not matter: the poorer states quickly lined up at the Commonwealth's doors. Western Australia, with its sprawling Outback and largely unexplored resource wealth, was the first to receive "relatively small" grants in 1910–11.[13] Two years later, the isolated island state of Tasmania, which dangled off the southeastern coast of the mainland, was the second to qualify, pocketing roughly £85,000 to £95,000 per year. In the mid-1920s, the procedure to determine the size of the grants changed. After years of complaints about political interference, Parliament shuffled the task to the Commonwealth treasury department and to special commissions established by successive federal governments.[14] In 1929–30, South Australia, with its empty plains, red deserts, and rugged coastline, joined the queue for cash.

Harmony remained stubbornly elusive. Australia's recourse to ad hoc solutions throughout the 1920s and early 1930s "had many weaknesses." Different people were appointed to different adjudicating bodies, and there was no consistent approach. "It was difficult, if not impossible," to establish a uniform formula. Everything was slapdash. Three states – South Australia, Western Australia, and Tasmania – became increasingly dissatisfied, and "the impact of the world depression, which reached its peak in or about 1931–32, increased their difficulties."[15]

The world's few federations were scrambling for ways to handle their still novel form of government in a changing world. There were new issues: state borrowing was becoming important – as Ottawa also ruefully discovered in the mid-1930s. What would happen if individual states declared bankruptcy? Would the credit rating of every member of the federation suffer? Would all taxpayers have to bail them out?

The Australians had to figure out what was wrong – but they did so one state at a time. In 1924, the Commonwealth Tariff Board described Western Australia as being on the "road to serfdom" and compared its position to that of the South after the Civil War.[16] In response, on 5 November 1924, Prime Minister Stanley Melbourne Bruce appointed the Royal Commission on the Finances of Western Australia as Affected by Federation. The Australian-born Bruce came from a wealthy merchant family and he had managed the family's import business, with the exception of his service in the First World War, until he entered cabinet in the early 1920s. He was generally pragmatic, but he was resolutely anti-socialist in a scrappily divided society. He was also determined to protect strong Australian manufacturers, to maximize trade and investment opportunities within the British Empire, and to forge a better relationship between the Commonwealth and its states. He wanted to fix the discontent in Western Australia.[17]

That was a hefty assignment. The three Royal Commissioners resolved to figure out what other federations were doing. They promptly obtained copies of the British Financial Mission report on Brazil, which had theoretically been a federation since 1891.[18] That thirty-nine-page report, which was presented in February 1924, singled out the federal government's ongoing battles with the Brazilian states over its loan guarantees for state infrastructure work. "The Brazilian Government should either make itself directly responsible for the [infrastructure] undertaking and arrange the finance directly," the report concluded, "or should refuse to give its guarantee where its control is difficult and limited."[19] The lesson was that states should not have the unfettered ability to run up tabs that could damage the central government.

The Royal Commission also managed to obtain a South African study from May 1923: the Baxter Commission report had examined financial relations between several provinces and the Union Government of South Africa, which had been a federation since 1909. The commission found no clear demarcation between federal and provincial responsibilities "since we live in a dynamic state" and no uniform way to finance those services.[20] This was sounding very familiar. Fiscal inequality among states in a federation was already a serious problem.

The subsequent Royal Commission report in September 1925 indicated that Canada remained a model: it cited Canadian policies on term limits for parliamentary members; and it looked at how Ottawa handled provincial demands for funds for technical education.[21] That was another small step in the very informative cross-pollination of ideas on federalism.

That report confirmed the Commonwealth government's concerns. State residents were talking angrily about secession, which a newspaper "of wide circulation ... sedulously fostered."[22] Commission chair Stephen Mills was deeply disturbed by such talk, "which ha[d] obtained a degree of acceptance that [could not] be dismissed as insignificant."[23] Commissioner John Entwistle actually endorsed the ferocious public mood: "In my opinion Western Australia should never have entered the Federation, but, having done so, there is, I feel convinced, only one complete and satisfactory remedy for her present disabilities, viz., Secession." Since that might not occur, he endorsed "relieving (at least to some extent) the present financial disabilities."[24]

The conclusions were harsh. The Commonwealth government's protectionist policies had hurt Western Australia's primary producers. But the federation's customs duties could not be lowered "without injuring the secondary industries of the Eastern States."[25] Given the balance of power with the wealthier states, that was unthinkable. Two commissioners recommended that Western Australia regain the right to impose its own tariff for twenty-five years. The third commissioner dismissed that notion.[26]

The fastest way to ease this dangerous dissatisfaction about inequality among the states – as it would be so often in Canada – was more money. But no one could agree on why Western Australia merited those funds. Many witnesses had argued that the state needed more money *because the federation was inherently unfair*. The commissioners dodged that explosive issue; instead, they decided that the state could use more cash *anyway* to meet such pressing needs as technical training.[27]

The very thought of such generous grants unsettled Bruce and his Commonwealth government. But many residents of Western Australia were British-born sheepherders and farmers and their families, and some were the descendants of transported convict labourers who had been put to work in the coalmines. The elites in Melbourne, which remained the capital until 1927, were wary of their disdain. Politicians had to do something about fiscal inequality if they wanted to keep their jobs – and preserve the peace – in that rowdy, sprawling state. The Commonwealth settled on a smaller grant than the majority recommended – but the funding stretched over five years starting in 1925–26.[28]

MARITIME DISCONTENT

In the anxious postwar world of the 1920s, the Maritimes was a region in ferment. All provinces had to provide better training for their more challenging workplaces. Education mattered: in 1933, in an appealing election promise, Angus L. Macdonald offered free textbooks for all children through grade 8. Every province had to improve basic public health care after the 1918–20 Spanish influenza epidemic, which killed Angus L. Macdonald's sister Margaret. Society was changing faster than the capacity of any government to address those needs.

Poorer provinces like the Maritimes could not cope. They could not afford the programs, such as the Old Age Pension, that the richer provinces and Ottawa espoused. And they resented their inferior fiscal position. In 1923, in Halifax, Liberal-Conservative MLA H.W.

Corning demanded a referendum on Nova Scotia's secession from Canada and the creation of an independent self-governing British dominion. Ottawa was violating the "spirit of the Confederation compact": Nova Scotia was not receiving fair treatment in "freight rates, railway shipping and other activities upon which the prosperity of the Province depended."[29] Worse, Nova Scotia "was forced to support the policy of protective duties that were mainly beneficial to upper Provinces, while increasing the cost of living at home with no balancing benefits."[30] Joseph Howe would have been proud. But such complaints – and the suggested remedies – were fraying Maritime society.

Prime Minister Mackenzie King did not understand Atlantic Canada and its already potent Maritime Rights movement. For decades, Maritime governments had grumbled about low subsidies, their diminishing political clout, and Ottawa's offhand neglect. King had heard those complaints for years. But he did not realize that the situation was far different in the 1920s because Maritimers nursed a new and dangerous grievance. Regional manufacturers had survived Ottawa's high tariff walls because the Moncton-based Intercolonial Railway had provided low-cost transportation since the mid-1870s. Maritime manufacturers could compete in Western and Central Canada because their basic freight rates were 20 to 50 percent lower than those in Ontario.[31] Capital investment in Maritime manufacturing had actually *quadrupled* between 1900 and 1920.[32]

When the war ended, however, the federal government combined the nation's struggling railways into one entity, and then clamped the well-regarded Maritime railway under the de facto jurisdiction of its Board of Railway Commissioners. When Central Canadian manufacturers and Prairie farmers demanded lower freight rates similar to those on the Intercolonial, Ottawa simply hiked Maritime rates. Worse, in 1920, the railway commissioners raised *national* freight rates by 40 percent. Between 1916 and September 1920, Maritime basic freight rates rose between 140 and 216 percent.[33]

Atlantic Canada seethed. Merchants were devastated. The protest against freight rates evolved into agitation that pulled together labour and business groups, along with farmers and fishers, *against* the rest of the country.[34] In the 1921 federal election, as Angus L. Macdonald campaigned for the Liberal candidate in Inverness, the Liberals exploited this anger. King captured twenty-five of the region's thirty-one ridings in a protest vote against Conservative rail-rate hikes. But typically, King dawdled – and the intensifying Maritime identity as a victim of Confederation's inequalities strengthened. In September 1923, Prince Edward Island voters replaced their Liberal government with a Conservative one.

By 1925, the price of inaction was apparent. In the late June provincial election, Angus L. campaigned for the government, finding himself in the "awkward position" of defending Nova Scotia's treatment within Confederation, claiming that he had never seen a "clear definition" of Maritime Rights.[35] He feebly supported higher railway rates with the claim that railway operating costs had also increased. And he contended – to little avail – that the Liberals had enacted tough regulations to boost mine safety.[36] (Incredibly, more than sixteen hundred men died in Nova Scotia coalmines between 1871 and 1939, which "conditioned a particular defiance in union workers.")[37] Few voters listened. Nova Scotia's Liberal government fell, and the new Conservative premier Edgar Rhodes promised to stop the flight of young people to other regions in search of better jobs.

In mid-August, New Brunswick voters also ousted the Liberals; the new Conservative premier John Baxter was a strong advocate of Maritime Rights, including freight-rate reductions. Three provincial Liberal governments had now fallen within three years. In the federal election of 29 October 1925, the Liberals slipped from twenty-three Maritime seats to six. It was only four short years since King had romped to victory by exploiting the very wave of discontent that now swamped him.

Voters in the three Maritime provinces – and their premiers – had sent a strong message. While Angus L. Macdonald watched from the backrooms, quietly building up his political markers, his Liberal colleagues reeled. The Nova Scotia Liberal Association represented both the federal party and the provincial party – so it was hard for party operatives to defend federal tariffs and transportation policies. After the wipeout, Macdonald joined other young Liberals in pushing for reforms, "promoting progress and development through infrastructure and education."[38] The party had to represent more than old-style patronage.

THE ROARING TWENTIES

Until the Depression arrived in Canada with a thump in 1929, the decade of the 1920s was marked by stark differences. Industrialists and the growing middle class were prospering. Wealthier families could purchase electric stoves and mechanical refrigerators; they could boil milk to protect their children from dangerous bacteria.[39] In contrast, a survey of Manitoba farm homes in 1922 indicated that roughly 60 percent still had wood-burning or coal-burning stoves. Few "had mechanical refrigerators or even iceboxes." A decade later, only 2 percent of those farm homes enjoyed the luxury of running water.[40] Many lower-income Canadians could see that prosperity had eluded them. There was "popular anger with social inequities."[41]

Canadian customs were changing rapidly. Maritime rumrunners assembled armed groups to supply alcohol to organized crime syndicates in the United States, where Prohibition lasted until 1933. Women operated blind pigs that served alcohol. There were cinemas that showed the latest silent hits. There were daring flappers and jazz.[42] There were shiny automobiles with their promise of independence; by 1929, there were more than 1 million cars in Canada.[43] After the grim years of war, there were celebrations in clubs and bars that could be almost frantic in their excesses.[44]

There were also hard times. In the early postwar years, many women who had taken jobs when the men enlisted found themselves pushed out of the labour market. Those who could find more work were once again relegated to traditional female jobs and low wages. Elizabeth Goudie of Labrador later recalled her arduous life as a domestic, starting at the age of fourteen. She earned two dollars a month to "do everything by hand; scrub, wash, bring wood and water, help to cook and mend clothing."[45] Women in manufacturing jobs were stuck in high-stress production lines: in one Winnipeg clothing factory, the "girls" were allowed only thirty minutes for lunch, "which they were compelled to eat in the workroom."[46] Although most provinces had set minimum standards for wages, hours, and conditions for female workers in industrial establishments, "abuses were rife."[47] Many women in clerical jobs were "relegated to subordinate positions that were routine, low-paying, and dead end."[48]

Although the persistent recession of the early 1920s eventually ended, prosperity was unevenly distributed. Historian Michael Horn estimates that more than half of the Canadian population was never anything but poor throughout the decade: the average annual wage of $1,200 in 1929 was $230 below the unofficial poverty line for families.[49] Different regions such as the Maritimes did not share in the heady rates of growth that cities such as Toronto and Montreal experienced in the latter half of the decade. The resentment was palpable.

KING PAYS ATTENTION

Such regional discontent was finally apparent to Prime Minister King, who would later bluntly summarize his peacemaking priorities: "We began with the Maritimes when they were in a state of insurgency."[50] The prime minister fell back on the reliable device of a royal commission. Theoretically, royal commissions can be viewed as "schemes of legitimation": their conclusions allow the state to take action – because that action has now become "thinkable, and therefore organizable."[51] In this case, King needed to prod his cabinet – and perhaps himself – into an understanding of the Maritime provinces' profound sense of economic inequality.

On 7 April 1926, the prime minister proudly unveiled his three-person Royal Commission, chaired by British industrialist Sir Andrew Duncan, to report on Maritime claims. It was "most undesirable," King declared, that Maritime residents should believe that their interests were "being knowingly prejudiced."[52] The Duncan Commission would scrutinize freight rates on the former Intercolonial Railway and look at how federal policies such as customs duties affected the three provinces. Maritimers were elated: it seemed that Ottawa was finally addressing their problems. Such scrutiny, the *Halifax Herald* reported, would "ensure a return of contentment and prosperity."[53]

On the day *after* that announcement, King grasped the depth of Maritime rage, which threatened social peace and his government's very survival. On the afternoon of 8 April, he met with a young man from Nova Scotia, whom he did not identify in his diary but who was probably a journalist. "Sinclair of N. S. astonished me by speaking of the strength of the secessionist movement in the Maritimes," King wrote: "It is a sort of council of despair."[54] Maritimers lacked markets, and "their people [were] leaving for the U.S. largely. There [was] need for radical change in freight rates & tariff policy."[55]

Chair Sir Andrew Duncan delivered his report in September 1926, although it was not tabled in the House of Commons until December. In a precedent that the Australians would later note, Duncan declared that the Maritimes provinces were partly responsible for their own woes. More important, in another precedent for Australia, he firmly refused to blame Confederation for the relatively unequal prosperity and development among the provinces: "We are unable to take the view that Confederation is, of itself, responsible for this fact ... much at least of what has happened within the Maritime Provinces must be related to *their* responsibility and not to the responsibility of the Dominion." Anyway, he added tartly, if the Maritimes have declined in some matters since 1867, they have made enormous advances in others. "And if the former are all to be ascribed to Confederation ... just as much must be the latter."[56]

That declaration set a significant precedent. Three decades later, the federal creators of equalization adopted Duncan's refusal to blame the very act of federation in 1867 for present-day inequalities. But if Duncan was stern, his commission's thirty-nine prescriptions were still generous. The commissioners called for an *interim* lump sum increase in the federal subsidy, pending in-depth federal examination. They also called for immediate freight rate reductions of 20 percent and renewed transportation subsidies for Maritime coal.[57] Although King worried that Duncan had "gone too far" on subsidies, the report suited his strategic requirements perfectly: "All I need to do is to stand firm on this report, and count on getting back Maritime support to keep us strong in future years."[58]

In the spring of 1927, however, King's cabinet objected to the cost of Duncan's plan. Maritime scholar Ernest R. Forbes argues that the cabinet "changed Duncan's program for Maritime rehabilitation into a plan for Maritime pacification."[59] King raised the region's annual subsidies by $1.6 million – "but presented them only as temporary grants conditional upon Maritime good behavior" – and cut most freight rates by 20 percent. King did not publicly confirm the subsidy increase as permanent until all provinces supported it later that year. In the interval, he was able to fend off additional claims.[60] He ignored many other proposals. But he shrewdly declared that he was adopting Duncan's measures "virtually in their entirety."[61] At the time, few Maritimers noticed the gulf between what he said and what he did.

But the times were prosperous. By early November of 1927, at a dominion-provincial conference, King could afford to placate all the poorer provinces. First, the nine provincial premiers endorsed the Duncan report, ensuring that those temporary grants became permanent.[62]

That special increase in subsidies to handle fiscal inequalities set a precedent for the first tentative and minuscule version of equalization in the tax-rental agreements of the 1940s: Maritimers would come to view this exception to the theoretical insistence on equal treatment for all provinces as part of their identity as Confederation partners.

At long last, harmony prevailed – temporarily. At that same 1927 conference, King also secured provincial agreement to transfer control over natural resources from Ottawa to the three Prairie provinces. That put them in a position of constitutional equality with the other six provinces after six decades of fierce disputes. The nine premiers also refrained from any objections to the return of the railway lands to British Columbia, which had surrendered them to Ottawa in the nineteenth century as a path for the transcontinental railway.[63]

The Duncan Commission became a model for nation building over the ensuing decades. Ottawa could act because an expert three-person panel had recommended it.[64] Although King also resorted to royal commissions as a way to stall for time, most commission hearings reinforced national bonds *anyway*: witnesses could articulate their frustrations to commissioners – and to their fellow Canadians. Theoretically at least, mutual understanding among the regions could grow. But it would be an uphill battle.

THE AUSTRALIANS TAKE ACTION

The Duncan Commission was also a milestone in the deepening relationship between Australia and Canada. On 27 July 1928, Australian prime minister Bruce telegrammed Prime Minister King: "Would be grateful for twelve copies Royal Commission on Maritime Claims. Would also be glad of information of action taken thereon. Similar inquiry here."[65] King replied promptly in the terse language of telegrams: "Forwarding today twelve copies report Royal Commission on Maritime Claims also Hansard containing statement government policy."[66] A day later, Bruce formally appointed the Royal Commission on the Finances of South Australia as Affected by Federation.[67]

Once again, the problem was the very structure of the federation. The economies of the individual states could not be equal because of their unequal circumstances. Prime Minister Bruce had adopted the practice "of making special or 'extra' grants to the less populous and prosperous states."[68] Now he needed to know how that slapdash approach was working. How had the financial fortunes of South Australia evolved since federation? After all, as a later Commonwealth Grants Commission memo reported, there was an "absence of any consistent or uniform approach to the problems of the weaker States."[69] Each state was assessed differently – and treated differently – but Bruce was at least attempting to examine one specific state.

Once more, the Australians set out to examine how the world's few federations were coping. In mid-October, anxious for information about the American approach to fiscal inequality, the Royal Commission on South Australia went through the requisite roundabout diplomatic channels: it asked Prime Minister Bruce to instruct Australian diplomats in the United States to find out. Their diplomatic letter to the US treasury department went unanswered for two months. Finally, the Australian diplomats in Washington received a reply that outlined the varying federal expenditures on direct payments to the states over two fiscal years, along with references to two academic studies. When an Australian official forwarded the US response to Canberra, he added wearily: "It is admitted that ... the information sent forward is – in most instances – wide of the mark."[70]

Still, the Royal Commission on South Australia now understood that the American federal government transferred funds – albeit in a haphazard fashion – to the states for such *specific* issues as rural roads. There were no general transfers for fiscal inequality among state governments. That American approach to handling inequality among federation members eventually became another (rejected) model for Canada.

Ironically, the report of the Royal Commission on South Australia appeared in August 1929, two months before the onset of the Great Depression. Australia was already mired in economic problems prior to the Wall Street crash because its high wages hindered its exports – and it imported many capital goods. The nation was on the brink of calamity. Australian historian Russel Ward dates the start of the Australian Depression to the autumn of 1928, when the nation's "grossly excessive dependence on world prices for wheat and wool and the drying up of overseas loan funds" meant trouble when wool and wheat prices started to tumble.[71] In 1929, British lenders adopted a grim view of the Australian capacity to service debt, as economist John K. Wilson observes, "and towards the end of the year new credit effectively stopped."[72]

The report on South Australia was succinct – and important. It recognized that the state had been facing "an acute and pressing problem" *before* the establishment of the Royal Commission in July 1928.[73]

But the commissioners did not blame the state's fiscal woes on the mere act of federation. Instead, they concluded that South Australia's problems arose "chiefly from her geographical position, her adverse natural conditions – climate, rainfall and natural configuration – and lack of natural resources."[74]

This was simply the way that federations operated:

> In every Federal form of Government the same phenomena appear. The advantages and disadvantages follow the course of nature, and distribute themselves unevenly as between the member States. To balance these natural inequalities, it is found necessary to make provision from time to time for some form of compensation. The latest instance of this is to be found in the Report of the Canadian "Royal Commission on Maritime Claims" published in 1927 ... The result was a recommendation of interim lump sum increased payments amounting to £325,000 per annum, in addition to many other suggestions affording relief ... The same principle is adopted in the United States of America [i.e., Washington also provided relief to the poorer states].[75]

The Australian report was important for Canada because it also dismissed the attempts of groups such as farmers to blame their plight on the disabilities of federation. Even pivotal complaints about the tariff were attributed to South Australia's natural inequalities, which put it at a disadvantage "from any policy aiming at the creation and maintenance of secondary industries over a large continent ... This inequality in the incidence of a tariff is inherent in all Federations."[76] The report added crisply that, a century ago, the Southern American states, which were the primary producing states, had sent similar complaints to Congress about the tariffs on the manufactured goods that they were forced to buy. The report's citation from the Southern States of America petition of 1831 did not mention that labour costs in a slave-owning plantation economy were far lower than those in the northern states. Nor did the commissioners themselves.[77] The very notion of dismantling tariff protection in Australia was not conceivable.

But the report did not stop there. It itemized eleven *benefits* that federation had brought to South Australia, including subsidies for industries, loans for railway construction, new infrastructure such as lighthouses, and payments for old-age pensions. It was apparent that the advantages were "of a most substantial character."[78] Still, the report called for a special grant of £500,000 per year for two years because the state "[was] worthy of sympathetic treatment."[79]

That proposal was generous. But it was another ad hoc solution to the ongoing problem of inequality. The commissioners could not find a general formula for the shifting circumstances among the states across the decades. They recommended that the Commonwealth government create a permanent body of specially qualified people "who would be able from time to time to inform the Commonwealth and the States authoritatively of the inter-actions of their policies and financial proposals."[80] It was a challenge: federations needed experts to handle fiscal inequality.

That report laid out new criteria for Canada's handling of fiscal inequality in the 1930s. The two nations were becoming so intertwined that one nation's report would cite the other's earlier report – back and forth – as they grappled with the challenges of federalism.

AUSTRALIA AND SOCIAL PEACE

Meanwhile, economic and social upheaval finally led to the ouster of Prime Minister Bruce. The conservative Australian had stalled on the introduction of employment insurance, child welfare, and other social reforms. When he finally decided to act in 1929, it was too late: he was swamped by the uproar over labour unrest at the northern coalfields in New South Wales. The owner of those mines, John Brown, was a "coal baron," shipowner, and racehorse breeder who despised unions. He treated his workers with severity – he even refused to let them buy the land on which their houses were built. When the price of coal dropped and his export markets dwindled, Brown demanded severe wage cuts. When the twelve thousand workers refused, he locked them out.[81] But lockouts under the new arbitration act were illegal unless the company was in a strike situation.[82]

Bruce made a futile bid to broker a settlement, stopping the prosecution of Brown. The state premiers from his own party turned on him. When he introduced legislation to abolish the Commonwealth Arbitration Court, dissidents within his own party ousted him. He lost the election to the Australian Labor Party – on 22 October 1929 – and his own seat.[83]

The new Labor prime minister James Henry Scullin was the child of Irish Roman Catholic immigrants. He had been a newspaper editor and a grocer. He was a non-smoker and a teetotaler, and he was an ardent supporter of his party's social justice platform. He backed the racist White Australia policy and endorsed the use of high tariffs to protect manufacturing. Scullin won office mere days before the New York stock market crashed, inheriting another thankless challenge in his already-depressed nation. He promptly "raised tariffs on imports, abandoned the gold standard, increased social service payments and reduced assisted immigration."[84] Despite his deputy leader's promise, he could not obtain higher wages for the miners, who were eventually forced back to work on the employers' terms.

But he did pay attention to the nagging problems of fiscal inequality. On 6 December 1929, after a deluge of complaints, Scullin asked the Parliamentary Joint Committee of Public Accounts to examine Tasmania's problems. The new prime minister was clearly anxious to shore up political support on the outlying island. When the committee finally reported on 7 August 1930, it had figured out another way to determine a state's plight: How severe was the state's taxation? The answer was "very severe." Even though Tasmania had imposed taxes that were nearly double the Australian average over the last five years, "the financial position was becoming acute."[85] In the mid-1920s, "taxation had overstepped the economic limit: the depression grew worse, and the exodus of population to the mainland reached unprecedented figures."[86] Still, the commission urged the state government to "carefully investigate" the possibility of increasing taxes on higher-income residents up to the Australian average.[87]

That proposed tax hike was probably important with regard to keeping the peace. But the committee had also learned from those earlier commissions. "It was inevitable that there would always be trouble in the financial relations between the Commonwealth and the States," the committee report observed dourly: "Similar troubles occurred in the United States of America, Canada, South Africa and Germany [Germany and South Africa were also federations]. Difficulties occurred particularly where there was a great diversity in the size, population, development and resources of the different States."[88] Misery had found company.

The Parliamentary Joint Committee also devoted a substantive section of its report to a "remarkable case parallel" between Tasmania and Canada's "treatment of these [Maritime] Provinces."[89] The circumstances surrounding the Duncan Commission were so similar that the conclusions were "very pertinent to the present situation of Tasmania."[90] In particular, the committee singled out the section that urged the central government to provide a sufficient minimum payment, "not in a spirit of meticulous bargaining, but in the broad spirit which arises from a feeling of their being met with sympathy and fairness rather than with narrow compromise."[91] Sharing could be a moral duty – *and* a pragmatic ploy.

The report added tartly that the Commonwealth government should eliminate ad hoc approaches. It should create a "permanent body ... to make a continuous study of the financial relations of the Commonwealth and the States."[92]

THE QUANDARY

Both Australia and Canada were groping their way towards a more permanent solution to inequality. The economic circumstances of individual states fluctuated – so federal governments needed a flexible system of transfers. Instead, Canada had a static, constitutionally entrenched system of fixed per capita subsidies.

When Ottawa extended special subsidies to poorer provinces in distress, such unusual treatment could upset the richer provinces. Few politicians considered the possibility of abolishing tariffs – especially after Sir Wilfrid Laurier's ill-fated bid to introduce free trade with the United States in 1911. So Canada remained an east-west construct that operated for the benefit of Central Canada at the expense of the poorer provinces on the peripheries.

The Australian system of special grants in response to individual state requests was equally contentious – largely because of the varying criteria. States made their case based "on the financial effects of federal policies" or their "adverse financial circumstances."[93] There *had* to be a better way: richer and poorer states – and richer and poorer taxpayers – needed the reassurance of independent appraisers with a comprehensive approach to the state's plight and the promise of a fair formula for resolution. Otherwise, grants might simply reward bad judgment or allow states to get away with not doing enough to help themselves.

In both nations, no one could find a satisfactory way to bring *balance* to the competing pressures. And no one could guarantee that the states with the most clout or the most powerful backers would not capture the bulk of the central government's attention and funds.

FEDERALISM AS THE DEPRESSION HITS

As the Depression settled heavily on Australia and Canada, all levels of government found themselves challenged to do more than they had ever deemed appropriate. Officials found their expertise and their governmental capacities tested to the utmost – and often failing. *Relatively* open economies such as those in Australia and Canada were vulnerable to price fluctuations in commodities such as wheat and wool. Their central governments were trapped amid radically different regional demands for tariff adjustments and currency devaluations. This was not the world of the late nineteenth and early twentieth centuries when the roles of business, labour, politicians, and personal responsibility were delineated – if frequently challenged. Politicians and bureaucrats were at sea.

The headlines captured the turmoil. In Australia, on 28 July 1930, the *Sydney Morning Herald*'s front-page news summary listed world events in one column. At the top, naturally, were the cricket scores, followed by the Davis Cup tennis results. Then came news of a terrible earthquake in Italy. The Australian Labor Party caucus was bitterly divided over economic strategy – which would eventually lead to the party's temporary undoing. An Australian Labor MP claimed, "Certain Labour [*sic*] members took money from private interests and got drunk in the House of Commons." There was little indication on the London Stock Exchange of interest in investment or speculative stocks. There were no grounds for hope for increased trade. The English market was glutted with soft fruits and apples – which Australia exported – and the prices were low. The industrial slump in Germany was deepening. A rare upbeat bulletin stood out: "Preparations for [English aviator] Miss Amy Johnson's welcome back to England are on a scale which will make it historic." Johnson was the first female pilot to fly solo from England to Australia.

And then came more unsettling domestic news. The unemployed, including "hunger-marchers," had held a conference at which a prominent Communist presided, "and the demands submitted for approval were of an extravagant nature." A Labor Council organizer, in turn, attacked the Communists for using the unemployed "for their own ends." Sydney merchants decried the higher duties on timber. Men working on relief projects went briefly on strike; one thousand men were expected to report back for duty in Sydney while one hundred men left for make-work projects in the countryside.

The very stability of the federation was threatened. The federal budget proposals had "given rise to talk of secession from the Commonwealth in both Victoria and South Australia." The Melbourne Chamber of Commerce president in Victoria singled out the "Federal Government's incapacity" as the reason for its threat. The attorney general of South Australia declared that his state would "have to consider unification or secession unless it [got] substantial relief."[94]

On that same day, in Canada, the *Globe* reported that Toronto was sweltering under a heat wave. The toll of weekend accidents and drownings in the province had set a new record for deaths and injuries. But the federal election, which was under way that day, dominated the headlines. The *Globe* endorsed the Liberals, supporting their tariff preferences for British Empire goods. Its news summary proclaimed that the recent federal Liberal budget would "have a profound effect in behalf of business expansion," citing new plants under construction in Canada to take advantage of those preferences.[95] In Regina, in a radio address, Finance Minister Charles Dunning called for an Unemployment Insurance scheme that the provinces would administer with Ottawa's cooperation. It was a belated conversion.

The *Globe* even ran a special address to "Madam Liberal," urging her to vote as a "matter of returning a Government, which, by low tariffs, will provide the home with the cheapest and best food, clothing, furniture, etc., and which will also give the maximum of employment to the family wage-earners." Voting would show loyalty to the Empire, while "Washing Will Wait."[96]

During the weekend before the Monday vote, the party leaders made their final pitches. In a two-hour address over the nationwide radio network, Prime Minister King reviewed his lengthy record, including those Empire trade preferences, the reduction of tariffs on producers and on consumer necessities, and "the removal of grievances in the Maritime Provinces." He insisted that Ottawa had been active in addressing unemployment: his government had offered to match the provinces and municipalities, dollar for dollar, "as soon as we are advised by the Provinces concerned that the unemployment, within its borders, is of such magnitude as to constitute an emergent condition requiring Dominion assistance."[97] The prime minister's blithe talk was out of touch with an increasingly desperate electorate.

Meanwhile, in an Ottawa campaign finale on Sunday, Conservative leader R.B. Bennett denounced "the tragedy of unemployment, and declared such a condition should not exist in Canada."[98] He called for reciprocal trade agreements and mutual preferences and promised relief for the unemployed. Indeed, he had vowed to do whatever was necessary to combat unemployment "or perish in the attempt."[99] It was a vow that would come to haunt him.

In Cape Breton, Angus L. Macdonald was awaiting the results in his first run for political office as a Liberal MP. He had been confident, probably over-confident, that he would do well on his familial turf. But he had changed in the two decades since he had left Cape Breton. As his first biographer John Hawkins noted, his speech and manners had altered: "He was more dignified and perhaps more withdrawn than he had been as a boy. He was a little out of touch, and appeared at times a little shy. Consequently some felt he was proud."[100] The Conservative incumbent won by 160 votes. It was Macdonald's "first major setback," and the only election that he would ever lose.[101] But he had attracted provincewide attention.

In Nova Scotia, little more than two months after his defeat as a federal candidate, Angus L. was nominated spontaneously as provincial Liberal leader – and won. Now he was working hard to ensure that the voters saw him as a credible alternative to the Conservative provincial government. During the first years of the 1930s, he criss-crossed his stricken province, boosted the organization in every constituency, and met regularly with his caucus although he did not have a seat.

His province was in trouble. The price of field crops and fresh fish plummeted by 50 percent from 1929 to the end of 1931. The lumber industry was crippled. Nova Scotia even had difficulty selling its famed apple exports. Coal production dropped from 7 million tons to 4 million tons in 1932.[102] Conservative premier Gordon Sidney Harrington, a former mayor of Glace Bay, had managed to settle Cape Breton disputes among the coalminers. But he faced mass unemployment and huge bills for relief. The public expected more than his government could possibly deliver.

Bennett won a huge majority – 135 seats to King's eighty-nine seats – although his share of the popular vote had risen little more than three percentage points. King viewed the results as "a great surprise ... I have gone down if I have with flying colours. A fine record of govt., a fine issue [sic], etc. & before more difficult times come."[103]

CONCLUSION

He was right about one thing: the times ahead would be harder. King blamed many factors, including lack of organization and poor publicity, for his defeat. But, as he conceded in his diary, "the extent of unemployment counted for very much."[104]

So many men and women were scrambling for any work, however temporary. So many children were hungry and leaving school to earn pennies. Between 1929 and 1932, dominion expenditures would increase by $132 million while revenues would decrease by $140 million "as tax revenues dried up ... [But] an increase of $132 million in Dominion expenditures was not large enough, nor sustained long enough ... to compensate for declining expenditures in the private sector."[105]

The leaders who took power during the first five years of the Depression struggled to understand, let alone cope with, their devastated world.

4

The Poorer Endanger the Richer, 1930–35

Austere and aloof, occasionally overbearing, Prime Minister R.B. Bennett was an unlikely revolutionary. He had dutifully supported unemployment insurance, labour unions, and old-age pensions throughout his political career. But he distrusted any threats to public order, including protests against his government's inability to ease unemployment. In the early 1930s, unsettled by the depths of the crisis, he told former prime minister Sir Robert Borden that Canada was "subject to the play of forces which we did not create and which we cannot either regulate or control." Any action beyond keeping "the ship of state on an even keel" could cause unthinkable consequences.[1] He was as reluctant to take drastic action as was his Liberal opponent, former prime minister Mackenzie King, who was waiting in the weeds for Bennett to defeat himself.

And then the pressures to change course became almost irresistible. The Tories lost provincial elections in Saskatchewan and Ontario in 1934, along with four of five federal by-elections in September.[2] That jarring message from the Canadian electorate stood in sharp contrast to the stirring rhetoric from American president Franklin Delano Roosevelt whose New Deal had created hope in millions of his countrypeople. Bennett's brother-in-law William Herridge, who was Canada's envoy to the United States, and his executive assistant Roderick K. Finlayson became convinced that daring reforms would also pull Canada out of its slump – and they inspired the prime minister. The two men worked with Bennett, crafting strong speeches that he delivered in five radio addresses in January 1935. "The old order is gone," he proclaimed, shocking many listeners. "If you believe things should be left as they are you and I hold irreconcilable views. I am for reform.

And, in my mind, reform means Government intervention ... It means the end of laissez-faire."[3]

It was a remarkable conversion after four and a half years in power, and it astonished his cabinet. The prime minister had not consulted them. As Bennett's biographer, historian John Boyko, explains, the man who was seen as a firm defender of capitalism and big business was now "boldly announcing that capitalism was broken, that corporate Canada had let the country down, and that radical reform was needed to put things right."[4] That appeal came too late, at least for Bennett. The only question was why he waited so long to conclude that so much was clearly wrong

THE HARD LIFE OF THE EARLY 1930S

Life was harrowing for many Canadians during Bennett's years in office. Between 1929 and 1933, gross national expenditure – that is, overall private and public spending – dropped by 42 percent. Population growth fell to its lowest level since the 1880s "through a combination of plummeting immigration and birthrates."[5]

The news was seemingly always bad. In June 1931, roughly 471,000 Canadian workers – or 18.6 percent of the labour force – were unemployed; by February 1932, as the results of the 1931 census trickled out, the Dominion Bureau of Statistics declared that a "conservative estimate of the unemployed ... would lie between 600,000 and 700,000."[6] By 1933, 30 percent of the workforce was unemployed, and one in five Canadians was dependent on government relief.[7] The rules for such assistance were strict: relief authorities confiscated goods from recipients that they deemed to be luxuries, such as cars, radios, and jewellery; they also seized telephones and liquor permits.[8]

Families were in turmoil. Women struggled to survive when their husbands lost their jobs. They stitched flour bags into clothing. They "substituted chicory or roasted grain for coffee, game for the butcher's cuts, and invented an endless variety of 'mock' dishes."[9] Unemployed men "frequently left their families to search for work elsewhere, and sometimes deserted them altogether rather than face the humiliation of failing to provide."[10] For family sustenance, women often sought work in traditional areas of female employment such as textile mills, piecework sewing, or restaurants; female participation rates in the labour force escalated. But "wages plummeted, working conditions deteriorated, union membership declined, and women's right to work was even more seriously challenged."[11]

They reached out to Bennett in desperation. A thirteen-year-old girl from Saskatchewan, Edwina Abbott, begged the prime minister for a coat because she had to walk four and a half miles to school every day in the cold. A Saskatchewan woman pleaded with Bennett in 1933 to purchase new underwear for her husband who was working outdoors in the bitter cold. She enclosed an order form from Eaton's department store in her name: "We have never asked for anything of anybody before." He complied with her request.[12]

Another Saskatchewan woman, Mrs C.L. Warden, told the prime minister in the winter of 1934 that she had three children and that they often survived on potatoes "for days at a time." She and her two oldest youngsters had abscesses in their teeth. Could they get them out "and have the town pay for the Dental Bill"? How much could they get from "Steady Relief"? She was five months pregnant and had not yet felt any stirrings of life, "I feel quite sure for lack of food."[13] A seventy-three-year-old New Brunswick man wrote to Bennett in 1935, explaining that he had sought relief that morning for himself and his sixty-eight-year-old wife, "and I had a hard time to get $3.00 worth," including a bag of flour and a gallon of paraffin oil but no tea: "It is a hard way to live so long in the party conservative and to be used that way."[14] Life seemed bereft of so much joy. But politicians did not know how to help them.

BENNETT AND THE PROVINCIAL PREMIERS

Prime Minister Bennett did meet frequently with the provincial premiers during his tenure – although little was seemingly accomplished. Their first gathering in April 1931 was devoted to the Statute of Westminster, which granted full legal freedom to British dominions except in areas where they chose to remain subordinate, such as Canada's right to amend its Constitution. That seems jarring. But the Bennett government had already appropriated $20 million for relief and infrastructure projects in 1930–31 and had then extended those provisions for 1931–32 with such unspecified amounts as "might be deemed expedient for relieving distress, providing employment and maintaining within the competence of Parliament, peace, order, and good government throughout Canada."[15] In the end, Ottawa would spend $42.7 million on relief that year.[16]

In April 1932, as the Depression deepened, the first ministers gathered in Ottawa for closed-door discussions about relief. After the conference, Bennett said that he had spelled out Ottawa's financial position – it had added $119 million to the 1931–32 federal debt – and he declared that the dominion was "not disposed to assume responsibility for the unemployment problem."[17] That assertion surely surprised many Canadians who remembered his ardent election vows. Instead, Ottawa would confine its spending to direct relief in emergency situations such as crop failure. The *Globe* correspondent William Marchington condescendingly noted that many provinces and municipalities had reached the "end of their tether" – but there was a limit to the number of useful public works that could be undertaken. Bennett's solution was tough: "No work, no relief."[18]

Despite Ottawa's stand, the poorer provinces did not *publicly* complain. Indeed, wealthy Ontario expressed guarded confidence in the economy: its attorney general, W.H. Price, even presumed to speak for the Western provinces by declaring that they "appeared to be quite optimistic" about the coming harvest and were grateful for past help "in their time of need by the Eastern Provinces."[19] Price implied that the need was presumably met. It was a small hint at the growing resentment among the wealthier provinces about Ottawa's generosity to their poorer kin. Ottawa would eventually relent – and spend $25.9 million on relief and employment projects in 1932–33.[20]

Economic and fiscal inequality could be dangerous in a downturn. In January 1933, at another Dominion-Provincial Conference, the rifts between the wealthier provinces of Ontario and Quebec and the poorer provinces, especially the Prairie provinces, were deepening. The delegates emerged with the recommendation that federal assistance to the provinces for direct relief should continue because of the "unprecedented economic conditions."[21] But there were no ringing *public* calls for additional federal help. The obscure phrasing of the resolutions is remarkable – and unintentionally revealing: "While some provinces desire an increase in the proportion [of relief] contributed by the Dominion, other provinces are satisfied with the present division and do not feel that an increase should be asked for."[22]

That public silence occurred because the first ministers were effectively deadlocked – and the poorer regions hoped to get more aid through private diplomacy. They also could not agree on constitutional changes that would establish federal Unemployment Insurance (Quebec and Ontario withheld consent).[23] Ultimately, Ottawa contributed $30.7 million to relief in 1933–34.[24]

The dissension remained unresolved at the next Dominion-Provincial Conference in January 1934. But that was when Nova Scotia premier Angus L. Macdonald finally joined his colleagues at the conference table – and nudged his way into the proceedings.

NOVA SCOTIA PREMIER ANGUS L. AND THE MARITIME PLIGHT

The best of the Depression-era premiers understood that the only way to survive in this challenging new world was to restructure the federation, formally or informally, shuffling the responsibilities or the revenues to accommodate pressures that the Fathers of Confederation had not anticipated. Perhaps it is not surprising that the new Joseph Howe became one of the most lucid and informed advocates for a revitalized federation. Indeed, Angus L. had "an admiration for Howe that bordered on fascination."[25] He read all of his predecessor's works, studied his life, and "was often seen gazing dreamily at the massive statue of Joseph Howe which stood outside his office" at the House of Assembly.[26]

Macdonald won power in August 1933 after a raucous election campaign. The Conservative government had passed legislation in 1931 that allowed provincially appointed registrars to prepare new lists of voters on the brink of an election. The Liberals feared that the law was designed to ensure that only Tories were on the list. When the Conservatives resisted efforts to amend the legislation, the Liberals turned it into a powerful election issue, rallying their supporters during desperate economic times. The key Dominion Steel and Coal Company had recently gone into receivership, putting thirty-two hundred jobs at risk (the company survived). The latest provincial budget foresaw an eighth consecutive year of deficits.[27]

Unable to raise funds through patronage, Liberal supporters had undertaken a "reasonably successful" fund-raising drive at the breweries and distilleries in Central Canada in June 1933.[28] Those firms contributed to both parties to ensure space for their products in the government-run liquor stores, which had opened in 1930 after voters endorsed the repeal of the Temperance Act. Macdonald won the election, taking twenty-two seats, leaving the battered Conservatives with eight. Although that victory "reflected the sins of the Conservatives more than the virtues of the Liberals," Macdonald proved to be "articulate, passionate, and popular."[29]

The new premier faced a dire situation. During the summer of 1933, forty thousand Nova Scotians were on direct or indirect relief. The government expected that seventy-five thousand people – or roughly one in seven residents – would be on relief during the winter. Conditions were even worse in Halifax and industrial Cape Breton, where 25 to 40 percent of the residents were dependent on relief.[30] Macdonald promptly diverted much relief spending into public works projects – although he had to provide supplemental direct relief.[31] He also agreed to participate in the Old Age Pension, contributing the requisite 25 percent of the cost.

THE GRIM LESSONS OF THE DEPRESSION

The Depression was slowly bringing home the flaws of unbridled capitalism to all battered provinces. Their citizenry needed help that only governments could provide. In the decades prior to this catastrophe, individual provinces had already started to expand their social programs. In 1914, Ontario introduced Workmen's Compensation, which allowed workers to collect an income when injured on the job. By 1919, five provinces had adopted such legislation.[32] Mothers' Allowances were introduced in Manitoba in 1916. By 1930, six provinces had adopted the program.[33] In 1927, Ottawa introduced the Old Age Pension, which picked up half of the cost of means-tested pensions to Canadians who were seventy and over; the provinces that agreed to join the plan picked up the other half. In 1931, Ottawa changed its contribution to 75 percent of the cost. By 1936, all provinces had joined.[34]

But the Old Age Pension would mark the limits of reform until the Second World War. Some Canadians were concerned that poorer individuals were asking for too much from their governments – even though, in retrospect, they were getting absurdly little. Demands for increased state aid jostled against the lingering characterizations of the poor as paupers who "were not simply poor but degraded, their character corrupted and their will sapped through reliance on charity."[35] Such harsh judgments were also applied to fellow provinces within the federation.

Those stereotypes lingered well into the twentieth century, intersecting disastrously with the structure of federalism itself. Those theoretically tidy compartments of federalism, which were never truly sealed off from each other, became an impediment to support for people and provinces hit by disastrous economic change. It was here that the fiscal inequalities among the provinces became brutally apparent: some provinces simply could not afford expanded social programs, even if they wanted them. The provincial economies were so unequal that joint action with Ottawa to remedy any social need – with the crucial exception of relief – was literally unthinkable. Also, the provinces had constitutional control over the "eleemosynary institutions," which aided the poor.[36]

But the Depression did witness the (very) slow growth in demands for federal remedies for the economic collapse. Social groups pushed for assistance – although their voices were largely ineffective. Provincial governments became increasingly aware of the inequalities among themselves. The premiers of the wealthier provinces of Quebec and Ontario were defensive. The poorer premiers were distressed – and their very presence at dominion-provincial conferences unsettled Bennett and then King. Those premiers understood that their societies were changing. And they knew that they could lose power if they could not secure more funds. Across the early years of the 1930s, they became an ever more desperate lot.

The debates became acerbic. Discussions about the level of taxation were not just about the defence of specific economic interests "but also about the morality of citizenship."[37] Surely, many Canadians asked each other, there was a limit to what the state could do without affecting its citizens' moral fibre? By the end of the 1930s, with so little evolution in the safety net through such despairing times, a leading charitable funding organization, the Community Chests, "seemed to have a chance of forestalling the welfare state ... [They] appear as both an alternative to the welfare state and its prototype."[38] Historian James Struthers notes that the expansion of social security in wartime only became possible because the number of people on relief had dropped, poor nutrition among the first enlisting soldiers had created concerns about children's health, and many experts feared that protests during wartime could disturb reconstruction in peacetime.[39]

It is significant that no province dared to ask for a specific federal program to remedy fiscal inequality during these early years of the

1930s. That was inconceivable. Instead, they asked for additional grants for unemployment relief or increased subsidies because of fiscal need. Sometimes, they argued – to no avail – that the political clout of other federation partners had relegated them to the role of underdogs. They did *not* address fiscal inequality as a permanent condition within the federation.

PREMIER MACDONALD MEETS HIS POORER KIN

Angus L. had plans for his beleaguered constituents. But the premier needed the funds to pay for such initiatives – or he had to induce Ottawa to accept responsibility for his poorer province's ills. On the eve of the next dominion-provincial conference in mid-January 1934, he joined a preliminary meeting of the Maritime premiers in Montreal. Those three premiers – New Brunswick's L.P.D. Tilley (the son of former premier Samuel Leonard Tilley), Prince Edward Island's William MacMillan, and Macdonald – asked Bennett to set up a Royal Commission to consider "a revision of the financial arrangements between the Dominion Government and the Maritime Provinces."[40]

Macdonald reiterated the trio's pleas at the conference itself. In fact, with his articulate approach, he almost stole the show. Ottawa should reassess its subsidies as the Duncan Report recommended. It should also establish a royal commission to consider the rearrangement of taxation sources because of the "dire necessity of all the provinces finding new sources of revenue."[41] The *Globe* could not resist the temptation to remark dourly: "Their [Maritime] requests are based upon moral rather than legal grounds."[42] Given the depths of the Depression, moral appeals remained difficult for Macdonald's Confederation partners.

In fact, the conference of January 1934 spent more time on the deepening fiscal plight of the three Prairie provinces and British Columbia. The Westerners were finally going public with their complaints. *Winnipeg Free Press* correspondent Grant Dexter privately confirmed to editor John Dafoe, the man he called "Chief," that Dafoe's hunch was correct: Westerners were angry. Very angry. "The western delegates are quite willing to talk and the belligerent attitude you noted in [Manitoba premier John] Bracken is very much in evidence among the others. I do think there will be a show-down and, perhaps, some serious fighting."[43]

A day later, that private distress was publicly confirmed. "West's Dire Straits Forcibly Presented at Premiers' Parlay," trumpeted the *Globe*'s headline for 18 January 1934. "Default on Bond Interest Faces Prairie and Coast Provinces Unless Federal Aid Is Forthcoming – Dominion Hopes to Stimulate Construction Industries."[44] Two days later, Prime Minister Bennett pointed out that the dominion government would have a deficit of more than $100 million in the current fiscal year.[45] But the case for the West was grim. As the *Globe* chronicled: "They have curtailed expenditures to the limit ... They cannot make further cuts without sacrificing their schools, hospitals or other essential services. Moreover, they have taxed their people until they have been threatened with a taxpayers' strike."[46]

All premiers finally recognized that the fiscal inequalities among the provinces were wrenching. Western resource control had not brought instant riches – partly because the administrative costs were high. Alberta's net gain would "not exceed $200,000 annually during the first five years of the 1930s."[47] By the end of the conference, Ottawa agreed to continue its aid to the Western provinces with the formal blessing of *all* participants, including wealthier Quebec and Ontario. Special ad hoc subsidies to alleviate desperate inequalities were becoming the norm. But there was no general principle, no formula, and no impartial adjudicator to determine the amount.

In response to Maritime pleas, Bennett also guardedly agreed to set up a subcommittee on Maritime Rights that would include an examination of tariff adjustments. He dawdled. In late July 1934, after a dominion-provincial meeting on relief, the three Maritime premiers – with Macdonald as "lead counsel" – stayed behind in Ottawa to lobby for an increase in subsidies.[48] Finally, on 14 September 1934, the prime minister set up a three-person royal commission under the chairmanship of former finance minister Sir Thomas White to deal "as speedily as possible" with the Duncan Commission's call for revised financial arrangements.[49]

But Macdonald could not wait for Bennett. He had promised to appoint a royal commission on his province's ills during the 1933 election campaign, and he had been searching for members for months. On 27 July 1934, he appointed his own three-person Royal Commission Provincial Economic Inquiry under the chairmanship of Leeds University economist John Harry Jones. The two other members were former Nova Scotia MP Alexander S. Johnston and political economist Harold Innis.

Their mission caught the zeitgeist of their Maritime age. They were to examine the effects of Ottawa's fiscal and trade policies on the province's economic life. They were to scrutinize "the adequacy of present financial arrangements" between Ottawa and the province "in the light of the powers, obligations, and responsibilities of the Dominion and Province" under the Constitution. And they were free to look at any other matter affecting the province's economic welfare or its relations with the dominion.[50] Those seemingly arcane questions seized the popular imagination. The commissioners dashed around the province, opening their hearings to large crowds in fishing villages, steel towns, and small agricultural communities. They inspected creameries and pulp and paper plants, learned the fine art of packing lobsters, and toured collieries.

Four months later, in early December, the Jones Commission issued a complex and occasionally disappointing report. Three main factors had contributed to the province's "relative economic decline: tariff policies, transportation costs, and centralized, protected industries."[51] The report carefully examined the problems – but there were no real solutions to catch the dispirited public's fancy. Harold Innis did not sign the main report, but he did issue a nearly one-hundred-page complementary report to strengthen the main report.[52]

Innis argued that two basic trends dominated Canada's economic history: centralization in the continental area and decentralization in the Maritimes: "Centralization has become increasingly marked and has been evident in transportation and banking particularly."[53] Central Canada's high tariffs had hampered Maritime reliance on the export of raw materials. During the Depression, "the burden of railway rates and customs duties became increasingly severe."[54] Innis even denounced "the callousness, lack of sympathy, and general disregard of broad policy, which has characterized federal supervision" of the Maritimes.[55] Ottawa should adopt a regional development policy and, *as in Australia*, assume the debts of the weaker provinces, especially the railway debts.[56] His conclusion was blunt: "Compensation is not enough."[57]

The Jones Report, including Innis's candid diagnosis, made little impression on Central Canada. The *Globe* commented glumly: "The unsatisfactory feature of the findings – but perhaps the inevitable one – is that most of Nova Scotia's troubles lie beyond her own control."[58] The newspaper urged other provinces to undertake similar studies to figure out how their subsidies were determined – and to demand changes, if necessary. Nothing much happened. The strains within the federation were evident – but not even Macdonald could remedy the general passivity.

MARITIME CALLS FOR ACTION

There was one fascinating outcome – although few noticed it at the time. Attached to the Jones Report was a twenty-three-page appendix – "Economic Inquiry – Financial Relations" – that Dalhousie University political scientist, Robert Alexander MacKay, had submitted to the commission on 26 September 1934. His paper examined fiscal inequalities from the province's entry into Confederation. Aggrieved Australians in the poorer states, especially Western Australia, would have felt thoroughly at home.

This future member of the Royal Commission on Dominion-Provincial Relations declared that struggling provincial governments should only receive federal money if they had a "reasonably efficient" administration, if their services were not "more extensive than those of other Provinces," and if they levied a "fair burden of taxation."[59] If a province passed those tests, "the Dominion is clearly under obligations to come to the aid of the Provinces."[60] Subsidies based on "fiscal need" were essential – and it was in the federation's self-interest to ensure that all provinces could fulfill their responsibilities.[61]

MacKay saw inequality as a perilous condition, which perhaps tempted him to go too far. He argued that his province could claim more subsidies if provincial revenues were "impaired by Dominion policies," notably federal tariffs and income taxes.[62] MacKay did *not* assert that this damage had occurred. But if it had, "Nova Scotia, it seems clear, has quite as good a claim for compensation by way of subsidies as had the western provinces for federal control of their lands or New Brunswick for loss of its right to levy export taxes on timber."[63] MacKay would later move away from that early claim for compensation for the inequities caused by federation.[64]

Finally, and perhaps most astonishingly, MacKay lamented the lack of "a suitable means for adjusting subsidies." Instead, any adjustments were left to dominion whims. But the history of subsidies made it "clear that *the principle of equality of treatment as between the Provinces is subordinate to the principle of fiscal need*."[65] The future royal commissioner was quietly building a case for equalization: How could poorer provinces be truly equal to the richer provinces if they could not afford to pay for similar services? Insistence on the equality of the provinces could not last.

THE WHITE COMMISSION

Two months after the Jones Report, the federal White Commission reported, less than five months after it had started its hectic examination of the Maritime provinces. Ever the shrewd lobbyist, Premier Macdonald had told the commission that "financial necessity" was the basis of "most if not all" federal revisions of the subsidy since Confederation. Ottawa had provided funds, he maintained, to meet the provinces' fiscal needs.[66] The White Commission firmly rejected that assertion, arguing that acceptance "would inevitably lead to conditions harmful and dangerous in the extreme." In other words, provinces could spend as much as they wanted and then demand money from Ottawa to meet their deficits. "Power to spend must entail responsibility for expenditures."[67]

Still, the report admitted that the three provincial governments had been "frugal" – and that they were handicapped by their "isolated economic position with respect to the rest of Canada, a stationary or declining population and less per capita wealth and taxable capacity than most if not all of the other provinces."[68] It added sagely that higher grants would not alone bring prosperity but they might "indirectly assist by promoting, through educational and public welfare services, economic efficiency or by reducing taxation within the Province and thus lessening the burden upon trade and industry."[69]

In effect, some form of equalization would benefit all Canadians. The White Commission agreed with the Duncan Commission's notion that it was not possible to ensure that every region of the country benefited equally from federation. "But *reasonable balance* is within accomplishment if there be periodic stocktaking."[70] It was stocktaking time. It recommended an increase in the subsidies for all three Maritime provinces, based upon "considerations of fairness and equity" and "the economic disadvantages to which the Maritime Provinces are particularly subject."[71]

This was an argument based upon the federation's moral obligation to its poorer members – but it was also a hardheaded decision. More remarkably, one of the three members of the White Royal Commission filed a dissenting report. The chief justice of the Prince Edward Island Supreme Court, John Alexander Mathieson, who was a former PEI premier, concluded that the main report minimized the actual fiscal needs of the provinces: the three Maritime provinces had been treated with "less justice and consideration" than the Western provinces. Fiscal inequality does breed envy, even among the poorer provinces.

There had been no equality of treatment for the Maritimes since Confederation. "One of the major problems facing Canada today is the devising of some general plan for the adjustment of Dominion and provincial financial relations," Mathieson maintained. "The practice which has existed from early days of dealing with single Provinces or groups of Provinces without due regard to the interests of all, may bring about a condition of grave unrest not free from danger to Canadian unity."[72]

The Bennett government listened, increasing Prince Edward Island's annual payments in the wake of the Duncan Commission's original recommendations from $125,000 to $275,000; New Brunswick's went from $600,000 to $900,000; and Nova Scotia's went from $875,000 to $1.3 million.[73]

THE CANADIAN-AUSTRALIAN CONTACTS CONTINUE

The close Canadian-Australian connection continued throughout the Depression. The two nations watched each other closely on so many common issues, including their efforts to implement Unemployment Insurance and to manage their currencies. In late 1933, the Australians told Canberra about Prime Minister Bennett's promise of an "economically independent" central bank, along with his "pride in the fact that the financial credit of Canada stood unchallenged."[74] (Australia had vested its Commonwealth Bank of Australia with central bank powers such as the ability to issue notes in the 1920s.) Most important, the financial disputes between the provinces and Ottawa – and among the provinces themselves – preoccupied Canberra.

Canada, in turn, watched Australia. At the 18–19 January 1934 Dominion-Provincial Conference, where Nova Scotia premier Angus L. Macdonald and the Western premiers pleaded for more funds for relief, there was another important theme running through the discussions that was largely overlooked at the time and certainly not mentioned to the press or the public: the situation in Australia. Even *Winnipeg Free Press* Ottawa correspondent Grant Dexter, who had extensive off-the-record access to politicians and bureaucrats, did not cite Australia in his chatty behind-the-scenes seven-page letter to his editor John Dafoe on 17 January 1934. Australia had not yet grabbed the public's imagination.

But senior bureaucrats were finally probing their fellow dominion's approach to the Depression. The federal package for Bennett's final conference in 1934 included a fourteen-page academic essay on how Australia had reduced real wages, slashed government expenditures, cut interest charges, expanded central bank credit to finance deficits and loans for necessary works, and depreciated its currency. Most measures were introduced as part of the so-called Premiers' Plan of 1931. "I do not suggest that Australian policy is the only way out," wrote University of Melbourne economist Douglas Copland, "but ... it has proved to be a way out at a time when less comprehensive action has not proved so successful in some countries ... The secret of Australia's attack on the depression lay in the combination of a courageous banking policy with drastic reductions in costs and government expenditure."[75]

There was more. The provincial delegates to that January 1934 conference also received an eleven-page federal memo on the consolidation of debts in Australia and the establishment of the Australian Loan Council. The document traced the Commonwealth's gradual approach to debt control from the first voluntary measures in 1924 to the formal constitutional adoption of the council in 1929.[76] The Commonwealth government had taken over all state debts and then put responsibility for all future federal or state borrowings under the Australian Loan Council. But the ingenious Australian solution to fiscal inequality was not an easy sell to Canada's suspicious provinces – especially the "have" ones. Those suggestions went nowhere.

Remarkably, the Australians still viewed the Dominion-Provincial Conference of 1934 as a sign of growing dominion-provincial agreement on the tricky issue of fiscal inequality. On 26 January 1934, their diplomats reported to Canberra that the five Eastern provinces had passed a resolution at that conference, "expressing appreciation of the difficulties of the grain-growing provinces of the west, and waiving objections to the continuation of the Federal loan policy." Bennett, they added, had vowed to keep financing the Western provinces – and to adopt a large public works policy. [77]

Presumably, Australian politicians took comfort from the news that their dominion's Depression-era misery had company. In Western

Australia alone, unemployment had been nearly 30 percent in 1932, wheat prices toppled, and the beleaguered state introduced an entertainments tax and a lotteries commission. All states were reeling. But, by 1933, Australia also had the fledgling Commonwealth Grants Commission to examine state applications for special assistance. The CGC initially decided that grants should enable claimant states "with reasonable effort, to put their finances in about as good order as that of the other states," but the grants "were not aimed at equalising incomes or living standards of individuals in the States."[78] By 1936, in its third report, the Grants Commission would refine that principle to ensure that states had "the amount of help found necessary to make it possible for that State by reasonable effort to function at a standard not appreciably below that of other States."[79] Canada would pay very close attention throughout this evolution.

THE STRUGGLE TO SURVIVE IN AUSTRALIA AND CANADA

Both nations were somehow coping with the strains on their societies – and their governments. Barely. Their newspapers were bewildering pastiches of vanishing lifestyles and grim realities. The differences between the richer and the poorer were rarely clearer. On 5 January 1934, the *Sydney Morning Herald* carried an advertisement for a clearance sale on maids' frocks in "popular summer weaves" along with ads for "startling new Studebakers."[80] Qantas Airlines had flown 2 million miles without an accident – which elicited acclaim in this new era of commercial flight.[81] Sir Hugh and Lady Poynter and their two daughters had returned from their five-month world tour, which "touched every continent and 'sailed the seven seas', and they had contrived to spend an enjoyable time in England as well."[82]

Others were struggling. Aborigines in the Northern Territory were fending off leprosy, tuberculosis, Chinese opium suppliers, and missionaries who interfered with native customs "without replacement by something just as useful."[83] The customs office was investigating the price of tea – in response to the suspicion that merchants were not passing along the recent reduction in customs' duties.[84] Most important, in headline Australian news, American president Franklin Delano Roosevelt had just told a joint session of Congress: "The hard beginning is over. We are definitely in [the] process of recovery."[85] Surely Australians, too, could have reason for hope.

Half a world away, in an era that was questioning the goodness of its gods, it remained news in the *Ottawa Journal* that fourteen women had made their vows to join the Roman Catholic sisterhood at St Joseph's Convent Chapel in Toronto.[86] The Ottawa branch of the Amputation Association of the Great War was planning its annual convention, having diverted its annual Christmas Cheer Fund from the traditional tree party "to provide needy comrades with baskets and other necessities."[87] Public health authorities in Ottawa heralded a "great triumph" for the campaign for immunization against diphtheria: there had been only eighty-eight cases in 1933, less than two-thirds of the number in 1932.[88]

The contrasts in Depression-era life in Canada were also dizzying. The paper's Woman's Realm section breezily declared that "Both Maid and Matron May Wear Velvet" – a distinction between married and unmarried women that seems almost unthinkable today.[89] The display of luxurious gowns was followed by several pages of huge advertisements for heavily discounted goods, ranging from clothes to furniture, that interim receiver Bryson-Graham Limited was offering in "The Biggest Shopping Event in Years."[90] It was a reminder that business bankruptcies remained frequent occurrences.

Governments dominated the news as they had in Australia – if only because they were the main agents of change in desperate times. The appointment of new deputy ministers in Ottawa vied for banner headlines with a major government scandal in France.[91] The gap between richer and poorer governments could be seen at a glance. Ontario premier George Henry announced that his province's 1933 year-end surplus was $476,000 instead of the anticipated deficit of nearly $3 million (this was fiscal year 1933–34). "It is largely the result of economy without impairment of efficiency in service," effused the *Ottawa Journal*.[92]

In contrast, the dominion government exited 1933 with a shortfall of more than $100 million, which was "not something for which the Government can be blamed." The newspaper summed up Ottawa's plight: "The Government has cut controllable expenditure to the bone; is running the country practically as cheaply as it was run before the war, this despite more services, a greatly increased interest overhead. What it couldn't avoid – no Government could – was the expenditure that had and has to be made for relief, the losses of the Canadian National [Railway], the tremendous curtailment of revenues."[93]

Those deficits were not Keynesian. Ottawa had not accepted the idea that fiscal policy could increase the level of demand or employment. Instead, as political scientist Robert M. Campbell argues: "Deficits in the 1930s were unintentional, reflecting declining revenues, and governments were encouraged by the business and financial community to control or eliminate them."[94] Bennett's deficits were reluctant. But they were a *very necessary* concession to his turbulent times.

YEAR-TO-YEAR SURVIVAL ON AN AD HOC BASIS

Ottawa was dispensing money to the provinces on an ad hoc and seemingly chaotic basis. On the eve of the Depression, Ottawa had transferred $16.5 million in statutory subsidies, grants, and conditional subsidies to the provinces. By 1934, that number was $55.9 million. A year later, it was $74 million.[95] In 1935, a Department of Labour publication took twenty-seven pages to itemize the numerous federal disbursements under relief legislation: they were almost $161 million between September 1930 and March 1935 – along with $81.8 million in outstanding loans and advances.[96] The payments and the programs varied drastically among provinces. But it was a lot of money: in his budget in mid-April 1934, Finance Minister Edgar Rhodes declared that tax revenues had netted $271.9 million in 1933–34 – but his government had spent $407 million.[97]

The federal contribution to relief and public works projects – which was in addition to subsidies – was a seemingly never-ending expense. They were "by far the most significant payments to the provinces ... While refusing to accept constitutional liability for relief the Dominion early recognized that the financial burden was of a magnitude far in excess of the capacity of at least six of the provinces."[98] In the first years of the Depression, Ottawa paid approximately one-third of the cost of relief, with the provinces and municipalities picking up the balance in roughly equal proportions. The federal government also paid for public works. After August 1934, the dominion adopted a "more pragmatic approach and granted money on a monthly basis which varied in amount with seasonal and other requirements."[99]

But even that pragmatic approach did not end Ottawa's assistance. In addition to its contributions for relief in all provinces, the federal government also made "substantial loans for relief and other purposes to the Prairie provinces and British Columbia. In all these amounted to about $175 million."[100] This figure did not include the later payments that were made between 1937 and 1941 to the desperate Prairie provinces – when the situation became even worse.

The federation could barely cope. Without a system of regular equalization, the provinces were left to rely on federal goodwill, whims, their regular subsidies, and political calculation.

BENNETT STRUGGLES TO CHANGE COURSE IN 1935

Two days after the last of the prime minister's dramatic radio addresses, his government's Speech from the Throne echoed his incendiary discourse. The speech outlined the failures of capitalism – and emphasized the pressing need for fairer treatment for Canada's beleaguered citizens. "In the anxious years through which you have passed, you have been the witnesses of grave defects and abuses in the capitalist system," the speech declared while his seriously divided cabinet listened. "Unemployment and want are proof of these ... New conditions prevail. These require modifications in the capitalist system to enable that system more effectively to serve the people."[101] Bennett promised legislation for unemployment insurance, minimum wages, old-age pensions, workplace reform, "and changes to regulate companies and to help farmers sell their products."[102] It was one of the most extraordinary turnarounds in Canadian political history. Some historians remain dubious that it was heartfelt.[103] But Bennett staked his re-election on the plan.

In effect, the prime minister was tackling the inequalities among citizens directly, irrespective of the unequal fiscal situations among the provinces, which were constitutionally responsible for social programs. He sought to expand the flimsy social security network gradually, over the horrified objections of hardline conservatives who accused him of socialism. He wanted to replace relief with the more dignified alternative of Unemployment Insurance, which would allow employers, employees, and the federal government to contribute to a fund that would support those who had lost their jobs because of the economic difficulties of their firms. As Boyko writes, the prime minister's Unemployment and Social Insurance Act constituted "a statement as clear as the July prairie sun that the government should care for and about the welfare of the governed."[104]

Meanwhile, behind the scenes, bureaucrats at the finance ministry and the new Bank of Canada were desperately searching for ways to shore up faltering provincial governments – without embroiling Ottawa in unsustainable financial obligations. Bennett had formally established the central bank in July 1934 – over the fierce objections of the chartered banks that "had to give up their profitable issue of bank notes in favour of a national currency ... [and] transfer their gold reserves to the Bank of Canada."[105]

The prime minister regarded the Bank of Canada as his finest domestic accomplishment. While Bennett talked revolution, his bureaucrats looked to other federations for inspiration. Something somewhere had to work. "No other industrial downturn in history was so massive or so persistent," Kenneth Norrie, Douglas Owram, and J. C. Herbert Emery observe in *A History of the Canadian Economy*.[106] Commodity markets had dwindled. Trade and credit had contracted, which was especially disastrous in a nation reliant on exports for a third of its Gross National Income.[107] The anxiety remained pervasive.

THE AUSTRALIANS WATCH WHILE BENNETT STUMBLES

In the spring of 1935, foreign affairs representatives in the Dominion of Canada, the Commonwealth of Australia, and the Union of South Africa agreed to exchange "in a more direct manner, current social, political, statistical and economic information ... as well as any general information that might be deemed interesting and useful to the other Dominions."[108] It was an interesting pact in tough times.

Meanwhile, Australian diplomats in Canada maintained their vigilance. But those diplomats did not tell their home country what was becoming apparent: no matter what Bennett did, and he had done much to change his strategy for dealing with the stark economic inequalities among Canadians during his last months in office, he could not revive his popularity. His New Deal did not capture the public's imagination, perhaps because "Bennett lacked the common touch; he was too often in thrall to his own deeply held convictions. Although his charity was vast, his capacity for mercy was limited."[109]

As well, for many Canadians still trapped in the Depression, Bennett's plan was a fascinating but not totally unfamiliar move: the prime minister and his officials had discussed unemployment insurance with provincial premiers for at least three years. But it remained an elusive measure in a federation that still could not figure out how to divide responsibilities and revenues among the different levels of government.

Throughout the spring of 1935, Bennett did not venture beyond relief grants and loans to the poorer provinces, along with money for public works projects, while his New Deal went through Parliament. It was a gamble. Liberal leader Mackenzie King watched with a mixture of glee and dread, first challenging Bennett to table the entire package and then pecking away at individual bills and *questioning the constitutional validity of key measures such as unemployment insurance.* But King shrewdly did not attempt to defeat the government. Bennett had to put his bills before the House – and on the line.

By the late spring, the prime minister was exhausted. He had endured an acute respiratory infection and a heart attack, struggled to handle the mounting frustration among unemployed single men in the relief camps, and overseen trade talks with the United States. When unemployed men deserted British Columbia camps in April 1935 to join a Vancouver protest, Bennett dismissed provincial and municipal pleas for help with the protesters: The prime minister had denounced the capitalist regime but he could not empathize with people whom he viewed as threats to law and order.[110] Somehow his government managed to present fourteen pieces of significant legislation, including Unemployment Insurance. "It was," says his biographer John Boyko, "a remarkable achievement."[111] But his New Deal package was also flawed. As political scientist W.H. McConnell would later write in the *Osgoode Hall Law Journal*: "The disjointedness and incoherence of the New Deal – its lack of unity or system – is attributable to Bennett's notorious penchant for one-man rule."[112]

THE BUREAUCRATS SEARCH FOR A BETTER WAY BEHIND THE SCENES

As Bennett struggled publicly, senior finance ministry bureaucrats privately scrounged for ideas. On 5 January 1935, as Bennett was in the midst of his radio addresses, Deputy Finance Minister W.C. Clark sent a memo to the prime minister's political advisor, R.K. Finlayson, suggesting a three-to-five-year federal guarantee for provincial loans. The idea was that the security of a federal guarantee would allow Western provinces, including British Columbia, to lower their interest costs – and still sell their bonds. "Indeed, it might make it possible for the provinces to finance all or a considerable portion of their unemployment relief expenditures without coming to us."[113]

There could be a hefty price, however, for this remedy. As Clark explained, that could include: "Probably, one: an agreement on the part of the province not to issue any new loans without approval of the Governor of the Bank of Canada and, possibly, two: an agreement on the part of the province to submit its budget for the general approval of the Governor of the Bank before presenting it to the Provincial Legislature."[114] Clark added that many bondholders assumed that the dominion would not let any province default. Interest rates were not lower, however, because there were enough skeptics to thwart much of the benefit to the Western provinces of that "implied moral guarantee."[115]

Clark had been deputy minister for less than three years when he wrote this politically naïve – almost shockingly naïve – memo. The next two years would upset many of his assumptions – including his notion that the provinces would be willing to accept federal budgetary oversight and his certainty that Ottawa would never allow a province to default. But at least the Ottawa wheels were now turning.

In mid-January 1935, the deputy governor of the Bank of Canada, J.A.C. Osborne, wrote to the Bank of England Overseas and Foreign Department, asking for more information on the Australian Loan Council, which had been mentioned at the Dominion-Provincial Conference of January 1934. Osborne was actually the secretary of the British Bank, on loan for up to five years to the fledgling Canadian institution. His colleague J. Fisher replied promptly, emphasizing an important difference between Australia and Canada: Australia had a constitutional amending formula. All six Australian states had ratified the surrender of key state powers to the federal authority for a loan council – and Australian voters had approved the idea in a referendum. Canberra had then passed the Financial Agreement Validation Act, 1929. So the adoption of a council had been relatively simple. Any similar agreement in Canada would require the approval of the dominion Parliament and every province – and that act, in turn, would require the consent of the British Parliament to become law. Unlike Australia, Canada did not have an amending formula.[116]

Fisher also advised Osborne that dramatic problems had developed quickly after the Australian act had passed. New South Wales governor Jack Lang had won office in October 1930, promising public works and markets for farmers. He vehemently opposed the Loan Council, arguing that it gave the central government too much power over the states. Lang was a huge man, "ruthless, calculating and shrewd, adept at short-term judgements that fostered his own interests, the model of the self-seeking house and land agent."[117] In March 1931, the former estate agent had arbitrarily reduced the interest rate on his state government's borrowings and suspended interest payments to British bondholders. The controversy had embroiled the entire federation and split the federal Labor Government.

The state of New South Wales duly defaulted, and the Commonwealth covered its tab. In January 1932, however, the United Australia Party under Prime Minister Joseph Lyons took power in the Commonwealth and promptly passed an act to seize the revenues of New South Wales in recompense. In response, the pugnacious Lang withdrew all state funds from government bank accounts. In May 1932, New South Wales governor Sir Philip Game dismissed Lang's government, which was massively defeated in the ensuing election in June 1932 as the unemployment rate hovered around 31 percent.[118] The High Court of Australia eventually upheld the validity of the 1932 federal act, which made the Commonwealth liable for state debts; and, crucially, it also upheld the Commonwealth's right to force a defaulting state to pay.[119]

Undeterred, the Bank of Canada kept researching models. It concluded that the South African provinces were "not a worry" for the central government because the Reserve Bank would not lend to them without the central government's approval: "There has even been talk of abolishing the Provinces altogether."[120] There were likely many occasions when the elite Ottawa bureaucrats envied the clout of the central governments in other federations.

Bank of Canada governor Graham Towers disregarded the Bank of England's warnings about loan councils. In a memorandum, he described a conversation on 16 May 1935 with British Columbia finance minister John Hart who wanted Ottawa to cut the interest rates on its loans to his province. Otherwise, he warned, "more drastic action" could occur.[121] Hart asked about the possibility of borrowing from the Bank, and Towers explained that such action was impossible. But, in that same memorandum, he also hinted that the Bank might exercise supervision to assist struggling provinces: "I mentioned that we [federal officials] visualized possible arrangements in which the Province, the Bank and the Province's chartered bankers would, in a sense, constitute a partnership" that would regulate the province's finances so that it could take full advantage of the improving securities markets.[122] Hart "did not think for political reasons the Province could submit to control by the Dominion Government but thought that such control could be given to the Bank of Canada."[123] Both Hart and Towers wisely did not commit themselves to the scheme.

Still, the Loan Council idea remained alive. In mid-1935, the new Bank of Canada secretary Donald Gordon even examined "the good features of Australia's Loan Council" in order to adapt them to Canada's constitutionally powerful provinces: an advisory council could approve provincial bond issues or it could *withhold approval* as a "disciplinary weapon" if any province ignored the council's recommendations. He added: "Now is the psychological time to do something."[124]

THE FEDERAL ELECTION OF 1935

Such discussions did not provoke action, nor did they seep into the press. The *politics* of the federal situation consumed the attention of Ottawa journalists. Against the terrible backdrop of the ongoing Depression, they were riveted by the upcoming election: How would King handle Bennett? How would Bennett, who was famously short-tempered and ill, handle the stress? Even *Winnipeg Free Press* journalist Grant Dexter, who was superbly well connected, did not mention the bureaucratic hunt for models – not even in his insider letters to his editor, John Dafoe.[125]

The Canadian New Deal – with its tangle of measures – could not save the prime minister. The government had lost the consent of the governed. Bennett ran on his record, insisting that unemployment had waned since 1930. He talked about the newly created Bank of Canada. He cited his efforts to force businesses "to improve wages and working conditions, and policies that had provided jobs and relief to desperate Canadians."[126] It was all in vain. As Mackenzie King told voters in Port Arthur, Ontario: "You have had five years of the Bennett Government. I wonder if any of you are as well off now as when it started?"[127] Resentment about inequality, even in comparison with one's own past, was in the air. The Liberal leader's slogan was: "King or Chaos."

On Election Day on 14 October 1935, the *Globe* headline trumpeted: "Canada Votes Today in Biggest Election in Her History." The number of parties – including the fledgling Co-operative Commonwealth Federation, which farm and labour leaders along with academics had founded in 1932 – and the number of candidates had set records.[128] Nearly 6 million people were eligible to cast a ballot. In the end, it was a Liberal landslide of 173 seats. The CCF took seven seats and a significant 8.9 percent of the popular vote. Bennett's so-called Liberal-Conservative Party won only thirty-nine seats. Significantly, Bennett took only one seat in Alberta, which was his own, one seat in Saskatchewan, and one seat in Manitoba. It was probably impossible for him to do better: despite Ottawa's ad hoc payments for relief and other needs, the West was lurching from crisis to crisis.

CONCLUSION

After nearly seven decades of turmoil and protest, the federation was no closer to a solution for sharing in 1935 than it had been in 1867. Bennett had staked his political career on remedying his dominion's plight. In the end, he had merely resorted to the tired old remedies of ad hoc subsidies and grants. It was now up to his successor to see if he could do any better with the plagues of poverty and glaring inequality.

5

King Stalls as the Depression Continues, 1935–37

Prime Minister Mackenzie King had never displayed much empathy for the individual victims of the Depression. His diary, which he kept from 1893 to 1950, remains one of the most astute and conniving political records in Canadian history. He had a genius for compromise and delay. But, even within the privacy of his own pages, he often wrote about social problems as political problems; even then, he usually wrote about his theories and not about the grim reality on the ground. Perhaps more telling, he recorded *his* feelings, not other people's feelings. In the October 1935 federal election, he had campaigned with a "safe and traditional platform" that included the promise of "moderation, faith in laissez-faire capitalism, a balanced budget and social legislation such as unemployment insurance," which the Liberal Party had first endorsed at its national convention in 1919.[1]

King had promised nothing radical – partly because he still blamed "the greed of individuals" instead of systemic problems for many of the nation's woes.[2] He also remained improbably wedded to the notion that the federal government was not responsible for the provinces' fiscal ills. So he had delivered nothing radical. He still did not understand the terrible power of fiscal and economic inequality among the provinces – or the political price to be paid for such inequality. Instead, he had stood back while his Conservative opponent, Prime Minister R.B. Bennett, defeated himself.

But, while King resisted pleas for further intervention in the economy, he also knew that he had to *appear* to be doing something, if only to set a new tone. He moved swiftly. Within two days of the 14 October 1935 election, he invited the premiers to Ottawa to deal with the "financial problems and constitutional difficulties" in Bennett's reform legislation, "much of which, it [was] feared, [was] invalid."[3] On 4 November, King and his cabinet passed an order-in-council to refer eight Bennett statutes to the Supreme Court of Canada, including Unemployment Insurance (UI).[4] King wanted clarification *before* implementation.[5]

Many groups were troubled over the legality of the UI measure – including provinces such as Ontario and New Brunswick and representatives of large industries such as the Canadian Manufacturers' Association, Canadian Pacific Railway (CPR) president Edward Beatty, and Canadian Bank of Commerce vice-president Sir Thomas White. Quebec premier L.A. Taschereau had referred to Bennett's New Deal as "a socialistic venture bordering on Communism" – but, perhaps surprisingly, he supported UI.[6] Even the federal government's own actuaries had reported to Parliament that the policy "has itself the tendency, for various reasons, to increase unemployment."[7] Privately, the prime minister referred to the laws as constitutionally "doubtful," so the referral to the Supreme Court was "a great step."[8] The canny politician did not want endless squabbles with the provincial leaders just before the upcoming Dominion-Provincial Conference. He wanted to sparkle on his return to the spotlight.

INEQUALITY AND ITS CHALLENGES

Ottawa and the provinces remained in ferment during this profound and baffling Depression. Politicians and officials spent months pondering the intricacies of their finances, their constitutional powers, and their fragile social supports. But these were desperate times – and any solutions beyond ad hoc subsidies were not readily apparent. Such subsidies could not permanently alleviate the ever-widening inequalities among federation members. The richer provinces were resentful of the eleventh-hour funding for the poorer provinces that their taxpayers unwittingly financed. The poorer ones could never get enough money – but the pleading, the trips to Ottawa, the ritual of polite-but-desperate-or-disdainful letters was exhausting.

The senior bureaucrats looked to other federations – to the United States, to Argentina, and *especially* to Australia – to figure out how they handled inequalities among states. Throughout the mid-1930s, they first singled out the Australian "Loan Council" as worthy of study: in 1929, the Commonwealth government had taken over all state debts and then put responsibility for all future federal or state borrowings under the council. When a Canadian version of the Loan Council did not win enthusiastic provincial approval, senior bureaucrats and their political masters eventually created a royal commission on *Re-confederation*. And every step of the way – from its Loan Council to its Commonwealth Grants Commission – the main model was Australia.

THE BANK OF CANADA GRASPS FOR IDEAS FOR THE FEDERATION

Two days before the Dominion-Provincial Conference, Bank of Canada deputy governor J.A.C. Osborne sent an oblivious memo to Deputy Finance Minister Clark, airily offering his views on procedure at the upcoming gathering. "Piecemeal negotiations" with individual provinces would no longer suffice – and the new Bank of Canada should offer advice to the politicians.[9] The dominion should simply accept liability for unemployment relief, old-age pensions, and non-sectarian education. "It would only be a question of administration" to decide how long the provinces should act as agents 'in carrying out Dominion [social] policy."[10] Then Canada could amend its Constitution. Ottawa could show each province how to "balance its budget on a lower level" while it reduced tariffs to revive trade and increase revenues. If that did not work, Ottawa could cut the number of provinces. If that did not work, "the Liberals could resign and let somebody else have a shot."[11] The letter was not intended as satire.

Clark probably hit the roof: only a rather condescending bureaucrat from the unitary state of Britain could have made such assertions. Osborne did not understand how the partners in the Canadian federation had to work *together*. In his biography of Bank of Canada governor Graham Towers, former government adviser Douglas H. Fullerton noted that Osborne "was regarded by the Bank staff as fair and impartial, but his English mannerisms and Bank of England traditions did not endear him to everyone."[12] King would never have contemplated such measures anyway: he had already referred Bennett's far less intrusive social legislation to the Supreme Court. And he was always hesitant about assuming more federal responsibilities.

The officials were perplexed. No one knew if the counter-cyclical prescriptions of British economist John Maynard Keynes would work: the politicians and bureaucrats at the very top of the Ottawa pecking-order could not be tempted to try them – although some were familiar with his work.[13] Finance ministry special assistant W.A. Mackintosh would lead a delegation to London in November 1942 to discuss Keynes's proposal for an international central bank, which the individual central banks would establish to clear payments.[14] But Canadian officials would not discuss his economic insights in depth with him in Ottawa until 1944–45.[15] Economists J. Stephen Ferris and Stanley L. Winer date the acceptance of Keynesian thought in Canada to Mackenzie King's White Paper on Employment and Income in 1945.[16] That paper was "aimed at addressing the perceived electoral strength of the Co-operative Commonwealth Federation (CCF) and the apparent incapacity of the Liberal Government to provide a clear alternative."[17] It was a relatively late conversion.

THE DECEMBER 1935 DOMINION-PROVINCIAL CONFERENCE

The conference ran from Monday, 9 December, to Friday, 13 December, and the proceedings were a remarkable example of King's ability to procrastinate under the guise of consultation. They also illustrate how heavily the federal government was relying on Australia's approach to provincial debt and fiscal inequalities. By now, most governments accepted that they were key players in tackling inequalities among themselves and their struggling citizens. They also recognized that their voters had just ousted the federal Conservatives – and those same voters were quite capable of turning on *them*.

Every premier knew that it was politically risky for the richer provinces to denounce the poorer provinces too strongly. Everyone remembered the March on Ottawa, when protesting residents of the relief camps and their supporters had set out for the capital. When the RCMP violently broke up that gathering in Regina on 1 July 1935, the incident reinforced the notion "that 'Iron Heel' Bennett had little concern for the working man."[18] As his biographer John Boyko notes: "Liberal papers and his political opponents were quick and ruthless in using [the strike, trek, and riot] as ammunition against him in the election that followed only months later, with the blood on Regina's streets still fresh in the nation's collective memory."[19]

But the first ministers were *very* far apart in their acceptance of any possible solution to the ongoing Depression beyond the continuation of federal relief contributions, ad hoc grants, and loans. They could not agree on a formal mechanism – they could not even envision such a mechanism – to remedy inequalities among their governments and their citizenry. There were entrenched and adamantly opposed interests among them. As *Le Devoir* noted, "never before, even in the worst moments of the financial crisis of 1931, have the financial difficulties which assail the federal, provincial and municipal governments been so clearly explained and so keenly felt ... One is seized with an understanding of the financial malady."[20]

Such difficulties ensured that the stalemate at this conference could not be attributed solely to Mackenzie King. After six full years of Depression, the provinces' disagreements allowed King to dodge most immediate demands for action. The conference did set up machinery to study problems that could not be resolved immediately. In the end, those supposedly permanent committees did not make much progress – and they eventually lapsed. The December 1935 conference was the eighth Dominion-Provincial Conference since Confederation – and it would be the last until the grim days of wartime in January 1941.

The focus was on revenues and responsibilities. King told the premiers that he wanted to figure out how the federation had changed since 1867, where "provincial responsibility should begin and federal responsibility should cease," and whether they could find "a formula for co-operation" wherever there were overlaps.[21]

Then the premiers spoke, and the differences between the richer and the poorer provinces were stark. Ontario Liberal premier Mitchell Hepburn had campaigned vigorously for King during the election but, as Hepburn's biographer John T. Saywell explains, King "saw only [Hepburn's] ambition" to replace him.[22] Their relationship, which would reach its nadir during wartime, was already fraying. As the premier from fat-cat Ontario, Hepburn discouraged Ottawa's interference in his province – but he would ask for an interest-rate cut on his loans.

Quebec premier L.A. Taschereau echoed that approach. "Confederation is pretty old now," he mused. "We have to face to-day problems that did not exist in 1867."[23] The provinces needed the right to levy indirect taxes such as sales taxes – and Ottawa should let them know "exactly where they [stood] on this matter."[24] With those broader taxing powers, Quebec could help itself.

Other premiers fretted about dependency. British Columbia premier T.D. "Duff" Pattullo complained that the virtue of self-reliance among seasonal workers had vanished: it was now "Eat, drink, and be merry, for to-morrow we go on relief." Instead of more relief, Ottawa should work with the provinces to fund the construction of public works to provide jobs.[25]

The Manitoba and Saskatchewan premiers confronted desperate inequalities. Manitoba premier John Bracken warned that, within the last ten years, the value of Manitoba's agricultural products had been halved. Within the last five years, Prairie farmers had lost $1 billion in purchasing power. Somehow, his government had provided food, clothing, and shelter for the needy, borrowing $35 million to ensure their survival. But seventy thousand people were still on relief – and the interest on the debt to pay for relief was $1.5 million per year. Bracken wanted to shuffle revenues or responsibilities.[26] "The needs of to-day cannot be met within the limitations of the constitution of sixty-eight years ago," he declared.[27]

Saskatchewan premier William Patterson recounted his devastating problems with drought, drifting soil, dust storms, plagues of grasshoppers, and fungal leaf rust. Eight thousand families had moved from the drought-stricken south to the north of the province, and, unless they could be helped to sustain themselves, they were "a permanent relief problem."[28] Ottawa, the province, and its municipalities had spent a staggering $105 million since 1929 on relief and agricultural assistance. Conditions had "reached proportions of a national calamity or a national catastrophe."[29] He, too, wanted constitutional change.

In contrast to his fellow Westerners, particularly in light of what would occur in less than five months, Alberta premier William "Bible Bill" Aberhart was publicly bland and duplicitous. "It has been our desire and our determination ... to handle our own problems and balance our budget," he maintained. Alberta might need federal public works, "but we are very desirous ... to help our people stand on their own feet."[30] Behind the scenes, in private appeals to Ottawa, the premier and his treasurer would tell a different story.

Most Maritime premiers understood that their problems had to take second place to the Prairie premiers' dismal plight (former prime minister Bennett had already raised their subsidies after the

White Royal Commission reported in February 1935). Nova Scotia premier Angus L. Macdonald merely hoped for "conclusions of common benefit to us all."[31] New Brunswick's Allison Dysart delivered deceptively mild platitudes that betrayed the depth of continuing Maritime anger: "It would be unfortunate indeed if in our deliberations we should seek to limit the discussion to the imaginary boundary lines that mark our geographical limits."[32] But, as historian Corey Slumkoski recounts, the province was a "stalwart defender of provincial rights" at this conference: Dysart (who was the lone holdout) refused to endorse a constitutional amendment to transfer sole responsibility for the unemployed to Ottawa.[33] Prince Edward Island's Walter Lea simply dismissed Ottawa's per capita assistance as "only small change."[34]

Then the premiers and their entourages broke into six subcommittees. They would not reconvene in a plenary session until mid-afternoon on their fifth and final day – when it would become clear what counter-revolutionary ideas lurked in Ottawa's briefing memoranda. Ottawa did *not* want to shuffle revenues or responsibilities to remedy inequality. King still had not accepted the extent of the provinces' woes. As King's biographer H. Blair Neatby observes, "King had convinced himself that Bennett's grants-in-aid to the provincial governments had encouraged extravagance and waste ... [The provinces] had almost certainly been reckless with relief funds because they were spending federal money."[35]

The real action at the conference took place at the subcommittee on financial questions, which Finance Minister Charles Dunning chaired. Dunning, who had strong connections to the Saskatchewan farming community, was an oddly unsympathetic chair. Born in England in 1885, Dunning had arrived on the Prairies as a penniless teenager, surviving as a transient farm labourer until he had secured a homestead. He joined farm organizations, and he honed his business skills as the general manager of the farmer-owned Saskatchewan Co-operative Elevator Company. By 1916, he was in the legislature; by 1922, he had been a very capable treasurer for six years when he also became premier. Farmers knew him as a sympathetic ally – and that was a formidable political asset when he left the Saskatchewan legislature to run for Parliament in 1926. Defeated in 1930, Dunning only returned to Ottawa *after* the 1935 election, when King convinced him that his skills were needed during the Great Depression. Perhaps he now owed his loyalty to King and the federal treasury: he was acclaimed as an MP shortly after the conference, on 30 December, in a by-election in a Prince Edward Island riding.

At the conference, Dunning made provocative suggestions about how Ottawa could ease provincial debt loads without increasing its special grants, including the adoption of a loan council based on the Australian model. And, while an abbreviated and watered-down version of those meetings was later presented to the full conference, other confidential memoranda show that progress on easing debts was shockingly minimal. Provinces had already raised taxes, introduced new taxes, and cut back services. But their debts were still increasing. As the subcommittee report privately conceded: "The financial relationships between the Dominion and the provinces are presently in a chaotic state. Constitutional difficulties and political uncertainties are obstacles to a solution. The effect is damaging."[36]

In another confidential memorandum, which summarized three days of private discussions, federal officials acknowledged the demands for renegotiated debt obligations. Nova Scotia premier Macdonald shrewdly asked about the Australian conversion plan for bondholders. Deputy Finance Minister W.C. Clark replied that only a small percentage of Australian bondholders were forced to convert their bonds to lower interest rates – "and their sacrifice was part of a comprehensive recovery scheme."[37] Macdonald stipulated that he preferred a redistribution of revenues and responsibilities to forced conversion anyway.[38] Alberta treasurer Charles Cockcroft then explained that Alberta had joined the committee "as a gesture of courtesy only, as they had already taken the first steps in working out their own conversion scheme."[39] His fellow politicians would soon find out – to their dismay – what the Albertans had devised.

The committee then considered the example of Australia, which would drive the federal search for more equality among governments throughout the remainder of the decade. As the committee report affirmed: "The parallel between the constitutional and financial problems of Canada and Australia draws attention to recent Australian measures."[40] Federal bureaucrats had provided Dunning with a thirteen-page memo on the Australian Loan Council. In 1929, Canberra had adopted the Financial Agreement Validation Act, which Australians had first ratified in a national referendum for insertion into the Constitution. This was the legislation that had provoked the fierce resistance from the governor of New South Wales in the early 1930s.

The Commonwealth had taken over all state debts and put the management of all future federal and state borrowings under the control of the newly reorganized Australian Loan Council. The council had been operating since 1923 – but only to prevent disastrous competition among the states in the money markets.

The dominion memo noted that future loans could be issued "either as direct obligations of the Commonwealth or as obligations of the States with the guarantee of the Commonwealth."[41] It added enviously: "Australia was fortunate to begin the depression with two effective instruments of financial control, namely, the Loan Council and the central or Commonwealth bank."[42]

Perhaps a Canadian version of the Loan Council could secure lower interest rates for the provinces. In his biography of Bank of Canada governor Graham Towers, former government adviser Douglas H. Fullerton maintained that Towers provided the memo on loan councils to Dunning on 2 January 1936. But, appended to the secret subcommittee report on financial questions, was a memo, "A Suggested Loan Council For Canada," which was also headed "D.P. 35 [i.e., Dominion-Provincial 1935]."[43] This was almost certainly the Towers memo, and it was provided to the dominion-provincial delegates.

Ottawa hoped that the Bank of Canada could eventually function as an "adequate instrument of control."[44] Dunning suggested that provinces "would require the approval of the Loan Council" for short-term borrowing, and Ottawa would have 50 percent of the council's voting power. That was unrealistic. As political scientists Daniel Béland and André Lecours note, provincial autonomy "was a crucial political idea early on ... Quebec premiers were, even in the early days, concerned with keeping the federal government at bay."[45] Privately, the memo conceded that, given the number of provinces, the differences in their financial strength, and the sensitivities around provincial rights, "it would seem that we have to contemplate an advisory rather than a compulsory body."[46]

Journalists were definitely aware of the bare bones of the Bank of Canada and finance ministry's approach to fiscal and economic inequality. The *Globe*'s Ottawa correspondent William Marchington praised the creation of the subcommittee on financial questions, which would consider "the creation of a National Finance Council" to reconstitute the federal, provincial, and municipal debt of between $6 and $7 billion. The scheme would offer comprehensive voluntary conversion, reconstituting "the internal debts of the various governmental bodies at lower rates of interest, but obligations to investors in other countries almost certainly would be unaffected."[47]

A day later, an editorial in the *Globe* lauded the idea of the National Finance Council, which could end "the constant claims for assistance and the demands for relief from certain obligations."[48] But it warned that relief costs were not the only drain on provincial treasuries. Provinces and municipalities had "plunged into prodigality before the relief problem became acute."[49] Rigid federal control should be imposed on their future expenditures: "Dominion credit must be retained, at whatever cost to Provinces and cities."[50]

In mid-week, the *Ottawa Journal* reported that Ontario premier Mitchell Hepburn was espousing federal refinancing of provincial debt, which would include "a reduction of interest rates on debts already outstanding and also [was] designed to improve public credit for future financing."[51] The premier estimated that this would result in an annual saving of approximately $16 million for his province. The idea of an expanded fiscal role for Ottawa – if only to refinance and guarantee existing provincial debts – was now definitely in the public realm. But the model of Australia received only brief mention in the press.

THE CANADIAN PUBLIC

More than eighty-five years later, it is impossible to miss the excitement in the journalists' stories about the Dominion-Provincial Conference of 1935. For once, it seemed, something might break the terrible spell that the Depression had cast on the nation. In retrospect, it was partly the hope that the new federal government could somehow spark revival. Most journalists in Ottawa understood that the federation was barely holding together as the poorer provinces struggled to pay their bills for interest charges and relief. Fiscal inequality among provincial governments could be tragic.

But there was also an air of unreality around their reports. Most Ottawa journalists were sympathetic to the federal government – and often oblivious to the rights and responsibilities of the provinces. Perhaps worse, there was a divide between the political speeches in the elegant Railway Committee Room on Parliament Hill and the on-the-ground lives of so many Canadians. The economic struggles of the latter received relatively scant attention. Historians Margaret Conrad and Alvin Finkel cite the life of a working-class Montreal woman who managed to keep her family fed because of the generosity of relatives. Her sister was married to a farmer so they had lots of vegetables; she would go to her mother's place, often for weeks at a time, sewing and knitting; her mother-in-law would feed the family, including her small daughter, and sometimes keep her for several days. "As soon as my little girl ate, I knew that everything would work out," the woman recounted.[52]

Other Montreal women had equally gripping stories of surviving poverty. One knitted mittens for fifteen cents and stockings for thirty-five cents: "It was no fortune. But for me it helped a lot." Another ignored the Roman Catholic Church's ban on contraceptives, believing that it would be better for the family if there were fewer children to feed and educate: "I told myself that the Good Lord sent me children but I did not want them to suffer later on. The big families always had miseries."[53]

Few Canadians had easy lives. Montreal garment workers staged a six-week strike in 1934, encouraged by their Industrial Union of Needle Trades Workers. Their gains were puny; within a year, their union was disbanded.[54] The fate of a Winnipeg immigrant woman was discussed in the House of Commons in January 1935, one month after she killed her two children and then killed herself with a strong germicide. She was despondent about her husband's failure to find work and the prospect of a poverty-stricken Christmas. Her note explained that she owed forty-four cents to the pharmacy for her poison.[55] It is difficult to imagine how the proposed National Finance Council or the Loan Council could have attracted the interest of those struggling souls.

AGREEMENT ELUDES THE CONFERENCE

In December 1935, the dominion-provincial delegates were having their own difficulties with such concepts. The trouble, of course, was that Ottawa's proposed Loan Council would be heavy-handed, no matter how advisory it appeared. Under the plan, the Dominion government would guarantee outstanding provincial debts *in return for* "the power to control future borrowing operations."[56] As the federal memo on the Australian Loan Council conceded, its "autocratic powers ... can scarcely be said to be in accord with democratic conditions."[57]

Much of the difficulty stemmed from the differences in constitutional powers within the two dominions. In the first two decades after federation, the Australian High Court had tended to interpret Commonwealth powers narrowly. That interpretation changed during the First World War and continued into the immediate postwar years. As a result, High Court decisions "greatly expanded the powers of the Commonwealth at the expense of the States ... [which] effectively reversed the intentions of the framers of the *Constitution*."[58] In contrast, Canada was designed to create a strong central government that held residual powers at the expense of the provinces. But Britain's Judicial Committee of the Privy Council "restrictively interpreted federal power over commerce and liberally interpreted provincial power over property and civil rights."[59] On fiscal issues especially, "the contrast between Australia's centralizing brand of federalism and Canada's competitive federalism is even more striking."[60] The lesson was clear: Ottawa could not simply impose a loan council on the provinces, no matter how advisory. The provinces could resist. And Ottawa politicians and officials were uneasily aware of their clout.

There were other models. The Canadian proposal also looked at the Bank of England's "centralized and highly flexible" approach to British treasury bills. But Britain, of course, was a unitary state. The memo then cited the state loan provisions in India, which retained its status as a colonial conquest: the Indian federation's new Constitution ensured that "the provinces [were] definitely more subordinate to the central government than the provinces in Canada."[61]

There seemed to be no way to help the poorer provinces dodge default without fundamental adjustments to their revenues and responsibilities. But the federation had no amending formula – and King would not accept radical change anyway. The prime minister had tried to adopt an amending formula during the Dominion-Provincial Conference of 1927. But his proposed approach, which differentiated between ordinary and fundamental amendments such as those that affected provincial and minority rights, found little support "and thus became a dead letter."[62] He tried again at this conference, suggesting that, if Parliament and two-thirds of the provinces with at least 55 percent of the national population agreed, Canada could amend its Constitution on matters directly affecting the provinces; unity was necessary for fundamental matters.[63] It was a half-hearted attempt, and the proposals were never adopted.[64]

Meanwhile, the fiscal situation in Alberta was becoming increasingly dire. During the federal election campaign of 1935, Premier Aberhart and his treasurer Charles Cockcroft had visited Ottawa to ask Bennett for a loan: the former prime minister advanced only $2.25 million to cover such emergency requirements as unemployment relief and interest charges until the end of October.[65] On 22 November, the King government sent another $1 million, partly to meet the cost of relief.[66] Just before the conference, acting Alberta premier Ernest Manning explained the province's difficulties in a letter to Canada's principal bond dealers, suggesting that its debt "might be refunded at lower interest rates."[67] As former senior bureaucrat Robert B. Bryce later wryly recounted: "This action, of course, destroyed what was left of the credit standing of the Alberta government and lent considerable urgency to the search for some solution to the debt problems of the western provinces generally."[68]

Perhaps most dramatically, a few days prior to the Dominion-Provincial Conference, "the Provincial Treasurer called in person [presumably at the federal finance ministry in Ottawa] and left a document ... setting forth certain suggestions."[69] He asked that the dominion *join* with the provincial government in negotiations with the province's bondholders for a reduction in interest rates and a change in the dates of maturity. Alberta also proposed that Ottawa guarantee Alberta's debt and that it should perhaps consolidate and refund the existing debts of Calgary and Edmonton.[70]

The delegates discussed that suggestion and similar ones behind closed doors at the committee on financial questions. Ontario premier Hepburn demanded that Ottawa convert its federal loans to the provinces to ones with lower interest rates. Even fat-cat Ontario was in trouble: "Debt interest and relief alone exceed revenue collections ... with the result that the debt of Ontario has increased each year for the past five years at an average rate of $40 million a year."[71] But Hepburn angrily rejected the idea of a loan council as inherently unfair to the wealthier provinces: "Ontario would not only have to pay its own share but its taxpayers would also pay over 40 per cent of Ottawa's share."[72] Even in such daunting times, the richer provinces objected to saddling their taxpayers with the poorer provinces' debts.

The moral appeal for more fiscal aid was reaching its limits. Both Ottawa and the provinces were "reluctant to part with sources of revenue," the *Globe*'s Marchington noted, but the provinces were "more clamorous than before for either a share of some of the Dominion income or for the assumption by the Dominion of more of their burdens."[73] He added that the proposed loan council generated "most of the contention" in "candid and lively debates" behind the scenes.[74] That centralizing prescription to fiscal inequality went nowhere.[75]

The provinces were understandably dubious about this radical federal power grab. The committee on financial questions did not embrace the Australian loan council: it shied away from the rigidities and the implications in both the Australian model and the Canadian proposal. Instead, it observed in the guarded tones that disagreement often elicits: "A non-political Loan Council, exercising its advisory functions in a proper manner, and re-enforcing its recommendations by publicity, could effectively improve the situation."[76]

That was faint praise. Although there was "no admission of defeat," they were deadlocked.[77] And Ottawa had no intention of tackling that impasse. On the last day of the conference, King strolled into a cabinet meeting before the final gathering. There, the prime minister found that "a considerable section" wanted to make large grants "to meet what they thought was expected by the public and the provinces at this time." King squashed their last-minute hopes of a federal rescue package for the provinces, the municipalities, or ordinary Canadians. "We had to do a number of unpleasant things," he warned them, "if the country was ever to get ahead, and now was the time to get down to rock bottom."[78] He did bow to cabinet pressure to increase Ottawa's relief grants to the provinces by 75 percent for three months. This was nowhere near to a solution. But cabinet finally agreed "that nothing would be approved or endorsed ... [and] no commitments of any kind would be made" with the exception of the offer to increase relief grants.[79]

When Hepburn discovered that Ottawa would not provide debt relief, he was disgusted: he departed before the concluding plenary session, leaving Attorney-General Arthur Roebuck to claim that the premier was "far from well." Within days, Hepburn would introduce the first provincial income tax "to raise between $12 and $14 million, the approximate cost of relief."[80] Meanwhile, Finance Minister Dunning reported that, given "the diversity and importance of the problems," the delegates could not reach unanimous agreement on the solutions.[81] Those problems were then deferred to meetings of the Permanent Committee on Financial Questions in mid-January.[82]

That committee did not – indeed, could not – come to any solutions for the unequal fiscal capacities of the provinces. They could not agree on the national loan council. Nor could they resolve any duplication of taxation. The premiers maintained that they could only balance their budgets – on their present scale – if Ottawa transferred "certain sources of revenue now belonging to or made use of by the Dominion." *Or*, if the dominion assumed "a larger portion of the cost of unemployment relief, and possibly certain other governmental services." *Or*, if Ottawa refinanced outstanding provincial and municipal debts – perhaps under dominion guarantee – so that annual interest charges could be reduced.[83] The first two measures would almost certainly have required constitutional change. The last request – refinancing those debts –unsettled Mackenzie King. He would not undertake such major commitments – despite Hepburn's anger.

In the end, Dunning declared that the real solution to the problems of public finance was an increase in national income.[84] He did not say how that could be accomplished. No one even mentioned the idea that Ottawa might create a program of permanent transfers to the poorer provinces. Such unconditional transfers were unthinkable – and basically unaffordable.

The conference did produce one seemingly innocuous measure that eventually brought huge headaches to King: another subcommittee unanimously approved the establishment of the Dominion Commission on Employment and Relief. As King told the conference in his concluding remarks, the commission's duty "would be by co-operation with public bodies and in other ways to find work for the unemployed."[85] He vowed to consult the provinces on the commission's personnel. He had basically deferred the problem of unemployment, too.

And that subdued outcome suited King perfectly. There was no pressure to do anything when Parliament and the provincial legislatures had not unanimously endorsed any major recommendation beyond the creation of an employment commission. The prime minister did unveil his grand proposal to raise relief grants "to a greater extent than has thus far been done." At the end of March, convinced that governments had to tighten their "indiscriminate relief process," King cut the relief grants that he had raised in December by 25 percent.[86] And so it went. For the next year, Ottawa did almost nothing to help its beleaguered citizenry as Canada plummeted towards the rock bottom that King had foreseen.

THE PUZZLE OF THE STALEMATE

It remains difficult to imagine why the first ministers could not do more. But even in the depths of the Depression, relief remained controversial among the recipients and the providers. During the summer of 1935, there had been a "wave of relief strikes" after Ontario disciplined municipalities that offered relief rates above the province's maximum ceilings.[87] Unemployed men and women protested in front of city halls, occasionally descending into violence, which could happen when food or clothing allowances were cut.[88] In North Bay in 1935, recipients "won emergency orders for bread and the right to choose where to redeem relief script."[89] But such successful protests were rare.

The contrary reaction could be seen in Ottawa during the week that the first ministers met. After an evening supper, Ottawa's social services commissioner, Major C.S. Ford, complained to the Men's Association of McLeod United Church that employment agencies made no effort to determine if employment was possible before supplicants were sent to the relief offices. The implication was that jobs were going unfilled. Ford added that Ontario's efforts to oversee the distribution of milk had added two cents to the price of milk – presumably to the price of each quart – which had added $48,000 to his relief budget.[90] King was uneasily aware of those conflicting views.

Historians have offered so many reasons for King's inaction during the mid-1930s. James Struthers concludes that King refused to act boldly against unemployment in the late 1930s because he viewed it as "primarily a provincial and local matter. The constitution provided the excuse but not the reason for [his] inaction."[91] Historian Roger Riendeau depicts King as highly responsive to voter pressure and polls.[92] The beleaguered provinces and their voters had not mustered enough collective clout in 1935 to demand – and get – action. At the end of the day, King knew that there were only seven CCF MPs.

But King also understood the constraints of the federal system only too well. The prime minister was a devious, calculating, and self-aggrandizing politician – but he was also shrewd. He recognized the need for balance that federations required – and he saw the implications when the Judicial Committee of the British Privy Council rejected most elements of Bennett's New Deal as unconstitutional. Political scientists Richard Simeon and Ian Robinson probably come closest to the truth: during the Depression, the prime minister adopted a strategy of "minimal federal activity, informed by his conviction that the principal threat to national unity lay in French-English conflict."[93] King was wary of triggering a fratricidal political war among the provinces and with Ottawa.

THE CRISIS DEEPENS

A month after the December 1935 Dominion-Provincial Conference, provincial representatives gathered in Ottawa for a meeting of the permanent committee on financial questions – and the model of the Australian Loan Council idea was revived. The discussion was "limited and vague."[94] The first province to buckle under the financial strain was Alberta. But it would only submit to a loan council if doing so would "not affect [its] autonomous rights ... We would sincerely trust that in the best interest of the whole Dominion situation no default would be forced upon us."[95]

Ottawa overlooked those caveats – and granted a federal loan of $1.58 million to meet bond maturities on 15 January 1936. But it warned the province that there would be no assistance with its upcoming 1 April maturity unless it accepted the Loan Council.[96] The two sides were at a standstill. Who was at fault? Former federal advisor Fullerton is brisk: Ottawa showed no "generosity of spirit ... Doctrinal, political, and constitutional considerations affected the federal position ... It was patronizing, condescending, and arrogant." The problem for the Prairie provinces was not so much economic mismanagement as "an abnormal and persistent combination of drought and seriously depressed world markets for wheat."[97]

Meanwhile, Bank of Canada bureaucrats were rethinking their Loan Council proposal. Research chief Alex Skelton was getting a better sense of the damage that a compulsory council based on the Australian model could cause in Canada. In a remarkable sixteen-page memorandum of 20 March 1936, Skelton explained that the plan "should be greatly modified, or better still, dropped entirely (if the Dominion Government can back out gracefully)."[98] Otherwise, the council would become a permanent institution. "[But] the general theories of federalism and of democracy, and the specific exigencies of Canadian politics, demand that the provinces shall always have an alternative."[99] Permanent federal oversight would be harmful.

The dangers of federal control over the poorer provinces' borrowing were enormous. Saskatchewan and Manitoba were teetering on the brink of catastrophe because the export markets for their agricultural products had dwindled. But the Western provinces objected to permanent usurpation of their powers; they viewed their difficulties as temporary while the council would be permanent; they also maintained that the dominion tariff policy had impoverished them – as opposed to their own policies. "Finally," wrote Skelton, "the provinces may question that the dictatorship of the Dominion will be a benevolent one." The Western provinces could point to tariffs "to illustrate the subordination of their interests to the politically dominant east." Then he cited the "additional fear" that "a province may suffer if it should be in the opposition political camp."[100]

His reasoning was explosive. If the dominion insisted on a loan council, the provinces might default on their interest payments. Or, the dominion might relax its supervision so the council would be ineffective. British Columbia and Alberta could simply opt for secession: "As independent states [they] could easily support their present debt structure and could gain other material economic benefits."[101] Or suppose, mused Skelton, that a province accepted the loan council and then a provincial rights party won the next election: "A serious effort by the Dominion to realize on its security might then lead to civil war."[102]

The scheme was risky. The dominion would assume a large liability; take responsibility for local problems that were fraught "with political friction and repercussions"; and bear the blame for encouraging partial default.[103] "To summarize," Skelton added, "effective and permanent Loan Council control would destroy the federal principle, and ineffective control would simply saddle the Dominion with new liabilities."[104]

He had a back-up plan: Ottawa should establish a national finance council, which would be a *voluntary* institution. It would include the federal finance minister, the nine provincial treasurers, and the Bank of Canada – and it would offer advice to any province that needed it. Its secretariat should have "knowledge of public finance theory and practice in general, and federal finance in particular (U. S. A., Australia, Argentine and other South America, etc. [*sic*])."[105] Although under political supervision, non-political management would control the council. The provinces would "nominally maintain complete autonomy, but in practice public opinion and money market sanctions would keep them in line."[106]

Skelton could not resist adding a centralist prescription. "The immediate problems of the provinces should be met by transferring emergency expenditures and certain social services to the Dominion," he wrote, "leaving the provinces with approximately balanced budgets and with the clear understanding that the Dominion has no further responsibility to them."[107]

The Ottawa bureaucrats could not yet envision a non-centralizing way to address the strained finances of poorer governments. Skelton's solution was more politically astute than an insistence upon a loan council along the lines of Australia. But Skelton had dramatic flair. His memo's wording in opposition to the Loan Council surely rattled the Ottawa elites.

LIFE REMAINS DIFFICULT FOR MOST CANADIANS

People and governments were still scrambling to get by, and the newspapers chronicled their search for solutions. In Alberta in early April 1936, the Social Credit government pushed through a 2 percent retail sales tax that applied to foodstuffs, with the exception of milk and bread, prompting opposition charges that it did not discriminate between the rich and the poor (the tax was rescinded in August 1937). Grain prices on the Winnipeg exchange fell one-eighth to one-quarter of a cent to new seasonal lows. The Hope Mission in Edmonton made an urgent appeal for funds as it offered garments, free meals, and free lodgings to nearly fifteen hundred families; more than eight hundred pairs of shoes were reconditioned in the mission's repair department and more than three thousand pairs were distributed to needy cases. The Women's International League for Peace and Freedom was holding a mass meeting in an Edmonton theatre to discuss "A Surrender to War or a Drive toward Peace?"[108]

Halfway across the country in Montreal, headlines trumpeted the $50 million that King was earmarking for relief and job creation for the 1936–37 fiscal year – which provinces and municipalities were expected to match. King also officially created the National Employment Commission, which would oversee public funds "in a time of great national emergency." Twenty-three charities, which were members of French Federated Charities, launched their annual appeal for funds; the Montreal-based group noted that in 1935 it had collected $305,689 for almost 63,000 people, which was an increase of 66 percent over the previous year. The Automotive Transport Association of the Province of Quebec sternly warned cash-strapped municipalities that they could not levy taxes on highway truck operators for the privilege of driving to and from their towns.[109] Problems were temporarily confronted but seemingly never solved.

ALBERTA DEFAULTS

Skelton's memo about a voluntary national finance council got Governor Towers's attention. But it came too late to rescind the ultimatum to Alberta. On 15 March, Alberta treasurer Cockcroft requested a federal loan of $2.85 million – or the province would default. On 17 March, Dunning replied that he had just read the premier's public announcement that he was reducing interest rates on those bonds – "apparently without reference to proposed loan council arrangement" – so "I do not see how I could justify to Parliament and the country the loan for which you are now asking."[110] Cockcroft had also suggested that Ottawa count the province's proposed settlement of $5 million for the use of its natural resources – a settlement that Alberta had previously spurned – against the new loans. Dunning refused: "As in the case of Saskatchewan the natural resources award would have to be offset against debts already owing by the provinces to the Dominion" – and Alberta owed almost $24.5 million.[111]

Dunning reiterated that Ottawa would not help unless it could oversee future provincial borrowings. The premier replied that he could not accept that condition. Meanwhile, Saskatchewan obtained Bank of Canada approval for loans because it agreed to accept the loan council – which would require a constitutional amendment to implement. On 1 April 1936, the Alberta government defaulted on its bonds.[112] That default would mark a generation of Depression-era Alberta politicians *and* their successors. A government of Prairie farmers who had taken pride in paying their debts was now effectively insolvent.

That drama would reverberate in Australia. On 22 June 1936, diplomats sent an unusually detailed five-page memo chronicling Alberta's lost struggle. In particular, they concentrated on Premier William Aberhart's refusal to go along with the federal demand for a loan council. The Australians were clearly fascinated by how their model – however modified – would *not* work in Canada.[113] The operation of a federation was an ongoing preoccupation in both nations.

THE PROVINCES AND OTTAWA
STILL CANNOT AGREE ON REMEDIES

Meanwhile, King and British Columbia premier Duff Pattullo were in an increasingly unpleasant standoff over the Loan Council. In mid-March, Pattullo told King that he did "not think any province should be placed in the position of either accepting proposal [sic] of the Dominion without modification or reservation or being left to its own devices."[114] On 1 May, King explained that Ottawa had amended its proposal to mollify provincial concerns that every loan would require federal approval. Instead, if a province joined the council, it would need Dominion approval before it could issue securities or incur debt *abroad*; if the debt or obligation were issued in Canada, the province could proceed without the council – but those securities or debts would not have Loan Council approval or its guarantee.[115]

King was doing everything that he could to control provincial spending without offering more money or powers to the poorer provinces. Indeed, the council would *restrict* provincial powers. But the federal guarantee of provincial debts would cut the interest payments that the poorer provinces had to pay. Pattullo was not buying it: "I think that the course you are pursuing is too rigid and inelastic, and that your policy will not effectuate the employment of the employable... However I have so many times explained the situation both by letter and conversation that there does not seem to be much use in pursuing the argument."[116]

Loan Councils as a solution to fiscal inequality were losing momentum – but Ottawa went through the motions anyway. On 1 May 1936, in his budget speech, Finance Minister Dunning said that the future remained "clouded" by the "uncertain" financial position of some provinces, especially the Western provinces. As the *Globe* reported, loans to the provinces had now reached $116.5 million – and it was Ottawa's intention "to proceed with the loan council scheme with some modifications."[117]

On 14 May 1936, King's government introduced a resolution in the House of Commons, asking the British Parliament to amend the BNA Act "to authorize the Dominion to guarantee provincial loans on specified conditions and to extend and clarify provincial taxing powers." It passed the next day. But the Senate delayed it, and eventually defeated it, to King's infinite relief.[118] As he confided in his diary on the day that he introduced it: "I confess that I do not like... the effort even indirectly to 'control' the provinces in any of their acts." Ottawa "might have been wiser simply to refuse to loan or guarantee" loans, even if that triggered bankruptcy, because such actions might only prolong the emergency.[119]

On 10 June 1936, a senior official at the Bank of Canada – almost certainly Towers – submitted a version of Skelton's proposed National Finance Council to Deputy Finance Minister Clark. A notation scrawled on the first page reads: "by draft – agreed with Johnson – subsequently modified a little by Clark but proposal turned down."[120] Johnson was almost certainly Treasury Solicitor David Johnson, who reported to Clark.[121] Skelton's clumsy mechanism to ease the fiscal pressures on the poorer provinces through voluntary measures, which would free more money for program spending, would not work.

THE MUTUAL INTEREST CONTINUES

The Australians were watching Canada closely because the parallels could be striking. On 9 June 1936, Trade Commissioner L.R. Macgregor sent a detailed memo chronicling the journey of the proposed Loan Council from the Dominion-Provincial Conference of December 1935, which sought a solution to "vexatious provincial financial questions," to its defeat in the Senate. "There appears, however, to be pronounced public support of the Senate's attitude," he explained, "although the Government has been threatening 'reform' of the Senate." He noted that Canadians could not amend their own Constitution because "the French-Canadian minority are jealous of the rights assured to them under that Imperial Statute."[122] The Australians really did not understand the force of provincial cultural and language rights – and the need for them – in Canada.

The fate of Bennett's New Deal also preoccupied the Australians. On 17 June 1936, Macgregor cabled Canberra when the Supreme Court of Canada rejected key elements of Bennett's package, including the Employment and Social Insurance Act. Macgregor noted that several Commonwealth ministries had expressed interest in the deal's fate.[123] In turn, Canberra officials informed Australian diplomats that two United Kingdom experts were scheduled to visit Australia to discuss the introduction of similar unemployment insurance: the Commonwealth government would appreciate "all the ideas and information on the subject it can procure" from Ottawa.[124]

The Australian diplomats also forwarded a 20 June 1936 article from the *London Times* headlined "Federal Powers in Canada," which referred to the Unemployment Insurance decision and to the United States Supreme Court decision that found elements of President Franklin Roosevelt's New Deal to be unconstitutional. "In Canada, as in the United States," the article noted pointedly, "necessary social and economic readjustments are hampered by a written Federal Constitution setting hard and fast boundaries to the authority of the national Government and Parliament."[125] The lesson for Canberra was clear: federalism itself – and its required constitution – was an impediment to the expansion of social programs to meet twentieth-century needs.

In any case, not everyone advocated the expansion of social security. The diligent Australians forwarded an extract from an article in *Industrial Canada* by Canadian Manufacturers' Association executive H.W. Macdonnell, who reviewed the state of social legislation in Canada. "The reason taxes are heavy is not because ambitious kings want to acquire new territory [as in the past]," Macdonnell explained, "but because we are spending money like drunken sailors on social services." People were losing their sense of self-reliance and thrift. Young people were letting their elderly relatives depend upon relief instead of supporting them: "The whole object and trend of this new point of view is to teach the individual not to rely on himself nor even look to his family, but to look to the State."[126]

That fear of dependency among individuals and provinces would run like a jarring contrapuntal melody alongside proposals to expand social security – and to tackle provincial fiscal inequality – throughout the ensuing decades. There would be little further expansion anyway – with the exception of Unemployment Insurance and Family Allowances in Canada in wartime – until federal health grants in 1948. The two federations were groping their way through tough times. Canada and Australia would become even closer over the remainder of the decade.

OTTAWA SEEKS NEW OPTIONS

After the defeat of the Loan Council and the rejection of the National Finance Council, Ottawa was scrambling to find a Plan B. In the summer of 1936, the Bank of Canada asked University of Toronto economist A.E. "Dal" Grauer – who had been a friend of Alex Skelton's from Oxford University – to study the distribution of taxing powers in Canada. His report on 30 August 1936 called for the centralization of income tax. "Wealth and income tends to arise in Ontario and Quebec," the report observed. So "it seems *equitable* ... that the main direct taxes on income and wealth (the income and death taxes) should be vested in the central government as an offset to these regional inequalities."[127]

This might be possible. Grauer suggested that the dominion could offer to share those revenues to induce provincial cooperation "on the understanding that the provinces would get more revenue than at present."[128] Ottawa could also make equal per capita payments to each province. That would elicit objections from the wealthier provinces because their taxpayers contributed more money per capita to Ottawa than did the taxpayers in the poorer provinces. Finally, "some of the provinces would certainly bring up the plea of special need."[129] Federal bureaucrats – or, at least, their advisors – were discussing the curse of unequal provincial revenues, even if they could not solve it.

Grauer's report opened a new path. Bank of Canada research chief Skelton and Governor Towers "rather quickly concluded" that the best way to improve the division of revenues and responsibilities "would be to set up a royal commission of inquiry."[130] After talks with Finance Minister Dunning and Deputy Finance Minister Clark, Towers drafted a succinct five-page memo, capturing the incipient pressures for expanded social security that were already jostling against provincial revenue-raising capacity to meet those new burdens.[131] "Social expenditures, including relief, have assumed an importance never contemplated 25 years ago – still less at time of Confederation."[132]

Dunning took the suggestion to King on Monday, 16 November. According to King's records, the prime minister pointed out that he had suggested a royal commission during the 1930 election campaign that would have looked *beyond* economic issues. Now the public might view any commission "as a way of avoiding facing the financial situation which has developed. I thought it better to seek to meet that situation some other way for the present at least."[133]

Undeterred, on 23 November 1936, Skelton wrote a dramatic seven-page memo, laying out "The Case for a Royal Commission Inquiry on Provincial Finances."[134] The Depression had driven home the liabilities of a sixty-year-old constitution that included "an extensive borderland where jurisdiction, taxation and expenditure may, and do, now overlap."[135] He wanted to replace "the present Topsy-like structure of Canadian public finance with one constructed on rational and business-like lines."[136] Other federations had different models: Australia enforced centralized control of all government borrowing; the United States concentrated "deficit financing in the hands of the federal body with the most elastic revenues, control of monetary policy, and the best credit."[137]

Canada could not keep drifting. "Serious strains" would soon plague the federation, including "secession or default of some of the more exposed units."[138] That, in turn, would "impoverish the central provinces and ruin their credit."[139] Central Canada should view constitutional overhaul as in its interests: continued federal "loans" to bankrupt provinces or purchases of provincial securities would be "only a palliative of the most deceptive kind, and Ontario and Quebec would have to bear the cost *with no compensating advantages.*"[140]

Two decades before formal equalization, Skelton captured the dangers of resentment among the richer provinces for their poorer kin. Sharing was not an idealistic venture: there had to be something more for every province. He concluded with a flourish: "Ostrich-like tactics will no longer do; 1937 should become as memorable a date in Canadian history as 1867."[141]

For months, this radical debate had gone on behind closed doors. But the fevered discussions among bureaucrats and politicians were about to percolate into the public realm.

OTTAWA ACCEPTS THAT IT HAS TO TAKE ACTION

On 9 December 1936, Dunning again welcomed the members of the Subcommittee on Financial Questions – now renamed the National Finance Committee – to Ottawa. It was this committee's first and only meeting, running from 9 to 14 December. And it was a game-changer. On the eve of the gathering, Bank of Canada governor Towers noted a "tendency towards progressive improvement" in dominion and provincial bond issues throughout the year.[142]

But such guarded optimism could not compete with the alarming news that Manitoba and Saskatchewan were on the brink of default. Manitoba premier John Bracken asked Towers how his province should go about reducing the interest on its bonds. Towers replied that the "final responsibility for taking a decision ... would rest with Manitoba."[143] That is: it would be Manitoba's fault. When Dunning suggested that the Bank of Canada could serve as the province's official financial advisor, Towers hastily demurred: the bank could not become an adviser just before a default – and Bracken agreed.[144] Towers's conversation with Saskatchewan premier W.J. Patterson went "along very much the same lines."[145]

In public, Dunning put a brave spin on the encounters. The proceedings were a "complete success" – even though there was "little progress" on such propositions as the "increased diversion of national revenues to the Provincial Treasuries and creation of a Royal Commission to study the whole picture of Dominion and Provincial relations under the Confederation pact."[146] Over the holidays, as the pressure escalated, the memoranda became charged with barely restrained alarm. On 4 January 1937, Towers wrote to Dunning that any offer of a temporary guarantee of interest on provincial bonds would be "a very dangerous form of liability for the Dominion."[147] Ottawa should offer temporary grants coupled with a royal commission investigation.[148] There had to be "some rearrangement of financial powers and responsibilities which [would] enable the various Governments to function more effectively within their own domains."[149] The financial bureaucrats were prowling departmental corridors, pushing hard for an in-depth look at the innards of Confederation.[150]

The debate continued. A day later, in a conversation with Dunning, Towers suggested ways to protect the dominion if Ottawa opted for a temporary guarantee of provincial bonds. In response, Dunning noted that Ottawa could perhaps offer to act as a financial advisor – if the province asked for assistance. But Dunning also affirmed his desire for a royal commission: "Even if one was not agreed upon at the present time, he hoped that it would come later, say after the Coronation [n.b., King George VI would be crowned on 12 May 1937]."[151]

The memos zipped back and forth. On Sunday, 10 January 1937, Skelton wrote that "a passive [federal] policy of non-interference" as Manitoba and Saskatchewan defaulted "would be neither virtuous, sound, or expedient."[152] Ottawa would be "sidestepping responsibilities which are properly those of the national government, i.e. widespread crop failure, national business depression and relief, loss of foreign markets, and *a moral responsibility* arising from the last six years' assistance."[153] The "most desirable alternative" was a royal commission.[154] In the interim, Saskatchewan would probably need an interim grant; Manitoba might be able to survive for the next six to nine months. If the province had to cut interest rates, Skelton suggested a dominion guarantee of repayment for itself and the bondholders.[155]

Throughout that chill Ottawa January, the bureaucrats kept writing to each other and to their political masters, suggesting and rejecting solutions. The Prairie provinces were in huge financial trouble – and the *relatively* wealthier Central Canadian provinces were oblivious or, perhaps worse, resentful of any additional federal commitments. This flurry of memos among the bureaucrats in their Ottawa office blocks was not a theoretical game. They were scrambling.

The stakes were incredibly serious: Canada's international credit rating; the fate of provincial governments with failing municipalities and desperate farmers; institutions with the accounts of thousands of ordinary Canadians that had purchased government bonds; the very ability of the federation to endure. The distance between those huge issues of fiscal inequality and the daily life of ordinary Canadians was surprisingly small – in mid-January, the Ottawa Children's Aid Society reported that its case load was growing by one new complaint per day: "The principal reason for the increased number of wards during the past several years, was due to people of limited means living under overcrowded conditions."[156] Governments could not find enough funds for struggling families.

On Monday, 11 January 1937, Bank of Canada secretary Donald Gordon wrestled with the prospect of a temporary provincial default: the dominion needed to provide "a strong gesture of compromise designed to show a recognition of an unusual situation and a desire to meet it in a fair minded and helpful way."[157] Gordon suggested that Ottawa guarantee the interest on any bonds that were turned in for a reduced interest rate for five years. Alberta could qualify for this plan as well if it opted for a *temporary* cut – as opposed to its *permanent* cut – in interest rates.[158]

On 12 January, the Bank of Canada's securities advisor K.A. "Ken" Henderson wrote a brutally frank memorandum about Western financial problems – and the notion of national sharing: "The Provincial economies have broken down in attempting to expand government services (including relief) during a period of reduced revenue ... *In times of depression it is much easier than at other times to develop a body of public opinion to the view that one should take from the 'haves' and give to the 'have-nots' without regard to the justice or the ultimate result of such action.*"[159] Now was the time for fiscal redistribution.

On that same day, a Bank of Canada official who was almost certainly Towers wrote a memo on the Prairie provinces' predicament – and then he rewrote it on 15 January at Dunning's request. As a notation says, Dunning wanted "only suggestions of procedure covering temporary guarantee of interest, and [so it] should not include discussion of the pros and cons."[160] The author concluded that the dominion should "not tacitly encourage and participate in a permanent cut" in interest rates.[161] Instead, it should make available "sufficient funds to cover the reduced interest on the securities concerned."[162]

The fiscal plight was now *very* clear. On Sunday, 17 January 1937, Towers, Dunning, and Deputy Finance Minister Clark met with Manitoba premier Bracken and Saskatchewan premier Patterson. Dunning and Clark toyed with the idea of a temporary reduction in interest rates coupled with the dominion's guarantee of those reduced rates. Someone – Towers did not record who – "suggested that the Bank of Canada should examine the situation to enable the Dominion to make up its mind."[163] Bracken wanted quick action. Towers concluded that both sides wanted "a quick whitewash and Dominion endorsement of rate cuts."[164] That would not happen.

Instead, on Monday, 18 January, Towers told Dunning and Clark that a dominion endorsement of interest rate cuts was dangerous, particularly if the dominion refused to appoint a royal commission. A day later, Bracken agreed to a Bank of Canada examination of his province's affairs. Privately, Towers had already upped the ante. "Our only recommendation is a cash grant and Royal Commission," he wrote that day to an undisclosed recipient, probably Clark. "Let the politicians take full responsibility for the selection of the alternative if they will not follow our advice."[165]

On Thursday, 21 January, the politicians and the bureaucrats sat down to deal with the overwhelming inequalities of federalism. Towers first met with Dunning and King to discuss the West's pressing debt crises. King asked Towers for a Bank of Canada report on the situation. Towers initially warned that such reports might embarrass the bank – and embroil it in political controversy. As King told his diary, Towers then "came back to the old idea of grants being made to the Provinces with a Commission to investigate financial relations."[166] King said that there was "no chance" of a commission – but he understood Towers's concern that such reports might embarrass the bank.[167] Later that day, Towers went back to King – and offered to do the reports. As Towers later explained: "In the circumstances it was more reasonable to accept this risk [of embarrassment] than to refuse an examination and probably precipitate immediate action on the part of the provinces."[168] King agreed.

With that reversal, the Bank of Canada acted. Towers sent Skelton on a lightning tour of two Prairie provincial capitals. In April, at the request of former prime minister R.B. Bennett and the Alberta government, Skelton also scrutinized that government's finances. The three reports were vivid – and devastating. In the Manitoba report, which was completed on 11 February 1937, Skelton concluded that, during most of the decade, the province had "made strong and commendable efforts" to balance its books, to limit its debt by raising taxes, and to control expenditures "without curtailing services to an extent which would not have been in the public interest."[169] But revenues "are not adequate, or are not sufficiently elastic, to enable the province to bear the burdens which modern practices of government and the force of the depression have placed upon it."[170]

The Saskatchewan report, which was completed on 6 March 1937, depicted the province as being in worse shape than Manitoba. One figure brought home the devastation: "The total relief expenditures since 1930 have exceeded the total ordinary revenues of the province for the same period."[171] Worse, the provincial government was picking up the costs of operational expenses for southern farmers in the drought areas, which amounted to "the prime costs of production for about one-half of its major industry."[172] The report depicted temporary financial aid as "justified."[173] It added: "We do not see any solution other than ... a complete enquiry into the financial powers and responsibilities of all our governing bodies."[174]

The final Alberta report, which appeared on 7 April 1937, briefly recapped the province's refusal to pay 50 percent of the interest on its bonds: "We can only deal with the situation as it is – not as it might have been in other circumstances. We find that Alberta can maintain its governmental services on as favourable a basis as Manitoba or Saskatchewan without receipt of additional assistance."[175] That was the not-so-subtle punishment for the debt-dodger. The Bank of Canada sent all three reports to the governor of the Commonwealth Bank of Australia.

In mid-February 1937, Towers delivered the bad news to Mackenzie King: Manitoba and Saskatchewan would default unless Ottawa assisted them. King understood that defaults could lead "to a worse condition than any up to the present,"[176] endangering Ottawa's credit rating and forcing up the interest rates on *its* bonds. Beset, King piously told his diary: "I have all along wanted a Commission on financial allocations and responsibilities of the provinces and the Dominion."[177] This was at variance with his reluctance to appoint a commission in 1936 – but it does reflect his call for a royal commission during the 1930 election. Once Ottawa's credit rating was endangered, King moved from theoretical approval to immediate action.

Four days before King informed the House of Commons of his decision, Towers wrote Bracken that he saw only one solution: "A comprehensive enquiry into the financial powers and responsibilities of all our governing bodies" and, pending the commission's report, the extension of temporary financial aid.[178]

The federal cabinet met at noon on 16 February 1937 and unanimously decided to appoint a royal commission – and to extend temporary aid to Manitoba and Saskatchewan. King announced to the House that afternoon that there would be a commission. The prime minister had left the decision until the last moment: the Manitoba legislature was due to meet the next day – and the province would likely have defaulted. Months later, King expanded his definition of the commission's task: it was to undertake "a re-examination of the economic and financial basis of Confederation and of the distribution of legislative powers in the light of the economic and social developments of the last seventy years."[179] The prime minister's world had changed – and, in his view, not necessarily for the better.

THE AUSTRALIANS FOLLOW THE DRAMA

The Australians were tracking Canada's ongoing woes. In late January 1937, the Judicial Committee of the British Privy Council rejected most of Bennett's New Deal package, including Unemployment Insurance, as unconstitutional. In their report to Canberra, the diplomats tucked an essay by McGill University constitutional expert Frank Scott, which denounced the decision. Scott noted that "every Dominion power" that Ottawa had invoked in favour of the legislation "was found to be inadequate."[180] Ottawa was permitted to use its emergency powers to impose temperance in 1878, Scott added bitterly, but the council would not accept the same argument when it came to remedies for unemployment and labour conditions.[181]

The diplomats also forwarded a disturbing article by University of Manitoba president Sidney T. Smith. It noted pointedly: "We cannot expect from the Privy Council an interpretation of the constitution that will enable the Dominion to take over some of the social services and the regulation of industrial activities which the provincial legislatures, with insufficient revenue, are unable to undertake." Such issues "were unknown in 1867, but many Canadians today would say they are of major importance."[182]

The Australians were clearly fascinated by Canada's inability to handle fiscal inequalities. The Royal Commission on Dominion-Provincial Relations attracted *huge* attention in Canberra – and it remained in the spotlight, even after the declaration of war in September 1939. King's announcement of the commission was forwarded to Australia. On 10 March 1937, assistant Australian trade commissioner R.R. Ellen wrote a detailed update: "The position in Canada is not unlike that in Australia in that the division of powers and responsibilities ... is the subject of much controversy. The administrative responsibilities of the Provinces and municipalities have grown beyond anticipations."[183]

Three months later, Trade Commissioner L.R. Macgregor updated Canberra. There were more than 27,000 taxing bodies, including municipalities, in Canada. The total indebtedness of its governing bodies was nearly $7.4 billion. The direct and guaranteed federal debt at the end of the 1936–37 fiscal year was $4.2 billion. For that same fiscal year, the Ontario government showed a surplus of $9.3 million. Indeed, Ontario premier Hepburn had announced that feat to "wild ovations" on 9 March 1937.[184] While other provinces were in trouble, the only province to default on three maturities amounting to $6.1 million was Alberta. There had been many municipal defaults. It was a perfect scene-setter for a federation trapped on the cusp of a modernizing world.[185]

THE ROYAL COMMISSION PROCEDURE

Three months before King finally accepted the need for a royal commission, Deputy Finance Minister W.C. Clark took Skelton's memo on the need for a royal commission, expanded it, and presented it as a fifteen-page memorandum, which he initialled. He added a list of possible members for the panel. As chairman, he suggested Ontario chief justice Newton Rowell, among others. Among the members – and he hoped to limit the membership to five – he proposed Quebec lawyer and future prime minister Louis St-Laurent "or a judge from the Province of Quebec." Ottawa could also consider University of British Columbia economist Henry Forbes Angus.

But Clark's first choice for membership was an Australian outsider, relatively unknown in Canada: "Professor L. F. Giblin: a very able practical economist who was one of the six economists responsible for the 'Premier's Plan' adopted in Australia in 1931 and largely responsible for Australian recovery; also a member of the Commonwealth Grants Commission and as such thoroughly familiar with the problems of relations between state and central governments in a federal country."[186] The Premiers' Plan, which the state and Commonwealth governments endorsed in June 1931, cut government spending and reduced the interest on government bonds. Although he did not become a commissioner, Giblin was a very influential presence from the start.

In a subsequent memo in Clark's files, which was not dated or signed, there is an outline of possible staff and studies, which Alex "Sandy" Skelton likely drafted during the spring of 1936. For the prestigious post of secretary, Clark recommended Skelton, who would be "ideal" as the head of the research staff because of his experience with provincial finance.[187] As an assistant to Skelton, Clark suggested future prime minister Lester Pearson, who was then first secretary at the Canadian High Commission in London. Among the research studies that the memo suggested, there was one that stood out: "A study of the working of Dominion subsidies to provinces [including] ... *the working of subsidies in other federal countries, the experience of Australia with the Commonwealth Grants Commission*, etc., etc."[188]

The direction of the Royal Commission secretariat was clear – even before it started: Australia would be the main model for remaking Canada. And Australian star Giblin would be a guide to its successful experiment in easing inequality.

CONCLUSION

After years of seeking solutions, Ottawa finally turned the problem of inequalities in federation revenues and responsibilities over to the experts. It was a start. But fiscal and economic inequality among governments was an insiders' problem. Most Canadians did not understand the implications: they simply wanted better lives.

6

The Poorer versus the Richer at the Royal Commission, 1937–40

The members of the Royal Commission on Dominion-Provincial Relations were determined to fix Canada, to pry into the innards of the federation, and to emerge with a plan that neatly shuffled revenues and responsibilities. They were not idealists – with the possible exception of their brilliant anglophone secretary Alex Skelton. They would likely have called themselves pragmatists or perhaps rationalists as they packed their bags to tour a nation plagued by poverty and inequality. Their hearings, along with their eventual report in May 1940, would provide the most gripping record of how Canada muddled through the terrible 1930s. Those hearings would also provide stark evidence that the gulf between the richer and the poorer provinces was too wide to span before the prosperity of the mid-1950s.

The chances were against the Royal Commission's success from the start – because different provinces espoused radically different approaches to federalism. Ottawa had already squandered three years in a futile push for a loan council, similar to the one in Australia, to constrain the borrowing of the poorer provinces – only to realize that even the poorest provinces were hesitant about surrendering permanent fiscal control. Meanwhile, many federal politicians and officials wanted *more*, not less, power and money – especially after Britain's Judicial Committee of the Privy Council ruled against Ottawa's proposed Unemployment Insurance.

The federation was a tangle of competing interests. But the feisty band of commissioners, their staff, and their journalistic entourage were indomitable. From 29 November 1937 to 1 December 1938, they criss-crossed the nation, listening to witnesses in every provincial capital, while recording 10,702 pages of evidence from eighty-five days of hearings. They read 427 briefs and ordered studies from thirty-six experts as well as in-depth looks at how other federations, especially Australia, handled fiscal inequalities.[1] Their job was to diagnose the problems and to recommend changes. It was a dramatic and often tense odyssey.

Their eccentric attendant through much of this physical and intellectual journey was Alex ("Sandy") Skelton, the first child of an early Canadian power couple, O.D. Skelton, who counselled prime ministers, and Isabel Skelton, who chronicled her society's neglected social history. Officially, his name was Douglas Alexander Skelton, born in Chicago on 25 July 1906. Unofficially, his name was sometimes Alex; usually, it was Sandy. Historian Doug Owram has included him among that circle of "Government Generation" intellectuals "who were not only active in observing and assessing the changing nature of the state in Canada but were also the proponents of, and participants in, that change."[2] Often inspired, never stodgy, continually curious about the Australian federation, always an advocate for a strong central government, Skelton frustrated and fascinated his commission colleagues. He could draw upon an intimidatingly wide circle of associates, who usually tolerated his outbursts of rebellion.

Skelton believed firmly in the power of governments as a force for economic good. But, as historians Barry Ferguson and Robert Wardhaugh explain, Skelton's view of Canada as an economic unit, which commission staff espoused, frustrated Commissioner John Dafoe. "Canada, of course, is not an economic unit," he told Skelton, "[it] was not one at the height of the effectiveness of the integrating policies; is now less than it then was an economic unit, and will go broke to-morrow if it is obliged to become an economic unit."[3] The tension between those two pivotal approaches to the Canadian economy ran throughout the commission's proceedings.

His presence as research director ensured that the commission's search for a renewed federation was exhaustive – and exhausting. The testimony fascinated the Australians, who saw their influence cited frequently. And it played out against a background of rising impatience with largely unregulated capitalism. The social-democratic Co-operative Commonwealth Federation, which was founded in 1932, had captured seven seats in the 1935 federal election. Throughout the latter half of the decade, its appeal – and its demand for a more equitable world – was growing, especially across the West.

The popularity of the CCF would eventually unnerve Prime Minister Mackenzie King.

The times demanded change – and many Canadians knew it. As the Bank of Nova Scotia's *Monthly Review* declared in June 1938: "The hearings have been followed with interest throughout the Dominion, for there has probably never been such a forum for public opinion on questions of national importance to Canada."[4] The commissioners were exploring unknown territory in the Canadian federal bargain. Buffeted by competing demands, then shaken by the loss of their key player, they soon lost their political compass.

THE ROYAL COMMISSION GETS UNDER WAY

Before the members could gather for their first full meeting, Chair Newton Rowell and Prairie Commissioner Dafoe held an informal gathering in Ottawa on 4 August 1937 with Skelton, along with finance ministry and Bank of Canada officials.[5] They needed hard data – and different perspectives. They set out a preliminary list of research studies and a proposed schedule of hearings.[6] Twenty-seven academics would eventually research the economy and nine would look at legal and constitutional affairs. Their emphasis was on the workings of federalism – and the search for better ways to handle economic inequalities. The ensuing scholarship would emerge as "the greatest research effort undertaken by a Canadian royal commission up to that time."[7]

The commissioners readied themselves for the trips ahead, trundling on and off trains, for public hearings.[8] They would have an avid national audience: *Winnipeg Free Press* editor Dafoe wanted to ensure that *all* anglophone Canadians knew what the commissioners were doing – and what they heard. He assigned his newspaper's legislative correspondent J.B. "Hamish" McGeachy to follow them across Canada and to file what became a syndicated column, "Confederation Clinic," under the byline J.B.M. While other journalists, such as Carl Reinke of the *Canadian Press*, also trailed after the commission, the hard-bitten McGeachy's reports managed to be both lively – *and* accurate – in terms of the operations of the federation.[9]

When the public hearings ended, McGeachy assisted Skelton and Commission Press Secretary Wilfrid Eggleston in the editing of the academic studies. He was surely an extraordinary companion. Journalist Peter Stursberg recalled meeting McGeachy, who was then the

Winnipeg Free Press correspondent in London, in a Fleet Street pub during the spring of 1939. McGeachy "looked like a pirate, a Captain Morgan reincarnated, with a Scots accent somewhat muffled by cigarettes and whiskey."[10] But, on the road with the commission, his comments on their adventures were lively and revealing.

In most capitals, provincial governments provided the most compelling and substantive evidence of the federation's fiscal inequalities. The richer provinces, such as Ontario and Quebec, forcefully expressed their reluctance to see Ottawa contribute more to the poorer provinces. The poorer provinces, such as Manitoba and Saskatchewan, vividly described their huge responsibilities, their insufficient revenues, and their crippling debts. During downtimes in Ottawa, the commissioners also heard from other important players, such as the Canadian Chamber of Commerce and the Canadian Welfare Council. Witnesses often mentioned Australia and, more rarely, other federations, such as Argentina, which also relied on commodity exports.

The commission was in pursuit of a more rational Canada.

ON THE ROAD

The commissioners were braced for unrelentingly bad news about life in the West. But, with the exception of Winnipeg's Dafoe, they found that it was even worse than they had anticipated. As a courtesy, their first witness on 29 November 1937 was Manitoba premier John Bracken, who had urged King in late 1936 to appoint the Royal Commission. The premier could be verbose, but he was always incisive about his province's unequal position within Canada. His statistics were compelling. The province's small number of provincial and municipal taxpayers were staggering under debt that equalled 98 percent of total annual income in 1933.[11] The total cost of relief alone in 1936 for Ottawa, the province, and its municipalities was $11.7 million – or 81.2 percent of Manitoba's ordinary expenditures.[12]

Bracken invoked the notion of justice: "From the earliest years of Confederation, there has arisen in province after province protests of inequity and claims for adjustment, large numbers of which have been found on examination to be just complaints."[13] Now Manitoba had joined that queue. "In presenting our case we shall feel that we are not less Canadian in spirit or in reality if we show that the economic picture ... is not just to those Canadians who happen to live here and is not in the interests of Canada as a whole."[14]

The lengthy Manitoba brief frequently cited Australia as an example of fairness in its treatment of states and citizens. Australia had depreciated its currency during the Depression: the Commonwealth Grants Commission had concluded that the positive effects of that currency depreciation had almost balanced the negative effects of the Australian tariff on resource producers. In a later private memo on the CGC, Commissioner Henry Angus would dispute Manitoba's claim that the CGC methodically toted up the effects of the tariff and the exchange rate: "This exaggerates the extent of its calculation."[15]

In contrast with Australia, the Manitoba brief asserted, Ottawa's exchange rate policies and tariffs to protect manufacturers were driving up the cost of farm production and impeding Western export sales. "For Canada, disability costs for the prairie provinces consist of the *sum* of tariff costs and exchange costs in contrast to the *difference* between the latter and the former, as for Australia."[16] Australia's efforts to achieve equality were ambitious: Ottawa's subsidies to the provinces were only one-quarter of the Commonwealth's subsidies to its states.[17] The Australians regarded even private debt as an impediment to economic recovery – so the Premiers' Plan of 1931 had cut interest rates across the board.

Bracken's plea was powerful. Although he half-heartedly suggested that Ottawa should abandon "the pretence of equality of treatment" in subsidies, he admitted that would be difficult.[18] Better still, he declared, Ottawa should cancel the province's debts for relief payments. And it could pick up "one-half of the cost of our social services, chiefly services relating to public welfare."[19] Manitoba was one of the few provinces that did not care what Ottawa did – as long as it did something. *Anything*.

The response was generally favourable, although francophone counsel Louis St-Laurent proved to be a difficult examiner (the commissioners, the two counsels, legal secretary Robert Fowler, and Skelton could ask questions). After several more witnesses, such as the Winnipeg Real Estate Board and the Winnipeg Board of Trade, correspondent McGeachy concluded that St-Laurent was "almost alarming ... His mind performs with speed and his questions come at the same rate. He pursues truth like an amiable but enthusiastic terrier after a rabbit."[20] McGeachy also decided that the provincial government had acquitted itself "with great care and elaboration ... All its briefs are documented and backed up with battalions of statistics."[21]

From the start, the hearings attracted an odd mixture of eminent scholars and full-blown eccentrics. After the first long day in Winnipeg, Wilfrid Eggleston, who had hesitantly abandoned journalism to act as Skelton's assistant for press relations, returned wearily to the hotel drawing room that he shared with Skelton. He found it "full of assorted characters and everybody seemed to be trying to talk at once."[22] Among them were three monetary cranks and a Swede who insisted on telling his life story and demonstrating his wrestling expertise. After he had shown a few holds to Skelton, "Sandy, who had been a noted athlete at Queen's [University] ... proceeded to fling the astonished Swede over his shoulder onto the chesterfield, on which sat an even more astonished professor of economics from the University of Manitoba."[23]

Such adventures were comic relief amid the tales of calamity – and Saskatchewan's plight was even worse than Manitoba's. Premier W.J. Patterson would win re-election in June 1938 – although the CCF would take ten seats – but he could already see his voters' discontent. In his introduction to his 434-page brief, the rattled premier promised to spell out the province's handicaps "by reason of its location and the physical conditions which apply to its basic industry of agriculture."[24] He pointedly added that Canada was so diverse that it was "difficult for Federal policies to apply with equal benefit to all sections of the nation."[25] The brief itself promised: "All this will be a very dark picture."[26]

And it was. The province's per capita income – with the exception of Prince Edward Island – was the lowest in Canada at two-thirds of the national average. The fiscal need of the province was "very great," while the existing arrangements for provincial support were "inherently faulty."[27] Roughly 407,600 people out of a population of 928,000 were now on relief. The premier expected that number to hit 500,000 before February, but at least there was "nobody starving or cold or homeless."[28]

His province's per capita provincial and municipal debt as a percentage of income was the highest in Canada.[29] Debt charges, including interest on borrowing for relief, consumed an astonishing 52 percent of ordinary revenues.[30] Residents had reached the end of their rope. They would "not readily tolerate further reduction or elimination of expenditures on education, hospitalization, care of the aged and destitute and other expenditures of a like character ... Saskatchewan cannot maintain, through periods of economic depression and crop failure, *the minimum standards of social and community services which are, by common consent, considered appropriate to Canada.*[31] Unnoticed then, those words were an early summary of the still unarticulated principle of equalization. The brief added that spending on social services in April 1936 was almost ten times higher than it had been in 1911.[32]

The provincial government could not stay afloat. Australia, once again, was cited with envy. That nation had learned during the early years of the Depression to concentrate on its national income – as opposed to Canada's continuing emphasis on "sound money." So Australia had depreciated its currency in 1931: "'Equality of sacrifice' while alleged to have potential anti-deflationary powers, was also considered an equitable and highly desirable goal in its own right."[33] The brief added bitterly that such devotion to equity did not exist in Canada: "The tacit assumption was that the economic distress could be localized, that the vulnerable groups must bear with fortitude *their unequal burdens*, sustained by the faith that their martyrdom was but the price of the sanctity of contract and of the credit of the Dominion."[34] Anyone who read the Saskatchewan brief understood that fiscal and economic inequality was dangerous. Or, as McGeachy observed, Manitoba witnesses were "polyannas by comparison with the Saskatchewan citizens. The story of bankruptcy told here is the most dismal the Commission will hear."[35]

Saskatchewan had a dizzying array of proposals. It wanted Ottawa to assume responsibility for that portion of the debt attributable to the payment of relief – because it was "incurred in the discharge of a national obligation."[36] Social services had to expand: Ottawa should take full responsibility for relief and for old-age pensions, which would have an eligibility age of sixty-five instead of seventy; it should consider health insurance; it should institute Unemployment Insurance; and it should enact a national labour policy. It should also increase its subsidies.[37] The commissioners should forget any prattle about parity among the provinces: equality "becomes an entirely useless word when … [certain national policies] have operated in the direction of a disastrous inequality for the majority of the provinces."[38] Saskatchewan was "the Cinderella of the Canadian Federation."[39]

The message from the Saskatchewan Urban Municipalities Association was even worse. Taxpayers faced "complete confiscation" of their homes because they could not afford the high property taxes that funded social services as well as relief for their unemployed neighbours.[40] The larger cities were also funding medical, optical, and dental care for families on relief.[41] The quality of infrastructure and schools was declining as the cost of relief decimated city budgets.[42] Municipal credit had been "completely" destroyed: no city had "been able to sell bonds on the open market since 1930"; some cities had defaulted; interest payments on bank loans and other debts were often "as much as the total relief costs in 1932."[43]

Most poignantly, the land that was once the source of Prairie wealth and pride "now [stood] as the symbol of liability."[44] Residents were growing poorer – and so were their governments. The hearings were so grim that Commissioner Henry Angus reminded Commissioner Joseph Sirois about Virgil's *Aeneid*: when Queen Dido asked Aeneas to recount his arduous journey, he replied, "Majesty, too terrible for speech is the pain which you ask me to revive."[45] Angus used the original Latin.

The commissioners listened in horrified fascination. In both provinces, they peered at the lines of despairing men who pleaded for jobs or handouts and the tarpaper shacks that housed their families. In Winnipeg, unemployed men were cleaning up the chilly riverbanks, paid with cash and relief vouchers.[46] In Regina, donations from across the nation had provided 80 million pounds of food for homes in drought-stricken southern Saskatchewan.[47] Cows and other livestock were starving on those prairies because ice had formed over the short stubble left from the disastrous crop year.[48] Temperatures were so cold that press assistant Eggleston had to buy a fur cap "for the first time in [his] life" to make the mile-and-a-half trek from the hotel to the Regina legislature with St-Laurent (and Eggleston lived in Ottawa!).[49]

It was almost impossible to imagine remedies for such desperate inequality. The commissioners were discovering that sharing among governments could be complicated. Their hearings would continue in Ottawa after the holidays. Meanwhile, King's problems were just getting worse – much as he wanted the Royal Commission to make them go away.

MACKENZIE KING'S WOES

The prime minister had his hands full. In December 1937, mere days after the Rowell-Sirois hearings in Regina finished, King learned of trouble ahead. The National Employment Commission, which he had established in April 1936 to placate the provinces, was about to recommend that Ottawa assume responsibility for *all* unemployed. The expense could have been crippling, destroying his government's reputation for fiscal prudence. The very idea of interference in areas of provincial constitutional responsibility appalled him. As historian James Struthers aptly notes: "In its final act the commission thus brought to a head the underlying tensions and contradictions which had surrounded Ottawa's involvement with the unemployed since its first contributions to relief at the end of the First World War."[50]

King was frantic. He turned to his idealistic labour minister Norman Rogers and was astonished to learn that Rogers supported that advice. "I pointed out that that meant the whole of relief," an alarmed King confided in his diary. "The Party would never escape that obligation on itself."[51] To his dismay, Rogers defended "the whole business as being the right thing."[52] Still, the next morning, at King's urging, Rogers spoke to British-born industrialist Arthur Purvis, who chaired the commission. Purvis defended his approach.

The crisis continued. That afternoon, King reminded his cabinet that Purvis was only supposed to look at unemployment on the ground – not the general problem of unemployment policy. By the letter of that mandate, King was correct. The commission had specific legal chores: to consider a possible apprenticeship program; to outline the conditions that would allow a province to qualify for relief funds; to examine employment for the disabled and ex-soldiers; to recommend public works that would provide employment; and to outline "comprehensive measures constituting a long-range plan of national development which may be proceeded with or not, as conditions warrant."[53]

The prime minister did not want to hear about the bigger picture. He viewed the report as a potential catastrophe. To his relief, cabinet backed him. But the impasse blighted King's Christmas. On 12 January 1938, he concluded that the dangers from the report were: "more disturbing than anything I have seen thus far in my public life," with the exception of the First World War.[54] In mid-January 1938, at Rogers's request, Purvis spoke with Royal Commission chair Rowell about what Rowell viewed as their apparently overlapping terms of reference. On 25 January, after all seven members of the Purvis Commission met with Rowell, Purvis agreed to cut much of the contentious material from his report.

King rejoiced. Rogers was isolated within cabinet. Purvis had backed down. The prime minister then declared that the Purvis Report should not be tabled until it was translated. By then, he reasoned, Parliament would be distracted with other problems. But the episode would leave him with an enduring mistrust of the finance ministry bureaucrats, especially those from the Queen's University economics department, such as W.A. Mackintosh and W.C. Clark. They had been working, King concluded dourly, to bring about constitutional change, "which [would] lead to a centralization of powers and away from the present order of things."[55] That distrust extended to the Rowell-Sirois Commission staff, including Secretary Alex Skelton, who had taken his undergraduate degree at Queen's.

Still, the prime minister had dodged a bullet. King had seen the corrosive conscription crisis split the nation during the First World War when Quebec was isolated in its opposition to enforced enlistment. He viewed the preservation of national unity as his primary job. And he was free – so far – to espouse that approach. As political scientists Richard Simeon and Ian Robinson observed, "As long as there was no clear English-speaking majority position on the appropriate role of the state, electoral politics left King with room to manoeuvre." The prime minister wanted to "avoid the kind of economic and social policy initiatives that [Quebec premier Louis-Alexandre] Taschereau denounced in 1935."[56] (Taschereau had opposed the efforts of younger Liberals under the leadership of Paul Gouin to abandon laissez-faire and adopt "an extensive scheme of labour and social legislation which would raise the incomes and provide greater economic security for the working class.")[57]

As the prime minister would observe when key cabinet ministers wanted to disallow Quebec's draconian Padlock Law to shut down the so-called communist media, which the Quebec Legislative Assembly had adopted in March 1937: "I took the view that in the last resort, the unity of Canada was the test by which we should meet all these things ... [We] had to consider, in our action, its effect upon the nation."[58] Although the prime minister disliked the Quebec legislation, he refused to disallow it. King's attitude provided a clue as to how he would eventually view the report from the Royal Commission on Dominion-Provincial Relations.

It was not until the late 1930s that the voices of those who saw the nation through the lens of social needs – and that group included key witnesses before the Rowell-Sirois Royal Commission – started to compete with the voices of those who espoused provincial language and cultural rights. Those advocates wanted Ottawa to take a more active role in social policy, arguing that only the federal government "possessed the fiscal resources and technical expertise to implement progressive social and economic policies."[59] But their voices were still weak.

In early 1938, King did not hear them. He did not want to upset the provinces, especially Quebec, by interfering in their constitutional responsibility for relief. He did not want Ottawa to centralize more power: in his view, such actions would only *destabilize* the federation. He now had a wonderful excuse for delay: the federal government had happily punted the fate of the unemployed employables to the Royal Commission (the commissioners would decide that Ottawa should assume responsibility for Unemployment Insurance but not relief). Why should Ottawa act until Rowell-Sirois reported?

THE COMMISSION CARRIES ON

While King dodged and feinted with Purvis and Rogers, the commissioners ploughed onward. They spent the last two weeks of January 1938 in Ottawa, querying witnesses from national organizations that chronicled Canada's inequalities. The Trades and Labor Congress demanded that labour and employment conditions "be uniform throughout Canada, for competition to be fair."[60] The commissioners were becoming wary of that word "fair" – which individual groups would define far differently.

The Canadian Medical Association wanted Ottawa to take responsibility for the "health of the casual and chronic unemployed."[61] As CMA general secretary T.C. Routley earnestly explained: "It does seem to us illogical to say to an unfortunate individual or family, the Government will provide you with a house and fuel to keep you warm, clothing to keep you covered, and food to sustain you, but, if you have the misfortune to become ill, then you must take your chances of living or dying, because so far as the Federal Government's responsibility goes, it washes its hands of the whole matter."[62] But the CMA shied away from a call for national health insurance even as it acknowledged that German chancellor Otto von Bismarck had introduced health insurance in 1883, future British prime minister David Lloyd George had done so in 1911 as chancellor of the exchequer, and forty nations now had similar plans. Instead, it called for studies on how each province might handle the issue, using the complications of federalism to dodge an unwanted policy.[63]

The Canadian Tuberculosis Association warned that, despite advances in health care, deaths were not declining among the Indigenous population: Aboriginals constituted 1 percent of the population – but 11 percent of the deaths from tuberculosis. Ottawa, which had constitutional responsibility for "Indians," should increase its spending on Indigenous health care by $500,000.[64] There was a pattern here: advocacy groups (even those that thought Ottawa was neglecting its duties) usually looked to Ottawa – *not* to the provinces – for solutions to those needs.

Then the commissioners swung east to Halifax and Charlottetown. They could be cynical about those parts of Maritime presentations that used any pretense to demand more money. One Nova Scotia municipality asked for roughly eighty dollars to cover the cost of an inquest into the death of a rumrunner shot at sea during a run-in with federal customs officers.[65] When the lawyer for one province – probably Nova Scotia – claimed that the province had lost heavily when it entered Confederation, Rowell pointedly compared the federation to a marriage: "Would it not be better to think twice before separating and to remember that you had taken each other for better or for worse?"[66] Silence ensued. When local residents later explained that the lawyer had gone through what was then a very rare divorce, stern Methodist Rowell was unrepentant. Improbably, Prince Edward Island wanted compensation for the profits that it might have made from liquor during Prohibition if it had remained outside Confederation.[67] That undoubtedly offended Rowell, too.

But the huge inequalities that existed in both provinces compared with the richer provinces horrified the commissioners. In Halifax, Premier Angus L. Macdonald's presentation – and its setting – had a remarkable effect on stalwart journalist McGeachy. The legislature was "a grimy structure which was saved with underprops from falling apart some years ago and stands in a slummy thoroughfare."[68] The nearby meeting room was decorated with a scrubby red carpet and a clock that chimed nine and then did not chime again. Premier Macdonald looked like "a bookkeeper with poetic aspirations."[69] But "when he speaks, the effect is astonishing. He is the first witness to testify with utter self-confidence, no fumbling for words or ideas."[70] While Westerners outlined their recent troubles, Nova Scotia chronicled grievances that were seventy years old, "something bred in the bone." Macdonald even "sounded a little world-weary."[71]

Macdonald wanted Ottawa to assume full responsibility for old-age pensions and mothers' allowances, perhaps through a constitutional amendment, because a poorer province "through no fault of its own cannot obtain sufficient revenue to support the normal standard [of services]."[72] He also wanted Ottawa to enact Unemployment Insurance.[73]

Then he turned to Australia. The premier parsed the principle of fiscal need, moving through the Duncan and White Royal Commission reports to the Australian Commonwealth Grants Commission. Macdonald maintained that if the Australians could accept fiscal need as a basis of adjustment, Canadians should admit that fiscal need "has been the determining factor as shown in practically all subsidy re-allocations."[74]

The Nova Scotia brief outlined how the CGC chose its personnel, demonstrated the scope of its inquiries, and included charts on the amounts of its annual grants. The premier even suggested that Canada create a permanent commission "patterned to some extent upon the Grants Commission in Australia": if provincial taxes were "appreciably above the normal rate" and government services were "appreciably below such normal standard," those conditions should be corrected "by an appropriate special grant."[75] This was a remarkable early effort at devising a system of equalization – based upon Australia.

In fact, the example of Australia ran throughout Nova Scotia's 141-page brief: it looked at its constitutional reform, the effect of its tariffs, the location of its industries, the establishment of its marketing agencies, and the introduction of regular Dominion-Provincial Conferences. In effect, Australia was the model for Angus L.'s lucid proposals – and those proposals would influence the commission's report.

As his testimony stretched into a second day, an impressed McGeachy depicted the premier's approach as "an essay on economic trends, with the odd illustrative statistic thrown in, which is the elegant way to do it."[76] Macdonald emphasized Nova Scotia's unequal position within the federation – because of the tariff, transportation costs, isolation, and the relative poverty of its resources. He insisted that Nova Scotians were "poorer than other Canadians, citing how little their taxes yield though high in rate and their shortage of radios and motor cars [Rowell could not resist observing that they had more boats]."[77] The journalist gravely noted Macdonald's contrast of "federal grants to Australian states, running to $20 a head, with the $3 a head Nova Scotia gets from Ottawa."[78] Wilfrid Eggleston was also impressed: "if he [Macdonald] had not been a Roman Catholic he might aspire to succeed Mackenzie King as Prime Minister of Canada."[79]

The commissioners had a rough ferry crossing to Charlottetown during a fierce blizzard. They waded through snowdrifts and then climbed three flights of stairs to the courthouse hearing room. Eggleston noticed that Dafoe was "boisterous," while Rowell was "delicate and frail."[80] The message that they heard, as seemingly always in Prince Edward Island in the 1930s, was grim. Public health services were so meagre that the government wanted Ottawa to take responsibility for communicable and preventable disease.[81] But the great fireplace in the commissioners' railway hotel was glowing as the blizzard raged. And the commissioners were shown "the very chairs sat in by the Fathers of Confederation in September, 1864."[82]

BACK ACROSS THE WEST

The troubles with inequality in the poorer provinces left the commissioners with little patience for the complaints of the wealthier provinces. Far worse, on the day that the commissioners set out for the West Coast, German chancellor Adolf Hitler invaded Austria. "Europe was rocked by the news, tension ran high, war seemed immanent; and nobody knew whether such inquiries as we were conducting still had any meaning," Eggleston recalled. "For the rest of the commission's existence it operated in an atmosphere of suspense and under darkening international skies."[83]

Their train chugged through the Rockies, crossing the Fraser River at New Westminster. By mid-March, they were in Victoria for ten long days crammed with hearings and social events. The commissioners flitted from a white-tie gala at Government House to another gala with the British Columbia cabinet. Commissioner Dafoe delivered a stern speech to the Canadian Institute of International Affairs, warning, "We are now in the early stages of World War II."[84]

At the hearings, British Columbia premier Duff Pattullo put a new spin on inequality: he argued that his province was also in an unequal position because Ottawa took out more tax money than it put into it. But he needed the money. His province was "still in a pioneering stage and dependent in the main on primary products for income."[85] Its expenses – especially for resource development and social services in "modern times" – were enormous.[86] Once again, Australia appeared in a province's narrative: "Canada, unlike Australia or the Argentine, had no special monetary policy planned to meet economic distress." So while Canada "relied on protection of her manufacturing industries to regain prosperity ... British Columbia suffered from this policy and received no special benefit."[87]

Pattullo's government faced political challenges. As the premier's biographer, historian Robin Fisher, observes, "The conditions of the depression decade had both raised people's expectations and increased government's responsibilities."[88] The premier espoused the probably unrealistic ideal of "socialised capitalism": capital should recognize "the duty and the desirability of giving larger consideration to the needs and welfare of society generally."[89] Governments, in turn, should redistribute that wealth. Ottawa should assume responsibility for unemployment relief and for health and welfare services for transients. It should participate in infrastructure and resource development projects. Ottawa should also make room for the province to increase its own income tax. "Inequalities and disabilities existing by reason of the application of the tariff and freight rates should be adjusted."[90]

But, and this was crucial, British Columbia was fed up with sharing with the Rest of Canada. Pattullo insisted that his province had "not been dealt with in a measure of parity in comparison with the treatment accorded to the other Provinces by the Dominion."[91] He submitted a statement of claim based on fourteen specific demands, starting with British Columbia's "debts and liabilities" that existed at the time of Union with Canada in 1871.[92] The premier even demanded that Ottawa pave the old wagon road that travellers had used before Ottawa constructed a railway across the province in the 1880s.[93] As Royal Commissioner Henry Angus later recalled, Pattullo freely confessed, behind the scenes, that he was itemizing vast numbers of needs so that he could later horse-trade with the federal government.[94]

His aim was clear: British Columbia did not want more of its citizens' federal tax dollars allocated to the poorer provinces. It wanted to send less money to Ottawa. Even "the local press" dismissed that approach "as narrow and parochial" – but the premier was undeterred.⁹⁵ As he would later tell the editor of the *Vancouver Province*: "The centralisers almost force one to appear in the light of a provincialist."⁹⁶ And Pattullo viewed the commissioners as centralizers.

The premier's presentation ran contrary to the views of the provincial CCF, which had snared almost 29 percent of the vote in the June 1937 election. As CCF MLA Dorothy G. Steeves later wrote, modern federations required "social planning, social security and provision for collective international agreement ... which can only be carried out by strong, centralized action." Steeves added that there was "vociferous public demand" in British Columbia for public health and hospitalization "to which even Liberal governments have to lend an ear."⁹⁷ Pattullo was undeterred.

McGeachy cast a dubious eye on most of the province's proposals – although he did report the province's claim that it was shortchanged in the queue for dominion aid. "This seems to be proved by the figures," McGeachy observed cautiously, adding that they were "presumably not cooked to excess."⁹⁸ Then he riffed on federal subsidies: "The subject is complicated. The system of federal subsidies in Canada is certainly one of the craziest arithmetical puzzles ever hatched in the hallucinated brains of public financiers. A long lifetime would be needed to get the hang of it."⁹⁹

Six days later, as the hearings stretched on, McGeachy noted pointedly that Pattullo believed that dominion grants should "not be based solely on either population or 'fiscal need' ... but on a survey of each province's economic position, including its share of the burden of tariff and income tax."¹⁰⁰ The premier was bold. But his ploy of asking for the moon would not work. Pattullo would talk compulsively about his disappointment with the Royal Commission for the remainder of his political life.¹⁰¹

Throughout the spring of 1938, the commissioners continued their weary slog across the nation. Only two provincial governments – Alberta and Quebec – had refused outright to cooperate. Both provinces just wanted Ottawa to leave them alone with enough revenue to fulfill their responsibilities. As well, Alberta was still irate over Ottawa's failure to provide assistance prior to its April 1936 default. Since then, the relationship had only grown worse. In 1937, Alberta premier William "Bible Bill" Aberhart had tried to restrict freedom of the press and to put the banks under provincial control. Lieutenant-Governor John C. Bowen had refused to sign those Social Credit bills into law, arguing that they were unconstitutional. He had referred them to the Supreme Court, which would eventually agree with Bowen. But the lieutenant-governor's principled conduct – he had been a Baptist minister – had infuriated Aberhart. The populist premier, who preached his blend of fundamentalism and Pentecostalism on a weekly radio show, objected to Ottawa's determination to uphold its constitutional rights. The federal government would disallow eleven Alberta statutes between 1937 and 1941.[102]

Aberhart also objected to the Royal Commission's very existence. When Prime Minister King formally announced the commission in mid-August 1937, Aberhart furiously telegraphed his objections to the personnel and the mandate. He detected renewed hints about the imposition of a loan council. "Other equally dangerous and undesirable possibilities for centralizing financial control and weakening the sovereignty of THE PEOPLE of each Province are, in our view, certain to arise from these particular terms of reference and this particular Commission."[103] Aberhart added a final shot: he was certain that King had moved with "precipitate haste" in announcing the commission so that it would coincide with Ottawa's recent disallowance of his provincial legislation.[104]

King rebutted every point. There were no hints of a loan council in his press release. He had first announced the commission in the House of Commons in February 1937. The commissioners had no mandate to change the Constitution. Finally, King could not ignore: "the offensive remark in your last paragraph ... Only to yourself will it be necessary to deny unequivocally that there was any connection" between the disallowances and the creation of the commission.[105]

There was no leeway for compromise. The premier refused to participate in the hearings in "bleak, stark, wintry" Edmonton as a blizzard blew "down Jasper Avenue and the north winds cut the flesh."[106] Although Rowell formally called on the premier in his hotel suite, the legislature actually voted to ignore the commission's presence; one MLA even declared, "The sooner the commission got out of town, the better."[107] But Aberhart's government did prepare a 377-page submission along with seventy-two pages of summaries and appendices, which it sent to Ottawa, which, in turn, forwarded it to the commission. That submission listed Alberta's complaints about the "faulty financial system" and touted its monetary magic, which promised to replace cash with credit notes.[108]

The province called for Ottawa to assume responsibility for unemployment relief and old-age pensions, to recognize the "disabilities borne by the Province" from national policies such as the tariff and freight rates, and to take responsibility for problems with the dominion's monetary policy.[109] Ottawa should offer grants for public health, education, mothers' allowances, and highway construction, pending "the transition period to a new economic order."[110] In effect, Alberta maintained that Ottawa had put the province in an unequal fiscal position – and it had to pay for it.

Despite the mercurial premier's absence, the commission's visit to Edmonton was certainly interesting. Under the guise of a frugality that seemed suspiciously like revenge, Aberhart cut off the utilities at Government House. The commissioners were guests at a luncheon there when Aberhart turned off the water to force the Bowen family to move. No lieutenant-governor would ever reside there again – although the Jacobean Revival-style building is now used for government dinners and receptions. McGeachy was irrepressible. As he noted: "In other capitals the visitors have had polite bids to lunch, or even dinner, from the powers that be. Here they live in a social vacuum."[111] McGeachy imagined Aberhart dining "in solemn solitude at the town's leading cafeteria."[112]

But the commissioners did receive a significant sixty-four-page brief from the Edmonton Chamber of Commerce, which effectively called for equalization. The chamber outlined the five disabilities "that rendered Alberta so vulnerable when the recent depression began."[113] Those included: the cost of pioneer development and railway branch lines, excessive freight costs, high interest rates, and Ottawa's high tariffs. The chamber noted that Australia and Argentina had depreciated their currencies during the Depression – in contrast to Canada.[114] Ottawa should assume many of Alberta's social responsibilities – ranging from unemployment relief to old-age pensions, from minimum wages to workmen's compensation – because the cost was crippling Alberta.[115] It should also increase its grants for education and transportation infrastructure.[116]

The most striking recommendation was buried in a wordy paragraph near the end of the chamber's brief. It demanded that Ottawa duplicate Australia's approach to fiscal inequality through the establishment of a permanent commission that would consider dominion subsidies and grants at regular intervals. The examination would "be automatic, non-political and based upon submissions by the various provinces as to what would constitute fair subsidies."[117] Surprisingly, there were many Canadians who knew about the Australian model – even if it would prove impossible to adopt in the federation of the 1930s.

THE TRAGEDY IN ONTARIO

The commissioners carried on, united in their growing camaraderie amid the constant complaints about inequality and unfair treatment from the poorer *and* the richer provinces. And then came their hearings in Ontario – and the week that they lost their chairman. Newton Rowell was the cornerstone of the commission, the chief justice of the Supreme Court of Ontario, and the link to Ontario's obstreperous and relatively wealthy Liberal government, which was deeply suspicious of the commission's doings.

When Ontario premier Mitchell Hepburn appeared on 2 May 1938, he seemed unsettled by Rowell's very presence. Commissioner Angus would later speculate that Hepburn was embarrassed. The premier mispronounced words. His jokes fell flat. He was rattled.[118] But that did not check Hepburn's anti-Ottawa diatribe. Ottawa should not have empowered a royal commission to handle the serious issue of designing the federation, fumed Hepburn. It should have called a dominion-provincial conference.[119] The commissioners should remember that $75 to $80 million of Ontario residents' tax dollars went to the Maritimes and the Prairies every year – which represented twenty-one dollars per capita.[120]

Ontario was doing its best: "It is almost incredible that the Prairie Provinces should now claim disability against the rest of Canada because the wheat-growers of the Prairie Provinces were not enabled to enter into competitive devaluation of currency with Australia," the premier declared.[121] Meanwhile, Prairie economists had proven that Nova Scotia's claim for compensation for the disabilities of the federation was incorrect. "Perhaps, one could not find a more striking illustration of the impracticalities of compensating provinces for the disabilities they claim (even the real ones) as a result of federal policy."[122] Provinces should not blame the federation for their fiscal woes.

Once again, Australia figured in a province's arguments. Ontario opposed any centralization of social programs. The provincial brief cited the Australian Commonwealth Grants Commission, which had observed that it was more efficient for provinces to administer social programs than to unify that administration in Canberra – or, the brief added, in Ottawa.[123] Ontario also objected to any attempt to compensate provinces for such disabilities as the tariff. As the brief noted tartly, Australia had rejected any claim for grants based on disabilities: the CGC had deplored "the validity of the whole basis of making claims on the grounds of the uneven effects of either individual or total federal policy."[124]

There was a limit to Ontario's generosity – and there should be a limit to Ottawa's redistribution – for the sake of national unity. "Equality between the Provinces is impossible ... and yet, somehow, we must get along together," the premier proclaimed. "The Provinces are fiscal entities; and governments, like individuals, must learn to manage within their means."[125] Ottawa should reduce its share of income tax because "it is poor politics, and worse economy, that one government should tax for another to spend."[126] The premier concluded with a smug remark: "A sense of sectional injustice has too long retarded the national aspirations of the Canadian people."[127] He wanted the poorer provinces to get over it.

It was an extraordinary performance – and a strong assertion of provincial rights – or, at least, the rights of the wealthier provinces. As McGeachy observed almost gleefully:

> The Great Hepburn, defender of hard-pressed Ontario against the idle rich of Saskatchewan and Manitoba ... looked as sleek and round as usual but less vivacious ... As his jokes fell like pancakes in a puddle, Mr. Hepburn was obviously unhappy though he never lost his aplomb ... He was expected to put up a battle for provincial rights but nobody supposed his statement would be quite as full of half-baked economics, appeals to prejudice, jumbled logic, and parish politics as it was.[128]

The journalist noted that Hepburn had divided the provinces into two apparently irreconcilable camps of richer and poorer. The premier viewed Western proposals to give new responsibilities and enlarged taxing powers to Ottawa as "nothing but an unashamed raid by the orphans of Confederation on the pockets of Central Canada."[129] McGeachy added: "It was a hilarious performance, but the atmosphere was pretty grim. The Commission was not amused."[130] Press Secretary Wilfrid Eggleston viewed the encounter between the "cocky" premier and the "aged" chief justice as "deplorably destructive and aggravating."[131] He was aghast.

It is important to remember that McGeachy was an employee of the *Winnipeg Free Press* and was presumably inclined to favour the prevailing Western viewpoint. But it appears that Hepburn really did go too far. Commissioner Angus recalled that Hepburn's "somewhat truculent presentation ... shocked the newsmen and deeply hurt the Chief Justice ... [He] was very distressed by the Commission's reception in his home province."[132] After Hepburn concluded, the dignified Rowell was sufficiently upset to make a brief statement: the commission was simply a "fact-finding body" that would issue recommendations for the consideration of a dominion-provincial conference.[133] No more. It had no power to change the Constitution. To add to Rowell's worries, he was also concerned about a case before his Ontario court.[134]

But Rowell did not hold grudges. He did appear at a dinner on Wednesday, 4 May 1938, that Hepburn threw for the commissioners and their staff along with his cabinet members at the King Edward Hotel. The party was sedate until the abstemious Rowell left. Then, as Maritime commissioner R.A. "Bert" MacKay told his horrified wife Kathleen, the scotch flowed freely while Hepburn and the dean of the Saskatchewan law school, Frederick Clinton Cronkite, sang an off-colour duet. There were more songs and stories. The commissioners who stayed for the party and their staff could "not help liking him [the premier], even though [they] might thoroughly disagree with him."[135] The commissioners were coming to understand the varying views of federalism – and the limits to remedying fiscal and economic inequality.

During the party, two Ontario cabinet ministers and deputy provincial treasurer Chester Walters apologized to MacKay for Hepburn's speech, which confirmed MacKay's view that Hepburn had formed a defensive alliance against Ottawa with Quebec premier Maurice Duplessis: "Circumstances were such that he [Hepburn] more or less had to do it (no doubt his bargain with Duplessis) though he thoroughly disliked it."[136] Hepburn himself "quit singing and remarked in my ear to the effect that Ontario wasn't so damned provincially minded and that we were all Canadians anyway."[137]

MacKay credited the party for the more conciliatory tone at the remaining commission hearings in Toronto. But Rowell was failing. His health could not stand the stress. Five days after Hepburn's diatribe, on 7 May 1938, Rowell suffered a heart attack followed by a crippling stroke. "He lost in a second the power of speech."[138] His colleagues were stricken. Rowell had been well acquainted with Dafoe before the commission, and he had bonded with the other three during their arduous cross-country trips. The commissioners had known that Rowell's health had never been good. In February 1938, Dafoe had even written to the American secretary general of the Institute of Pacific Relations: "I am a bit apprehensive as to whether his strength will be equal to the task."[139] They noticed that he rationed his energy. But the hearings were difficult, as Dafoe also noted: "the task is so complex and overwhelming that it takes pretty much full possession of my mind and my energies."[140]

Rowell was probably beyond help after the heart attack and the stroke. In his absence, Sirois became acting chair. He would become chair when Rowell resigned in November 1938. By early August, Rowell could read a little – and apparently understand what was said to him. And that was all. But he would not die until November 1941, trapped in his silent netherworld. As his biographer Margaret Prang observes: "Not a few wondered whether his encounter with the brash and vulgar Hepburn had contributed to his illness."[141]

The commissioners were reeling, but they somehow carried on. They finished their hearings in Toronto and then continued in mid-May to Quebec City. Prior to the hearings, the province had even refused to provide fiscal statistics.[142] Once there, the commissioners met with formidable assertions of provincial cultural and linguistic rights. Despite francophone counsel Louis St-Laurent's pleas, Quebec premier Duplessis refused to appear as a witness – or to answer any of the twenty-three questions that Saint Laurent had submitted. (Sample: "What is the view of the Quebec Government as to the inclusion in the Canadian Constitution of safeguards for fundamental rights of citizenship, such as freedom of speech, of the press, of assembly, and of access to the Courts?")[143]

Instead, on the Quebec government's behalf, lawyer Emery Beaulieu read an eleven-page memo that endorsed Ontario premier Hepburn's opposition to any centralization, depicting it as a feature "in countries that we call totalitarian."[144] How dare Ottawa ask a royal commission to look into provincial finances? "Under our federal system, each province, in its own sphere, constitutes an autonomous state, enjoying all the prerogatives of a sovereign state and not subject to federal power," Beaulieu read in French.[145] If Quebec recognized the Royal Commission's authority, it would have to "consent to sacrifice the prerogatives of provincial autonomy."[146]

Ottawa was *not* entitled to examine Quebec's financial position. If it wanted to pry into the nation's finances – and it should because Confederation had "prejudicially affected" Ontario and Quebec – it should work with the provincial legislatures. Provinces needed higher subsidies – and Ottawa should free up more tax room for provinces to raise their own revenues. Duplessis thanked Hepburn for dismissing the complaints of the West about federation.[147] Quebec was willing to share with other provinces – *but* it would not abridge its rights under "the fallacious pretense of working for the common weal."[148]

The Fathers of Confederation "belonging to two great races and two parties" had designed the federation to protect the rights of minorities.[149] Quebec would protect its distinct identity of francophone culture, religion, and language – and any federal interference would damage the Confederation pact. It was an unmistakable warning. *Le Devoir* printed the entire text of Beaulieu's statement under the headline, "Ottawa Should Have Started by Consulting All the Provinces."[150] This statement demonstrates why any postwar efforts to centralize revenues would fail.

The ever-curious McGeachy confirmed that Hepburn and Duplessis – "the Jonathan and David of Canadian politics" – had collaborated on their approach to the commission: "On learning that Mitch's address to the Commission was to be a snooty repudiation of all responsibility to be helpful, Maurice agreed to co-operate on that basis."[151] *Le Devoir* journalist Léopold Richer noted that the commission could recommend anything that it wished, but "the federal government will think twice before recommending constitutional reforms ... no federal party will know what to do in the face of the combined opposition of Ontario and Quebec."[152]

That was a prescient insight. The next day, the commission heard from four witnesses, including the Montreal Board of Trade, the Montreal division of the Chamber of Commerce, and lawyer Hector Lalonde from *La Société Saint-Jean-Baptiste de Montréal*. The Société's brief was a fierce affirmation of the province's rights: "In fact, and in law, Canada is a mixed nation: it constitutes two races, two cultures, two civilizations ... We wish to review the consistency of this phenomenon back through the double Canadian personality generated from this national equality."[153]

Then the Société scrolled through time from Jacques Cartier's voyage in 1534 to the present. Ottawa should not interfere: the province could only preserve "its moral and spiritual heritage – culture and civilization" if "its political climate allows it to grow in its innate fashion." If Ottawa wanted to do a "great service," it would support the economic recovery and stop trying to centralize "the administration of social laws."[154] It was a discreet warning that the absent Duplessis surely cheered.

But the Quebec premier was not without politesse. The commissioners had lunch at Government House on the same day – and the premier sat next to the bilingual Angus. "He was quite genial and, in a somewhat malicious way, witty," Angus recalled.[155] The commissioners still hoped that Duplessis would relent and testify. The premier then invited everyone to dinner at the Chateau Frontenac. They accepted, again. Still hoping. It was a rowdy evening. As historian Dale C. Thomson notes: "An ardent baseball fan, Duplessis proved expert in knocking out electric light bulbs with champagne glasses."[156] The party continued throughout the night. Angus recalled that St-Laurent had asked, after Hepburn's Toronto party, what the people of Ontario would say about their leaders' conduct. Now he could not resist posing the same question to the dignified St-Laurent.[157] He did not record the answer.

Duplessis never did appear before the commission. As his biographer Conrad Black explains, he and Hepburn were annoyed with Ottawa for its refusal to authorize provincial hydroelectric exports to the United States. This would remain a "considerable irritant to federal-provincial relations for many years."[158] But Duplessis would curtail his drinking during 1942, and he quit altogether in 1943. He would become one of the key proponents of provincial rights who would force Ottawa to find a better way to share with the provinces.

After those tough hearings in Quebec City, the constitutional and fiscal gulfs within the federation were much clearer to the commissioners. To their relief, their last stop was Fredericton, where they gathered within the "dreamy leisurely Arcadian atmosphere" of the legislature buildings, beside the St John River.[159] Liberal MLA and lawyer Walter Jones languidly read New Brunswick's tart denunciation of the dominion.[160] Ottawa should abandon the principle of equality among the provinces when calculating federal subsidies: it was "quite apparent from the record that the grants to the provinces have always been based upon the principle of fiscal need ... [But] the fiscal need of one province may be quite different from the fiscal need of another province."[161]

New Brunswick had been treated unfairly. "Wealth is centralized in one or two provinces and the *future of the Dominion* depends upon a proper adjustment of revenue, and the consideration of the resources of one province as compared with other provinces," the brief declaimed. "We do not advocate a redistribution of all the wealth in Canada but ... the burden should fall upon the provinces which have most profited by the operation of the Confederation system."[162] It was another early version of equalization.

The province needed money to expand social programs. Its illiteracy rates were the highest in Canada.[163] Fewer than 8,500 of 92,000 children of secondary school age were actually attending school.[164] The province spent half as much per pupil as did Ontario.[165] Ottawa should set the standards for education and then hand over the cash for those programs to the provincial government, which would administer them. If the outcome was unsatisfactory, Ottawa could assume control because there would be an agreement that would permit such dominion action when necessary.[166]

But the brief stumbled on the vital question of revenues. McGeachy was baffled by its earnest suggestion that "income tax, sales tax, and succession duties should all be reserved for the provinces."[167] When the commissioners asked "how the Dominion could find the money to finance social services if deprived of these sources, [the province's lawyer] was not sure."[168]

Other witnesses guardedly backed the impoverished province. The Union of New Brunswick Municipalities related the plight of the failing pulp-and-paper town of Newcastle. The town had spent $3,300 on education in 1901 and $33,000 in 1931 – "with practically no increase in population."[169] The New Brunswick Teachers' Association appealed for federal funds "to equalize educational opportunities" within the province.[170] Those were the laments of the impoverished who could never raise enough money on their own.

NATIONAL BLUEPRINTS

When the hearings resumed in Ottawa in late May, there were more witnesses with detailed schemes to overhaul the nation. It was an indication of how the Royal Commission's mission had gripped the nation's imagination. The Canadian Welfare Council (CWC) emphasized the key role of the state in the security of the individual. Citizens should be able to find employment that would provide "at least the essential elements of survival."[171] When that was impossible, the state should "assure directly or indirectly the provision of the minimum sustenance which life demands."[172] Intriguingly, the council viewed better social security as the remedy for "the persisting and increasing nature of dependency" within the nation.[173] It outlined a system of contributory and non-contributory services that different levels of government could administer: Ottawa could handle Unemployment Insurance, health insurance, and old-age pensions.[174]

A few days later, on 30 May 1938, the five-person delegation from the Canadian Chamber of Commerce bustled into the hearing room at the Board of Railway Commissioners to present what it characterized as a national business standpoint on Canada's problems. Perhaps unsurprisingly, the chamber called for balanced budgets, smaller government, and federal old-age pensions. But chamber representative H.W. Morgan also called for the creation of a loan council similar to the Australian Loan Council: if a province needed to borrow to meet its obligations, the loan council could approve the loan, which would ensure a lower rate of interest.[175] Even more surprisingly, the chamber called for a permanent grants commission – similar to the Australian Grants Commission – to investigate the needs of provinces that applied for subsidies.[176] The fiscal plight of the poorer provinces – and the Australian solutions – had certainly attracted public attention.

The commissioners were also treated to one of Research Director Skelton's pranks. He slotted Tim Buck, general secretary of the Communist Party of Canada (CPC), into the witness line-up – just before the appearance of the president of the National Research Council of Canada, temporarily retired Major-General Andrew McNaughton, who would later command the Canadian armed forces in Europe. Skelton might have wished to provoke fireworks. But the commissioners likely disappointed him because they approached both witnesses with fascination.

Buck was an extreme centralizer in the quest for social security: he wanted Ottawa to provide everything from Unemployment Insurance and relief to housing and labour standards. He also wanted Ottawa to assume control over *all* companies, which were now the "complete dictators of the economic life of the country."[177] He told the commissioners that his brief did not represent his party's final goal, which was "the collectivization of industry, mines, railways and factories."[178] But he did reassure them that "armed struggle" had been eliminated as a policy instrument from the CPC's constitution.[179] When the commission's anglophone counsel James McGregor Stewart asked if extreme views on one side provoked extreme views on the other – "if fascism was not the fruit of communism" – Buck denied that Communists were extreme. "I'm a very conservative individual," he maintained.[180]

Despite such jousting, the commissioners were more interested in Buck's parsing of the national income, which used Dominion Bureau of Statistics figures to underline the ongoing inequality among Canadians. Roughly thirty-six hundred people – or six-tenths of 1 percent of the population – had pocketed more than 25 percent of total Canadian income in 1934.[181] In contrast, 3.4 million people – that is, 90 percent of the employed – received 51 percent of the national income.[182] Remarkably, the commissioners questioned Buck for much of that sunny June day.

In contrast, Major-General McNaughton of the National Research Council was relatively brief – but he did offer a stout defence of organized scientific research in Canada. The need was "so great" that there was ample scope for national and provincial research bodies.[183]

THE INTERNATIONAL MODELS

The workings of the Australian federation remained endlessly fascinating to Canadians. In May 1938, the Bank of Nova Scotia devoted its entire *Monthly Review* to an examination of the Commonwealth Grants Commission: "There can be no doubt that it has achieved its primary purpose of saving the three States from extreme financial embarrassment ... It does not seem to have contributed to extravagance on the part of the States and the method used to determine the grants should be protection against such a development in the future."[184]

The Royal Commission itself asked for numerous reports on international models. There were many analyses of Australia. There were several on Argentina, Switzerland, and the United States. Several of those reports were filed informally with commission records – and were not recorded as official research studies. But, officially and unofficially, the Royal Commission was diligent.

Perhaps the most significant clue to the commissioners' thoughts occurred just before the hearings commenced. As the chairman of the Institute of Pacific Relations and one of the founders of the Canadian Institute of International Affairs, Commissioner John Dafoe knew many foreign dignitaries. On 24 November 1937, he wrote to his Australian friend, the chairman of the Commonwealth Grants Commission, F.W. Eggleston. "I note that in the studies that are being carried on by our economic and taxation experts, much attention is being paid to experiments, if I may call them so, which are being carried out by Australia. There is, I think, exceptional interest in the work of the Special Grants Commission [sic] of which I note you are chairman."[185]

The cordial reply, which did not arrive until April 1938, probably startled Dafoe. Eggleston sent copies of CGC reports and newspaper supplements. And he added a rueful observation. "A good many financial authorities from [North] America have been in Australia recently," Eggleston wrote. "They all express interest and general approval of our principles, but say they would not do in United States of America or Canada as the case may be." Eggleston did not quite understand the reason for this rejection. "But [I] presume that it is because of the different financial situation of the Constitutional members, especially as to debit. My theory is that in a Federation it is most unlikely that the operation of various factors will produce equality, *and this must be rectified after careful assessment.*"[186]

Meanwhile, Secretary Alex Skelton started to produce international experts for the commissioners' Ottawa hearings. On 28 January 1938, they interviewed former German chancellor Heinrich Brüning on the operation of federalism during the then vanished Weimar Republic. Richer states, such as Hanover and Prussia, were compelled to transfer part of their income tax. This was redistributed based on "the population, the expenditure for education and for welfare, for unemployment benefit and everything like that." It was noteworthy that the money did not come from the central government – but as "a special grant out of the pocket of the rich industrial states."[187]

On 21 April 1938, the commissioners heard from University of London law professor Ivor Jennings, who explained how the unitary state of England handled the division of powers among lower levels of government. When commission lawyer Carl Goldenberg asked if the national government's provision of services reflected "the fact that local taxation is not sufficiently flexible or elastic to meet modern needs," Jennings first dodged the question with the weary assertion that local authorities always demanded new grants whenever new services were established.[188] When Goldenberg asked again, Jennings agreed tersely.

On 25 May 1938, mere weeks after Rowell became incapacitated, Skelton even produced the famed Swedish economist Gunnar Myrdal who described his nation's taxation system along with its relatively new social support systems. The "big trouble" was the great variation in the tax rates among different counties and communities: Stockholm had large corporations and numerous rich people, so "we have a rather low taxation and still we can go on with very large expenditures, while in poorer country districts the taxation is high and the standard of expenditure is low."[189] The solution was "to give much more percentage of rate to the poor districts."[190] He added dolefully that Sweden still had "not solved that problem."[191] But it was a fascinating look at the struggle to remedy inequality in a unitary state.

Then came experts on American federalism. The acting director of the US Budget Bureau, D.W. Bell, discussed the division of powers between states and the federal government in education, highways, social services, and relief. The under secretary for the treasury, Roswell Magill, reviewed the taxation aspects of federal finance. In October 1938, the research director of the Rockefeller Center in New York, Canadian-born Bryce M. Stewart, outlined how the United States handled unemployment insurance and basic social services such as old-age assistance – and what the nation should have done differently.[192]

The thousands of pages on federalist models in the Royal Commission files remain astonishing. Calgary lawyer H.E. Crowle, who was on contract to the commission, wrote a fourteen-page report on Argentina: "Argentina is in the happy position ... of having a federation whose federal government is in a very real sense the dominant government."[193] Crowle also wrote studies on marketing and price control in Switzerland, New Zealand (which was/is not a federation), and Sweden and Denmark.[194] There was more. Crowle wrote eighty-one pages on such topics as Australian banking and the Premiers' Plan.[195] He also penned a nine-page report on Australia's financial history, including the workings of the Loan Council. He marvelled at "the extent of the powers given to the Australian Federal Parliament ... by the amendment of the Constitution [in 1929]."[196]

Other researchers pried into every aspect of federalism. University of Toronto dean of law W.P.M. Kennedy compared the distribution of legislative powers over welfare, taxation, labour, treaty-making, and residual powers in Argentina, Australia, the United States, and Switzerland. His meticulous forty-seven-page section on Australia concluded that the federation had endured "inadequate distribution of powers, their conflicts, duplication of governmental machinery and a host of uncoordinated services," which extra-constitutional conferences had largely remedied.[197] Kennedy's 166-page report likely dashed any notion that Australia had devised the perfect federation. But Kennedy did *not* examine federal payments to the states to remedy inequality, which were becoming the focus of the commission's studies.

The Royal Commission was fascinated with inequality. Skelton asked one of his former researchers at the Bank of Canada to do a special report on the Commonwealth Grants Commission. As John Dafoe later told Henry Angus in a chatty letter from Winnipeg on 5 July 1938: "Jimmy Coyne who has been making a detailed study of the operation of the Grants Commission tells me (he is here on his holidays) that his paper runs to 225 pages ... A Grants Commission on the Australian model would never do for Canada and I don't think it will have a welcome for much longer in Australia."[198] So much for prescience. That "Jimmy" would replace Towers as Bank of Canada governor in 1955: he would be in office when Ottawa introduced equalization legislation – *albeit based upon a different approach* – in 1956. And the Australian Commonwealth Grants Commission is still in operation.

Coyne's meticulous report for the Royal Commission, "Federal-State Financial Relations in Australia, July 1938," eventually ran to 185 pages, including a twenty-four-page summary. It reviewed everything from the early constitutional approach to state inequality through to the establishment of the CGC and the Premiers' Plan.[199] Coyne also wrote a seventy-nine-page report entitled "Federal-Provincial Financial Relations in the Argentine Republic," which bears the inscription: "It was thought that a summary of recent public finance history in the Argentine, similar to that prepared for Australia, would be useful."[200] It was also dated July 1938, and it analyzed federal and state government functions as well as federal and state taxation.

Commissioner Henry Angus also wrote a concise (and lively!) twenty-page summary of Federal Finance in Australia, covering the evolution of the CGC and the Loan Council from 1901 to 1937. The economist drew broad lessons from Australian legislation and from each annual CGC report. His criticism could be trenchant: Angus explained that, in its fourth year, the CGC had adopted the same qualifications for aid as in previous hearings, but it had offered to entertain other arguments. "The result is another very long report with almost incredible repetition."[201] The solution was always elusive.

By then, Dafoe was already wary of any attempt to transplant the Australian model without adjustments. As he told CGC chair Eggleston in a revealing hand-written letter on 5 July 1938 – the same day that he told Angus about Coyne's visit – the Royal Commission had sparked Canadian debate about the state of the federation: "There has been more discussion and study of our national difficulties and problems in the last six months than in the previous 15 years. There has been a revelation of conflicting interests and loyalties that has shocked and stirred up opinion, which is all to the good." Dafoe added pointedly: "Australia has figured largely in the discussions ... But Australia and Canada are very different propositions."[202]

On 9 January 1939, in a remarkable letter to Australian academic and writer Sir James Barrett, Dafoe observed that he hoped the commission could make "some contribution to the adjustment of a situation already dangerous and likely to become more so if adjustments are not made." The commission had paid close attention to Australia, but Dafoe did not think the studies were "of much value ... [with regard to] suggesting solutions." Australia was an island with a "homogenous population, and with an increasing sense of danger calling for unity of action." That dominion was perhaps heading towards a unitary government with the states "maintaining only a shadowy existence." Dafoe added: "Nothing like this is either possible or desirable in Canada for reasons which would take me a long time to set out. At the same time there must be a considerable strengthening of federal powers in some respects in Canada."[203]

In reply, Sir James firmly disputed Dafoe's diagnosis. The two dominions might be different politically, but Australians viewed federal politicians as extravagant spenders who imposed irritating taxes. Referenda to extend federal control had been "decisively rejected," and "the people [understood] the State government and they dislike[d] Canberra."[204] He added that the premier of Ontario (Mitchell Hepburn) had visited Australia "and was reported to have stated that Canada would be insolvent in three years."[205]

THE PROBLEM OF FISCAL NEED

One fundamental issue remained unresolved. As Skelton told Dafoe on 22 July 1938, the research team had "not yet done any of the work you suggested on possible fiscal need formulae and [could] do very little" until the reports on federal finances and national income were completed and analyzed.²⁰⁶ It was impossible to find remedies for fiscal need without an understanding of the cost of government operations.

As the Canadians knew, the Commonwealth Grants Commission accepted fiscal need as a basis for assistance. But the CGC had repeatedly refused to recognize the disabilities that the mere act of federation had imposed on individual states as a justification for grants. In early 1938, in its fifth report, the CGC explained, with some asperity, that it had rejected such arguments – and that states should stop making them. Suppose, the report added, that grants were awarded on the basis of those disabilities? The more prosperous states might then qualify for a grant – even though their wealth "would mean that other favorable influences had counterbalanced the unfavorable effect of the item of federal policy shown to be adverse."²⁰⁷

If states wanted to claim for disabilities, they would also have to count the benefits of federation. And that would be difficult. Individuals as well as states felt the effects of federal policies such as the tariff. But it would be "absurd" to compensate a claimant state "because some of its citizens suffered, and not to compensate other States or individuals affected in a similar way."²⁰⁸

The sixth CGC report, which appeared in early 1939, was equally vehement: "We are convinced that it is impracticable to assess special grants on the basis of disabilities arising from federation and from the operation of federal policy ... *We believe that our method of assessing grants on the basis of financial needs* has much to commend it."²⁰⁹ That report emphasized the crucial role of such assistance within a federation: "If a federal system is to work effectively, some equalizing adjustment such as we have attempted is required ... and all federations are now being forced to recognize the need for some equalizing distribution of federal resources."²¹⁰ Although neither the fifth nor the sixth report mentioned Canada, Australian diplomats in Ottawa had ensured that Canberra was well aware of Canada's examination of fiscal inequalities.

The commissioners had decided that the determination of fiscal need – however defined – would be the key. But there were problems. As Angus explained, chronic impoverishment "raised the abstract question wheter in a federal state regional inequalities of wealth were radically different from regional inequalities within a unitary state."²¹¹ He was not certain that they were. But he added cynically: "An attempt to compensate for regional disadvantages even if the local economy were barely viable seemed as inevitable politically as it was unsound economically."[212] But the disabilities of federation could not justify subsidies: "It was impossible to disentangle the comparative benefits and burdens of Confederation province by province."[213]

They were groping for wisdom. Ottawa now funded many provincial activities – so it was active in the lives of its citizens. As Skelton wrote to Dafoe: "It is no longer sufficient to set the scene and let the play go on; the state must now take a direct hand in the part of every individual actor." Then he added a remark that some provinces might have viewed as a threat: "And whether there are lines enough to go round or not, the play must go on. This particular development in political philosophy has obviously the greatest importance to public finance and Dominion-provincial relations."[214] Skelton clearly assumed that Ottawa would direct the play.

But how could the commissioners possibly redesign Confederation when the partners agreed on almost nothing? Perhaps worse, like Mackenzie King, the commissioners were beginning to worry about the controlling views of their own staff – especially after an unsettling lunch with Research Director Skelton. They accepted that Skelton and the assistant research director, economist John Deutsch, would write large portions of their report's initial draft. They admired both men. But they were troubled by their staff's Ottawa-centric approach – and their determination to promote Ottawa's clout within the federation.

Commissioner MacKay would later note that Skelton had a close circle of advisors, starting with his father, the most powerful bureaucrat in Ottawa, O.D. Skelton, who was under-secretary of state for external affairs. Alex Skelton could also reach out to Bank of Canada governor Towers, Deputy Finance Minister Clark, and Queen's University economist W.A. Mackintosh, who was doing work for the commission.[215] Those same officials had advocated stronger federal control over the provinces through a loan council before the Royal Commission was appointed. They had advised Skelton when he drafted the research program in 1937. And they were still there, supporting Skelton.

The commissioners were afraid of being cut out of the loop. As Angus later remarked, Skelton and Deutsch "worked admirably together but not very easily with anyone else."[216] Skelton had accompanied Rowell when he visited the provincial governments at the outset of the commission. He knew ministers and civil servants in every provincial capital – and he was in "far closer contact" with the Ottawa elites than anyone except Rowell.[217] And they had lost Rowell.

They were right to worry. After Rowell had his stroke, Skelton invited the four remaining commissioners to a meeting at Ottawa's Roxborough Hotel with his legendary father Oscar, Deputy Finance Minister Clark and himself. There, as Angus recalled, Skelton explained that the commissioners were "taking too much into their own hands."[218] They should stick to their regional hearings – which Skelton viewed as "little more than a formality" – while the staff wrote the report. Angus remained calm and firm. The commissioners were not "a mere façade."[219] They would do the job that they were asked to do – not what Skelton wanted them to do. The younger Skelton later admitted, "He had been a damn fool."[220]

But he had done it. The commissioners took that lunch to heart. Thereafter, they were on their guard against any attempt by Skelton and Deutsch to impose their views on the report. Economist Angus strongly disputed what he called the "literary thesis" of Deutsch, who wanted the report to depict "an emasculated federal government surrounded by virile provinces." With the support of his fellow commissioners, Angus rebutted that approach with his explanation of Ottawa's philosophy during the 1920s: "Fashionable indolence and emasculation are not the same thing."[221]

But the commissioners struggled to design new roles for Ottawa and the provinces without drastically upsetting the balance. After Skelton's rash bid to control the report, the commissioners took steps to ensure that his strong views on centralization would not dominate theirs. During the winter of 1938–39, they "met daily to consider drafts prepared by our secretariat and to go over them line by line and sometimes word by word."[222] Angus shared a room at the Roxborough Hotel with commissioner Mackay. Then MacKay spent the hot summer of 1939 in Ottawa, revising and editing, as the nation slipped towards war. While MacKay worked in Ottawa, Dafoe and Sirois consulted each other by mail. The commissioners met only once at Murray Bay, Quebec, during the summer of 1939.

It was perhaps a mark of how strongly most commissioners now felt about inequality that, just before King George VI and Queen Elizabeth visited Ottawa in May 1939, MacKay penned a disgusted letter to his spouse Kathleen. In the previous week, there had been "a group of single unemployed who had been turned out of shelter because appropriation had come to an end, and who insisted on interviewing the mayor and the govt., and parading with placards such as 'We are Canada's lost generation.' 'We fought for king and country and now we starve.' And so on." MacKay added in dismay: "It is significant that the unveiling of the [new] war memorial is a morning-dress-top-hat affair."[223]

AUSTRALIA AND THE AUSTRALIAN STAR WITNESS

The Australians watched virtually every major Canadian move throughout these years. On 12 January 1938, Trade Commissioner L.R. Macgregor penned a ten-page memorandum that itemized seventeen pivotal political issues, including the complexities of Canadian federalism. He included the upcoming opening of Parliament, which was expected to be so fractious that Finance Minister Charles Dunning had remarked, "the very structure of Confederation is facing a crisis."[224] Macgregor examined the Prairie provinces, Alberta's Social Credit government, the tension between Ottawa and the Ontario government, the alliance between Quebec premier Maurice Duplessis and Ontario premier Mitchell Hepburn, and the dominion's renewed push for a constitutional amendment to establish Unemployment Insurance.

Pivotally, in Macgregor's discussion of the Rowell-Sirois Royal Commission, he underlined Canada's difficulties with the structure of its federation. "There has been a frequent citing of Australian precedents, particularly in such matters as the setting up of the Australian Loan Council, various aspects of the Financial Rehabilitation Scheme, depreciation of currency, etc."[225] As in Australia, the Depression had ensured that federations could no longer ignore fiscal inequalities among their members when provincial obligations to their citizenry were so great. Macgregor even pulled out a pivotal excerpt from commissioner Dafoe's recent address to the Canadian Club in Vancouver: "The Canadian federation has stood the strain of time better than the other federal systems of the English-speaking world, though it still has inherent weaknesses."[226] It was a dubious assertion.

On 21 March 1938, in a perfect example of cross-pollination, the Australian external affairs secretary told the Australian trade commissioner that the Commonwealth Grants Commission would be starting its annual hearings into states' claims on 11 April. Would there be "any objection to quotation at hearings from Canadian briefs and submissions forwarded by you?"[227] In the end, there would be no reference to Canada in the commission's fourth, fifth, or sixth reports. But it is likely that the commissioners cited Canada during their questioning of state witnesses.

The monitoring about fiscal inequality was relentless. On 19 May 1938, Australian diplomats sent a book review along with two copies of an American study entitled "The Administration of Canadian Conditional Grants," which the Public Administration Service of the Social Science Research Council in Washington had published. American political scientist Luella Gettys criticized the "relatively slight and ineffective degree" of dominion supervision of federally aided activities. She added: "The idea that the Dominion might effectively provide administrative leadership ... seems to have made little headway."[228] Gettys did not grasp the degree of fierce provincial autonomy in Canada – and the resistance to federal supervision. Still, the Australian diplomats assumed that the work "may prove of interest" to Canberra.[229]

They were assiduous. On 9 June 1938, they singled out Finance Minister Dunning's move to nationalize the Bank of Canada as a completely publicly owned institution (King's government had already amended the Bank of Canada Act in 1936 to ensure majority federal ownership and a majority of federal directors).[230] A week later, they sent Dunning's fifty-six-page budget speech of 16 June 1938 to Canberra, drawing pen lines along the side of the document to emphasize Canada's desire for bilateral trading relationships with the United States and the United Kingdom as well as with all countries of the British Commonwealth.[231]

Dunning saw increased trade as the answer to Canada's enduring economic pain. The finance minister also went out of his way to dismiss the "frequent controversy" over Australian cuts in the interest rate on its outstanding bonds: in 1931, the Australian rates were much higher than the Canadian rates; in 1938, the Australian rates remained higher than the Canadian rates – because Canada had followed "a different and more normal policy."[232] The constant comparisons with Australia had clearly stung Dunning.

What remains striking today, however, is his rejection of Keynesian economics: "The experience of several countries with expansionist policies during the last few years has proven that only a rise in the rate of new investment can provide a durable basis for an upswing in business activity ... Government expenditures cannot take the place of private enterprise."[233]

The rejection of Keynes was not universal. But support was concentrated among the more junior members of the finance ministry and younger Canadian academics. None of them had enough power to challenge their departmental masters. A.F.W. Plumptre, who would become assistant deputy finance minister in 1954, had studied under Keynes at Cambridge, but, in the last half of the 1930s, he was still a university lecturer and economic analyst. Robert Bryce, who had also studied under Keynes, would not become powerful within the ministry until wartime. Another Keynesian, W.A. Mackintosh, who did research for the Rowell-Sirois Commission, would later become special assistant to the deputy finance minister. But he would not join the department until 1939. It was only in October 1942 that Mackintosh led a finance ministry delegation to consult with Keynes in Britain.[234]

The Canadian examination of the Australian experience culminated with the appearance of L.F. Giblin on 8 August 1938.[235] The commissioners were fascinated as Giblin outlined the CGC's quirky approach to the analysis of fiscal need, including its comparison of taxation levels and its disapproval of reckless over-spending, notably in Tasmania. But it would take many more debates to shape their final report.

THE DELAY IN PUBLICATION OF
THE ROYAL COMMISSION REPORT

It was a small miracle that the Royal Commission report even appeared amid the disruptions of war. Since 10 September 1939, when Canada had declared war on Germany, little else mattered in Ottawa except the war effort, at home and abroad. Commissioner MacKay captured the capital with a cynical eye in a letter to his wife Kathleen on 14 October 1939: "There is an air of suppressed excitement and purposeful activity everywhere. What a pity we could not have shown the same activity and enthusiasm for getting rid of unemployment, or finding decent housing, or suppressing diseases and social evils." [236] The hearings had deeply affected him.

But time was slipping away. In January 1940, five months before the report's debut, Ottawa anticipated a key recommendation: King espoused Unemployment Insurance. In March, the prime minister persuaded the last reluctant premiers to cooperate. On 10 June 1940, after agreements with every province, the Canadian Constitution was amended to grant responsibility for Unemployment Insurance to Ottawa. The subsequent Unemployment Insurance Act, 1940, would be fast-tracked through both Houses of Parliament and would receive Royal Assent on 7 August 1940. It would take effect on 1 July 1941.

Such speed aroused the commissioners' envy. They were still working on their report into the eighth month of the war. In mid-December 1939, MacKay told Kathleen that Skelton and Deutsch were behind schedule and that "it was probably impossible to herd them on."[237] In early March, Skelton abruptly left with his powerful father O.D. Skelton by rail to New York City, then on a ship to Havana and Vera Cruz, and then to Mexico City, where he planned to stay ten days. When Skelton airily informed Sirois of the trip, he was stunned: "Would I expose myself to an action in damages," Sirois wrote MacKay, "if I expressed to you my opinion that they are all gone crazy in Ottawa."[238] His colleagues were equally unsettled. "It would be charitable to assume," Dafoe wrote to Angus, "that Skelton père, going on a much-needed vacation, carried off Alex, but ... I still feel a degree of exasperation over the mishaps and delays of the closing stages of the work of the Commission."[239]

Even Prime Minister King fretted about the schedule. After a formal dinner at the prime minister's residence, King took Sirois aside for long-winded remarks about the timing of the report and the timing of the federal election, which was held in late March of 1940. As Angus recalled: "His [King's] long tortuous statement was followed by a gruff voice with something of a French accent. 'If I understand you correctly, Mr. Prime Minister, you want us to report not too soon and not too late.' Mr. King was a bit taken aback by this paraphrase of his carefully chosen words and, with at least an appearance of embarrassment said, 'Yes, yes, quite so.'"[240]

But would the commission's massive report remain relevant? Legal secretary Robert Fowler told Commissioner Dafoe that he believed "nearly all the conclusions [were] strengthened rather than weakened by the advent of war."[241] Dafoe agreed: "The impact of war upon our economy will be to strengthen the view that *Canada has got to be a nation* in every sense of the word."[242] Both men understood that they were engaged in a nation-building exercise amid a society in turmoil.

In turn, officials in the Bank of Canada and the finance ministry finally convinced themselves that the report would survive amid the wartime news. On 8 May, eight days before the prime minister tabled it in Parliament, Bank of Canada governor Towers wrote to King's special assistant L.W. Brockington, emphasizing the report's benefits for efficiency *and* equity in wartime and peacetime: "Existing difficulties – and, for the moment, I am not referring to the war – *and the much larger part played by governments in the lives of individuals*, have produced a situation where inefficient organization has a very definite effect on the standard of living of the people." Canadians had to insist "on efficient organization of our whole governmental setup."[243]

Today we would refer to Towers's notes as "talking points" for King. The debates were agonizing. As Alex Skelton later explained: "The Commission decided, after deliberation, to complete the Report exactly as it would have been completed had War not been declared." The recommendations were written "with the possibility of emergencies in mind and are, it is hoped, sufficiently flexible to be adjusted to any situation which the War may produce."[244]

CONCLUSION

In the end, despite the commissioners' assertion that "national unity and provincial autonomy" were not competitors for citizens' allegiance, their search for a remedy for fiscal need would inevitably lead towards plans to centralize revenues. Historians Barry Ferguson and Robert Wardhaugh emphasize that Dafoe wanted "to recognize regional differences and to reconstruct federal finance so that the 'unjust' and rigid 'mathematical equality between the provinces' would be swept aside.[245]

But the commission's solutions to such problems would be controversial. As Commissioner Angus maintained, in Dafoe's view, Canada was not a compact among the provinces. It was not an agreement between two nations: Quebec with its distinct identity and the Rest of Canada. Instead, Dafoe saw only one country. That vision could be difficult on occasion – and oddly limiting. During the dark days before the Munich agreement to carve up Czechoslovakia in September 1938, Dafoe's group of "Winnipeg Liberals" wanted to impose sanctions on Germany. "Mackenzie King with his solicitude for Canadian unity would never threaten war to avoid war," Angus mused. But the Winnipeg Liberals would have done so "and would have assumed that Canadian unity was not worth preserving if it could not stand the strain."[246]

Dafoe *tried* to control his preconceived notions. "[He] never called his opinions by the foolish adjective 'unalterable,'" recalled Angus. "He had a journalist's acceptance of hard facts – a sort of retroactive tolerance that can be a most valuable political quality."[247] But Dafoe had already talked about the establishment of "certain minimum standards" for provinces and people before the hearings even commenced.[248] In the end, the Winnipeg editor helped to convince his fellow commissioners – to King's dismay – that the survival of the nation depended on reclaiming a strong role for Ottawa within the federation. Skelton and Deutsch no doubt assisted in this endeavour.

Ironically, the commission itself would strain Canadian unity. And the commissioners, once dubbed "The Fathers of Re-Confederation," would never grasp why.[249]

7

Inequality in Wartime, 1940–44

In mid-May 1940, Canadians were distraught. The nation was at war with Germany – for the second time in twenty-two years. The news from abroad was ominous. On 9 April, the Nazis had invaded Norway and Denmark – and were handily defeating Allied troops. On 10 May, they launched their Blitzkrieg against the Netherlands, Belgium, and France, starting the encirclement of the Allied armies that would push them towards the Channel ports. On that same day, British prime minister Neville Chamberlain resigned – and Winston Churchill replaced him. In Ottawa, Prime Minister Mackenzie King cabled Chamberlain and Churchill. Then he met with Royal Commission chairman Joseph Sirois, anglophone secretary Alex Skelton ("Skelton's son"), and francophone secretary Adjutor Savard, who presented him with a specially bound copy of their massive report. The ceremony was brief, almost cursory.

The prime minister was distracted. He toddled off to a press conference where he explained that he had just received the report, and he offered to make it public on Monday, 13 May, or Thursday, 16 May. The journalists agreed on Thursday at noon as the release date, when the report would also be presented to Parliament (it would be sent to provincial governments on Thursday morning). They asked for immediate copies, which they pledged not to publicize. Subsequent news reports explained that King had delayed the report's release for three days "because of the new crisis in Europe."[1] That was true.

Six days later, King tabled the Royal Commission report with a perfunctory flourish. Then he did nothing about it for weeks. The Royal Commission on Dominion-Provincial Relations – with its "three principal volumes of more than two hundred pages each, together with twenty-nine additional volumes of appendices and other data, a total of thirty-two crimson-covered quarto volumes containing some 3,855 pages, with an attractive format and plenty of statistics, though without graphs and maps" – was seemingly forgotten.[2]

But appearances were deceptive. Behind the scenes, many Canadians – and many Australians – were drawn to the report as a possible remedy for the divisiveness of federalism. The report's key recommendations constituted a remarkably coherent blueprint for how a twentieth-century federation might work to ensure relative equality among its members. *Theoretically*. As political scientist Peter Leslie notes, "The report is a useful reference point because of the comprehensiveness and the internal coherence of its recommendations."[3]

It was in the real political world that the trouble soon became evident.

THE REPORT

After so many hearings and studies, the commissioners had settled on a plan for the ideal federation. Ottawa should centralize revenues from income taxes and succession duties; and assume responsibility for unemployed employables and old-age pensions, labour legislation, and advances to farmers and primary industries. There should be regular dominion-provincial conferences, along with a secretariat to oversee federal-provincial machinery; and there should be grants for highway and conservation expenditures along with supplementary emergency grants for abnormal economic conditions.

Ottawa should take over current provincial debts. It should include all future provincial debts in any calculation of emergency aid – *if* the proposed advisory Dominion Finance Commission had approved such provincial borrowing. (This proposal was clearly the non-compulsory version of the loan council that Skelton had first considered in 1936.)

Most important, provinces would receive "lump sum, annual, unconditional National Adjustment Grants for the support of education and welfare at an average national standard."[4] Ottawa would assess each province's spending to determine its per capita fiscal needs in comparison with the national average. The commission had a "precise idea" of what provincial autonomy meant: "the master-solution of the report was aimed at ensuring that each province was put in a financial position to provide, if it chose, a level of provincial services at average national standards without subjecting its citizens to provincial taxation above the national average."[5]

The Royal Commission had finally jettisoned the dangerous fiction that all provinces were theoretically equal: poorer provinces would require more financial assistance. As historian James Struthers observes: "It was this call for a redistribution of the nation's wealth and the establishment of national standards in social services that earned Rowell-Sirois its reputation as a blueprint for the Canadian welfare state."[6] More important, the National Adjustment Grants would become another model for equalization, albeit with a different formula for establishing entitlements. In many modern federal systems, such as the United States, Australia, Switzerland, and Canada, "the basic constitutional design [of some form of equalization] preceded the development of the expanded role of government implied in the 'welfare state.'"[7]

The report was nudging Canada towards this crucial first step in expanding social security. The grants were *"designed to make it possible for every province to provide for its people services of average Canadian standards."*[8] "In effect but without saying so," the commission proposed that Canada espouse "the centerpiece of fiscal federalism in Australia, adopted in 1933."[9]

There were differences, largely because the National Adjustment Grants were pegged to provincial spending in *specific* areas. Poorer provinces and municipalities would receive funds for their joint per capita spending on public welfare and education – "after adjustment in some cases for costs of living and other local circumstances" – in comparison with the national average.[10] The grants would also compensate poorer provinces for their average annual expenditures on highways, agriculture, and the public domain. Recipients would have to tax their citizens at an average standard of severity.[11] Provinces could not charge low taxes, provide inferior services, cry poor, and pocket federal grants. The cost of future loans could only be included in the calculation of the grants if the proposed Dominion Finance Commission approved the borrowing.[12]

Theoretically, the provinces were free to spend their National Adjustment Grants within any of those vaguely specified policy areas. But the commissioners cherished the dream of enticing the provinces to adopt better spending priorities. In an ideal world, their voters could force change upon their politicians – or change the politicians. "The freedom of action of a province is in no way impaired ... But no provincial government will be free from the pressure of the opinion of its own people."[13] The report defended the grants with the same argument that had convinced commission chairman Sirois to support them: "They illustrate the Commission's conviction that provincial autonomy in these fields must be respected and strengthened, and that the only true independence is financial security."[14]

There was another breakthrough: the report bridged the gulf between the dangerous avowals that the mere act of federation had created disabilities – and the very real poverty that federal policies had inadvertently created. Grants should "be justified on moral grounds, as a question of decency and social justice," observes political scientist David Milne: "Although the commission was careful to dismiss the notion that the Dominion was directly responsible as such to a province for the adverse effects of federal policy on it, it nonetheless argued that Ottawa should support a province in fiscal need, particularly where part of the cause can be shown to flow from federal policy."[15]

The commissioners recognized how much their society had changed. From 1874 to 1937, total per capita government expenditures had "increased by eleven times."[16] The cost of education and public welfare had gone from "the almost negligible figure of $4 million to $360 million."[17] Ottawa's share of the total cost of government had fallen from two-thirds to less than one-half – and that included federal contributions to the provinces for relief and old-age pensions.[18]

The provinces' limited tax base had left them in an impossible position: they could not afford what they now had to deliver. As historian Frank Underhill, one of the founders of the CCF, later wrote, the report captured a nation that was unusually dependent on outside forces, caught up in the international system of trade and finance, and scrambling to deal with the huge fiscal inequalities among its members. The disparities were especially striking within provinces, such as wheat-exporting Saskatchewan, that were most dependent on international markets. Underhill approvingly quoted the report: "Our 'boundless resources' are worth only what we can sell them for ... Economically, Canada can be compared to a string of beads, and they are not all pearls."[19]

THE FATE OF THE COMMISSIONERS

The commissioners had worked so hard to achieve a unified vision. When they were finalizing their report, Sirois had considered writing a minority opinion – because he wanted to preserve the provinces' right to impose income taxes and, especially, succession duties.[20] After prolonged discussions with francophone counsel Louis St-Laurent and anglophone counsel James McGregor Stewart, however, Sirois conceded that only a national government could effectively aid "Canadians in need in every part of the country."[21] (The commissioners also believed that Sirois acquiesced because he replaced his confessor with someone "who assured him that he could safely follow his conscience in constitutional and financial matters.")[22] Thereafter, Sirois never wavered in his defence of the report's call for federal Unemployment Insurance and centralized tax collection – because that would allow Canadians to share with one another.

But Sirois also presciently argued that "Quebec must never stand in the way of the other provinces doing as they wished but should be free to stand out."[23] His colleagues listened. In early January of 1940, Angus told an ailing Dafoe that a recent Ottawa meeting with the secretariat had been "exasperating" – because they had bogged down in changing phrases that Sirois viewed as open to attack from Quebec. But he also captured the admiration that Sirois had inspired: "I feel that Dr. S. has gone so much further than we ever thought possible that one should do something to meet his wishes."[24]

The commissioners stood by their conclusions throughout their lifetimes.

Four months after the report's debut, King appointed Sirois as chairman of Ottawa's new Unemployment Insurance Commission. It was the PM's gesture of respect for Sirois's brave work. But the sixty-one-year-old Sirois did not live long enough to take up his duties: he died of what was probably congestive heart failure in a Quebec City hospital in mid-January 1941. His fellow commissioner, Henry Angus, who was fluently bilingual, understood why the Rowell-Sirois Report did not figure prominently in the Quebec tributes to him. "The Commission service was only a very small (and not well understood) part of Dr. Sirois's life," he explained to Commissioner R.A. MacKay, who attended the service.[25] Angus later remarked: "In his way Dr. Sirois was as good a Canadian as [Commissioner John] Dafoe with perhaps a greater appreciation of the difficulties of unity."[26]

The others watched their report's fate with disquiet. On 9 January 1944, John Dafoe died suddenly in Winnipeg. As Angus reflected: "Dafoe said he was willing to live to be a hundred – but no more – and he quite evidently expected to achieve this age."[27] Alex Skelton drowned in Nigeria in July 1950 in an apparent suicide. He was forty-four. Angus and MacKay worked together at the Department of External Affairs in Ottawa. MacKay was Ottawa's permanent representative to the United Nations when equalization was finally introduced in the mid-1950s. He eventually returned to teaching at Carleton University and died in Ottawa in 1979. Angus also lived to see the introduction of equalization – just after he retired as the first dean of graduate studies at the University of British Columbia. A building on the UBC campus is named in his honour. He celebrated his one-hundredth birthday in 1991. He would remember the commission with great fondness – and unexpected realism. As he mused to Dafoe in early 1940: "Someday I should like to hear what the P.M. really thinks of it."[28] That would never occur.

THE REPORT'S DEBUT AMID THE NEWS OF WAR

The report's reception was initially bumpy. After its publication on 16 May 1940, it was seemingly submerged amid the news of the Nazi advance. With the exception of the first day of headlines, it was largely relegated to the back pages. On 20 May, Canada and Britain called for a day of prayer to ask for "strength and victory."[29] That same day, the Nazis reached the English Channel.

One day later, remarkably, Ontario premier Mitchell Hepburn charged that King had withheld publication of the report "to draw people's attention away from [Canada's] lack of war effort."[30] If that was King's intention – and it almost certainly was not – it did not work. But Hepburn's attack sparked a national proliferation of anti-King bumper stickers and posters, criticizing the federal war effort and embroiling the report in a highly politicized discussion.[31] On 28 May, as Belgium surrendered, King told Senate Government Leader Raoul Dandurand "that not only Britain but France could be defeated in this war." He added grimly that Dandurand "turned visibly white."[32]

The news was almost incessantly grim. On 14 June 1940 German forces occupied Paris. On 22 June, France and Germany signed an agreement to divide France, with Italy taking a small zone in the southeast. Canadians watched flickering newsreel footage of German chancellor Adolf Hitler in his greatcoat arrogantly touring Paris, sweeping past the Arc de Triomphe, the Eiffel Tower, Napoleon's Tomb, and the Sacre Coeur. On 25 June, in a rare snippet of good news, Canada's minister to France, Lieutenant-Colonel Georges Vanier, reached safety in London after a warship rescued him from a tiny sardine fishing vessel in the Bay of Biscay. It was little wonder that Canadians flocked to the theatres to watch Dorothy Lamour in her famed sarong alongside Bing Crosby and Bob Hope in the comedy *Road to Singapore*. Brief moments of escapism were cherished.

But the Rowell-Sirois Report somehow stayed alive. Abroad, it fascinated the Australians who pored over its proposals and its reception. At home, it became an underground sensation. In late 1940, constitutional expert Frank Underhill marvelled that the report "has been out of print since early last summer ...This is something that never happened to any book of any contemporary Canadian professor, and is encouraging."[33] Improbably, it was percolating across the nation, slowly reaching an audience. Academics, politicians, and social advocates recognized its "daring and dramatic" presentation of "thorough research, keen analysis, skillful presentation, and masterful writing."[34] The numbers alone were in its favour: there had been eighty-five days of public hearings in ten cities with more than ten thousand pages of evidence, 154 briefs from municipal groups and public administration organizations, and many witnesses.[35] Too many people had put too much effort into its study of revenues and responsibilities, including the defenders of provincial rights (who were alarmed) and the advocates of expanded social security (who were intrigued) to let it slip away.

THE PROBLEMS WITH THE REPORT

The commission's daring concepts could be mesmerizing. More than eight hundred orders for the massive report were placed within three months.[36] But the first serious qualms appeared soon after its publication. At least one commissioner, economist Henry Angus, had expected them. The replacement of subsidies with adjustment grants would open deep divides between the richer and the poorer provinces. As provincial politicians and bureaucrats did the arithmetic, they would come up with "a rather disconcerting result ... At the outset every province except Ontario would benefit" by receiving more in benefits than it lost in revenues. But "the recommendations were made by a Commission on which Ontario had no representation." Worse, the grants "took no account of the need for developmental expenditures" or whether Ottawa should make the grants "where the return would be greatest or where the need for greater income was most intense."[37]

The report should clearly explain that there would be winners and losers. Otherwise, Angus argued, "opposition could be aroused in Ontario for what would appear a large financial benefit to Quebec."[38] He was prescient. Grants based on national average spending would be too open-ended. The wealthier provincial governments would object loudly at dominion-provincial conferences over the next fifteen years: they needed *their* taxpayers' money for their own needs; and they resented what they perceived as unduly generous federal spending on their poorer kin. Ironically, the report could not implement equalization without threatening national unity.

The report simply could not work in the edgy Canadian federation. In the commission's ideal world, there were no messy provincial identities to interfere with its constitutional redraft. To determine adjustments grants, for one, Ottawa would have to monitor and evaluate each province's spending and taxation. Such intrusiveness was unthinkable. The recommendations were "not only politically unacceptable, they were intrinsically unworkable."[39]

As well, the commissioners could not see beyond their terrible times to imagine the return of prosperity. As former finance official Ronald M. Burns noted only two decades later, the commissioners took "a surprisingly short-term view," and it was a pivotal mistake: "The 1930's could not be typical ... It was in the general recasting of our political life in the economic terms of the 1930's ... that the main weakness lay."[40] Perhaps worse, their "political innocence" was baffling: such centralizing recommendations "could never have been acceptable" to many provincial governments.[41] Burns darkly blamed "prominent staff members" for the commission's approach – and those members no doubt included Alex Skelton and John Deutsch.[42] The loss of their politically adept chairman Newton Rowell had damaged the commissioners' political judgment.[43]

AUSTRALIA KEEPS WATCH

The Australians did not yet have the same pressures on their doorstep that Canada now experienced with U-Boats in the Atlantic. Australian troops were only brought home gradually from the Mediterranean and the Middle East in early 1942 as the Japanese swept through Southeast Asia. But every step of the way, throughout the war and into peacetime, they watched their sister dominion.

On the cusp of summer in 1940, new high commissioner Sir William Glasgow noted: "'Hitler weather' appears to have reached Ottawa from across the Atlantic in the past few days and the brilliant sunshine seems to mock the gloom which assails us."[44] In a separate memo, Glasgow, who had attained the rank of major-general in the First World War, outlined the mobilization: "Canadian armed forces were now on duty in Newfoundland and the first contingent of a Canadian expeditionary force had already landed in Iceland for the purpose of maintaining the security of the North Atlantic sea lanes."[45]

The High Commission's most wrenching enclosure to Canberra was customarily among the dreariest. Not this time. Almost three months after the Liberals had won another majority government in late March 1940, Minister of Finance J.L. Ralston delivered his budget "at the most critical hour in history." His outlook was grim: "The Hun is hammering at the gate ... A new 'Dark Ages' may not be the figment of a wild imagination."[46] The minister delivered hard medicine: he raised income taxes, levied a so-called 2 percent "salary tax," and imposed a 10 percent tax on all imports. His economic forecast in late June 1940 might "meet conditions probably more unforeseeable than those of any period in our history."[47] But, he added firmly, Canada would "fail neither the Commonwealth nor the cause."[48] Notably, the finance minister did *not* mention the Royal Commission report – or its possible implications for his bottom line.

But the Royal Commission report fascinated the Australians. They clearly hoped that it would be seen as a remedy for political instability – especially in wartime. And they were not heartened by the ensuing rhetorical fracas. Throughout 1940, there were dozens of memos about the report back and forth between Canberra and Ottawa. On 14 May 1940, two days before the report was officially tabled, the Australian external affairs secretary in Canberra wrote to the High Commission in Ottawa to ask for copies. On 7 June, the High Commission managed to procure one copy of the report – along with a three-page summary from the *Monetary Times* – for Canberra.[49] It also sent a four-page memorandum from High Commission secretary Nöel Deschamps, which parsed the report's history and its recommendations.[50] On 18 July, Secretary Deschamps ruefully told Canberra that the report was "out of print and [would] not be available for another six weeks."[51]

The Australians in Canberra were impatient: they wanted nine copies for distribution.[52] In early August, Deschamps wearily explained that the three volumes of the report itself were out of print – and there had been no authorization for reprinting "in spite of the fact that 800 orders for the Report have been received."[53] On that same day, he sent nine complete sets of appendices and special studies via ocean mail, with the exception of the detailed statements of dominion-provincial public finance statistics, which were selling at fifty dollars per set. By late August, "as a result of pressure on the Prime Minister's [King's] Office," four copies were secured – and forwarded to Canberra.[54] In mid-November, Deschamps finally obtained five more copies – "only now made available by the King's Printer."[55] The report was an improbable hit in Australia.

INTEREST GROWS AT HOME

The Rowell-Sirois Report was also gaining traction within Canada. In September 1940, the Ryerson Press published an eleven-thousand-word summary of the report, which would go into four printings by January 1941. The authors – Dalhousie University historian S.A. Saunders and researcher Eleanor Back – also wrote a slightly smaller, rather disjointed pamphlet criticizing the report.[56] And perhaps this was understandable: Secretary Alex Skelton had experienced great difficulties with most of the regional studies for the commission – "very mixed nature and inferior quality" – and he and Saunders had clashed.[57]

In November 1940, the *Canadian Forum* devoted seven pages to three essays on key aspects of the report, including Frank H. Underhill's pivotal observation: "Incidentally, though there was not a single Marxian who got within miles of the commission's deliberations save when Tim Buck appeared to present the Communist party brief, the whole report in almost every sentence, every paragraph, every volume, is a powerful exercise in the economic interpretation of history."[58]

The avid analysis continued. In December 1940, the Bank of Nova Scotia's *Monthly Review* devoted all four pages to a consideration of the report that reflected the anxieties of wartime and the economic pressures of maintaining troops at home and abroad. The commission's conclusions appeared "workable and suitable to the needs of the Canadian federation as we know them to-day ... The alternative, indeed, appears to be – drift."[59] As it was, the state of dominion-provincial relations was "undoubtedly ... conducive to friction and inefficiency in Canadian economic life and may thus be regarded as hampering the war effort."[60] The National Adjustment Grants would bring "greater stability in provincial expenditures and revenues."[61]

That same month, the Canadian Association for Adult Education and the Canadian Institute of International Affairs jointly published a slim booklet, *Confederation Marches On: A Comment on the Rowell-Sirois Report*. It was the work of the commission's legal secretary, Toronto lawyer R.M. Fowler, who stressed that the report's debut on 16 May 1940 "may some day be regarded as a day equal to July 1st, 1867, in significance to Canadians."[62] Fowler was well aware of the competition for attention: "As the German legions thundered into France, the news of battle almost succeeded in driving from the headlines of Canadian newspapers an event of supreme national importance."[63] He wanted to keep the report alive.

That was emphatically not how Mackenzie King viewed the report: he wanted to postpone any consideration of it during wartime. He certainly was not interested in the report's call for roughly equalized grants to the provinces in return for their key tax revenues. He wanted provincial tax revenues to prosecute the war, *not* to subsidize the poorer provincial governments. And he would never endanger national unity in wartime to accomplish the permanent constitutional changes that the commission recommended.

But the report would not go away. King was buffeted between two forces. In favour of the report were many senior bureaucrats at the Bank of Canada and the finance ministry, along with a few cabinet ministers. That group included Bank of Canada governor Graham Towers; former Rowell-Sirois research director Alex Skelton, who was now back at the Bank of Canada; Deputy Finance Minister Clifford Clark; finance ministry special advisor W.A. Mackintosh; Finance

Minister J.L. Ilsley; and Mines and Resources Minister T.A. Crerar.[64] Skelton's powerful father O.D. Skelton, who was under secretary of state for external affairs, supported them.

Their motives were mixed. Some of the younger members of the commission staff, such as Skelton, "had become persuaded of the virtues of the Keynesian doctrine ... [The report] would transfer to Ottawa precisely those taxes that would be needed to implement a set of policies for economic stabilization."[65] Those officials concluded that too many provincial players had "exacerbated the decline and retarded recovery ... It seemed unjust, as far as the mandarins were concerned, that governments and individuals in some provinces should struggle just to survive while others continued to live in relative comfort."[66] There was also the seldom-acknowledged factor of self-interest: more funds would expand Ottawa's power within the federation.

On the other side were less powerful finance ministry officials, including tax expert Ken Eaton and departmental solicitor Ross Tolmie, and income tax commissioner Fraser Elliott. More important, the clear majority of cabinet did not want to implement the report, at least not during wartime.[67] They had King's ear. As the prime minister later recounted, there was strong cabinet opposition to the briefing documents on the report from his special assistant Leonard Brockington and deputy principal secretary J.W. Pickersgill, "with the Bank of Canada in the background."[68] He added with grim satisfaction: "It was interesting how the point of view of the intelligentsia by whom I am surrounded ... was attacked from the entire cabinet circle."[69] The intelligentsia wanted King to push for complete implementation of the report. The majority of the cabinet wanted King to be conciliatory during discussions with the provinces and *not* to dictate the adoption of its terms. That approach suited King perfectly. And that is what he would do.

KING'S SCORNED INTELLIGENTSIA PUSH FOR IMPLEMENTATION

The high-level bureaucratic and political push to implement the Rowell-Sirois Report had commenced within three months of its tabling. In mid-September, under pressure from Bank of Canada governor Towers, Finance Minister Ilsley presented cabinet with several options: "postpone action until after the war; hold a Dominion-provincial conference; or implement, as a wartime measure, the report's most urgent recommendations."[70] King appointed a cabinet subcommittee under Ilsley to consider those choices. Ilsley went back to cabinet with a report of dissension among the provinces.[71]

King then read a letter to cabinet that he had received from Manitoba premier John Bracken, who was "strongly recommending" a conference.[72] But the ministers were also uneasily aware of Ontario premier Hepburn's private message: he was "unalterably opposed" to the report – "and would fight it to the limit."[73] Given that inflammatory rhetoric, the cabinet resolved that a conference would be "unwise." King should explain to Parliament "why holding of conference [sic] at this time was likely to be of little avail."[74] King noted that, if there had been a possibility of agreement at a conference, he would "probably have arranged for one forthwith notwithstanding the possibility of criticism of diverting our energies from the war effort."[75] He was equivocating – even with himself.

In early November, however, Ilsley came back to cabinet with a modified proposal for a conference – and cabinet agreed. What had changed? As historian J.L. Granatstein explains: "The warnings of impending financial disaster from Ilsley's Department could not be ignored; the pressing demands of Premier Bracken, supported by his fellow Manitoban, [federal Resources Minister] Crerar, could not readily be delayed further; and the federal government would be on much stronger ground if it could appear to the public as having been balked by provincial obstinacy."[76]

Some poorer provinces wanted the reassurance of equality and extra cash, especially in wartime. The richer provinces were appalled at the very possibility of losing the revenues from their income taxes and succession duties. The Bank of Canada files include multiple newspaper articles about Hepburn's rage. One from mid-November reads, "Hepburn May Call Election for Test of Public Opinion on Issue of Sirois Report," which conveyed Ontario's objection to being "forced to swallow unfair provisions."[77]

King agreed to the conference. But he confided his misgivings to his diary: "I confess I have little hope of getting anything of the Dominion-Provincial conference, nor am I personally wholly satisfied that the Sirois report should be accepted holus bolus." He felt "a bit suspicious about a report not according with more democratic views that should be made to prevail once this war is over. It will require careful study in advance."[78] His instincts were right.

By mid-December, with the exception of Resources Minister Crerar, cabinet members essentially concluded that the upcoming conference "would amount to nothing."[79] King suspected that Hepburn wanted to form a coalition against him to assume the leadership of the federal party – and that he would use the upcoming conference to boost his chances.[80] Ever shrewd, the prime minister told his ministers: "We would have to construct a mattress that would make it easy for the trapeze performers as they dropped to the ground one by one. I have never believed that the conference could succeed at this time of war." But he had also concluded that he had to proceed: "Were the government not to make the attempt, it would be blamed for whatever financial disasters will follow, as it certainly will, in the course of the next year or two."[81]

THE HOME FRONT

While King schemed, Canadians were rallying to support the troops, collecting everything from bones and rags to waste fats as salvage, investing in Victory Bonds, and opening their doors to British children sent across the Atlantic for safety. Women painted seams down the back of their legs to emulate scarce stockings; they stretched one pound of minced beef, which was deemed "one coupon" meat, to serve patties to six people; they knit sweaters, scarves, mittens, and socks to "help the gallant people of Britain."[82] After the collapse of France and the retreat from Dunkirk, before the armed forces started recruiting women in mid-1941, women from coast to coast were forming auxiliary paramilitary groups. "None, however, was given official recognition."[83] Others were training as drivers or nurses for the Red Cross – the first unit had completed the course in Montreal in April 1940.

The feeling of urgency was widespread. Farmers, dairy workers, and fishers were producing wheat, flour, bacon and ham, dried and fresh eggs, cheese, canned meats, canned salmon and herring, and fish oil to send to Britain.[84] In 1939, Canada had virtually no war industry. By the end of the war, 1.1 million men and women – roughly one-tenth of the population – "working in war plants had turned out 900,000 rifles, 794,000 motor vehicles for military purposes, 244,000 light machine guns, 16,000 aircraft of nearly 80 different types and 486 navy vessels plus 391 cargo vessels and 3,500 craft for various support purposes, all necessary to the war effort."[85] The work was tough – and distractions such as movies were prized.

There was little time to pay attention to federal-provincial discussions of the report from the Royal Commission on Dominion-Provincial Relations.

THE DOMINION-PROVINCIAL CONFERENCE 1941

The Dominion-Provincial Conference of 1941 is dismissed today as a failure. After opposition from two relatively wealthy provinces – Ontario and British Columbia – and from monetary renegade Alberta, the dominion dropped its half-hearted proposal to implement the Royal Commission report. Instead, Finance Minister Ilsley simply proclaimed Ottawa's right to assume control of provincial revenues from income taxes and succession duties, invoking the power of the War Measures Act. After the conference broke up acrimoniously, Ilsley concluded tax rental deals with all provinces for the duration of the war plus one year.

But the Dominion-Provincial Conference of 1941 does epitomize why Ottawa *had* to back away from the commission's proposal to centralize revenues and provide explicit adjustment grants to the poorer provinces. Otherwise, amid ongoing emotional debates about conscription, the federal government would have been pinned between the budding influence of social security advocates such as social scientist Leonard Marsh and his *Report on Social Security for Canada 1943*, on the one hand, and the fierce protectors of provincial rights and fiscal autonomy, on the other.

Decades later, it is difficult to imagine the atmosphere as the premiers arrived in Ottawa for their gathering in the House of Commons. The Battle of the Atlantic was under way. More than twenty-eight hundred ships had attempted the crossing in convoys from Halifax with food, personnel, and matériel in 1940 as German wolf packs prowled the North Atlantic. Another thirty-one hundred would set out in 1941, including many that were now ploughing through ferocious winter storms.[86] By May 1945, more than forty-six hundred servicemen and servicewomen from the Royal Canadian Navy, the Canadian Merchant Navy, and the Royal Air Force would be dead at sea.[87] In France, the Germans were so confident that they were tearing down the Maginot Line, the massive French fortification system, to make room for small farms. In Britain, the few survivors of the Royal Air Force's Canadian squadron were crossing the English Channel to harry German troop formations in occupied France.[88] A fight among the first ministers over constitutional changes seemed jarring.

It could not end well. The three principal protectors of provincial rights – Ontario, Alberta, and British Columbia – were vocal in their opposition. Their stance came at a price: they were pilloried as petty-minded politicians who guarded their turf at the expense of the war effort. But they clearly represented the limits of generosity within the federation – and the vital need to respect each province's constitutional rights and responsibilities. British Columbia premier Duff Pattullo maintained that the adjustment grants would "lower the general standard of development … [leaving British Columbia] to turn the treadmill of mediocrity in perpetuity."[89] Alberta premier William Aberhart, who was still broadcasting his weekly Bible show, detected a plot "by the money powers to increase centralized control of our national life while our attention is fully occupied with the prosecution of the war effort."[90] Six years before Alberta's major discovery of oil at Leduc, he remained as wary of Ottawa as Jason Kenney is today: he asked for Ottawa's help in renewing his bonds at a lower interest rate, and, if that help were forthcoming: "we will be able to get along and look after our own problems."[91]

Ontario premier Mitchell Hepburn, who loathed King (and vice versa), delivered a lengthy denunciation of Ottawa, including the recent budget's increase in federal income tax. Worse, there were already complaints that Quebec would be "getting preferred treatment" with the adjustment grants.[92] "To me it is unthinkable that we should be fiddling while London is burning," he added. "This is a peace-time document, and we believe honestly and sincerely that the time to discuss it is not now."[93] As historian P.E. Bryden notes, even though both governments were Liberal, the relationship with Ottawa was "on an extremely shaky footing."[94]

The remaining six provinces were divided. There were three relatively neutral premiers – of Quebec, New Brunswick, and Nova Scotia – who depicted themselves as listeners. Quebec premier Adélard Godbout owed his return to power in October 1939 to the intercession of Mackenzie King's ministers, who declared that they "would resign unless the Liberal party received a vote of confidence from Quebecers at the provincial level."[95] That was a huge favour. In return, the former agronomist toned down the vehement defence of provincial rights that former premier Maurice Duplessis had espoused. Instead, Godbout stipulated that such wartime tax measures should not remain "the permanent future of Canada."[96] Quebec had the right to maintain a vibrant language and culture: "A scrupulous respect for provincial rights is essential to Canadian unity and Canadian progress."[97] *Le Devoir* was fascinated. Godbout's statement was "neither fish nor fowl" (*ni chair ni poisson*), while Hepburn had effectively "torpedoed a dangerous movement destined to accentuate the centralization of Ottawa's powers." The sub-headline was "Mr. Hepburn Throws His Bomb."[98]

Nova Scotia premier A.S. MacMillan was a newcomer to the first ministers' table, replacing Angus L. Macdonald when he became federal defence minister for naval services in July 1940. MacMillan had become wealthy from forestry and construction before winning a seat in the House of Assembly in 1925 – and then a place in Macdonald's cabinet in 1933. He had sat through the worst of the Depression – and it had confirmed his province's traditional views. Almost predictably, he blamed Confederation for Nova Scotia's descent into near poverty since the mid-nineteenth century. Federal policies in transportation, settlement, and tariffs "were formulated primarily to assist the economic development of the central and western provinces."[99] National Adjustment Grants, however, would provide "sufficient finances to meet and care for our provincial responsibilities ... with average severity of taxation."[100] He wanted some form of equalization, but he was not an outright cheerleader for the report.

New Brunswick premier J.B. McNair, who was also a relative rookie, complained that the commission had rejected his province's demand for special treatment. McNair was a lawyer who had been first elected in 1935. Premier A.A. Dysart put him in cabinet as attorney general and, when Dysart retired in March 1940, the balding and bespectacled McNair succeeded him. He was a shrewd and smart politician, but Montreal bankers "were threatening to foreclose" on his province.[101] Perhaps that was why he cautiously said that it was too "early" to form an opinion on the report.[102]

Then there were three provinces that largely supported the report because their budgets were so strained and their inequality was so glaring. For Manitoba premier John Bracken, Prince Edward Island premier Thane A. Campbell, and Saskatchewan premier W.J. Patterson, the proposed National Adjustment Grants were models of sharing. Their taxes were almost unreasonably high; they could not afford to deliver comparable social services to their citizenry. Their political fates could hang on their ability to secure more funds from Ottawa. These three premiers argued that the nation would be stronger through sharing.

It had been the same old song for years. Bracken warned that if they did not implement the report, they would "be encouraging a drift toward disunity."[103] Manitoba could not "maintain an average Canadian standard of social and educational services, and at the same time pay these relief costs and service [its] debt."[104] Bracken's Progressives had worked amiably with the provincial Liberals from his first victory in 1922 – and the two parties had merged in 1932. In 1940, his party had formed a coalition with the Conservatives, the CCF, and the Social Credit in a non-partisan government. He was restrained – but he needed those grants.

Prince Edward Island premier Thane A. Campbell emphasized that his poor agricultural province had dutifully paid the interest on its bonds while Alberta had defaulted. Campbell had been a Rhodes Scholar and a prominent lawyer, who had sat in the Legislative Assembly since 1931. When premier Walter Lea died in 1936, Campbell had succeeded him. He insisted that the National Adjustment Grants would be in every government's interest, rich or poor: "There are very many transactions to which both parties to every one of them are winners ...The man who parts with his money is not by any means always the loser."[105] But Campbell did have a resentful caveat: because PEI had the lowest per capita debt among the provinces, "it would seem that we shall be called upon to *share* the burden of those provinces whose per capita debts are higher than ours."[106]

Saskatchewan premier W.J. Patterson viewed the report as a godsend because: "[if Ottawa and the provinces] are not functioning effectively and to the maximum of their capacity we cannot effectively, or at least as effectively as we should, prosecute our war effort, nor can we as effectively deal with the problems which will arise after the war."[107] This was the exact opposite of Ontario premier Hepburn's reasoning: all Canadians should "enjoy a somewhat comparable measure of service and attention from the government under which they happen to live."[108] Patterson was a lawyer who had set up a small-town financial and insurance agency. He had sat in the legislature since 1921, and he vehemently opposed government deficits. But he would lose to Tommy Douglas and the Co-operative Commonwealth Federation in 1944, largely because the CCF promised a more socially active government.

THE UNBRIDGEABLE GULF BETWEEN THE RICHER AND THE POORER PROVINCES

The 1941 Dominion-Provincial Conference was a failure. The differences among the participants were impossibly wide. But the discussions were a microcosm of the conflicting impulses that prevailed throughout the nation. Then and now. On the afternoon of the second day, Finance Minister Ilsley explained that Ottawa needed roughly $1 billion per year for the war effort. That was twice the size of its largest total peacetime budget – and larger than the combined total of all annual federal, provincial, and municipal expenditures in peacetime. He had supported the report because the divisions within Canada were "economic divisions, *not racial and religious divisions.*"[109]

And now came the tough news. Since the provinces could not agree among themselves, Ottawa would use its power to invade the provincial fields of corporate and personal income taxes and succession duties. Canada needed a tax system "which will enable us to distribute the burden as fairly as human ingenuity can devise over the people of Canada as a whole, whatever region they may live in or whatever economic class they may represent – and fairness in taxation means, in my opinion, 'in accordance with ability to pay.'"[110] Ilsley was not aiming to provide better social services: he aspired for relatively equal levels of taxation in all provinces to wage war. And he was explicit: "Under the War Measures Act we may do what is necessary as a war measure."[111]

King concluded with the offer to reconvene if the nine provinces could reach unanimity. The conference closed with the singing of the national anthem. The headlines were huge: "Conference of Premiers Collapses; Ontario Group Walks Out of Meeting; Ilsley Says Gasoline Rationing Near."[112] As King calculated, the blame fell on the renegades.

The royal commissioners were confounded – especially because of the resistance from Hepburn, Pattullo, and Aberhart. Henry Angus in Vancouver wrote to his fellow commissioner, R.A. (Bert) MacKay in Halifax: "Personally I think a definite bust-up was much better than prolonged and fruitless debate. The three stalwarts are strange bed-fellows and they face something of an anti-climax in explaining how they have helped to win the war."[113] Alex Skelton shared their dismay. As he told *Winnipeg Free Press* Ottawa correspondent Grant Dexter, the politicians had lost the chance to centralize revenues permanently. Instead, they had adopted "a poor second best [plan] ... buying out the 'sons-of-bitches.'"[114]

That reaction was at odds with King's. As the prime minister confided with brutal frankness, he was "distinctly relieved and happy" about the result: "While, to appearances, it has been a failure, in reality it has served the purpose ... of avoiding attack for not having called the conference, and particularly what would certainly have followed, invasion of provincial sources of revenues." It was a triumph: "We have now got the pledge of the provinces to let us take their revenues if we need them – a tremendous achievement."[115]

The reputations of the three dissenting premiers did suffer. Aberhart would die in May 1943 – still a polarizing renegade. As Pattullo's biographer Robin Fisher notes, "those two days in Ottawa were to determine the course of the rest of his political career."[116] Branded as a saboteur of the wartime effort, Pattullo would emerge from his October 1941 election with a minority government and a rebellious caucus – and resign in early December. Hepburn was pilloried, although his biographer John T. Saywell notes that he was "not contrite": "He was so incensed by the criticism of his stand at the Conference that the government placed large ads in provincial newspapers."[117] But Hepburn had made dangerous enemies in Ottawa and within his own caucus. He would resign as premier in October 1942. King rejoiced.[118]

MACKENZIE KING, THE HOME FRONT, THE AUSTRALIANS, AND THE REPORT

The cautious King never shared the fascination with the Royal Commission's report. Although he was in frequent touch with Australia as a sister dominion-in-arms, their exchanges were never about the report. Initially, the relationship was cooperative: after the outbreak of the war, the two nations developed the British Commonwealth Air Training Plan – and agreed to exchange high commissioners. So far, so good.

The Australians avidly followed the drama at the 1941 Dominion-Provincial Conference – and they sympathized with King's *apparent* goals. They did not understand the prime minister's devious strategy – so they did not view the outcome as a federal win. Instead, in a lengthy account to the external affairs secretary in Canberra, High Commissioner Sir William Glasgow emphasized the political instability that Hepburn, Aberhart, and Pattullo had created, making "the proceedings lively from the outset."[119] While some commentators blamed King for calling the conference in wartime, the "majority of responsible newspapers" condemned the trio "for destroying national unity."[120]

Ever mindful of the need for national unity, especially in wartime, Glasgow admiringly singled out Quebec premier Godbout's declaration: "We come here as Canadians with as strong a spirit of Canadianism as anyone has."[121] He did not stress the fiscal inequality among the provinces, although he noted that King had linked implementation of the report – or, at least, discussion of the report – with a more effective war effort. The implied lesson was that federations were particularly tricky creatures in wartime. Glasgow would likely have been shocked to learn that King saw the report as a danger to national unity.

At home, most Canadians were struggling with wartime shortages, and many were likely too distracted to see through King's ruse. By the summer of 1941, intrepid families in West Edmonton were planting Victory Gardens. They staked out vacant lots, tilled the soil with spades and forks, and put in radishes, lettuce, beans, corn, peas, potatoes, squash, and pumpkins. By late summer, the harvest was so huge that it was hard to give away: gardeners took "baskets of vegetables to work and put them on a desk and people would take their pick." They canned and pickled and dried their crops until "there weren't enough bottles around, and to make more they'd have to take glass materials away from what they called the vital war effort – which probably meant panes of glass in the windows of barracks at army camps." By then, however, many "didn't want to see another cabbage or cob of corn."[122]

Meanwhile, the wily King made an unusually careless blunder, straining Canada's relationship with Australia. When he recalled High Commissioner Charles J. Burchell in July 1941, he selected a disastrous replacement, Major-General Victor Odlum. In January 1942, Odlum impulsively promised Canadian military aid to Australia without authorization.[123] When a desperate Australia gratefully accepted, and the new Labor government of Prime Minister John Curtin took heart, King did not initially contradict his high commissioner. The drawn-out disappointment with King's stalling – External Affairs Minister Herbert Evatt even flew to Ottawa in April 1942 to discuss the deal despite his paralyzing fear of flying – and King's eventual rejection of the deal would plague diplomatic relations until King retired in 1948, and the Australians defeated their Labor government in 1949.[124]

But High Commissioner Glasgow did manage to establish a tenuous truce in 1944. After all, the two nations were allies in the war. They received each other's visiting delegations – although King's diaries reflect his mixed reactions to those contacts.[125] King *never* discussed the Commonwealth Grants Commission with Australia during those years – even though there are several hundred references to Australia sprinkled throughout his diaries from 1939 to the end of the war and its aftermath. He had escaped relatively unscathed from the 1941 conference – and he did not want to deal with fiscal inequality in wartime.

THE BANK OF CANADA CLINGS TO THE REPORT – IN DESPERATE TIMES

Unlike King, many Bank of Canada and finance ministry officials were deeply disappointed when the 1941 conference disintegrated. They did not want to abandon its federation blueprint. Mere days after the conference failed, on 20 January 1941, the bank's deputy chief of research, J.R. Beattie, outlined a devious strategy to resolve the impasse. "The most serious objection made at the Conference to the implementation of the Report was that permanent measures were not justified to meet a temporary situation ... [But] all the recalcitrant or doubtful provinces said that they were willing to take any action, or bear any burden, which was necessitated by the war, for the duration of the war." Thus temporary tax rental deals were doable so Ottawa could finance the war with "*a minimum degree of equity.*"[126]

The appeal for fiscal equity was a relatively new argument. If Ottawa imposed those three taxes *at the same rates* across the nation, the burden could be shared equally. Taxpayers in different provinces would not be envious. Ottawa could provide "temporary assistance" to those provinces that surrendered control.[127] In the short term, Ottawa should ensure that the word "temporary" was "plastered all over the agreement."[128] In the longer term, "it would greatly facilitate final adoption of the Report if any temporary arrangements which have to be made could conform to the broad outline of [the Royal Commission] proposals as closely as possible."[129]

This is extraordinary. Despite strong objections from the three dissenting premiers and King's private objections, some Ottawa officials had not given up hope that they could implement the Royal Commission report in peacetime. They did not understand that the federation was changing rapidly. The tax rental deals were temporary – and they would stay temporary. King had secured the funds to fight the war while escaping the report's messy constitutional recommendations. He was safe. If the prime minister had known that Bank of Canada officials were still plotting to centralize key revenues permanently, he would have shaken the grey columns of the bank's elegant granite headquarters, which opened in 1938.

THE TAX RENTAL DEALS AND THE WAR

The tax rental agreements provided Ottawa with money for the armed forces. In return, the poorer provinces secured barely adequate compensation for their needs. All provinces preserved their constitutional right to key revenues – in return for a temporary loss of control. Provincial officials might argue with federal officials about the details of their one-on-one deals. But they would not bother Mackenzie King about the Rowell-Sirois Report throughout the tough years of the war. Instead, Ottawa "aimed to ensure that a single tax base and a single schedule of rates applied uniformly across the country ... It would equip Ottawa to pursue a Keynesian stabilization policy, an intent announced in 1945."[130]

The principle of fiscal equality did not preoccupy Ottawa. But politicians and bureaucrats were also aware that they could not slide into peacetime with the same catastrophic nonchalance that they exhibited after the First World War. Activists inside and outside government wanted a better world. They earnestly studied plans for health care, for employment, for income security, for better pensions. But few tackled or even enunciated the primary problem: it was virtually impossible to establish social programs if the poorer provinces could not pay their share. In the end, during the latter years of the war, Prime Minister King acted unilaterally, earmarking funds for families, not provinces.

Few Canadians followed the slow march towards those obscure tax rental deals anyway – if only because there was so much else to worry about. By the time the last deal was signed in May 1942, the news was still grim – and the fighting was seemingly endless.[131] The Russians were waging a ferocious tank battle with the Axis powers around Kharkov in Ukraine, struggling to advance into the Caucasus. They would lose that encounter. American bombers were targeting Japanese bases in northern New Guinea. American lieutenant-general Joseph Stilwell arrived in northeastern India, leading more than four hundred people to safety across treacherous mountain trails as the Japanese occupied Burma. Manhattan held its first total blackout of the war. The historic British city of Bath was struggling to recover from devastating German bombing raids in late April and early May.[132] Even the movies reflected the new world: the Alfred Hitchcock thriller *Saboteur* was playing at an Ottawa cinema.[133]

Fiscal equality was way below the radar. One after another, all provinces signed tax deals that ran until a year after the end of the war. The provinces refrained from levying personal and corporate income taxes and succession duties. In turn, they received grants based on one of two mechanisms. Under the first option, grants were based on the revenues collected in 1941 within a province's boundaries from those three taxes. Quebec, Ontario, Manitoba, British Columbia, and (initially) Alberta selected this option, which political economist Thomas Courchene describes as "the antithesis of equalization" because it was based on each province's tax collection.[134]

Under the second option, grants were based on the net cost of servicing the province's debt in 1940–41 – minus the succession duties that it collected in that year. Four poorer provinces – Saskatchewan and the three Maritime provinces – selected this option. The existence of the two options was fascinating in itself: "It is possible to argue that the availability of a choice of options embodied some consideration of fiscal need," notes Courchene.[135]

Former senior finance official R.M. Burns noted that Ottawa "had always been reluctant to acknowledge fiscal need per se as a basis for grants to the provinces, preferring adjustments to statutory subsidies or special grants to acknowledge any fundamental disabilities within the federation."[136] But the grants that Ottawa had bestowed on the Maritimes in the late 1920s and the mid-1930s – in response to the Duncan and White reports – had already recognized special needs, at least indirectly. Now, officially, Ottawa crossed this rhetorical bridge: the rental agreements effectively replaced the special grants to the West and the awards to the Maritimes with subsidies based on *existing* fiscal need. Ottawa also guaranteed that provincial revenues from liquor and gasoline would not fall below the level of 1940.

In effect, the tax rental deals established a vital point: the poorer provinces would now get *extra* revenues in return for cooperating with Ottawa – although no province could ignore the deals. "It was the war that changed everything," Burns remarks: "On both patriotic and constitutional grounds, the Dominion's unlimited authority under wartime emergencies was fully established."[137] Although Prime Minister King would not live to realize it, he had taken the first tiny steps towards equalization.

THE AUSTRALIAN-CANADIAN INTEREST IN WARTIME

Despite the strains between their prime ministers, the Australian fascination with Canada continued throughout the war – and into peacetime. Australian diplomats paid special attention to Canadian unity – perhaps because instability plagued their own political parties. In April 1941, the High Commission's official secretary Noël Deschamps forwarded a lengthy report from the *Montreal Gazette* along with an emphatic covering letter, outlining the speech of Montreal cardinal Jean-Marie-Rodrigue Villeneuve to a prestigious Toronto audience. The cardinal had appealed for national unity, denying the existence of "any strong separatist movement" in Quebec."[138] Deschamps depicted the speech as "an authoritative statement of the French Canadian attitude at the present time."[139]

The interest was mutual. In early 1942, horrified Canadians watched the fierce but futile resistance that Australian troops put up against Japanese troops in Malaya, Java, and Singapore. As *Montreal *Gazette* columnist L.S.B. Shapiro wrote in the language of the time: "the Jap is at Australia's gate."[140] The Imperial Order of the Daughters of Empire in Canada launched an appeal to raise $50,000 to purchase a Hurricane fighter for the Australians.[141] Ottawa sent films such as the Canadian Red Cross documentary *There Too Go I*.[142] It fostered links for members of the Empire Parliamentary Association.[143] It procured drawings for the installation of tank guns and sent sample components for the Bren gun.[144] The Canadian Broadcasting Corporation in cooperation with the Australian Broadcasting Corporation aired *The Anzac News Letter* every Sunday for Australian and New Zealand airmen in training across the Canadian West.[145] In turn, the Australians sent five of their short films, including *Australia Has Wings* and *Keeping the Fleet at Sea*.[146]

Australia's high commissioner Glasgow, who had arrived in Canada in early March 1940, finally managed to ease relations (King had suggested that Australia and Canada exchange high commissioners on 3 September 1939 for "strengthening" cooperation in wartime).[147] As the *Australian Dictionary of Biography* explains, Glasgow eventually won the trust of King and his key ministers with his fierce advocacy for closer liaison on Pacific strategy. In March 1944, the two dominions concluded an agreement for "mutual aid," setting up a mission under Sir William's supervision. Canada "provided two merchant ships" and Lady Glasgow launched one of them. "In August 1943 and September 1944, Glasgow attended the Quebec conferences between Churchill and Roosevelt," where the British prime minister and his staff briefed him – and where he spoke about Australia's concerns. Astonishingly, the Australian account adds: "Canadian government advisers recommended Glasgow for consideration as governor-general."[148]

CANADIANS STRUGGLE TO MAINTAIN MORALE

Across wartime Canada, governments were struggling to maintain harmony and determination. Taxes were sky high. Farmers and organized labour were worn out from the increased demand for their services. The wage-and-price freeze imposed in mid-October 1941 and effective on 1 December 1941 was meeting resistance.[149] Canadians suspected each other of making windfall profits. Affordable housing was often a single room in a home; shelter was often "far too small or dilapidated."[150] Landlords faced charges of rent gouging as workers migrated to industrial centres.[151]

Coupon rationing, introduced in 1942 and 1943, limited the availability of milk, butter, sugar, tea, coffee, meat, lard ... the lists were endless.[152] Clothing and footwear were in short supply because production plants were geared to the military.[153] There were stampedes to purchase silk stockings.[154] Gasoline was rationed from April 1942 to August 1945.[155] There were coal shortages, partly because of labour shortages.[156] "Increased industrial and military demand, transportation bottlenecks, and labour deficiencies" created fuel shortages; in response, consumers cut up fences, street signs, and park benches.[157] One Toronto resident even destroyed an old piano on a freezing February day. Most Canadians followed the rules, but they suspected that there was extensive cheating and black market activity. They were also concerned about the "moral decline" in their communities.[158] Their sacrifices sometimes seemed futile. Their societies were under stress.[159]

Some Canadians were making illicit money. An Ottawa basement was cut into four suites that "you could only charitably call cubicles, with one toilet, one washtub, for four families or four couples ... No pets. No parties after 11 p.m. No replacing 40-watt bulbs with 100-watt bulbs. No children in some places." Two Alberta brothers who carried freight southeast of Edmonton were able to purchase gas-ration books on the black market by giving a quarter of their gross take every week to two men who travelled throughout the Prairie provinces every three months, which "was sure a lesson in free enterprise." Two cousins shot twenty steers near Calgary, poaching them on a night "dark as a hundred feet down a well and with a wind blowing."[160]

The prospect of peace seemed illusory.

THE BATTLE FOR
EXPANDED SOCIAL SECURITY PERSISTS

While many Canadians struggled to remain upbeat, social activists resolved to seize an opportunity. Organizations such as the National Council of Women of Canada, which was a pivotal, if relatively privileged, voice for Canadian women, and the Canadian Congress of Labour envisaged a better world. Those activists maintained that there had to be a way to expand social security across the nation – even though the provinces were responsible for education, health care, and relief, Their voices – especially within anglophone Canada – became increasingly persuasive. Key federal social policies in wartime emerged as "a strategic compromise" in response to economic and political challenges.[161] Politicians had to do something to preserve stability *and* their own jobs.

But in a "symbolic change in thinking," Canadians were also shifting their views on what the state owed its citizens "from charity to entitlement." This was "a central metaphorical turn in the construction of the welfare state."[162] The reformers nurtured a sentiment that had been percolating over the last few decades: the state owed aid to its struggling citizens as a moral duty.

The idea evolved slowly in Canada. As early as the 1920s, the premiers of the Australian states had stoutly defended the continuation of their per capita payments from the Commonwealth as a "moral right."[163] In the United States, the notion of an individual's moral right to state aid appeared during the 1930s, reinforced with an implicit threat. In June 1935, US president Franklin Roosevelt told Congress that the federal tax system was contributing to an "unjust concentration of wealth and economic power ... Social unrest and a deepening sense of unfairness are dangers to our national life which we must minimize by rigorous methods."[164] That same year, Roosevelt introduced the landmark Social Security Act, which provided pensions for the elderly and unemployment insurance – and enabled states to make more adequate provision for dependent children.[165]

Historian David M. Kennedy is succinct: "Security was the leitmotif of virtually everything the New Deal attempted ... Its cardinal aim was not to destroy capitalism but to devolatize it, and at the same time to distribute its benefits more evenly."[166] A year later, on 27 June 1936, Roosevelt accepted his party's nomination with a paean to the role of government in hard times: "There is a mysterious cycle in human events. To some generations much is given. Of other generations much is expected. This generation of Americans has a rendezvous with destiny."[167]

That notion of the state's moral obligation to its citizens grew in strength as wartime sacrifices engendered dreams of a better world. Canadian activists were well aware of the report that social reformer William Beveridge had submitted to the British Parliament in

November 1942, which proposed a minimum standard of living for all citizens. Surely this dream was also possible for Canadians?

Ottawa grappled with the challenges in typically Canadian style: plans for expanded social security grew amid a sea of impenetrable acronyms, multiple committees, and fierce rivalries. In September 1939, the cabinet had created the Economic Advisory Committee comprised of officials to oversee the war.[168] That committee was eventually drawn into planning for peacetime. In September 1941, the cabinet formally recognized the existence of the Advisory Committee on Reconstruction, which the principal of McGill University, Cyril James, chaired while social scientist Leonard Marsh served as research advisor.[169] That committee agreed on three assumptions: social security measures would foster a healthy economy and full employment; the postwar years could bring "considerable economic and social dislocation"; and, perhaps most important, "inevitably, the state and the bureaucracy would have to continue to exercise in the post-war world at least a portion of the powers they had assumed to handle the wartime emergency."[170]

Such declarations appealed to National Health Minister Ian Mackenzie. The Vancouver MP was a social activist but his historical reputation remains deeply marred. King had moved Mackenzie out of the defence ministry in mid-September 1939 after journalists uncovered "wasteful spending, patronage, costly land flips and sheer incompetence" in his department.[171] In the national health ministry, Mackenzie continued his pattern of supporting almost every anti-Asian proposal in the British Columbia legislature (1920–1930) and then in Parliament, which he entered in 1930. The only exception occurred in 1929, when Mackenzie supported "the extension of the provincial franchise to Asian veterans of the First World War."[172] He was one of the key proponents within cabinet in the internment of Japanese Canadians during the war.

King was careful around Mackenzie. He viewed him as an overly sensitive and proud Scot, who drank too heavily.[173] Mackenzie, in turn, knew that his transfer out of defence in wartime was "an obvious vote of non-confidence" in his ability.[174] Aware of reform ideas from his time in the BC legislature, he resolved to advocate extended social security as "a means by which he could enhance his own portfolio and demonstrate to King his importance as a colleague."[175] In late September 1941, the minister was nagging King about health insurance, whether through the provinces supplemented by federal assistance or through federal legislation.[176]

The release of the James committee's "extremely modest" interim report in the autumn of 1942 prompted its researcher Leonard Marsh to act on his own. The British-born social scientist took inspiration from John Maynard Keynes and from his mentor, Sir William Beveridge, and he was a founding member of what became the League for Social Reconstruction in 1931.[177] In less than two months, Marsh cobbled together a proposal of more than 250 pages, which was presented to the House of Commons Committee on Reconstruction in March 1943. It called for a comprehensive minimum of care that included unemployment assistance, employment retraining, health insurance, and children's allowances.[178]

Such reports caught the public's attention. In May 1943, an *International Labour Review* (*ILR*) of the Marsh report offered a succinct assessment: "Social security has become identified with that better world for which they [Canadians] are fighting."[179] In a hint at the continuing anxiety about dependency, however, the *ILR* analysis added: "Social insurance benefits must be less than the earnings of the self-supporting individual, while social assistance payments must be less than the earnings of the unskilled worker."[180] There was cautious optimism.

But the James committee report had also triggered a turf war between Mackenzie and his health ministry officials and officials in the finance ministry and the Bank of Canada.[181] The James committee had aroused this opposition when it called for the creation of a new portfolio to handle reconstruction that Mackenzie would presumably head.[182] In December 1942, Mackenzie pointedly reminded the cabinet's Committee on Reconstruction that Canada had subscribed "immediately" to the Atlantic Charter, which US president Franklin Roosevelt and British prime minister Winston Churchill had endorsed in August 1941.[183] It vowed to ensure that "all the men in all lands may live out their lives in freedom from fear and want."[184] Mackenzie maintained that the prime minister: "has repeatedly underlined and emphasized the determination of this country to establish for all our people security from the great fears which haunt the majority of mankind from infancy to the grave – the fear of ill health, the fear of unemployment, the fear of hunger, and the fear of an impoverished old age."[185]

Both Mackenzie and the James committee had driven home "the necessity of planning for reconstruction."[186] But the bureaucracy moved slowly. In February 1942, the cabinet had appointed a formal advisory committee on health insurance, which worked under Mackenzie's oversight. In late 1942, the 558-page Advisory Committee Report, with two draft bills, was complete. In early 1943, Prime Minister King swung behind the idea, using the Speech from the Throne to call for a "comprehensive national scheme of social insurance."[187] Anxious to retain the lead, Mackenzie persuaded his cabinet colleagues to refer the report to the all-party Special House Committee on Social Security, which first met in March 1943.[188]

The two draft bills were fascinating: one outlined how to keep federal fiscal control over the provinces through conditional grants for health care; the second provided draft legislation for each province to establish a commission to administer health insurance.[189] Ottawa would pay three-fifths of the provincial cost; the provincial governments would pay the remaining amount through a tax of twelve dollars imposed on each adult.[190] Mackenzie craftily argued that socialism had become "a national political menace." So the Liberals should defuse any appeal from the CCF by holding a dominion-provincial conference to consider draft health legislation "as soon as possible."[191]

The concept retained its appeal. In January 1944, in the Speech from the Throne, Ottawa promised to provide "federal assistance in a nation-wide system of health insurance" after "suitable agreements" with the provinces.[192] In May 1944, provincial ministers and bureaucrats met in Ottawa to discuss the draft health insurance bills – and how to meet those costs. According to a later federal summary, most provinces "indicated their strong desire that health insurance should be proceeded with by stages and that any scheme adopted should be flexible enough to permit the provinces to build on the varying services in each province."[193]

The movement towards expanded social security was seemingly gathering momentum. But the minister was losing his bureaucratic battle to oversee those postwar plans: in January 1943, finance ministry officials had adeptly switched the wartime concerns of the Economic Advisory Committee to peacetime, creating a rival subcommittee on reconstruction.[194] They also challenged the health ministry's cost estimates for health insurance. The cabinet swung against Mackenzie's plans, and his influence waned. Still, King's biographer Allan Levine says that Mackenzie "redeemed himself" as a progressive thinker in the prime minister's eyes in the health portfolio.[195] It was an ironic coda to a chequered career.

THE AUSTRALIANS KEEP TRACK

The Australians remained fascinated, reporting to Canberra on Ottawa's proposed reconstruction measures. Ottawa wanted to establish the men and women of the armed forces "in useful and remunerative employment after the war."[196] It aimed to secure "adequate income and full employment after the war for primary producers."[197] Perhaps most important: "Government believes that a comprehensive national scheme of social insurance, which will constitute charter of social security for whole of Canada, should be worked out at once. It proposes early appointment therefore of Select Committee to examine and report on most practicable measures of social insurance, including national system of health insurance."[198] It was a glowing summary and, as the Australians surely sensed, an impossible dream.

It is important to note that all of those Canadian reports dealt with inequality among people. They did *not* tackle the glaring fiscal and economic inequalities among provinces, which remained a basic barrier to social reform. Ottawa politicians and officials could dream – and the Australians could avidly report those dreams – but they still lacked the practical fiscal mechanism to implement those programs. Provinces could not expand social programs until there was relative fiscal equality among them.

THE YEARNING FOR A BETTER WORLD

The Liberal government was aware that Canadians wanted them to win the war – *and* the peace. Perhaps the Canadian Teachers' Federation best captured this yearning in an August 1943 report: it embraced the idea of the Good Life, which American educator George S. Counts had propounded during the 1930s. "A true democracy can be content with nothing less than what has become generally known as The Good Life for all the people ... That somehow, as a result of this terrible struggle, this Good Life may be attained fully or in large part by the millions of plain folk who comprise the

Democratic nations ... this is what our boys are fighting for."[199] The federation called for "a comprehensive and all-inclusive plan of Social Security for all citizens ... covering unemployment, health, accidents, marriage, childbirth, allowance for children and retirement for the aged."[200] And they looked to Ottawa to deliver this package. So did the Montreal local of the National Council of Women, which implored civic governments to ask Ottawa for a "greatly expanded" housing program.[201]

Other groups wanted to strengthen the resources of the provinces in the postwar era. The Canadian Congress of Labour (CCL) wanted more funds for education. In a memorandum to Ottawa, the CCL explained that "the wide diversity in educational standards, in text books, and curricula in Canada" was a source of disunity. Ottawa should provide financial assistance to the provinces "which will enable them to raise educational standards to the highest possible level."[202]

Federal officials knew they were in a sticky situation, trapped between the aspirations of many Canadians and the constitutional provisions for strong provincial identities. While the war news continued to dominate the headlines, they were already considering the financial landscape in peacetime. Could Ottawa retain the revenues that it had? What would happen to the dreams of the Good Life? In December 1943, an unsigned Bank of Canada memo on postwar finance finally spelled out the problem, which few acknowledged: "It seems clear that the provinces cannot finance any major extension of welfare services out of their own resources."[203]

Worse, if the tax rental agreements with their mildly equalized grants ended, some provinces would "find it difficult or impossible to finance even the present level of services."[204] This might be ominous: "Welfare, like prosperity, or peace, is indivisible."[205] The memo suggested one of two courses: "Transfer the constitutional responsibility for certain welfare services (such as health insurance?) from the provinces to the federal government," which would require a constitutional amendment.[206]

Or, alternatively, Ottawa could transfer federal funds to the provinces "on the basis of need, which will provide adequate checks against misuse of funds but will not encroach upon the essentials of provincial autonomy."[207] This approach could be politically risky, however, because the payments would be pegged to provincial spending. "It would be difficult to define welfare services in sufficiently objective and specific terms, and determine their cost closely enough, to make effective supervision of the relevant provincial expenditures possible."[208] Provinces could spend large amounts of money "which they did not have to take the onus of raising from their electors." Worse, "regional groups ... [could] block legitimate national policies if they so desired."[209] The clear implication was that it was safer to put more responsibility for social security in Ottawa's hands – along with the funds to expand those programs.

Clearly, Bank of Canada officials had not abandoned their plan to absorb those provincial taxes permanently and perhaps take over the administration of key social programs. Once again, no one dared to raise the prospect of non-conditional transfers to the poorer provinces. And no one suggested that transfers could be linked to tax revenues as opposed to spending needs. Genuine equalization was not contemplated. But the pressure for action on social issues was strong.

MORE WOMEN ENTER THE WARTIME WORKFORCE

While the federal government prepared for peace, the war demanded ever more resources, sparking personnel shortages. In March 1942, Mackenzie King had unveiled a plan to bring women into the war industries. The publicity campaign urged: "Roll up your sleeves for Victory."[210] By October 1943, an estimated 261,000 women were employed in war production, "directly or indirectly." By mid-1944, the Department of Labour estimated that one out of every four workers in war industries was a woman, doing what Ottawa depicted as their patriotic duty on a temporary basis.[211] In Regina, the employment representative for an Eastern Canadian munitions plant told the *Regina Leader Post* that he was offering thirty-five cents per hour for a forty-five-hour week as a starting wage, plus time-and-a-half for overtime, along with board of seven dollars per week and rooms in dormitories. The plant even offered movies every Thursday night with a fifteen-cent admission.[212]

Women were also entering the armed services. By January 1942, the first group of officers for the Royal Canadian Air Force, Women's Division, had been trained, and they were ready for postings across Canada, including Camp Borden and Brantford in Ontario. As the employment shortages grew more severe, the number of their trades expanded from eight in 1941, including cooks and clerks, to fifty in 1942, "and reached sixty-five by the end of the war."[213] The Women's Royal Canadian Naval Service was established in July 1942, posting women to naval establishments and ports across Canada, eventually opening up thirty-nine trades for women, including supply assistants and the almost inevitable cooks.[214]

PUBLIC PRESSURE ON MACKENZIE KING

By 1943, Mackenzie King did not need a sign from the heavens to discern a political threat to his government. In August 1943, the CCF became the official opposition in Ontario when the Conservatives won the provincial election. That same month, the CCF snared two of four seats in federal by-elections. In September 1943, a Gallup Poll showed that the CCF held a one-percentage-point lead over both the Liberals and the Conservatives.[215] In June 1944, former MP Tommy Douglas and his CCF became the first social democratic government in Canada when he won the Saskatchewan election.

The electorate was impatient – but plans for expanded social security with the provinces were stalled. Instead, the prime minister opted to deliver payments to individual Canadian through family allowances, which were hugely convenient substitutes. The money would go to families with children, especially large families, providing income maintenance. It would relieve pressure from labour groups to drive up wages, which would fuel inflation. And putting cash into the pockets of low-income consumers would increase employment while allowing, and often forcing, women to leave their wartime jobs in peacetime. Like his finance ministry officials, King was already fretting about the transition from war to peace. "Economic policies now dominated social welfare issues," observes historian Doug Owram.[216]

In his diary, King emphasized the connection between the economy and family allowances, describing a cabinet meeting with Deputy Finance Minister W.C. Clark in January 1944: "He [Clark] made a very fine presentation, stressing among other things how serious might be the solution of some other questions, e. g. relief, housing and the like, unless family allowances measure were introduced [sic]. He also touched upon the necessity of this measure if wage stabilization and price ceiling were to be maintained."[217] Direct federal transfers to individuals could deter social democrats;

they could also promote economic vitality during the fearfully anticipated postwar downturn.[218]

But the ever-cautious King remained wary of firm commitments to health insurance. Even after the CCF won the Saskatchewan election on 15 June 1944, the prime minister remained "uneasy about the financial ramifications of health insurance."[219] In August of 1944, he decided against a dominion-provincial conference that would consider the two draft bills on health care from the Special Committee on Social Security. He argued that he should wait until after the next federal election. In January 1945, in an unusual Speech from the Throne that *closed* the session in anticipation of the election, Ottawa again repeated its intention to adopt health insurance as soon as "suitable arrangements" could be made with the provinces at a post-election dominion-provincial conference.[220] King's "strategic delay" ensured that those ambitious plans started to lose momentum.[221]

But King could not relax. The prime minister scraped through the June 1945 federal election. The CCF won twenty-eight seats with 15.6 percent of the popular vote. That was less than many party stalwarts had expected after Douglas's win in Saskatchewan. But King understood that the electoral threat had not gone away.

THE AUSTRALIANS PREPARE FOR POSTWAR RECONSTRUCTION

The Australians were working on postwar planning – and the Canadians were following *their* efforts. The Bank of Canada Archives contain the summary of an address that Australia's director-general of postwar reconstruction, H.C. Coombs, delivered during the summer of 1944. Coombs – who was an economist and the most important civil servant of his generation – had a warning for his listeners. "There is a great danger that when the war itself is over we will be tired by the mental and spiritual strain of years of war and will be unwilling to strive further," he declared. "There is a danger that ... when we realize that we have gained only the opportunity to work for these objectives, there will be disillusion, and cynicism."[222]

The situation in Australia was challenging. The wartime willingness to make radical changes could "melt in the face of hostile criticism of interests adversely affected and we will not be 'allowed' to have the changes which alone can make fruitful the victory won."[223]

Australian society was "war weary and to some extent psychologically unstable, but nevertheless anxious for change and willing to be inspired into social unity for a common purpose."[224] The first objective should be "a high and stable level of employment."[225] Coombs added pointedly: "The history of the depression years completely destroyed the belief that insecurity is an effective stimulus to endeavor."[226] Government had an important role in preserving prosperity and hope. It was a lesson that many in both nations were now heeding.

KEYNESIAN POLICIES GAIN CREDENCE

There was another factor at play as official Ottawa considered its postwar world: the Keynesians were edging into control within the Government Generation. Keynes himself visited Canada three times in 1944–45. His former students at Cambridge University – future deputy finance minister Robert Bryce and future assistant deputy finance minister A.F.W. Plumptre – were attracting respectful attention when they spoke about his views in Ottawa.[227]

Even those who had not formally embraced the doctrine now realized that "under-employment was not self-correcting in capitalist economies."[228] Employers, veterans' organizations, trade unions, and individual men and women now grappled with the role of the state in fostering employment, arguing over "the varying rights of citizenship and property."[229] What would happen if Ottawa lost control of that huge pot of tax revenues that could be useful in a downturn? In May 1944, Ottawa tapped its best resource on dominion-provincial financial relations to handle such problems: it named Alex Skelton as the secretary of a committee to prepare for a postwar dominion-provincial conference.[230]

Skelton worked fast. Within a month, he had produced an eleven-page memorandum, which summarized the changing world for people and governments. "The war has greatly expanded our administrative capacity and general 'know-how' of taking effective preventive measures against some forms of economic distress which were formerly considered to be acts of God," he wrote.[231] Government should "for economic reasons, [be] thinking of the distressed citizen as a consumer and potential producer as well as for social reasons (thinking of him as a human being)."[232] It should provide a "rock-bottom minimum of economic security." [233] Skelton always tried to look out for the underdog – but he also could not resist the chance to promote Ottawa's expertise.

In turn, the provinces "must be in a position to provide roughly comparable services to their residents with no great disproportion in their respective burdens of taxation."[234] Skelton warned that the provinces would want more money to renew the tax rental deals because their citizenry would demand more services in peacetime. Poorer provinces should receive special assistance – *as long as* Ottawa retained control of those three taxes so that "full employment, high national income, and social security programmes are to be developed on an effective scale."[235]

The bottom line was clear: Ottawa should renew the tax rental deals – and provide equalizing compensatory grants. It should also assume more responsibility for social programs such as training, rehabilitation, and health services, bearing in mind the "economic value of adequate social security measures in maintaining consumption."[236] Skelton could not abandon the centralizing approach to revenues in the Rowell-Sirois Royal Commission Report and the tax rental deals. Nor could he abandon his wish to expand federal social responsibilities.

THE WAR NEARS AN END

Finance ministry bureaucrats wrestled with those crucial issues during the hard winter of 1944–45 while Allied troops fought their way through Europe and across the Pacific Islands, By early May 1945, as the war in the Pacific continued, the war in Europe was over. Seven weeks later, Canadian service personnel were coming home from Europe, disembarking in Halifax – although future ships would also dock in Montreal or Quebec City. In Bavaria, Allied Forces captured nineteen former Nazi henchmen who had run Buchenwald concentration camp, including Commandant Hermann Pister (who would die of a heart attack in prison in September 1948); the men were posing as former prisoners of war with identification papers that they had forced their Jewish inmates to fill out for them. With the Russians in control of Eastern Europe, Britain decided to pay the current expenses of the Polish Foreign Army in London.[237] At Canadian theatres, Betty Grable was starring as *The Pin Up Girl*, a romantic comedy spun around the tale of returning US naval heroes.[238] It was fluffy fare for audiences who still waited in fear for a telegram announcing a relative's death in the Pacific War.

The times were turbulent. In late July 1945, while British prime minister Sir Winston Churchill was at the Potsdam Conference with US president Harry Truman and Soviet Communist Party general secretary Joseph Stalin, he learned that he had lost the British election to Labour leader Clement Attlee, who took his place at the table. By early August, the three leaders had concluded their discussions: they reasserted their demand for Japan's unconditional surrender; Russia would receive 10 to 15 percent of German industrial equipment in the Allies' western zones; and the trial of Nazi wartime criminals would commence in the autumn. By 4 August 1945, American bombers flying out of Guam had dropped more than 3 million leaflets on Japanese cities, outlining the "surrender or else" ultimatum from Potsdam.[239]

In Ottawa throughout those last tough weeks, federal officials were working hard. Among the files of W.A. Mackintosh in the Queen's University Archives there is an outline of federal fiscal policy for the upcoming Dominion-Provincial Conference. The unknown author had a bedrock Keynesian assumption: "Some level of government must take final responsibility for maintaining a high level of employment" – and that was Ottawa.[240] In times of economic downturn, Ottawa "could speed up programs of national development and useful public investment to take up the slack ... the Dominion must expect, and be able to manage, substantial deficits at such periods."[241]

There were competing pressures. Ottawa had three "generally agreed"-upon social security objectives: old-age pensions, family allowances, and "large grants to the provinces to provide health insurance benefits."[242] But taxes could not go sky high. The dominion had to balance "equity or fairness" with "the effects of taxes on incentives – production and employment."[243] Properly done, Ottawa could "maintain prosperity within a modern, progressive and democratic society."[244] The policy paper was a flat-out power grab cloaked in practical prose: "[Ottawa] cannot hope to succeed if it must contend and compete with other governments imposing taxes of the same kind on the same incomes or businesses."[245] Ottawa should keep corporate and personal income tax revenues and succession duties after the war – in return for continued transfers.

Almost from the start, this plan for fiscal centralization was disruptive. It threatened the identity of the more powerful provinces – Quebec and Ontario – for radically different reasons. But it could not do much about fiscal equity.

CONCLUSION

In peacetime, Canada would be no closer to sharing among governments than it had been in wartime. And sharing was the remedy for fiscal and economic inequality along with the huge holes in the social security network. Mackenzie King was relieved when he fended off the recommendations of the Rowell-Sirois Report. He did not want to intrude permanently into provincial turf, nor did he want to tamper with Quebec's distinct identity. He was also averse to piling up postwar debts.

But, as the war ended, King had to face the provinces with his own idealistic but half-hearted proposals for the new world. While Canadians waited expectantly for the Good Life, he stepped into his toughest round of federal-provincial negotiations. And he would find few friends on his side during this seemingly endless odyssey.

8

Mackenzie King's Last Showdowns, 1945–48

Canada was still at war when Prime Minister Mackenzie King assembled the weary premiers in Ottawa on 6 August 1945. Abroad, American Super Fortress bombers were targeting Japanese industrial and railway infrastructure.[1] At home, in Mount Hope, Ontario, four pilots on a routine training mission died in a mid-air collision near the Royal Canadian Air Force wireless school.[2] But signs of tentative hope and celebration were everywhere. American and Canadian tourists were thronging into Northern Ontario, buying out the beer stores, scooping up baked goods and fresh fruit, and occupying virtually every available hotel room.[3] The main headline in the *Globe and Mail* was "Ottawa Ends Liquor Curb," heralding the lifting of restrictions on wartime liquor supplies and alcohol strength, which had been imposed in December 1942.[4] The nation was clearly on the cusp of peace.

And with that hope of peace came, perhaps almost predictably, the resumption of the often prickly talks about revenues, responsibilities, and the difficult art of sharing between the prime minister and the premiers. King launched those discussions with an idealistic Green Paper for social security, and he would spend the next three years fending off provincial demands for its implementation. Cautious by nature, he could never bring himself to commit to such expensive cradle-to-grave promises as per capita health insurance for family doctors or universal old-age pensions. As historian Alvin Finkel concludes, although Ottawa would blame Quebec and Ontario for the impasse with the provinces, it "cynically and successfully manipulated" the outcome "because it did not want to undertake the expenses implied in the reform proposals."[5]

More important, however, fiscal inequality among the provinces prevented the adoption of expansive national programs. King would not implement the Green Paper until all provinces signed renewals of the tax rental deals. Ontario and Quebec would not sign the deals – for different reasons. And the other provinces would not sign new tax rental deals until they knew how much money they would get in return. The deals "took into account differences in fiscal capacity through per capita payments (implicit equalization)," notes health policy expert Gregory P. Marchildon, "and [they] provided minimum base grants to poorer provinces."[6] Even then, the poorer provinces would lack sufficient funds for their share of those costly social programs. But, in the early postwar years, governments did not address the elephant in the room: fiscal and economic inequality among federation members.

It was not just economics that separated the participants. As a key player, Quebec premier Maurice Duplessis firmly defended his province's constitutional right to collect and control its own revenues. Quebec had cooperated with Ottawa in wartime. But it would not cede its rights in peacetime, especially not for the limited per capita amounts in compensation that the federal government initially offered. Quebec needed money for roads, health, education, agriculture, and settlement, and, as Duplessis remarked scathingly on the opening day of the Dominion-Provincial Conference, the provinces "are fit to deal with their own affairs and so Ottawa with its own affairs."[7] The premier would never budge from that position.

Worse, a simmering feud between King and Ontario premier George Drew, whose Progressive Conservative government had replaced the Liberals in 1943, disrupted the proceedings. Although ambitious federal politicians and bureaucrats wanted to augment Ottawa's peacetime capabilities and responsibilities, the recalcitrant Drew was planning "his own brand of reconstruction based on a fusion of more traditional economic principles and provincial rights." As historian Marc J. Gotlieb recounts, the premier would not accede to a tax rental process that "threatened radically to alter the traditional distribution of power." The conference only "exacerbated Drew's personal dislike for Mackenzie King to the point where the premier was scarcely able to restrain it."[8]

It is tempting to speculate that Ottawa could have saved itself a decade of difficulties if it had simply resisted the Keynesian temptation to centralize key tax revenues in case of a postwar downturn. Many premiers from the poorer provinces, which eventually signed deals, would not stop pestering King to call another dominion-provincial conference to consider expanded social security. Some premiers, especially Ontario's Drew, would engage in lengthy feuds with him. King made small concessions with the provision of health care grants. But the prime minister would not escape the incessant pressures until he left office in late 1948.

THE DOMINION-PROVINCIAL CONFERENCE OPENS

King and the nine premiers knew that the coming peace could be almost as difficult as the wartime home front. They were braced for a recession, even as their impatient voters demanded a finer world. Each premier was determined to use the Reconstruction Conference in the House of Commons Chamber to highlight his province's needs.[9] Each premier wanted his share of headlines.

But from the beginning, on that rainy August Monday, Ottawa stole the show.

Canadians were warned. As the *Globe and Mail* explained, "Expect Ottawa to Ask Extended Tax Control."[10] That oblique headline was shorthand for Ottawa's decision to ask for a renewal of the tax rental deals. The provincial delegates believed that Ottawa was "adamant" about its "assumption of sole taxing powers ... [which] would amount to a continuation of the wartime tax agreements."[11] The *Globe and Mail*'s Ottawa correspondent added that the premiers were guardedly prepared to cooperate: "[But] there is no suggestion any one Province is prepared to fall within the Dominion lap and take any old thing that is offered in return. Every Province is jealous of its autonomy."[12] As federal bureaucrat Alex Skelton had warned in June 1944, most provinces wanted more compensation if Ottawa pressed for renewals. The focus was largely on money – and it would remain so.

Still, the yearning for the Good Life was almost visceral when King opened the proceedings. He outlined his government's ambitious plans for a "progressive and secure standard of living based on remunerative employment for all who are able and willing to work." That promise was coupled with Green Paper proposals for "a comprehensive system of social insurance, partially federal and partially provincial."[13] The package included per capita grants for health insurance to cover family doctors' bills, visiting nursing services, and hospital care; health grants for public health and preventative medicine; universal old-age pensions for those who were seventy and over; and unemployment assistance to those who had exhausted their UI benefits or who were not eligible for UI. As historian Alvin Finkel observes, there was "growing public demand for significant state intervention in the marketplace," partly because wartime planning had "largely eliminated unemployment and restrained inflation."[14] Surely such security could continue in peacetime

It was clear that the Green Paper would take time to implement. A secret federal brief for the conference noted flatly: "It is significant that the nations which have not adopted health insurance include Australia, the United States and Canada. *All three of these nations are federations*, where the power to deal with health is a matter of local concern, of the states and provinces."[15] King surely realized that full implementation would require decades. And that was almost certainly fine with him.

Perhaps he glimpsed the impasse ahead. The 1945–46 Dominion-Provincial Conference is now virtually forgotten. On the opening day, King told the premiers that their gathering "may well be the most important Canadian Conference since Confederation."[16] He was wrong. But it was certainly the longest. The premiers met for five days in plenary sessions from 6 to 10 August. They created a coordinating committee that met for ten days throughout the fall and winter of 1945–46 into the spring of 1946. The record of their federal-provincial statements – which does not include every policy document – spans 624 large pages.

They accomplished nothing. Their talks were inconclusive. They made virtually no progress on the big issues of provincial fiscal inequality, social security, and postwar infrastructure that were facing the nation. The conference remains valuable because there was little doubt where the individual premiers stood: they spelled out the barriers to equalization – and to most social programs – that would persist over the ensuing decade. The gaps between the richer provinces of Ontario and British Columbia and the poorer provinces of Nova Scotia and New Brunswick were enormous – and they did not narrow over the nine-month marathon.

The transcript traces an arc from initial cordiality to outright incivility. On 2 May 1946, New Brunswick premier J.B. McNair plaintively mused that the Fathers of Confederation "never envisaged the possibility that eighty years after the Union was created, at a meeting such as this, the citizens in the different provinces would be talked about as though they were so many different peoples."[17] The delegates had started with so much optimism and determination. In the end, federal health minister Brooke Claxton lamented that the politicians had put "too much emphasis" on the tax provisions.[18]

That was exactly what happened – but it was understandable. The premiers could never agree on national social programs until they established their budgetary bottom lines. How much revenue would they surrender in response to Ottawa's offer to rent their corporate and personal income taxes and their succession duties? How much would they receive in return? And, most crucially, would Ottawa recognize the fiscal needs of the poorer provinces?

The ghosts of the Rowell-Sirois Report and the Australian Commonwealth haunted the proceedings. It remains astonishing how many premiers and ministers cited the Commonwealth government's annual grants to all states for wartime tax rentals as well as the Commonwealth Grants Commission allocations to the poorer states based on fiscal need. Politicians brandished varying figures, contradicting each other on exchange rates and Australian taxes. Arguably, the worst side of every delegate emerged at one time or another. As long as Ottawa insisted on centralizing revenues, there was probably no other possible outcome.

AUSTRALIA PREPARES FOR PEACETIME

The Australians foresaw a long struggle ahead in the Pacific War. But by 6 August they were also wrestling with domestic priorities and problems. Federal authorities were considering the abolition of all restrictions on passenger rail travel.[19] Workers at Commonwealth government munitions factories in New South Wales – which were closing – were imploring the state government to switch to the production of civilian goods to preserve their jobs.[20] In the Melbourne suburbs, vigilante bands of ex-servicemen were violently seizing empty houses – and installing returned soldiers and their families in them.[21] As always, as the war edged towards an end, the potential winners and losers were elbowing each other aside: politicians were debating the new allotment of petrol rations and asking why so much supply was granted to private motorists.[22] Perhaps most jarring were the newspaper ads: the *Sydney Morning Herald* ran advertisements for women's fashions in "lovely peppermint white tailored neckwear" in incongruous proximity to the daily lists of army and air force casualties.[23] The wartime allies of Canada and Australia were in uneasy sync on the cusp of a different world.

THE OPENING DAYS OF THE CONFERENCE BRING DRAMA

Mackenzie King had opened the proceedings with aplomb, but he was soon distracted. At noon, he received a note from Munitions Minister C.D. Howe, which stated that a bomb had been dropped. The prime minister confirmed the meaning of the word "bomb" with Howe – but he remained silent until a wire-service report verified US president Harry Truman's assertion. At 1:00 p.m., King adjourned the proceedings for lunch, explaining that he had a "world shaking announcement."[24] Then he told the participants about the atomic bomb that had been dropped on Hiroshima. There was "dead silence."[25] It was a civic holiday in Ontario. There were no newspapers. So, when the session resumed that afternoon, King read statements from politicians around the world, including one from former British prime minister Winston Churchill. The news "created mixed feelings in my mind and heart. We were now within sight of the end of the war with Japan."[26]

The event drove the conference, which had opened with such grand intentions, off the nation's front pages. Understandably. "Jap Morale Shaken by Allies Atomic Bomb," shouted the *Ottawa Journal* headlines on 7 August. "Considerable Damage Is Admitted" was the news out of Guam, which relayed Tokyo's description of the devastation in Hiroshima. Uranium company stock rose on the Toronto stock exchange. Ironically, stock prices fell on Wall Street as traders viewed the bomb "as meaning a quicker-than-expected end of the Japanese war." The transition to peace was almost all-consuming. While global experts debated the weight of the atomic bomb's explosive charge, the American military government in Frankfurt, Germany, was directing all civil governments to remove Nazi names from public places. In Ottawa, the First Canadian Army commander, General Harry Crerar, arrived to an ecstatic welcome and a state luncheon at the Chateau Laurier Hotel.[27] The conference delegates joined the welcoming throng and the luncheon.

The politicians simply could not compete with this startling brew of terror and euphoria. On the second day of the conference, as King greeted Crerar, Finance Minister J.L. Ilsley spelled out Ottawa's plans. Federal postwar obligations were onerous: Ottawa had to finance substantial deficits "when necessary"; it had to adjust the tax system to foster investment and employment; it had to offer "a dependable financial basis" to all provinces; and, most important, *it had to bring balance* to the federation. "Post-war financial arrangements ... should make possible at least an adequate minimum standard of services in all provinces while not denying to any province the advantages which its resources give to it nor the freedom to establish its own standards."[28] It was an implicitly equalizing goal.

Ilsley's approach was also unreservedly Keynesian: "In carrying out its [dominion] employment policy it will at times be necessary for large deficits to be incurred while at the same time expenditures are being increased or taxation reduced in order to aid employment." If Ottawa occasionally ran a deficit, "it should be in a position to recapture in periods of high employment and vigorous business activity revenue from rising incomes and profits."[29]

The finance minister offered to implement this approach in return for continued control over key provincial tax revenues. In compensation, Ottawa dangled per capita grants of twelve dollars to every province, based on the 1941 census, which would increase or decrease with the value of the Gross National Product.[30]

And then the quarrels commenced.

THE CONTINUING DEBATES ABOUT FAIRNESS

At the heart of the discussions, running through every session, was the debate around how to handle fiscal inequality. Each premier had a view. And each premier made sure that the others heard him (they were all male in those fraught days). In his lengthy opening statement, Manitoba premier Stuart Garson, who had close ties with King's government, said Ottawa had to increase its per capita grants – and provide national adjustment grants to poorer provinces "on the basis of fiscal need."[31] Saskatchewan premier Tommy Douglas, the former CCF MP who would introduce provincewide hospital insurance in January 1947, maintained that social security measures "should be raised to a minimum standard" so that "no Canadian shall be penalized" because of where he or she lived.[32]

And so it continued. Some provinces simply wanted a higher per capita grant. In late November of 1945, Alberta premier Ernest C. Manning, who had continued the *Back to the Bible Hour* radio broadcasts of his predecessor William Aberhart, told the Conference Coordinating Committee that the proposed grant was "inadequate ... insufficient to meet post-war requirements."[33] Other provinces wanted a version of the National Adjustment Grants that the Rowell-Sirois Commission had proposed for poorer provinces. New Brunswick asked for "a special allowance or fiscal need subsidy" that would allow local and provincial services "to be raised to the average standard prevailing throughout Canada" without raising taxes.[34] Nova Scotia demanded that Ottawa recognize the principle of fiscal need – and then set up a permanent commission similar to the Australian Commonwealth Grants Commission.[35]

Ontario premier Drew had little patience for those demands – or for Ottawa's attempt to centralize his tax revenues. In early January, he became the only premier to table a counter-proposal: the wartime tax agreements should lapse without renewal; the provinces should retain their tax revenues for social security and economic development; and 10 percent of provincial tax revenues from "full-scale post-war production" should go into a national adjustment fund, which a dominion-provincial coordinating committee would oversee.[36] Under the Ontario plan: "[the poorer provinces] will not be without some freedom to meet unusual conditions which because of the limited aspect of their economy – I mean limited in the particular nature of the economy – do present special problems."[37]

That daring plan, directly counter to Ottawa's fiscal centralization schemes, put the cat among the poorer provincial pigeons. It was also a "bombshell" surprise for the federal government. Historian P.E. Bryden says that Health Minister Claxton was reportedly "vitriolic." He considered Drew's proposals to be "uneconomic, impossible of implementation, unacceptable to other provinces, and drafted solely with a view to the selfish interests of Ontario."[38] Saskatchewan premier Douglas complained that Ontario's proposals "do not represent fiscal need at all, but are rather a source of federated poor-box, into which contributions will be made by the provinces, and the poor relations will line up at Christmas time to get a handout from the fund."[39] Manitoba premier Garson was even more emphatic. "His [Drew's] is the viewpoint of a rich, powerful and populous central province." So many firms, including banks and steel mills that did business in Manitoba, "are all owned and controlled, and they have their head office in his province."[40] Ontario was a fat cat.

Drew was outraged. "The overwhelming majority of every dollar produced in Ontario is made by the work, the brain and the vigour of the people of Ontario," he declared, arguing that more than 85.5 percent of the federal tax revenues collected in Canada came from Ontario, Quebec, and British Columbia.[41] Any tax rental deal "must have due regard for the heavy share which will come from the people of Ontario."[42] When Ontario finally attached very complicated figures to its proposal – the province wanted Ottawa to withdraw from other tax fields as well – Finance Minister Ilsley was aghast: the plan would add $100 million per year to Ottawa's tab "as a minimum applied to all the provinces."[43]

Ilsley also ruled out subsidies based on fiscal need as "the worst kind of subsidy" because the provinces would have to make the case for need based on a detailed examination of their spending and severity of taxation. But Ottawa did raise its offer to fifteen dollars per capita from twelve dollars per capita – and that was where it would stay. When King announced the increased $50 million to the premiers, however, "it was not nearly enough to satisfy the critics." Drew shrewdly demanded that the discussion focus on the federal proposals, not Ontario's submissions, "as a way of ensuring that he would not be blamed for any breakdown of negotiations."[44]

But the conference participants were at an impasse. They could not heal the breaches between the richer and poorer provinces. Indeed, more than seven decades later, the conference remains noteworthy because it re-emphasized, and probably deepened, the divisions among them. Two of the nine provinces – Quebec and Ontario – fiercely resisted any extension of the wartime tax rental agreements. The situation disintegrated to such an extent that Ontario premier Drew cited German chancellor Adolf Hitler's *Mein Kampf* to illustrate the dangers of centralizing revenues, and Quebec premier Duplessis declared that the federal proposals would give birth to "little Hitlers."[45]

The canny Duplessis, whose Union Nationale had regained power in Quebec in August 1944, had no objection to federal help for the Maritimes, and he vowed to work with them to secure that help: "The Maritime provinces contributed a lot to the weal of this country, in every walk of life and in every human endeavor."[46] But he would not consent to the continued centralization of his revenues: "Temporary payments, or so-called generous subsidies, cannot compensate for permanent rights, and once those rights are impaired or abandoned the results may be disastrous ... The province of Quebec is always in favour of cooperation, always against complicity."[47] That stand, which would endure for the next decade, ensured that Quebec would play a "truly pivotal role" in the creation of equalization.[48] The premier actually left before the start of the last afternoon session in May 1946. As *Le Devoir* reported, his supporters planned an "enthusiastic reception" at the train station; one admirer praised "his defence of our rights ... without bending" at the conference.[49]

Meanwhile, during that final brutal week, Ontario premier Drew maintained that the Commonwealth government had just renewed its rental of all state income taxes in return for an astonishing 18.5 percent of the revenues. That worked out to £40 million for the states or close to $200 million Canadian dollars for a population of 7.5 million people. The states had secured "a very much larger percentage of [Commonwealth] income tax."[50]

Drew and King were political enemies: the Ontario premier, who was a lawyer from southwestern Ontario, had been fiercely critical of King's cautious approach to conscription – as well as his overall handling of the war. So his challenge to the proposed tax rental renewals was another red flag. Health Minister Claxton, who was an idealistic if thin-skinned Montreal lawyer, countered that, in Australia, the states raised "a very large percentage of their revenue from income tax," so their compensatory grants had to be larger. The Commonwealth government raised funds from other sources, such as taxes on real estate. Given that situation, Ottawa's proposals were "reasonable, fair and comprehensive."[51] Also, he added tartly, the current rate of exchange put the size of the Australian grants at C$144 million, not the C$200 million that Drew alleged.[52]

A day later, Finance Minister J.L. Ilsley argued that the Commonwealth had increased its grants to the states by only 17 percent, whereas the dominion proposals increased grants by 59 percent.[53] Nova Scotia premier Angus L. Macdonald, who had returned to provincial politics in August 1945, pointedly interjected that the Commonwealth government was "still making [additional] grants under the Commonwealth Grants Commission." And then he gave the exact 1944–45 figures for South Australia, Western Australia, and Tasmania.[54]

Drew responded that land taxes constituted only 1 percent of the Commonwealth government's revenues.⁵⁵ The issue – which was a symbol of the general ill will – would not go away. Health Minister Claxton returned to the topic in what was virtually the last hour. Unlike Canada, the Commonwealth government had established "a very wide, almost comprehensive system of social security for which it pays."⁵⁶ Canada was well behind in the provision of social security.

THE CONFERENCE FAILS

In the end, the provinces disagreed with each other – and *all* provinces objected to the size of Ottawa's proposed grants. Claxton was dashed, and his lament for the loss of Ottawa's dreams and schemes was eloquent: "Far from being 'Ottawa,' we who represent the Federal government here represent the people who elected us ... we represent the people of all of Canada, of every province, of every part, and of every race. In these discussions sometimes it is very easy to refer to others as 'they.'"⁵⁷

The Dominion-Provincial Conference adjourned on 1 May 1946 with little agreement on anything – and no firm date for a further meeting. The premiers returned to their provincial capitals, nurturing grievances. Many were anxious to pin the blame on others. Historian James Struthers singles out Drew and latterly Duplessis for the impasse because both provinces wanted to regain their fiscal autonomy. Ontario wanted to off-load "as many of its costs as possible onto the federal treasury and [to prevent] ... raids by weaker provinces on its wealth."⁵⁸

In his diary, King had two scapegoats. First, he blamed the Bank of Canada for its continued push to centralize revenues. Second, he concluded incorrectly that the provinces would eventually wane in relative power, even though "that [was] still a long way off."⁵⁹ Meanwhile, Ottawa should let the provinces resume control "over certain fields of taxation," interfering only to maintain "certain standards."⁶⁰

Claxton, King added sourly, but probably sagely, had made "too many commitments in the matter of social reform, particularly any commitments for legislation involving more in the way of taxation by a levy on all classes."⁶¹ Now, King noted, social legislation would have to "follow on later" – which was the prime minister's code for postponing action.⁶² He felt "neither elation nor depression ... The failure to reach agreement is only part of the spirit of the times ... The world is full of hate and unrest and strife. The spirit of the devil let loose."[63] King vowed to warn Ilsley against the imposition of further taxes: attention should be focused on veterans and on immediate needs, such as housing, while deferring further social programs.[64]

In effect, Claxton had tried to go too fast in a difficult federation with fiscally and economically unequal provinces. The timing simply was not right. As historian P.E. Bryden notes, early postwar efforts to create "a coherent system of equalization were destined to failure until two preconditions were met: the federal government began into tap into Ontario's rich fiscal capacity, and Ontario agreed on a political level to this form of redistribution."[65] In effect, the Ontario economy had to generate more revenue for Ottawa – and for the provincial government – before sharing would become acceptable.

That was certainly one of the key reasons for the débacle. The 1945–46 Dominion-Provincial Conference set the tone for the postwar years of the 1940s, ensuring that there was little expansion of the social safety net. The powerful federal government could not even contemplate the creation of genuine equalization: that is, *non-conditional* federal grants to the poorer provinces based upon an apparently neutral formula. Ottawa still wanted to centralize revenues, albeit temporarily, to maintain control of the purse strings, to smooth out economic cycles – and to influence how the bulk of the money was spent. Instead of funding social programs, the prime minister put federal funds towards national reconstruction projects such as highways and towards defence measures to combat Communism.

But King remained caught between the defenders of provincial identity and the lobbyists for universal social programs, which now included some provincial premiers, such as Saskatchewan's T.C. Douglas. In the years ahead, the voices of those groups would become louder. The 1945–46 Dominion-Provincial Conference had fuelled the aspirations of many Canadians for better social security. That vision would not abate.

But, first, Ottawa had to learn to let go.

THE AUSTRALIANS DO BETTER

The Australians also faced problems with postwar reconstruction. At a Commonwealth-state conference during late 1942, Canberra had asked for constitutional amendments to "enable a return to a stable peacetime footing."[66] The states agreed to transfer fourteen legislative powers for such matters as commodity marketing and corporate regulation to Canberra for a trial period of not less than five years. But they would not consent to permanent constitutional amendments. Even that limited measure did not pass unanimously in the state legislatures. A follow-up referendum in August 1944 secured acceptance only in South and Western Australia. And that was the end of that constitutional initiative. A Bank of Canada memorandum on Australia speculated that there was an "underlying desire that the States shall remain sovereign states and that the federal government [in Australia] should remain weak [the Commonwealth government was actually not weak]."[67]

But that unsigned postwar memorandum – which, based on internal indications, dates to 1945 – also examined the remarkable extent of Australia's social security benefits. Prior to 1945–46, the Commonwealth had transferred money into its National Welfare Fund for unemployment and sickness benefits (which began in 1944), old-age pensions, and child benefits. It is worth remembering that Canberra had introduced the Child Endowment Act, 1941, to provide a small weekly payment to each citizen "who supported more than one child under 16 years of age, the sum being increased according to the number of children supported. There was no means test."[68]

The expansion of other social services was tougher. In 1938, Canberra had proposed a national health insurance scheme – but "the medical profession rejected the range of services to be covered and the proposed remuneration arrangements."[69] The legislation was not implemented. In 1944, the Commonwealth government passed another law to cover the cost of prescription drugs – but pharmacists challenged the law and it was found unconstitutional.[70]

The Hospital Benefits Act, 1945, survived a legal challenge: it subsidized public hospitals on the condition that they provided certain free services. But the federal Labour government was rattled by the High Court rejection of pharmacare – and it was uneasily aware that the Australian public (like the Canadian public) had high expectations of the state in peacetime. In 1946, it passed a constitutional amendment to transfer power over "pensions and social services of all kinds including medical, dental and hospital benefits" to the Commonwealth government.[71]

The amendment faced ratification under a tough process, which required approval "by an absolute majority of people and by a majority of the electors in a majority of the six States."[72] It sailed through: more than 54 percent of the electors and all six states approved the measure.[73] Starting in 1945–46, the Commonwealth government collected contributions for social security along with payroll taxes to fund health and social services, including care in public hospitals and the cost of medical prescriptions.

Australia was well ahead of Canada, and the comparison underlined the complications and sensitivities of provincial rights. The contrast was vivid, despite Australia's failure to transfer, even temporarily, key state powers such as corporate regulation to Canberra. Australia had managed the near impossible in a federation: it had introduced health care insurance and pharmacare despite the strains of postwar adjustment.

The most pressing worry in Australia was now economic. The Bank of Canada rather smugly summarized the Australian situation: "For some time at least the level of demand will be in excess of the resources available to produce goods and services and conflict will arise between investment goods or consumption goods, public investment or private." In the long run, investment would "contribute more to the maintenance of the standard of living than would the satisfaction of the full demand for consumption goods after the war."[74] Australia would have to continue rationing and price controls until "a new balance" was achieved.[75]

In turn, the Australians examined Canada's situation. In late May 1945, they noted that Ottawa was about to remove 80 percent of the wartime controls on business and industry. But Munitions Minister C.D. Howe warned that price controls would remain "for months, and maybe years ... After the battles of Europe and Asia, we will still have the battle of inflation.[76] In early September 1945, High Commission diplomats passed on the news that Canada was reintroducing meat rationing in order to share supplies with southern Europe, including Greece, Albania, and Yugoslavia, where "very many deaths are still taking place due to starvation."[77] Victory did not always bring peace.

TOMMY DOUGLAS AND THE POSTWAR PRESSURE FOR EXPANDED SOCIAL SECURITY

Tommy Douglas saw so many sides to Mackenzie King. When Douglas first encountered the prime minister in 1935, he was an impatient member of Parliament, barely thirty-one years old, representing his rural Saskatchewan riding for the Co-operative Commonwealth Federation. He watched a politician, whose speeches could last four hours or longer, when "ninety percent of the rural people [in Douglas's riding] were on relief." Douglas was taken aback: "We'd just come through the Regina riot, and had this feeling of urgency that we ought to be doing something. And here I was, catapulted into the House of Commons and watching this stout, courteous, elderly gentleman talking for hours."[78] Meanwhile, across the border, US president Franklin Roosevelt was offering "dynamic leadership ... rallying the people of the United States behind his great campaign against poverty, against a nation ill-fed, ill-clad, and ill-housed."[79]

In later years, Douglas witnessed a more estimable side to King's character. In 1939, in "one of the most moving scenes in Parliament," he watched the prime minister rise in the House of Commons to praise CCF MP J.S. Woodsworth – just before the long-time Social Democrat spoke in opposition to the declaration of the Second World War.[80] King warned MPs that they should be respectful: Woodsworth "had been the conscience of the Canadian Parliament for a quarter of a century; men of his calibre were an ornament to any Parliament and he hoped Mr. Woodsworth would be listened to accordingly."[81] Douglas was impressed.

But there was one facet of King's character that Douglas always understood. As he explained decades later, the prime minister "wrote his speeches with a back door in every sentence, so that he could back out of anything. Every sentence was qualified by another sentence, which gave him a perfect escape."[82] In the postwar years, as the premier of Saskatchewan at the endless Dominion-Provincial Conference, Douglas became determined to close the escape hatch. He had thoroughly approved of King's Green Paper proposals to expand social security – and its tax rental deals to centralize revenues.

He endorsed Ottawa's Keynesian approach to the economy to maintain full employment and economic growth. He also concluded that the tax rental deals were fair: "There are a great many corporations that make their money in our [have-not] provinces but don't pay corporation taxes, income taxes, or inheritance taxes in our province."[83] If those tax revenues remained centralized in return for generous federal grants, there might be enough money to expand social security. Douglas set out to convert the very recalcitrant prime minister to expanded social security, using his own promises to trap him.

But King had abandoned those Green Paper proposals after the failure of the Dominion-Provincial Conference. The prime minister remained relieved. He was unwilling to tread too heavily on the provinces' constitutional turf, and he was cautious about assuming more expensive and expansive responsibilities. The Green Paper plan on health insurance alone committed Ottawa to covering three-fifths of the cost at an estimated $150 million.[84] King's government eventually signed tax rental renewals with seven of the nine provinces; only Quebec and Ontario refused to participate. In turn, Douglas resolved to hold King to his Green Paper. But the prime minister had reached his limits.

SOCIAL ACTIVISM STARTS TO STRENGTHEN

Throughout the early postwar years, King wanted to preserve cash for spending on infrastructure during downturns and for defence during the Cold War. In turn, advocacy groups and their political supporters, such as Douglas, tailored their pleas for expanded social programs to counter Ottawa's resistance. Douglas argued that improved old-age pensions would smooth out the fiscal cycle, funnelling cash to poorer Canadians to spend during recessions. The compensatory grants in the tax rental deals would flatten out regional downturns, ensure economic stability, and strengthen national ties. Social programs would also deepen resistance to Communism and loyalty to the Canadian way of life.

Such arguments made little impact. But as federal politicians and officials worked to renew the wartime tax rental deals for 1947–52, they were uneasily aware that they were running out of string. The Green Paper had aroused hopes that social advocates could not abandon. Advocacy groups, some provincial premiers, and other politicians and academics, especially those in the Rest of Canada, became an increasingly persistent force. Budgetary trade-offs became progressively more difficult. But Ottawa could not find a compromise between the defenders of provincial rights and the activists for social security. Non-conditional equalizing grants to the poorer provinces remained inconceivable.

The pressure for expanded social security had actually deepened before the 1945–46 Dominion-Provincial Conference officially failed. In March 1946, in an important intervention, the Canadian Welfare Council lauded Ottawa's conference proposals, especially its Green

Paper. The federal government recognized that social security played an important role in "achieving high employment and adequate standards of living."[85] There was so much to do. Unemployment Insurance benefits were inadequate: Ottawa should boost wage rates in depressed areas and industries, which would automatically raise UI payments. But the fear of dependency remained vivid. "Insurance benefits must obviously be somewhat less than wage rates," the Welfare Council observed, "some of which are now very low indeed."[86] Ottawa should also offer grants to the provinces for a national health program, social assistance payments, and employment retraining.

Then it added a crucial, and prescient, caveat: Ottawa's transfers *"must guarantee that the poorer provinces have sufficient revenues to carry on their essential services of education, health, welfare, conservation, highways, etc., at a reasonable level."*[87] Such grants were pivotal for social reform – and Ottawa should "give the poorer provinces larger Dominion grants, on a per capita basis, than the richer provinces – which should freely accept such treatment in the interests of national unity and welfare."[88] But the council still linked such grants to *specific* initiatives.

The Welfare Council was also an early convert to the language of social rights, as opposed to social needs. It put a high priority on the redesign of the old-age pension, including the lowering of the age of qualification from seventy to sixty-five and the elimination of the despised means test. There were "great numbers of independent, hardworking, self-respecting people in Canada who can and do avoid 'relief' and other means-test schemes during their working lives, but cannot avoid the ignominy of the means-test after they retire from active work unless there are provided for them pensions *as a matter of right*."[89] That was one early voice among a growing chorus that was starting to talk about the *right* to social security when describing the requirements for the postwar world.

ON THE CUSP OF PROSPERITY

Life was easier for Canadians in their postwar world, and optimism was rising. Many had viewed the conflict as the Good War – that is, the just cause that had vanquished evil. That sentiment made any continuing privations at home and abroad easier to handle. By the fall of 1945, as the number of available ships escalated, Canada was bringing home one thousand military personnel per day of the roughly

500,000 stationed outside Canada. By March 1946, the process was essentially finished.[90] More than 40 percent of Canadian males between the ages of eighteen and forty-five had joined the military during the war, even though only 6 percent had any prewar military experience, mostly in the militia.[91]

The readjustment to civilian life after six years of war could be unnerving. Returning soldiers, particularly those who had been prisoners of war, found a radically different world from their Spartan, occasionally rowdy and often dangerous existence. Tales of infidelity, at home and abroad, haunted their families. One returning veteran found books inscribed "To my darling May, from John" along with another man's bankbook in her purse.[92] Many women were unhappy with their house-bound world after their independence in the workforce. Large numbers of women eventually returned to work, usually after their children were in school, and "typically found themselves streamlined into low-paying female job ghettos."[93] Canadian society was evolving in ways that many could scarcely grasp. The "traditional, conservative, and patriarchal postwar order" had largely vanished after six years of war with its legacy of "wartime black markets, strikes, rising illegitimacy, infidelity, VD, delinquency, divorce, quickie marriages, women in coveralls and khaki, and battle-hardened servicemen."[94]

But after the wild exhilarations and abject sorrows of wartime, there were many rewards, including the simple pleasures of stability. The veterans came home to a generous package of benefits, including free vocational training or university education or assistance in starting a farm or business.[95] The economy remained strong, and the dangerous spectre of inflation seemed under control. Many Canadian families managed to re-establish secure home lives. Jobs were plentiful. Social mobility seemed within grasp. Most men and women could glimpse a better world that they could almost touch.

Consumers were already seeing progress. Before the war ended, in March 1944, Canada had suspended meat rationing (which was temporarily reimposed in 1945), partly because large herds born in the early 1940s could no longer be held back from market. Alcohol rationing ended in August 1945 – although provincial liquor outlets often retained quotas. Rationing stopped slowly because Canada was shipping food to devastated postwar Europe: the last ration book was issued in September 1946.[96] Historian Jeffrey A. Keshen cites surveys showing that 21 percent of Canadians planned to buy a new car at the first opportunity and 22 percent wanted a new appliance.[97] Shortages in consumer goods such as clothing continued, but many Canadians were initially patient. There were exceptions: when Canada reapplied meat rationing in September 1945, coal miners in Alberta and British Columbia took a "work holiday" to demand a double ration of red meat. But Canadians knew that the worst was over.[98]

THE INCREASED PRESSURE FOR SOCIAL SECURITY

Many Canadians were aware of the calls for expanded social security from a formidable array of largely anglophone activists. At the annual National Council of Women (NCW) gathering in June 1946, local affiliates promoted cherished causes. The council was a non-partisan institution, founded in 1893 by fifteen hundred women under the presidency of Lady Ishbel Aberdeen, the spouse of the governor general, along with several prominent Canadian suffragists.[99] In the post-Second World War era, it was a federation of largely middle-class women who had the ear of still-condescending governments because the NCW was considered respectable.

Their causes were diverse. The delegates from Windsor, Ontario, called for the "early" resumption of the Dominion-Provincial Conference to hammer out constitutional amendments to meet "present day ideas of social services and ... modern economic conditions."[100] The resolution did not specify what that might entail – or how the first ministers could address the huge fiscal inequalities among the provinces. But the yearning was there.

The NCW's Vancouver affiliate called for subsidized rental housing for low-income Canadians, citing the proposals of the housing subcommittee of the Advisory Committee on Reconstruction.[101] That controversial wartime subcommittee had called on Ottawa to pick up the full tab for subsidies to low-income renters – and to loan money to municipalities to construct new public housing units. It also urged Ottawa to provide annual subsidies to local authorities to ensure that rents stayed low.[102] Those were big dreams.

The NCW from Peterborough, Ontario, wanted Ottawa to "enact some measure of National Health Insurance to be enforced along the same lines as Unemployment Insurance to replace the haphazard non-continuous form of Compulsory Insurance now in effect with the different employers."[103] The resolution implied that Canadians would pay for their health insurance through payroll deductions. There was no mention of the provinces, which were responsible for hospitals and health care, or of provincial inequality.

Other groups were also singing from the same idealistic if constitutionally addled songbook. In October 1947, the seventh annual convention of the Canadian Congress of Labour requested "a comprehensive social security plan for Canada," the abolition of the means test for the old-age pension, and a national program for low-rental housing.[104] The CCL was formed in 1940 as a merger between the All-Canadian Congress of Labour and the Canadian section of the Congress of Industrial Organizations, which was expelled from the Trades and Labor Congress of Canada at the request of squabbling American unionists.[105] Most of its founding members were social democrats who believed strongly that unions should be involved in politics. In 1945, the union had formally aligned itself with the CCF. But their resolution made no mention of what level of government would pay for programs – or what level of government would administer them. Fiscal inequalities among provinces were simply ignored.

In March 1948, the CCL reflected its members' hopes with another nudge: it regretted that Ottawa had not proceeded with the Green Paper of 1945, including "health insurance, increased old age pensions, unemployment assistance and similar benefits."[106] The CCL welcomed Health Minister Paul Martin's reassurance that the proposal had not been abandoned, "but it is obvious that a programme of the nature proposed is urgently needed."[107] Once again, there was no mention of provincial fiscal inequalities or the source of funding for those programs.

The inequalities among people and provinces remained glaring. In mid-1948, the Canadian Council of Churches, on behalf of ten churches and three affiliated groups, asked Prime Minister King to work with the provinces to enact "a comprehensive scheme of social insurance" that would "constitute a charter of social security for the whole of Canada."[108] The churches added that the social security program should be financed on a contributory basis "for all appropriate items, [and] participated in by the Dominion and all Provincial Governments."[109] There was no mention of how the poorer provinces would pay for programs that personal contributions alone could not cover.

Those major groups targeted the prime minister along with the dominion government in general. But federalism seemingly confused them. At best, they urged Ottawa to work with the provinces. Or they urged Ottawa to act on its own. Or they called upon taxpayers to pay through contributions to public insurance plans. But it is striking today that those advocacy groups did not tackle the huge challenge of federalism: fiscal inequality among the provinces. It was apparently up to governments to figure out how social programs could apply across the nation when poorer provinces could not afford them.

The voices of these disparate groups were becoming stronger. The federal Liberals could not completely ignore the public expectations that they had aroused, especially because many Canadians knew what other nations had done for their postwar citizenry. In a report on a roundtable at the University of Toronto in May 1948, social work professor John S. Morgan offered a blunt warning: public opinion in Canada accepted the "need in a complex industrial society for programs of social security" that would protect people "against the main hazards of modern times on a predictable insurance basis."[110] In response, he insisted, the dominion government had increasingly assumed responsibility for social welfare.[111]

But Morgan also understood the complications that dominion control would entail. There was a "battle of wits and words" at the roundtable over the difficulty of establishing adequate social security in a federal state: "The constitutional issues were recognized."[112] Most delegates concluded that contributory insurance schemes should be a federal operation.[113] Perhaps Ottawa could use grants to fund other nationwide but provincially administered programs. Morgan made no mention of how the poorer provinces could pay their share. So far, all levels of government had "shirked the problem" and concealed the "the real costs of having no integrated plan for social security... patching and repairing the neglect of [Canada's] human resources."[114] But the Canadian people wanted "something more constructive and more positive."[115]

MACKENZIE KING'S POSTWAR WORLD

Throughout his last years in power, Mackenzie King paid little attention to fiscal inequality or social programs. He was exhausted from the war – and from the need to ensure that the peace remained calm, prosperous, and safe. His heart was quietly failing, and his blood pressure was high. He sought solace in a world of spirits that included his beloved mother and the late US president Franklin Roosevelt. He was seemingly incapable of inspiring deep affection among the voters. And his instincts were usually to resist the more activist government that many Canadians now craved.

He took refuge in continuity. He sought to preserve the ethnic composition of Canadian society in the postwar era – even though Canada's increasing participation in world affairs ensured a "selectively more open" immigration policy.[116] On 1 May 1947, he told the House of Commons that Ottawa would encourage the immigration of those who could "advantageously be absorbed in our national economy" and who would not "make a fundamental alteration in the character of our population." In particular, King ruled out "any considerable Oriental immigration."[117] But Canada needed skilled and unskilled labour, and the economies of many still devastated European countries could not support their workers. Despite King's cautious approach, between 1946 and 1962, Canada admitted almost 2.15 million immigrants, or roughly 126,600 per year.[118]

More than a third of those immigrants were from Britain. Many others were so-called "displaced persons" who had fled the Soviet takeovers in Eastern Europe, often with only a handful of belongings. Former journalist Barry Broadfoot recorded the stories of such postwar arrivals. There was the small family that escaped from Latvia, clambering aboard a fishing boat to Sweden and then onto a Red Cross ship to Halifax and finally to a displaced persons camp in Ajax, Ontario. The federal government assigned them to work on a sugar beet farm in Alberta, but their six-year-old son got measles so, to their relief, they could not get on the train. Instead, the family picked fruit in Niagara Falls orchards. The harvesters included the grandfather, who was a former Latvian railways minister before the war; the university-trained father, who spoke English; the mother, who had somehow managed to pack one small suitcase before they fled their home; and the son, who was thrilled to earn three dollars in one week in the orchard but who later recollected, "There was a lot of culture shock. A lot."[119]

Meanwhile, the veterans were coming home to a better world. On 1 October 1941, the federal Liberal government had issued an order that promised rehabilitation assistance to all veterans and specified that military service would constitute insurable employment under the Unemployment Insurance Act of June 1940.[120] The package of benefits was generous – so they could restart their lives. But their domestic fates were mixed. Some service members returned to what Broadfoot dubbed, "Happily Ever After." One Calgary man came home to "quite a party" because everyone brought ration coupons for liquor to his parents' house. His father presented him with a car. His mother packed a picnic lunch. Then he drove past a woman cycling up a hill that he had taken to dances in high school. He took her on his picnic. They got engaged that day – despite the objections of their parents. "There was somebody up there watching us," he happily recollected decades later.[121]

Others were left with what Broadfoot called "Broken Hearts, Broken Dreams." One man recounted the fate of his buddy in the service corps who married on an embarkation furlough and then headed overseas after a few days with a young woman that he "hardly knew." His friend returned three years later to realize that he and his wife "didn't have one damn thing to say to each other ... There was an awful lot of unhappy couples after the war."[122]

Canadians were looking for stability – and not always finding it.

MACKENZIE KING AND THE RENEWED TAX RENTAL DEALS

The prime minister wanted peace and prosperity. And he could not tolerate any more messy conferences with the provinces after May 1946. The second round of the tax rental deals, which ran from 1947 to 1952, were done through one-on-one negotiations. They contained adjustments for fiscal need, partly because the compensatory grants offered more money per capita for each percentage point of tax than the poorer provinces could collect on their own. As Finance Minister J.L. Ilsley explained in 1947, the payments ensured that the "weaker provinces would share equally" from productivity gains in the three taxation fields.[123] Quebec did not sign the rental deals on constitutional principle; Ontario did not sign because it objected to the amount of compensation and the loss of autonomy.

But Saskatchewan premier Tommy Douglas had joined the chorus of activists who were calling for expanded social programs, especially for health care. The premier, who is now honoured as the founder of Medicare, started his campaign mere weeks after the 1945–46 Dominion-Provincial Conference dissolved. On 29 June, he told Ilsley that his province would sign a tax rental deal, and he called for immediate steps "to establish social security on a national basis."[124] When Ilsley's answer was vague, Douglas wrote to King, arguing that his proposed social security program had been left at "loose ends."[125] On 15 July 1946, King responded that he was waiting for "sufficient acceptance" of the tax rental deals.[126] That was a ploy – and Douglas recognized it.

Douglas would always speak for many of the poorer, more left-leaning provinces after his Depression-era experience as a Baptist minister and an ardent proponent of the social gospel. He wanted more federal money for social security, and he was impatient with Quebec's insistence on autonomy over its revenues. He would never comprehend Quebec's resistance to Ottawa's push for revenue centralization, nor would he ever grasp the depth of Quebec premier Maurice Duplessis's social conservatism.

It was an unexpected and somewhat unsettling side to an estimable politician. He later maintained that Canadians "had wasted a lot of time arguing about federal grants for education, highways, and the development of natural resources."[127] Ottawa should have divided the revenues from income taxes and succession duties in the postwar era more fairly, or made more room for the provinces to apply those taxes. Provinces should be able to accept non-conditional federal grants *"without any strings attached* ... The sources of [provincial] revenue have not kept pace with the increasing responsibilities laid on our [provincial] doorstep."[128] His inability to understand Quebec's distinct society would persist throughout the ensuing decade.

To Mackenzie King's dismay, other provinces joined this campaign. On 5 July 1946, New Brunswick premier John McNair told Ilsley of his "regret" at the postponement of the social security proposals, suggesting that the expansion of old-age pensions could be implemented separately.[129] Nova Scotia premier Angus L. Macdonald telegrammed Ilsley, pointedly asking for the details of Ottawa's proposed health care grants and its assistance for the unemployed employables. On 5 July, Ilsley told Macdonald that health care grants were "not included in the present [tax rental] offer" and that unemployment assistance was "necessarily dependent upon agreement of all the provinces" with that offer.[130] In mid-October, Macdonald told King that it seemed "illogical" to settle the tax rental deals with individual provinces "and then to confer on dependent matters the dignity of consideration by a general conference."[131] King replied that a conference would serve no "useful purpose" unless "the attitude of certain provincial governments has altered."[132]

The prime minister had found his "back door": he could not recall the premiers to discuss social security until *all* of the tax rental deals were signed. And he used that excuse. Repeatedly. In early October, Alberta premier Ernest C. Manning made a "personal appeal" to King to recall the Dominion-Provincial Conference because the issue "so vitally concerns the welfare of the people of Canada as a whole."[133] Once again, King argued that there could be no conference until there were tax rental deals with every province.

Douglas tried again. He asked King to recall the conference to discuss "social security, unemployment, health insurance and old-age pensions ... these matters cannot be delayed indefinitely ... It should be possible to find certain minimum services at least on which all the provinces and the Federal Government could agree to proceed."[134] King ducked again – with politely expressed regret.

SOME PROVINCES DO NOT GIVE UP

There were other reasons for Ottawa's hesitancy in expanding social spending. The federal government wanted to conserve its available cash to protect Canada against another Depression. Finance Minister Douglas Abbott, who moved from the national defence portfolio to replace Ilsley in December 1946, perfectly captured Ottawa's conversion to Keynesian economics on 24 January 1947. The minister outlined the progress in negotiating tax rental deals – and then he asserted Ottawa's aims: "It was the Dominion Government's hope ... that all governments would be in a position to act effectively to prevent a repetition of the calamitous days of the 30s ... Tax agreements are desirable ... to meet the challenge of possible post-war deflation and depression."[135] The Lennoxville Quebec-born Abbott had served overseas during the First World War, and his memories of the recession following that conflict remained vivid.

Douglas dropped the issue of expanded social security for ten months. Then, in mid-August 1947, he again tackled King. He reminded the prime minister of his exact words in his telegram on 15 July 1946: "As soon as there is a sufficient acceptance of the proposed tax agreements we shall be ready to explore in a general conference or otherwise the possibility of working out mutually satisfactory arrangements" in public investment and social security.[136] Since seven provinces had now signed tax rental deals with Ottawa, surely King should call a conference "immediately to work out details for implementing proposals regarding old age pensions health insurance unemployment and public investment."[137] In the cryptic language of telegrams, the premier went straight to the point.

King replied the next day, also by telegram, referring Douglas to Finance Minister Abbott's budget speech on 29 April 1947. Then, Abbott had said the government still hoped to secure provincial approval for its proposals at the 1945–46 conference, including the "development of an efficient and flexible tax system designed to promote the expansion of employment and incomes, as well as a comprehensive program for the co-operation of the Dominion and provincial governments in the field of public investment and social security."[138] Now, King told Douglas in telegraph shorthand, "I am doubtful if government would be prepared to go beyond position stated by Mr. Abbott in Parliament."[139] It was a long-winded way of saying "No."

Those discussions took place as other premiers argued with King about the resumption of the conference or their tax rental deals. Ontario premier Drew became embroiled in a nasty four-month exchange with King: the premier wanted the prime minister to recall the conference; the prime minister insisted that the premiers had to agree on the tax rental deals *before* he would recall the Conference to discuss "mutually satisfactory arrangements relating to public investment and social welfare."[140] It was hardball.

The animosity crackled in their exchanges. Ontario insisted that the federal compensatory grants for the surrender of its tax revenues were so low that it could not meet its responsibilities. Drew wanted a conference to negotiate while Ottawa was putting "unfair pressure" on needy provinces through one-on-one deals.[141] By mid-October, Drew was so irate that he released his correspondence with King – although the posturing in those letters indicates that had clearly been the aim of both politicians all along.[142] For the next decade, Ontario premiers simply walked away from Ottawa's tax rental deals (from 1947 to 1952) *or* they drove hard bargains for compensation (from 1952 to 1957).

Quebec objected to the tax rental deal on constitutional grounds – although Premier Duplessis was more polished than Drew in his rejection. In peacetime, Duplessis initially *seemed* willing to allow Ottawa to collect income taxes – but he set impossible conditions upon any potential deal. He concluded that if he actually surrendered access to revenues that he had the constitutional right to collect, he could no longer protect Quebec's rights, including its unique approach to social policy.

The issue was particularly important for Quebec. The province had introduced corporate income taxes in 1884.[143] It would introduce personal income taxes in 1954, partly as a gesture of defiance against Ottawa. But Duplessis flatly refused to surrender his province's right to collect succession duties. As he argued in late April 1946, that tax was associated with "traditions, traditions of loyalty, traditions of family life, traditions with regard to estates and who should inherit estates ... [It] forms part of our soul, and the soul is indivisible."[144] In effect, Quebec was unwilling to surrender one of its hegemonic roles in the cultural life of its citizens: it wanted to remain the primary presence during the legal rites of generational change. Nine months later, the premier formally ruled out a tax rental deal at a press conference: "To participate in the violation of the federative pact ... would be complicity, not collaboration."[145] The province would not sign another accord.

Other provinces squabbled over which province had secured the better tax rental pact with Ottawa. But many premiers agreed with the reassuring economic logic behind the deals. As Manitoba premier Stuart Garson argued on 26 January 1946, the pacts ensured that Ottawa had enough money to smooth out economic downturns: "One of the surest ways to destroy our federal system" would be to ensure that "no government has the authority and the ability ... to prevent the return of the industrial unemployment and the low farm incomes which were so typical of the pre-war conditions."[146] Garson remembered the Depression on the Prairies only too well – and he wanted Ottawa to have funds for stimulus.

But federal politicians and bureaucrats surely dreaded the renewal of the five-year deals with their one-on-one disputes and their impossible dreams. The issue of revenue centralization split the participants between the "haves" and "have nots" – *and* between the defenders of provincial rights and the proponents of expanded social security. These were not tidy splits: individual provinces adopted nuanced approaches to Ottawa and to each other. Despite changes in their political leadership, however, provincial governments kept generally consistent positions over the postwar decade. During King's last years in power, the federation was at an uncomfortable impasse.

FEDERATIONS REQUIRE EQUALIZATION TO SURVIVE

Many politicians and bureaucrats now understood what was to blame for this postwar stalemate: the very nature of federalism itself – especially Canadian federalism with its strong provincial identities. As Premier Douglas and the Saskatchewan government shrewdly maintained on 6 August 1945 – the day *after* that failed conference commenced: "The federal system of government cannot be commended as giving a maximum of convenience ... [But] A federal union is certainly to be preferred to no union at all ... it seems reasonable to urge that the federal system should be made as workable as possible."[147] Without an equalization program in place, Douglas was wasting his time.

More than two years later, social reformer Harry Cassidy summarized that lesson in an influential report on Canadian social security, which he wrote at the request of Health Minister Paul Martin. The University of Toronto sociologist outlined the huge gaps in social security coverage. And he stressed how far Canada lagged behind other developed nations: the United States with its Social Security Act, 1935; New Zealand with its Social Security Act, 1938; Great Britain's extensive postwar program based on the report of social reformer Sir William Beveridge; and Australia's postwar reforms.

Canada was far behind – because its federal system was extremely difficult: "A major reason for Canada's delay in building social services up to good modern standards has been the acute conflict between the Dominion and the provinces regarding finances and legislative jurisdiction." Many provinces were reluctant "to move forward vigorously on social security measures" until Ottawa and the provinces could agree on their roles. But dominion action was clearly difficult as long as some provinces objected to federal infringement "upon their traditional jurisdiction over health and welfare and as long as they [were] unwilling to agree to redistribution of the tax fields."[148]

It was a pivotal observation. Cassidy recognized the nation's quandary: Ottawa could not unilaterally barge onto the provincial turf of social programs, at least not in all provinces; but many poorer provinces lacked sufficient funds to implement roughly comparable programs to any in the richer provinces without impossibly high tax rates. Cassidy had a solution: Ottawa "should be actively interested in all aspects of social security. It should assist and encourage those parts of the program which are administered by the provincial and local governments by means of financial grants and technical services."[149] He did not explicitly address the need for equalizing grants; instead, he maintained, "minimum standards of service should be general throughout the country."[150] His advocacy eventually prompted Martin to push King to take small steps towards expanded health care.

AUSTRALIA AND INEQUALITY IN THE POSTWAR WORLD

As Canada worked through the complications of federalism, the Australians monitored the process – and the Canadians watched them enviously in return. When Bank of Canada researcher W. Elwynne Scott visited Australia for six weeks during the autumn of 1946, he produced a fourteen-page chronicle of Australian life, including its weather, its housing and trade policies, its industrial strategies, its living standards, and the decrepitude of its automobiles: "I had a couple of thrilling rides in a 1925 Ford touring and a 1921 Italian car of forgotten ancestry which made Alex Skelton's car look like a streamlined model."[151]

Scott concluded that Australia was "an ideal country for the little man. He can get enough to eat, decent housing and clothes and have reasonable leisure time. He is not 'pushed around' or made to feel particularly inferior in his occupation and he is not made unhappy by the sight of great wealth in the hands of the few."[152] By then, of course, Australia had developed a social security network. Canada's sister dominion had dealt with fiscal inequality among state governments in 1933 – and Canberra had summoned up sufficient constitutional power to create social programs.

KING FINALLY TAKES ACTION

In May 1948, Health Minister Martin warned the prime minister that the public was becoming more critical of his government's failure to provide health care funding. After reading Martin's letters, King confided to his diary that he had already been considering the proclamation of a nationwide social security minimum that could be "identified with my life's effort."[153] That might have been true. Then again, the prime minister was capable of self-deception in his diary – and he had not acted.

But Martin's warning about the possibility of electoral shifts stung him. In January 1948, he had indicated that he would resign later that year. Now, he worried that his inaction on social policy might have put the Liberal government at risk. A day after those musings, he told key ministers that health care would provide "a human side" for the Liberals in the upcoming election campaign.[154] Then he told the entire cabinet that he was aiming "in the direction of national minimum ... [That] would perhaps obviate having to take up other bits of social reform at present. *I did not want the party to do more than it really should.*"[155]

That was typical King: cautious to the end. But when he read a statement of his health care policy to the House of Commons on Friday, 14 May 1948, he was met with almost universal applause. He would start with federal health care grants totaling $30 million per year to all provincial governments – even if he did not have tax rental accords with Ontario and Quebec. Ottawa earmarked the money for surveys of the health status and needs of Canadians, hospital construction, and free diagnosis and treatment of selected disorders such as tuberculosis.[156] He "obtained Quebec's approval [for the grants] through personal diplomacy with its premier, Maurice Duplessis."[157] Ontario would also accept the federal funding. Federal efforts were minimal, far short of the Green Paper that Ottawa had championed with such aplomb in 1945. But it was a start. More important, those grants did *not* require matching grants from the provinces. So King did not have to tackle the issue of provincial fiscal inequality and the need for equalizing grants.

KING RETIRES ... SLOWLY

King's goodbye was prolonged, partly because he wanted to exceed the time in office of other prime ministers, and partly because he was superstitious about auspicious numbers. On 7 June 1946, he surpassed Prime Minister Sir John A. Macdonald's record time in office. In late January of 1948, he announced his retirement, calling for a leadership convention in the summer. On 20 April 1948, amid congratulatory "telegrams, flowers, and lots of reflection on the meaning of life," he exceeded the tenure of Britain's first prime minister, Sir Robert Walpole.[158]

The Liberal convention took place from 5 to 7 August 1948, which were the exact dates of the convention that had selected King in 1919. But King did not step down. With St-Laurent's consent, he toddled off to the United Nations General Assembly meeting in Paris and the Commonwealth prime ministers' conference in London. Back in Ottawa on 7 November, he finally resigned on Monday, 15 November. As his biographer Allan Levine notes briskly, "the age of Mackenzie King ended with heartfelt farewells and a huge sigh of relief from just about everyone in Ottawa."[159] Even then, he did not resign as an MP until his successor Louis St-Laurent dissolved Parliament for an election in April 1949.

He bequeathed a nation that was thriving amidst its newfound prosperity. In November 1948, as St-Laurent was sworn in as prime minister, Ottawa department stores were running full page advertisements for warm winter coats, toy train sets, and winter boots with the once almost unthinkable luxury of sheepskin linings. After years of wartime deprivation, the descriptions alone were enticing: "Exciting selling: Slenderizing Dark-Seam Nylons, $1.75." The Royal Winter Fair opened in Toronto with more than seventeen thousand livestock and poultry along with the "First Canadian Post-War Appearance" of the RCMP Musical Ride, fashion shows "for the ladies," and a flower show.[160] After wartime shortages, consumers could get coal – "as much of next winter's supply as your bin will hold" – in the size and grade they wanted.[161] The *Edmonton Journal* congratulated Alberta's Social Credit government on its expected 1948–49 oil revenues of $16 million. It predicted that revenues would grow as proven areas were expanded so that the government would "be 'sitting pretty' financially, very pretty indeed."[162] Many Canadian families were finally sitting pretty, too, and their confidence was fuelling a surprising Baby Boom.

But social programs for health care, pensions, and education were not expanding as Ottawa had so grandly promised during the heady days at the war's end.

CONCLUSION

After the stress of wartime, and the challenge of ensuring stability in the postwar era, Mackenzie King simply ran out of enthusiasm for more social change. He had introduced Unemployment Insurance and Family Allowances in wartime. Shortly before he retired, he offered federal grants for health care projects to the provinces.

But he did not contemplate the expansion of social programs through federal-provincial cooperation. So he did not have to face the fiscal and economic inequalities among the poorer and the richer provinces. He had done what he could comfortably handle – but most of his alluring Green Paper remained unfulfilled.

It was time to take comfort in his accomplishments – and to slip away. He would die on 22 July 1950. It would be up to St-Laurent to devise new social programs for the nation, along with the equalization program to support them.

9

The Compromise, 1948–57

It was that astute politician J.W. Pickersgill who summed up Louis St-Laurent's approach to governing with an apt comparison to his predecessor. Whenever Mackenzie King detected an almost insoluble problem, he did nothing until everyone agreed there was a problem. So when King found a solution, even if it was not first-rate, everyone concluded that King was a great statesman. In contrast, St-Laurent often found a solution before most Canadians, including some of his ministers, even knew there was a problem. And where did this talent get St-Laurent? "The verdict of the Canadian people was that Canada was an easy country to govern, and that anybody could govern Canada," declared Pickersgill as he comforted St-Laurent in the months after his election loss in June 1957, "and they decided to let anybody try."[1] That was a swipe at the new Progressive Conservative prime minister John Diefenbaker. St-Laurent remained inconsolable.

Pickersgill perceived what so many Canadians did not recognize, then and now. The deceptively avuncular corporate lawyer had dragged Canadian federalism, and some resistant premiers, from the nineteenth into the twentieth century. The prime minister came late to politics, relatively unscathed by partisan discord, and he brought an analytical approach to the nation's predicaments. When he recognized that the tax rental deals with the provinces had become a threat to federation unity, he changed his strategy. Instead of pacts with individual provinces to collect three key taxes, St-Laurent devised and oversaw the search for an alternative system that preserved the federation.

He was involved every step of the way, sometimes leaving the lead to Finance Minister Walter Harris, but always on top of the file, and pivotal to the solution. He sat through long meetings with premiers from the wealthier provinces who resented the amount of money that Ottawa wanted to transfer to their poorer kin. He negotiated with premiers from the poorer provinces who remained unsatisfied with their share of federal funds. He dealt with premiers who simply did not understand Quebec's desire to preserve its rights and responsibilities.

It was a thankless undertaking. No province – with the possible exception of Quebec – was content. But equalization ensured that the poorer provinces could deliver roughly similar levels of services for roughly similar levels of taxation. With their revenue needs (partly!) met, even the poorer provinces could now introduce and support social programs such as hospital care and, eventually, Medicare that Ottawa would partly fund.

At first glance, this ingenious transfer scheme looked simple – partly because federal cabinet members opted for a formula that they could explain to their constituents if they were pushed. But, during the months before and after the enabling legislation received royal assent on 31 July 1956, federal politicians were rarely pushed because most Canadians did not understand what St-Laurent had accomplished. Ottawa and the provinces were dealing with a flourishing Baby Boom, surges of anxious immigrants, more women entering the workforce, economic booms and brief busts, and unrelenting demands for improved infrastructure and expanded social security. The federation could no longer tolerate the huge fiscal inequalities among its partners.

Equalization grants addressed that plight. They were non-conditional, and they were calculated using an apparently neutral formula. Provinces did not have to fill out application forms. The program's very existence resolved a difficult confrontation with Quebec, which had refused to allow Ottawa to collect its taxes in peacetime. As a result, it had lost generous compensatory federal grants.

It was a masterful scheme. But the years between Mackenzie King's retirement on 15 November 1948 and the distribution of the first federal cheques on 1 April 1957 were turbulent. Ottawa and the provinces squabbled. Quebec nationalism revived. The Communist threat ensured that defence spending took priority in the federal budget to the dismay of social activists in the Rest of Canada who became increasingly assertive and occasionally hostile. The Maritime provinces were deeply unsatisfied with the size of their grants. Ontario premier Leslie Frost resented the fact that his richer province did not qualify for equalization, and he demanded an increased share of personal income tax under the tax rental deals for infrastructure and services. After an unsatisfactory First Ministers' Conference to discuss equalization and the tax rental deals in early March 1956, Frost was ominous: "It will not be too long before the Federal Government regrets the action it took today."[2] The premier was effectively invoking provincial rights against what he viewed as a federal revenue grab.

St-Laurent did not properly address those damaging complaints of unfair treatment, partly out of concern for Ottawa's bottom line. In retaliation, in late April 1957, Frost threw his powerful campaign team behind Progressive Conservative leader Diefenbaker. The premier made supportive speeches in different communities, occasionally on the platform with the Tory leader, lauding him as the "only one man who can find that just solution [of the tax sharing problem] for the little men and the little women of Canada."[3] Equalization, that well-meaning remedy for the ills of fiscal federalism, became an improbable issue in the June 1957 federal election, and it contributed to St-Laurent's loss. It was a deeply ironic dénouement for the prime minister's ingeniously modern remedy for sharing.

LOUIS ST-LAURENT BECOMES PRIME MINISTER

Advocacy groups drew new resolve when King retired, assuming that his successor would be more amendable to change. What about the Green Paper on social security? When would Ottawa work with the provinces to implement such plans as unemployment assistance for those who had exhausted their Unemployment Insurance? What about health and hospital insurance? Many groups did not care if such programs were under federal or provincial constitutional jurisdiction. Some groups understood intuitively that Ottawa and the provinces had to collaborate in some manner if such programs were to function effectively. Others wanted Ottawa to pick up the tab. *Very* few recognized the huge impediment of fiscal and economic inequality among federation members. Talk of equalization was *always* a government insiders' game.

But St-Laurent's very presence seemed to promise a new era. The new prime minister was a dignified lawyer, the son of an anglophone mother and a francophone father, who had learned to speak English because his wife refused to speak French. Louis St-Laurent, in turn, learned to read and write in English first, before he attended a local

French-language separate school in Quebec's Eastern Townships. He was bilingual and bicultural, and a firm exponent of harmony among francophones and anglophones. As a scholarly lawyer in the 1920s and 1930s, he had often pleaded cases on behalf of the governments of Quebec and Canada; he had also argued for minority rights such as the Jewish demand for representation on Montreal's Protestant Board of School Commissioners.[4]

He was a Liberal supporter but not an overtly partisan presence in his province. In December 1941, when Mackenzie King needed to replace his trusted justice minister Ernest Lapointe who had died in November, he turned to St-Laurent. By May 1942, he was Quebec's senior minister. In 1946, he agreed to King's plea that he remain in politics despite the formidable financial and personal challenges. He moved to the external affairs portfolio, earning his officials' respect and gratitude.[5]

He was King's logical successor at a time of cautious optimism. Four-and-a-half months after he took his oath of office as prime minister, at midnight on 31 March 1949, the impoverished colony of Newfoundland joined the federation as the tenth province after two divisive referenda. St-Laurent had been the head of those negotiations in the summer of 1947 and during the fall of 1948 – and he had been "Newfoundland's strongest supporter in the King cabinet."[6] Canada now proudly stretched from its western to its eastern to its northern seas. A day later, radio commentator Joey Smallwood, who had cajoled dubious Newfoundlanders into Canada, became his province's first premier (a position he would hold for almost twenty-three years). A few days after that, Canada joined the North Atlantic Treaty Organization, which was another step towards the nation's growing prominence as a middle power in an increasingly menacing postwar world.

But St-Laurent did not initially tackle the challenge of expanding social programs, partly because the provinces were still divided on the next round of tax rental deals. The international situation was also fraught. From the early years of the postwar era, with the Red Army already in control of much of Eastern Europe, fears about the spread of Communism preoccupied the West, especially after the Soviet Union acquired the atomic bomb. Those sentiments deepened with the Korean War, which stretched from June 1950 to July 1953. Canada participated in that conflict at the behest of the United Nations Security Council. It also beefed up its defence budget in response to the perceived Communist threat, setting up yet another tug-of-war between spending on social security and spending on defence.

Undaunted, many advocacy groups and politicians portrayed this tension as artificial, arguing that a strong society was a strong defence. In February 1949, the Canadian Teachers' Federation (CTF) urged St-Laurent to earmark federal funding for education to address the fiscal inequalities across provinces and municipalities. The federation was founded in Calgary in July 1920 with representatives from the four Western provinces and Ontario; it soon expanded to include Quebec and the Maritimes. By 1948, it had a central office in Ottawa – and it had become a respected voice on educational and social justice issues. Now the CTF lamented the inequities that plagued children from birth: "Surely, the educational opportunity of the Canadian child should not depend entirely upon the wealth of the province of his birth, the real property of his municipality and the generosity of the individual property owner."[7]

The teachers' federation *did* understand the Constitution: it specified that control over education should remain with the provinces. But Ottawa should provide "a straight per pupil capita grant" to the provinces as long as they did not lower their own educational spending.[8] It added pointedly: "To the degree that the education of Canadian boys and girls is deficient or insufficient, we reduce the prosperity of our nation and *increase the vulnerability of our national security*."[9]

In March 1949, University of Toronto sociologist Harry Cassidy suggested to Justice Minister Stuart Garson that Ottawa should hold a series of dominion-provincial conferences on specific issues, especially social security. Ottawa could consider a constitutional amendment that would allow the federal government to administer contributory social insurance measures. It should also introduce a program to assist those whose Unemployment Insurance payments had expired. "As economic conditions become more difficult the old 'relief' problems of the 1930s will reappear," Cassidy warned.[10] He was one of the few experts who acknowledged the constitutional problems of expanding social security. But, by putting the onus on Ottawa, he simply skated over potential objections from provinces such as Quebec.

A few days later, the Canadian Congress of Labour made its ninth annual presentation to the federal government with the pointed observation that "our recommendations in the past have not been as effective as we had wished."[11] It was a clear challenge to St-Laurent: the CCL called for "free medical, hospital and dental services, as well as sickness and accident insurance."[12] Although Ottawa was cooperating with the provinces and municipalities – this was a reference to King's national health grants – there had been "undue delay" in the implementation of a national health insurance scheme.[13] After all, there were superb models to emulate: Ottawa should examine "the British system of social security."[14] Old-age pensions were "particularly urgent." Few workers had "pension plans of any kind, and most of these plans [were] altogether inadequate for health and decency. Millions of Canadian citizens have nothing to look forward to at the end of their working lives but destitution or penury."[15]

The author of this memo, presumably the CCL's brilliant research director and future senator Eugene Forsey, called for constitutional amendments so that Ottawa could institute a nationwide social security program. Social programs "are of common interest to the Canadian people" and could only be dealt with "in an adequate manner" if such amendments were made.[16] Thus, the CCL ignored the major problem of provincial fiscal inequality with the simple expedient of putting the onus on Ottawa – in spite of the problems that could arise with the provinces, particularly Quebec.

In response, St-Laurent hastily assured the delegates that they could take credit for recent modifications in labour and social legislation. They remained impatient and implacable. A few days later, when Ottawa refused to provide funding for low-rental housing, CCL president A.R. Mosher was mildly menacing: "Unless the Government can offer something better than this, the Canadian people are bound to show their resentment."[17]

Individual Canadians underlined those frustrations in letters to St-Laurent. Madame P. Emile Ouellet wrote from Matane County, Quebec, on 9 April 1949, begging the prime minister to "tax the rich instead of the poor, so that we might be able to live a little better. When a man with a family and who has worked hard all his life reaches the age of 50 without having been able to accumulate any savings or to own a house, there is no social security ... We lack clothing, food and housing ... all the stores are loaded down with fruit and meat. All that is lacking is money."[18] The promised postwar boom did not extend to everyone.

Canadians were engaged in this debate. At a University of Toronto expert roundtable in May 1949, social work professor John S. Morgan was emphatic in his summary of the talks – and the language of rights was emerging here, too. "Social security was seen to be ... an essential protection of individual rights in human society."[19] The participants emphasized the importance of employment for human dignity, adeptly linking a healthy economy with a healthy society. Ottawa's challenge was to devise unemployment assistance for employables who had exhausted their benefits: "But" added Morgan with a flourish, "there are fiscal problems and constitutional difficulties in relating political and administrative responsibilities to financial capacity."[20] The experts had finally grasped the central problem of fiscal inequality within the federation – but they could not solve it.

In the six months since St-Laurent had taken office, the advocacy was becoming frequent and often fierce.

AUSTRALIA KEEPS TRACK

Australian diplomats watched avidly. Across the postwar decades, they deluged Canberra with catalogues of current Canadian legislation, updates on provincial and federal politics, lists of prominent civil servants and politicians – in February 1950 the Bank of Canada's new deputy governor James Coyne was a "refreshing anomaly" – and the texts of budgets and speeches from the throne.[21] The topic of federalism, particularly social security within a federation, retained its endless fascination.

The Australians were far ahead of Canada in the implementation of Social Security – but they also understood the careful balance that such programs entailed. Tucked into the High Commission's files was a pivotal address that Canadian finance minister Douglas Abbott gave on 5 January 1949 to the annual lunch of the Canadian Women's Club of New York. The minister provided an overview of Canada's progress in 1948: "It is safe to say that the average Canadian today enjoys a standard of living at least half as high again as he did before the war, and a good deal higher than at any time in the past."[22]

The fourteen-page speech was remarkable because Abbott boasted about the Liberal government's advances in social equity *as a boost for economic efficiency*. Social security

> strengthens the economy, increases production by assuring a more intelligent and more healthy population, lessens the haunting worry of unemployment and family illness that might otherwise impair morale and productivity, makes systematic provision in advance against the inevitable contingencies and to that

extent makes it unnecessary when adversity comes for the state to step in with improvised and expensive construction or other remedial programs."[23]

This was a major shift from federal attitudes prior to the Second World War. Abbott admitted that the division of responsibilities for social programs within the federation could be difficult. Still, "even though progress has not been as rapid as some might have wished," he maintained, "it has been substantial."[24] With improved old-age pensions, unemployment insurance, and family allowances, federal spending on social security had multiplied tenfold over the previous ten years. The Australians likely gloated about their more adaptable federation and their superior programs. They certainly understood that Canada had made almost negligible progress in the expansion of social security since the end of the war.

ST-LAURENT WINS THE ELECTION – AND THE LOBBYING BEGINS AGAIN

After seven months in power, St-Laurent handily won his first election as prime minister in late June 1949 with more than 49 percent of the vote. The CCF, the Progressive Conservatives, and the Social Credit parties actually lost seats. All three opposition parties supported a national health insurance program. Immediately after the election, 80 percent of respondents told pollsters that they backed a government-funded health plan to which they would make monthly contributions.[25]

Saskatchewan premier Tommy Douglas did not waste a minute. The premier knew from first-hand experience what a hospital stay could cost. In 1944, en route to visit Canadian troops in Europe, he had become seriously ill on the train to Ottawa. He was lucky: the military had recently released penicillin for civilian use, which saved his life. But he was saddled with a hospital bill of just under $1,000. "This gives you some idea of why hospital insurance certainly appealed to me," he later recounted ruefully. "I had to borrow the money."[26] Mackenzie King *did* send a car to bring him home from the hospital.

By mid-July, Douglas was pushing St-Laurent to reconvene the 1945–46 Dominion-Provincial Conference to deal with the Green Paper. "The problems which the Federal Government recognized as crying for attention then are even more pressing now," he wrote on 15 July 1949.[27] Saskatchewan had implemented hospital insurance in January 1947, which was "placing a very heavy financial burden upon the individual taxpayer and upon the provincial treasury."[28] Douglas wanted to discuss a similar plan for all Canadians, so that "some system of prepaid health services [could be] established in some of the provinces at least."[29]

He also wanted to talk about health insurance, universal old-age security, federal contributions of 50 percent to pensions for those between the ages of sixty-five and seventy – and the maintenance of full employment. St-Laurent replied almost five weeks later on 18 August – "after a much appreciated holiday" – with the cautionary observation that he first had to renew the tax rental deals for 1952–57. Anyway, "more progress can be made ... [through] frank discussions with individual provincial administrations about separate concrete questions."[30] It was a polite brush-off. It seemed as if nothing had changed since the Dominion-Provincial Conference had broken up so acrimoniously in May 1946.

Other premiers wistfully remembered the Green Paper. In early August 1949, Manitoba premier Douglas Campbell asked St-Laurent to resume the earlier conference. But he was cautious: "Our first concern in Manitoba would be ... to insure the financial stability of the provinces and to develop sound productive policies on public investment, on development and conservation of natural resources, on social security measures of various sorts, and on measures designed to encourage industrial and agricultural development generally."[31] The Liberal-Progressive premier, who would spend a record forty-seven uninterrupted years in the legislature, was a "lifelong believer in small government."[32] Now he wanted Ottawa and the provinces to work together "to improve the general welfare of Canada."[33] The poorer provinces clearly had a realistic idea of what their voters wanted, what their governments could afford – and *what they needed from Ottawa* to make up the difference. He, too, got nowhere initially.

ST-LAURENT FINALLY TACKLES THE DOMINION-PROVINCIAL FILES

Eventually, St-Laurent moved unhurriedly to work. He was a corporate lawyer but, more important, he had been the francophone counsel to the Rowell-Sirois Royal Commission. He understood perfectly that the Constitution was an impediment to any reshuffling of federal and provincial revenues and responsibilities. Perhaps worse, as St-Laurent grasped, Canada had no amending formula: convention *seemingly* dictated that all governments had to assent to major changes – and the approval of the British Parliament was then required.

So the prime minister embarked on a series of federal-provincial conferences, starting with the amending formula. It was a calculated move to address that basic problem. But only constitutional experts could love this gambit: most Canadians did not understand the relationship between the Constitution and the expansion of social security. There could be few advances in social security if the poorer provinces could not afford them. Their initial gathering in Ottawa in January 1950 was the first conference devoted exclusively to the patriation of the Constitution with an amending formula. It was also the first that Newfoundland attended since it had joined Canada in 1949. The conference failed.

There were now two parallel tracks running through federal-provincial discussions. On one side were the appeals for expanded social security, largely within anglophone Canada, which were growing more insistent. In July 1950, the Canadian Federation of Business and Professional Women's Clubs petitioned Ottawa for "a retirement pension plan without a means test."[34] That would remove an expense from the provinces – which had covered 25 percent of the cost of pensions for low-income seniors over seventy since 1931 – and put the onus on Ottawa. There was no immediate response. The elegant St-Laurent understood the issue in theory – but he floated above those women's real world.

On the other side were the increasingly tricky negotiations with the provinces for the third round of five-year tax rental deals. British Columbia was wealthier than most, but it became increasingly resentful. The province had always maintained that Ottawa did not take into account its *special* revenue needs – or its far greater reliance on income taxes before the Second World War. In 1950, Premier Bjorn "Boss" Johnson pressed that complaint with newfound vigour. The Liberal premier headed a coalition government of Liberals and Conservatives, which had won a huge electoral victory in 1949. Johnson, who ran a building-supply firm in Victoria, had the larger caucus so he was premier.

The British-born Conservative leader Herbert Anscomb, perched atop a divided party, took the finance portfolio. Anscomb was a fiscal conservative who had introduced a 3 percent sales tax in 1948. And he was blunt in his dealings with Ottawa. In February 1950, in his budget speech, he declared that the province "was prepared to help the have-not provinces ... [but] felt it must put its own interests first."[35] He eventually secured generous treatment in the next rental deal. But such continued complaints about Ottawa's generosity to the poorer provinces ensured that the relationship was often tense and occasionally bitter.

THE FIRST MINISTERS STRUGGLE FOR HARMONY

St-Laurent and the premiers met again in late September in the Quebec Legislative Assembly. Once again, they discussed constitutional patriation and their deadlocked hunt for an amending formula. Once again they failed.

But the prime minister did pull out a plum for the social activists. In January, he had proposed a third conference for late 1950 – and he had asked the premiers for suggestions on the agenda. Six provinces inundated his office with ideas, including medical and hospital insurance, unemployment assistance for employable and unemployable persons, and the adoption of a minimum standard for educational opportunity. Newfoundland deferred to its peers. Quebec did not respond but federal officials cited Premier Maurice Duplessis's frequent references to "the problems relating to the exclusive rights of the provinces in the matter of insurance, unemployment, and radio broadcasting, etc., etc."[36] (The prime minister should have paid more attention to that warning.)

Many provinces did recognize the fiscal inequalities among their governments. New Brunswick, Prince Edward Island, and Saskatchewan asked for National Adjustment Grants. Ontario airily proposed subsidies based on fiscal need to "assure a *minimum* standard of public services."[37] Prince Edward Island wanted an overhaul of federal subsidies coupled with the "transfer of certain existing services to federal jurisdiction."[38] Saskatchewan proposed federal assistance to the provinces for capital financing, while Manitoba wanted a review of federal grants "in the light of increasing municipal costs."[39] It was an expansive and expensive list.

Their efforts were largely in vain. St-Laurent's senior civil servants had almost certainly seen the Bank of Canada's review of Social Security payments in late June 1950. Those payments had an effect on those who received them and those who funded them through insurance contributions and taxes. If the benefit rates were too high in relation to the earnings among potential beneficiaries, "some individuals might work less, and make less provision for their own future security, than they should or otherwise would."[40] As well, the higher taxes that would be required to pay for benefits might impair the incentive to work or invest.

The effects of any new programs could only be determined "over a period of time."[41] Programs such as family allowances had already increased the purchasing power of the recipients by nearly five times the amount that social programs had provided in 1938. Total personal expenditure on consumer goods and services had nearly tripled since the prewar years.[42] Canadians had more money in their pockets – and that money could buy so much more. The Bank of Canada clearly viewed further expansion of social security as a gamble.

Four months later, the Privy Council Office produced a seventeen-page report on the history of federal- provincial relations since Confederation, detailing the constitutional provisions, the dominion-provincial meetings, the departmental meetings, the administrative collaboration, the royal commissions, the delegations of administrative power, and the proposals for cooperative machinery.[43] It was exhaustive – and no doubt exhausting for its readers. But its pivotal first appendix examined the cooperative federation machinery in the United States and Australia, including the premiers' frequent conferences, the Loan Council, and the Grants Commission.[44] Australia remained a strong model for reform.

Perhaps overwhelmed by the challenges, St-Laurent took refuge in fiscal and political prudence. In October 1950, he limited the conference agenda, citing the "uncertainty" around international economic conditions – and the failure to resolve the constitutional limitations on Ottawa's role in social security.[45] The third First Ministers' Conference of 1950 would be restricted to discussions of the tax rental deals and old-age security with possible subcommittees on other issues.

Discouraged, Tommy Douglas wrote again: St-Laurent was hesitant to expand social security because of the cost of defence. "[But] the home front is equally as important as the international front ... The best way to defend democracy is to remove those social and economic forces that tend to undermine it."[46] That argument went nowhere.

St-Laurent replied that the majority of premiers were willing to restrict their discussions to his agenda. Douglas reluctantly agreed – but he reserved the right to push for the expansion of the agenda after they had handled those items. If that did not happen, they should create subcommittees to produce reports for another conference in 1951: it was "the very least that ought to be done."[47]

St-Laurent could not escape the activists. In November 1950, superintendent reverend J. Lavell Smith of the Queen Street and Church of All Nations in Toronto, which was affiliated with the United Church of Canada, asked the Interdepartmental Conference Committee to remember "that we still have the unemployed with us, in considerable numbers." His church was a block away from the Unemployment Insurance Office in downtown Toronto. "And on these wintry days, we are having, numbers of men come to us, looking for a meal, a pair of shoes and overcoat, or a night's lodging." It was an "ever present problem."[48]

Two weeks later, in December 1950, Elizabeth DeWitt, secretary to the board of directors of the Visiting Homemakers Association of Toronto, asked that the conference consider assistance for the unemployed employables who had exhausted their unemployment insurance: "Last winter a number of families which were known to our agency suffered hardships due to the present policy of not giving assistance to unemployed employable persons when it was impossible for them to secure work in this area."[49] The association had already forwarded a similar plea to the Ontario government.

Neither the Reverend Smith nor Ms DeWitt suggested which level of government should pay for such social assistance – or administer it. Nor did they deal with the fiscal inequalities among the provinces. That was perhaps because they lived in relatively wealthy Ontario – but it is more likely that they did not even consider this challenge. The problem of the unemployed employables who had exhausted their UI would become worse as the economy faltered in the mid-1950s.

THE DOMINION-PROVINCIAL CONFERENCE OF DECEMBER 1950

The groups that wanted the conference participants to expand Social Security would have been shocked to learn that their efforts were largely futile. In January 1950, the cabinet shelved unemployment assistance because that was a provincial or municipal responsibility – and Ottawa was theoretically committed to full employment.[50] Senior bureaucrats confirmed that decision on 27 November 1950, noting that unemployment rates were not above normal – and Ottawa had already widened unemployment insurance coverage.[51] In late November, a federal cabinet committee also postponed any expansion of health care because of the cost. As St-Laurent observed, "In the light of the present international situation and the obligations of the government it would not be desirable to attempt any such things now."[52]

The only suggestion that the cabinet could not dismiss was an expansion of the old-age pension. On 7 November 1950, Finance Minister Douglas Abbott argued that a contributory plan, which would cost more than $200 million, would fuel inflation.[53] His colleague, Health Minister Paul Martin, countered that the Liberals had campaigned on this proposal, which they had also advocated in 1945. A joint parliamentary committee had reported favourably on the issue in June 1950 to all-party acclaim. If the government did not expand the program, there would be huge pressure to raise the actual amount of the pension – which would also prove costly. Anyway, relatives were already spending heavily on their elderly: federal payments would simply be a substitute for that spending, not inflationary new spending.[54] Martin got everyone's attention – and consent.

At the conference in early December 1950, the participants concentrated on old-age pensions that Ottawa would administer and that would not be based upon need. They created a subcommittee on old-age security that split the approach: Ottawa would administer the contributory system with no means test for those aged seventy and over; Ottawa and the provinces would share the costs of pensions for those between the ages of sixty-five and sixty-nine, based upon a means test, but the provinces would administer them. Martin declared that this expensive proposal, which would triple federal and provincial contributions to the elderly, had strong public support: "it was felt that the general public was prepared to pay directly for this important improvement in its domestic security."[55]

But there was a catch. A constitutional amendment was required to shift responsibility for old-age pensions to Ottawa. The premiers were generally amenable: even Quebec premier Duplessis agreed to refer the required amendment to the Legislative Assembly. But Duplessis insisted on the insertion of a clause asserting that the measure would not affect "the operation of any law present or future of a provincial legislature" in relation to old-age pensions.[56] The Quebec defenders of provincial rights had brushed up against the advocates for expanded social security – and they had guardedly yielded, partly because the federal payments, which went directly to elderly individuals, relieved obligations on the provincial treasury, which had been paying one-quarter of the cost for those aged seventy and over. To provide partial funding for the measure, Ottawa settled upon the Old Age Security Tax.[57] The Old Age Security Act took effect on 1 January 1952.

PREDICTABLY, NO ONE WAS SATISFIED

The times were oddly dissonant. Many Canadians could see their standard of living gradually improving. They could purchase convenient appliances and stylish clothes, buy everything that was missing from their Depression-era upbringing for *their* children, invest in a home and buy a car to take the family for Sunday drives. The *Ottawa Citizen* was stuffed with full-page ads for sofas, clothing, garden furniture, bedroom suites, cribs, and electric refrigerators with freezers equipped with ice-cube trays and "true, honest, Automatic Defrost."[58] Canada seemed like paradise to new arrivals: in late May, a boatload of young women from the United Kingdom, where rationing would persist for another three years, arrived at Ottawa's Union Station, smiling broadly, ready to start their new jobs as maids.[59] Ontario premier Leslie Frost, who had succeeded George Drew as premier in 1949, was promising to consider unconditional grants to the province's municipalities, arguing that federal grants should also be "free and unallotted."[60] The genial small-town lawyer was wrestling with the challenges of prosperity.

Society was changing as the Korean War persisted. For the first time since the end of the Second World War, the RCAF took down the "Men Only" sign at its downtown Ottawa recruiting office, and the first women enlisted within hours.[61] In early June of 1951, the United Nations was struggling to secure Communist consent to a cease fire in Korea along the lines of the 38th parallel, where the boundary would eventually be established in 1953.[62] A Royal Canadian Air Force pilot from Mont Joli, Quebec, back from six months in the Korean war zone, described how he shot down a Russian-manufactured MIG that swooped out of Manchuria. He then escaped a second pursuer: Communist pilots "were no great shakes."[63] US president Harry S. Truman signed a $6.4 billion supplementary appropriation bill with the bulk of the money earmarked for military hardware such as tanks and aircraft.[64]

The Korean War and the continuing Communist threat preoccupied Ottawa. In April 1951, the 360,000-member Canadian Congress of Labour reminded St-Laurent that it was stoutly backing efforts to combat Communism abroad. Its press release added: "There was also need for a social and economic program in Canada itself to give Canadians a full realization of their opportunities and *the necessity to fight* to preserve those conditions."[65] Eleven months later, the CCL asked Ottawa to restore price and rent controls, impose an excess-profits tax, deal with unemployment, and take action on housing, especially the "greatest need" for low-rental housing.[66] It put special emphasis on health insurance as "the biggest gap in our social security system. It is high time it was filled."[67] It called for a parliamentary inquiry "leading to immediate and effective action."[68] It did not explain how the poorer provinces would pay for their share.

St-Laurent countered with a well-practised argument: "He [St-Laurent] said that Canada is doing what it can to prevent a third World War, but that our share of the joint effort amounted to nearly two billion dollars, which was almost fifty per cent of the entire [federal] budget of the nation."[69] The defence tab was so high that Ottawa could not meet the CCL's demands. Union leaders were exasperated.

The public mood was evident. The use of commercial health insurance and voluntary prepayment plans was rapidly expanding. Canadians clearly wanted protection against medical and hospital bills, "and were willing to pay for it."[70] By 1950, government-run hospital insurance existed in four provinces – Saskatchewan, British Columbia, Alberta, and Newfoundland – and all were without federal subsidy. The expense was onerous. As policy expert Malcolm G. Taylor noted, "[provincial] leaders and members of parliament constantly reminded the federal government that the time had come for the 1945 offer [the Green Paper] to be fulfilled."[71]

There was, however, one powerful group that consistently backed St-Laurent in his efforts to curb social spending: the Canadian Chamber of Commerce. Across the 1950s, the voluntary federation, representing more than 650 boards of trade and local chambers in ten provinces, always argued for restraint. In February 1951, the chamber explained that demands for expanded social security "must be viewed carefully in the light of new and additional financial burdens for National Defence."[72] Any extra spending should go only to defence "until the threatening clouds which are on the horizon have been dissipated."[73]

It repeated that mantra throughout the ensuing years. On 5 February 1954, the chamber urged restraint to preserve Ottawa's economic health – and to curb the role of the state in meeting individual social needs: "Careful distinction must be drawn between what is socially desirable as an ultimate aim and that which can be achieved without damaging the system which makes our social welfare advances possible."[74] That appeal to self-sufficiency was out of step with public opinion, at least within anglophone Canada.

THE QUARREL WITH QUEBEC COMMENCES

Such often-conflicting pressures eventually ensnared St-Laurent in a dangerous vise. On 1 June 1951, the Royal Commission on National Development in the Arts, Letters and Sciences – otherwise known as the Massey Commission – reported after more than two years of work. Almost three weeks later, in response to its recommendations, the prime minister offered $7 million in per capita federal grants to Canadian universities – or roughly fifty cents per student. St-Laurent stressed that the money was "a necessary supplement" to existing provincial funding – and the universities should use it "to maintain quality rather than to increase facilities."[75]

The Quebec government reacted with distrust. But Quebec's francophone universities pushed Ottawa to negotiate a deal with the Duplessis government. They wanted the money from "this audacious and unprecedented scheme" of statutory nonconditional grants.[76] Duplessis initially yielded. For the 1951–52 year, a joint Quebec-Ottawa committee administered the funds for Quebec – and the provincial representative counter-signed the cheques. But, as historian Michael Behiels relates, this approach could not last: "Sensitive to the loud outcry from nationalist circles and hoping perhaps to keep Quebec universities under his government's political control, Duplessis refused to renew the arrangement after 1952."[77] The skirmish was among the first in a fight that would eventually lead to equalization.

Quebec was leading the postwar provincial resistance to Ottawa's use of its spending power, which was effectively an anti-Rowell-Sirois movement. The assertion of provincial rights was as old as Confederation itself. But this powerful Quebec nationalist movement was developing throughout the 1950s because of the clash of two postwar forces.

Ottawa's decision "to forge ahead with Keynesian-inspired fiscal and monetary policies and the creation of a highly centralized social welfare state" was changing federal-provincial relations. Neo-nationalists viewed this new federalism as "a serious threat to provincial autonomy and therefore to the French-Canadian nation."[78] Ottawa was nudging into Quebec's place in the cultural heart of French Canada, encroaching on its right to protect its language and culture.[79]

Quebec was the only province that did not sign the third tax rental agreement – the second postwar deal – that ran from 1952 to 1957. Ontario did sign – much to Quebec's chagrin – so "Quebec found itself alone in the fight for the autonomy of the provinces."[80] Other provinces, such as British Columbia, drove hard bargains. But Quebec was the provincial rights force pressing on St-Laurent. Ottawa did offer an abatement of 7 percent on corporate taxes and 5 percent on personal income taxes to Quebec taxpayers (it had offered an abatement of five percentage points to Ontario and Quebec for the 1947–52 tax rental deals).[81] But Duplessis refused to create a provincially administered personal income tax – "no matter how small."[82] The province lost more than $76 million in revenue from compensatory grants between 1947 and 1952 because of Duplessis's line-in-the-sand on the tax rental deals.[83]

The premier fought back. In 1953, he established the pivotal provincial Royal Commission of Inquiry on Constitutional Problems, which Judge Thomas Tremblay chaired. In late 1953, well before the commissioners' final report, they urged Duplessis to resist Ottawa's fiscal domination. The province was experiencing "an increasingly difficult time finding enough revenue to finance all of the highways, bridges, schools, and hospitals that were required."[84] In 1954, Duplessis finally introduced a provincial income tax equal to 15 percent of the federal rate. It was a direct challenge: Quebec taxpayers would be hit with "double taxation" unless Duplessis could accomplish "the difficult task" of convincing the St-Laurent government to allow them to deduct their provincial tax from their federal tax.[85] Duplessis also contended that Quebec had priority in the field of direct taxation. "A lively struggle ensued between the two governments."[86]

Duplessis had strong support among Quebec groups. In January 1954, the Quebec Division of the Canadian Manufacturers' Association told the Tremblay Commission that there were many good reasons to resist the tax rental deals, including the association's nightmare scenario: "Such a centralized system would provide a government of socialistic tendencies with a ready-made instrument of attack not only on provincial prerogatives but on free enterprise as well."[87]

Duplessis also cultivated the prelates and priests of the Roman Catholic Church. He "prolonged the significance of the Church in matters that have subsequently become secular: education, hospitalization, public assistance."[88] In turn, "the higher clergy" approved of Duplessis for reasons that "were generally rooted in ideology, or at least policy, especially provincial autonomy and Duplessis's incessant representation of himself as the more Catholic candidate."[89]

The stage was set for Quebec's battle with Ottawa that would reappear so strongly during the Quiet Revolution.

ST-LAURENT INITIALLY DEEPENS THE PROBLEM

After months of fierce skirmishes, St-Laurent delivered a particularly tough challenge to Duplessis at the Quebec Reform Club on 18 September 1954. He was open to suggestions to settle the dispute – but he refused to recognize Quebec's claim to priority over direct taxes. He also made a startling assertion: "Quebec is a province like the others."[90] Journalist Bruce Hutchison maintained that St-Laurent did not consult his cabinet before he made those off-the-cuff remarks, which offended many Quebecers.[91] The reaction startled St-Laurent: he knew that the situation was untenable. He had not created the impasse with Quebec but he had certainly deepened it. The dispute was now a threat to national unity.

St-Laurent *had* to find a gracious exit. The two men met privately at Montreal's Windsor Hotel on 5 October 1954 to draft the outlines of a compromise.[92] In January 1955, the prime minister told his cabinet that the only solution was to make an offer that would be available to *all* provinces. As the cabinet records reveal, the prime minister concluded: "No matter how far the Federal government went, the government of Quebec would not be satisfied ... [but] Any serious Federal proposal, even though it might not satisfy Mr. Duplessis, would at least show the people of Quebec that the Federal authorities had honestly tried hard to meet their point of view and had sought to relieve, at least in part, those who suffered from double taxation."[93]

Accordingly, Ottawa offered to reduce its income tax by 10 percent for all provinces where a provincial income tax was levied – and to apply that move retroactively to Quebec for 1954. On 19 January

1955, Duplessis accepted this truce. In a subsequent telephone call with St-Laurent, he also agreed to delete the assertion of provincial priority in direct taxation from the provincial income tax act.[94] That scuffle "had wider significance. For the first time since the war, Ottawa had to draw back and temper its new national policy [of tax rental accords and compensatory grants] to take the demands of a province into account."[95]

THE AUSTRALIANS LAUD CENTRALISM

St-Laurent's initially belligerent response to the tense situation with Quebec impressed the Australians, particularly High Commissioner Sir Douglas Copland, who was an academic and an economic analyst. In a "confidential" five-page memorandum to Australia's external affairs minister R.G. Casey, Copland outlined the standoff over jurisdictions. Under the heading "The Measure of the Man," Copland reviewed St-Laurent's career as well as the political situation in Quebec: "In all federations there are usually one or more units who find it difficult to fit into the federal structure. This is probably more so in Canada than in any other modern federation, because the Province of Quebec is jealous of its French origin, its language, its culture and, above all, its religion ... The law in Australia on [taxation] is much more uncompromising than it is in Canada."[96]

Then Copland considered the reputations of St-Laurent (who was "the most distinguished living French Canadian") and Duplessis – who wanted to position himself as "the defender of the faith, the upholder of French culture in Canada, the guardian of autonomy."[97] The two men had clashed on several occasions throughout the autumn, Copland reported, but it was St-Laurent's defiant speech at the Quebec Reform Club on 18 September that impressed the high commissioner. "He [St-Laurent] was able to show ... that, above all, the path to glory was to drop any policies and practices that would divide the nation into a minority of little Canadians and a majority of those who believed in the expansion of Canada as one nation."[98]

The Australian did not grasp the importance or the force of provincial identity in Canada. But economist Copland was also a source for Canada's files on Australia. The Bank of Canada Archives include a thirty-page paper on post-1945 Australian economic policy and economic development that the High Commissioner delivered to the American Philosophical Society in Philadelphia in 1953. Copland surveyed everything from national income to wage movements to Australia's administrative structure. His prose was dense; he included multiple lists of statistics; he did not address the workings of the Commonwealth Grants Commission.

But when he outlined the development of social policy in Australia, he added a fierce observation: such programs had not evolved as part of an economic strategy – nor was their impact on the economy as a whole taken into account. "It is not easy to do this in a unitary state," he added. "[It is] still more difficult in a federal structure where governments may be jealous of their prerogatives and unduly concerned with their own immediate interests."[99] That insight into the important if difficult connection between economic policies and social programs would have resonated in Canada.

THE TREMBLAY REPORT, QUEBEC, AND EQUALIZATION

The five-volume Tremblay Royal Commission report on federalism brought sociological depth to Quebec's resistance. More important, although almost overlooked at the time, it singled out fiscal inequality as a huge impediment to the expansion of social services within the federation. Tabled in 1956, it espoused a complicated plan: all provinces should take over the taxation of revenues earned within their boundaries; they should also agree to cooperate on the taxation of revenues earned from interprovincial trade; and, finally, Ottawa or the provinces through a special fund should send money to the Maritime provinces for "social equalization ... to assure them the same services as the rest of the country" – as long as all provinces endorsed such transfers.[100]

The report did not grapple with the impractical, and probably impossible, chore of distinguishing revenues earned from trade within the province from revenues earned from trade with other provinces. But it did explain that it was necessary "to assure the really handicapped provinces of social services in conformity with the minimum standards of the country as a whole."[101] Significantly, the report added that the Constitution "makes no provision for equalization in any form." Ottawa's claim to handle such measures was "an interpretation of its powers which, in our opinion, is inadmissible (the 'unlimited' taxing power and the 'absolute' spending power). It is essential that this situation be regularized."[102] In effect, the Tremblay Report called for a system of equalization payments that the provinces would organize – and Ottawa might administer. Duplessis was able to set aside those recommendations with the excuse that Ottawa had responded to his demands. In reality, "its conclusions went farther than he had wished, especially with respect to the province's assumption of social programs and to educational reform."[103]

But the report's statement of principles would become an operational manta. "By reason of its history, as well as of the cultural character of its population, Quebec is not a province like the others, whatever may be said to the contrary." That was a direct shot at St-Laurent's assertion that Quebec was like the others. Instead, Quebec "speaks in the name of one of the two ethnic groups which founded Confederation ... It is the only one able to represent one of these two partners, just as it alone may determine its reasons for refusing federal largesse."[104]

The Tremblay Report's assertion that Quebec was one of the two founding partners of the Confederation compact would persist across the decades.

CANADIANS BECOME INCREASINGLY RESTLESS

Throughout the mid-1950s, many middle-income Canadians eagerly adopted a new way of life. The first enclosed shopping mall opened in West Vancouver in September 1950. By the fall of 1953, the largest shopping centre in Canada was in northeast Montreal, and dozens more were springing up and sprawling out. Suburban housing tracts were appearing on the outskirts of major cities. The first comprehensive one, which was called Don Mills, was constructed in 1954 to the northeast of downtown Toronto. Those developments were making "modern technology available to the average Canadian," broadening the "standardized North American middle-class lifestyle."[105] Families could afford these new homes for their growing families. They lived side by side in neighbourhoods where they could find friends who often shared their wartime and postwar experiences, and their children could attend the new public schools that provincial governments were scrambling to build.

Items that were once luxuries were now widespread. Advertisements in the *Ottawa Journal* urged consumers to switch from coal to oil furnaces, eliminating the sooty bins and acrid smoke. An advertisement entitled "Let's Eat Out" listed local restaurants, urging families to "make it a 'Once-a-Week' habit."[106] With the growing popularity of cheaper Chinese restaurants and pizzerias, many families could now afford that treat. General Motors proudly announced the opening of another Ottawa dealership that would carry Pontiacs, Buicks, Vauxhalls, and GMC trucks with their "sensational" new 1955 models.[107] Admiral announced its "Triumph: You've Never Seen It So Big" Super Giant 21-inch TV.[108] Five-piece bridge sets were selling fast at Eaton's department store.[109] Completely automatic home washing machines and dryers were now available, which were huge improvements on wringer washers.

International tensions abated. An armistice ended the Korean War on 27 June 1953. Sixteen months later, in October 1954, Canada celebrated the ninth anniversary of the day that the United Nations charter took effect.[110] In an editorial in late October, the *Ottawa Journal* proudly marked the twelfth anniversary of the Allied victory at El Alamein in the North African desert "when the forces of the enemy had appeared irresistible."[111] For a generation that vividly remembered the war, so much had altered for the better.

The very demographics of Canada were changing. More women were slipping into the workforce, and more were starting to live on their own or with other women of their own age before they married. The high marriage rates in the immediate aftermath of the war were gradually declining.[112] Almost one-third of the immigrants from 1945 to 1961 were from the British Isles, but roughly 15 percent were from Italy.[113] Others flocked from Germany, the United States, the Netherlands, Poland, and southern Europe.

Canada was flourishing – and Canadians could mostly congratulate themselves. But, with the exception of the expansion of old-age security and the per capita grants to postsecondary institutions in the early 1950s, little had changed for so many who faced serious illness or dismal poverty. The promises of the 1945 Green Paper remained mostly unfulfilled.

ADVOCACY IN THE 1950S

In the mid-1950s, social advocates were out of patience. Many groups now demanded expanded social programs – but few addressed the challenge of fiscal inequality. As a rule, their views resembled those of sociologist Harry Cassidy: they wanted Ottawa to find the money for social security for the provinces or to launch the programs on its own dime. It was up to governments to devise the missing link of equalization.

The onus was on Ottawa. The years from 1949 to 1957 were "hardly a stable time economically," but there was also "considerable economic vibrancy."[114] By the mid-1950s, despite the occasional slowdowns, the mood was upbeat – and exasperated.[115] The Canadian Congress of Labour was vehement after the 1953–54 federal budget cut taxes – but refused to adopt national health insurance with the "excuse" that Canada could not afford it.[116] "The workers of Canada are becoming weary of procrastination and excuses on this subject, the more so since the drop in defence expenditure is removing one of the chief excuses of recent years."[117]

Labour unions could rarely control their members' votes. But they could capture the zeitgeist. In mid-November 1954, the CCL called for the creation of "an industrial pension plan" that would cover all workers through a fund of employer-employee contributions "administered by the government with pension credits accruing regardless of the changes in employment."[118] It was an early vision of the Canada Pension Plan, which the first ministers eventually established in 1965 (Quebec created a parallel Quebec Pension Plan). The first pensions were paid in January 1967.

In December 1955, in a presentation to St-Laurent and his cabinet, the Trades and Labor Congress (TLC) of Canada, which represented more than 600,000 affiliated members, "urgently requested immediate action to implement a nation-wide health insurance scheme."[119] Founded in 1883, the TLC had survived the fierce skirmishes among competing national and international unions across the decades. Delegates at its annual convention had called for health insurance "in the full knowledge of the constitutional difficulties ... A nation-wide health insurance scheme should be government-subsidized, contributory and cover every Canadian citizen; and include medical, surgical, dental and optical care, hospitalization, provision of artificial limbs where necessary, psychiatric treatment, and competently supervised mental homes."[120] It was a shopping list from the frustrated.

Canada was now more than a decade behind its fellow dominion, Australia, in expanding social programs. Politicians could aspire. Ordinary Canadians and advocacy groups could demand. But Canada was moving so gradually that in April 1962 the minister of St Paul's United Church in Toronto would warn the Royal Commission on Health Services that many unskilled immigrants from southern Italy who worked hard at temporary jobs for fifty or sixty cents an hour and who lived in crowded boarding houses with few essentials were becoming ill. They really needed state-funded health care.[121] In June 1964, that commission, also known as the Hall Commission, would recommend Medicare. It was difficult to adjust the mechanics of federalism to meet Canadian needs.

ST-LAURENT LOOKS FOR ANOTHER WAY

By 1955, federal politicians and bureaucrats knew that they had to rethink their approach to the tax rental deals, if only to halt Quebec's isolation. In his later book on those agreements, federal bureaucrat R.M. Burns dated the official birth of equalization to the aftermath of St-Laurent's settlement with Duplessis. In a *pivotal* letter to the other premiers after that pact, on 14 January 1955, St-Laurent explained that Ottawa was not wedded to the principle of the tax rental deals "to the exclusion of any better alternative arrangement if one could be found."[122]

But Ottawa "had no intention of abandoning the *objective* of the tax rental agreements which is to make it financially possible for all provinces, whatever their tax base, to perform their constitutional functions themselves and *to provide a reasonable Canadian level of provincial services without an abnormal burden of taxation*. That is the foundation of the policy of the federal government."[123] Burns, who was then director of the federal-provincial relations division in the finance department, emphasized: "This was the first official acknowledgement by the federal government of its adoption of equalization as a basic and explicit principle ... since its acceptance of the Rowell-Sirois recommendations in 1941."[124]

That is true. There had been adjustments to the Maritime provinces' subsidies in the 1920s and 1930s in the name of generosity. But St-Laurent's letter, which recognized the concept of fiscal inequality among the provinces and how to measure it in terms of the tax revenues required to perform necessary services, was also an explicit recognition of ideas that the federal bureaucracy had quietly mulled since 1941, whenever the tax rental agreements came up for renewal (senior finance and Bank of Canada officials had also worked behind the scenes with the Rowell-Sirois Commission).

A subsequent history of fiscal events during the mid-1950s by former Privy Council clerk Robert B. Bryce downgraded the influence of the Rowell-Sirois Report on the creation of equalization. Bryce conceded that the report "did have an important but indirect effect in leading to the tax rental agreements."[125] But he argued that the proposed National Adjustment Grants did not "have any significant influence on the introduction" of equalization in 1957.[126] Instead, St-Laurent simply wanted to separate the "fiscal need" element of the individual provincial tax rental deals from the estimated yield of key taxes in each province: this was "Prime Minister St. Laurent's own decision, reached after lengthy discussions with Finance, and it reflected his view that the inclusion of such a subsidy in the tax rental agreements was seriously unfair to Quebec ... I was the secretary to the Cabinet at the time and very much involved in the discussions on the subject."[127]

That assertion that the proposed National Adjustment Grants did not have "any significant influence" on the introduction of equalization is questionable. St-Laurent had been the francophone counsel to the Royal Commission on Dominion-Provincial Relations. He had befriended Joseph Sirois and convinced him to join the commission. He had endured its arduous hearings. He had asked questions of the witnesses. And, in the end, he had convinced Sirois to accept *all* of the commission's recommendations, including the call for National Adjustment Grants. Sirois later argued that adequate revenues were necessary for true provincial autonomy. More remarkably, as historian P.E. Bryden points out, the federal bureaucrat who espoused equalization in 1955 was J.J. Deutsch, who had been the assistant research director and then the research director for the Rowell-Sirois Commission and who was then secretary of the Treasury Board.[128] She asserts that equalization was Deutsch's "brainchild" – although she does not make the connection of Deutsch to Rowell-Sirois.[129]

In his memoirs, St-Laurent's former Clerk of the Privy Council, J.W. Pickersgill, who was now in cabinet but still involved as an advisor on equalization, maintained that the prime minister worked closely with Deutsch on the introduction and development of equalization.[130] He did *not* mention Robert Bryce in this regard (Bryce did, however, summarize cabinet discussions of the varying formulas).

The cabinet records also show that the prime minister wanted to be closely involved in the introduction of equalization. In mid-March of 1955, St-Laurent set up the nucleus of a cabinet committee to work with an interdepartmental committee of bureaucrats to plan for upcoming federal-provincial discussions on the tax rental deals and equalization as well as unemployment assistance. St-Laurent was the chair of this committee along with Finance Minister Walter Harris and Justice Minister Stuart Garson.[131] The three politicians first oversaw preparations for a preliminary meeting with provincial representatives in late April.[132] They agreed that fiscal arrangements would be the "main item, of course" on the agenda.[133] The full conference was scheduled to kick off on 3 October 1955.

During the summer of 1955, finance ministry bureaucrats took over. On 17 June, an unnamed bureaucrat outlined "some possible lines of approach" that included "Plan C – Equalization Payments Applicable to All Provinces." Among the advantages of Plan C, Ottawa "could not be held to ransom" by provincial governments because Ottawa alone would determine equalization payments. As well, the use of revenues from income taxes and succession duties as a formula to establish grants to the poorer provinces "generally produces results easier to understand and to explain."[134] The choice was blunt: if Ottawa wanted "absolute and formal control," it should retain the tax rental deals, "and Ontario's signature would become essential"; if ending the fiscal isolation of Quebec was far more pivotal, Ottawa could drop the tax rental deals, minimizing "the possibility of a recurrence of the recent personal income tax imbroglio with Quebec."[135]

The memorandum made other terse observations. Wealthy Ontario did not regard the tax rental deals "as a sound approach [to the federation's fiscal problems] ... but only as a temporary expedient."[136] Ottawa would have to raise its concessions to secure that province's consent. Other provinces would then demand similar concessions. And that would further isolate and penalize Quebec.[137] As well, the tax rental approach could "invite some provinces to become fiscally irresponsible": whenever they needed more money, rather than raising taxes, they might "look to the Federal Government for increased grants."[138]

On 30 August, R.M. Burns summarized Ottawa's dilemma in a five-page memorandum. As he saw it, "the stone over which the agreements have stumbled has been the heavy penalty falling on Quebec for non-compliance and this equalization plan has the very considerable merit of providing a possible solution."[139] Premier Duplessis would likely accept the grants because "they would be unconditional and would involve no form of agreement."[140]

But Burns was backing away from the seemingly radical course of Plan C. He wanted to preserve as much of the tax rental deals as possible because that "might at least have the merit of salvaging some of the control and much of the tidyness [sic] that has existed since 1941."[141] The deals would survive one more round – but the times were changing. Twenty-five years later, Burns was still ruefully reflecting on why Ottawa grew "more flexible, some might even have said less self-confident" as the October 1955 conference approached.[142] His words were a lament for a lost time from a baffled fiscal centralist:

> No longer was there over-riding concern with central fiscal and economic controls which had been considered so vital from 1941 on. Whether this was a conscious conversion to a new spirit of federalism, a response to Quebec demands, a realistic assessment of changing provincial and public attitudes, a reaction to the political hazards of Keynesian management, or merely an unwillingness to continue to be pushed by the provinces to provide more revenue at federal political expense is not determinable. Undoubtedly all these factors influenced different people at different times. *The important point is that willingness to relinquish a measure of control existed*, even though it was not unanimous ... The basic ground rules were changing and the ideas that were sacrosanct in the 1941–52 period were no longer inviolable in 1955–56.[143]

Meanwhile, other officials were examining other models to remedy fiscal inequality. In early September, Economic Policy Division official E.A. Oestreicher prepared a thirty-two-page package for Deputy Finance Minister K.W. Taylor. He concluded:

- The Australian Commonwealth Grants Commission: "The most important criticism ... refers to the complexity of its method."[144]
- The Rowell-Sirois Report's proposed National Adjustment Grants, which were based on fiscal expenditures: "The basic dilemma is that the secular growth in national income encourages demands for an expansion of governmental activities." That is, voters could force provinces to spend more, and provinces would then demand more from Ottawa.[145]
- The controversial Ontario proposal for sharing from the Dominion-Provincial Conference of 1945–46: "An unusual feature of this proposal is that the funds ... are raised by provincial governments solely and are to be administered jointly with the federal government."[146]

- The American system of variable grants for specific programs such as public health and hospital construction: "In certain instances, the poorer states cannot really afford to take advantage of the federal offer. If they do, it sometimes results in a distortion of their services in favour of those subsidized by the federal government."[147]

By mid-September, the bureaucratic studies reached cabinet. St-Laurent "liked the plan" for equalization.[148] John Deutsch was "its main advocate" within the bureaucracy.[149] Finance Minister Harris, however, was receiving conflicting advice about equalization "from highly competent and respected senior advisors in his department."[150] This is evident from Burns's memo in late August in favour of the retention of the tax rental deals. Initially, Harris brought ambiguous advice to cabinet. He explained that the principle behind the tax rental deals was still sound – but it "would not *seem* to be in the national interest" to isolate Quebec.[151] The cabinet could replace the tax rental deals with equalization based on the fiscal capacity in two or three provinces with the highest tax potential *or* in the wealthiest province *or* on the national average.[152] Harris was torn. Pickersgill recounted that St-Laurent "became impatient with Harris for the only time in their close relationship that I can recall."[153] After many talks with Pickersgill and others, Harris did come to support equalization whole-heartedly.

Ottawa's tense relationship with Quebec ensured that it could not use spending needs as the basis for equalization. Ottawa had "relatively good data" on revenue-raising capacity but "much weaker" data on provincial spending. To obtain spending data, Ottawa would have been too intrusive – and the consultative process might have broken down; unit costs across the provinces differed for everything from public service salaries to capital expenditures; officials could not decide if there should be a difference between so-called controllable costs and uncontrollable costs; it would be difficult to disentangle the presence of other federal transfers from provincial spending; and the total provincial population might not produce "a reasonable result" for individual expenditure items.[154] It would be a risky business.

But equalization based on tax revenues was also difficult. There were ominous hints of the trouble during that pivotal cabinet discussion on 21 September 1955, which senior officials, including Deutsch and Burns, eventually joined. One "disturbing political problem" was that Quebec would get more than $40 million "while no payment was made to Ontario."[155] British Columbia and Prince Edward Island would receive less money under any future formula than under the tax rental deals (this was fixable).[156] And New Brunswick wanted the formula to recognize "the lower tax potential of certain provinces in other taxation fields as well."[157] All of the Atlantic provinces wanted more cash. St-Laurent did not pay enough attention to those issues, perhaps because there was little opportunity or money to fix two of the three of them.

But St-Laurent maintained his support for the basic proposal. As Pickersgill remarked, "it could be implemented without formal agreements with any provincial government, and would, therefore, leave the federal government free to determine, on its own, how great the equalization payments would be."[158] Significantly, Pickersgill added: "The opponents of the new plan in the bureaucracy objected to it on the ground that all the provincial governments would be free to impose any taxes they liked and the simplicity and the convenience of having a single personal income tax all over Canada might disappear."[159] Pickersgill dismissed this argument because Quebec already had its own income tax, calculated on a different basis.

This loss of federal control *appealed* to equalization's supporters. The grants could restore harmony and preserve the federation. But "it was characteristic of St.-Laurent's leadership that he left the management of the debate on equalization entirely to Harris and did not himself say a word during the enactment of a measure *for which he was uniquely responsible*."[160] In effect, St-Laurent drove this process. But he shunned the spotlight.

SOCIAL CITIZENSHIP ALSO ON THE TABLE

The push for expanded social security continued as Ottawa grappled with provincial needs. In late April 1955, Ottawa and the provinces discussed federal contributions for the unemployed employables. The first ministers concluded that it would be "impractical and invidious" to separate the hard-core unemployed, one by one, from everyone on relief. So they decided to remove the hard-core unemployed of "say 1 or 1.5 or 2 percent of the total population" from the list of those eligible for federal help.[161]

In mid-June, as the equalization discussions proceeded, Ottawa and many provinces tentatively agreed on a deal on unemployment assistance: the federal government would pay 50 percent of the costs of provincial relief whenever the number of people on relief exceeded 0.45 percent of a province's population (in Nova Scotia, the limit was set at 0.30 percent because of the depressed economic conditions). This excess group was deemed to represent the unemployed employables.[162]

The Unemployment Assistance Act passed on 11 July 1956, but it was retroactive to July 1955 since six provinces had signed agreements with Ottawa.[163] Ontario premier Leslie Frost refused to initial the deal, contending that Ottawa should pay 50 percent of the entire relief tab.[164] It was not until the new Progressive Conservative government removed the ceiling in December 1957 that Ontario joined.[165] In mid-1959, Quebec signed the deal – and its participation was made retroactive to 1958.[166] For the first time, Quebec adopted an assistance program for needy people who were not in hospital: "All provinces had signed agreements by 1959."[167] This federal contribution would eventually become the Canada Assistance Plan of 1966, which would contribute to the cost of *all* provincial welfare payments.

THE FEDERAL-PROVINCIAL CONFERENCE, OCTOBER 1955

The participants at the First Ministers' Conference in early October 1955 understood that they had put off the solution to provincial fiscal inequality – and therefore hindered the expansion of social security – for far too long. This conference was the discussion that St-Laurent had been preparing for since he first joined the Rowell-Sirois Commission in 1937. But the public plaudits were muted.

There was so much else to intrigue and delight Canadians as the first ministers huddled in conclave. On the evening that the conference opened, American evangelist Billy Graham urged an overflow Ottawa crowd of twenty-three thousand people, which included Alberta premier E.C. Manning and Newfoundland premier Joey Smallwood, to pray every day, read the Bible, go to church on Sundays, and bear witness to the Gospel. On the second day, the underdog Brooklyn Dodgers won the World Series in the final seventh game, beating the superstar New York Yankees. The coverage of both events dominated the front pages; a photo of Dodgers' pitcher Johnny Podres pushed a photo of St-Laurent, Alberta premier Manning, Ontario premier Frost, and Quebec premier Duplessis onto page two in the *Ottawa Journal*.[168]

There were so many other distractions. The Canadian Daily Newspaper Publishers Association boasted that circulation had hit "A New All Time High" of 3,867,000 despite competition from television, radio, magazines, and other media.[169] Canadian Pacific was offering train trips from Montreal to Vancouver and Toronto to Vancouver with scenic domes for all passengers and deluxe dining cars that offered the "surroundings of a luxurious hotel dining room."[170] *The Glenn Miller Story*, with James Stewart as the wartime bandleader who disappeared over the English Channel en route to Paris in December 1944 was playing at local theatres.[171] The new 1956 Ford Thunderbird with its elaborate tail fins and "thrilling" engine was finally available for test-driving.[172] RCA Victor now advertised a "deep image" television with a twenty-one-inch screen and a phonograph that could connect to the cabinet.[173]

A dominion-provincial conference that concentrated on the tax rental deals and equalization seemed stubbornly out of step with such heady times. The events on the first day were open; the next three days were closed. But, wherever the politicians appeared, they demonstrated the ongoing divide between the defenders of provincial rights, who wanted to preserve their fiscal and social bailiwicks, and the advocates of social security, who wanted Ottawa to continue fiscal centralization to redistribute funds, especially to the poorer provinces. Those were very clear-cut differences.

At the opening on Monday, 3 October, the prime minister was dignified, eloquent – and prepared to resolve the public's impatience. "Second only to national security are the demands of social security, *which the public expects of both Canada and the provinces in great measure*," he declared.[174] Fiscal arrangements were "the heart of our problem ... The public now expects both levels of government to do things which require high taxes."[175] He paid tribute to the Rowell-Sirois Commission for its "serious and scholarly effort," which included the call for constitutional changes that "were found impossible to accept."[176]

As yet, Ottawa had no definitive proposal. But it favoured payments based upon the yield of a set of standard taxes "to bring the revenue per capita up to some specified level defined in terms of what all provinces or certain provinces might obtain from those sources."[177] Provinces could continue the tax rental deals if they wished. Ottawa would likely provide a stabilization guarantee to ensure that no province lost money on any new deal. The bottom line was clear: Ottawa wanted "*to ensure that there will not be any first-class or any second-class kind of Canadian citizen.*"[178]

The premiers had mixed reactions. Ontario Premier Frost, who had brought thirty-three experts to the talks, warned that overly large subsidies to the poorer provinces could "destroy enterprise and productivity in the province from which the revenue is taken."[179] Ontario needed its tax revenues because it had to spend more on infrastructure to make money from economic development. But Frost also proposed expanded health and hospital insurance: Ottawa, the provinces, and the patients would share the costs of the provincially administered system. St-Laurent gravely responded that Ottawa might participate in a stage-by-stage program that would build up hospital infrastructure and then introduce hospital insurance – *if* the provinces with the majority of the population agreed.[180]

Quebec premier Duplessis remained adamantly opposed to the tax rental deals.[181] And he took a cynical view of Ottawa's need to centralize revenues. At an in-camera session, he pointed out that the temporary tax rental agreements appeared to have become permanent, with Ottawa's rationale changing from wartime needs to postwar reconstruction to defence. He observed with asperity: "if the provinces were to survive they must have breathing space."[182]

The federation was endlessly divergent. New Brunswick premier H.J. Flemming proposed that Ottawa bring the poorer provinces, including New Brunswick, up to 85 percent of the per capita personal income of Canada for the preceding three years.[183] The difference between New Brunswick and Ontario, let alone Quebec, was stark.

British Columbia premier W.A.C. Bennett insisted that he would only renew his tax rental deal if Ottawa recognized that "under the present formula we are not receiving a fair or adequate share."[184] Bennett had grown up in poverty in New Brunswick, moved to British Columbia in 1930, and established a chain of hardware stores. Dubbed "Wacky" by friends and foes, he won seven straight elections, starting in 1952.[185] Now he insisted that his province had "the right to substantially increased federal assistance ... No area [should] fall below the national average in the matter of social and educational services."[186] In fact, his province was wealthy – but Bennett wanted more.

Saskatchewan premier T.C. Douglas had just celebrated the golden anniversary of the province's creation in 1905. Governor General Vincent Massey – who had become Canada's first Canadian-born governor general in 1952 – kicked off the ceremonies in May with the official opening of the new Royal Saskatchewan Museum of natural history "dedicated to the pioneers of the province."[187] More than five hundred communities had written local histories and collected pioneer artefacts. The closing ceremonies were held on Labour Day with Prime Minister St-Laurent and several former premiers, including Charles Dunning and James Gardiner, in attendance.[188] Douglas could remember the 1930s "when the dust and the grasshoppers and the drought had us all down."[189] He was into his third term in office, and he wanted to honour the "vision and imagination and courage of the pioneers."[190]

Now he seconded New Brunswick's plea for equity. First ministers had an obligation to decide "what adjustment grants or equalization payments should be paid to the less favoured provinces to permit an equitable minimum standard of government services across Canada."[191] He was convinced that the majority of Canadians wanted "adequate levels of education, health and welfare services and economic development in all parts of Canada."[192] He eloquently dismissed St-Laurent's plea that Ottawa needed to earmark large amounts of revenue for defence: "The so-called 'cold war' is more than a contest of armaments; it is also a conflict of ideas ... [The greatest defence] is a happy and contented people who enjoy an increasing measure of protection against sickness, unemployment and want ... people who have a stake in the democratic way of life."[193]

The tax rental deals should continue because Ottawa needed sufficient revenues to fulfill its "responsibility for maintaining high levels of employment and income."[194] Douglas was a Keynesian.[195] He did not understand that the federation could no longer survive such fiscal centralization. Ottawa would renew the tax rental deals for one more term with those provinces that wanted to participate – but the end of such control was nigh.

There was one last grace note. After more than six years in Confederation, Newfoundland premier Joseph Smallwood declared that Newfoundlanders would "infinitely prefer" to finance their essential public services from natural resource taxes "rather than by dependence on a hand-out from the benevolent Federal government in Ottawa."[196] The fear of dependency haunted these discussions.

After four days of wrangling, the participants emerged with a vague message. Ottawa had proposed "a system of equalization payments to be made unconditionally by the Federal government to those provincial governments whose tax potential in the fields of personal income taxes, corporation taxes and succession duties was below some defined level."[197]

Ottawa had made the hard choice – and opted for equalization based on tax revenues. More than a decade later, Ottawa equalization expert Douglas H. Clark, who was the best of his bureaucratic generation on this topic, conceded: "The concept of fiscal need grants is superior to the concept of revenue equalization grants ... [but] very little progress has been made in our ability to make intergovernmental comparisons concerning the costs of and needs for public expenditures."[198] Roughly fifty years after the 1955 conference, University of Alberta economist Bev Dahlby added that Canada avoided Australia's system because it was difficult to define need – and provinces could distort their spending.[199] In effect, the federal government feared that provinces could game the system, exaggerating their needs to pocket more funds.

THE FORMULA

Four weeks after the conference adjourned, a senior federal official – who seems to have been R.M. Burns – summarized the provincial positions and posed twelve detailed policy challenges, including the possibility of extra payments for the Maritimes. He concluded that, if equalization payments were based upon tax collections in the wealthiest or the two wealthiest provinces, then "equalization can probably provide sufficient [revenues] for all provinces."[200] Officials clearly lacked acute political instincts for the seriousness of the Maritime dilemma.

Burns viewed Ontario with some derision as a poor-little-rich-kid regime. "While not opposing equalization as a principle or method, Ontario seemed to feel that the Federal adoption of the idea had gone too far."[201] That was a protest that would resound across the decades –and affect St-Laurent's re-election chances – until Ontario needed equalization, too.

When Burns turned to Quebec, he was smug. Duplessis left the impression "that there would be no basic objection in principle to the equalization formula." But Duplessis "did not seem prepared to recognize or accept the fact that on a basis of personal income per capita or tax collection per capita, Quebec was below the national average of provinces."[202] Despite its pride, Quebec would receive equalization.

There were more tart observations. Manitoba wanted to retain the tax rental deals, but it wanted its per-capita payments to be higher.

The province believed "the long-term interests of the economy were best served by some form of central control of tax policy."²⁰³ Manitoba also proposed *"supplementary fiscal need payments* where these were necessary."²⁰⁴

Saskatchewan premier Douglas agreed with Manitoba: he wanted to retain the tax rental deals, basing the rental arrangements "on equalization to the highest provinces with growth provisions."²⁰⁵ But he would penalize any provinces that did not sign rental deals by withholding any supplementary or equalization payments. Rather remarkably, Douglas wanted Ottawa to create "an incentive" for those who signed the deals as a "tangible reward in compensation."²⁰⁶ As Burns later wrote, Douglas rattled federal officials with his suggestion that only provinces that signed the deals should get the grants, "a bias the Government of Canada had been trying to avoid in the new approach."²⁰⁷

In the end, Burns was upbeat. "Equalization as an idea on principle seemed to get fairly general acceptance whether as a basis for payment under [tax rental] agreements or otherwise."²⁰⁸ There were caveats. Ontario and British Columbia felt the idea "could be carried too far"; New Brunswick and Saskatchewan wanted to extend the compensation to cover the revenues from other tax fields.²⁰⁹ There was also "a very strong body of opinion" that extra grants might be needed for the poorest provinces.²¹⁰ A cynic might say that it was business as usual within the fractious federation. A deal seemed possible.

THE DEBATE NEARS AN END

Equalization went back to the full cabinet twice during December 1955. On 7 December, the ministers weighed approaches that might placate New Brunswick and Nova Scotia. Should they adopt a two-pronged formula that used the average per capita personal income in the four wealthiest provinces – *as well as* the revenues from the three taxes – to determine equalization? "In effect, this would mean the payment of an additional subsidy."²¹¹

They decided that an extra grant of fifty cents per capita for every $100 below the average per capita personal income in the four provinces would only aggravate Quebec because "it would be said that ... federal authorities recognized they had taxed more than they should in the three main fields."²¹² Perhaps worse, the proposal to determine grants based on personal income "was arbitrary in nature and could be criticized as derisively small ... [and] seemed so full of problems."[213] They abandoned the notion. But St-Laurent and his ministers would regret this failure to address Maritime grievances.

Two weeks later, cabinet ministers went back to their original plan, playing with formulas. What about using the average yield of those three taxes from Ontario, British Columbia, and a sufficient portion of Quebec to bring the total up to one-half of the Canadian population? That would not work. "Equalizing to the top half was a difficult concept to understand and almost impossible to explain in public."[214] Ministers quailed at the very thought.

They wrestled with the mechanics of an equalization formula: How could they explain the needs of strangers – let alone their moral rights – to their fellow Canadians? What would happen if they based their calculations on the per capita average collections in the five wealthier provinces "to keep the equalization grants as low as possible?"[215] The use of the two wealthier provinces of Ontario and British Columbia as a base would mean higher equalization payments: How would the richer provinces and the West accept a formula that delivered $40 million to Quebec "if that was justified?"[216]

The cabinet decided to take a chance on the simpler formula, using only the two wealthiest provinces as the basis for their calculations, concluding that no provincial government with the possible exception of Ontario would offer much objection to the higher level of generosity: "The advantages of trying to keep this [equalization] grant [of $40 million to Quebec] a little below that figure by averaging to the top half [of the provinces] were far outweighed *by the disadvantages of adopting a formula which would be inexplicable.*"[217] They seriously underestimated the strength of Ontario's objections and its appeal to provincial rights.

The discussions were reaching an end. In early January, at three separate meetings, cabinet revised a letter outlining Ottawa's basic approach, which St-Laurent eventually sent to the provincial premiers.[218] The prime minister offered an amendment, which cabinet rejected because it might have committed future parliaments to financial obligations. But it was an indication of his involvement.[219] The cabinet also clarified the huge innovation of equalization: if a province did not rent its taxes, it would still receive increased grants, which would "guarantee a measure of stability in this sector."[220]

The plan was ready. St-Laurent now moved into the spotlight. The 10 January 1956 Speech from the Throne singled out the proposals to the provinces on fiscal relations.[221] One day later, the prime minister tabled Ottawa's letters to the premiers in the House of Commons. One day after that, during the debate on the Speech from the Throne, he outlined the basic approach under which every province except Ontario would receive equalization grants. "It has seemed to us that a system of applying a kind of provincial means tests ... would not be acceptable or workable in a country with our history and traditions," St-Laurent explained in his reply to Conservative leader George Drew's criticism. "We want something more objective than a provincial means test."[222] That is, Ottawa did not want to pry into what each province was spending to determine the size of its grants. Instead, it would look at what it had the capacity to collect in tax revenues.

The prime minister's demeanour was low-key, and it puzzled journalist George Bain. "There was no fire, and very little that was new ... Most parliamentary observers rated it one of his poorest performances. He sounded like a man who was tired or bored, or both."[223] St-Laurent was likely exhausted. As his biographer Dale C. Thomson noted, he was not in an "imaginative frame of mind" from early December onward. He was suffering from "the fatigue that appeared to recur annually, making his burdens seem almost unbearably heavy."[224]

On 15 February, the prime minister led the discussion on fiscal arrangements in cabinet. The ministers agreed that any reference to fiscal need in an invitation to the premiers for a follow-up meeting should not be seen "as a permanent refusal in principle of the proposals put forward by the Maritime provinces, although no definite commitments should be made."[225] Ottawa "was not in a position to make any further commitments or to accept another concept of fiscal need."[226] Cabinet also decided that Finance Minister Harris would discuss key technical issues with federal officials – and then brief St-Laurent and key regional ministers in-depth on the answers.[227] The prime minister was taking an abiding interest in equalization, even its detailed workings.

He should have seen the disasters ahead. Ottawa had promised in October 1955 to hold a final conference on fiscal arrangements, so the cabinet reluctantly scheduled another federal-provincial meeting for March.[228] The ensuing one-day gathering broke up acrimoniously. Behind closed doors, Ontario premier Frost warned: "There is no recognition in the formula of the fact that it costs money to earn money ... We simply cannot afford many of the services the other provinces now have."[229] He demanded the return of "at least $100 million more from these three main tax fields."[230] In public, he delivered a terrible verdict: "Today's lack of foresight will bring this country to the brink of economic disaster."[231]

The Maritime premiers were equally unsettled by the small size of their grants. New Brunswick's Hugh John Flemming explained that nothing extra had been done for his region, "in which the rate of economic growth has been so low." He demanded "a supplementary formula" that considered how little the province raised from its other taxes.[232] But he did counter Frost's assertions with a firm endorsement of equalization: "Our people are citizens of Canada ... They expect Canadian standards of health services; they expect Canadian standards of educational services; they expect roads built to Canadian standards; and they expect a way of life which is not too dissimilar from the way of life enjoyed by Canadians in other provinces."[233] Nova Scotia premier Henry D. Hicks lamented the limitations of the formula because it fell "far short of equalizing per capita revenue from all sources."[234]

St-Laurent had already ruled out the Maritime pleas. And he could not convince Frost to change his mind about the limits of generosity. But St-Laurent did not need Frost's consent to send equalization cheques from the federal government to the poorer provinces. On 14 June, cabinet changed the wording of the bill "to make clear that a tax rental agreement was not a required feature" of equalization.[235] That is, Quebec would receive equalization even though it did not sign a tax rental deal. On 12 July, federal ministers rejected Frost's demand for an additional $250 million for the provinces, including $100 million more for Ontario in its tax rental deal: "The Federal government had gone as far as it could."[236] To compensate, Frost reluctantly revived the province's corporation tax along with some previously discontinued levies.[237]

Ottawa's enabling legislation passed without amendment at the end of July 1956. In 1957–58, equalization payments were $139 million, including a $46.4 million peace offering to Quebec.[238] It was a godsend for the poorer provinces, although the Maritimes remained unhappy with the size of their grants. The new program commenced as the tax rental agreements reached their last renewal. All provinces signed the 1957–62 tax rental deals, except Ontario and Quebec. Ontario rented only its personal income tax, but it remained unsatisfied with its share of the tax that Ottawa collected. Quebec stayed out of this last postwar pact – finally without penalty.[239] There would be no more deals. The first cheques went out on 1 April 1957.

THE DÉNOUEMENT FOR ST-LAURENT

Almost forgotten now, equalization was then seen as pivotal to St-Laurent's career. As Pickersgill noted, the prime minister "regarded the settlement of the tax-sharing problem ... as more essential to the continued unity and growth of Canada than the construction of the [Trans Canada] pipeline ... [It was] a measure for which he [St-Laurent] was uniquely responsible."[240] The federal government had finally found a non-intrusive way to remedy fiscal and economic inequality among the provinces.

But St-Laurent had seriously underestimated the extent of Ontario premier Frost's dissatisfaction. Indeed, Frost turned his quest for a higher percentage of the personal income taxes in his tax rental deal into an issue during the June 1957 federal election. Frost had previously worked well with St-Laurent. Now, he went to war, denouncing "what he regarded as the pig-headedness of the St.-Laurent government."[241] The premier spoke frequently on behalf of the federal Tories. At a rally with Diefenbaker at Toronto's Massey Hall in late April, he explained that he had turned against the federal Liberals because "this province is vitally interested in what is happening down at Ottawa, with special reference to the question of taxation."[242]

Frost shrewdly coupled his demands with the stipulation that the "chronically poor" Atlantic provinces should also get an extra adjustment grant, "which softened the overt tax-grab component" of his plan.[243] "So effective was Frost at driving home his twin messages – more tax room for the wealthier provinces, equalization grants for the poorer provinces – that fiscal concerns became identified as a key battlefield in the federal election," notes historian P.E. Bryden.[244] Frost introduced Progressive Conservative leader John Diefenbaker at a Toronto rally with the declaration: "It is not a matter of the Federal Government giving Ontario or the Provinces anything. That is the patronizing attitude in Ottawa. All that we ask is a reasonable part of our own."[245] Diefenbaker reinforced the theme. At a rally in Trois-Rivières, Quebec, for one, he promised "more just" fiscal arrangements, and "termed sacred the provinces' rights under confederation."[246]

It was electoral dynamite. In a Gallup poll of almost two thousand Canadians in May 1957, the Liberals had the support of 37.9 percent compared to the Conservatives at 26.3 percent.[247] That represented an increase in the Liberal lead from 35.2 percent in March 1957 (the Conservatives had also increased their standing from 23.3 percent).[248] But St-Laurent lost the election. There were many reasons for the defeat, such as the perception of Liberal arrogance. But Frost almost certainly made the difference: in Ontario, the Liberals plummeted from fifty-one seats to twenty-one seats. Four Ontario cabinet ministers lost their ridings, including Finance Minister Harris. The *Globe and Mail* concluded that the electorate agreed "with the Frost-Diefenbaker contention that the provinces and municipalities deserved a better share of tax revenues."[249] The Tories gained one seat in New Brunswick and swept ten of the twelve seats in Nova Scotia, which had been a Liberal bastion.

Diefenbaker got the message. His new government provided grants-in-aid for the Atlantic provinces in mid-November 1957.[250] In late January 1958, after Frost sent stern reminders to Diefenbaker of his political debts, the federal Conservatives raised every province's share of the personal income tax that Ottawa collected.[251]

The social activists paid virtually no attention to St-Laurent's breakthrough in resolving provincial inequality. Few realized what equalization had accomplished. Or, if they did, they wanted more federal money for the provinces anyway – and they would link that demand with specific social spending. It was almost as if the advocates were unaware of the miracle of equalization. That was an irony that generations of beleaguered politicians and bureaucrats would have appreciated.

CONCLUSION

Equalization did not magically unite the partners in the Canadian federation. There would be many more battles ahead among Ottawa and the provinces over provincial autonomy, fiscal sharing, and the expansion of social citizenship. Saskatchewan would soon ask that Ottawa include petroleum and natural gas revenues in the formula calculation.[252] But the days of fiscal centralization were temporarily creaking to an end. Now nine provinces, including British Columbia, were cashing non-conditional cheques based upon a neutral formula (obviously, since British Columbia was the poorer of the two wealthiest provinces used in the formula, it received a relative pittance of $5.5 million, too).[253] Poorer provinces could count on regular transfers that raised their revenues to the per capita fiscal capacity of Ontario and British Columbia. It worked.

Perhaps the best summary of the miracle of equalization came from Prime Minister Lester Pearson, who recognized that sharing had brought freedom to the federation, allowing provincial governments to devise their own versions of social programs. On 31 March 1964, he told the first ministers that equalization was the key to a better world. He spoke in government jargon – but he captured the possibilities on the eve of the nation's centenary:

> We believe that in the past shared-cost programs have been essential to remove the obstacles created by the uneven fiscal capacity of the provinces and the competing demands on provincial treasuries ... *However, changing conditions – including, above all, the development of our system of equalization of revenues in the shared tax fields – now offer us more alternatives than we had in the past.* It is appropriate, therefore, to consider whether some of the shared programs should now be changed, with federal withdrawal and a full assumption of provincial responsibility.[254]

Quebec accepted Pearson's offer as a new way to fund specific social programs. Ottawa lowered its income taxes by several percentage points while Quebec raised its taxes by the equivalent amount. Ottawa then equalized this amount from each percentage point of provincial tax to bring it up to federal levels. The federation had not solved inequality. But it had found a remedy that, however briefly, satisfied (almost) every government. And, almost unnoticed, Pearson attributed the evolution of social security to this unlovely program that only an accountant could love.

The federation partners now had their fiscal peace treaty.

Conclusion

Fiscal inequality can destroy federations. The wealthier provinces have the money to provide better services while imposing lower taxes. The poorer provinces struggle to fund basic care. They keep raising taxes – but they can never catch up. Jealousy eats into their politicians and their voters. They blame Ottawa and their fellow citizens in the richer states, convinced that federal policies are rigged against them. They see wealthier provinces – just across an invisible border – doing so much better that the contrast can be visible, even in road quality or schools. Their citizens consider moving when they need better services such as health care.

Equalization is sharing with a wry twist. If federations do not share, if they do not ease the fiscal and economic inequalities among their members, they may not survive. In theory, federal sharing is a moral act, whereby money is given freely to a provincial government as a *right* of social citizenship. Those ideals are still cited as a legitimate defence for Canada's huge federal transfer program of equalization, which ensures that all provinces can provide relatively equal levels of services for relatively equal levels of taxation. And that remains the foundational ideal.

But the reality is that equalization is also a hardheaded bargain that ties Ottawa along with the richer and the poorer provinces into a skein of calculated trade-offs. The formula is complex, but *theoretically* beyond any political interference that would tamper with payments. Provincial treasurers can figure out their annual entitlements – and they can usually budget ahead for several years because the amounts remain relatively stable and stabilized. The federal government – with the sometimes grudging consent of the wealthier provinces – hands out the cash that it collects from taxpayers in all provinces. It cannot tell the poorer recipients how to spend the money. There are no application forms. It is not a beloved social program like Medicare or an obvious lifesaver such as federal transfers for postsecondary education.

Instead, it is a practical system that took decades to develop after close consideration of important models such as the Australian Commonwealth Grants Commission. It is designed to keep the peace. When richer provinces such as Alberta and Saskatchewan object to the generosity of the transfers or to Ottawa's apparent stinginess with their governments, or when poorer provinces such as New Brunswick hint about the need for more funds, federal politicians should take those complaints seriously. For almost sixty-five years, Canada has survived such unsettling criticisms with good luck and adept politicking. As political scientists André Lecours and Daniel Béland observe, "In virtually all federal systems, equalization triggers some discontent amongst the federal units."[1] The trick is to treat every province with respect. Not all complaints can be resolved, at least not permanently. So far, however, despite mutual resentments among the poorer and the richer provinces, sharing has largely worked.

There is now relative fiscal equity across provincial boundaries. An Environics Institute report in 2015 concluded that Canadian public schools "are among the best in the world at helping to level the playing field between rich and poor children, and Canada is one of only a very few high-immigration countries that show no significant achievement gap between immigrants and non-immigrants."[2] The effect can be seen in a comparison with the United States, which has no comparable equalization program: in no Canadian province "does spending per student fall below 90 percent of the national average, or rise above 120 percent. In contrast, spending in the US falls below 90 per cent of the national average in 22 states ... [It] rises above 120 per cent in 11 states."[3]

Prime Minister Louis St-Laurent and his Liberal government adopted equalization in 1956 to soothe the tensions within the federation, especially with Quebec, which would not allow Ottawa to collect its key taxes after the Second World War. Ottawa could – and eventually would – tinker with the equalization formula across the decades, usually to include the revenues from more taxes in its calculations. But equalization was sharing without the messy process of federal ad hoc handouts, subsidies, and loans that had prevailed in the past. There were few complaints, partly because few Canadians understood the system – or grasped its importance in the funding of social services in the poorer provinces. There were few compliments because the intricacies of equalization were a mystery – even to many federal and provincial cabinet ministers. And that remains just the way that most insiders like it.

Alberta's denunciations of Ottawa are often alarming – and widely misunderstood within the province and across the nation. But equalization has saved the federation. The poorer provinces could participate in the expansion of social programs such as Medicare because they finally had the funds. The principle, which was embedded in the Constitution in 1982, has become a pivotal fiscal tie that binds every province to Ottawa and to each other.

HISTORIC ROOTS

Sharing among the federal and provincial governments was not a novelty when the first equalization cheques went out on 1 April 1957. Throughout the first ninety years of Confederation, the partners had haggled, fretted, and feuded over inequality and inequity. Ottawa provided subsidies to all provinces, which were theoretically equal. But those subsidies could be quietly manipulated to send extra cash to the poorer ones: negotiators offered extra cash to the Maritimes as an inducement to join Confederations. It was an unsatisfactory, often slapdash and inherently unfair solution for inequality – if only because the extra payments were minimal and the decisions were often ad hoc.

Meanwhile, Ottawa effectively implemented a "systematic consolidation and centralization of [fiscal] power."[4] Poorer provinces often blamed the very act of federation for their plight – and demanded special subsidies for their inherently unequal fiscal status and their fiscal needs. Subsidies, in effect, became economic *and* political acts that tacitly addressed inequality. But there were limits to Ottawa's power. The richer provinces resented Ottawa's largesse with *their* taxpayers' funds. They invoked the fiction that all provinces were purportedly equal. Their ire restrained overt federal bids to buy popularity with flashy announcements in poorer provinces.

Ottawa could usually maintain a temporary peace. But the Confederation bargain had not foreseen the diminution in the value of the fixed subsidies across time, the loss of traditional social supports from churches and extended family, and the growth of provincial responsibilities. By the late 1920s and into the 1930s, as the role of governments in Canadian society escalated, Ottawa scrambled to help provinces provide minimal services such as relief for their citizenry.

Amid the iron grip of the Depression, however, it was difficult to maintain this approach for the federation's poorer members in the Prairies and the Maritimes. Politicians and bureaucrats realized that the division of revenues and responsibilities within the federation was not working. And after decades of close contact with their fellow dominion of Australia, they had the ingenious example of the Australian Commonwealth Grants Commission, which had found a far less contentious way to ease federation resentments.

THE SHAPE OF A SOLUTION

In Depression-era Canada, there was no thought of espousing federal non-conditional transfers to the poorer provinces – and there was not enough money to do much anyway. But by the mid-1930s, federal bureaucrats and politicians – as well as some remarkable provincial politicians such as Manitoba premier John Bracken and Nova Scotia premier Angus L. Macdonald – knew that the Australian Commonwealth government was sharing federal funds with the poorer states. They kept tabs on Canada's sister federation, and the interest was mutual.

The Canadians were diligent. They scrutinized the workings of the Australian Loan Council: under an agreement in 1929, the Commonwealth government took over all state debts and then put responsibility for future federal or state borrowing under the council. They knew that, under the so-called Premiers' Plan of 1931, Australia had reduced real wages, slashed government expenditures, cut interest charges, expanded central bank credit to finance deficits and loans for necessary works, and depreciated its currency.

Most important, Bank of Canada and finance ministry officials were aware of Australia's brush with the risks of inequality. When the residents of Western Australia voted to secede in 1933, federal politicians created the Commonwealth Grants Commission to transfer funds based largely on fiscal need to the poorer states. All states accepted the commission's decisions because it operated at arm's length from Canberra – and the formula appeared to be politically neutral. In turn, the Australians followed Canada's political and economic issues – but they were particularly interested in the increasingly desperate efforts of the Western provinces during the 1930s to avoid default. It was clear that the Canadian federal system was not working.

Throughout the mid- to late 1920s and well into the 1930s both Canada and Australia set up commissions to probe the inequalities that were creating such profound dissatisfaction and near ruin. Royal commissions in each nation started to cite reports from its sister dominion. Each inquiry asked if the poorer states were put in an inferior position by the very structure and provisions of the federation. Each asked if central governments should treat their members equally in the distribution of subsidies or if they should ease fiscal inequality.

As the Depression-era pressures increased, Prime Minister Mackenzie King finally set up the Royal Commission on Dominion-Provincial Relations. That commission studied how other federations, especially Australia, tackled fiscal inequalities. The resulting report, which was tabled in wartime in May 1940, called for Ottawa to centralize key provincial tax revenues and to provide National Adjustment Grants for key areas of provincial spending. Such revisions in revenues and responsibilities would have entailed radical change – and Prime Minister King eschewed that approach. But the call for National Adjustment Grants did provide another model for equalization. In effect, the report made a breakthrough when it concluded that the poorer provinces should be able to provide roughly comparable services at roughly comparable levels of taxation.

After three provinces rejected the Royal Commission's report in January 1941, Ottawa unilaterally centralized key provincial revenues from income taxes and succession duties – and sent compensatory grants to the provinces, which were minimally equalized. In peacetime, the federal government fought to keep control of those revenues, embracing the Keynesian notion that it should spend during economic downturns. Quebec resisted Ottawa's fiscal centralization schemes in peacetime. It fiercely defended its decision on constitutional grounds, but deeply resented the loss of generous compensatory grants.

The situation became untenable. Quebec was dangerously alienated. Other provinces played hardball during tax rental negotiations. Meanwhile, politicians and bureaucrats became increasingly sensitive to the lobbying for expanded social security, especially within the Rest of Canada. There was an eerie absence of concern about fiscal inequality: civil society groups wanted progress on social security but they did not see the elephant in the federal-provincial room. The first ministers discussed national programs for hospital care and social assistance while the poorer provinces explained that they could barely meet their existing social responsibilities, let alone their citizens' often-eloquent demands.

Ottawa could no longer ignore the danger to national unity that the five-year tax rental deals posed as they neared another expiry date in 1957. Nor could Ottawa and the provinces ignore the calls from social advocates for expanded social care. It was a stalemate.

THE HEART OF THE STRUGGLE

Equalization was a long time coming because Ottawa and the provinces were embroiled in a battle over the division of revenues and responsibilities. Ottawa wanted a strong central government with control over the lion's share of the tax revenues. Remarkably, many politicians and officials did not accept or even understand the strength of provincial rights. Quebec wanted to protect its cultural and linguistic responsibilities through control of its own tax revenues. Richer provinces such as Ontario wanted to preserve their taxpayers' revenues for *their* purposes – and they objected to the size of Ottawa's subsidies to their poorer kin.

It was impossible to simply emulate the Commonwealth Grants Commission. For more than 130 years, Australia and Canada have been "rivals, allies, and models."[5] But the central government in Australia had far more power than the states – and the cultural differences among the states were far less marked. Canada had to find its own way, drawing inspiration from the Australian model but staking out an approach that worked for this federation.

Commonsense prevailed. At least two initial conditions for reform were necessary. First, there had to be a changing of the guard in Ottawa: Mackenzie King was too cautious about increased federal spending – and exceedingly wary of projects such as nationwide hospital insurance that might set Ottawa on a collision course with Quebec. Second, his successor, Prime Minister Louis St-Laurent, had to moderate his support for fiscal centralization. St-Laurent had spent his political career within the Ottawa establishment, absorbing its centralizing approach to fiscal federalism.

By the mid-1950s, however, that mind-set was simply too risky. Ottawa could not barge into areas of provincial jurisdiction such as hospital care – and run national programs. But the poorer provinces could not create programs that were roughly similar to those in the richer provinces without extra funding or impossible levels of taxation. St-Laurent was also uneasily aware that the tax rental agreements – which Quebec would not sign – had awakened a nationalist resistance to Ottawa's policies.

The prime minister backed down. He separated the grants that compensated the poorer provinces for their revenue needs from the tax rental deals. In January 1955, St-Laurent settled the tax dispute with Quebec – and informed the other provinces that Ottawa's primary aim was to "make it financially possible for all provinces, whatever their tax base, to perform their constitutional functions themselves and to provide a reasonable Canadian level of provincial services without an abnormal burden of taxation."[6] The tax rental deals were nearing their end.

The prime minister was involved in the settlement. He had been the francophone counsel for the Royal Commission on Dominion-Provincial Relations. He worked closely with the treasury official J.J. Deutsch, who had been the assistant research director – and then the research director – of that Royal Commission. Both St Laurent and Deutsch were well aware of the Australian model and the National Adjustment Grants.

St-Laurent oversaw the search for a formula as the chair of a three-person cabinet committee to prepare for federal-provincial talks. Unlike the Australian model, his government did not link equalization with provincial spending. Nor did it link the size of the grants to specific provincial spending, as the Royal Commission had advocated. Instead, equalization compensated provinces for inequalities in fiscal capacity based upon the average per capita collection from three major taxes in the two wealthiest provinces of British Columbia and Ontario. All provinces were brought up to that level, which included a payment for British Columbia.

ST-LAURENT'S FATE

The amounts of the equalization grants did not please everyone. Ontario objected to its compensation for renting its personal income taxes. The Maritime provinces grudgingly accepted their cheques –

but they wanted more money for their special needs. During the June 1957 federal election campaign, Ontario premier Leslie Frost astutely combined his demands with the Maritime complaints. As a result, "fiscal concerns became identified as a key battlefield."[7] The unlikely issue of fiscal and economic inequality had its (brief) moment of fame – and, partly for that reason, St-Laurent lost to Progressive Conservative John Diefenbaker.

In November 1957, Diefenbaker's government provided extra grants to the hard-pressed Atlantic provinces. In January 1958, it mollified Ontario by returning a larger share of its personal income tax revenues, moving from 10 to 13 percent (that decision applied to all provinces that had rented their personal income taxes).[8] Only then, with relative peace among the federation members, could all governments finally accept the program. As historian P.E. Bryden maintains, "a coherent system of equalization" was only possible when "the federal government began to tap into Ontario's rich fiscal capacity, and Ontario agreed on a political level to this form of redistribution."[9] In effect, the Ontario economy had to generate more wealth for Ottawa – *and* for the provincial government – before such formal sharing became generally acceptable.

THE BARGAIN

Equalization has been a deft compromise. Fiscal disparities among federation members can create regional identities that become bred in the bone, instilling expectations and resentments in succeeding generations. They can disrupt economic efficiency and equity – if only because populations in poorer regions could receive inferior standards of services that ill-prepare them for their social and economic world *or* they could move to another province for better care. As economists Anwar Shah and Robin Boadway observe, equalization transfers "create one of those rare instances in economics when equity and efficiency considerations coincide."[10]

The precise reasons for inequality may only capture the attention of the initiates – those politicians and civil servants within the inner circles of government finance. But the discourse of inequality can seep throughout the federation, arousing envy within the poorer provinces and acrimony within the wealthier provinces. If a nation-state is the geographic area over which citizens are prepared to share – to paraphrase sociologist Raymond Breton – then the vitality of the equalization program is an important indicator of the health of the nation-state.

Equalization heralded the introduction of new social programs. In July 1956, before the first cheques were in the mail, Ottawa agreed to pick up the tab for a portion of provincial social assistance for those who had exhausted their unemployment insurance benefits. In 1957, Ottawa agreed to fund half of the costs of a specific set of provincial hospital and diagnostic services: provinces would get 25 percent of their per capita costs and 25 percent of the national per capita costs. The plan would take effect on 1 July 1958 – *if* six provinces representing a majority of Canadians agreed to participate. A few days later, six provinces signed up – and hospital coverage commenced on 1 July 1958.

There were more innovations. In 1966, Ottawa introduced the formal Canada Assistance Plan, which picked up half of the costs of social assistance benefits and services. That same year, Ottawa passed the innovative Medical Care Act, which initially paid 50 percent of the national average costs for insured medical services on an equal per capita basis. By 1972, all provinces had embraced Medicare. In 1967, Ottawa introduced a cost-sharing agreement on postsecondary education: provincial governments could accept 50 percent of the operating costs of such institutions or a specific per capita amount.

Ottawa applied the principle of equalization with imagination. In 1964, it established the so-called interim agreement on specific shared-cost programs. It allowed the provinces to occupy tax room that it had vacated – and then it ensured that the provincial revenue from those tax points was equalized. Provinces could operate their own programs in exchange for a tax abatement, *an equalization payment to bring the province up to what it would have received from those tax points*, and an operating cost adjustment. Only Quebec accepted this arrangement.

In effect, equalization became the key to another quiet revolution. Indeed, it was an almost unnoticed revolution. But, without this transfer program, the social security network could not have expanded. The wealthier provinces could count on equalization as a back-up plan if their fortunes changed (Ontario briefly qualified in the late 1970s – and it was a recipient province in the twenty-first century). The poorer provinces could provide relatively similar levels of services for relatively similar levels of taxation.

The equalization mechanism is not perfect. It is an adjustable fiscal creation, neither inherently good nor bad. But it is immensely useful.

Poorer provinces may flirt with dependency. For example, fiscal analysts have wondered aloud if New Brunswick has rejected fracking because it is politically easier to pocket equalization than to earn those controversial resource revenues.[11] Richer provincial governments have become resentful, most recently with Alberta premier Jason Kenney's denunciation of the generous payments to Quebec. But somehow, so far, the power of non-conditional sharing has pulled the nation through.

Equalization is a program that should be adjusted to ensure its survival. But equalization is also a principle that should be cherished. It is a gift from the generation that came home from the Second World War to make a better world.

Notes

INTRODUCTION

1 Jason Kenney interview, posted on YouTube, 24 August 2017. https://www.youtube.com/watch?v=hITOA02BEpM.
2 Ibid.
3 "Bill Morneau Requests Quick Review of Provinces' Calls for Expanded Stabilization Pogram," *Globe and Mail*, 17 December 2019, https://www.theglobeandmail.com/politics/article-health-care-stabilization-transfers-top-provinces-requests-to/.
4 The survey was conducted by the Environics Institute for Survey Research in partnership with policy think tanks across Canada. It was conducted in January 2019 with a representative sample of 5,732 Canadians ages eighteen and over.
5 Brown, *Equalization*, 5.
6 Courchene, *Social Canada in the Millennium*, 13. Courchene attributes a portion of this insight into the relatively diminished influence of class in Canada to social policy analyst Keith G. Banting in his "Neoconservatism in an Open Economy."
7 As quoted in the federal budget speech of Finance Minister Walter Harris, 14 March 1957, 8, http://publications.gc.ca/collections/collection_2016/fin/F1-23-1-1957-eng.pdf.
8 Béland and Lecours, "Fiscal Federalism and American Exceptionalism," 302.
9 Ibid., "Accommodation and the Politics of Fiscal Equalization in Multinational States," 347.
10 Political scientist Ronald L. Watts has briefly documented the history of pre-modern federal systems from ancient Israeli tribes and Indigenous confed-

eracies in North America in 1200 BCE through the Roman Empire, mediaeval Italy, Germany, and Switzerland. Both Watts and Malcolm M. Feeley and Edward Rubin attribute the first explicitly modern discussion of federalism to the seventeenth-century political philosopher Johannes Althusius.
11 Watts, *Comparing Federal Systems*, 3rd ed., 3. Watts summarizes the history of nineteenth- and twentieth-century federations.
12 Donaghy, *Parallel Paths*.
13 Canada, *Report of the Royal Commission on the Constitution*, 74, 81.
14 Donaghy, *Parallel Paths*.
15 McKenzie and MacMillan, "Introduction," in MacMillan and McKenzie, *Parties Long Estranged*, 3.
16 Béland et al., *Fiscal Federalism and Equalization Policy in Canada*, 18.
17 Banting, "Neoconservatism in an Open Economy," 153.
18 Watts, *Comparing Federal Systems*, 3rd ed., 3.
19 Feeley and Rubin, *Federalism*, 1.
20 The Constitution Act, 1867, clause 92, subsection 2. Note that sales taxes have subsequently been deemed to be direct taxes.
21 Ibid., clause 91, subsection 24.
22 Ibid., subsection 3.
23 Silver, *French-Canadian Idea of Confederation*, 50.
24 Bélanger, Readings in Quebec History, last updated August 2000, http://faculty.marianopolis.edu/c.belanger/quebechistory/readings/special.htm.
25 First Nations were largely ignored then: their consent was not sought – even though their peoples represented another major component of the nation. Instead, the Constitution granted control over "Indians, and lands reserved for the Indians" to Ottawa. It was only in 1982 that existing Aboriginal and treaty rights were affirmed – along with rights that could be acquired in future land claims agreements. See Constitution Act, 1867, clause 91, section 24; Constitution Act, 1982, clause 35.
26 Weir and Skocpol, "State Structures," in *Bringing the State Back In*, 108.
27 Esping-Andersen, "Three Political Economies," 145–8.
28 History of Pensions and Other Benefits in Australia, Australian Department of Social Security, http://www.abs.gov.au/ausstats/abs@.nsf/94713ad445ff1425ca25682000192af2/8e72c4526a94aaedca2569de00296978!OpenDocument.
29 Skocpol, *Protecting Soldiers and Mothers*, 10.
30 US Social Security Administration, Historical Background and Development of Social Security, https://www.ssa.gov/history/briefhistory3.html.

31 Bryden, "Pooling Our Resources," 401.
32 Ibid., "Obligations of Federalism," 76.

CHAPTER ONE

1 As quoted from the *Daily Mirror*, 24 September 1962, in Field, *Lyndhurst Falkiner Giblin*, 17. Field is a former premier of Tasmania.
2 According to his friends, Giblin was initially denied access to the bank's elevators after his appointment in October 1935 because the lift operators refused to believe that he was entitled to enter the second-floor boardroom. See Bartley, "Giblin and the Commonwealth Bank," 56. See also Field, *Lyndhurst Falkiner Giblin*, 7.
3 Royal Commissioner J.W. Dafoe to Commonwealth Grants Commission Chairman F.W. Eggleston, 5 July 1938, National Archives of Australia, MS 423, 1, 55, p. 2.
4 Ward, *History of Australia*, 205–6.
5 Musgrave, "Western Australian Secessionist Movement," 104.
6 Besant, "Two Nations, Two Destinies," 216.
7 The Dominion League, State Library of Western Australia. This site says the league was founded in July 1930, http://www.slwa.wa.gov.au/federation/sec/049_domi.htm.
8 Ward, *History of Australia,*" 205–6.
9 "W. A. Secession: Petition Disallowed Committee's Report Minority Request," *Mercury*, 25 May 1935, 14, https://trove.nla.gov.au/newspaper/article/30087998.
10 Bartley, "Giblin and the Commonwealth Bank," 61.
11 Besant, "Two Nations, Two Destinies," 216.
12 Field, *Lyndhurst Falkiner Giblin*, 22.
13 Bird, *Federal Finance in Comparative Perspective*, 141.
14 "Special Grants in the Australian Federation," *Bank of Nova Scotia Monthly Review*, May 1938. The National Archives of Australia, Canada – Internal Politics, ser. A 981, CAN 24, pt. 1, barcode 173375. p. 4. I am also grateful to Bank of Nova Scotia archivist Andrea McCutcheon for confirming this report – and supplying other monthly reviews.
15 Brown, "Giblin and the Grants Commission," 55.
16 Besant, "Two Nations, Two Destinies," 296.
17 Brown, "Giblin and the Grants Commission," 55.
18 Unpublished autobiography of H.F. Angus, chap. 7, Library and Archives Canada (hereafter LAC), MG 30, ser. E274, vol. 1, 274.

19 *Report of the Royal Commission on Dominion-Provincial Relations*, 9.
20 Gower, "Note on Canadian Unemployment since 1921," http://www.statcan.gc.ca/pub/75-001-x/1992003/87-eng.pdf.
21 Commission press secretary Wilfrid Eggleston, for one. See Eggleston, *While I Still Remember*, 229.
22 Keith Stewart, "Movie-Go-Round," *Toronto Daily Star*, 22 July 1938, 13.
23 "Tone Leaves 'Ambitious' Joan: Love Walks Out of Stars' Home," *Toronto Daily Star*, 20 July 1938, 19.
24 "Throat Infection Keeps Quints Abed," *Globe*, 8 August 1938.
25 "Palais Royale," ad in *Globe*, 8 August 1938, 8.
26 "Free to the Public: Christian Science Reading Rooms," ad in *Globe*, 8 August 1938, 2.
27 Campbell, *Respectable Citizens*," 80.
28 Courchene, *Equalization Payments*, 17.
29 Grant, *W. A. Mackintosh*, 145–51; Wardhaugh, *Behind the Scenes*, 62, 122. Robert Skidelsky, "Keynes and Canada," Toronto seminar, 6 November 2001.
30 Dominion-Provincial Conference, 1935, 13 December 1935, in *Dominion-Provincial Conferences*, 63.
31 Ferguson and Wardhaugh, "Impossible Conditions of Inequality," 3.
32 Bank of England Advisor Raymond Kershaw to Bank of Canada Governor Graham Towers, 2 September 1937, Bank of Canada Archives, Secretary's Fonds, Royal Commission on Dominion-Provincial Relations, B95-291, 1.
33 Bank of Canada Governor Graham Towers to Bank of England Advisor Raymond Kershaw, 10 September 1937, Bank of Canada Archives, Secretary's Fonds, Royal Commission on Dominion-Provincial Relations, B95-29, 1.
34 Margaret E. Prang entry on Newton Wesley Rowell, *Dictionary of Canadian Biography*, http://www.biographi.ca/en/bio/rowell_newton_wesley_17E.html.
35 Unpublished autobiography of H.F. Angus, chap. 7, LAC, MG 30, series E274, vol. 1, 260.
36 Ibid., 261.
37 John Dafoe to Resources Minister T.A. Crerar, 21 April 1937, University of Manitoba Archives, John Dafoe Fonds, box 14, fol. 1, 2, 4.
38 Unpublished autobiography of H.F. Angus, chap. 7, LAC, MG 30, ser. E274, vol. 1, p. 262. MacKay claims, however, that Alexander Skelton organized the research plan. Enclosure to R.M. Fowler from R.A. MacKay, unpublished memoir of R.A. MacKay, LAC, MG 30, ser. E159, vol. 10, file: Correspondence and Personal Reminiscences of the Rowell-Sirois Commission, 1963. As well, backing this assertion that Rowell offered the general outlines – and

Skelton put them into effect. See John Dafoe to Alexander Skelton (who was still at the Bank of Canada), 27 August 1937, University of Manitoba Archives, John Dafoe Fonds, box 5, fol. 1. 1–2.
39 Thomson, *Louis St. Laurent*, 95.
40 Ibid.
41 Newton Rowell to John Dafoe, 23 November 1937. As quoted in the entry for Joseph Sirois in the *Dictionary of Canadian Biography*, http://www.biographi.ca/en/bio/sirois_joseph_17E.html.
42 *The Argus* editor Edward Cunningham to John Wesley Dafoe, 9 March 1926, correspondence, Dafoe Papers, LAC, MG 30, D45, p. 1.
43 Thomson and Dafoe, "Bibliography of J. W. Dafoe."
44 Royal Commissioner J.W. Dafoe to Commonwealth Grants Commission Chairman F.W. Eggleston, 5 July 1938, National Archives of Australia, MS 423, 1, 55. 2.
45 Ferguson and Wardhaugh, "Impossible Conditions of Inequality," 5.
46 Cook, *Politics of John W. Dafoe*, 223.
47 John Wesley Dafoe to Sir James Barrett, 9 January 1939, correspondence, Dafoe Papers, LAC, MG 30, D45, 2.
48 Unpublished autobiography of H.F. Angus, chap. 7, LAC, MG 30, ser. E274, vol. 1, 256.
49 Ibid., 269.
50 As quoted in Waite, *Lives of Dalhousie University*, 2:55.
51 R.A. MacKay, "Some Personal Reminiscences of the Rowell-Sirois Commission," 26 July 1963, LAC, MG 30, vol. 10, ser. E159, file: Correspondence and Personal Reminiscences of the Rowell Sirois Commission 1963, 1–7.
52 "The Political Ideas of William Lyon Mackenzie," *Canadian Journal of Economics and Political Science* 3, 1 (1937): 3.
53 Diary of William Lyon Mackenzie King, 2 December 1938, 3, http://www.bac-lac.gc.ca/eng/discover/politics-government/prime-ministers/william-lyon-mackenzie-king/Pages/item.aspx?IdNumber=19655&.
54 Research Director D.A. Skelton to Royal Commissioner Henry Forbes Angus, 21 August 1937, Royal Commission on Dominion-Provincial Relations, LAC, C-6988, RG 33, ser. 23, 15. See also File: Angus, H.F., LAC, RG 33, ser. 23, vol. 71.
55 Fransen, "Unscrewing the Unscrutable," v.
56 Ibid.
57 Ibid.
58 *Report of the Royal Commission on Dominion-Provincial Relations*, 1:245. http://publications.gc.ca/collections/collection_2016/bcp-pco/Z1-1937-2-1-2-eng.pdf.

59 Ibid.
60 Ibid.
61 Ibid.
62 Rowell-Sirois Commission Secretary Alex Skelton to Commissioner John Dafoe, 12 September 1938, John Dafoe Fonds, University of Manitoba Archives, box 14, fol. 3, 3.
63 Unpublished autobiography of Henry Angus, chap. 7, LAC, MG 30, ser. E274, vol. 1, 266–7.
64 Professor R.O. Macfarlane, "An Historical Approach to the Canadian Constitution: Extracts from a Broadcast of the Kelsey Club, Winnipeg over the Network of the Canadian Broadcasting Corporation Recently," in *Monetary Times*, 30 October 1937, National Archives of Australia, Canada Constitutional, ser. A981, CAN 13, pt. 2, barcode 173360, 1.
65 Memorandum for the Australian Trade Commissioner, Canada, from W.R. Hodgson, 16 December 1937, National Archives of Australia, Canada Constitutional, ser. A 981, CAN 13, pt. 2, barcode 173360, 1.
66 Treasury Department Assistant Secretary to the Department of External Affairs Secretary, 11 August 1938, National Archives of Australia, Canada Constitutional, ser. A 981, CAN 13, pt. 2, barcode 173369, 1.
67 Prime Minister J.A. Lyons to Prime Minister William Lyon Mackenzie King, 24 December 1937, as quoted in Acting Secretary of the Treasury to Secretary Department of External Affairs in Canberra, with copy to Australian Trade Commissioner, 18 March 1938, National Archives of Australia, Canada Constitutional, ser. A 981, CAN 13, pt. 2, barcode 173360. n.p. within file but page 2 of letter.
68 Prime Minister J.A. Lyons to Prime Minister William Lyon Mackenzie King, 1 February 1938. King's private secretary H.R.L. Henry forwarded the letter to Alex Skelton, LAC, microfilm reel C-3735, vol. 253, reference number MG 26-J1, P. 215501.
69 Royal Commission Secretary Alex Skelton to Commonwealth Bank of Australia London Manager A.H. Lewis, 2 May 1938, LAC, RG 33, ser. 23, vol. 71, 1.
70 Commonwealth Bank of Australia London Manager A.H. Lewis to Royal Commission Secretary Alex Skelton, 18 May 1938, LAC, RG 33, ser. 23, vol. 71, file: Witnesses Called, 1.
71 Ibid.
72 Fullerton, *Graham Towers and His Time*, 111, 113.
73 "Confidential Memorandum: Royal Commission on Economic Basis of Confederation," by W.C. Clark, 7 December 1936, LAC, RG 19, E 2 C, vol. 22, file 101-85-15 General File, 1–2.

74 "Extract: Memorandum re: Conversation with Mr. Armstrong of Australia," 17 April 1937, Bank of Canada Archives, Secretary's Fonds, Royal Commission on Dominion-Provincial Relations, B95-291, ASK 1939, 1.
75 Bank of Canada memo, 3 May 1937, appears to be initialed by J.A.C. Osborne, Bank of Canada Archives, Department of Bank Operations Fonds, Secretary's Fonds, Royal Commission on Dominion-Provincial Relations, B95-291, ASK 1939, 1.
76 Telegram from L.F. Giblin to Royal Commission Secretary D.A. Skelton, Cunard White Star *Andania*, 5 August 1938, LAC, RG 33, ser. 23, vol. 71, 1–4.
77 Royal Commissioner R.A. MacKay to Kathleen MacKay, 9 August 1938, LAC, MG 30, ser. E159, vol. 10, file: Sirois Commission: Personal Letters, MacKay to his wife Kathleen, 1937–38, 2.
78 "Some Personal Reminiscences of the Rowell-Sirois Commission," 26 July 1963, correspondence and personal reminiscences of R.A. MacKay, LAC, MG 30, vol. 10, ser. E159, 2.
79 Former legal secretary R.M. Fowler to former commissioner R.A. MacKay, 6 August 1963, correspondence and personal reminiscences of R.A. MacKay, LAC, MG 30, vol. 10, ser. E159, 3.
80 Clark University Economist J.A. Maxwell to Royal Commission on Dominion-Provincial Relations Secretary Alec Skelton, 3 October 1938, LAC, MG 30, ser. E159, vol. 8, 1. See also LAC, RG 33, ser. 23, vol, 71, file: Witnesses Called, 1.
81 Royal Commission on Dominion-Provincial Relations, transcripts of public hearings, 1937–38, testimony of 8 August 1938, LAC, RG 33/23, vol. 16, 1–59, microfilm reel C-6989. The digital version of his testimony is missing online.Thanks to LAC reference archivist Sophie Tellier I found it on microfilm reel C-6989.
82 Ibid.
83 Ibid., 3.
84 Ibid., 5–6.
85 Ibid., 3.
86 Ibid., 8.
87 Ibid.
88 Ibid., 8–9.
89 Ibid., 9.
90 Ibid.
91 Ibid., 12.
92 Ibid., 14.
93 Ibid.
94 Ibid., 16.

95 Bird, *Federal Finance in Comparative Perspective*, 141 (emphasis in original).
96 Ibid., 142.
97 Royal Commission on Dominion-Provincial Relations, transcripts of public hearings, 1937–38, testimony of 8 August 1938, 16.

CHAPTER TWO

1 Howe, *Confederation in Relation to the Interests of the Empire*, 6.
2 Ibid., 34.
3 Ibid., 35.
4 Ibid., 21–2.
5 Ibid., 10.
6 Government of Canada, the London Conference, December 1866–March 1867, https://www.bac-lac.gc.ca/eng/discover/politics-government/canadian-confederation/Pages/london-conference.aspx.
7 Waite, *Life and Times of Confederation*, 49.
8 Heaman, *Tax, Order, and Good Government*, 44. She quotes Reformer George Brown on the tough consultations that reached agreement on the issue at the Quebec City meetings during the fall of 1864.
9 Heaman describes Sir John A. Macdonald's notion of accountability to the citizenry as "a quasi-patrician one, studiously ignorant of and callous towards the scantily propertied." See Heaman, *Tax, Order, and Good Government*, 460.
10 Heaman, *Tax, Order, and Good Government*, 58
11 Ibid., 58.
12 As cited in Ibid.
13 Premier Charles Tupper to Finance Minister Alexander Galt, 13 December 1864, as quoted in Ormsby, "Letters to Galt," 166.
14 Phillip Buckner on Sir Charles Tupper, *The Canadian Encyclopedia*, https://www.thecanadianencyclopedia.ca/en/article/sir-charles-tupper/.
15 Newfoundland Liberal Party leader Ambrose Shea to Finance Minister Alexander Galt, 15 December 1864, in Ormsby, "Letters to Galt," 167.
16 Niko Block on Sir Ambrose Shea, *The Canadian Encyclopedia*, https://www.thecanadianencyclopedia.ca/en/article/sir-ambrose-shea/.
17 Ibid.
18 Liberal Assemblyman Edward Whelan to Finance Minister Alexander Galt, 17 December 1864, in Ormsby, "Letters to Galt," 168.
19 Ian Ross Robertson on Edward Whelan, *The Canadian Encyclopedia*, https://www.thecanadianencyclopedia.ca/en/article/edward-whelan/.

20 As quoted from 10 December 1864, in Waite, *Life and Times of Confederation*, 240.
21 Ibid.
22 C.M. Wallace on Sir Samuel Leonard Tilley, *The Canadian Encyclopedia*, https://www.thecanadianencyclopedia.ca/en/article/sir-samuel-leonard-tilley/.
23 Trotter, "British Finance and Confederation," 89–96.
24 Moore, *1867*, 115.
25 Silver, *French-Canadian Idea of Confederation*, 50.
26 "Review of Dominion Provincial Financial Arrangements," John James Deutsch Fonds, no name, revised August 1955, Queen's University Archives, box 81, file 770, 2.
27 Tilley emerged from that June 1866 election as provincial secretary, yielding the premiership to his fellow pro-Confederation advocate Peter Mitchell. But he remained the primary New Brunswick negotiator in London, to Mitchell's chagrin.
28 Norrie, Owram, and Emery, *History of the Canadian Economy*, 143.
29 "Review of Dominion Provincial Financial Arrangements," Deutsch Fonds, 3. See also J. Murray Beck on Joseph Howe, *Dictionary of Canadian Biography*, http://www.biographi.ca/en/bio/howe_joseph_10E.html.
30 Ibid.
31 Ibid.
32 Buckner, Sir Charles Tupper, *The Canadian Encyclopedia*.
33 "Review of Dominion Provincial Financial Arrangements," Deutsch Fonds, 4.
34 Buckner, Sir Charles Tupper, *The Canadian Encyclopedia*.
35 Stevenson, *Fiscal Federalism*, 3.
36 "Review of Dominion Provincial Financial Arrangements," Deutsch Fonds, 4.
37 Bakvis, "Political Parties," 6–7.
38 Macintyre, *Concise History of Australia*, 4th ed., 4.
39 Documents of Reconciliation, Council for Aboriginal Reconciliation, http://www5.austlii.edu.au/au/orgs/car/docrec/policy/brief/terran.htm.
40 Macintyre, *Concise History of Australia*, 4.
41 Documents of Reconciliation, Council for Aboriginal Reconciliation.
42 Hodgins, Wright, and Heick. *Federalism in Canada and Australia*, 174.
43 Macintyre, *Concise History of Australia*, 95.
44 Sir Robert Garran, *Memories of Federation – The First Convention and After*, ABC radio presentation, broadcast January 1951, National Archives of Australia, ser. SP369/1, G/2/2, barcode 3244610. p. 1.

45 Ibid.
46 Ibid., 2.
47 Quotes in this paragraph from Moore, *1867*, 128.
48 Bill Parenteau, "'Care, Control and Supervision': Native People in the Canadian Atlantic Salmon Fishery, 1867–1900," in Conrad and Finkel, *Nation and Society*, 81.
49 Gillian Creese, "Exclusion or Solidarity? Vancouver Workers Confront the 'Oriental Problem,'" in Conrad and Finkel, *Nation and Society*, 103.
50 Sarah-Jane (Saje) Mathieu, "North of the Colour Line: Sleeping Car Porters and the Battle against Jim Crow on Canadian Rails, 1880–1920," in Conrad and Finkel, *Nation and Society*, 121–2.
51 Laurent J. Thibault, "Manufacturing in Canada," in *The Canadian Encyclopedia*, https://www.thecanadianencyclopedia.ca/en/article/manufacturing.
52 E.W. Humphrys, "Hydroelectricity," in *The Canadian Encyclopedia*, https://www.thecanadianencyclopedia.ca/article/hydroelectricity
53 Thibault, "Manufacturing in Canada."
54 I have borrowed the phrase from Armstrong and Nelles, *Monopoly's Moment*.
55 Interprovincial Conference, 1902, in *Dominion Provincial and Interprovincial Conferences from 1887 to 1926*, 42.
56 "Review of Dominion Provincial Financial Arrangements," Deutsch Fonds, 4.
57 Resolution 17, Interprovincial Conference in 1887 in Quebec City, in *Dominion Provincial and Interprovincial Conferences from 1887 to 1926*, 24.
58 "Review of Dominion Provincial Financial Arrangements," Deutsch Fonds, 3–4.
59 As quoted in Milne, "Equalization and the Politics of Restraint," in Boadway and Hobson, *Equalization: Its Contribution*, 182.
60 Resolution 17 (3), Interprovincial Conference, 1887, *Dominion Provincial and Interprovincial Conferences from 1887 to 1926*, 24.
61 Ibid., 25.
62 Ibid.
63 Garran, *Memories of Federation*, 2.
64 Ibid.
65 Ibid., 3.
66 Deakin, *Federal Story*, 28. Deakin did not specify which Canadian conference.
67 *Report of the Royal Commission on the Constitution*, 74.
68 Ibid.

69 Ibid., 77, 78.
70 Ibid., 81.
71 Ibid., 88. Canada would not abolish appeals to the Judicial Committee of the British Privy Council until 1949.
72 Moon and Sharman, *Australian Politics and Government*, 184.
73 Musgrave, "Western Australia Secessionist Movement," 97.
74 Besant, "Two Nations, Two Destinies," 228.
75 Musgrave, "Western Australia Secessionist Movement," 98.
76 Federation of Australia, National Library of Australia, https://www.nla.gov.au/selected-library-collections/federation-of-australia.
77 Musgrave, "Western Australia Secessionist Movement," 97.
78 Ibid., 99.
79 British North America Act, 1907. Schedule attached to the act, Enactment no. 14.
80 Letter from Richard McBride tabled at the Interprovincial Conference, 1906, in *Dominion Provincial and Interprovincial Conferences from 1887 to 1926*, 61.
81 Report from the Representatives of Nova Scotia, New Brunswick, Prince Edward Island, Quebec, Ontario, and British Columbia, "Minutes of the Proceedings in Conference between the Members of the Government of Canada and of the various Provincial Governments assembled at Ottawa, in the Senate Chamber (Victoria Memorial Museum), November 1918," in *Dominion Provincial and Interprovincial Conferences from 1887 to 1926*, 98 (emphasis mine).
82 Ottawa's 1912 boundary extension tucked portions of the Northwest Territories into northern Quebec, Ontario, and Manitoba. The Maritimes were not contiguous to this land.

CHAPTER THREE

1 Henderson, *Angus L. Macdonald*, 35.
2 Ibid., 33.
3 Ibid., 19.
4 Many of the details in this paragraph are from Macdonald's biographer. See Henderson, *Angus L. Macdonald*.
5 Forbes, *Maritime Rights*, viii.
6 Conrad and Finkel, *History of the Canadian Peoples*, 2:200, 211.
7 As quoted in Prentice et al., *Canadian Women*, 255.
8 Henderson, *Angus L. Macdonald*, 17.

9 Ibid.
10 J. Harvey Perry, "Foreword," in Hanson, *Australian Commonwealth Grants Commission*, i.
11 Dr [J.A.] Maxwell, "The Work of the Commonwealth Grants Commission," in *Commonwealth Grants Commission – Work of Memoranda by Dr. Maxwell*, 8 December 1944, National Archives of Australia, ser. A2770, 24, barcode 209883, 1.
12 Commonwealth of Australia Constitution Act, 1900, sec. 96.
13 Dr [J.A.] Maxwell, "Work of the Commonwealth Grants Commission," 1.
14 Ibid., 1.e
15 Ibid., 1.
16 Musgrave, "Western Australian Secessionist Movement," 100–1. Australia drew many unsettling lessons from the American South.
17 Heather Radi, entry on Stanley Melbourne Bruce, *Australian Dictionary of Biography*, http://adb.anu.edu.au/biography/bruce-stanley-melbourne-5400.
18 Wheare, *Federal Government*, 22.
19 Report submitted to His Excellency the President of the United States of Brazil, 23 February 1924, Brazil – Report of British Financial Mission, National Archives of Australia, ser. CP660/17, bundle 1/Brazil, barcode 261855, 34.
20 J.H. Botha, "Financial Problems of Provincial Government in South Africa," *South African Journal of Economics* 1, 2 (1933), https://onlinelibrary.wiley.com/doi/pdf/10.1111/j.1813-6982.1933.tb02572.x.
21 *Report of the Royal Commission on the Finances of Western Australia as affected by Federation*, National Archives of Australia, west stack, call no. Nf336.941 R425, enumeration c.1. lxiv, cxxv.
22 Ibid., x.
23 Ibid.
24 Ibid.
25 Ibid., vii.
26 Ibid., cxi.
27 Ibid., x
28 Jim Hancock and Julie Smith, *Financing the Federation* (Adelaide: South Australian Centre for Economic Studies, 2001), 29, https://www.adelaide.edu.au/saces/publications/reports/consultancy/FinancingtheFederation.pdf.
29 As paraphrased in "Wants Nova Scotia Separate Dominion: Conservative Member of N. S. Assembly Moves That Province Secede," *Globe*, 20 April 1923. 1
30 Ibid.

31 Forbes, "The Origins of the Maritime Rights Movement," in Forbes, *Challenging the Regional Stereotype*, 102.
32 Ibid.
33 Ibid., 103.
34 Ibid., 113.
35 Henderson, *Angus L. Macdonald*, 29.
36 Ibid., 29–30.
37 Palmer, *Working-Class Experience*, 198.
38 Henderson, *Angus L. Macdonald*, 33.
39 Conrad and Finkel, *History of the Canadian Peoples*, 2:186.
40 Ibid.
41 Ibid.
42 Ibid., 202.
43 "In Search of the Canadian Car," Canadian Science Technology Museum, http://www.canadiancar.technomuses.ca/eng/frise_chronologique-timeline/1920/.
44 Conrad and Finkel, *History of the Canadian Peoples*, 2:202.
45 Prentice et al., *Canadian Women*, 221.
46 Ibid., 224.
47 Ibid.
48 Ibid.
49 As quoted in ibid., 192.
50 Prime Minister Mackenzie King to Professor Norman McLeod Rogers (Queen's University), 25 January 1930, LAC, Prime Ministers' Fonds, C2322, vol. 180, MG 26 J1, 153886.
51 Ashforth, "Reckoning Schemes," 1.
52 "Sir Andrew Duncan Heads Commission of Investigation," *Halifax Herald*, 8 April 1926, LAC, Prime Ministers' Fonds, C3457, vol. 102, MG 26 I, 58487.
53 Ibid.
54 Diary of William Lyon Mackenzie King, 8 April 1926, http://www.bac-lac.gc.ca/eng/discover/politics-government/prime-ministers/william-lyon-mackenzie-king/Pages/item.aspx?IdNumber=9805&.
55 Ibid.
56 Duncan, *Report of the Royal Commission on Maritime Claims*, 9, 10 (emphasis mine).
57 Ibid., 19, 22, 35.
58 Diary of William Lyon Mackenzie King, 22 September 1926, http://www.bac-lac.gc.ca/eng/discover/politics-government/prime-ministers/william-lyon-mackenzie-king/Pages/item.aspx?IdNumber=10123&.

59 Forbes, *Maritime Rights*, 176.
60 Ibid.
61 Ibid., 177.
62 Official précis for Wednesday morning, 9 November 1927. See *Dominion-Provincial Conferences: November 3–10, 1927; December 9–13, 1935; January 14–15, 1941*, 23–6.
63 Ibid.
64 Ashforth, "Reckoning Schemes," 1.
65 S.M. Bruce to Prime Minister, Ottawa, Canada, 27 July 1928, in *General, 1928–29 Royal Commission on Finance of South Australia*, National Archives of Australia, ser. A460, E5/36, barcode 90417, 20.
66 Mackenzie King to Prime Minister, Canberra, 1 August 1928, in *General, 1928–29 Royal Commission on Finance of South Australia*, National Archives of Australia, ser. A460, E5/36, barcode 90417, 18.
67 Ibid., 3.
68 Ward, *History of Australia*, 205.
69 "The Work of the Commonwealth Grants Commission," in Commonwealth Grants Commission memo, 8 December 1944, National Archives of Australia, ser. A2770, file 24, barcode 209883. p. 1. It is important to note that the individual commissions only perpetuated the problem of lack of coherence in their own way.
70 Official Secretary D.M. Dow, Office of the Commissioner for Australia in the USA, New York, to Secretary, Prime Minister's Department, Canberra, 14 December 1928, *General, 1928–29 Royal Commission on Finances of South Australia*, National Archives of Australia, ser. A460, E5/36, barcode 90417, 3.
71 Ward, *History of Australia*, 163.
72 John K. Wilson, "Government and the Evolution of Public Policy," in Ville and Withers, *Cambridge Economic History of Australia*, 342.
73 *Report of the Royal Commission on the Finances of South Australia*, 7.
74 Ibid., 18.
75 Ibid.
76 Ibid., 26.
77 Ibid.
78 Ibid., 31.
79 Ibid., 37.
80 Ibid., 33.
81 J.W. Turner, entry on John Brown, *Australian Dictionary of Biography*, http://adb.anu.edu.au/biography/brown-john-5388.
82 Ward, *History of Australia*, 167.

83 Heather Radi, entry on Stanley Melbourne Bruce, *Australian Dictionary of Biography*, http://adb.anu.edu.au/biography/bruce-stanley-melbourne-5400.
84 J.R. Robertson, entry on James Henry Scullin, *Australian Dictionary of Biography*, http://adb.anu.edu.au/biography/scullin-james-henry-8375.
85 Report of the Joint Committee of Public Accounts on the General Question of Tasmania's Disabilities, the Parliament of the Commonwealth of Australia, 7 August 1930, National Archives of Australia, West stack, call no. Nf336.946A938, enumeration N pbk c. 1, 16.
86 Ibid.
87 Ibid., 46.
88 Ibid., 37.
89 Ibid.
90 Ibid.
91 As quoted from the Report of the Royal Commission on Maritime Claims in ibid., 37. Quote taken from Duncan, *Report of the Royal Commission on Maritime Claims*, 19.
92 Report of the Joint Committee of Public Accounts on the General Question of Tasmania's Disabilities, the Parliament of the Commonwealth of Australia, 7 August 1930, 46.
93 *Commonwealth Grants Commission*, 31.
94 All news items in "Summary" in the *Sydney Morning Herald*, 28 July 1930, late edition, 1, https://www.newspapers.com/image/124099872.
95 "What It Means to Canada," and "Budget a Business-Builder," *Globe*, 28 July 1930, 1.
96 "Loyalty to Empire to Be Shown Today by Women Voters: Marking of Ballot Is Job of Prime Importance Today – Washing Will Wait," *Globe*, 28 July 930, 14.
97 Coast-to-Coast Radio Message Sounds Final Call to Canadians to Mark Ballots for Empire Trade: Premier King, Speaking from Laurier House to Millions of Citizens, Enunciates Great Doctrine of Empire Commerce, and Asks Support for 'May Day' Budget; Campaign Ends; Voters to Decide," *Globe*, 28 July 1930, 1 and 10.
98 "Ottawa Meeting Marks Last Stage of Tory Campaign: Bennett Assails New Zealand Butter and Soviet Coal Importations, Thanks All Electorate: Night of Rain as Conservatives Wind Up Their Speechmaking," *Globe*, 28 July 1930, 1 and 2.
99 R.B. Bennett, 9 June 1930, https://www.collectionscanada.gc.ca/primeministers/h4-3281-e.html.

100 Hawkins, *Life and Times of Angus L.*, 94.
101 Ibid., 101.
102 Ibid., 146–7.
103 Diary of William Lyon Mackenzie King, 29 July 1930, 174 and 175, https://www.bac-lac.gc.ca/eng/discover/politics-government/prime-ministers/william-lyon-mackenzie-king/Pages/item.aspx?IdNumber=12384.
104 Ibid., 29 July 1930, 175, https://www.bac-lac.gc.ca/eng/discover/politics-government/prime-ministers/william-lyon-mackenzie-king/Pages/item.aspx?IdNumber=12385.
105 Norrie and Emery, *History of the Canadian Economy*, 328.

CHAPTER FOUR

1 P.B. Waite, "Bennett, Richard Bedford, 1st Viscount Bennett," *Dictionary of Canadian Biography*, vol. 17, http://www.biographi.ca/en/bio/bennett_richard_bedford_17E.html.
2 Ibid.
3 Ibid.
4 Boyko, *Bennett*, 363–4.
5 James Struthers, "Great Depression" in *The Canadian Encyclopedia*, https://www.thecanadianencyclopedia.ca/en/article/great-depression#.
6 Struthers, *No Fault of Their Own*, 61–2.
7 Struthers, "Great Depression."
8 Prentice et al., *Canadian Women*, 236.
9 Ibid., 237.
10 Ibid., 236.
11 Ibid., 233.
12 Conrad and Finkel, *History of the Canadian Peoples*, 2:210.
13 Mrs C.L. Warden from Lambert Saskatchewan to Prime Minister R.B. Bennett, as quoted in Conrad and Finkel, *History of the Canadian Peoples*, 2:237.
14 As quoted in ibid, 2:210.
15 Survey of Federal Relief Activities since 1930, reprinted from the *Labour Gazette*, May 1935, LAC, RG 47, vol. 60, file: Conferences 1935, 2.
16 Ibid., 24.
17 William Marchington, "Joint Public Works as Relief Measure to Be Discontinued: Dominion Will Confine Operations to Direct Assistance to Unemployed, Ottawa Learns – Provincial Delegates Confer with Federal Government; No Work, No Help, Is to Be Slogan," *Globe*, 11 April 1932, 1–2.
18 Ibid.

19 Ibid.
20 Survey of Federal Relief Activities since 1930, 24.
21 Resolutions of Dominion-Provincial Conference, Ottawa, 17–19 January 1933, LAC, RG 47, vol. 67, p. 1.1001
22 Ibid., 1.
23 William Marchington, "Insurance Snag," *Globe*, 19 January 1933, 2.
24 Survey of Federal Relief Activities since 1930, 24.
25 Hawkins, *Life and Times of Angus L.*, 103.
26 Ibid.
27 Henderson, *Angus L. Macdonald*, 51–2.
28 Ibid., 52. Henderson says that Macdonald cited the franchise scandal successfully in each of his next four elections.
29 Ibid., 56.
30 Ibid., 59.
31 Ibid., 60.
32 Ontario, Alberta, British Columbia, Nova Scotia, New Brunswick, in Conrad and Finkel, *History of the Canadian Peoples*, 2:89.
33 Manitoba, Saskatchewan, Alberta, British Columbia, Ontario, and Nova Scotia (1930), in Veronica Strong-Boag, "'Wages for Housework': Mothers' Allowances and the Beginnings of Social Security in Canada," in Blake and Keshen, *Social Welfare Policy in Canada*, 124.
34 Bothwell, Drummond, and English, *Canada since 1945*, 163.
35 Fraser and Gordon, "Genealogy of Dependency," 316.
36 British North America Act, 1867, clause 92, sec. 7.
37 Tillotson, *Contributing Citizens*, 25.
38 Ibid., 21.
39 Struthers, *Limits of Affluence*, 108–9. Struthers writes about Ontario – but those conditions were applicable across the nation.
40 Letter of the Three Maritime Premiers to the Prime Minister of Canada, 16 January 1934, as quoted in *Report of the Royal Commission on Financial Arrangement*, vi. See also "Maritime Subsidy Held Inadequate," *Globe*, 16 January 1 1934, 3.
41 "Ask Provinces to Look After Own Financing: Desire of Federal Government Is to Shift Responsibility Back Gradually," *Ottawa Journal*, 18 January 1934, 4.
42 "Commission May Untangle West's Finance: Seek Cause and Cure of Fiscal Muddles in Four Provinces ... Maritime Rights Also Reopened," *Globe*, 19 January 1934, 1.
43 *Winnipeg Free Press* Ottawa correspondent Grant Dexter to *Winnipeg Free*

Press editor John Dafoe, 17 January 1934, University of Manitoba Archives, John Dafoe Fonds, box 8, fol. 1, 1–2.
44 Headlines in the *Globe*, 18 January 1934, 1.
45 The 1934–35 deficit was actually more than $125 million. See Di Matteo, *Federal Fiscal History*, 82, 87, https://www.fraserinstitute.org/sites/default/files/federal-fiscal-history-canada-1867-2017.pdf.
46 "All Governments Meet Obligations, Premiers Decide: Permit No Default in Canada, Determination as Parlay Ends – Against Western Probe," *Globe*, 20 January 1934, 1.
47 Boothe and Edwards, *Eric J. Hanson's Financial History of Alberta*, 97.
48 Henderson, *Angus L. Macdonald*, 66.
49 White, *Report of the Royal Commission on Financial Arrangements*, vi.
50 Province of Nova Scotia, *Report of the Royal Commission*, 4.
51 Henderson, *Angus L. Macdonald*, 63.
52 The commissioners were pleased that his more historical approach led to "the same general conclusions and recommendations." See Province of Nova Scotia, *Report of the Royal Commission*, 25.
53 "Complementary Report of Dr. Harold A. Innis, Halifax, October 24, 1934," in Province of Nova Scotia, *Report of the Royal Commission*, 151.
54 Ibid., 152.
55 Ibid., 225.
56 Innis made that reference to Australia.
57 Province of Nova Scotia, *Report of the Royal Commission*, 225–6.
58 "The Ills of a Province," *Globe*, 10 December 1934, 6.
59 R.A. MacKay, "Economic Inquiry – Financial Relations," in Province of Nova Scotia, *Report of the Royal Commission*, 37.
60 Ibid., 37.
61 Ibid., 36.
62 Ibid., 39.
63 Ibid., 40.
64 He was a commissioner with the Royal Commission on Dominion-Provincial Relations, which rejected that approach. See chapters 3 and 4.
65 Province of Nova Scotia, *Report of the Royal Commission*, 37 (emphasis mine).
66 White, *Report of the Royal Commission on Financial Arrangements*, 5.
67 Ibid., 6.
68 Ibid., 12.
69 Ibid., 20
70 Quotation from the Duncan Commission in White, *Report of the Royal Commission on Financial Arrangements*, 20 (emphasis mine).

71 Ibid., 20.
72 Chief Justice J.A. Mathieson (Prince Edward Island), memorandum of dissent, 16 February 1935, in White, *Report of the Royal Commission on Financial Arrangements*, 23–4.
73 Ibid., 4, 21. See also, "Review of Dominion Provincial Financial Arrangements," John James Deutsch Fonds, no name, rev. 1955, Queen's University Archives, box 81, file 770, 8.
74 L.L.O. Note – 15.12.33, "The Central Bank for Canada," National Archives of Australia, Canada – Internal Politics, ser. A981, CAN 24, pt. 1, barcode 173375, unnumbered pages within file.
75 University of Melbourne economist Douglas Copland, "Economic Adjustment in Australia," *Lloyds Bank Limited Monthly Review* 4, 46 (1933): 450. See also LAC, C-1-4, correspondence and proposals for discussions 1934, RG 47, vol. 67.
76 "Commonwealth of Australia: Consolidation of Debts of Commonwealth and Its Constituent States and Establishment of Australian Loan Council," LAC, C-1-4, correspondence and proposals for discussions 1934, RG 47, vol. 67, 1–11.
77 L.L.O. Note – 25- 1-34, "Finance," in National Archives of Australia, Canada – Internal Politics, ser. A981, CAN 24, pt. 1, barcode 173375, unnumbered pages within file.
78 *Commonwealth Grants Commission*, 31.
79 Ibid.
80 "Maids' Frocks Clear," classified ad for Hordern Brothers' Great Summer Sale, and "They're Here: Startling New Studebakers for 1934," in *Sydney Morning Herald*, 5 January 1934, 2, 5.
81 "Aviation: Praise for Qantas – Safe Commercial Flying," *Sydney Morning Herald*, 5 January 1934, 10.
82 "Sir Hugh and Lady Poynter," *Sydney Morning Herald*, 5 January 1934, 4.
83 "Far North Land: How the Missions Work. Happiest Places in the Territory – Problem of White Man's Diseases," *Sydney Morning Herald*, 5 January 1934, 10.
84 "Tea Prices: Customs Investigation," *Sydney Morning Herald*, 5 January 1934, 10.
85 "United States: Mr. Roosevelt, Address to Congress, 'Building on Ruins,'" *Sydney Morning Herald*, 5 January 1934, 9.
86 "Many Candidates Join Sisterhood," *Ottawa Journal*, 5 January 1934, 2.
87 "Preparing Plans for Convention," *Ottawa Journal*, 5 January 1934, 4.
88 "Down Diphtheria," *Ottawa Journal*, 5 January 1934, 8.
89 "Both Maid and Matron May Wear Velvet," *Ottawa Journal*, 5 January 1934, 9.

90 "Bryson-Graham's Interim Receiver's Sale," *Ottawa Journal*, 5 January 1934, 11, 12, 22.
91 "Important Changes Made in Government Posts," *Ottawa Journal*, 5 January 1934. 1.
92 "Public Finance," *Ottawa Journal*, 5 January 1934, 8.
93 Ibid.
94 Campbell, *Grand Illusions*, 11.
95 Courchene, *Equalization Payments*, 17.
96 "Survey of Federal Relief Activities since 1930," *Labour Gazette*, May 1935, LAC, RG 47, vol. 60, file, Conferences, 1935, 24.
97 "The Budget," *Globe* (editorial), 19 April 1934, 6.
98 *Review of Dominion Provincial Financial Arrangements*, John James Deutsch Fonds, n. name, rev. August 1955, Queen's University Archives, box 81, file 770, 8.
99 Ibid., 9.
100 Ibid.
101 Speech from the Throne, 17 January 1935, as quoted in Brodie, "Three Stories of Canadian Citizenship," 52.
102 Boyko, *Bennett*, 379.
103 Forster and Read, "Politics of Opportunism," 347.
104 Boyko, *Bennett*, 380.
105 Waite, "Bennett, Richard Bedford."
106 Norrie, Owram, and Emery, *History of the Canadian Economy*, 317.
107 Struthers, "Great Depression."
108 W.R. Hodgson, assistant secretary of the Australian External Affairs Department, to the Officer-in-Charge, Territories Branch, Prime Minister's Department, 2 May 1935, in Territories - Exchange of Information with Canada and South Africa, National Archives of Australia, ser. A518, DB112/1, barcode 102498, 1
109 Waite, "Bennett, Richard Bedford."
110 Boyko, *Bennett*, 331.
111 Ibid., 390.
112 McConnell, "Judicial Review," 40.
113 Deputy Finance Minister W.C. Clark to R.K. Finlayson, 5 January 1935, LAC, RG 19, vol. 3986, file: Prov. Financial (Conf. File) P-1-10-1, 2.
114 Ibid., 2.
115 Ibid., 3.
116 Bank of Canada Archives, Department of Bank Operations Fonds, Research Fonds, box 2, file 3, Provincial Financing 1-1, vol. 1 – Loan Councils and National Finance Council Confidential, J. Fisher of the Overseas and For-

eign Department of the Bank of England to Bank of Canada Deputy Governor J.A.C. Osborne, 28 January 1935, 1–3.
117 Bede Nairn, John Thomas (Jack) Lang, *Australian Dictionary of Biography*, http://adb.anu.edu.au/biography/lang-john-thomas-jack-7027.
118 Ibid.
119 Bank of Canada Archives, Department of Bank Operations Fonds, Research Fonds, box 2, file 3, Provincial Financing 1-1, vol. 1 – Loan Councils and National Finance Council Confidential. J. Fisher of the Overseas and Foreign Department of the Bank of England to Bank of Canada Deputy Governor J.A.C. Osborne, 28 January 1935, 1–3.
120 Bank of Canada Archives, Department of Bank Operations Fonds, Research Fonds, box 2, file 4, File: PF1-1, vol. 1 – Provincial Financing – General 1934–January 1937, "South Africa" memo of 10 July 1935, initials from Bank of Canada governor Graham Towers and Deputy Governor J.A.C. Osborne, 1.
121 Bank of Canada Archives, Department of Bank Operations Fonds, Graham Tower's Fonds, "Memorandum of conversation with Honourable John Hart, Minister of Finance for the Province of British Columbia, May 16, 1935," box 2, file 1, Tower's Memoranda 1935–37, 1–51, 2. Please note documents say "Tower's."
122 Ibid., 1.
123 Ibid., 2.
124 Bank of Canada Archives, Department of Banking Operations Fonds, Research Fonds, "Memorandum to the Governor," 22 July 1935, box 2, file 3, PF1-1 vol. 1 – Loan Councils and National Finance Council Confidential, 4, 2.
125 See 1935 letters from *Winnipeg Free Press* Ottawa correspondent Grant Dexter to Editor John Dafoe of 4 January, 7 January, 12 January, 14 January, 21 January, 23 January, 11 July, etc., John Dafoe Fonds, University of Manitoba Archives, box 8, fol. 1.
126 Boyko, *Bennett*, 401.
127 Glassford, *Reaction and Reform*, 181.
128 "Canada Votes Today in Biggest Election in Her History," *Globe*, 14 October, 1935, 1.

CHAPTER FIVE

1 Levine, *King*, 224. See also https://www.mapleleafweb.com/features/employment-insurance-canada-history-structure-and-issues.html.
2 William Lyon Mackenzie King, 27 February 1933, House of Commons, as quoted in Struthers, *No Fault of Their Own*, 139.

3 William Marchington, "Conference of Premiers in November: Cabinet to Discuss Bennett Acts," *Globe*, 17 October 1935, 1.
4 McConnell, "Judicial Review of Prime Minister Bennett's New Deal," 41. See also Diary of William Lyon Mackenzie King, 4 November 1935, 5, http://www.bac-lac.gc.ca/eng/discover/politics-government/prime-ministers/william-lyon-mackenzie-king/Pages/item.aspx?IdNumber=16549.
5 Finkel, *Business and Social Reform*, 89–91, 95.
6 McConnell, "Judicial Review of Prime Minister Bennett's New Deal," 47n25. See also Finkel, *Business and Social Reform*, 91.
7 "Many Safeguards Held Necessary in New Legislation, Actuaries Point to Operating Weaknesses in Insurance in Report to House," *Ottawa Journal*, 15 February 1935, 12–13.
8 Diary of William Lyon Mackenzie King, 4 November, 1935, 5, http://www.bac-lac.gc.ca/eng/discover/politics-government/prime-ministers/william-lyon-mackenzie-king/Pages/item.aspx?IdNumber=16549.
9 Bank of Canada Archives, Department of Banking Operations Fonds, enclosure of 3 December 1935 with covering letter of 7 December 1935 from Bank of Canada Deputy Governor J.A.C. Osborne to Deputy Finance Minister W.C. Clark, box 2, vol. 1, file: PF1-2, vol. 1 – Dominion-Provincial Conferences – 1935–November 1945, 2.
10 Ibid., 3.
11 Ibid., 3–5.
12 Fullerton, *Graham Towers and His Times*, 84.
13 Grant, *W. A. Mackintosh*, 145–51; Wardhaugh, *Behind the Scenes*, 62, 122; Robert Skidelsky, "Keynes and Canada," Toronto seminar, 6 November 2001, copy in possession of author.
14 Grant, *W. A. Mackintosh*, 240. See also "The Keynes Plan," in *The International Monetary Fund 1945–1965 – Twenty Years of International Monetary Cooperation*. Vol. 3: *Documents*, ed. J. Keith Horsefield (Washington: International Monetary Fund, 1969), 3.
15 Skidelsky, "Keynes and Canada," 1.
16 Ferris and Winer, *Searching for Keynes*, 2, https://papers.ssrn.com/sol3/papers.cfm?abstract_id=437403.
17 Grant, *W. A. Mackintosh*, 17.
18 Boyko, *Bennett*, 345–6.
19 Ibid., 346.
20 "Les difficultés d'ordre financier sont considérables," *Le Devoir*, 10 December 1935, 1 (my translation from clipping).
21 Prime Minister Mackenzie King, Proceedings of Opening Day Plenary Ses-

sion at Dominion-Provincial Conference 1935, in *Dominion-Provincial Conferences*, 9.
22 Saywell, "Just Call Me Mitch," 223.
23 Premier L.A. Taschereau, Proceedings of Opening Day Plenary Session at the Dominion Provincial Conference 1935, in *Provincial-Dominion Conferences*, 11.
24 Ibid., 12.
25 Premier T.D. Pattullo, 13 December 1935, Closing Plenary Session of the Dominion Provincial Conference 1935, in *Provincial-Dominion Conferences*, 56.
26 Premier John Bracken, Proceedings of Opening Day Plenary Session at the Dominion Provincial Conference 1935, in *Provincial-Dominion Conferences*, 13.
27 Ibid., 14.
28 Premier W.J. Patterson, Proceedings of Opening Day Plenary Session at the Dominion Provincial Conference 1935, in *Provincial-Dominion Conferences*, 18–19.
29 Ibid., 19.
30 Premier William Aberhart, Proceedings of Opening Day Plenary Session at the Dominion Provincial Conference 1935, in *Provincial-Dominion Conferences*, 21.
31 Premier Angus L. Macdonald, Proceedings of Opening Day Plenary Session in Dominion-Provincial Conference 1935, in *Provincial-Dominion Conferences*, 12.
32 Premier Allison Dysart, Proceedings of Opening Day Plenary Session in Dominion-Provincial Conference 1935, in *Provincial-Dominion Conferences*, 13.
33 Slumkoski, "... A Fair Show and a Square Deal," 126–7.
34 Premier Walter Lea, Proceedings of Opening Day Plenary Session in Dominion-Provincial Conference 1935, in *Provincial-Dominion Conferences*, 17.
35 Neatby, *William Lyon Mackenzie King*, 3:156.
36 Report of Subcommittee on Financial Questions, Dominion-Provincial Conference 1935, miscellaneous general file, LAC, RG 47, vol. 62, 9.
37 Bank of Canada Archives, Department of Bank Operations Fonds, Provincial Financing Fonds, box 2, vol. 1, file: PFI – 2 the Dominion-Provincial Conferences, 1935–November 1945, confidential memorandum by S. Skelton, 15 December 1935, 4.
38 Ibid., 6.

39 Ibid., 5.
40 "Australian Reforms," Report of Subcommittee on Financial Questions, Dominion-Provincial Conference 1935, miscellaneous general files, LAC, RG 47, vol. 62, 3.
41 "The Australian Loan Council," Dominion Provincial Conference 1935, Secret, D.P.C. 35 (F) 1935, miscellaneous general file, LAC, RG 47, vol. 62, 2.
42 Ibid., 4.
43 "A Suggested Loan Council for Canada," Dominion Provincial Conference 1935, Secret, D.P. 35 (F) no. 5, miscellaneous general file, LAC, RG 47, vol. 62, 1.
44 Ibid., 5.
45 Béland and Lecours, "Ideational Dimension of Federalism," 9.
46 "A Suggested Loan Council for Canada," Dominion Provincial Conference 1935, Secret, D.P. 35 (F) no. 5, miscellaneous general file, LAC, RG 47, vol. 62, 6–7.
47 William Marchington, "Way Opened for Changing B. N. A. Act," *Globe*, 10 December 1935, 1–2.
48 "The Program at Ottawa," *Globe*, 11 December 1935, 4.
49 Ibid.
50 Ibid.
51 "Hepburn Urging Refunding on Lower Interest Basis," *Ottawa Journal*, 11 December 1935, 1.
52 Conrad and Finkel, *History of the Canadian Peoples*, 2:261.
53 Ibid., 261.
54 Prentice et al., *Canadian Women*, 238.
55 As cited in ibid., 256.
56 "A Suggested Loan Council for Canada," Dominion Provincial Conference 1935, Secret, D.P. 35 (F) 1935, miscellaneous general file, LAC, RG 47, vol. 62, 6.
57 The Australian Loan Council: Dominion Provincial Conference 1935, Secret D.P.C. 35 (F), Dominion-Provincial Conference 1935, miscellaneous general file, LAC, RG 47, vol. 62, 7.
58 Musgrave, "Western Australia Secessionist Movement," 101 (emphasis in original).
59 Gérald A. Beaudoin, "Distribution of Powers," *The Canadian Encyclopedia*, https://www.thecanadianencyclopedia.ca/en/article/distribution-of-powers.
60 Lecours and Béland, "Institutional Politics of Territorial Redistribution," 107.
61 "A Suggested Loan Council for Canada," Dominion Provincial Conference 1935, Secret D.P. 35 (F) 1935, miscellaneous general file, LAC, RG 47, vol. 62, 5.

62 Dupras, "The Constitution of Canada," Library of Parliament, January 1992, http://publications.gc.ca/Collection-R/LoPBdP/BP/bp283-e.htm.
63 Ibid.
64 Ibid.
65 "Summary of Assistance Requested of and Given by the Dominion to Province of Alberta since September 3, 1935," memo dated 26 February 1937, LAC, RG 19, vol. 3985, file: Provincial Matters – Alberta – miscellaneous – P – 1-1-10, N.N., 1.
66 Ibid., 1.
67 Fullerton, *Graham Towers and His Times*, 4.
68 Bryce, *Maturing in Hard Times*, 182.
69 "Summary of Assistance Requested of and Given by the Dominion to Province of Alberta since September 3, 1935," memo dated 26 February 1937, LAC, P-1-1-10, Provincial Matters – Alberta – miscellaneous – P – 1-1-10, RG 19, vol. 3985, N.N., 2.
70 Ibid., 2–3.
71 "The Dominion-Provincial Conference, December 1935 – Sub-Conference on Financial Questions," 15 December 1935, confidential memorandum by "Mr. S. Skelton," Bank of Canada Archives, Department of Bank Operations Fonds, Provincial Financing Fonds, box 2, file PF1 – 2, vol. 1 – Dominion-Provincial Conferences 1935 – November 1945, 1–2.
72 Saywell, *"Just Call Me Mitch,"* 249.
73 "Hepburn Returns Dissatisfied with Ottawa Parley," *Globe*, 14 December 1935, 1–2.
74 Ibid.
75 "The Dominion-Provincial Conference, December 1935 – Sub-Conference on Financial Questions," 15 December 1935, confidential memorandum by "Mr. S. Skelton," Bank of Canada Archives, Department of Bank Operations Fonds, Provincial Financing Fonds, box 2, file PF1 – 2, vol. 1, Dominion-Provincial Conferences 1935–November 1945, 10.
76 Report of Subcommittee on Financial Questions, Dominion-Provincial Conference 1935, miscellaneous general file, LAC, RG 47, vol. 62, 9.
77 "Hepburn Returns Dissatisfied with Ottawa Parley."
78 Diary of William Lyon Mackenzie King, 13 December 1935, http://www.bac-lac.gc.ca/eng/discover/politics-government/prime-ministers/william-lyon-mackenzie-king/Pages/item.aspx?IdNumber=16728&.
79 Ibid.
80 Saywell, *"Just Call Me Mitch,"* 252.
81 Finance Minister Charles Dunning, Report of the Sub-Committee on Financial Questions, in *Dominion-Provincial Conferences, 1935*, 45.

82 "Summary of Assistance Requested of and Given by the Dominion to Province of Alberta since September 3, 1935," memo dated 26 February 1937, LAC, P-1-1-10, Provincial Matters – Alberta – miscellaneous – P – 1-1-10, RG 19, vol. 3985, N.N., 3.
83 Report of the Sub-Committee on Financial Questions, in *Dominion-Provincial Conferences, 1935*, 44.
84 Finance Minister Charles Dunning, Report of the Sub-Committee on Financial Questions, in *Dominion-Provincial Conferences, 1935*, 45.
85 Prime Minister Mackenzie King, Dominion-Provincial Conference, 1935, Proceedings of Closing Plenary Session, 13 December 1935, in *Provincial-Dominion Conferences*, 63.
86 As quoted in Struthers, *No Fault of Their Own*, 148.
87 Campbell, *Respectable Citizens*, 238n43.
88 Ibid., 157.
89 Ibid., 158.
90 "Urges Greater Use of Agencies: Major C. S. Ford Gives Talk on Relief and Unemployment," *Ottawa Journal*, 11 December 1935, 2.
91 Struthers, *No Fault of Their Own*, 10.
92 Riendeau, *Brief History of Canada*, 234. As Riendeau notes about King's conduct in wartime: the prime minister became "even more interested in social welfare measures when a public opinion poll in September 1943 indicated that the CCF [Co-operative Commonwealth Federation] had edged past the Liberals and Conservatives in popularity."
93 Simeon and Robinson, *State, Society, and the Development*, 82.
94 Bank of Canada Archives, Department of Bank Operations Fonds, Research Fonds, "The National Finance Council" memo, 21 January 1936, file 2B-400, vol. 1, box 1, signed ASk (Alex "Sandy" Skelton), 1.
95 "Summary of Assistance Requested of and Given by the Dominion to Province of Alberta since September 3, 1935," memo dated 26 February 1937, LAC, P-1-1-10, Provincial Matters – Alberta – miscellaneous – P – 1-1-10, RG 19, vol. 3985. N.N., 4.
96 Ibid., 4.
97 Fullerton, *Graham Towers and His Times*, 75–6.
98 Bank of Canada Archives, Department of Bank Operations Fonds, Research Department Fonds, Recommendations on Dominion-Provincial Relations, box 2, file PF1, vol. 1, Provincial Financing – general 1934 – January 1937, signed A. Skelton, 20 March 1936, covering letter on Federal-Provincial Finances, memorandum, 1.
99 Ibid., 9.

100 Ibid., 5–6.
101 Ibid., 6.
102 Ibid.
103 Bank of Canada Archives, Department of Bank Operations Fonds, Research Department Fonds, Recommendations on Dominion-Provincial Relations, box 2, file PF1, vol. 1, Provincial Financing – general 1934–January 1937, signed A. Skelton, 20 March 1936, 6.
104 Ibid., 7.
105 Ibid., 8, 11.
106 Ibid., 11.
107 Ibid., 1.
108 All stories from the *Edmonton Journal*, 4 April 1936, 3, 12, 14, 15.
109 All stories from the *Montreal Gazette*, 4 April 1936, 1, 4.
110 "Summary of Assistance Requested of and Given by the Dominion to Province of Alberta since September 3, 1935," memo dated 26 February 1937, LAC, P-1-1-10, Provincial Matters – Alberta – miscellaneous – P – 1-1-10, RG 19, vol. 3985. N.N., 4–5.
111 From correspondence read by Finance Minister Charles Dunning to the House of Commons on 1 April 1936 as quoted in *Eric J. Hanson's Financial History of Alberta*, ed. Boothe and Edwards, 175.
112 "Summary of Assistance Requested of and Given by the Dominion to Province of Alberta since September 3, 1935," memo dated 26 February 1937, LAC, P-1-1-10, Provincial Matters – Alberta – miscellaneous – P – 1-1-10, RG 19, vol. 3985, N.N., 6.
113 Memorandum from Australian Trade Commissioner in Canada, L.R. Macgregor, to the Secretary, Department of External Affairs, 22 June 1936, National Archives of Australia, Canada: Internal Politics, ser. A981, CAN 24, pt. 1, barcode 173375, n.p. in file, 1–5.
114 Premier T.D. "Duff" Pattullo to Prime Minister Mackenzie King, 14 March 1936, LAC, RG 19, vol. 3986, file: Provincial Matters British Columbia 1936, P 1-2-1, 2.
115 Prime Minister Mackenzie King to Premier T.D. "Duff" Pattullo, 1 May 1936, LAC, RG 19, vol. 3986, file: Provincial Matters British Columbia 1936, P 1-2-1, 2–3.
116 Premier T.D. "Duff" Pattullo to Prime Minister Mackenzie King, 6 May 1936, LAC, RG 19, vol. 3986, file: Provincial Matters British Columbia 1936, P 1-2-1, 2.
117 "Budget Review Shows Brighter Outlook: But Dunning Sees Difficult Economic Problems to Solve," *Globe*, 2 May 1936, 8.

118 Bryce, *Maturing in Hard Times*, 189.
119 Diary of William Lyon Mackenzie King, 14 May 1936 (emphasis in original), https://www.bac-lac.gc.ca/eng/discover/politics-government/prime-ministers/william-lyon-mackenzie-king/Pages/item.aspx?IdNumber =16986&.
120 Bank of Canada Archives, Department of Bank Operations Fonds, Research Fonds, "National Finance Council, June 10, 1936," box 2, vol. 1, file: PF 1-1 vol. 1 – Loan Councils and National Finance Council Confidential, 1.
121 Bryce, *Maturing in Hard Times*. On page 227, Bryce describes the staffing of Clark's office.
122 Memorandum from Australian Trade Commissioner in Canada, L.R. Macgregor, to the Secretary, Department of External Affairs, 9 June 1936, National Archives of Australia, Canada: Constitutional, ser. A981, CAN 13, pt. 2, barcode 173360, n.p. in file, 1–2.
123 Three-page memorandum and cable from Australian Trade Commissioner in Canada, L.R. Macgregor, to the Secretary, Department of External Affairs, both dated 17 June 1936, National Archives of Australia, Canada: Constitutional, ser. A981, CAN 13, pt. 2, barcode 173360, n.p. in file, 1–4.
124 Memorandum from the Secretary, Department of External Affairs, to Australian Trade Commissioner in Canada, L.R. Macgregor, 18 June 1936, National Archives of Australia, Canada – Internal Politics, ser. A981, CAN 24, pt. 1, barcode 173375, 1.
125 "Federal Powers in Canada," *London Times*, 20 June 1936, National Archives of Australia, Canada: Constitutional, ser. A981, CAN 13, pt. 2, barcode 173360, n.p. in file, 1.
126 "A Review of Social Legislation in Canada: Motives Which Have Led to the Passing of Social Legislation – Some of the Enactments," by H.W. Macdonnell, Secretary of the Industrial Relations Department of the Canadian Manufacturers' Association, July 1936, along with covering memorandum by Assistant Australian Trade Commissioner R.R. Ellen to the Secretary, Department of External Affairs, 10 July 1936, National Archives of Australia, Canada: Internal – pt. 1, ser. A981, CAN 21, pt. 1, barcode 173371, n.p. in file, three pages in total.
127 Bank of Canada Archives, Department of Bank Operations Fonds, Research Fonds, "The Distribution of Taxing Powers in Canada," by A.E. Grauer, 30 August 1936, box 1, file 1, file 28-170, vol. 1, 49 (emphasis mine).
128 Ibid., 57.
129 Ibid. (emphasis mine).
130 Bryce, *Maturing in Hard Times*, 190.
131 Bank of Canada Archives, Department of Bank Operations Fonds, Graham

Tower's Fonds, "Memorandum: Notes on a Possible Commission of Enquiry, Confidential, Original sent to Mr. Dunning with Letter," 20 October 1936, box 2, file 1, file: PF4, vol. 1 – Provincial Financing – Manitoba 1936–41, 1.
132 Ibid., 2.
133 Diary of William Lyon Mackenzie King, 16 November 1936, http://www.bac-lac.gc.ca/eng/discover/politics-government/prime-ministers/william-lyon-mackenzie-king/Pages/item.aspx?IdNumber=17409&.
134 Bank of Canada Archives, Department of Bank Operations Fonds, Research Fonds, "The Case for a Royal Commission Inquiry on Provincial Finances," 23 November 1936. ASk [Sandy Skelton], 23 November 1936, box 1, vol. 1, file 2B – B400, 1.
135 Ibid., 3.
136 Ibid.
137 Ibid., 4.
138 Ibid., 5.
139 Ibid., 6.
140 Ibid., 6–7 (emphasis mine).
141 Ibid., 7.
142 Bank of Canada Archives, Department of Bank Operations Fonds, Graham Tower's Fonds, "Review Covering (A) Dominion and Provincial Financing during Recent Past (C) Trend of Interest Rates – Long Term and Short Term (B) Present Condition of Investment Market and Probable Immediate Future, for Dominion-Provincial Conference, December 1936" [sic], box 2, File: Tower's Memoranda 1935–37, no. 1-61, 1.
143 Bank of Canada Archives, Department of Bank Operations Fonds, Graham Tower's Fonds, "Memorandum of Conversations with Provincial Representatives at the Time of National Finance Committee Meetings and Subsequently – December 9–14, 1936," box 2, file 1: Tower's Memoranda, 1935–37, no. 1-61, 1.
144 Ibid., 2.
145 Ibid., 3.
146 William Marchington, "Finance Parley Like Locarno: Ottawa Highlights," *Globe*, 15 December 1936, 5.
147 Bank of Canada Archives, Department of Bank Operations Fonds, Research Department Fonds, Bank of Canada Governor Graham Towers to Finance Minister Charles Dunning, confidential letter of 4 January 1937, box 2, file: PF1, vol. 1 – Provincial Financing – general 1934–January 1937, 1.
148 Ibid., 3.
149 Ibid., 4.

150 In his 16 June 1938 budget speech, Finance Minister Charles Dunning referred to "substantial" federal, provincial, municipal, and private corporation bond sales in 1937 that raised almost $702 million – of which $476 million was earmarked for refunding. Despite the "heavy volume" of dominion financing in 1937, he added, interest yields on bonds were low. See Canada: Budget Speech delivered by Hon. Chas. A. Dunning, Minister of Finance, Member for Queens, Prince Edward Island, in the House of Commons, 16 June 1938, National Archives of Australia, Canada – Internal Politics, ser. A 981, CAN 24, pt. 1, barcode 173375, 54–5, 12. I am grateful to historian Shirley Tillotson, who confirmed that the federal bond prospectus in 1937 makes it "very clear that the Dominion is NOT taking any responsibility for provincial bond issues." In other words, Ottawa might have discussed the possibility of supporting provincial bonds *in theory* – but the idea went nowhere in reality.

151 Bank of Canada Archives, Department of Bank Operations Fonds, Research Department Fonds, "Memorandum of Conversation with Mr. Dunning, Tuesday, January 5/37," box 2, file: PFI vol. 1 – Provincial Financing – general 1934–January 1937, 1–2.

152 Bank of Canada Archives, Department of Bank Operations Fonds, Research Department Fonds, "Provincial Default: The Alternatives, January 10, 1937," signed ASk (Skelton), box 2, file: PFI vol. 1 – Provincial Financing – general 1934–January 1937, 1 (emphasis mine).

153 Ibid., 1.

154 Ibid., 2.

155 Ibid., 3.

156 "Children's Aid Society," *Ottawa Journal*, 14 January 1937, 10.

157 Bank of Canada Archives, Department of Bank Operations Fonds, Research Department Fonds, "Western Provinces, January 11, 1937," confidential memo by Secretary Donald Gordon, box 2, file: PFI, vol. 1 – Provincial Financing – general 1934–January 1937, 1.

158 Ibid., 2.

159 Bank of Canada Archives, Department of Bank Operations Fonds, Research Department Fonds, "Western Financial Problems," Bank of Canada securities advisor K.A. (Ken) Henderson, 12 January 1937, box 2, file: PFI, vol. 1 – Provincial Financing – general 1934–January 1937, 1–2 (emphasis mine).

160 Bank of Canada Archives, Department of Bank Operations Fonds, Research Department Fonds, "Notes on Prairie Provinces Situation Based on Decision That a Temporary Guarantee of Interest Is the Type of Arrangement Which Should Be Attempted," first written on 12 January 1937. Covering memo

written 15 January 1937, box 2, file: PF1, vol. 1 – Provincial Financing – general 1934–January 1937, 1.
161 Ibid., 2.
162 Ibid., 3.
163 Bank of Canada Archives, Department of Bank Operations Fonds, Research Department Fonds, "Memorandum of Conversations, Sunday, January 17, 1937 – Conversation with Messrs. Dunning, Bracken, Patterson and Clark," box 2, file: PF1, vol. 1 – Provincial Financing – general 1934–January 1937, 1.
164 Ibid., 1.
165 Bank of Canada Archives, Department of Bank Operations Fonds, Research Department Fonds, "Bank of Canada and the West," 19 January 1937, handwritten notation "Written by the Governor," box 2, file: PF1, vol. 1 – Provincial Financing – general 1934–January 1937, 1.
166 Diaries of William Lyon Mackenzie King, 21 January 1937, https://www.bac-lac.gc.ca/eng/discover/politics-government/prime-ministers/william-lyon-mackenzie-king/Pages/item.aspx?IdNumber=17626&.
167 Ibid.
168 Bank of Canada Archives, Department of Bank Operations Fonds, Research Department Fonds, "Memorandum of Two Conversations with Mr. King on Thursday, Jan. 21/37," box 2, file: PF1, vol. 1 – Provincial Financing – general 1934–January 1937, 1.
169 Summary of the Bank of Canada report on the financial position of Manitoba, 12 February 1937, Douglas Alexander Skelton Fonds, Queen's University Archives, box 1, file 17, 22.
170 Ibid., 24.
171 Summary of the Bank of Canada report on the financial position of Saskatchewan, March 1937, Douglas Alexander Skelton Fonds, Queen's University Archives, box 1, file 17, 19.
172 Ibid., 23.
173 Ibid., 27, 28.
174 Ibid., 28.
175 Summary of the Bank of Canada report on the financial position of Alberta, 7 April 1937, Douglas Alexander Skelton Fonds, Queen's University Archives, box 1, file 17, 41–2.
176 Diaries of William Lyon Mackenzie King, 16 February 1937, https://www.bac-lac.gc.ca/eng/discover/politics-government/prime-ministers/william-lyon-mackenzie-king/Pages/item.aspx?IdNumber=17682&.
177 Ibid., https://www.bac-lac.gc.ca/eng/discover/politics-government/prime-

ministers/william-lyon-mackenzie-king/Pages/item.aspx?IdNumber
=17682&.
178 Bank of Canada Archives, Department of Bank Operations Fonds, Provincial Financing – Manitoba, Research Department Fonds, Bank of Canada Governor Graham Towers to Premier John Bracken, 12 February 1937, box 2, file: PF4, vol. 1 – Provincial Financing – Manitoba, 1936–41, 3.
179 "Terms of Reference," *Report of the Royal Commission on Dominion-Provincial Relations* 1:9.
180 F.R. Scott, "The Privy Council and Mr. Bennett's 'New Deal' Legislation," extract from *Canadian Journal of Economic and Political Science* 3, 2 (1937), National Archives of Australia, Canada – Internal Politics, ser. A981, CAN 24, pt. 1, barcode 173375, 1.
181 Ibid., 4.
182 "Privy Council Decisions" by University of Manitoba president Sidney T. Smith in the *Winnipeg Free Press*, 5 February 1937, National Archives of Australia, Canada: Constitutional, ser. A981, CAN 13, pt. 2, barcode 173360, n.p. in file, 1.
183 Assistant Australian Trade Commissioner R.R. Ellen to the Secretary, Department of External Affairs, 10 March 1937, National Archives of Australia, Canada: Constitutional, ser. A981, CAN 13, pt. 2, barcode 173360, n.p. in file, 1.
184 Saywell, *"Just Call Me Mitch,"* 294.
185 Memorandum from Australian Trade Commissioner in Canada, L.R. Macgregor, to the Secretary, Department of External Affairs, 10 June 1937, National Archives of Australia, Canada: Constitutional, ser. A981, CAN 13, pt. 2, barcode 173360, n.p. in file, 1–2.
186 W.C. Clark, "Confidential Memorandum: Royal Commission on Economic Basis of Confederation," 7 December 1936, LAC, RG 19, E2 C, vol. 22, file: 101-85-15, general file, 12.
187 "Royal Commission on Dominion-Provincial Relations," LAC, RG 19, E2 C, vol. 22, file: 101-85-15, general file, n.d., 3.
188 Ibid., 5 (emphasis mine).

CHAPTER SIX

1 Fransen, "Unscrewing the Unscrutable," v.
2 Owram, *Government Generation*, x.
3 Ferguson and Wardhaugh, "Impossible Conditions of Inequality," 14.
4 "'His Majesty's Right Trusty and Well-Beloved': Royal Commissions – A Method of British Democracy," in Bank of Nova Scotia *Monthly Review* 12, 6

(1938): 4. I am grateful to Bank of Nova Scotia archivist Andrea McCutcheon for supplying these monthly reviews.
5 In the beginning, D.A. Skelton was head of research and anglophone secretary. Eventually, John Deutsch took over as research chief.
6 Research Director D.A. Skelton to Royal Commissioner Henry Forbes Angus, 21 August 1937, Royal Commission on Dominion-Provincial Relations, LAC, RG 33, ser. 23, vol. 71, file: Angus, H.F., 1.
7 Fransen, "Unscrewing the Unscrutable," v.
8 Ibid., v.
9 Skelton told Dafoe that when he showed them to Australian federalism expert L.F. Giblin in August 1938, the Australian pronounced them "as a really first-rate achievement, in journalism of the best kind, – which is rare these days." See Rowell-Sirois Commission Secretary Alex Skelton to Commissioner John Dafoe, 12 September 1938, John Dafoe Fonds, University of Manitoba Archives, box 14, fol. 3, 3.
10 Stursberg, *Those Were the Days*, 159.
11 "Manitoba's Case – The Effects of Declining Income," in Manitoba's Case: A Submission Presented to the Royal Commission on Dominion-Provincial Relations, LAC, RG 33/23, vol. 1, pt. 5, 2–4. The premier did not specify the number of income-tax payers.
12 "Analysis of Manitoba's Treasury Problem," in Manitoba's Case: A Submission Presented to the Royal Commission on Dominion-Provincial Relations, LAC, RG 33/23, vol. 1, pt. 7, 56, http://heritage.canadiana.ca/view/oocihm.lac_reel_c6980/292?r=0&s=6.
13 "Introduction," in Manitoba's Case: A Submission Presented to the Royal Commission on Dominion-Provincial Relations, LAC, RG 33/23, vol. 1, pt. 1, 2, http://heritage.canadiana.ca/view/oocihm.lac_reel_c6980/29?r=0&s=6.
14 Ibid., 5.
15 "Comments by Prof. Henry Forbes Angus on Federal Finance in Australia," for the Royal Commission on Dominion-Provincial Relations, LAC, RG 33, ser. 23, vol. 71, file Angus, H.F., 11.
16 "The Effects of Federal Monetary Policy," in Manitoba's Case: A Submission Presented to the Royal Commission on Dominion-Provincial Relations, LAC, RG 33/23, vol. 1, pt. 3, 32 (emphasis in original), http://heritage.canadiana.ca/view/oocihm.lac_reel_c6980/119?r=0&s=6.
17 "Dominion and Provincial Budgets, in an Examination of Certain Proposals for the Readjustment of Dominion-Provincial Finance Relations," in ibid., 14–15.
18 "Analysis of Manitoba's Treasury Problem," in ibid., 48.
19 "Manitoba's Case – Summary and Recommendations," in ibid., 52–6, http://heritage.canadiana.ca/view/oocihm.lac_reel_c6980/345?r=0&s=6.

20 J.B. McGeachy, "Confederation Clinic: 1867–1937," signed J.B.M. in *Winnipeg Free Press*, 1 December 1937, 11.
21 Ibid.
22 Eggleston, *While I Still Remember*, 223.
23 Ibid., 224.
24 Premier W.J. Patterson, Foreward [*sic*] to Province of Saskatchewan, Submission to the Royal Commission on Dominion-Provincial Relations, 1937, LAC, RG 33/23, vol. 2, i, http://heritage.canadiana.ca/view/oocihm.lac_reel_c6980/847?r=0&s=4.
25 Ibid.
26 Introductory to Province of Saskatchewan Submission to the Royal Commission on Dominion-Provincial Relations, 1937, LAC, RG 33/23, vol. 2, 3.
27 Province of Saskatchewan, Submission to the Royal Commission on Dominion-Provincial Relations, 1937, LAC, RG 33/23, vol. 2, 15.
28 Wellington Jeffers, "Relief Problems Acute, but None Uncared For," *Globe and Mail*, 11 December 1937, 1.
29 Province of Saskatchewan Submission to the Royal Commission on Dominion-Provincial Relations, 1937, LAC, RG 33/23, vol. 2, 72.
30 Ibid., 35.
31 Ibid., 46, emphasis mine, http://heritage.canadiana.ca/view/oocihm.lac_reel_c6980/874?r=0&s=5.
32 Ibid., 274, http://heritage.canadiana.ca/view/oocihm.lac_reel_c6980/991?r=0&s=5.
33 Ibid., 243.
34 Ibid., 244 (emphasis mine).
35 J.B. McGeachy, "Confederation Clinic: 1867–1937," *Winnipeg Free Press*, 11 December 1937, 21.
36 Province of Saskatchewan Submission to the Royal Commission on Dominion-Provincial Relations, RG 33/23, vol. 2, 331.
37 Ibid., 333–4.
38 Ibid., 14.
39 Ibid., 285.
40 Brief of the Saskatchewan Urban Municipalities Association to the Royal Commission on Dominion-Provincial Relations, LAC, RG 33/23, vol. 3, 7.
41 Ibid., 11.
42 Ibid., 14.
43 Ibid., 15.
44 Ibid., 16, http://heritage.canadiana.ca/view/oocihm.lac_reel_c6981/199?r=0&s=5.
45 Unpublished autobiography of H.F. Angus, chap. 7, LAC. MG 30, ser. E274,

vol. 1, File: H.F. Angus Autobiography 1966, 275–6. Translation is from Virgil, *The Aeneid*, trans. W.F. Jackson Knight (Harmondsworth, Middlesex, UK: Penguin Books, 1978), 51.
46 "Work for Jobless," *Globe and Mail*, 19 November 1937, 17.
47 "80,000,000 Pounds of Food for Drought-Stricken Are Distributed," *Globe and Mail*, 15 November 1937, 15.
48 "Cows Starve as Ice Forms: Icy Crust over Saskatchewan Grazing Range Creates Acute Situation," *Globe and Mail*, 1 December 1937, 8.
49 Eggleston, *While I Still Remember*, 226.
50 Struthers, *No Fault of Their Own*, 175.
51 Diary of William Lyon Mackenzie King, 20 December 1937, http://www.bac-lac.gc.ca/eng/discover/politics-government/prime-ministers/william-lyon-mackenzie-king/Pages/item.aspx?IdNumber=18593&.
52 Ibid., http://www.bac-lac.gc.ca/eng/discover/politics-government/prime-ministers/william-lyon-mackenzie-king/Pages/item.aspx?IdNumber=18594&.
53 "*Unemployment and Relief in Canada: Issued as a Supplement to the Labour Gazette*," April 1936 (Ottawa: J.O. Patenaude, Printer to the King's Most Excellent Majesty, 1936), National Archives of Australia, Canada – Economic and Financial, ser. A981, CAN 18, pt. 1, barcode 173366, 4.
54 Diary of William Lyon Mackenzie King, 12 January 1938, http://www.bac-lac.gc.ca/eng/discover/politics-government/prime-ministers/william-lyon-mackenzie-king/Pages/item.aspx?IdNumber=18685&.
55 Diary of William Lyon Mackenzie King, 25 January 1938, http://www.bac-lac.gc.ca/eng/discover/politics-government/prime-ministers/william-lyon-mackenzie-king/Pages/item.aspx?IdNumber=18721&.
56 Simeon and Robinson, *State, Society*, 82.
57 As quoted in ibid., 71.
58 Diary of William Lyon Mackenzie King, 6 July 1938, http://www.bac-lac.gc.ca/eng/discover/politics-government/prime-ministers/william-lyon-mackenzie-king/Pages/item.aspx?IdNumber=19223.
59 Simeon and Robinson, *State, Society*, 83.
60 Analysis of Trades and Labour Congress brief in Digest of Briefs and Evidence for the Rowell-Sirois Commission, LAC, RG 33, ser. 23, vol. 60, file FA 33-20, pt. 2, 105 (his capital letters).
61 Analysis of Canadian Medical Association brief in Digest of Briefs and Evidence for the Rowell-Sirois Commission, LAC, RG 33, ser. 23, vol. 60, file FA 33-20, 210.
62 Canadian Medical Association before the Royal-Commission on Dominion-Provincial Relations, 21 January 1938, LAC, RG 33/23, vol. 4, 11.

63 Ibid., 13, 17.
64 Canadian Tuberculosis Association at the Royal-Commission on Dominion-Provincial Relations, LAC, RG 33/23, vol. 4, pp. 3, 15.
65 Unpublished autobiography of H.F. Angus, chap. 7, LAC, MG 30, ser. E-274, vol. 1, file: H.F. Angus Autobiography 1966, 278.
66 Ibid., 261.
67 Ibid., 278. This reference does not appear in the commission's analysis of the evidence, no doubt because the commission dismissed it out of hand.
68 J.B. McGeachy, "Confederation Clinic: 1867–1937," *Winnipeg Free Press*, 4 February 1938, 11.
69 Ibid.
70 Ibid.
71 Ibid.
72 Submission by the Government of the Province of Nova Scotia to the Royal Commission on Dominion-Provincial Relations, February 1938, LAC, RG 33/23, vol. 6, 38.
73 Ibid., 43.
74 Ibid., 72.
75 Ibid., 24–6.
76 J.B. McGeachy, "Confederation Clinic: 1867–1937," *Winnipeg Free Press*, 5 February 1938, 19.
77 Ibid.
78 Ibid.
79 Eggleston, *While I Still Remember*, 227.
80 Ibid., 229.
81 Analysis of Prince Edward Island Brief in Public Health, Digest of Briefs and Evidence for the Rowell-Sirois Commission, LAC, RG 33, ser. 23, vol. 60, file FA 33-20, 208.
82 Eggleston, *While I Still Remember*, 228.
83 Ibid., 229.
84 Ibid., 230–2. In early September 1939, Dafoe told Eggleston that he had seen war coming for four or five years: "but I never thought it would arrive in my lifetime" (254).
85 Brief of the Province of British Columbia to the Royal Commission on Dominion- Provincial Relations, LAC, RG 33/23, vol. 8, 177, http://heritage.canadiana.ca/view/oocihm.lac_reel_c6984/148?r=0&s=5.
86 Ibid.
87 Ibid., 318–19.
88 Fisher, *Duff Pattullo*, 320.
89 Ibid., 215.

90 Brief of the Province of British Columbia to the Royal Commission on Dominion-Provincial Relations, the Royal Commission on Dominion-Provincial Relations, LAC, RG 33/23, vol. 8, 351.
91 Province of British Columbia, Claim for Readjustment of Terms of Union, presented by Hon. T.D. Pattullo, Attorney-General Hon. G. McG. Sloan, Minister of Finance Hon. John Hart to the Royal Commission on Dominion-Provincial Relations, LAC, RG 33/23, vol. 8, 31.
92 Ibid., 32–3.
93 Unpublished Autobiography of Henry Angus, chap. 7, LAC, MG 30, ser. E274, vol. 1, file: H.F. Angus Autobiography 1966, 277.
94 Ibid., 278.
95 Fisher, *Duff Pattullo*, 322.
96 As quoted in ibid.
97 Dorothy G. Steeves, "A British Columbia View," in "The Sirois Report – A Discussion of Some Aspects," *Canadian Forum*, November 1940, 238.
98 J.B. McGeachy, "Confederation Clinic: 1867–1937," *Winnipeg Free Press*, 18 March 1938, 13.
99 Ibid., 13.
100 Ibid., 24 March 1938, 14.
101 Fisher, *Duff Pattullo*, 357–8.
102 Palmer, *Alberta: A New History*, 274.
103 Premier William Aberhart to Prime Minister Mackenzie King, 26 August 1937, LAC, file: Provincial Matters – Alberta – miscellaneous P 1-1-10, RG 19, vol. 3985, 3.
104 Ibid., 4.
105 Prime Minister Mackenzie King to Premier William Aberhart, 31 August 1937, LAC, RG 19, vol. 3985, file: Provincial Matters – Alberta miscellaneous, P 1-1-10, 4.
106 Eggleston, *While I Still Remember*, 233.
107 Ibid., 233, 234.
108 *The Case for Alberta: Dominion/Provincial Relations 1938*, pt. 11 (Edmonton: A. Shnitka, King's Printer, Government of Alberta, 1938), 25.
109 Ibid., 375–6.
110 Ibid., 377–8.
111 J.B. McGeachy, "Confederation Clinic: 1867–1937," *Winnipeg Free Press*, 31 March 1938, 13.
112 Ibid.
113 Brief of the Edmonton Chamber of Commerce to the Royal Commission on Dominion-Provincial Relations, LAC, RG 33/23, vol. 9, 39, http://heritage.canadiana.ca/view/oocihm.lac_reel_c6985/90?r=0&s=5.

114 Ibid., 42.
115 Ibid., 52.
116 Ibid.
117 Ibid., 63.
118 Unpublished autobiography of Henry Angus, chap. 7, LAC, MG 30, ser. E274, vol. 1, file: H.F. Angus Autobiography 1966, 262.
119 Statement of Honourable Mitchell F. Hepburn to the Royal Commission on Dominion-Provincial Relations, April 1938, LAC, RG 33/23, vol. 12, 25.
120 Statement by the Government of Ontario to the Royal Commission on Dominion- Provincial Relations, LAC, RG 33/23, vol. 12, 21.
121 Statement of Honourable Mitchell F. Hepburn to the Royal Commission on Dominion-Provincial Relations, April 1938, LAC, RG 33/23, vol. 12, 16, http://heritage.canadiana.ca/view/oocihm.lac_reel_c6986/550?r=0&s=4.
122 Ibid., 21.
123 Statement by the Government of Ontario to the Royal Commission on Dominion-Provincial Relations, LAC, RG 33/23, vol. 12, 13, http://heritage.canadiana.ca/view/oocihm.lac_reel_c6986/584?r=0&s=6.
124 Ibid., 79.
125 Statement of Honourable Mitchell F. Hepburn to the Royal Commission on Dominion-Provincial Relations, April 1938, LAC, RG 33/23, vol. 12, 3 May 1938, 11.
126 Ibid., 10.
127 Ibid., 21.
128 J.B. McGeachy, "Confederation Clinic: 1867–1937," *Winnipeg Free Press*, 3 May 1938, 13.
129 Ibid.
130 Ibid.
131 Eggleston, *While I Still Remember*, 235, 236.
132 Unpublished autobiography of Henry Angus, chap. 7, LAC, MG 30, ser. E274, vol. 1, file: H.F. Angus Autobiography 1966, 261–2.
133 Digest of Briefs and Evidence for the Royal Commission on Dominion-Provincial Relations, FA 33-20 (ser. 23), pt. 2, 12. And "Conference Necessary before Commission's Findings Acted Upon," *Globe and Mail*, 3 May 1938, 2.
134 Unpublished autobiography of Henry Angus, chap. 7, LAC, MG 30, ser. E274, vol. 1, file: H.F. Angus Autobiography 1966, 262.
135 Royal Commissioner R.A. MacKay to his wife Kathleen MacKay, 8 May 1938, LAC, MG 30, ser. E159, vol. 1D, file: Royal Commission – personal letters – Mackay to his wife Kathleen, 1937–38, 8.
136 Ibid., 7.

137 Ibid.
138 Eggleston, *While I Still Remember*, 238.
139 John Wesley Dafoe to Edward C. Carter, 24 February 1938, John Wesley Dafoe, correspondence, LAC, MG 30, D45, 1.
140 John Wesley Dafoe to Edward C. Carter, 16 February 1938, John Wesley Dafoe, correspondence, LAC, MG 30, D45. 1.
141 Prang, *N.W. Rowell*, 496.
142 Eggleston, *While I Still Remember*, 238.
143 "Questions on Which the Commission Would Be Glad to Have the Views of the Government of Quebec," Royal Commission on Dominion-Provincial Relations, LAC, RG 33/23, vol. 13, 5, http://heritage.canadiana.ca/view/oocihm.lac_reel_c6987/329?r=0&s=5.
144 Statement of Province of Quebec to the Royal Commission on Dominion-Provincial Relations, LAC, RG 33/23, vol. 13, 7.
145 Ibid., 2 (my translation).
146 Ibid., 3.
147 Ibid., 8.
148 "Quebec Denies Power of Dominion to Probe Provincial Finances," *Globe and Mail*, 13 May 1938, 15.
149 Statement of Province of Quebec to the Royal Commission on Dominion-Provincial Relations, LAC, RG 33/23, vol. 13, 10.
150 *Le Devoir*, 12 May 1938, 1 (my translation).
151 J.B. McGeachy, "Confederation Clinic: 1867–1937," *Winnipeg Free Press*, 13 May 1938, 12.
152 Léopold Richer, "Sur l'accueil plûtot frais de l'Ontario et du Québec à la commission Rowell," *Le Devoir*, 13 May 1938, 1–2 (my translation).
153 Brief of the Société Saint-Jean Baptiste de Montréal, Royal Commission on Dominion-Provincial Relations, LAC, RG 33/23, vol. 13, 3 (my translation).
154 Ibid., 26, 28 (my translation).
155 Unpublished autobiography of Henry Angus, chap. 7, LAC, MG 30, ser. E274, vol. 1, file: H.F. Angus Autobiography 1966, 281.
156 Thomson, *Louis St. Laurent*, 101.
157 Unpublished autobiography of Henry Angus, chap. 7, LAC, MG 30, ser. E274, vol. 1, file: H.F. Angus Autobiography 1966, 281.
158 Black, *Render unto Caesar*, 156.
159 Eggleston, *While I Still Remember*, 241.
160 McGeachy depicted the reader as a lawyer while Eggleston remembered him as an academic.
161 Submission by the Government of the Province of New Brunswick to the

Royal Commission on Dominion-Provincial Relations, pt. 1, LAC, RG 33/23, vol. 13, 10, http://heritage.canadiana.ca/view/oocihm.lac_reel_c6987/345?r=0&s=4.

162 Ibid., 11 (emphasis mine).
163 Ibid., 37.
164 Digest of Briefs and Evidence for the Royal Commission on Dominion-Provincial Relations, Submission by the Government of the Province of New Brunswick to the Royal Commission on Dominion-Provincial Relations FA 33-20 (ser. 23), pt. 2, 50.
165 Submission by the Government of the Province of New Brunswick to the Royal Commission on Dominion-Provincial Relations, pt. 1, LAC, RG 33/23, vol. 13, 36.
166 Ibid., 39.
167 J. B. McGeachy, "Confederation Clinic: 1867–1937," *Winnipeg Free Press*, 19 May 1938, 15.
168 Ibid.
169 Digest of Briefs and Evidence for the Royal Commission on Dominion-Provincial Relations, FA 33-20 (ser. 23), pt. 2, Union of New Brunswick Municipalities to the Royal Commission on Dominion-Provincial Relations, 51.
170 Brief of the New Brunswick Teachers' Association to the Royal Commission on Dominion-Provincial Relations, LAC, RG 33, ser. 23, vol. 14, 7.
171 "Welfare Services for the Canadian People," the submission of the Canadian Welfare Council to the Commission on Dominion-Provincial Relations, Ottawa, LAC, RG 33/23, vol. 14, 5.
172 Ibid.
173 Ibid., i–ii.
174 Ibid., 18.
175 H.W. Morgan, Representative of the Canadian Chamber of Commerce, to the Royal Commission on Dominion-Provincial Relations, LAC, RG 33, ser. 23, vol. 14, 8.
176 Ibid.
177 "Toward Democratic Unity for Canada," Submission of the Dominion Committee, Communist Party of Canada, to the Royal Commission on Dominion-Provincial Relations, ed. Alderman Stewart Smith, n.p., n.d., 41.
178 "Reds Peaceful, Buck Declares: Tells Rowell Commission. Violence Dropped as an Instrument of Policy: Describes Party's Goal," *Globe*, 2 June 1938, 3.
179 Ibid.
180 Ibid.

181 Submission of the Dominion Committee, Communist Party of Canada, to the Royal Commission on Dominion-Provincial Relations, LAC, RG 33, ser. 23, vol. 14, 17.
182 Ibid., 27.
183 "Reds Peaceful, Buck Declares: Tells Rowell Commission. Violence Dropped as an Instrument of Policy: Describes Party's Goal," *Globe*, 2 June 1938, 3.
184 "Special Grants in the Australian Federation," the Bank of Nova Scotia *Monthly Review*, Toronto, May 1938, National Archives of Australia, Canada – Internal Politics, ser. A 981, CAN 24, pt. 1, barcode 173375, 4.
185 Royal Commissioner J.W. Dafoe to Commonwealth Grants Commission Chairman F.W. Eggleston, 24 November 1937, National Archives of Australia, MS 423, 15.9.1.
186 Commonwealth Grants Commission Chairman F.W. Eggleston to Royal Commissioner J.W. Dafoe, 22 April 1938, University of Manitoba Archives, John W. Dafoe Fonds, box 14, fol. 4. p. 2 (emphasis mine).
187 Evidence of former German Chancellor Heinrich Brüning to the Royal Commission on Dominion-Provincial Relations, 28 January 1938, LAC, RG 33, ser. 23, vol. 20, 3743–4, http://heritage.canadiana.ca/view/oocihm.lac_reel_c6991/751?r=0&s=6.
188 Evidence of University of London Law Professor Ivor Jennings to the Royal Commission on Dominion-Provincial Relations, 21 April 1938, LAC, RG 33, ser. 23, vol. 25, 6714D–5D, http://heritage.canadiana.ca/view/oocihm.lac_reel_c6993/1043?r=0&s=6.
189 Evidence of Stockholm University Political Economy Professor Gunnar Myrdal to the Royal Commission on Dominion-Provincial Relations, 25 May 1938, LAC, RG 33, ser. 23, vol. 28, 9142.
190 Ibid., 9143, http://heritage.canadiana.ca/view/oocihm.lac_reel_c6995/712?r=0&s=4.
191 Ibid.
192 Evidence of New York's Rockefeller Center Research Director Bryce M. Stewart to the Royal Commission on Dominion-Provincial Relations, 20 October 1938, Royal Commission on Dominion-Provincial Relations, LAC, C-6988, RG 33, ser. 23, vol. 30, 9988–10077.
193 H.E. Crowle, "Comparative Federalism: Report on the Republic of Argentina," Report for the Royal Commission on Dominion-Provincial Relations, LAC, RG 33, ser. 23, vol. 60, file: H.E. Crowle Report of the Republic of Argentina, 1.
194 Ibid., 15–42. Please note that the reports on New Zealand, Switzerland, Denmark, and Sweden are attached to the Argentina file.

195 H.E. Crowle, "Comparative Federalism: "Preliminary Report on Banking in Australia"; "Transportation in Australia"; "Commercial Law in Australia: Final Report on Marketing and Price Control"; "Preliminary Report on Insurance and on Corporations in Australia"; "Preliminary Report on Incorporation and Regulation of Corporations in Australia"; "Commercial Law in Australia"; "Preliminary Report on Australian Refunding Agreements." See H.E. Crowle, Australia: Comparative Federalism, Royal Commission on Dominion-Provincial Relations, LAC, RG 33, ser. 23, vol. 60, file: Crowle, H.E Australia Comparative Federalism, 1–81 in total.

196 Ibid., 8.

197 University of Toronto Dean of Law H.P.M. Kennedy, "Report on Aspects of Comparative Federal Laws," LAC, RG 33, ser. 23, vol. 38, file: RG 33 23 38: Study of Federal Constitutions W.P M. Kennedy, 55.

198 John Dafoe to Henry Angus, 5 July 1938, University of Manitoba Archives, John W. Dafoe Fonds, box 14, fol. 1, 3-4.

199 "Federal-State Financial Relations in Australia, July 1938," Royal Commission on Dominion-Provincial Relations, LAC, RG 33, ser. 23, vol. 59, file: Coyne, J.E., "Federal State Financial Relations in Australia," 1–24 (summary) and 1–159 (full report).

200 "Federal-Provincial Financial Relations in the Argentine Republic, July 1938," Royal Commission on Dominion-Provincial Relations, LAC, RG 33, ser. 23, vol. 59, file: Coyne, J.E., Federal-Provincial financial relations in the Argentine Republic, 1–82.

201 "Comments by Prof. Henry Forbes Angus on Federal Finance in Australia," for the Royal-Commission on Dominion-Provincial Relations, LAC, RG 33, ser. 23, vol. 71, file: Angus, H.F, 15.

202 Royal Commissioner John W. Dafoe to Commonwealth Grants Commission Chairman F.W. Eggleston, 5 July 1938, National Archives of Australia, MS 423, 1/55, 2.

203 John Wesley Dafoe to Sir James Barrett, 9 January 1939, Dafoe Correspondence, LAC, MG 30, D45, 1–2

204 Sir James Barrett to John Wesley Dafoe, 14 February 1939, Dafoe Correspondence, LAC, MG 30, D45, 1.

205 Ibid., 2.

206 Research Director Alexander Skelton to Commissioner John Dafoe, 22 July 1938, John W. Dafoe Fonds, University of Manitoba Archives, box 14, fol. 3, 2.

207 Fifth Report (1938) of the Commonwealth Grants Commission, applications made by the States of South Australia, Western Australia, and Tasmania for Financial Assistance in 1938–39 from the Commonwealth under

Section 96 of the Constitution (Canberra: L.F. Johnston, Commonwealth Government Printer, 1938), National Archives of Australia, ser. AWM68, 3DRL 8052/129, pt. 1A, barcode 496892, 41.
208 Ibid.
209 *Sixth Report (1938) of the Commonwealth Grants Commission, Applications Made by the States of South Australia, Western Australia, and Tasmania for Financial Assistance in 1939-40 from the Commonwealth under Section 96 of the Constitution* (Canberra: L.F. Johnston, Commonwealth Government Printer, 1939), National Archives of Australia, ser. CP211/2, 69/12, barcode 250523, 10–11 (emphasis mine).
210 Ibid., 78.
211 Unpublished autobiography of Henry Angus, chap. 7, LAC, MG 30, ser. E274, vol. 1, file H.F. Angus autobiography 1966, 282.
212 Ibid.
213 Ibid., 284.
214 Research Director Alexander Skelton to Commissioner John Dafoe, 21 December 1938, John W. Dafoe Fonds, University of Manitoba Archives, box 14, fol. 3, 2.
215 R.A. MacKay, "Some Personal Reminiscences of the Rowell-Sirois Commission, July 26, 1963," LAC, MG 30, vol. 10, file: Correspondence and Personal Reminiscences of the Rowell-Sirois Commission 1963, 1–2.
216 Unpublished autobiography of Henry Angus, chap. 8, LAC, MG 30, ser. E274, vol. 1, file H.F. Angus autobiography 1966, 308.
217 Unpublished autobiography of Henry Angus, chap. 7, LAC, MG 30, ser. E274, vol. 1, file H.F. Angus autobiography 1966, 270.
218 Ibid., 271.
219 Ibid., 270.
220 Ibid., 271.
221 Henry Angus to John Dafoe, 21 February 1940, University of Manitoba Archives, John Dafoe Fonds, box 14, fol. 2, 1.
222 Unpublished autobiography of Henry Angus, chap. 7, LAC, MG 30, ser. E274, vol. 1, file H.F. Angus autobiography 1966, 282.
223 Commissioner R.A. MacKay to Kathleen MacKay, 14 May 1939, LAC, MG 30, ser. E159, vol. 10, file: Sirois Commission – personal letters – MacKay to his wife Kathleen 1939–40, 3.
224 Australian Trade Commissioner L.R. Macgregor to the Department of External Affairs Secretary, memorandum on political conditions in Canada, 12 January 1938, National Archives of Australia, Canada – Internal pt. 1, ser. A981, CAN 21, pt. 1, barcode 173371, 1.
225 Ibid., 6–7.

226 Ibid., 10.
227 "Draft Cablegram to Australian Trade Commissioner, Canada," from Australian External Affairs Secretary, 21 March 1938, National Archives of Australia, Canada: Constitutional, ser. A981, CAN 13, pt. 2, barcode 173360, 1.
228 Gettys, *Administration of Canadian Conditional Grants*. Quotations are from the review in the *Annals of the American Academy of Political and Social Science*, November 1938, 324.
229 Australian Trade Commissioner L.R. Macgregor to the Secretary of the External Affairs Department, 19 May 1938, National Archives of Australia, Canada – Internal pt. 1, ser. A981, CAN 21, pt. 1, barcode 173371, 1.
230 Extract from *Toronto Daily Star*, 9 June 1936, National Archives of Australia, Canada – Internal Politics, ser. A 981, CAN 24, pt. 1, barcode 173375, 1.
231 Canada: Budget Speech delivered by Hon. Chas. A. Dunning, Minister of Finance, Member for Queens, Prince Edward Island, in the House Of Commons, 16 June 1938, National Archives of Australia, Canada – Internal Politics, ser. A 981, CAN 24, pt. 1, barcode 173375, 54–5.
232 Ibid., 12–13.
233 Ibid., 8.
234 Dimand, "Comment," 126.
235 I am indebted to Tasmanian parliamentary archivist Sarah Ravanat and to former Tasmanian premier Michael Field, now chancellor of the University of Tasmania, for assistance with the biographies of Giblin and his father, former Tasmanian premier William Robert Giblin.
236 Royal Commissioner R.A. MacKay to his spouse Kathleen MacKay, 14 October 1939, LAC, MG 30, ser. E159, vol. 10, file: Sirois Commission – personal letters, MacKay to his wife Kathleen, 5–6.
237 Ibid., 15 December 1939, 2.
238 Royal Commission Chairman Joseph Sirois to Commissioner R.A. MacKay, 5 March 1940, MG 30, ser. E159, vol. 8, Rowell Sirois Correspondence 1938–40, 1.
239 Royal Commissioner John W. Dafoe to Royal Commissioner Henry F. Angus, 29 March 1940, University of Manitoba Archives, John W. Dafoe Fonds, box 14, fol. 1, 1 (my insertion of grave accent in "père").
240 Unpublished autobiography of Henry Angus, chap. 7, LAC, MG 30, ser. E274, vol. 1, file H.F. Angus autobiography 1966, 268.
241 Commission Legal Secretary Robert Fowler to Commissioner John W. Dafoe, 24 September 1939, University of Manitoba Archives, John W. Dafoe Fonds, box 14, fol. 2, 2.
242 Commissioner John W. Dafoe to Commission Legal Secretary Robert

Fowler, 30 September 1939, University of Manitoba Archives, John W. Dafoe Fonds, box 14, fol. 1, 1 (emphasis mine).
243 Bank of Canada Archives, Department of Bank Operations Fonds, Secretary's Fonds, Bank of Canada Governor Graham Towers to L.W. Brockington, Special Assistant to Prime Minister Mackenzie King, 8 May 1940, Royal Commission on Dominion-Provincial Relations, box 1, file B95-291, 2 (emphasis mine).
244 D.A. Skelton, "Sirois Report and the War," confidential memorandum, 24 July 1940, John James Deutsch Fonds, Queen's University Archives, box 109, fol. 1295.
245 Ferguson and Wardhaugh, "Impossible Conditions of Inequality," 15.
246 Unpublished autobiography of Henry Angus, chap. 7, LAC, MG 30, ser. E274, vol. 1, file H.F. Angus autobiography 1966, 265.
247 Ibid., 266.
248 As quoted from a letter from John Dafoe to Research Director Alex Skelton, 27 August 1937, in Cook, *Politics of John W. Dafoe*, 225.
249 "Wide Revision of Canada's Fiscal Structure Advocated," *Gazette*, 17 May 1940, 12, National Archives of Australia, Canada Constitution, ser. A 981, CAN 13, pt. 1, barcode 173359, 12.

CHAPTER SEVEN

1 "Report to Wait Until Thursday: Will Now Be Released Day Parliament Opens, New Crisis Cause," *Globe and Mail*, 11 May 1940, 5.
2 Bank of Canada Archives, Department of Bank Operations Fonds, "Canadian Federalism in Transition," Albert Lepawsky, Public Administration Review, autumn 1940, *Journal of the American Society for Public Administration*, article filed 1 November 1940 in Secretary's Fonds, box 1, file 291, 9.
3 Leslie, *National Citizenship and Provincial Communities*, 13.
4 Lepawsky, "Canadian Federalism in Transition," 77.
5 Smiley, "Rowell-Sirois Report," 56.
6 Struthers, *No Fault of Their Own*, 205.
7 Brown, *Equalization on the Basis of Need*, 2.
8 *Report of the Royal Commission on Dominion-Provincial Relations*, 2:125, (emphasis mine).
9 Leslie, *National Citizenship and Provincial Communities*, 15.
10 *Royal Commission on Dominion-Provincial Relations*, 2:125.
11 Ibid.
12 Ibid.

13 Ibid., 84.
14 Ibid., 125.
15 Milne, "Equalization and the Politics of Restraint," 186.
16 *Report of the Royal Commission on Dominion-Provincial Relations*, 1:245, http://publications.gc.ca/collections/collection_2016/bcp-pco/Z1-1937-2-1-2-eng.pdf.
17 Ibid.
18 Ibid.
19 Underhill, "Sirois Commission as Historians," 235.
20 Letter from R.M. Fowler to R.A. MacKay, 6 August 1963, LAC, MG 30, ser. E 159, vol. 10, file: Correspondence and Personal Reminiscences of the Rowell-Sirois Commission 1963, 4.
21 Thomson, *Louis St. Laurent*, 102.
22 Unpublished autobiography of Henry Angus, chap. 7, LAC, MG 30, ser. E 274, vol. 1, file H.F. Angus autobiography 1966, 283. Angus attributes the story to the commission's francophone secretary Adjutor Savard. See also: Letter from R.A. MacKay to R.M. Fowler, 9 August 1963, LAC, MG 30, ser. E 159, vol. 10, file: Correspondence and Personal Reminiscences of the Rowell-Sirois Commission 1963, 1–2.
23 Unpublished autobiography of Henry Angus, 267.
24 H.F. Angus to John Dafoe, 3 January 1940, University of Manitoba Archives, John Dafoe Fonds, box 14, fol. 2, 1.
25 H.F. Angus to R.A. MacKay, 28 January 1941, LAC, MG 30, ser. E 159, vol. 8, 1.
26 Unpublished autobiography of Henry Angus, 267.
27 Ibid., 264.
28 Henry Angus to John Dafoe, 21 February 1940, University of Manitoba Archives, John Dafoe Fonds, box 14, fol. 3, 2.
29 "Canada Sets Day for Prayer," *Globe and Mail*, 20 May 1940, 17.
30 "Hepburn Holds Sirois Report Is Red Herring: Charges King Intended to Blind Dominion to Lack of War Effort," *Globe and Mail*, 22 May 1940, 5.
31 Saywell, *"Just Call Me Mitch,"* 450. Years later, in March 1945, Hepburn confessed that he probably erred in attacking King "in a personal way." See Levine, *King*, 361.
32 Diary of Prime Minister William Lyon Mackenzie King, 28 May 1940, ://www.bac-lac.gc.ca/eng/discover/politics-government/prime-ministers/william-lyon-mackenzie-king/Pages/item.aspx?IdNumber=21703&.
33 Underhill, "Sirois Commission as Historians," 233.
34 Bank of Canada Archives, Department of Bank Operations Fonds, "Canadian Federalism in Transition," 9.
35 Ibid.

36 Australian High Commission Secretary Nöel Deschamps to the Secretary, Department of External Affairs, 2 August 1940, Canada: Constitution, National Archives of Australia, ser. A981, CAN 13, pt. 1, barcode 173359, 1.
37 Unpublished autobiography of H.F. Angus, 285. Once Rowell left, of course, Ontario had no representation.
38 Ibid., 287.
39 Leslie, *National Citizenship and Provincial Communities*, 19.
40 Burns, "Royal Commission on Dominion-Provincial Relations," 153–4.
41 Ibid., 154.
42 Ibid.
43 Ibid.
44 Australian High Commissioner to Canada T.W. Glasgow to External Affairs Minister, Canberra, 20 June 1940, National Archives of Australia, Australian High Commissioner in Canada – memoranda from, ser. A461, D348/1/15, barcode 1950707, 1. This is memo no. M. 9/ 40.
45 Australian High Commissioner to Canada T.W. Glasgow to External Affairs Minister, Canberra, 20 June 1940, National Archives of Australia, Australian High Commissioner in Canada – Memoranda from, ser. A461, D348/1/15, barcode 1950707. This is a separate memo from Glasgow to the Australian external affairs minister: it was also written on 20 June 1940 but it is no. M. 10/ 40, 2.
46 Budget Speech, delivered by Honourable J.L. Ralston, Minister of Finance, Member for Prince, Prince Edward Island, in the House of Commons, 24 June 1940, National Archives of Australia, Canada: Economic and Financial, ser. A981, CAN 18, pt. 2, barcode 173367. 1.
47 Ibid., 14.
48 Ibid., 32.
49 "Dominion-Provincial Relations," extract from "Monetary Times 18-5-40, National Archives of Australia, Canada: Constitution, ser. A981, CAN 13, pt. 1, barcode 173359, 1–3.
50 Memorandum to the Secretary, Department of External Affairs, from Australian High Commission Secretary Nöel Deschamps, 7 June 1940, National Archives of Australia, Canada: Constitution, ser. A981, CAN 13, pt. 1, barcode 173359, 1–4.
51 Australian High Commission Secretary Nöel Deschamps to the Secretary, Department of External Affairs, 18 July 1940, National Archives of Australia, Canada: Constitution, ser. A981, CAN 13, pt. 1, barcode 173359, 1.
52 Draft Telegram to High Commissioner, Ottawa, from External, 8 August 1940, Canada: Constitution, National Archives of Australia, ser. A981, CAN 13, pt. 1, barcode 173359, 1.

53 Australian High Commission Secretary Nöel Deschamps to the Secretary, Department of External Affairs, 2 August 1940, National Archives of Australia, Canada: Constitution, ser. A981, CAN 13, pt. 1, barcode 173359, 1.
54 Australian High Commission Secretary Nöel Deschamps to the Secretary, Department of External Affairs, 28 August 1940, National Archives of Australia, Canada: Constitution, ser. A981, CAN 13, pt. 1, barcode 173359, 1.
55 Australian High Commission Secretary Nöel Deschamps to the Secretary, Department of External Affairs, 14 November 1940, National Archives of Australia, Canada: Constitution, ser. A981, CAN 13, pt. 1, barcode 173359, 1.
56 Saunders and Back, *Rowell-Sirois Commission*, 1:45, 37.
57 Commission Secretary Alex Skelton to Commissioner John W. Dafoe, 23 June 1938, University of Manitoba Archives, John W. Dafoe Fonds, box 14, fol. 3, 1.
58 Underhill, "Sirois Commission as Historians."
59 "The Rowell-Sirois Report: A Brief Survey of Its Financial Recommendations," *Monthly Review* (Bank of Nova Scotia) 14, 12 (1940): 4. I am grateful to Bank of Nova Scotia archivist Andrea McCutcheon for these reports.
60 Ibid.
61 Ibid., 2.
62 Fowler, *Comment on the Rowell-Sirois Report*, 1.
63 Ibid.
64 Fransen, "Unscrewing the Unscrutable," 417.
65 Leslie, *National Citizenship and Provincial Communities*, 17.
66 Fransen, "Unscrewing the Unscrutable," 451-2.
67 Ibid., 417.
68 Diary of William Lyon Mackenzie King, 9 January 1941, 2.
69 Ibid.
70 Fullerton, *Graham Towers and His Times*, 153.
71 Granatstein, *Canada's War*, 164-5.
72 Diary of William Lyon Mackenzie King, 22 October 1940, 2.
73 Ibid.
74 Ibid.
75 Ibid.
76 Granatstein, *Canada's War*, 165.
77 Bank of Canada Archives, Department of Bank Operations Fonds, "Sirois Report Spells $10,000,000 Annual Loss to Ontario: Hepburn May Call Election for Test of Public Opinion on Issue of Sirois Report," *Evening Telegram*, Toronto, 15 November 1940, n.p., Secretary's Fonds, box 1, file B95-291.
78 Diary of William Lyon Mackenzie King, 6 December 1940, 2.
79 Ibid., 1.

80 Ibid.
81 Diary of William Lyon Mackenzie King, 13 December 1940, 2.
82 Bruce, *Back the Attack!*, 3–8.
83 Ibid., 22.
84 Broadfoot, *Six War Years*, Author's summary, xii.
85 Ibid, xii.
86 Kimber, *Sailors, Slackers and Blind Pigs*, 84.
87 http://www.veterans.gc.ca/eng/remembrance/history/second-world-war/battle-atlantic.
88 Headlines, *Ottawa Journal*, 14 January 1941, 1.
89 Premier Duff Pattullo, Dominion-Provincial Conference, 14–15 January 1941, in *Dominion-Provincial Conferences*, 39.
90 Premier William Aberhart, ibid., 59.
91 Ibid., 61.
92 Premier Mitchell Hepburn, ibid., 15.
93 Ibid., 15–16.
94 Bryden, "Justifiable Obsession," 10–11.
95 Dirks, *Failure of L'Action Libérale Nationale*, 142.
96 Premier Adélard Godbout, Dominion-Provincial Conference, 14–15 January 1941, 17.
97 Ibid., 82.
98 Léopold Richer, "Elle paraît marcher vers un échec éclatant,"*Le Devoir*, 15 January 1941 (my translation).
99 Premier A.S. MacMillan, Dominion-Provincial Conference, 14–15 January 1941, 17.
100 Ibid., 18.
101 Slumkoski, "Fair Show and a Square Deal," 135.
102 Premier J.B. McNair, Dominion-Provincial Conference, 14–15 January 1941, 19.
103 Premier John Bracken, Dominion-Provincial Conference, 14–15 January 1941, 23.
104 Ibid., 25.
105 Premier Thane A. Campbell, Dominion-Provincial Conference, 14–15 January, 1941, 44.
106 Ibid., 48 (emphasis mine).
107 Premier W.J. Patterson, Dominion-Provincial Conference, 14–15 January 1941, 51.
108 Ibid., 54.
109 Finance Minister James Ilsley, Dominion-Provincial Conference, 14–15 January 1941, 71, 73 (emphasis mine).

110 Ibid., 73.
111 Ibid., 75.
112 "Conference of Premiers Collapses; Ontario Group Walks Out of Meeting; Ilsley Says Gasoline Rationing Near," *Ottawa Journal*, 15 January 1941, 1
113 Henry Angus to R.A. MacKay, 28 January 1941, LAC, MG 30, ser. E 159, vol. 8, file: Rowell-Sirois Correspondence, 1938–41, 1.
114 *Winnipeg Free Press* correspondent Grant Dexter to Editor John Dafoe, 13 May 1941, as quoted in Fransen, "Unscrewing the Unscrutable," 464.
115 Diary of William Lyon Mackenzie King, 15 January 1941, 3.
116 Fisher, *Duff Pattullo*, 334.
117 Saywell, *"Just Call Me Mitch,"* 462.
118 Ibid., 493.
119 Australian High Commissioner to Canada Sir William Glasgow to Australian External Affairs Secretary in Canberra, 30 January 1941, National Archives of Australia, Australian High Commissioner in Canada – memoranda from, ser. A461, D348/1/15, barcode 1950707, 1.
120 Ibid., 2.
121 Ibid., 1.
122 Broadfoot, *Six War Years*, 34–5. In the early 1970s, Broadfoot travelled across Canada, recording roughly 340,000 words for this oral history. Unfortunately, the speakers are not identified.
123 Perras, "She Should Have Thought of Herself First," 128–9.
124 Ibid., 144.
125 I went through *every* reference to Australia in King's diaries from 1938 through to 1949.
126 Bank of Canada Archives, Department of Bank Operations Fonds, memorandum from Bank of Canada Deputy Chief of Research J.R. Beattie, 20 January 1941, Secretary's Fonds, B95, file 291, 1 (emphasis mine).
127 Ibid., 1.
128 Ibid., 2.
129 Ibid., 3.
130 Leslie, *National Citizenship and Provincial Communities*, 19.
131 Campbell, "J. L. Ilsley and the Transformation of the Canadian Tax System," 658.
132 All news taken from the *Ottawa Journal* on 23 May 1942, 1–3, including "Manhattan Performs Miracle in First Total Blackout," 2.
133 Ibid., 24.
134 Courchene, *Equalization Payments*, 27.
135 Ibid., 27.
136 Burns, *Acceptable Mean*, 29.

137 Ibid., 35.
138 High Commission Official Secretary Noël Deschamps to External Affairs Department Secretary, memorandum on Cardinal Villeneuve's speech, 24 April 1941, National Archives of Australia, Canada – Internal, pt. 1, ser. A981, CAN 21, pt. 1, barcode 173371, 1.
139 Ibid., 1.
140 L.S.B. Shapiro, "Lights and Shadows: A Letter to Australia," *Montreal Gazette*, 25 March 1942, National Archives of Australia, Canada – Relations with Australia, ser. A981, CAN 32, barcode 173383, 1.
141 Cablegram from the High Commissioner's Office to the Australian Prime Minister, 16 March 1942, National Archives of Australia, Canada – Relations with Australia, ser. A981, CAN 32, barcode 173383, 1.
142 Letter from Canadian Trade Commissioner L.M. Cosgrave to Secretary of External Affairs, Canberra, 23 November 1942, National Archives of Australia, Australian High Commissioner in Canada – misc. letters forwarded, ser. A 981, AUS 161, barcode 172972, 1.
143 Letter from Australian High Commission Official Secretary Noël Deschamps to Secretary of External Affairs, Canberra, 12 November 1942, National Archives of Australia, Australian High Commissioner in Canada – misc. letters forwarded, ser. A 981, AUS 161, barcode 172972, 1.
144 High Commission Official Secretary Noël Deschamps to External Affairs Department Secretary, 11 November 1942, re: installation of tank guns, 1; High Commission Secretary W.R. Hodgson on behalf of the John Inglis Company of Toronto to the Manager, Small Arms Factory, Lithgow, NSW, 14 October 1942, re: sample components of the Bren gun, 1. Both letters in National Archives of Australia, Australian High Commissioner in Canada – misc. letters forwarded, ser. A 981, AUS 161, barcode 172972.
145 CBC Prairie Region Press Representative C.E. L'Ami to Australian High Commission Secretary Noël Deschamps, 16 July 1941, National Archives of Australia, ser. A981, CAN 37, barcode 173387, 1.
146 Memorandum from Canberra to Official Secretary Noël Deschamps, 21 February 1941, National Archives of Australia, ser. A981, AUS 152, barcode 172964, 1.
147 Cablegram from the Prime Minister, Ottawa, to Prime Minister's Department, Canberra, 3 September 1939, National Archives of Australia, Australian High Commission in Canada, general, ser. A981, AUS 151, pt. 1, barcode 1026429, 1.
148 Ralph Harry on Sir Thomas William Glasgow (1876–1955), *Australian Dictionary of Biography*, http://adb.anu.edu.au/biography/glasgow-sir-thomas-william-6397.

149 Keshen, *Saints, Sinners, and Soldiers*, 57.
150 Ibid., 76–7.
151 Ibid., 76.
152 Ibid., 106–8.
153 Ibid., 104.
154 Ibid., 105.
155 Ibid., 98.
156 Ibid., 103.
157 Ibid., 104, 103.
158 Ibid., 120.
159 Ibid. For list of products, see https://wartimecanada.ca/essay/eating/food-home-front-during-second-world-war and https://www.chronicallyvintage.com/2011/06/look-back-at-canadian-ration-coupon.html.
160 Broadfoot, *Six War Years*, 191, 194–5, 196–7
161 Stephen, *Pick One Intelligent Girl*, 9. Stephen said that she was paraphrasing Struthers – but her summary is more succinct.
162 James Struthers, "Family Allowances, Old Age Security, and the Construction of Entitlement in the Canadian Welfare State, 1943–1951," in Neary and Granatstein, *Veterans Charter*, 179.
163 Premier J.A. Lyons (Tasmania), who would later become Australian prime minister, had supported his case with the claim that "the effect [of abolition] would be much more serious on the smaller states." See May, *Financing the Small States*, 13.
164 Kennedy, *Freedom from Fear*, 275.
165 https://www.ssa.gov/history/briefhistory3.html.
166 Kennedy, *Freedom from Fear*, 365, 372.
167 Ibid., 281.
168 Diary of William Lyon Mackenzie King, 14 September 1939, 4.
169 Grant, *W.A. Mackintosh*, 270.
170 Owram, *Government Generation*, 282.
171 Levine, *King*, 301.
172 Sunahara, *Politics of Racism*, 16n28, 178.
173 Levine, *King: William Lyon Mackenzie King*, 301.
174 Owram, *Government Generation*, 279.
175 Ibid., 279.
176 Health Minister Ian Mackenzie to Prime Minister Mackenzie King, 29 September 1941, LAC, RG 2, ser. 18, vol. 5, file D-21-5 1941, 1.
177 Marsh, *Report on Social Security*.
178 Ibid. See also John I. Clark, review of Leonard Marsh, "Report on Social

Security for Canada 1943," book review in *Canadian Public Policy* 1, 4 (1975): 587–9.
179 "Social Security Planning in Canada: Dr. L. C. Marsh's Report on Social Security for Canada, Health Insurance Legislation," *International Labour Review* 47, rev. 591 (May 1943): 592.
180 Ibid., 595
181 Owram, *Government Generation*, 282.
182 Ibid., 283–4.
183 Chairman Ian Mackenzie from the minutes of Proceedings of the Committee on Reconstruction, special joint meeting, 4 December 1942, LAC, MG 28, ser. I103, vol. 195, file: Federal Government, House of Commons, Special Committee on Reconstruction and Re-establishment 195-16, 5.
184 Quotation from the Atlantic Charter, http://avalon.law.yale.edu/wwii/atlantic.asp.
185 Chairman Ian Mackenzie from the minutes of Proceedings of the Committee on Reconstruction, 5.
186 Owram, *Government Generation*, 286.
187 Ibid., 290.
188 Naylor, *Private Practice, Public Payment*, 111–12.
189 Ibid., 109–10.
190 National Health Minister Brooke Claxton, Plenary Session of the Dominion-Provincial Conference, August 6, 1945. *Dominion-Provincial Submissions*, 88.
191 Naylor, *Private Practice, Public Payment*, 120.
192 The Speech from the Throne, 27 January 1944, 5, https://www.poltext.org/sites/poltext.org/files/discours/tcan1944.pdf.
193 National Health Minister Brooke Claxton, Plenary Session of the Dominion-Provincial Conference, 6 August 1945, in *Dominion-Provincial Submissions*, 88.
194 Owram, *Government Generation*, 286,
195 Levine, *King*, 344.
196 Cablegram to the External Affairs Department, the full Cabinet and multiple ministries from the Australian High Commissioner's Office, 29 January 1943, National Archives of Australia, Canada – Internal: Canadian War Policy – summary of speech regarding, ser. A989, 1943/125/4/1, barcode 183417, 1
197 Ibid.
198 Ibid.
199 Canadian Teachers' Federation, *Education: The Keystone of Democracy*, Report

of the Reconstruction Committee of the Canadian Teachers' Federation, adopted August 1943, LAC, MG 28, vol. 11, File: Briefs, Pamphlets re: Federal Aid., 7.
200 Ibid., 11.
201 Montreal Local Council, Resolutions of the National Council of Women, LAC, MG 28, ser. I25, vol. 85, file: Resolutions, Correspondence 9143-1944, file 2, 3.
202 Memorandum submitted to the dominion government by the Canadian Congress of Labour, 24 April 1945, LAC, MG 28, vol. 171, file 171-16, circular letter 74, memorandum to the dominion government, 3.
203 Bank of Canada Archives, Department of Bank Operations Fonds, "Post-War Provincial Finance," unsigned memorandum of 10 December 1943, Research Fonds, box 1, file 28-500, vol. 1, 1.
204 Ibid., 8.
205 Ibid., 12.
206 Ibid., 16.
207 Ibid.
208 Ibid.
209 Ibid., 16–17.
210 Bruce, *Back the Attack!*, 55.
211 Ibid.
212 Ibid., 66.
213 Ibid., 75.
214 Ibid., 93.
215 Keshen, "Getting It Right the Second Time Around," 66.
216 Owram, *Government Generation*, 312.
217 Diary of William Lyon Mackenzie King, 13 January 1944, 2, http://www.bac-lac.gc.ca/eng/discover/politics-government/prime-ministers/william-lyon-mackenzie-king/Pages/item.aspx?IdNumber=26408&.
218 That downturn would not happen: there would be "but limited use of the Keynesian instruments in the period prior to the Korean War. Aggregate demand conditions were healthy after the war." See Campbell, *Grand Illusions*, 70.
219 Naylor, *Private Practice, Public Payment*, 131.
220 Health Minister Brooke Claxton, Plenary Session of the Dominion-Provincial Conference, 6 August 1945, in *Dominion-Provincial Submissions*, 88
221 Naylor, *Private Practice, Public Payment*, 131.
222 Bank of Canada Archives, Department of Bank Operations Fonds, "The Economic Aftermath of War," summary of address by Dr H.C. Coombs, the Summer School of the Australian Institute of Political Science, 1944, International Department Fonds, file 4E-110 vol. 1, 4.

223 Ibid., 4–5.
224 Ibid., 5.
225 Ibid.
226 Ibid., 6.
227 Robert Skidelsky, "Keynes and Canada," Toronto seminar, 6 November 2001, 1 of 9.
228 Owram, *Government Generation*, 295. Owram quotes J.F. Parkinson, "Some Problems of War Finance," *Canadian Journal of Economics and Political Science* 6, 3 (1940): 415.
229 Stephen, *Pick One Intelligent Girl*, 20.
230 Corolyn Cox, "'Sandy' Skelton Faces His Second Dominion-Provincial Conference," *Saturday Night*, 13 May 1944. n.p.
231 D.A. Skelton, "Dominion Preparations for Dominion-Provincial Conference," 15 June 1944, Queen's University Archives, W.A. Mackintosh Fonds, box 3, file 76, 10.
232 Ibid., 8.
233 Ibid.
234 Ibid., 2.
235 Ibid., 2, 3.
236 Ibid., 5, 9.
237 Headlines, *Ottawa Journal*, 30 June 1945. All stories on 1.
238 Rialto ad, *Ottawa Journal*, 30 June 1945, 6.
239 "3,000,000 Surrender Leaflets Dropped," *Ottawa Journal*, 4 August 1945, 1.
240 "Points for Inclusion in a Statement on Dominion Fiscal Policy and the Importance to It of the Dominion-Provincial Arrangements Proposed," 9 July 1945, Queen's University Archives, W.A. Mackintosh Fonds, box 3, file 70, 1.
241 Ibid., 2.
242 Ibid., 1.
243 Ibid., 3.
244 Ibid.
245 Ibid.

CHAPTER EIGHT

1 "580 Superforts from Marianas Hit Jap Industry," *Globe and Mail*, 6 August 1945, 2.
2 "Four Airmen Die as Planes Crash Near Hamilton," *Globe and Mail*, 6 August 1945, 1.
3 "Tourists Pour North, Jam Camps, Resorts," *Globe and Mail*, 6 August 1945, 4.

4 "Ottawa Ends Liquor Curb: Cuts in Quotas and Strength Are Restored," *Globe and Mail*, 6 August 1945, 1.
5 Finkel, "Paradise Postponed," 120.
6 Marchildon, "Understanding Equalization," as quoted in Béland et al., *Fiscal Federalism and Equalization Policy in Canada*, 18.
7 Quebec premier Maurice Duplessis, Plenary Session of the Dominion-Provincial Conference, 6 August 1945, Dominion-Provincial Conference (1945), Dominion and Provincial Submissions and Plenary Conference Discussions, 531.
8 Gotlieb, "George Drew and the Dominion-Provincial Conference," 27.
9 The *Globe and Mail* reported that Ottawa set aside 170 rooms in the Parliament Buildings for the conference in addition to the House of Commons chamber. See Kenneth C. Cragg, "Expect Ottawa to Ask Extended Tax Control," *Globe and Mail*, 6 August 1945, 1.
10 Ibid.
11 Ibid.
12 Ibid.
13 Prime Minister Mackenzie King, Plenary Session of the Dominion-Provincial Conference, 6 August 1945, in *Dominion and Provincial Submissions and Plenary Conference Discussions*, 5, 6.
14 Finkel, "Paradise Postponed," 122.
15 "Social Security," in *The Dominion Proposals for High Employment and National Welfare*, Secret, Dominion-Provincial Conference on Reconstruction, August 1945, LAC, RG 2, ser. 18, vol. 37, file: D-40 1945 (July–August), pt. 2, 12 (emphasis mine).
16 Prime Minister Mackenzie King, Plenary Session of the Dominion-Provincial Conference, 6 August 1945, in Dominion-Provincial Conference (1945), *Dominion and Provincial Submissions and Plenary Conference Discussions*, 7.
17 Premier J.B. McNair, Plenary Session of the Dominion-Provincial Conference, 2 May 1946, in Dominion-Provincial Conference (1945), *Dominion and Provincial Submissions and Plenary Conference Discussions*, 561.
18 Health Minister Brooke Claxton, Plenary Session of the Dominion-Provincial Conference, 3 May 1946, in Dominion-Provincial Conference (1945), *Dominion and Provincial Submissions and Plenary Conference Discussions*, 621.
19 "All Rail Bans May Go," *Sydney Morning Herald*, 6 August 1945, 3.
20 "Change-Over from War Industry," *Sydney Morning Herald*, 6 August 1945, 2.
21 "Violent Seizure of Houses Raises Problem: Procedure Criticised," *Sydney Morning Herald*, 6 August 1945, 4.

22 "Petrol Scale Criticised," *Sydney Morning Herald*, 6 August 1945, 4.
23 Army and air force casualty lists and advertisement in *Sydney Morning Herald*, 6 August 1945, 4.
24 Diary of William Lyon Mackenzie King, 6 August 1945, 2, http://www.bac-lac.gc.ca/eng/discover/politics-government/prime-ministers/william-lyon-mackenzie-king/Pages/item.aspx?IdNumber=28648&.
25 Ibid.
26 Ibid.
27 Headlines, *Ottawa Journal*, 7 August 1945, 1.
28 Finance Minister J.L. Ilsley, Plenary Session of the Dominion-Provincial Conference, 7 August 1945, in Dominion-Provincial Conference (1945), *Dominion and Provincial Submissions and Plenary Conference Discussions*, 112–13.
29 Ibid., 113.
30 Ibid., 115.
31 Premier Stuart Garson, Plenary Session of the Dominion-Provincial Conference, 7 August 1945, in Dominion-Provincial Conference (1945), *Dominion and Provincial Submissions and Plenary Conference Discussions*, 161.
32 Premier T.C. Douglas, Plenary Session of the Dominion-Provincial Conference, 7 August 1945, in Dominion-Provincial Conference (1945), *Dominion and Provincial Submissions and Plenary Conference Discussions*, 179. On Saskatchewan's progress towards hospital care, see C. Stuart Houston and Merle Massie, "Four Precursors of Medicare in Saskatchewan," in Marchildon, *Making Medicare*, 143.
33 Brief submitted by the Government of Alberta, presented by Premier Ernest C. Manning, to the Coordinating Committee, 26 November 1945, Dominion-Provincial Conference (1945), *Dominion and Provincial Submissions and Plenary Conference Discussions*, 209.
34 Submission of the Government of New Brunswick on certain proposals of the Dominion, 24 January 1946, Dominion-Provincial Conference (1945), *Dominion and Provincial Submissions and Plenary Conference Discussions*, 313.
35 Submission by the Government of Nova Scotia, 26 January 1946, Dominion-Provincial Conference (1945), *Dominion and Provincial Submissions and Plenary Conference Discussions*, 316–17.
36 Submissions [sic] by the Government of the Province of Ontario, 8 January 1946, Dominion-Provincial Conference (1945), *Dominion and Provincial Submissions and Plenary Conference Discussions*, 240–3.
37 Premier George Drew, Plenary Session of the Dominion-Provincial Confer-

ence, 29 April 1946, in Dominion-Provincial Conference (1945), *Dominion and Provincial Submissions and Plenary Conference Discussions*, 408.
38 As quoted in Bryden, "Justifiable Obsession," 28, 29-30.
39 Premier T.C. Douglas, Plenary Session of the Dominion-Provincial Conference, 30 April 1946, Dominion-Provincial Conference (1945), *Dominion and Provincial Submissions and Plenary Conference Discussions*, 479.
40 Premier Stuart Garson, Plenary Session of the Dominion-Provincial Conference, 29 April 1946, Dominion-Provincial Conference (1945), *Dominion and Provincial Submissions and Plenary Conference Discussions*, 427.
41 Premier George Drew, Plenary Session of the Dominion-Provincial Conference 1 May 1946, Dominion-Provincial Conference (1945), *Dominion and Provincial Submissions and Plenary Conference Discussions*, 520-1.
42 Ibid., 521.
43 Finance Minister J.L. Ilsley, Plenary Session of the Dominion-Provincial Conference, 2 May 1946, Dominion-Provincial Conference (1945), *Dominion and Provincial Submissions and Plenary Conference Discussions*, 574.
44 Bryden, "Justifiable Obsession," 30-1.
45 Premier George Drew and Premier Maurice Duplessis, Plenary Session of the Dominion-Provincial Conference, 1 May 1946, in Dominion-Provincial Conference (1945), *Dominion and Provincial Submissions and Plenary Conference Discussions*, 515, 530.
46 Premier Maurice Duplessis, Plenary Session of the Dominion-Provincial Conference, 1 May 1946, in Dominion-Provincial Conference (1945), *Dominion and Provincial Submissions and Plenary Conference Discussions*, 529.
47 Premier Maurice Duplessis, Plenary Session of the Dominion-Provincial Conference, 1 May 1946, in Dominion-Provincial Conference (1945), *Dominion and Provincial Submissions and Plenary Conference Discussions*, 528.
48 Milne, "Equalization and the Politics of Restraint," 190.
49 "Réception enthousiaste préparée pour M. Duplessis," D.N.C. Québec, *Le Devoir*, 3 May 1946, 3.
50 Premier George Drew, Plenary Session of the Dominion-Provincial Conference, 2 May 1946, in Dominion-Provincial Conference (1945), *Dominion and Provincial Submissions and Plenary Conference Discussions*, 580.
51 Health Minister Brooke Claxton, Plenary Session of the Dominion-Provincial Conference, 2 May 1946, in Dominion-Provincial Conference (1945), *Dominion and Provincial Submissions and Plenary Conference Discussions*, 581.
52 Health Minister Brooke Claxton to Premier George Drew, Plenary Session of the Dominion-Provincial Conference, 2 May 1946, in Dominion-Provincial Conference (1945), *Dominion and Provincial Submissions and Plenary Conference Discussions*, 580-1.

53 Finance Minister J.L. Ilsley, Plenary Session of the Dominion-Provincial Conference, 3 May 1946, in Dominion-Provincial Conference (1945), *Dominion and Provincial Submissions and Plenary Conference Discussions*, 585.
54 Premier Angus L. Macdonald to Finance Minister J.L. Ilsley, Plenary Session of the Dominion-Provincial Conference, 3 May 1946, in Dominion-Provincial Conference (1945), *Dominion and Provincial Submissions and Plenary Conference Discussions*, 585.
55 Premier George Drew, 3 May 1946, in Dominion-Provincial Conference (1945), *Dominion and Provincial Submissions and Plenary Conference Discussions*, 592.
56 Health Minister Brooke Claxton, Plenary Session of the Dominion-Provincial Conference, 3 May 1946, in Dominion-Provincial Conference (1945), *Dominion and Provincial Submissions and Plenary Conference Discussions*, 619.
57 Ibid., 622.
58 Struthers, *Limits of Affluence*, 126.
59 Diary of William Lyon Mackenzie King, 3 May 1946, 2. http://www.bac-lac.gc.ca/eng/discover/politics-government/prime-ministers/william-lyon-mackenzie-king/Pages/item.aspx?IdNumber=29527&.
60 Ibid.
61 Ibid.
62 Ibid., 3.
63 Ibid.
64 Ibid., 2–3.
65 P.E. Bryden, "The Obligations of Federalism: Ontario and the Origins of Equalization," in Anastakis and Bryden, *Framing Canadian Federalism*.
66 Bank of Canada Archives, Department of Bank Operations Fonds, "Post-War Planning in Australia," International Department Fonds, file 4E-110 vol. 1, 1.
67 Ibid., 4.
68 Ward, *History of Australia*, 255.
69 "Roles and Responsibilities in Health," Issues Paper 3, December 2014 (Canberra: Commonwealth of Australia), 5, https://ahha.asn.au/sites/default/files/docs/policy-issue/rotf_issues_paper_3_-_roles_and_responsibilities_in_health.pdf.
70 Ward, *History of Australia*, 292.
71 Ibid., 276.
72 Ibid., 72.
73 "Roles and Responsibilities in Health," Issues Paper 3, 6.
74 Bank of Canada Archives, Department of Bank Operations Fonds, "Post-War Planning in Australia," International Department Fonds, file 4E-110, vol. 1, 36.

75 Ibid.
76 "Price Control in Canada: May Stay for Years," *Sydney Morning Herald*, 22 May 1945, American section, Canada, Internal Affairs – Economic General, National Archives of Australia, ser. A1066, A45/1/3/1, barcode 186955, n.p.
77 "Meat for Europe, The [Canadian] Wartime Prices and Trade Board" press release, 10 September 1945, American section, Canada, Internal Affairs – Economic General, National Archives of Australia, ser. A1066, A45/1/3/1, barcode 186955, 2.
78 Thomas, *Making of a Socialist*, 94.
79 Ibid., 94–5.
80 Ibid., 124.
81 Ibid.
82 Ibid., 347.
83 Ibid., 217.
84 National Health Minister Brooke Claxton, Plenary Session of the Dominion-Provincial Conference, 6 August 1945, in Dominion-Provincial Conference (1945), *Dominion and Provincial Submissions and Plenary Conference Discussions*, 88. Claxton said that the total cost based on the 1941 census was $250 million.
85 "Dominion-Provincial Relations and Social Security," Canadian Welfare Council brief presented to the Government of Canada, March 1946, LAC, MG 28, ser. I 103, vol. 358, file: Social Security Canada 1946, 2.
86 Ibid., 8.
87 Ibid., 3–4 (emphasis mine).
88 Ibid., 4.
89 Ibid., 5 (emphasis mine).
90 Keshen, *Saints, Sinners, and Soldiers*, 262–3.
91 Ibid., 256.
92 Bruce, *Back the Attack!*, 161.
93 Keshen, *Saints, Sinners, and Soldiers*, 283.
94 Ibid., 286.
95 Ibid., 280–1, 272.
96 https://www.chronicallyvintage.com/2011/06/look-back-at-canadian-ration-coupon.html.
97 Keshen, *Saints, Sinners, and Soldiers*, 116.
98 Ibid., 118.
99 Veronica Strong-Boag and Diane Macdonald, National Council of Women of Canada, in *The Canadian Encyclopedia*, https://www.thecanadianencyclopedia.ca/en/article/national-council-of-women-of-canada.

100 Resolutions: Annual Meeting Niagara Falls, 3–7 June 1946, National Council of Women, LAC, MG 28, ser. I 25, vol. 89, file: resolutions 1945–46, file 2, 4.
101 Ibid., 3
102 Bacher, *Keeping to the Marketplace*, 169–70.
103 National Council of Women Resolutions, Annual Meeting, Niagara Falls, 3–7 June 1946, LAC, MG 28, ser. I 25, vol. 89, file: resolutions 1945–46, file 2, 7.
104 "CCL Holds Canada's Greatest Labour Convention," *Canadian Congress of Labour News Bulletin No. 16*, 17 October 1947, LAC, MG 28, ser. 103, vol. 173, file: New Bulletin 1947, 173-7, 1–2.
105 Irving Abella on the Canadian Congress of Labour in *The Canadian Encyclopedia*, https://www.thecanadianencyclopedia.ca/article/canadian-congress-of-labour/.
106 Memorandum submitted to the Dominion Government by the Canadian Congress of Labour, 5 March 1948, LAC, MG 28, ser. l 103, vol. 173, file: News Releases, January–June 1948, 173–24, 4.
107 Ibid.
108 Memorandum for Right Honourable W.L. Mackenzie King from the Canadian Council of Churches, LAC, RG 19, ser. E– 2–C, vol. 226, file: 164 SS 1949, n.d., 2. This was tucked in a 1949 file – but it dates from mid-1948.
109 Ibid., 2.
110 John S. Morgan, *A Meeting of Minds: A Report on the Round Table on Social Security, held at the University of Toronto, May 8–11, 1948*, reprinted from *Canadian Welfare*, July 1948, LAC, MG 28, ser. I 103, vol. 358, file: Social Security Canada, Morgan John S., a Meeting of Minds, 1948, 6.
111 Ibid., 5.
112 Ibid., 10.
113 Ibid.
114 Ibid., 11.
115 Ibid.
116 Kelley and Trebilcock, *Making of the Mosaic*, 312.
117 Ibid., 312.
118 Ibid., 313.
119 Broadfoot, *Immigrant Years*, 11. Broadfoot did oral histories of so many pivotal eras in Canada but, sadly, his interviews were anonymous.
120 Peter Neary, "Introduction," Neary and Granatstein, *Veterans Charter*, 6.
121 Broadfoot, *Veterans' Years*, 89–90.
122 Ibid., 120–1.

123 Burns, *Acceptable Mean*, 74.
124 Premier T.C. Douglas to Finance Minister J.L. Ilsley, 29 June 1946, Dominion-Provincial Conference, correspondence since the budget of 1946 on matters of substance regarding tax agreements with the provinces, LAC, RG 19, vol. 538, file (1) 135-0-167, 1946, 52.
125 Premier T.C. Douglas to Prime Minister Mackenzie King, 12 July 1946, Dominion-Provincial Conference, correspondence since the budget of 1946 on matters of substance regarding tax agreements with the provinces, LAC, RG 19, vol. 538, file (1) 135-0-167, 1946, 53.
126 Prime Minister Mackenzie King to Premier T.C. Douglas, 15 July 1946, Dominion-Provincial Conference, correspondence since the budget of 1946 on matters of substance regarding tax agreements with the provinces, LAC, RG 19, vol. 538, file (1) 135-0-167, 1946, 54.
127 Thomas, *Making of a Socialist*, 218.
128 Ibid., 218–19 (emphasis mine).
129 Premier John B. McNair to Finance Minister J.L. Ilsley, 5 July 1946, Dominion-Provincial Conference, correspondence since the budget of 1946, on matters of substance regarding tax agreements with the provinces, LAC, RG 19, vol. 538, file (1) 135-0-167, 1946, 41.
130 Finance Minister J.L. Ilsley to Premier Angus L. Macdonald, 5 July 1946, Dominion-Provincial Conference, correspondence since the budget of 1946 on matters of substance regarding tax agreements with the provinces, LAC, RG 19, vol. 538, file (1) 135-0-167, 1946, 27.
131 Premier Angus L. Macdonald to Prime Minister Mackenzie King, 16 October 1946, Dominion-Provincial Conference, correspondence since the budget of 1946 on matters of substance regarding tax agreements with the provinces, LAC, RG 19, vol. 538, file (1) 135-0-167, 1946, 28.
132 Prime Minister Mackenzie King to Premier Angus L. Macdonald, 22 October 1946, Dominion-Provincial Conference, correspondence since the budget of 1946 on matters of substance regarding tax agreements with the provinces, LAC, RG 19, vol. 538, File (1) 135-0-167, 1946, 29.
133 Premier Ernest C. Manning to Prime Minister Mackenzie King, 8 October 1946, Dominion-Provincial Conference, correspondence since the budget of 1946 on matters of substance regarding tax agreements with the provinces, LAC, Dominion-Provincial Conference, RG 19, vol. 538, file (1) 135-0-167, 1946, 59.
134 Premier T.C. Douglas to Prime Minister Mackenzie King, 13 November 1946, Dominion-Provincial Conference, correspondence since the budget of 1946 on matters of substance regarding tax agreements with the provinces, LAC, RG 19, vol. 538, file (1) 135-0-167, 1946, 55.

135 "Text of Abbott Offer for Tax Agreements," *Globe and Mail*, 25 January 1947, 2.
136 Telegram from Premier T.C. Douglas to Prime Minister Mackenzie King, 13 August 1947, LAC, RG 2, vol. 76, file D40 1947–49, Dominion-Provincial Relations, 1. Douglas put "quote" and "end quote" around King's previous message.
137 Ibid., 2.
138 "Minister Says Ottawa Still Wants Agreement," *Globe and Mail*, 30 April 1947, 12.
139 Telegram from Prime Minister Mackenzie King to Premier T.C. Douglas, 14 August 1947, LAC, RG 2, vol. 76, file D40 1947–49, Dominion-Provincial Relations, 1.
140 Prime Minister Mackenzie King to Premier George Drew, 27 September 1946, Dominion-Provincial Conference, correspondence since the Budget of 1946 on matters of substance regarding tax agreements with the provinces,. LAC, RG 19, vol. 538, file (1) 135-0-167, 1946, 10.
141 Premier George Drew to Prime Minister Mackenzie King, 16 October 1946, Dominion-Provincial Conference, correspondence since the budget of 1946 on matters of substance regarding tax agreements with the provinces, LAC, RG 19, vol. 538, file (1) 135-0-167, 1946, 17.
142 Ibid., 18.
143 J. Thomas McCallum, "A Trip Down Tax Memory Lane: Reflections on the Evolution of Taxation and Tax Rates," *CGA Magazine*, January–February 2008, the Chartered Professional Accountants of Canada, 46.
144 Premier Maurice Duplessis, 29 April 1946, Plenary Session of the Dominion-Provincial Conference, 1945–46, in *Dominion and Provincial Submissions and Plenary Conference Discussions*, 413.
145 "Avoid Friction over Tax Deals, Duplessis Warns," *Globe and Mail*, 3 February 1947, 15.
146 Statement of Premier Stuart Garson to the Coordinating Committee Meeting, 26 January 1946, in *Dominion and Provincial Submissions and Plenary Conference Discussions*, 319.
147 Saskatchewan Replies ... to the Dominion Government Proposals delivered to the Dominion-Provincial Conference on Reconstruction, 6 August 1945, with covering letter from Premier T.C. Douglas, LAC, RG 19, vol. 536, file 135-0-167 (1), 1944–45, 84.
148 Harry M. Cassidy, *A Canadian Program of Social Security: A Report to the Honourable Paul Martin, Minister of Health and Welfare*, 16 December 1947, LAC, RG 19, vol. 440, file 108-8-1, 4.
149 Ibid., 30.

150 Ibid., 202.
151 Bank of Canada Archives, Department of Bank Operations Fonds, "Australia: A General Memorandum Based on October-November Visit 1946," 25 February 1947, signed with initials W.E.S., International Department Fonds, file 4E-110, vol. 2, 4–5.
152 Ibid., 14.
153 Diary of William Lyon Mackenzie King, 11 May 1948, 2. http://www.bac-lac.gc.ca/eng/discover/politics-government/prime-ministers/william-lyon-mackenzie-king/Pages/item.aspx?IdNumber=32089.
154 Ibid., 12 May 1948, 1.
155 Ibid., emphasis mine.
156 Naylor, *Private Practice, Public Payment*, 153.
157 Implementing the National Health Grants, in *Making Medicare: The History of Health Care in Canada, 1914–2007*, History Museum, Government of Canada site, https://www.historymuseum.ca/cmc/exhibitions/hist/medicare/medic-3h17e.html.
158 Levine, *King*, 388.
159 Ibid., 391.
160 *Ottawa Journal*, 15 November 1948, 5, 9, 15, 32.
161 *Marpole-Richmond Review* (Richmond, BC), 17 November 1948, 4.
162 "Alberta's Revenue from Oil," *Edmonton Journal*, 13 November, 1948, 4.

CHAPTER NINE

1 Pickersgill, *My Years with Louis St. Laurent*, 328.
2 William Kinmond, "Meeting Was Abortive: Premier Frost Declares," *Globe and Mail*, 10 March 1956, 1.
3 Graham, *Old Man Ontario*, 332.
4 Robert Bothwell, *Dictionary of Canadian Biography* entry on Louis-Stephen St-Laurent, http://www.biographi.ca/en/bio/st_laurent_louis_stephen_20E.html.
5 Ibid.
6 Ibid.
7 Canadian Teachers' Federation to Prime Minister Louis St-Laurent, 3 February 1949, LAC, MG 28, vol. 10, file: Briefs to Govt. C.T.F., 1938–61, 3.
8 Ibid., 7.
9 Ibid., 3 (emphasis mine).
10 Harry M. Cassidy, Director of the University of Toronto School of Social Work, to Justice Minister Stuart Garson, 17 March 1949, LAC, RG 2, vol. 126, file D-40 (vol. 1), 1949 Dominion-Provincial Relations, 3.

11 Memorandum submitted to the Government of Canada by the Canadian Congress of Labour on Friday, 25 March 1949, LAC, MG 28, ser. I 103, vol. 282, file: Annual Memorandum to Federal Government (Canadian Congress of Labour), 1943–56, 1.
12 Ibid.
13 Ibid.
14 Ibid., 2.
15 Ibid.
16 Ibid.
17 News release, 30 March 1949, Canadian Congress of Labour, LAC, MG 28, ser. l 103, vol. 173, file: News Release, Refusal of Federal Government, 173-70, 2.
18 Mrs P. Emile Ouellet to Prime Minister Louis St-Laurent, 9 April 1949 [PMO translation], LAC, RG 19, ser. E-2-C, vol. 226, file 164 SS, 1949, 1.
19 John S. Morgan, "Foundations of Economic Security: A Report on the Second Round Table organized by the School of Social Work and the Department of Extension in the University of Toronto, held in Toronto May 28, 29 and 30, 1949," reprinted from *Canadian Welfare* 25, 4 (1949), LAC, MG 28, ser. I 103, vol. 358, file: Social Security Canada, Morgan John S., 1949, 15.
20 Ibid., 12.
21 Memorandum, Canadian personalities: Mr J.E. Coyne for the External Affairs Secretary in Canberra from the High Commission Official Secretary, 21 February 1950, National Archives of Australia: Canada – Internal – Personalities, ser. A1838, 229/1/3, pt. 1, barcode: 1603792, 1.
22 "Report on Canada in 1948: Address by the Honourable Douglas Abbott, Minister of Finance, at the Annual Luncheon of the Canadian Women's Club of New York, January 15th, 1949," National Archives of Australia: Canada – Internal – General, ser. A1838, 229/1/1, pt. 1, barcode: 1603769, 2.
23 Ibid., 8.
24 Ibid., 9.
25 "Making Medicare: The History of Health Care in Canada, 1948–1958," Canadian Museum of History, https://www.historymuseum.ca/cmc/exhibitions/hist/medicare/medic00e.html.
26 Lewis, *Making of a Socialist*, 188.
27 Premier T.C. Douglas to Prime Minister Louis St-Laurent, 15 July 1949, LAC, RG 19, ser. E 21, vol. 3442, file: Correspondence between Dominion and Provinces re Conference, 1.
28 Ibid., 2.
29 Ibid.
30 Prime Minister Louis St-Laurent to Premier T.C. Douglas, 18 August 1945,

LAC, RG 19, ser. E 21, vol. 3442, file: Correspondence between Dominion and Provinces re Conference, 1.

31 Premier Douglas Campbell to Prime Minister Louis St-Laurent, 6 August 1949, LAC, RG 19, ser. E 21, vol. 3442, file: Correspondence between Dominion and Provinces re Conference, 1.

32 Memorable Manitobans, Douglas Lloyd Campbell (1895–1995), the Manitoba Historical Society, http://www.mhs.mb.ca/docs/people/campbel_dl.shtml.

33 Premier Douglas Campbell to Prime Minister Louis St-Laurent, 6 August 1949, LAC, RG 19, ser. E 21, vol. 3442, file: Correspondence St-Laurent between Dominion and Provinces re Conference, 1.

34 Forbes, *With Enthusiasm and Faith*, 60.

35 As paraphrased in Burns, *Acceptable Mean*, 94.

36 "Items for the agenda as proposed by provincial governments," Interdepartmental Committee on the Federal-Provincial Conference, confidential, F-P (G) document 14, 9 September 1950, LAC, RG 19, ser. E21, vol. 3442, file: Cabinet Committee on the Dominion-Provincial Conference, 1950, 1.

37 Ibid., 1–3. Quotation from 1 (emphasis mine).

38 Ibid., 1.

39 Ibid., 2.

40 Federal Social Security Payments, Bank of Canada memorandum, 28 June 1950, LAC, RG 2, vol. 126, file D-40 (vol. 1), 1949–50 (July) Dominion-Provincial General Relation 1950, General Conference, 5. There is no name on the memorandum.

41 Ibid., 5.

42 Ibid., 3.

43 A Report on Federal-Provincial Co-operation, Federal-Provincial General Conference 1950, Privy Council Office, October 1950, LAC, RG 2, ser. 18, vol. 151, file D-40-D (vol. 2) 1950 filed separately (FPG) documents, 1–17. Notation says F.P. (G) document no. 19.

44 Appendix I, a Report on Federal-Provincial Co-operation, Federal-Provincial General Conference 1950, Privy Council Office, October 1950, LAC, RG 2, ser. 18, vol. 151, file D-40-D (vol. 2) 1950 filed separately (FPG) documents. pps. 1-17. Notation says F.P. (G) document no. 19, 16.

45 Prime Minister Louis St-Laurent to Premier Leslie M. Frost, 11 October 1950, LAC, RG 19, ser. E21, vol. 3442, file: Correspondence between Dominion and Provinces re: Conference, 2.

46 Premier T.C. Douglas to Prime Minister Louis St-Laurent, 26 October 1950. LAC, RG 19, ser. E21, vol. 3442, file: Correspondence between Dominion and Provinces re: Conference, 1.

47 Premier T.C. Douglas to Prime Minister Louis St-Laurent, 20 November 1950, LAC, RG 19, ser. E 21, vol. 3442, file: Correspondence between Dominion and Provinces re: Conference, 1.
48 Reverend J. Lavell Smith, Superintendent of the Queen Street and Church of All Nations, the United Church of Canada, to R.G. Robertson, Secretary of the Inter-Departmental Committee of the Federal-Provincial Conference, 25 November 1950, LAC, RG 2, vol. 149, file D-40 vol. 1 (a) 1950–51, dominion-provincial relations – general, 1.
49 Elizabeth DeWitt, Secretary to the Board of Directors of the Visiting Homemakers Association of Toronto to R.G. Robertson, Secretary of the Inter-Departmental Committee of the Federal-Provincial Conference, 7 December 1950, LAC, RG 2, vol. 149, file D-40 vol. 1 (a) 1950–51, dominion-provincial relations – general, 1.
50 Cabinet Committee on the Dominion-Provincial Conference, 3 January 1950, secret, LAC, RG 2, ser. 18, vol. 151, file: D-40-M (vol. 1) and 2 1949–50, dominion-provincial relations, 3.
51 Interdepartmental Committee on Social Security, 27 November 1950, secret. RG 19, ser. E-2-C, vol. 92, file 135-0-167, general file, 1-2.
52 Cabinet Committee on Federal Provincial Relations, 28 November 1950, secret, LAC, RG 19, ser. E 21, vol. 3442, file: Cabinet Committee on the Dominion-Provincial Conference 1950, 3.
53 Cabinet Committee on Federal-Provincial Relations, 7 November 1950, secret, LAC, RG 19, ser. E 21, vol. 3442, file: Cabinet Committee on the Dominion-Provincial Conference 1950, 2.
54 Ibid., 3.
55 Committee on Old Age Security, Federal-Provincial Conference, December 1950, confidential, LAC, RG 2, vol. 149, file: D-40 (vol. 1), 1950 August, 1–2.
56 Linteau et al., *Quebec since 1930*, 281. See also, section 94A, Constitution Act, 1982.
57 The earmarked tax, which took effect in 1952, was actually a composite of three taxes: one on manufacturers' selling price or the duty-paid value of all items covered by the federal sales tax, one on personal income, and one on corporate income. See http://publications.gc.ca/Collection-R/LoPBdP/MR/mr58-e.htm.
58 "A New Kind of 2-Door Refrigerator with True Automatic Defrost," in Philco ad in the *Ottawa Citizen*, 1 June 1951,16.
59 "Ottawa's Gain," *Ottawa Citizen*, 1 June 1951, 19.
60 "Frost Announced Conference Planned to Ease Tax Load on Local Govts," *Ottawa Citizen*, 1 June 1951, 17.
61 "RCAF Takes Down Sign 'Men Only,'" *Ottawa Citizen*, 1 June 1951, 18.

62 "Lie Talks Peace on Visit to City: Says Time Ripe for Cease-Fire," *Ottawa Citizen*, 1 June 1951, 1. Trygve Haivdan Lie was UN secretary-general.
63 "Canadian Pilot Tells of Korean Jet Battle," *Ottawa Citizen*, 1 June 1951, 1.
64 "Signs Bill for Army 'Hardware' Tanks and Planes," *Ottawa Citizen*, 1 June 1951, 19.
65 Canadian Congress of Labour news release, 11 April 1951, LAC, MG 28, ser. I 103, vol. 174, file: News Releases 1951, 174-2, 2 (emphasis mine).
66 News release, Canadian Congress of Labour, 27 March 1952, LAC, MG 28, ser. I-103, vol. 174, file: News Releases 1952, 174-3, 2.
67 Ibid., 3.
68 Ibid.
69 Canadian Labour Congress Circular Letter no. 279, 28 March 1952, LAC, MG 28, ser. I 103, vol. 172, file: Circular Letters 1952, 172-87, 2.
70 Taylor, "Health Insurance," 77.
71 Ibid.
72 "Submission to the Minister of Finance and the Minister of National Revenue regarding Canada's Fiscal Policy, the Income Tax Act and the Dominion Succession Duty," Canadian Chamber of Commerce, 23 February 1951, LAC, RG 19 E2C, vol. 116, file 164-B-1951 A, 4.
73 "Ibid.
74 "Submission to the Minister of Finance and the Minister of National Revenue regarding Canada's Fiscal Policy, the Income Tax Act, the Excise Tax Act, and the Dominion Succession Duty Act," Canadian Chamber of Commerce, 5 February 1954, LAC, RG 19 E2C, vol. 116, file: 164 B 1950 A, 25.
75 "Universities to Receive $7,000,000 Ottawa Aid: CBC Also to Get Help," *Globe and Mail*, 20 June 1951, 3.
76 Behiels, *Prelude to Quebec's Quiet Revolution*, 206.
77 Ibid.
78 Ibid., 185, 186.
79 Simeon and Robinson, *State, Society*, 125, 129, 140–5.
80 Claude Bélanger, Department of History, Marianopolis College, http://faculty.marianopolis.edu/c.belanger/quebechistory/federal/taxrent.htm.
81 Ibid.
82 Behiels, *Prelude to Quebec's Quiet Revolution*, 196.
83 Ibid., 199.
84 Ibid.
85 Ibid.
86 Linteau et al., *Quebec since 1930*, 282.
87 Memorandum of Submissions to the Royal Commission of Inquiry on Constitutional Problems, 27 January 1954, Canadian Manufacturers' Associ-

ation Incorporated, Quebec Division, LAC, RG 19, vol. 624, file: 164#201 to 282, 12.
88 Black, *Render unto Caesar*, 401.
89 Ibid., 399.
90 As quoted in Black, *Duplessis*, 436. J.W. Pickersgill quotes a slightly different version of the remarks: St-Laurent believed "that the province of Quebec can be a province like any other." See Pickersgill, *My Years with Louis St. Laurent*, 256.
91 Hutchison, *Mr. Prime Minister*, 300.
92 Behiels, *Prelude to Quebec's Quiet Revolution*, 204.
93 Cabinet conclusions, 13 January 1955, top secret, RG 2, Privy Council Office, ser. A-5-a, vol. 2657, access code: 12, 4. (p. 1 of online document), http://www.bac-lac.gc.ca/eng/discover/politics-government/cabinet-conclusions/Pages/item.aspx?IdNumber=14090 .
94 Cabinet conclusions, 20 January 1955, top secret, RG 2, Privy Council Office, ser. A-5-a, vol. 2657, access code: 12, 4 (p. 1 of online document).
95 Linteau et al., *Quebec since 1930*, 282.
96 "The Measure of the Man: Confidential," with covering letter dated 6 December 1954, High Commissioner Sir Douglas Copland to External Affairs Minister R.G. Casey, National Archives of Australia, Canada – Internal – General, ser. A1838, 229/1/1, pt. 1, barcode: 1603769, 1.
97 Ibid., 2.
98 Ibid., 5.
99 Bank of Canada Archives, Department of Bank Operations Fonds, Sir Douglas Copland, "Economic Policy and Economic Development in Australia from 1945: A Study in Economic Administration," International Department Fonds, file: 4E-110, vol. 2, 8.
100 Kwavnick, *Tremblay Report*, 218.
101 Ibid.
102 Ibid.
103 Michel Sarra-Bournet, *Dictionary of Canadian Biography*, http://www.biographi.ca/en/bio/duplessis_maurice_le_noblet_18E.html.
104 Kwavnick, *Tremblay Report*, 166.
105 Owram, *Born at the Right Time*, 74.
106 Ad in *Ottawa Journal*, 23 October 1954, 34.
107 Ad in *Ottawa Journal*, 25 October 1954, 8.
108 Ibid., 10.
109 Ad in *Ottawa Journal*, 23 October 1954, 4.
110 "'Precarious and Uneasy Peace' Nine Years after UN Founded," *Ottawa Journal*, 23 October 1954, 3. The actual anniversary was on Sunday, 25 October.

111 "El Alamein, the First Bright Spot," *Ottawa Journal*, 23 October 1954, 6.
112 Prentice et al., *Canadian Women*, 319.
113 G.A. Rawlyk, Canada's Immigration Policy, 1945–62, in *Dalhousie Review*, 288, https://dalspace.library.dal.ca/bitstream/handle/10222/58908/dalrev_vol42_iss3_pp287_300.pdf?sequence=1.
114 Campbell, *Grand Illusions*, 93–4.
115 Ibid., 93.
116 News release, Canadian Congress of Labour, 20 February 1953, LAC, MG 28, ser. I-103, vol. 172, file: Circular Letters 1953, 172-90, 1.
117 News release, Canadian Congress of Labour, 12 November 1954, LAC, MG 28, ser. I-103, vol. 174, file: News Releases 1953–55, 174-4, 4–5.
118 Ibid., 5.
119 Press release, Trades and Labor Congress of Canada, 14 December 1955, LAC, MG 28, ser. I 103, vol. 282, file: Annual Memorandum to Cabinet (Trades and Labor Congress) 1955, 282-17, 1.
120 Ibid., 3–4.
121 Conrad and Finkel, *History of the Canadian Peoples*, 2:301.
122 Letter from Louis St-Laurent to all provincial premiers with the exception of Premier Maurice Duplessis, 14 January 1955, as quoted in Burns, *Acceptable Mean*, 111–12.
123 Ibid., emphasis mine.
124 Ibid., 112.
125 Bryce, *Maturing in Hard Times*, 218.
126 Ibid.
127 Ibid., 269.
128 P.E. Bryden, "The Obligations of Federalism," in Anastakis and Bryden *Framing Canadian Federalism*, 81.
129 Ibid. Historian Robert Bothwell, political economist Ian Drummond, and historian John English also declare that equalization was Deutsch's "brainchild." See Bothwell, Drummond, and English, *Canada since 1945*, 152.
130 Pickersgill, *My Years with Louis St. Laurent*, 309. Pickersgill says that Deutsch was with the finance ministry but he was actually with the Treasury Board.
131 Federal-Provincial Conference, preparation, cabinet conclusions, 18 March 1955, top secret, LAC, RG 2, ser. A-5-a, vol. 2657, file 14236, 10.
132 Ibid.
133 Federal-Provincial Conference 1955, preliminary meeting of 26 April, unemployment assistance, cabinet conclusions, 20 April 1955, LAC, RG 2, ser. A-5-a, vol. 2657, file 14290, 2. A second meeting with provincial representatives in Ottawa on 20–21 June concentrated on unemployed employables.

134 "Federal-Provincial Fiscal Relations: Some Possible Lines of Approach," 17 June 1955, confidential, Interdepartmental Committee for the Federal-Provincial Conference 1955, LAC, RG 19, vol. 3880, file: 5515-04 (55/2)-2, 8–9.
135 Ibid., 9–10.
136 Ibid., 2.
137 Ibid., 3.
138 Ibid.
139 "Some Problems in Application of an Equalization Formula," initialed RMB, 30 August 1955, title: Plenary Conferences Conference, 3 October 1955, agenda – briefing material, LAC, RG 19, vol. 3880, file 5515-04 (55/2) -2, 1. The memo runs for five pages.
140 Ibid., 2.
141 "Ibid., 5.
142 Burns, *Acceptable Mean*, 122
143 Ibid., emphasis mine.
144 "Fiscal Need Grants" (signed E.A. Oestreicher), Plenary Conferences Conference, 3 October 1955, agenda – briefing material, LAC, RG 19, vol. 3880, file 5515-04 (55/2)-2, 11.
145 Ibid., 21.
146 Ibid., 22–3.
147 Ibid., 27.
148 Pickersgill, *My Years with Louis St. Laurent*, 309.
149 Ibid.
150 Ibid.
151 Federal-Provincial Conference: fiscal arrangements, cabinet conclusions, 21 September 1955, top secret, LAC, RG 2, ser. A-5-a, vol. 2658, file: 14579, 21 (emphasis mine).
152 Ibid., 21.
153 Pickersgill, *My Years with Louis St Laurent*, 310.
154 Clark, "Canada's Equalization Program," 104–5.
155 Federal-Provincial Conference: fiscal arrangements, cabinet conclusions, 21 September 1955, top secret, LAC, RG 2, ser. A-5-a, vol. 2658, file: 14579, 24.
156 Ibid., 23.
157 Ibid., 20.
158 Pickersgill, *My Years with Louis St. Laurent*, 309.
159 Ibid.
160 Ibid., 312 (emphasis mine).
161 Federal-Provincial Conference 1955, preliminary meeting, 27 April 1955 –

afternoon session, confidential, title: Plenary Conferences Conference, 3 October 1955, agenda – briefing material, LAC, RG 19, vol. 3880, file: 5515-04 (55/2)-2, 2.
162 John E. Osborne, Special Advisor on Policy Development, Department of National Health and Welfare, *The Evolution of the Canada Assistance Plan, Appendix to the Nielsen Task Force Report on the Canada Assistance Plan, 1985*, ed. federal bureaucrat Gilles Seguin, on Canada Social Research Links, http://www.canadiansocialresearch.net/capjack.htm.
163 Fowler, "Unemployment Assistance Act (1956)," 30, 33.
164 Ibid., 36–7; and Struthers, *Limits of Affluence*, 175.
165 Struthers, *Limits of Affluence*, 178.
166 Linteau et al, *Quebec since 1930*, 236.
167 Osborne, *The Evolution of the Canada Assistance Plan*.
168 "Dodgers Win World Series" and "With 687 Decisions for Christ Billy Graham Makes History," *Ottawa Journal*, 4 October 1955, 1
169 Ad in *Ottawa Journal*, 4 October 1955, 3.
170 Ibid., 9.
171 Movie ads in *Ottawa Journal*, 4 October 1955, 25.
172 Ad in *Ottawa Journal*, 4 October 1955, 26.
173 Ibid., 4.
174 Prime Minister Louis St-Laurent, Proceedings of the Federal-Provincial Conference 1955, Ottawa, 3 October 1955, Plenary Conferences Conference, 3 October 1955, summary record of proceedings, LAC, RG 19, vol. 3880, file: 5515-04 (55/2)-3, 8 (emphasis mine).
175 Ibid., 13.
176 Ibid., 14.
177 Ibid., 17.
178 Ibid., 18 (emphasis mine).
179 "Frost Brings 33 Experts to Parley: Leads All Others," *Ottawa Journal*, 4 October 1955, 2; and Premier Leslie Frost, Proceedings of the Federal-Provincial Conference 1955, Ottawa, 3 October 1955, Plenary Conferences Conference, 3 October 1955, summary record of proceedings, LAC, RG 19, vol. 3880, file: 5515-04 (55/2)-3, 21.
180 "Door Opened by Federal Gov't to Sharing in Health Insurance: But Run by Provinces," *Ottawa Journal*, 4 October 1955, 2.
181 Premier Maurice Duplessis, Proceedings of the Federal-Provincial Conference 1955, Ottawa, 3 October 1955, Plenary Conferences Conference, 3 October 1955, summary record of proceedings, LAC, RG 19, vol. 3880, file: 5515-04 (55/2)-3, 37.

182 Federal-Provincial Conference 1955, 4 October 1955 – morning session, federal summary of Premier Maurice Duplessis at the In-Camera Proceedings, confidential, Plenary Conferences Conference, 3 October 1955, summary record of proceedings, LAC, RG 19, vol. 3880, file 5515-04 (55/2)-3, 2.

183 Appendix E, Province of New Brunswick, attached to the Proceedings of the Federal-Provincial Conference, Ottawa, 3 October 1955, Plenary Conferences Conference, 3 October 1955, summary record of proceedings, LAC, RG 19, vol. 3880, file: 5515-04 (55/2)-3, 117–26.

184 Premier W.A.C. Bennett, Proceedings of the Federal-Provincial Conference 1955, Ottawa, 3 October 1955, Plenary Conferences Conference, 3 October 1955, summary record of proceedings, LAC, RG 19, vol. 3880, file: 5515-04 (55/2)-3, 76.

185 Patricia E. Roy, *Canadian Encyclopedia*, https://www.thecanadianencyclopedia.ca/en/article/william-andrew-cecil-bennett.

186 Premier W.A.C. Bennett, Proceedings of the Federal-Provincial Conference 1955, Ottawa, 3 October 1955, Plenary Conferences Conference, 3 October 1955, summary record of proceedings, LAC, RG 19, vol. 3880, file: 5515-04 (55/2)-3, 76–7.

187 Thomas, *Making of a Socialist*, 319.

188 Ibid., 319–20.

189 Ibid., 321–2.

190 Ibid., 320.

191 Premier T.C. Douglas, Proceedings of the Federal-Provincial Conference 1955, Ottawa, 3 October 1955, Plenary Conferences Conference, 3 October 1955, summary record of proceedings, LAC, RG 19, vol. 3880, file: 5515-04 (55/2)-3, 81.

192 Ibid.

193 Ibid., 91.

194 Ibid., 82.

195 Ibid.

196 Premier Joseph R. Smallwood, Proceedings of the Federal-Provincial Conference 1955, Ottawa, 3 October 1955, Plenary Conferences Conference, 3 October 1955, summary record of proceedings, LAC, RG 19, vol. 3880, file: 5515-04 (55/2)-3, 98.

197 Press communiqué, 6 October 1955, app. F, Proceedings of the Federal-Provincial Conference 1955, Ottawa, 3 October 1955, Plenary Conferences Conference, 3 October 1955, summary record of proceedings, LAC, RG 19, vol. 3880, file: 5515-04 (55/2)-3, 127–8.

198 Douglas H. Clark, "The Concept and Calculation of Fiscal Need and Rev-

enue Equalization Grants with Specific Reference to Canada," Ottawa, February 1968, Federal-Provincial Relations Division: equalization fiscal needs, LAC, RG 19, vol. 5512, file 5628- 04 pt. 1, 3.
199 Dahlby, "Fiscal Equalization," 4.
200 "Points for Decision," signed RMB (Burns), 3 November 1955, Plenary Conferences Conference, 3 October 1955, summary record of proceedings, LAC, RG 19, vol. 3880, file 5515-04 (55/2)-3, 14.
201 "Summary of Provincial Viewpoints on Fiscal Matters as Expressed at 'In Camera' Session," proceedings of the Federal-Provincial Conference, Ottawa, 3 October 1955, Plenary Conferences Conference, 3 October 1955, summary record of proceedings, LAC, RG 19, vol. 3880, file: 5515-04 (55/2)-3, 1. The initials "RMB" and the date "3 11 55" are at the bottom of this document.
202 Ibid., 2.
203 Ibid., 4.
204 Ibid. (emphasis mine).
205 Ibid., 5.
206 Ibid.
207 Burns, *Acceptable Mean*, 146.
208 "Summary of Provincial Viewpoints on Fiscal Matters as Expressed at 'In Camera' Session," Proceedings of the Federal-Provincial Conference, Ottawa, 3 October 1955, Plenary Conferences Conference, 3 October 1955, summary record of proceedings, LAC, RG 19, vol. 3880, file: 5515-04 (55/2)-3, 6.
209 Ibid.
210 Ibid., 7.
211 Federal-provincial fiscal arrangements, cabinet conclusions, 7 December 1955, LAC, RG 2, ser. A-5-a, vol. 2659, file 14742, 23.
212 Ibid., 25.
213 Ibid., 26.
214 Federal-provincial fiscal arrangements, cabinet conclusions, 21 December 1955, LAC, RG 2, ser. A-5-a, vol. 2659, file 14769, 13.
215 Ibid., 14.
216 Ibid.
217 Ibid., 15 (emphasis mine).
218 Federal-provincial fiscal arrangements, cabinet conclusions, 3 January 1956 and 5 January 1956, LAC, RG 2, ser. A-5-a, vol. 5775, files 14777, 14779, and 14797, pps. 2–4 (3 January) 2–3 (5 January) and 13 (later on 5 January 5). Cabinet decided on 5 January 1956 that all ten letters would bear the date of 7 January 1956.
219 Federal-provincial fiscal arrangements, cabinet conclusions, 5 January 1956, LAC, RG 2, ser. A-5-a, vol. 5775, file 14797, 13.

220 "Letter to Provincial Premiers," from Prime Minister Louis St-Laurent, 6 January 1956, confidential, LAC, MG 28, ser. I 103, vol. 171, file: D-60 1956–57 drafts – (Privy Council Office) – official correspondence, 4.
221 Speech from the Throne, 10 January 1956, 21, https://www.poltext.org/sites/poltext.org/files/discoursV2/Canada/CAN_DT_XXXX_22_03.pdf.
222 George Bain, "PM Says Offer Based on Picture of Nation's Needs," *Globe and Mail*, 13 January 1956, 1–2. Bain's article is dated 12 January 1956.
223 Ibid., 2.
224 Thomson, *Louis St. Laurent*, 412–13.
225 Federal-provincial fiscal arrangements, possible resumption of conference, cabinet conclusions, 15 February 1956, LAC, RG 2, ser. A-5-a, vol. 5775, file 14882, 3.
226 Ibid., 3.
227 Ibid., 4.
228 Ibid., 3. The record indicates: "If it were not for the statement in the [October] communiqué, the Federal government could probably have proceeded to implement its proposals without a further conference. It now seemed necessary, however, to offer an opportunity for such a meeting to the provincial governments."
229 Premier Leslie Frost, Plenary Conferences Conference, 9 March 1956, formal statements, LAC, RG 19, vol. 3880, file 5515-04 (56/1)-4, 3, 7.
230 Ibid., 7.
231 William Kinmond, "Meeting Was Abortive, Premier Frost Declares," *Globe and Mail*, 10 March 1956, 1. The headline was "5 Hours of Disagreement: Ottawa Ends Tax Talks, $640,000,000 Limit, Harris Tells Provinces," *Globe and Mail*, 10 March 1956, 1.
232 Premier Hugh John Flemming, Plenary Conferences Conference, 9 March 1956, formal statements, LAC, RG 19, vol. 3880, file 5515-04 (56/1)-4, 2, 10.
233 Ibid., 17.
234 Premier Henry D. Hicks, Plenary Conferences Conference, 9 March 1956, formal statements, LAC, RG 19, vol. 3880, file 5515-04 (56/1)-4, 1.
235 Legislation. Federal-Provincial Tax-Sharing Arrangements Bill, cabinet conclusions, 14 June 1956, LAC, RG 2, ser. A-5-a, vol. 5775, file 15157, 2.
236 Fiscal arrangements with provinces, request from the Premier of Ontario, cabinet conclusions, 12 July 1956, LAC, RG 2, ser. A-5-a, vol. 5775, file 15203, 16.
237 Graham, *Old Man Ontario*, 322.
238 Courchene, *Equalization Payments*, 37.
239 Burns, *Acceptable Mean*, 157.
240 Pickersgill, *My Years with Louis St. Laurent*, 310, 312.

241 Graham, *Old Man Ontario*, 322.
242 "Always Backs a Winner: Frost Pledges Support to Diefenbaker Drive," *Globe and Mail*, 26 April 1957, 5.
243 Bryden, "The Obligations of Federalism," in Anastakis and Bryden, *Framing Canadian Federalism*, 86.
244 Ibid.
245 Ibid.
246 Langevin Cote, "Unity Under PC's: Diefenbaker Defends Rights of Provinces," *Globe and Mail*, 5 June 1957, 7. (This is presumably Côté, although the *Globe and Mail* did not punctuate it.)
247 Canadian Gallup Poll, May 1957, no. 258, https://search1.odesi.ca/#/details?uri=%2Fodesi%2Fcipo-258-E-1957-05.xml.
248 Canadian Gallup Poll, March 1957, no. 256, http://odesi2.scholarsportal.info/documentation/Gallup/mar1957-256.txt.
249 Grey Hamilton, "Liberals Hit by Landslide in Ontario," *Globe and Mail*, 11 June 1957, 1.
250 Cabinet Committee on the Dominion-Provincial Conference 1957, 19 November 1957, confidential, Dominion-Provincial Conference 1957–58, LAC RG 22, vol. 121, file 83-2-7, 3.
251 Graham, *Old Man Ontario*, 337.
252 Burns, *Acceptable Mean*, 155.
253 Courchene, *Equalization Payments*, 37.
254 Opening Statement of Prime Minister Lester B. Pearson at the Federal-Provincial Conference in Quebec City, 31 March – 2 April 1964, app. B, conditional grants and shared cost programs, in notes on Federal-Provincial Plenary Conference at Quebec City, 31 March –2 April 1964, LAC, RG 19, vol. 3884, file 5515-04 (64/1)-3, 53 (emphasis mine).

CONCLUSION

1 Lecours and Béland, "Federalism and Fiscal Policy," 570.
2 Parkin, *International Report Card*, iv.
3 Ibid., 26.
4 Heaman, *Tax, Order, and Good Government*, 460.
5 McKenzie and MacMillan, "Introduction," in MacMillan and McKenzie, *Parties Long Estranged*, 7.
6 Letter from Louis St-Laurent to all provincial premiers with the exception of Premier Maurice Duplessis, 14 January 1955, as quoted in Burns, *Acceptable Mean*, 111–12.

7 P.E. Bryden, "The Obligations of Federalism," in Anastakis and Bryden, *Framing Canadian Federalism*, 87.
8 Bothwell, Drummond, and English, *Canada since 1945*, 237.
9 Bryden, "Obligations of Federalism," in Anastakis and Bryden, Framing Canadian Federalism, 76. Bryden does not note Ontario's increased share of PIT.
10 As cited in Shah, "Fiscal Need Approach," 100.
11 Eisen and Milke, *Nova Scotia, New Brunswick, and the Equalization Policy Crutch*, https://www.fraserinstitute.org/studies/nova-scotia-new-brunswick-rely-on-equalization-while-shunning-resource-development.

Bibliography

Abbott, George M. "Pattullo, the Press, and the Dominion-Provincial Conference of 1941," *BC Studies* 111 (Autumn 1996) : 37–59.

Abrams, Philip. "Notes on the Difficulty of Studying the State." *Journal of Historical Sociology* 1, 1 (1988): 58–89.

Adamoski, Robert, Dorothy E. Chunn, and Robert Menzies, eds. *Contesting Canadian Citizenship: Historical Readings*. Peterborough, ON: Broadview Press, 2002.

Aitken, Hugh G.J., John J. Deutsch, W.A. Mackintosh, Clarence L. Barber, Maurice Lamontagne, Irving Brecher, Eugene Forsey. *The American Economic Impact on Canada*. Durham, NC: Duke University Press, 1959.

Anastakis, Dimitry, and P.E. Bryden, eds. *Framing Canadian Federalism*. Toronto: University of Toronto Press, 2009.

Anderson, Benedict, *Imagined Communities: Reflections on the Origin and Spread of Nationalism*, rev. ed. London: Verso, 1991.

Armstrong, Christopher. *The Politics of Federalism: Ontario's Relations with the Federal Government, 1867–1942*. Toronto: Ontario Historical Studies Series, 1981.

Armstrong, Christopher, and H.V. Nelles, *Monopoly's Moment: The Organization and Regulation of Canadian Utilities, 1830–1930*. Philadelphia: Temple University Press, 1986.

Ashforth, Adam. "Reckoning Schemes of Legitimation: On Commissions of Inquiry as Power/Knowledge Forms." *Journal of Historical Sociology* 3, 1 (1990): 1–22.

Bacher, John C. *Keeping to the Marketplace: The Evolution of Canadian Housing Policy*. Montreal and Kingston: McGill-Queen's University Press, 1993.

Bakvis, Herman. "Political Parties, Party Government and Intrastate Federalism in Canada." In *Parties and Federalism in Australia and Canada*, ed. Campbell Sharman. Canberra: Federalism Research Centre, Australian National University, 1994.

Bakvis, Herman, and Campbell Sharman. "Australian Fiscal Federalism." *Policy Options*, December 1991.
Bakvis, Herman, and Grace Skogstad, eds. *Canadian Federalism: Performance, Effectiveness, and Legitimacy*. Don Mills, ON: Oxford University Press, 2002.
Bakvis, Herman, and William M. Chandler, eds. *Federalism and the Role of the State*. Toronto: University of Toronto Press, 1987.
Banting, Keith G. "Neoconservatism in an Open Economy: The Social Role of the Canadian State." *International Political Science Review* 13, 2 (1992): 149–70.
– *The Welfare State and Canadian Federalism*, 2nd ed. Montreal and Kingston: McGill-Queen's University Press, 1987.
Barman, Jean. *The West beyond The West: A History of British Columbia*. Toronto: University of Toronto Press, 1995.
Barnhart, Gordon L., ed. *Saskatchewan Premiers of the Twentieth Century*. Regina: Canadian Plains Research Centre, University of Regina, 2004.
Bartley, T.J. "Giblin and the Commonwealth Bank." In *Giblin: The Scholar and the Man*, ed. Douglas Copland, 56–63. Melbourne: F.W. Cheshire, 1960.
Behiels, Michael D. *Prelude to Quebec's Quiet Revolution: Liberalism versus Neo-Nationalism, 1945–1960*. Montreal and Kingston: McGill-Queen's University Press, 1985.
Béland, Daniel, and André Lecours. "Accommodation and the Politics of Fiscal Equalization in Multinational States: The Case of Canada." *Nations and Nationalism* 20, 2 (2014): 337–54.
– "Fiscal Federalism and American Exceptionalism: Why Is There No Federal Equalisation System in the United States?" *Journal of Public Policy* 34, 2 (2014): 303–29.
– "The Ideational Dimension of Federalism: The 'Australian Model' and the Politics of Equalisation in Canada." *Australian Journal of Political Science* 46, 2 (2011): 199–212.
Béland, Daniel, André Lecours, Gregory P. Marchildon, Haizhen Mou, and M. Rose Olfert. *Fiscal Federalism and Equalization Policy in Canada*. Toronto: University of Toronto Press, 2017.
Bercuson, David. J. *The Secret Army*. Toronto: Lester and Orpen Dennys, 1983.
– *True Patriot: The Life of Brooke Claxton, 1898–1960*. Toronto: University of Toronto Press, 1993.
Besant, Christopher W. "Two Nations, Two Destinies: A Reflection on the Significance of the Western Australian Secession Movement to Australia, Canada and the British Empire." *University of Western Australia Law Review* 20, 2 (1990): 209–310.

Betcherman, Lita-Rose. *Ernest Lapointe: Mackenzie King's Great Quebec Lieutenant.* Toronto: University of Toronto Press, 2002.
Bird, Richard M. *Federal Finance in Comparative Perspective.* Toronto: Canadian Tax Foundation, April 1985.
Bird, Will R. *These Are the Maritimes.* Toronto: The Ryerson Press, 1959.
Black, Conrad. *Duplessis.* Toronto: McClelland and Stewart, 1977.
– *Render unto Caesar: The Life and Legacy of Maurice Duplessis.* Toronto: Key Porter Books, 1998.
Black, Edwin R. *Divided Loyalties: Canadian Concepts of Federalism.* Montreal and Kingston: McGill-Queen's University Press, 1975.
Blake, Raymond B. *Canadians at Last: Canada Integrates Newfoundland as a Province.* Toronto: University of Toronto Press, 1994.
– "Mackenzie King and the Genesis of Family Allowances in Canada, 1939–44." In *Social Welfare Policy in Canada. Historical Readings*, ed. Raymond B. Blake and Jeff Keshen, 233–54. Toronto: Copp Clark Ltd., 1995.
Blake, Raymond B., and Jeff Keshen, eds. *Social Welfare Policy in Canada: Selected Readings.* Toronto: Copp Clark, 1995.
Blindenbacher, Raoul, and Abigail Ostien Karos, eds. *Dialogues on the Practice of Fiscal Federalism: Comparative Perspectives.* Ottawa: Forum of Federations, 2006.
Boadway, Robin. "Fiscal Equalization: The Canadian Experience." In *Fiscal Federalism and Political Decentralization: Lessons from Spain, Germany and Canada*, ed. Nuria Bosch and José M. Duran, 109–36. Cheltenham, UK: Edward Elgar, 2008.
Boadway, Robin, and Paul A.R. Hobson. *Equalization: Its Contribution to Canada's Economic and Fiscal Progress.* Kingston: John Deutsch Institute for the Study of Economic Policy, Queen's University, 1998.
Boadway, Robin, and Ronald L. Watts. *Fiscal Federalism in Canada, the U.S.A., and Germany,* Working Paper 2004 (6). Kingston: IIGR, Queen's University, 2004.
Boothe, Paul. Quoted in *Toolkits and Building Blocks: Constructing a New Canada*, ed. Richard Simeon and Mary Janigan, 21–2, 119–20. Toronto: C.D. Howe Institute, 1991.
Boothe, Paul, and Heather Edwards, eds. *Eric J. Hanson's Financial History of Alberta: 1905–1950.* Calgary: University of Calgary Press, 2003.
Bosch, Núria, and José M. Durán, eds. *Fiscal Federalism and Political Decentralization: Lessons from Spain, Germany and Canada.* Cheltenham, UK: Edward Elgar, 2008.
Bothwell, Robert. *Canada and Quebec: One Country, Two Histories,* rev. ed. Vancouver: UBC Press, 1998.
Bothwell, Robert, Ian Drummond, and John English. *Canada since 1945:*

Power, Politics, and Provincialism. Toronto: University of Toronto Press, 1981.
Boyko, John. *Bennett: The Rebel Who Challenged and Changed a Nation*. Toronto: Key Porter Books, 2010.
Broadbent, Edward, ed. *Democratic Equality: What Went Wrong*. Toronto: University of Toronto Press, 2001.
Broadfoot, Barry. *The Immigrant Years: From Europe to Canada, 1945–1967*. Vancouver: Douglas and McIntyre, 1986.
– *Six War Years, 1939–1945: Memories of Canadians at Home and Abroad*. Toronto: Doubleday Canada, 1974.
– *The Veterans' Years: Coming Home from the War*. Vancouver: Douglas and McIntyre, 1985.
Brodie, Janine. "Three Stories of Canadian Citizenship." In *Contesting Canadian Citizenship: Historical Readings*, ed. Robert Adamoski, Dorothy E. Chunn, and Robert Menzies, 43–66. Peterborough, ON: Broadview Press, 2002.
Brooks, Stephen and Marc Ménard, *Canadian Democracy: A Concise Introduction*. Don Mills, ON: Oxford University Press, 2013.
Brown, Douglas M. *Equalization on the Basis of Need in Canada*. Kingston: Institute of Intergovernmental Relations: Queen's University, 1996.
Brown-John, Lloyd. *Federalism and Cultural Pluralism: The Canadian Experience*. Barcelona: Institut de Ciències Polítiques i Socials, 1995.
– *Federalism and Decentralization*. Fribourg, Switzerland: International Association of Constitutional Law, 1987.
– "Self-Determination, Autonomy and State Secession in Federal Constitutional and International Law." *South Texas Law Review* 90, 3 (1999): 567–601.
Brown-John, Lloyd C., ed. *Centralizing and Decentralizing Trends in Federal States*. Lanham, MD: University Press of America Inc., 1988.
Bruce, Jean. *Back the Attack! Canadian Women during the Second World War – at Home and Abroad*. Toronto: Macmillan of Canada, 1985.
Bryce, Robert B. *Maturing in Hard Times: Canada's Department of Finance through the Great Depression*. Kingston and Montreal: McGill-Queen's University Press, 1986.
Bryden, P.E. *"A Justifiable Obsession": Conservative Ontario's Relations with Ottawa, 1943–1985*. Toronto: University of Toronto Press, 2013.
– *Planners and Politicians: Liberal Politics and Social Policy, 1957–1968*. Montreal and Kingston: McGill-Queen's University Press, 1997.
– "'Pooling Our Resources': Equalization and the Origins of Regional Universality, 1937–1957." *Canadian Public Administration* 57, 3 (2014): 401–18.
Buckner, Phillip. "CHR Dialogue: The Maritimes and Confederation: A Reassessment." *Canadian Historical Review*, 71 1 (1990): 1–45.

Burgin, Angus. *The Great Persuasion: Re-Inventing Free Markets since the Depression*. Cambridge, MA: Harvard University Press, 2012.

Burns, R.M. *The Acceptable Mean: The Tax Rental Agreements, 1941–1962*. Toronto: The Canadian Tax Foundation, 1980.

– "The Royal Commission on Dominion-Provincial Relations: The Report In Retrospect." In *Canadian Issues: Essays in Honour of Henry F. Angus*, ed. Robert M. Clark, 143–57. Toronto: University of Toronto Press, 1961.

Burns, R.M., ed. *One Country or Two*. Montreal and Kingston: McGill-Queen's University Press, 1971.

Cahill, Barry. *The Thousandth Man: A Biography of James McGregor Stewart*. Toronto: The Osgoode Society for Canadian Legal History, University of Toronto Press, 2000.

Cairns, Alan C. "The Governments and Societies of Canadian Federalism." *Canadian Journal of Political Science* 10, 4 (1977): 695–75.

Cameron, David, and Richard Simeon. "Ontario in Confederation: The Not-So-Friendly Giant." In *The Government and Politics of Ontario*, 5th ed., ed. Graham White, 148–85. Toronto: University of Toronto Press, 1997.

Campbell, Colin. "J.L. Ilsley and the Transformation of the Canadian Tax System, 1939–1943," *Canadian Tax Journal* 61, 3 (2013): 633–70.

Campbell, Lara. *Respectable Citizens: Gender, Family, and Unemployment in Ontario's Great Depression*. Toronto: University of Toronto Press, 2009.

Campbell, Robert M. *Grand Illusions: The Politics of the Keynesian Experience in Canada, 1945–1975*. Peterborough: Broadview Press, 1987.

Carty, R. Kenneth and W. Peter Ward, eds. *Entering the Eighties: Canada in Crisis*. Toronto: Oxford University Press, 1980.

Casey, R.G. *A Delicate Mission: The Washington Diaries of R. G. Casey, 1940–42*, ed. Carl Bridge. Canberra: National Library of Australia, 2008.

Christie, Nancy. *Engendering the State: Family, Work, and Welfare in Canada*. Toronto: University of Toronto Press, 2000.

Clark, Douglas H. "Canada's Equalization Program: In Principle and in Practice." In *Equalization: Its Contribution to Canada's Economic and Fiscal Progress*, ed. Robin W. Boadway and Paul A.R. Hobson, 83–156. Kingston: John Deutsch Institute for the Study of Economic Policy, Queen's University, 1998.

Clark, Robert M, ed. *Canadian Issues: Essays in Honour of Henry Angus*. Toronto: University of Toronto Press, 1961.

Clarke, Patricia. *Eilean Giblin: A Feminist between the Wars*. Clayton, Victoria: Monash University Publishing, 2013.

Coleman, William D. *The Independence Movement in Quebec, 1945–1980*. Toronto: University of Toronto Press, 1984.

Coleman, William, Selwyn Cornish, and Alf Hagger. *Giblin's Platoon: The*

Trials and Triumphs of the Economist in Australian Public Life. Canberra: The Australian National University, 2006.

The Commonwealth Grants Commission: The Last 25 Years. Braddon, Canberra, ACT: The Commonwealth Government, Commonwealth Grants Commission, 2009.

Communist Party of Canada, Dominion Committee. *Toward Democratic Unity for Canada*. Submission to the Royal Commission on Dominion-Provincial Relations. Toronto: n.p., n.d.

Conrad, Margaret, and Alvin Finkel. *History of The Canadian Peoples*. Vol. 1 *Beginnings to 1867*. 5th ed. Newmarket, ON: Pearson Education Canada, 2005.

– *History of the Canadian Peoples*. Vol. 2: *1867 to the Present*, 5th ed. Newmarket, ON: Pearson Education Canada, 2008.

Conrad, Margaret, and Alvin Finkel, eds. *Nation and Society: Readings in Post-Confederation Canadian History*. Toronto: Pearson Longman, 2004.

Constitution Acts 1867 to 1982: A Consolidation. Ottawa: Department of Justice Canada, Canadian Government Publishing Centre, 1986.

Cook, Ramsay, *The Maple Leaf Forever: Essays on Nationalism and Politics in Canada*. Toronto: Macmillan of Canada, 1977.

– *The Politics of John W. Dafoe and the Free Press*. Toronto: University of Toronto Press, 1963.

Cook, Ramsay, ed. *French-Canadian Nationalism: An Anthology*. Toronto: Macmillan of Canada, 1969.

Cook, Ramsay and Réal Bélanger, eds., *Canada's Prime Ministers, Macdonald to Trudeau – Portraits from the Dictionary of Canadian Biography*. Toronto: University of Toronto Press, 2007.

Copland, Douglas, ed. *Giblin: The Scholar and the Man*. Melbourne: F.W. Cheshire, 1960.

Corry, J.A. *Difficulties of Divided Jurisdiction: A Study Prepared for the Royal Commission on Dominion-Provincial Relations*. Ottawa: J.O. Patenaude I.S.O., Printer to the King's Most Excellent Majesty, 1939.

Coucill, Irma. *Canada's Prime Ministers, Governors General and Fathers of Confederation*. Markham, ON: Pembroke Publishers, 2005.

Courchene, Thomas J. *Equalization Payments: Past, Present and Future*. Toronto: Ontario Economic Council, Special Research Report, 1984.

– "Intergovernmental Transfers and Canadian Values: Retrospect and Prospect." *Policy Options*, May 2010, 32–40.

– *Refinancing the Canadian Federation: A Survey of the 1977 Fiscal Arrangements Act*. Toronto: The C.D. Howe Research Institute, 1979.

– "A Short History of Equalization." *Policy Options*, March 2007, 22–9.

– *Social Canada in the Millennium: Reform Imperatives and Restructuring Principles*. Toronto: C.D. Howe Institute, 1994.

- *Subnational Budgetary and Stabilization Policies in Canada and Australia.* Chicago: University of Chicago Press, National Bureau of Economic Research, January 1999.
Craig, Gerald M., ed. *Lord Durham's Report: An Abridgement.* Toronto: McClelland and Stewart, 1963.
Creighton, D.G. *British North America at Confederation: A Study Prepared for the Royal Commission on Dominion-Provincial Relations 1939.* Ottawa: Roger Duhamel, Queen's Printer and Controller of Stationery, 1963.
- *The Forked Road: Canada 1939–57.* Toronto: McClelland and Stewart, 1976.
Crowley, Terry. *Marriage of Minds: Isabel and Oscar Skelton Reinventing Canada.* Toronto: University of Toronto Press, 2003.
Dafoe, John Wesley. *The Imperial Press Conference: A Retrospect with Comment.* Winnipeg: Manitoba Free Press (first published prior to 1923, printed in Great Britain by Amazon).
Dahlby, Bev. *Fiscal Equalization: Country Experiences.* Munich: Ifo Institute, DICE Report 1, 2008.
Deakin, Alfred. *The Federal Story: The Inner History of the Federal Cause.* Melbourne: Robertson and Mullens, 1944.
Dexter, Grant. *Ottawa at War: The Grant Dexter Memoranda, 1939–1945,* ed. Frederick W. Gibson and Barbara Robertson. Winnipeg: The Manitoba Record Society Publications, 1994.
Diefenbaker, John G. *One Canada: Memoirs of the Right Honourable John G. Diefenbaker – The Crusading Years, 1895 to 1956.* Toronto: Macmillan of Canada, 1975.
- *One Canada: Memoirs of the Right Honourable John G. Diefenbaker – The Years of Achievement, 1956 to 1962.* Toronto: Macmillan of Canada, 1976.
- *One Canada: Memoirs of the Right Honourable John G. Diefenbaker – The Tumultuous Years, 1962 to 1967.* Toronto: Macmillan of Canada, 1977.
Dimand, Robert W. "Comment: Expectations, Confidence and the Keynesian Revolution." In *The State of Interpretation of Keynes,* ed. John B. Davis, 123–9. New York: Springer Science + Business Media New York, 1994.
Di Matteo, Livio. *A Federal Fiscal History: Canada, 1867–2017.* Vancouver: The Fraser Institute, 2017.
Dirks, Patricia. *The Failure of L'Action Libérale Nationale.* Montreal and Kingston: McGill-Queen's University Press, 1991.
Djwa, Sandra. *The Politics of the Imagination: A Life of F.R. Scott.* Toronto: McClelland and Stewart, 1987.
Dominion-Provincial Conferences: November 3–10, 1927; December 9–13, 1935 and January 14–15, 1941. Ottawa: Reprinted by Edmond Cloutier King's Printer, 1951.

Dominion Provincial and Interprovincial Conferences from 1887 to 1926. Ottawa: Reprinted by Edmond Cloutier King's Printer, 1951.

Dominion-Provincial Conference (1945), Dominion and Provincial Submissions and Plenary Conference Discussions. Ottawa: Edmond Cloutier, Printer to the King's Most Excellent Majesty, 1946.

Dominion-Provincial Conference 1957: Ottawa, November 25th and 26th, 1957. Ottawa: Edmond Cloutier, Queen's Printer and Controller of Stationery, 1958.

Donaghy, Greg. *Parallel Paths: Canada-Australian Relations since the 1890s.* Ottawa: Department of Foreign Affairs and International Trade, 1995.

Dummit, Christopher. "Empire Man: A New Look at the Complicated Life and Work of Donald Creighton." *Literary Review of Canada* 23, 7 (2015): 7.

Duncan, Sir Andrew Rae. *Report of the Royal Commission on Maritime Claims.* Ottawa: F.A. Acland, Printer to the King's Most Excellent Majesty, 1926.

Dupras, Daniel. *The Constitution Of Canada: A Brief History of Amending Procedure Discussions*, Law and Government Division, Library of Parliament, Government of Canada, January 1992. http://publications.gc.ca/Collection-R/LoPBdP/BP/bp283-e.htm.

Dyck, Rand. "The Canada Assistance Plan: The Ultimate in Co-Operative Federalism." In *Social Welfare Policy in Canada: Historical Readings*, ed. Raymond B. Blake and Jeff Keshen, 326–39. Toronto: Copp Clark Ltd., 1995.

Eggleston, Wilfrid. *While I Still Remember.* Toronto: The Ryerson Press, 1968.

Eisen, Ben, and Mark Milke. *Nova Scotia, New Brunswick, and the Equalization Policy Crutch.* Vancouver and Halifax: Fraser Institute and The Atlantic Institute for Market Studies, 2014.

Engelmann, F.C. and M.A Schwartz. *Canadian Political Parties: Origin, Character, Impact.* Scarborough, ON: Prentice-Hall, 1975.

English, John. *The Life of Lester Pearson.* Vol. 1: *Shadow of Heaven, 1897–1948.* Toronto: Lester and Orpen Dennys, 1989.

– *The Life of Lester Pearson.* Vol. 2: The Worldly Years, 1949–1972. Toronto: Vintage Canada, 1993.

Esping-Andersen, Gøsta. "The Three Political Economies of the Welfare State." In *Power Resources Theory and the Welfare State: A Critical Approach*, ed. J. O'Connor and G. Olsen, 145–8. Toronto: University of Toronto Press, 1998.

Fahrni, Magda, and Robert Rutherdale. *Creating Postwar Canada, 1945–1975.* Vancouver: UBC Press, 2008.

Federal-Provincial Conference 1955: Preliminary Meeting, Ottawa, April 26, 1955. Ottawa: Edmond Cloutier, Queen's Printer and Controller of Stationery, 1955.

Federal-Provincial Conference 1960: Ottawa, July 25th, 26th and 27th, 1960. Ottawa: Roger Duhamel, Queen's Printer and Controller of Stationery, 1960.

Federal-Provincial Conference 1963: Ottawa, November 26th, 27th, 28th and 29th, 1963. Ottawa: Roger Duhamel, Queen's Printer and Controller of Stationery, 1964.

Feeley, Malcolm M. and Edward Rubin. *Federalism: Political Identity and Tragic Compromise*. Ann Arbor: University of Michigan Press, 2008.

Field, Michael. *Lyndhurst Falkiner Giblin, 1872–1951: Economist, Eccentric, and Hero*. Unpublished. Hobart: Tasmanian Parliamentary Library, 1994.

Ferguson, Barry, and Robert Wardhaugh. "'Impossible Conditions of Inequality': John W. Dafoe, the Rowell-Sirois Royal Commission, and the Interpretation of Canadian Federalism." *Canadian Historical Review* 84, 4 (2003): 551–84.

Ferguson, Barry, and Robert Wardhaugh, eds. *Manitoba Premiers of the 19th and 20th Centuries*. Regina: Canadian Plains Research Centre, University of Regina, 2010.

Ferns, H.S. *Reading from Left to Right: One Man's Political History*. Toronto: University of Toronto Press, 1983.

Ferris, J. Stephen, and Stanley L. Winer. *Searching for Keynes: An Essay on the Political Economy of Fiscal Policy, with Application to Canada, 1870–2000*. CESIFO Working Paper No. 1016, category 2: Public Choice, August 2003 (rev. June 2004).

Finkel, Alvin. *Business and Social Reform in the Thirties*. Toronto: James Lorimer and Co., 1979.

– "Origins of the Welfare State in Canada." In *Social Welfare Policy in Canada: Historical Readings*, eds Raymond B. Blake and Jeff Keshen, 221–43. Toronto: Copp Clark Ltd., 1995.

– "Paradise Postponed: A Re-examination of the Green Book Proposals of 1945." *Canadian Historical Association* 4, 1 (1993): 120–42.

– *The Social Credit Phenomenon in Alberta*. Toronto: University of Toronto Press, 1989.

– *Social Policy and Practice in Canada. A History*. Waterloo: Wilfrid Laurier University Press, 2006.

Fisher, Robin. *Duff Pattullo of British Columbia*. Toronto: University of Toronto Press, 1991.

Forbes, Elizabeth (Bess), compiler. *With Enthusiasm and Faith: History of The Canadian Federation of Business and Professional Women's Clubs – La Fédération Canadienne des Clubs de Femmes de Carrieres Libérales et Commerciales – 1930–1972*. Published by the Canadian Federation of Business and Professional Women's Clubs, 1974.

Forbes, E.R. *Challenging the Regional Stereotype: Essays on the 20th-Century Maritimes*. Fredericton, NB: Acadiensis Press, 1989.

– *Maritime Rights: The Maritime Rights Movement, 1919–1927 – A Study in Canadian Regionalism*. Montreal and Kingston: McGill-Queen's University Press, 1979.

Forsey, Eugene A. *How Canadians Govern Themselves*, 7th ed. Ottawa: The Library of Parliament, 2010.

Forster, Donald and Colin Read, "The Politics of Opportunism: The New Deal Broadcasts." *Canadian Historical Review* 49, 3 (1979): 324–49.

Foucault, Michel. "Two Lectures." In *Power/Knowledge: Selected Interviews and Other Writings, 1972–1977*, ed. Colin Gordon, 78–108. New York: Pantheon, 1980.

Fowler, Douglas Weatherbee. "The Unemployment Assistance Act (1956): Its Implications for Social Security and Public Welfare Administration in Canada." MA thesis, University of British Columbia, 1958.

Fowler, R.M. *A Comment on the Rowell-Sirois Report*. Toronto: The Canadian Association for Adult Education and the Canadian Institute of International Affairs, December 1940.

Fransen, David. "'Unscrewing the Unscrutable': The Rowell-Sirois Commission, the Ottawa Bureaucracy, and Public Finance Reform 1935–1941." PhD diss., University of Toronto, 1984.

Fraser, Nancy, and Linda Gordon, "A Genealogy of Dependency: Tracing a Keyword in the U.S. Welfare State." *Signs* 19, 2 (1994): 309–36.

Friesen, Gerald. *The Canadian Prairies: A History*. Toronto: University of Toronto Press, 1987.

Fulbrook, Mary. *A History of Germany, 1918–2008: The Divided Nation*, 3rd ed. Chichester, West Sussex, UK: Wiley-Blackwell, 2009.

Fullerton, Douglas H. *Graham Towers and His Times*. Toronto: McClelland and Stewart, 1986.

Gagnon, Alain-G. and Hugh Segal, eds. *The Canadian Social Union without Quebec: 8 Critical Analyses*. Montreal: Institute for Research on Public Policy, 2000.

Galligan, Brian, ed. *Federalism and the Economy: International, National and State Issues*. Canberra: Federalism Research Centre, Australian National University, 1993.

Gettys, Luella. *The Administration of Canadian Conditional Grants*. Washington: Public Administration Service, 1938.

Glassford, Larry A. *Reaction and Reform: The Politics of the Conservative Party under R. B. Bennett, 1927–1938*. Toronto: University of Toronto Press, 1992.

Gordon, H.S. "A Twenty-Year Perspective: Some Reflections on the Keynesian Revolution in Canada." In *Canadian Economic Policy since the War: A Series of Six Public Lectures in Commemoration of the Twentieth Anniversary of the White Paper on Employment and Income of 1945 Delivered at Carleton University September-November 1965*, ed. S.F. Kaliski, 23–46. Montreal: Canadian Trade Committee, Private Planning Association of Canada, 1966.

Gordon, Linda. *Pitied but Not Entitled: Single Mothers and the History of Welfare*. Cambridge, MA: Harvard University Press, 1994.

Gordon, Walter. *A Political Memoir*. Toronto: McClelland and Stewart, 1977.

Gotlieb, Marc J. "George Drew and the Dominion-Provincial Conference on Reconstruction of 1945–6." *Canadian Historical Review* 66, 1 (1985): 27–233.

Gower, Dave. "A Note on Canadian Unemployment since 1921." *Perspectives on Labour and Income* 4, 3 (1992): article 3, 1–2.

Graham, Roger. *Old Man Ontario: Leslie M. Frost*. Toronto: University of Toronto Press for The Ontario Historical Studies Series, 1990.

Granatstein, J.L. *Canada's War: The Politics of the Mackenzie King Government, 1939–1945*. Toronto: University of Toronto Press, 1990.

– *The Ottawa Men: The Civil Service Mandarins, 1935–1957*. Toronto: Oxford University Press, 1982.

Granatstein, J.L., Irving M. Abella, T.W. Acheson, David J. Bercuson, R. Craig Brown, and H. Blair Neatby. *Nation: Canada since Confederation*, 3rd ed. Toronto: McGraw-Hill Ryerson, 1983.

Grant, Hugh. *W.A. Mackintosh: The Life of a Canadian Economist*. Montreal and Kingston: McGill-Queen's University Press, 2015.

Grauer, A.E. *Public Assistance and Social Insurance: A Study Prepared for the Royal Commission on Dominion-Provincial Relations*. Ottawa: J.O. Patenaude, Printer to the King's Most Excellent Majesty, 1939.

Groenewegen, Peter, and Bruce McFarlane. *A History of Australian Economic Thought*. New York: Routledge, 1990.

Hannay, James. *The Life and Times of Sir Leonard Tilley: Being a Political History of New Brunswick for the Past Seventy Years (1897)*. St John, NB: Reprinted from the Cornell University Library, 2016.

Hanson, Eric J. *Financial History of Alberta 1905–1950*, ed. Paul Boothe and Heather Edwards. Calgary: University of Calgary Press, 2003.

– *Fiscal Needs of the Canadian Provinces*. Toronto: The Canadian Tax Foundation, 1961.

Hawkins, John, *The Life and Times of Angus L*. Windsor, NS: Lancelot Press, 1969.

Heaman, E.A. *Tax, Order, and Good Government: A New Political History of*

Canada, 1867–1917. Montreal and Kingston: McGill-Queen's University Press, 2017.

Heeney, Arnold. *The Things That Are Caesar's: Memoirs of a Canadian Civil Servant*, ed. Brian D. Heeney. Toronto: University of Toronto Press, 1972.

Henderson, George Fletcher. *Federal Royal Commissions in Canada, 1867–1966: A Checklist*. Toronto: University of Toronto Press, 1967.

Henderson, T. Stephen. *Angus L. Macdonald: A Provincial Liberal*. Toronto: University of Toronto Press, 2007.

Hillmer, Norman, ed. *O.D. Skelton: The Work of the World, 1923–1941*. Montreal and Kingston: McGill-Queen's University Press, 2013.

– *O.D. Skelton: A Portrait of Canadian Ambition*. Toronto: University of Toronto Press, 2015.

Hodgins, Bruce W., Don Wright, and W.H. Heick. *Federalism in Canada and Australia: The Early Years*. Waterloo: Wilfrid Laurier University Press, 1978.

Hooper, Paul F. "The Institute of Pacific Relations and the Origins of Asian and Pacific Studies." *Pacific Affairs* 61, 1 (1988): 98–121.

Howe, Joseph. *Confederation in Relation to the Interests of the Empire*. London: Edward Stanford, 1866.

Hutchison, Bruce. *Mr. Prime Minister: 1867–1964*. Don Mills, ON: Longmans Canada, 1964.

Ignatieff, Michael. *The Needs of Strangers*. New York: Picador, 2001.

Innis, Harold A. *Political Economy in the Modern State*. Toronto: Ryerson Press, 1946.

Johnson, A.W. *Dream No Little Dreams: A Biography of the Douglas Government of Saskatchewan, 1944–1961*. Toronto: University of Toronto Press, 2004.

Johnston, Richard and Campbell Sharman, eds. *Parties and Party Systems: Structure and Context*. Vancouver: UBC Press, 2015.

Jones, Benjamin T. *Republicanism and Responsible Government: The Shaping of Democracy in Australia and Canada*. Montreal and Kingston: McGill-Queen's University Press, 2014.

Keirstead, W.C. "The Basis of Provincial Subsidies." In *Papers and Proceedings of the Canadian Political Science Association* 3 (1931): 134–61.

Kelley, Ninette, and Michael Trebilcock. *The Making of the Mosaic: A History of Canadian Immigration Policy*. Toronto: University of Toronto Press, [1998] 2000.

Kendle, John. *John Bracken: A Political Biography*. Toronto: University of Toronto Press, 1979.

Kennedy, David M. *Freedom from Fear: The American People in Depression and War, 1929–1945*. New York: Oxford University Press, 1999.

Kent, Tom. *Getting Ready for 1999: Ideas for Canada's Politics and Government.* Halifax: The Institute for Research on Public Policy, 1989.

Kent, Tom. *A Public Purpose.* Kingston and Montreal: McGill-Queen's University Press, 1988.

Keshen, Jeff. "Getting It Right the Second Time Around." In *The Veterans Charter and Post-World War II Canada*, eds Peter Neary and J.L. Granatstein, 62–84. Montreal and Kingston: McGill-Queen's University Press, 1998.

Keshen, Jeffrey A. *Saints, Sinners, and Soldiers: Canada's Second World War.* Vancouver: UBC Press, 2004.

Kessler-Harris, Alice. *In Pursuit of Equity: Women, Men, and the Quest for Economic Citizenship in 20th-Century America.* New York: Oxford University Press, 2001.

Kimber, Stephen. *Sailors, Slackers and Blind Pigs: Halifax at War.* Toronto: Doubleday Canada, 2002.

Kwavnick, David. *Organized Labour and Pressure Politics: The Canadian Labour Congress, 1956–1968.* Montreal and Kingston: McGill-Queen's University Press, 1972.

Kwavnick, David, ed. *The Tremblay Report.* Toronto: The Carleton Library, McClelland and Stewart, 1973.

La Forest, Gerard V. *The Allocation of Taxing Power under the Canadian Constitution.* Toronto: Canadian Tax Foundation, 1967.

Laporte, Pierre. *The True Face of Duplessis.* Montreal: Harvest House Limited, 1960.

LaMarsh, Judy. *Memoirs of a Bird in a Gilded Cage.* Toronto: Pocket Book, 1970.

Lazar, Harvey, ed. *Canadian Fiscal Arrangements: What Works, What Might Work Better.* Kingston: School of Policy Studies, McGill-Queen's University Press, 2005.

Lecours, André, and Daniel Bédard. "Federalism and Fiscal Policy: The Politics of Equalization in Canada." *Publius: The Journal of Federalism* 40, 4 (2009): 569–96.

– "From Secessionism to Regionalism: The Changing Nature of Territorial Politics in Western Australia." *Journal Regional and Federal Studies* 29, 1 (2019): 25–44.

Lecours, André, and Daniel Béland. "The Institutional Politics of Territorial Redistribution: Federalism and Equalization Policy in Australia and Canada." *Canadian Journal of Political Science* 46, 1 (2013): 93–113.

Lepawsky, Albert. "Canadian Federalism in Transition." *Public Administration Review* 1, 1 (1940): 76–81.

Leslie, Peter M. *National Citizenship and Provincial Communities: A Review of Canadian Fiscal Federalism*. Kingston, ON: Institute of Intergovernmental Relations, Queen's University, 1988.

Levine, Allan. *King: William Lyon Mackenzie King – A Life Guided by the Hand of Destiny*. Vancouver: Douglas and McIntyre, 2011.

Linteau, Paul-André, René Durocher, Jean-Claude Robert, and François Ricard. *Quebec since 1930*. Toronto: James Lorimer, 1991.

Little, Margaret. *No Car, No Radio, No Liquor Permit: The Moral Regulation of Single Mothers in Ontario 1920–1997*. Toronto: Oxford University Press, 1998.

MacGregor, James G. *A History of Alberta*, rev. ed. Edmonton: Hurtig, 1981.

Macintyre, Stuart. *A Concise History of Australia*, 4th ed. Port Melbourne, Victoria: Cambridge University Press, 2016.

Mackintosh, W.A. *The Economic Background of Dominion-Provincial Relations*. Toronto: McClelland and Stewart, 1964. Originally published in 1939 as app. 3 of the Rowell-Sirois Report.

MacMillan, Margaret, and Francine McKenzie, *Parties Long Estranged: Canada and Australia in the Twentieth Century*. Vancouver: UBC Press, 2003.

Mancuso, Maureen, Richard G. Price, Ronald Wagenberg, eds. *Leaders and Leadership in Canada*. Toronto: Oxford University Press, 1994.

Marchildon, Gregory P. "Understanding Equalization: Is It possible?" *Canadian Public Administration* 48 (3): 420–8.

Marchildon, Gregory P., ed. *Making Medicare: New Perspectives on the History of Medicare in Canada*. Toronto: University of Toronto Press, 2012.

Marsh, Leonard. *Report on Social Security for Canada 1943*. Toronto: University of Toronto Press, 1975.

Marshall, Dominique. *The Social Origins of the Welfare State: Quebec Families, Compulsory Education, and Family Allowance, 1940–1955*. Trans. Nicola Doone Danby. Waterloo, ON: Wilfrid Laurier University Press, 2007.

Marshall, T.H. "Citizenship and Social Class." In *Inequality and Society*, ed. Jeff Manza and Michael Sauder, 148–54. New York: W.W. Norton and Co., 2009.

Martinez-Vazquez, Jorge, and Bob Searle. *Fiscal Equalization: Challenges in the Design of Intergovernmental Transfers*. New York: Springer Science and Business Media, Inc., 2007.

Mathews, R.L. and W.R.C. Jay. *Federal Finance: Intergovernmental Financial Relations in Australia since Federation*. Melbourne: Thomas Nelson (Australia) Ltd., 1972.

Maxwell, J.A. "Notes and Memoranda on Some Appendices to the Rowell-Sirois Report." In *Canadian Journal of Economics and Political Science* 7, 2 (1941): 244–67.

May, R.J. *Australia: Financing the Small States in Australian Federalism*. London: Oxford University Press, 1971.
– *Federalism and Fiscal Adjustment*. London: Oxford University Press, 1969.
McCallum, J. Thomas. "A Trip Down Memory Lane: Reflections on the Evolution of Taxation and Tax Rates." In *CGA Magazine*, January–February 2008, Chartered Professional Accountants of Canada.
McConnell, W.H. "The Judicial Review of Prime Minister Bennett's New Deal." *Osgoode Hall Law Journal* 6, 1 (1968): 39–86.
McGeachy, J.B. *A Touch of McGeachy*. Toronto: The Financial Post, 1962.
McNaught, Kenneth, *A Prophet in Politics: A Biography of J.S. Woodsworth*. Toronto: University of Toronto Press, 1959.
Melnyk, George, ed. *Riel to Reform: A History of Protest in Western Canada*. Saskatoon: Fifth House Publishers, 1992.
Milne, David. "Equalization and the Politics of Restraint." In *Equalization: Its Contribution to Canada's Economic and Fiscal Progress*, ed. Robin W. Boadway and Paul A.R. Hobson, 175–203. Kingston: John Deutsch Institute for the Study of Economic Policy, Queen's University, 1998.
Mitchell, David J. *WAC: Bennett and the Rise of British Columbia*. Vancouver: Douglas and McIntyre, 1983.
Moon, Jeremy and Campbell Sharman, eds. *Australian Politics and Government: The Commonwealth, the States and the Territories*. Cambridge, UK: Cambridge University Press, 2003.
Moore, Christopher. *1867: How the Fathers Made a Deal*. Toronto: McClelland and Stewart, 1997.
Morley, J. Terence, Norman J. Ruff, Neil A. Swainson, R. Jeremy Wilson, and Walter D. Young. *The Reins of Power: Governing British Columbia*. Vancouver: Douglas and McIntyre, 1983.
Morton, Desmond. *Social Democracy in Canada: NDP*, 2nd ed.. Toronto: A.M. Hakkert Ltd., 1977.
Morton, W.L. *Manitoba: A History*, 2nd ed. Toronto: University of Toronto Press, 1967.
Musgrave, Thomas. "The Western Australian Secessionist Movement." *Macquarie Law Journal* 3 (2003): 95–129.
Nathan, Richard P., and Margarita M. Balmaceda. "Comparing Federal Systems of Government." In *Decentralization, Local Governments, and Markets: Towards a Post-Welfare Agenda*, ed. Robert J. Bennett, 59–77. New York: Clarendon Press, 1990.
Naylor, David C. *Private Practice, Public Payment: Canadian Medicine and the Politics of Health Insurance, 1911–1966*. Montreal and Kingston: McGill-Queen's University Press, 1986.

Neary, Peter, and J.L. Granatstein, eds. *The Veterans Charter and Post-World War II Canada*. Montreal and Kingston: McGill-Queen's University Press, 1998.

Neatby, H. Blair. *The Politics of Chaos: Canada in the Thirties*. Toronto: Macmillan of Canada, 1972.

– *William Lyon Mackenzie King*. Vol. 2: *1924–1932 – The Lonely Heights*. Toronto: University of Toronto Press, 1963.

– *William Lyon Mackenzie King*. Vol. 3: *1932–1939 – The Prism of Unity*. Toronto: University of Toronto Press, 1976.

Nordlinger, Eric A. *On the Autonomy of the Democratic State*. Cambridge, MA: Harvard University Press, 1981.

Norrie, Kenneth, Douglas Owram, and J.C. Herbert Emery. *A History of the Canadian Economy*, 4th ed. Toronto: Thomson Nelson, 2008.

O'Connor, Julia S. "Gender, Class, and Citizenship in the Comparative Analysis of Welfare State Regimes: Theoretical and Methodological Issues." In *Power Resources Theory and the Welfare State: A Critical Approach*, 209–28. Toronto: University of Toronto Press, 1998.

O'Farrell, Clare. *Michel Foucault*. Los Angeles: Sage, 2005.

O'Leary, Grattan. *Grattan O'Leary: Recollections of People, Press, and Politics*. Toronto: Macmillan of Canada, 1977.

Oliver, Peter C. *The Constitution of Independence: The Development of Constitutional Theory in Australia, Canada, and New Zealand*. Oxford: Oxford University Press, 2005.

Orloff, Ann Shola. "Gender and the Social Rights of Citizenship: A Comparative Analysis of Gender Relations and Welfare States." *American Sociological Review* 58, 3 (1993): 303–28.

Ormsby, Margaret A. *British Columbia: A History*. Toronto: Macmillan, 1958.

Ormsby, W.G. "Letters to Galt Concerning the Maritime Provinces and Confederation." *Canadian Historical Review* 34, 2 (1953): 166–9.

Owram, Douglas. *Born at the Right Time: A History of the Baby Boom Generation*. Toronto: University of Toronto Press, 1996.

– *The Government Generation: Canadian Intellectuals and the State, 1900–1945*. Toronto: University of Toronto Press, 1986.

Palmer, Bryan D. *Working-Class Experience: The Rise and Reconstitution of Canadian Labour, 1800–1980*. Toronto: Butterworth, 1983.

Palmer, Howard, with Tamara Palmer. *Alberta: A New History*. Edmonton: Hurtig, 1990.

Palmer, Howard, and Donald Smith, eds. *The New Provinces: Alberta and Saskatchewan, 1905-1980*. Vancouver: Tantalus Research Ltd., 1980.

Parkin, Andrew. *International Report Card on Public Education: Key Facts on Canadian Achievement and Equity*. Toronto: The Environics Institute, 2015.

Peach, Ian, ed. *Constructing Tomorrow's Federalism: New Perspectives on Canadian Governance*. Winnipeg: University of Manitoba Press, 2007.
Pearson, Lester B. *Mike: The Memoirs of the Right Honourable Lester B. Pearson*. Vol. 1: *1897–1948*. Toronto: University of Toronto Press, 1972.
– *Mike: The Memoirs of the Right Honourable Lester B. Pearson*. Vol. 2: *1948–1957*. Toronto: University of Toronto Press, 1973.
– *Words and Occasions*. Toronto: University of Toronto Press, 1970.
Pedersen, Susan. *Family, Dependence, and the Origins of the Welfare State: Britain and France, 1914–1945*. Cambridge, UK: Cambridge University Press, 1995.
Perras, Galen. "'She Should Have Thought of Herself First': Canada and Military Aid to Australia, 1939–45." In *Parties Long Estranged: Canada and Australia in the Twentieth Century*, ed. Margaret MacMillan and Francine McKenzie, 124–50. Vancouver: UBC Press, 2003.
Perry, J. Harvey. *A Fiscal History of Canada: The Postwar Years*. Toronto: The Canadian Tax Foundation, 1989.
– "Foreword" to Eric J. Hanson, *Australian Commonwealth Grants Commission: A Quarter Century of Fiscal Judgement*. Toronto: Canadian Tax Foundation, 1960.
Pickersgill, J.W. *My Years with Louis St. Laurent: A Political Memoir*. Toronto: University of Toronto Press, 1975.
Pickersgill, J.W. ed. *The Mackenzie King Record*. Vol. 1: *1939–1944*. Toronto: University of Toronto Press, 1960.
Pickersgill, J.W. and D.F. Forster, eds. *The Mackenzie King Record*. Vol. 2: *1944–1945*. Toronto: University of Toronto Press, 1968.
– *The Mackenzie King Record*. Vol. 3: *1945–1946*. Toronto: University of Toronto Press, 1970.
– *The Mackenzie King Record*. Vol. 4: *1947–1948*. Toronto: University of Toronto Press, 1970.
Pierson, Ruth Roach. "Gender and the Unemployment Insurance Debates in Canada, 1934–1940." *Labour/Le Travail* 25 (Spring 1990): 77–103.
Piven, Frances Fox, and Richard A. Cloward. *The Breaking of the American Social Contract*. New York: The New Press, 1967.
– *Regulating the Poor: The Functions of Public Welfare*. New York: Vintage Books, 1993.
Plumptre, A.F.W. *Three Decades of Decision: Canada and the World Monetary System, 1944–1975*. Toronto: McClelland and Stewart, 1977.
Porter, Ann. *Gendered States: Women, Unemployment Insurance, and the Political Economy of the Welfare State in Canada, 1945–1997*. Toronto: University of Toronto Press, 2003.
Pottle, Herbert L. *Newfoundland, Dawn without Light: Politics, Power and the People in the Smallwood Era*. St John's: Breakwater, 1979.

Prang, Margaret. *N.W. Rowell: Ontario Nationalist.* Toronto: University of Toronto Press, 1975.
Prentice, Alison, Paula Bourne, Gail Cuthbert Brandt, Beth Light, Wendy Mitchinson, and Naomi Black. *Canadian Women: A History.* Toronto: Harcourt Brace Jovanovich, 1988.
Proceedings of the Conference of Federal and Provincial Governments, Ottawa, December 4–7, 1950. Ottawa: Edmond Cloutier, Queen's Printer and Controller of the Stationery, 1953.
Province of Nova Scotia. *Report of the Royal Commission: Provincial Economic Inquiry.* Halifax: Provincial Secretary, King's Printer, 1934.
Québec's Traditional Stands on the Division of Powers, 1900–1976. Quebec City: Government of Quebec, Ministry of Inter-governmental Affairs, 1979.
Quiring, Brett. *Saskatchewan Politicians: Lives Past and Present.* Regina: Canadian Plains Research Centre, University of Regina, 2004.
Rea, J.E. *T. A. Crerar: A Political Life.* Montreal and Kingston: McGill-Queen's University Press, 1997.
Reid, Darrel R. *Bibliography of Canadian and Comparative Federalism, 1980–1985.* Kingston: Institute of Intergovernmental Relations, Queen's University, 1988.
Rennie, Bradford J., ed. *Alberta Premiers of the Twentieth Century.* Regina: Canadian Plains Research Centre, University of Regina, 2004.
Report of the Royal Commission on the Constitution Together with Appendixes and Index. Canberra: H.J. Green, Government Printer, 1929.
Report of the Royal Commission on the Finances of South Australia as Affected by Federation Together with Appendices. Canberra: H.J. Green, Government Printer, the Parliament of the Commonwealth of Australia, 1929.
Report of the Royal Commission on Financial Arrangements between the Dominion and the Maritime Provinces. Ottawa: J.G. Patenaude, Printer to the King's Most Excellent Majesty, 1935.
Report of the Royal Commission on Dominion-Provincial Relations, Vol. 1: *Canada: 1867–1939*; Vol. 2: *Recommendations*; Vol. 3: *Documentation*. Ottawa: Edmond Cloutier, Queen's Printer and Controller of Stationery, 1954.
Richards, John, and Larry Pratt. *Prairie Capitalism: Power and Influence in the New West.* Canada in Transition Series. Toronto: McClelland and Stewart, 1979.
Riendeau, Roger. *A Brief History of Canada.* Markham, ON: Fitzhenry and Whiteside, 2000.
Rintala, Marvin. *Creating the National Health Service: Aneurin Bevan and the Medical Lords.* New York: Routledge, 2003.

Roberts, Edward. *How Newfoundlanders Got the Baby Bonus: Stories from Our Imperfect Past.* St John's: Flanker Press, 2013.

Robertson, Heather. *More Than a Rose: Prime Ministers, Wives and Other Women.* Toronto: Seal Books, 1991.

Robin, Martin. *Pillars of Profit: The Company Province, 1934–1972.* Toronto: McClelland and Stewart, 1973.

– *The Rush for Spoils: The Company Province, 1871–1933.* Toronto: McClelland and Stewart, 1972.

Roy, Patricia E., ed. *A History of British Columbia: Selected Readings.* Toronto: Copp Clark Pitman Ltd., 1989.

Rudin, Ronald. *Making History in Twentieth-Century Quebec.* Toronto: University of Toronto Press, 1997.

Saunders, S.A. and Eleanor Back. *The Rowell-Sirois Commission.* Part 1: *A Summary of the Report.* Toronto: The Ryerson Press, 1940.

– *The Rowell-Sirois Commission.* Part 2: *A Criticism of the Report.* Toronto: The Ryerson Press, 1940.

Saywell, John T. *"Just Call Me Mitch": The Life of Mitchell F. Hepburn.* Toronto: University of Toronto Press, 1991.

Scott, Frank and Michael Oliver, eds. *Quebec States Her Case.* Toronto: Macmillan of Canada, 1964.

Shah, Anwar. "A Fiscal Need Approach to Equalization." *Canadian Public Policy* 22, 2 (1996): 99–115.

Sharman, Campbell, ed. *Parties and Federalism in Australia and Canada.* Canberra: Federation Research Centre, Australian National University, 1994.

Sharp, Mitchell. *Which Reminds Me ... A Memoir.* Toronto: University of Toronto Press, 1994.

Silver, A.I. *The French-Canadian Idea of Confederation, 1864–1900.* Toronto: University of Toronto Press, 1982.

Simeon, Richard. *Federal-Provincial Diplomacy: The Making of Recent Policy in Canada.* Toronto: University of Toronto Press, 1972.

– "We Are All Smiley's People: Some Observations on Donald Smiley and the Study of Federalism." In *Federalism and Political Community: Essays in Honour of Donald Smiley,* ed. David P. Shugarman and Reg Whitaker, 1–4. Peterborough, ON: Broadview Press, 1989.

Simeon, Richard, ed. *Must Canada Fail?* Montreal and Kingston: McGill-Queen's University Press, 1977.

Simeon, Richard, and Ian Robinson. *State, Society, and the Development of Canadian Federalism.* Toronto: University of Toronto Press, 1990.

Skocpol, Theda. *Protecting Soldiers and Mothers: The Political Origins of Social Policy in the United States.* Cambridge, MA: Belknap Press of Harvard University Press, 1992.

Slater, David. "Setting the Scene: The Post-WWII Canadian Economy," *Canadian Business Economics* (Winter/Spring 1997): 6–13.
Slater, David and R.B. Bryce. *War, Finance and Reconstruction: The Role of Canada's Department of Finance 1939–1946*. Ottawa: David W. Slater, 1995.
Slumkoski, Corey. "'... A Fair Show and a Square Deal': New Brunswick and the Renegotiation of Canadian Federalism, 1938-1951." *Journal of New Brunswick Studies* 1 (2010): 124–42.
– *Inventing Atlantic Canada: Regionalism and the Maritime Reaction to Newfoundland's Entry into Canadian Confederation*. Toronto: University of Toronto Press, 2011.
Smallwood, Joseph R. *I Chose Canada: The Memoirs of the Honourable Joseph R. "Joey" Smallwood*. Toronto: Macmillan of Canada, 1973.
– *The Time Has Come to Tell*. St John's: Newfoundland Book Publishers Ltd., 1967.
Smiley, Donald V. *Canada in Question: Federalism in the Seventies*. Toronto: McGraw-Hill Ryerson, 1972.
– "Federal States and Federal Societies, with Special Reference to Canada," *International Political Science Review* 5, 4 (1984): 443–54.
Smiley, Donald V. ed. *The Rowell/Sirois Report*, book 1. Toronto: McClelland and Stewart, 1964.
Smith, Denis. *Gentle Patriot: A Political Biography of Walter Gordon*. Edmonton: Hurtig, 1973.
Stark, Kirk J. "Rich States, Poor States: Assessing the Design and Effect of a U.S. Fiscal Equalization Regime." *Tax Law Review* 63 (January 2011): 957–1009.
Starr, Richard. *Equal as Citizens: The Tumultuous and Troubled History of a Great Canadian Idea*. Halifax: Formac Publishing, 2014.
Steeves, Dorothy G. "A British Columbia View." In *The Sirois Report – A Discussion of Some Aspects*, *Canadian Forum*, November 1940.
Stephen, Jennifer. *Pick One Intelligent Girl: Employability, Domesticity and the Gendering of Canada's Welfare State, 1939–1947*. Toronto: University of Toronto Press, 2007.
Stevens, Geoffrey. *Stanfield*. Toronto: McClelland and Stewart, 1973.
Stevenson, Garth. *Ex Uno Plures: Federal-Provincial Relations in Canada, 1867–1896*. Montreal and Kingston: McGill-Queen's University Press, 1993.
Stevenson, Garth. *Unfilled Union: Canadian Federalism and National Unity*, 4th ed. Montreal and Kingston: McGill-Queen's University Press, 2004.
Strayer, Barry L. *Canada's Constitutional Revolution*. Edmonton: University of Alberta Press, 2013.
Strinati, Dominic. *An Introduction to Theories of Popular Culture*. London: Routledge, 1995.

Struthers, James. *The Limits of Affluence: Welfare in Ontario, 1920–1970.* Toronto: Ontario Historical Studies Series, 1994.
– *No Fault of Their Own: Unemployment and the Canadian Welfare State 1914–1941.* Toronto: University of Toronto Press, 1983.
Stursberg, Peter. *Those Were the Days: Victoria in the 1930s.* Victoria, BC: Horsdal and Schubart, 1969.
Sunahara, Ann Gomer. *The Politics of Racism: The Uprooting of Japanese Canadians during The Second World War.* Toronto: James Lorimer, 1981.
Szalay, Michael. *New Deal Modernism: American Literature and the Invention of the Welfare State.* Durham, NC: Duke University Press, 2000.
Taylor, Graham D. *The Rise of Canadian Business.* Toronto: Oxford University Press, 2009.
Taylor, Malcolm G. "Health Insurance: The Roller-Coaster in Federal-Provincial Relations." In *Federalism and Political Community: Essays in Honour of Donald Smiley*, ed. David P. Shugarman and Reg Whitaker, 73–92. Peterborough, ON: Broadview Press, 1989.
Thomas, Lewis H., ed. *The Making of a Socialist: The Recollections of T.C. Douglas.* Edmonton: University of Alberta Press, 1982.
Thomson, Dale C. *Louis St. Laurent: Canadian.* Toronto: Macmillan, 1967.
Thomson, Inga, and Marcella Dafoe. "Bibliography of J. W. Dafoe (1866–1944)." *Canadian Journal of Economics and Political Science* 10, 2 (1944): 213–15. doi:10.2307/137501.
Tillotson, Shirley. *Contributing Citizens: Modern Charitable Fundraising and the Making of the Welfare State, 1920–1966.* Vancouver: UBC Press, 2008.
Trofimenkoff, Susan Mann, *The Dream of Nation: A Social and Intellectual History of Quebec.* Toronto: Macmillan of Canada, 1982.
Trotter, R.G. "British Finance and Confederation." *Report of the Annual Meeting of the Canadian Historical Association* 6, 1 (1927): 89–96.
Underhill, Frank H. "The Sirois Commission as Historians." In the Sirois Report – A Discussion of Some Aspects, *Canadian Forum*, November 1940.
Upholding the Australian Constitution: Proceedings of the Sixth Conference of the Samuel Griffith Society. Vol. 6, November 1995. Mulgrave, Vic.: The Samuel Griffith Society, 1996.
Ville, Simon, and Glenn Withers, eds. *The Cambridge Economic History of Australia.* Port Melbourne: Cambridge University Press, 2015.
Waite, P.B. *The Life and Times of Confederation, 1864–1867: Politics, Newspapers, and the Union of British North America.* Toronto: University of Toronto Press, 1962.
– *The Lives of Dalhousie University.* Vol. 2: *1925–1980.* Montreal and Kingston: McGill-Queen's University Press, 1998.
Walsh, Cliff, and Norm Thomson. *Federal Fiscal Arrangements in Australia:*

Their Potential Impact on Urban Settlement. Canberra: Federal Research Centre, Australian National University, 1994.

Ward, Russel. *The History of Australia: The Twentieth Century*. New York: Harper and Row, 1977.

Wardhaugh, Robert A. *Mackenzie King and the Prairie West*. Toronto: University of Toronto Press, 2000.

– *Behind the Scenes: The Life and Work of William Clifford Clark*. Toronto: University of Toronto Press, 2010.

Watts, George S. *The Bank of Canada: Origins and Early History*. Ottawa: Carleton University Press, 1993.

Watts, Ronald L. *Comparing Federal Systems in the 1990s*. Montreal and Kingston: McGill-Queen's University Press, 1998.

– *Comparing Federal Systems*. 3rd ed. Montreal and Kingston: McGill-Queen's University Press, 2008.

Weir, Margaret, and Theda Skocpol. "State Structures and the Possibilities for 'Keynesian' Responses to the Great Depression in Sweden, Britain, and the United States." In *Bringing the State Back In*, ed. Peter B. Evans, Dietrich Rueschemeyer, and Theda Skocpol, 107–63. Cambridge, UK: Cambridge University Press, 1999.

Wheare, K.C. *Federal Government*, 3rd ed. London: Oxford University Press, 1953.

White, Sir Thomas. *Report of the Royal Commission on Financial Arrangements between the Dominion and the Maritime Provinces*. Ottawa: J.O. Patenaude, 1935.

Wolfe, David A. "The Rise and Demise of the Keynesian Era in Canada, 1930–1982." In *Readings in Canadian Social History*. Vol. 5: *Modern Canada, 1930–1980s*, ed. M.S. Cross and G.S. Kealey, 46–79. Toronto: McClelland and Stewart, 1984.

Wright, J.F.C. *Saskatchewan: The History of a Province*. Toronto: McClelland and Stewart, 1955.

Young, Walter D. *The Anatomy of a Party: The National CCF, 1932–1961*. Toronto: University of Toronto Press, 1969.

Index

Abbott, Douglas, 239–40, 253–4, 260; depicts social security as boost for economic efficiency, 253–4
Abbott, Edwina, 81
Aberdeen, Lady Ishbel, 233
Aberhart, William "Bible Bill," 108, 115, 122; rejects Loan Council, 122; quarrels with Mackenzie King, 150–2; denounces Royal Commission report at Dominion-Provincial Conference 1941, 190–4; fallout from failure of Dominion-Provincial Conference 1941, 194
Advisory Committee on Health Insurance, 205; two draft bills, 205
Advisory Committee on Reconstruction, 203; housing subcommittee, 233
Alberta, 25; economic troubles in 2019, 3–4; resource control, 87; default, 132; Australia's view of Alberta, 133, 169; at Dominion-Provincial Conference, 1935, 108–10; economic crisis 1935–36, 115, 119–20, 122, 129, 131; rejects Royal Commission but submits brief, 138, 150–2; denounces Royal Commission report at Dominion-Provincial Conference 1941, 190–3; signs first tax-rental deal, 198; growing oil revenues, 245
amending formula, Australia, 52, 99; rejects Canada's model of no formula, 52
amending formula, Canada, 99; attempts to establish one, 114; failures in 1950, 256–7
Angus, Henry F., 18, 25, 27–8, 133; reaction to witnesses, 142, 149, 153–5, 158; examines Australia's CGC for Royal Commission, 139, 164; on fiscal need, 166–7; on D.A. Skelton and John Deutsch, 167–8; editing Royal Commission report, 168–9; predicts report's divisive effect, 181–2; on Dafoe, 173–4, 180; on Joseph Sirois, 172, 179–80; reaction to failure of

Dominion-Provincial Conference, 194; death, 180
Anscomb, Herbert, 256–7
Anzac News Letter, 200
Argentina, 9, 104, 114, 120, 138, 149, 152; studies of, 161, 163, 164
Armstrong, Alfred Norman, 33
Atlantic Canada, 41, 48, 64; initial objections to equalization, 12–13
Atlantic Charter, 204
Attlee, Clement, 213
Australia, 12–13, 35–6, 69–72, 75, 88, 92–3, 104–6, 170, 242, 258, 292–3; close relationship with Ottawa, 9, 68–9, 92–3, 124, 292–5; Royal Commission on Dominion-Provincial Relations, 31–2, 133–6, 138–9, 140–1, 147–9, 152–4, 160, 161–5, 166–70, 176–7, 183–4; key model for Canadian equalization, 5, 9–10, 13, 22, 25, 29–30, 71–2, 104, 136, 146, 284, 290–5; settlement of the island as so-called "terra nullius," 46; constitutional models of Canada and the United States, 51–2; steps toward federation, 46–7, 51–4; social security, 72–3, 124; early remedy for fiscal inequality, 15–18, 60–3, 69–72, 74, 120, 161, 170, 176–7, 242, 292–5; 1935 agreement to exchange information with Canada and South Africa, 97; Loan Council as model for Canada, 101, 104, 110–13, 116, 119–21, 124, 127, 134–5; Atlantic Canada, 124, 258; chronicles Alberta's default, 122, 131; rejection of Bennett's Unemployment Insurance, 124–5, 132–3; Premiers' Plan, 34, 134; Royal Commission studies Loan Council and Commonwealth Grants Commission, 161–4; diplomats cite Royal Commission's numerous references to Australia, 169–70; reaction to failure of Dominion-Provincial Conference 1941, 195; wartime relationship with Canada, 196, 199–200; Australian premiers defend moral right to federal grants, 202; examines Ottawa's postwar plans for social security, 206; cited at Dominion-Provincial Conference 1945–46, 215–19, 222–4; reconstruction efforts, 210–11, 219–20, 226–8; on Canada's renewed price controls, 228; postwar social security, 218–19, 226–8, 253–4, 266–7; Canadian Privy Council examines its federation, 258; on internal Canadian federation disputes, 266–7
Australian Labor Party, 72, 75, 100
Australian Loan Council, as model for Canada, 101, 104–5, 110–13, 116, 119–21, 124, 127, 134–5, 292

Back, Eleanor, 184
Bain, George, 284
Bank of Canada, 29, 97, 99, 101, 105–6, 164, 210; studies Prairie Provinces, 23, 131; contacts with Commonwealth Bank of Australia, 131; and Royal Commission, 125–31, 137, 167, 172–3, 185–7, 271; Australian interest, 33, 91, 292; nationalization, 170;

and South Africa, 100; Loan Council, 99–101, 110–11, 119–21, 122, 124; preserve Royal Commission report for postwar implementation, 196–7; social security, 204, 207–8; tacitly advocates continuation of postwar tax rental deals, 207–8; tracks Australia's reconstruction, 210–11; King blames for failure of Dominion-Provincial Conference, 1945–46, 225; and Australia's postwar challenges, 225, 227–8, 243, 265–6; review of social security payments, 257–8

Bank of Nova Scotia *Monthly Review*, 137, 161, 185

Banting, Keith, 10

Barrett, Sir James, 27, 165

Battle of the Atlantic, 189

Baxter, John, 65

Beattie, J.R., 196–7

Beatty, Edward, 104

Beaulieu, Emery, 156–7

Beck, J. Murray, 44–5

Behiels, Michael, 263

Béland, Daniel, 7, 111, 290

Bell, D.W., 163

Bennett, R.B., 79–81, 131; election win 1930, 76–7; meetings with premiers, 81–3, 92; and Maritime premiers, 86–7, 91; opposition to his New Deal, 21–2; anger with R.A. MacKay, 28; New Deal, 96–8, 124, 132; and Bank of Canada, 91, 97; Dominion-Provincial Conference 1934, 92–3; illness, 98; election loss, 101–2, 103; King refers New Deal to Supreme Court, 103–4; fallout from March on Ottawa, 1935, 106–7

Bennett, W.A.C., at Dominion-Provincial Conference 1955, 279

Beveridge, Sir William, 202–3, 204, 242

Bird, Richard M., 37

Bismarck, Otto von, 145

Black, Conrad, 158

Boadway, Robin, 296

Board of Railway Commissioners, 64, 160

Borden, Sir Robert, 25, 79

Bowell, Mackenzie, 9

Bowen, John C., 150–1

Boyko, John, 80, 96, 98, 106–7

Bracken, John, 23, 30, 86, 108, 292; on possible default, 127–8, 130, 132; witness at Royal Commission, 138–9; advocates implementation of Royal Commission report, 187; at Dominion Provincial Conference 1941, 192; calls for National Adjustment Grants, 192

Brazil, British Financial Mission report of 1924, 61–2

Breton, Raymond, 296–7

British Columbia, 18, 25, 27–8, 50, 54, 96, 98, 133, 233; return of railway lands, 69; at the Dominion-Provincial Conference, 1934, 86; at the Dominion-Provincial Conference, 1935, 108; and federal help, 96, 98–9, 100–1, 120, 123; at Royal Commission, 148–50; at Dominion-Provincial Conference 1941, 189–94; at Dominion-Provincial Conference, 1945–46,

218, 223; first tax rental deal, 198; demands more compensation for third tax rental, 256–7, 264; equalization, 276, 287–8, 295; at Dominion-Provincial Conference 1955, 279, 282–3
British Commonwealth Air Training Program, 195
British North America Act, 1867, division of responsibilities, 11
Broadfoot, Barry, 236–7
Brockington, L.W., 173, 186
Brown, John, 72
Bruce, Stanley Melbourne, 61, 69, 72
Brüning, Heinrich, 162
Bryce, Robert B., 115, 171, 211, 271–2
Bryden, P.E., 13, 190, 222, 226, 272, 286, 296
Bryson-Graham Limited, 94
Buck, Tim, 160–1, 184
Burchell, Charles J., 196
Burns, Ronald M.: on Royal Commission report, 182; on fiscal need in tax-rental deals, 199; on tax-rental compromise, 271, 275; on Quebec and equalization, 273–4, 281–2
Butler, Richard Layton, 17

Campbell, Douglas, 255
Campbell, Robert M., 95
Campbell, Thane: at Dominion-Provincial Conference, 1941, 192; calls for National Adjustment Grants, 192
Canada, 5, 7, 14, 144, 172–3, 178, 180–1, 208–9, 236, 269, 274, 290; as federation, 9, 11, 27, 64, 74–5, 91, 114, 125–7, 135, 137, 141, 150, 153, 157, 159, 169–71, 177, 250; in Depression, 18, 21, 23, 75, 79, 105, 117, 129, 135, 149, 152, 292; at Confederation, 47–8; as constitutional model for Australia, 51–2, 60, 62, 73–4; economy, 48–9, 66–7, 88–90, 188–9, 193, 199–201, 211–12, 222–5, 232–3, 239; federal election, 1935, 76–7; 1935 agreement to exchange information with South Africa and Australia, 97; wartime relationship with Australia, 196, 199–200, 220; mutual interest with Australia, 5, 32, 35–7, 69–70, 93, 99–100, 110–11, 124–5, 132–3, 148, 152–3, 160, 162, 165, 169–71, 177, 183–4, 199–200, 206, 224–5, 243–4, 266–7, 281, 292–3; social security, 6, 12, 177, 189, 201–3, 206, 224–5, 228, 231, 235, 253–4, 271–2, 278, 295; federal election 1957, 286–7
Canada Assistance Plan, 277, 297
Canada Pension Plan, 270
Canadian Association for Adult Education, 185
Canadian Chamber of Commerce, 138; at Royal Commission, 160; cites Australia, 30, 160; urges restraint on social security, 262–3
Canadian Chamber of Commerce, Montreal division, 157
Canadian Congress of Labour, 201–2; on education, 207; demands comprehensive social security, 234, 251–2; argues that social security bolsters security,

262; calls for national health insurance and pension plan, 270
Canadian Council of Churches, demands comprehensive social security, 234
Canadian Federation of Business and Professional Women's Clubs, 256
Canadian Institute of International Affairs, 27, 148, 161, 185
Canadian Manufacturers' Association, 104, 125; Quebec division, 264–5
Canadian Medical Association, 145–6
Canadian Pacific Railway (CPR), 104
Canadian Teachers' Federation: advocacy for the Good Life, 206–7; calls for comprehensive social security, 206–7; demands more federal funds for provincial education, 251
Canadian Tuberculosis Association, 146
Canadian Welfare Council, 138, 159–60; lauds Green Paper, urges equalized subsidies but fears dependency, 230–1; espouses social rights, 231
Casey, R.G., 266
Cassidy, Harry, 242–2, 251
Chamberlain, Joseph, 53
Chamberlain, Neville, 175
Child Endowment Act, 227
Churchill, Sir Winston, 20, 175, 200, 204, 213, 220
Civil War, Algeria, 4
Civil War, Canada, threat of, 120
Civil War, Switzerland, 9

Civil War, US, 61
Clark, Douglas H., 281
Clark, W.C., 33, 98–9, 105, 110, 124, 126, 130, 133, 144, 167; suggests guarantee of provincial loans, 98–9, 110, 124; support for Royal Commission, 126, 133–4; King distrusts, 144; advocates implementation of Royal Commission report, 185; advocates family allowances, 209–10
Claxton, Brooke, 219, 222, 224–6
Cockcroft, Charles, 110, 115, 122
Collier, Philip, 17
commodity trade, 75, 97, 137–8, 227
Commonwealth Bank of Australia, 15, 32, 34, 131; assumes central bank powers in the 1920s, 91
Commonwealth Grants Commission (CGC): introduction, 9, 15, 17–18, 70, 258, 292; rough formula in 1938, 37; aims to equalize, 93; as model, 105, 134, 139, 208, 274, 290, 292, 294; in Bank of Nova Scotia *Monthly Review*, 161; at Royal Commission, 147, 153, 162, 163–4, 169–70; requests briefs from Royal Commission, 169–70; at Dominion-Provincial Conference, 1945–46, 219, 220–4; and fiscal need, 166
Commonwealth Tariff Board, 61
Communism, 104; as threat, 226, 230, 248, 250–1, 262
Communist Party of Canada, 34; at Royal Commission, 160–1
Community Chests, 85
Congress of Industrial Organizations (CIO), 234

Conrad, Margaret, 112
Conservative parties. *See* Progressive Conservative parties
Constitution Act, 1907, 54
Cook, Ramsay, 27
Coombs, H.C.: on postwar Australian challenges, 210–11
Co-Operative Commonwealth Federation (CCF), 22, 30, 101–2, 106, 112, 118, 136–7, 140, 150, 178, 192–3, 193, 205, 221, 229, 234; popularity in wartime, 209; in 1935 election, 102; in 1945 federal election, 210; in 1949 election, 244
Copland, Sir Douglas, 92; assesses Maurice Duplessis and Louis St-Laurent, 266–7; on social policy, 266–7
Corning, H.W., 63–4
Counts, George S., 206
Courchene, Thomas J., 198
Coyne, James "Jimmy," 165, 253; studies Argentina and Australia for Royal Commission, 164
Crerar, Gen. Henry Duncan "Harry," 220–1
Crerar, T.A., 25, advocates implementation of Royal Commission report, 186–8
Cronkite, Frederick Clinton, 155
Crowle, H.E., 163
Cunningham, Edward, 27
Curtin, John, 196

Dafoe, John, W., 15, 25–7, 37, 86, 92, 101, 169; work on Royal Commission, 29, 31, 37, 138, 148, 156, 164–5, 167, 168, 173–4, 179–80; trip to Australia, 27; on Canada's economy, 136, 137; predicts war, 148; correspondence with F.W. Eggleston, 161–2, 165; correspondence with Sir James Barrett, 165; reaction to D.A. Skelton's vacation, 172; timing of Royal Commission report, 172; death, 180
Dahlby, Bev, 281
Dandurand, Senator Raoul, 180
Deakin, Alfred, 51
dependency, 13, 21, 27, 50, 108, 125, 160; concern about people and provinces, 13, 84, 108, 204, 231, 280, 298; Bank of Canada fears, 257–8
Depression, 12–13, 20–2, 28, 31, 58, 75, 78, 82–6, 88, 91–2, 95, 104, 238–9, 250, 292–3; federal election 1935, 101; and Mackenzie King's government, 103, 107, 109, 112, 118, 126, 128–9, 131; at Royal Commission, 139, 149, 152, 179; in Australia, 16, 61, 70, 75, 92–3, 111, 141, 152, 179, 211
Deschamps, Noël, 184, 199
Deutsch, John James, 13, 167–8, 172, 174, 182; tax rental compromise, 272–5, 295
DeWitt, Elizabeth, 259
Dexter, Grant, 86, 91, 101, 194
Diefenbaker, John, 5, 247, 249, 296; addresses demands of Ontario and Atlantic Canada, 286–7, 296
disabilities of federation, 55, 62, 71, 89, 149, 151–2, 153–4, 166–7, 178, 199; CGC refusal to recognize, 166
Dominion Bureau of Statistics, 80, 161

Dominion Commission on Employment and Relief, 117
Dominion Finance Commission, 176-7
Dominion League of Western Australia, 16
Dominion-Provincial Conference, 1931, 81
Dominion-Provincial Conference, 1932, 82
Dominion-Provincial Conference, 1933, 82; deadlock between poorer and richer provinces, 82-3
Dominion-Provincial Conference, 1934, 86-7; plight of Prairie Provinces and British Columbia, 87; citations of Australian Premiers' Plan and Loan Council, 91-3
Dominion-Provincial Conference 1935, 23, 106-12; lack of progress, 115-17
Dominion-Provincial Conference, 1941, 189-94
Dominion-Provincial Conference, 1945-46, 215-26; federal goals including renewed tax-rental deals, 213-14, 215-19, failure and consequences, 225-6
Dominion-Provincial Conference, 1950, 260-1; federal cabinet rejects discussion of health care and unemployment assistance, 259-60; on old-age pensions, 260-1
Dominion-Provincial Conference, 1955, 277-81
Dominion Steel and Coal Company, 83

Douglas, T.C.: forms CCF Saskatchewan government, 193, 209-10, at Dominion-Provincial Conference, 1945-46, 221-2, 226; on Mackenzie King, 228-9; espouses Keynesian tax-rental deals and Green Paper, 229-30, 279-82; pushes for expanded social security, 230, 237-40, 258-9; diagnoses trouble with federalism, 242; pushes Louis St-Laurent for conference on Green Paper, 254-5; at Dominion-Provincial Conference 1955, 278-3; does not understand Quebec, 282
Drew, George, 261, 284; feud with Mackenzie King, 216-217, 224; at Dominion-Provincial Conference 1945-46, 216-17, 222-5; cites Australia and CGC, 224-5; repeated clash with King, 240
Duncan, Sir Andrew, 67-8
Dunning, Charles, 23, 76, 122, 126-30, 129-30, 280; at Dominion-Provincial Conference 1935, 109-11, 116-17, 122; Australia cites his views, 169-70; budget 1936, 123; budget 1938 cites Australia and rejects Keynesian approach, 170-1
Duplessis, Maurice, 155, 158, 169, 190, 266, 273; refuses to answer Royal Commission's questions, 156; and Mitchel Hepburn, 157, 159; dinner for Royal Commission, 158; at Dominion-Provincial Conference 1945-46, 216-19, 223-4, 225; rejects second tax-

rental deal, 240–1; defends Quebec's rights, 257, 263–5, 268; agrees to health care grants, 244; agrees to federal old-age pensions, 260–1; pact with Louis St.-Laurent, 265–6, 271; at Dominion-Provincial Conference 1955, 277–9, 281

Dysart, Allison, 109, 191

Eaton, Ken: opposes implementation of Royal Commission report, 186

Economic Advisory Committee, 203; switched to peacetime issues, 205–6; challenge health insurance costs, 205–6

economy, 29; nineteenth and early twentieth century, 40, 48–9; in 1920s–30s, 57–8, 94, 97, 136–7, 166–7; during Second World War, 172, 188–99, 203, 209; postwar, 222, 226, 232, 253, 267, 270, 282, 296

Edmonton Chamber of Commerce, cites Australia and Argentina, 152–3

Eggleston, Sir Frederic William, 162, 165

Eggleston, Wilfrid, 137, 140, 142, 148, 154, 161–2

Ellen, R.R., 133

Elliott, Fraser: opposes implementation of Royal Commission report, 186

Emery, J.C. Herbert, 97

employment, 57, 76, 81, 95, 106, 117, 118, 121, 123, 124, 143, 145, 148, 198, 203–4, 206, 209, 211–12, 213, 217, 221, 229, 231, 236, 240, 253, 255, 260, 270, 280; women, 66, 80–1, 248; in wartime production and armed services, 208–9; lose postwar jobs, but many eventually rejoin work force, 232, 269

Entwistle, John, 62

Environics, Canadian attitudes toward equalization, 4–5, 290

equalization, 3–5, 6–7, 14, 45–6, 68–9, 90, 96, 141, 159, 164, 180, 198–9, 218, 224, 226, 267–8, 291, 294–8; formula renewal 2019, 4; definition, 5–7; Australia as model, 9–10, 17–18, 35, 37, 60, 147, 152; Constitution Act, 1982, 13; development of, 10, 12, 247–9, 263; and Louis St-Laurent, 13, 26, 31, 246, 248, 263, 271–2, 286; federal consideration of options and problems, 273–6; National Adjustment Grants, 13, 24, 89, 127, 177, 182, 191, 272–3, 293, 295; and tax-rental deals, 216; formula based on fiscal capacity for three taxes at Dominion-Provincial Conference 1955, 278–83; cabinet consideration of approaches, 1955–56, 272–3, 275–6, 278–80, 282–4; legislation adopted, first cheques go out, 285–6; permits expansion of social security, 242, 285, 287–8, 297; objections, 284–7, 290–1

Evatt, Herbert, 196

family allowances, 10, 13, 125, 209–10, 213, 246, 254, 258; as an economic tool, 209–10

Federal Council, 51

Index

federal expenditures, 30, 78, 80, 81–3, 87, 90, 94–6, 112, 120–1, 170–1, 193, 221, 270, 274, 281; Royal Commission summary, 178, 182; in Australia, 27, 92, 292

federalism, 9, 11, 29, 72, 75, 85, 114, 119, 130, 135, 137, 155, 162–4, 169, 176–7, 247, 249, 264, 267, 271, 274, 294; as impediment to social security, 7–8; 124–5, 146, 218, 235, 242–3, 255; in United States, 70; in Australia, 31, 62, 114, 125, 176–7

Ferguson, Barry, 136, 173

Ferris, J. Stephen, 106

Financial Agreement Validation Act, 1929, Australia, 99–100, 110

Finkel, Alvin, 13, 215, 218

Finlayson, Roderick K., 79, 98

fiscal capacity, 5–6, 13, 216, 226, 275, 288, 295–6

fiscal inequality, 30, 40–1, 54, 57, 59, 82, 85–6, 91, 104–5, 122, 129, 133, 170, 187–8, 196, 244, 274–5, 289, 293–4; effect on social services, 8, 85, 216, 235, 244, 253, 269, 271, 277; in Australia, 60–3, 72–3, 152, 187, 195, 235; in United States, 70; Dominion-Provincial Conference 1934, 91–2, 112, 116; theme at Dominion-Provincial Conference 1941, 189; effect of tax-rental deals in wartime, 198; Bank of Canada recognizes as barrier to social security, 207–8; at Dominion-Provincial Conference 1945–46, 218, 221–5; and Quebec, 267

fiscal need, 50, 55, 86, 90, 165–7, 257, 272, 291; and Royal Commission, 140, 150, 158–9, 165–6, 173, 178; and Maritimes, 90–1, 100, 147, 158–9; in Australia, 17, 166–7, 181, 292; tacitly acknowledged with tax-rental deals, 198–9, 237; at Dominion-Provincial Conference, 1945–46, 219, 222–3; British Columbia wary of too much sharing, 257; cannot use to calculate equalization, 275, 281–2, 284

Fisher, J., 99–100

Fisher, Robin, 149, 194

Flemming, Hugh John: at Dominion-Provincial Conference 1955, 279; at federal-provincial meeting 1956, 285

Forbes, Ernest R., 68

Ford, Major C.S., 118

Forsey, Eugene, 252

Fowler, Robert M., 34–6, 139, 185; timing of Royal Commission report, 172

Frost, Leslie, 262; opposes Ontario's treatment with equalization, 248–9; supports John Diefenbaker and Atlantic Provinces in 1957, 249, 286–7, 296; initial refusal to join Unemployment Assistance, 277; at Dominion-Provincial Conference 1955, 277–9; at federal-provincial meeting, 1956, 284–5; federal cabinet rejects demands, 285

Fullerton, Douglas H., 33, 105, 111, 119

Gallup Polls, 209; 1957, 286–7

Galt, Alexander, 42

Game, Sir Philip, 100
Gardiner, James, 280
Garran, Sir Robert, 46–7, 51
Garson, Stuart, 221, 222–3, 241, 251; endorses second tax-rental deal, 241
Germany, 9, 11, 51, 73, 75, 171, 173, 175, 181, 220, 269; health insurance, 145
Gettys, Luella, 170
Giblin, Eilean, 34
Giblin, L.F., 15–20, 31, 32–4, 133–4; Royal Commission testimony including comparisons between Australian states and Canadian provinces, 35–8, 171
Glasgow, Sir William, 183, 195; slowly repairs relations with Canada, 196, 200
Godbout, Adélard: at Dominion Provincial Conference 1941, 190–1; cited by Australians, 195
Goldenberg, Carl, 162
Gouin, Paul, 144
Gordon, Donald, 129; on Loan Council, 101
Gotlieb, Marc J., 216
Goudie, Elizabeth, 66
Granatstein, J.L., 187
Grauer, A.E. "Dal," 125–6
Great Britain. *See* United Kingdom
Green Paper for Social Security, 215–16, 217–18, 244, 246; aroused hopes, 229–30, 234, 249, 254–5, 262, 279

Hall Commission. *See* Royal Commission on Health Services
Harrington, Gordon Sidney, 77
Harris, Walter, 247, 273, 275–6, 284, 287
Hart, John, 100–1
Hawkins, John, 77
health care grants, 217, 238, 244
health insurance, 13, 141, 145–6, 207; in the United Kingdom, 12, 145–6, 204; growing demand for, 160, 233–4, 239–40, 252, 254–5, 262, 270; federal-provincial officials discuss two draft bills in 1944, 205–6; delays action on health insurance, 210; as goal at Dominion-Provincial Conference, 1945–46, 213–15, 218; in Australia, 227–8; costs in Green Paper, 230; federal cabinet rejects discussion in 1950, 260
Henderson, K.A. "Ken," 129
Henry, George, 94
Hepburn, Mitchell, 107, 112, 133, 156, 181; at 1935 Dominion-Provincial Conference, 115–17; in front of Royal Commission, 153–5, 157; cites Australia, 153–4; dinner for Royal Commission, 155, 158; visit to Australia, 165; attacks King, 180; opposes implementation of Royal Commission report, 187–8; denounces report at Dominion-Provincial Conference, 190–3; fallout from failure of Dominion-Provincial Conference, 1941, 194–5
Herridge, William, 79
Hicks, Henry D.: at federal-provincial meeting 1956, 285
High Court of Australia, 46, 52, 100; approach to state powers, 114, 227

Hiroshima, 220
Hitler, Adolf, 29, 148, 181, 183; cited at Dominion-Provincial Conference 1945–46, 223
Horn, Michael, 66–7
Hospital Benefits Act, 227
hospital insurance, 13, 294; growing demand for, 150, 249, 257, 262, 279; in Saskatchewan, 221, 254–5; in four provinces, 262
House of Commons Committee on Reconstruction, 204
Howe, C.D., 220, 228
Howe, Joseph, 39–40, 44–6, 55–6, 58, 83
Hutchison, William Bruce, 265

Ilsley, J.L., 226, 237–8, 239; advocates implementation of Royal Commission report, 185–6, options on implementation of report, 186–7; takes control of provincial revenues in wartime, 189, 193; calls for tax-rental renewals with Keynesian goals, 221, 237; rejects Ontario plan and fiscal need, 223; cites Australia, 224; renews tax-rental deals, 237
immigration, 80, 236, 269, 290; in Australia, 73
Imperial Order of the Daughters of Empire, 200
income inequality, Canada, 66–7, 161
India, Canada examines its state loan provisions, 114.
Industrial Union of Needle Trades Workers, 113
Innis, Harold, 87–9

Institute of Pacific Relations, 25, 156, 161
Intercolonial Railway, 64–5, 67
International Labour Review, 204

James, Cyril, 203, release of report, 204–5
Jennings, Ivor, 162
Johnson, Amy, 75
Johnson, Bjorn "Boss," 256
Johnson, David, 124
Johnston, Alexander S., 87
Jones Commission Report. *See* Royal Commission Provincial Economic Inquiry (Nova Scotia)
Jones, John Harry, 87–9
Jones, Walter, 158–9
Judicial Committee of the British Privy Council, 21, 114, 118, 132

Kennedy, David M., 202
Kennedy, W.P.M., 163–4
Kenney, Jason, 5–6, 14, 17, 190, 298; on equalization and Quebec, 3–4, 14
Kershaw, Raymond, 24
Keshen, Jeffrey A., 232–3
Keynes, John Maynard, 15, 22, 32–3; proposal for an international central bank, 105; growing influence in Ottawa, 211, 213
Keynesian approach, 22, 186, 204, 216, 229, 274, 280; not accepted in 1930s, 95, 106, 170–1; tax-rental deals in wartime, 197; growing influence in Ottawa, 211, 213, 264, 293; Ottawa's espousal, 221, 239
King, William Lyon Mackenzie, 18, 23–4, 57–8, 85, 103–5, 121, 123,

137, 170, 196, 201–2, 238–9; and Australia, 32–3, 69; and Maritimes, 65–9; last appeal in 1930 election, 76–8; election win, 1935, 98, 101–2; search for amending formula, 114; White Paper on Employment and Income, 106; caution at Dominion-Provincial Conference 1935, 23, 106–12, 115, 117, 118–19; King's cautious approach to Quebec, 118–19, 145; and Loan Council, 121, 123–4; and Royal Commission, 19, 23–4, 26–7, 29, 38, 126, 128, 130–2, 133, 138, 151, 167, 171–2, 173–4, 179; and National Employment Commission, 23, 117, 121, 142–4; opposition to Queen's University economists and intelligentsia, 144, 186; timing of Royal Commission report, 172, 180, 185–6; tables Royal Commission report, 175–6; handling of Royal Commission report, 185–8, 214; Dominion-Provincial Conference, 1941, 189–94, 195; tax-rental deal, 197–8, 199; with Australians, 196, 200; and comprehensive social insurance in 1943 and 1944, 205, 210; and family allowances, 209–10; wartime manpower, 208; at Dominion-Provincial Conference 1945–46, 215–18, 220–1; feud with George Drew, 216–17, 224, 240; diagnoses Conference failure, 225–6; and Tommy Douglas, 228–30, 238–40; failing health, 235–6, immigration stance, 236; and health-care grants, 243–4, 245; last days in office, 244–5; death, 246
Korean War, 250–1, 261–2, 269

Lalonde, Hector, 157–8
Lang, Jack, 99–100
Lapointe, Ernest, 26, 250
Laurier, Sir Wilfrid, 25, 54, 74
Lea, Walter, 109
League for Social Reconstruction, 204
Lecours, André, 7, 111, 290
Lefort, Gwen, 59
Leslie, Peter, 176
Levine, Allan, 206, 245
Lewis, A.H., 32–3
Liberal Parties, 28, 42, 59, 103, 191; Maritime gains in 1921, 64–5; Maritime losses in 1923–25, 65
Lloyd George, David, 145
Loan Council, 36, 151, 258; in Canada, 113; Australian Loan Council as model, 60, 92, 99–100, 100–1, 104–5, 114, 120–1, 123–4, 125, 135, 160, 163–5, 169, 176, 258, 292; at Dominion-Provincial Conference 1935, 110–11, 115–17; Ottawa insists on Council, 119, 122; Senate rejects Council, 123–4
London Conference on Confederation, 40
Lyons, J.A., 17, 32, 33

Macdonald, Angus L., 22, 30, 57–9, 63–5, 71, 77, 191, 292; admiration for Joseph Howe, 83; becomes premier, 83–4; at Dominion-Provincial Conference, 1934, 86–7, 89, 91; and Royal Commission Provincial Economic Inquiry, 87–9; insists on fiscal need at White Commission, 90; at Dominion-Provincial Conference 1935, 108–10; before royal commission and citing Australia, 146–8; at Dominion-Provincial Conference 1945–46, 224; calls for expanded social security, 238–9

Macdonald, Sir John A., 50, 244

Macdonald, Margaret, 63

MacFarlane, R.O., 31

Macgregor, L.R., 124, 133, 169–70

MacKay, Robert, 28–9, 34–5, 194; R.B. Bennett's anger, 28; and the Royal Commission Provincial Economic Inquiry, 89–90; at Mitchell Hepburn's dinner, 155; editing Royal Commission report, 167–9, 171–2, 179; death, 180

Mackenzie, Ian, 203–4; embroiled in internal turf war over reconstruction, 204–5; oversees advisory cabinet committee on health insurance, 205; influence wanes, 205–6

Mackenzie, William Lyon, 29

Mackintosh, W.A., 106, 144, 167, 171, 213; advocates implementation of Royal Commission report, 185

MacMillan, A.S.: at Dominion Provincial Conference, 1941, 191; calls for National Adjustment Grants, 191

MacMillan, Margaret, 9

MacMillan, William, 86

Magill, Roswell, 163

Manitoba, 292; share of equalization, 7, 18, 23, 35, 49–50, 55, 84, 102; Depression-era plight, 66, 86, 108; on brink of default, 119–20, 127–8, 130–2; at Royal Commission, 138–41, 144; brief cites Australia, 139; Dominion-Provincial Conference, 1941, 187, 192; tax-rental deal, 198; Dominion-Provincial Conference, 1945–46, 221–3, 241; advocates Conference resumption, 255, 257; Dominion-Provincial Conference 1955, 281–2

Manning, Ernest C., 115, 222, 239, 267

March on Ottawa, 106–7

Marchildon, Gregory P., 216

Marchington, William, 82, 111, 115–16

Maritime provinces, 73, 76, 223, 267; objections to equalization in 1957, 6, 248, 284, 295; economies in the 1930s, 59–60, 63–5, 67–8; concerns about Confederation, 39–41, 44–5; complaints about subsidies, 47, 271; at Dominion-Provincial Conference, 1934, and subsequent Commissions, 86–91; tax-rental deals, 198; at Dominion-Provincial Conference 1955, 278–83

Maritime Rights Movement, 55, 58–9, 63–5

Marsh, Leonard, 189, 203–4; puts together report, 204

Martin, Paul, 234, 242–3, 260; warns Mackenzie King, 243–4

Massey, Vincent, 279–80

Massey Commission. *See* Royal Commission on National Development in the Arts, Letters and Sciences
Mathieson, John A., 90–1
Maxwell, J.A., 35, 42
McBride, Richard, 54
McConnell, W.H., 98
McGeachy, J.B. "Hamish," 31, 137–9, 141, 146–8, 150, 152; on Mitchell Hepburn, 154–5; on Quebec's attitude, 157; on New Brunswick, 159
McKenzie, Francine, 9
McLelan, Archibald W., 45
McNair, J.B.: at Dominion Provincial Conference 1941, 191; at Dominion-Provincial Conference 1945–46, 218–19; calls for expanded social security, 238
McNaughton, Andrew, 160–1
Medicare, 237, 248, 270–1, 290–1, 297
Mercier, Honoré, 50
Mills, Stephen, 62
Milne, David, 178
Mitchell, Sir James, 16
Montreal Board of Trade, 157
Moral Appeals for Financial Assistance, 50, 55, 74, 85, 86, 90, 99, 115, 128, 156, 178, 201, 202, 283, 289
Morgan, H.W., 160
Morgan, John S., 235, 252–3
Morneau, Bill, 4
Mosher, A.R., 252
Mothers' Allowances, 84, 147, 152
Mowat, Oliver, 43
Myrdal, Gunnar, 163

National Adjustment Grants (NAGs), 176–8, 185, 272, 293; calls for at Dominion-Provincial Conference, 1941, 191–2; calls for at Dominion-Provincial Conference, 1945–46, 221–2; demands from New Brunswick, Prince Edward Island, and Saskatchewan, 257; as model for equalization, 274
National Council of Women of Canada, 201–2, 233–4; Montreal branch calls for postwar housing, 207; Windsor, ON, affiliate wants constitutional renewal, 233; Vancouver affiliate wants rental subsidies and more public housing, 233
National Employment Commission, 23, 117, 121, 142–4
National Finance Committee, 127–8
National Finance Council, 111–12, 113, 120, 122; rejection of, 124–5
National Research Council, 160–1
National Welfare Fund, 227
NATO (North Atlantic Treaty Organization), 250
Neatby, Blair H., 109
New Brunswick, 35, 49, 65, 89, 104, 238, 257, 287, 298; importance of equalization, 7, 290; on joining Confederation, 40–1, 43–5; ousts provincial Liberals, 65; at Dominion-Provincial Conference, 1934, 86; at Dominion-Provincial Conference, 1935, 109; extra subsidy, 91; brief to Royal Commission, 158–9; at Dominion-Provincial Conference, 1941, 190–1; at Dominion-Provincial Conference, 1945–46, 218, 222;

demands expanded equalization, 276, 285; at Dominion-Provincial Conference, 1955, 278–82

New Brunswick Teachers' Association, 159

Newcastle, NB, 159

Newfoundland and Labrador, 183, 256, 257, 277; economic troubles in 2019, 4; objections to Confederation, 42; enters Confederation, 250; hospital insurance, 262; at Dominion-Provincial Conference, 1955, 277, 280

New South Wales, 37, 46, 51; labour unrest, 72, 219; default, 99–100, 110

New Zealand, 163, 200, 242

Norrie, Kenneth, 97

Nova Scotia, 22, 30, 49, 56, 57–9, 65, 89, 91, 287, 292; anti-Confederation sentiments, 39–40, 41–3, 44–5, 46, 63–4; Depression-era conditions, 59–60, 77, 84; Maritime claims, 67–8; at Dominion-Provincial Conference, 1934, 83, 87, 91; at Dominion-Provincial Conference, 1935, 109–10; before royal commission, 146–8, 163; citing Australia, 147, 222; at Dominion-Provincial Conference, 1941, 190–1; at Dominion-Provincial Conference, 1945, 218, 222, 224; and social security, 238, 277; and equalization, 282, 285

Odlum, Victor: blunders with Australians, 196

Oestreicher, E.A., 274–5

Ogilvie, Albert, 17

Old-Age Pension, 30, 58, 63, 79, 84, 96, 105, 141, 147, 152, 160, 176, 230, 231, 234, 238–40, 252, 254–5; federal program, 213, 215, 218, 258–61, 269; in Britain, 12; in Australia, 71, 227

Old-Age Security Act, 261

Ontario, 13, 64, 79, 84–5, 94, 101, 104, 118, 126–7, 133, 208–9, 215, 244, 257, 261, 277, 283–4, 295, 297; objections to equalization, 6, 12, 248, 275–6, 280–2, 283–8, 294, 296; in Depression, 18, 20, 82–3; on Confederation bargain, 40–1, 43, 45, 47, 49, 165; at Dominion-Provincial Conference, 1934, 87; at Dominion-Provincial Conference, 1935, 107, 112, 115; and Royal Commission, 35, 138, 153–5, 156–7, 159, 169, 180–2; dinner for Royal Commission, 155, 158; denounces Royal Commission report, 187; at Dominion-Provincial Conference, 1941, 189–93; first tax-rental, 198; at Dominion-Provincial Conference, 1945–46, 215–18, 222–6; proposals for 1945–46 Conference, 222–3, 274; stays out of second tax-rental deals, 214, 230, 237; urges recall of 1945–46 Conference, 240; third tax-rental deals, 264; at Dominion-Provincial Conference, 1955, 277, 279–83, 281–2; at federal-provincial meeting, 1956, 284–5; rents only personal income tax in 1957, 273, 285

Ontario proposals for Dominion-Provincial Conference, 1945–46, 222–3; as model for equalization, 274–5
Osborne, J.A.C., 33–4; asks for information on Australian Loan Council, 99–100; advice for politicians in 1935, 105
Ouellet, Mme P. Emile, 252
Owram, Douglas, 97, 136, 209

Padlock Law, 144
Parkes, Sir Henry, 51–2
Parliamentary Joint Committee of Public Accounts on Tasmania, 73–4; cites United States, Canada, South Africa, and Germany, but especially Royal Commission on Maritime Claims, 73–4
Patterson, William, 108; at Dominion-Provincial Conference, 1935, 108; on possible default, 128, 130; witness at Royal Commission, 140–1; at Dominion-Provincial Conference, 1941, 192–3; calls for National Adjustment Grants, 192–3; defeat in 1944, 193
Pattullo, Thomas Dufferin "Duff," 108, 123; at Dominion-Provincial Conference, 1935, 108; and Loan Council, 123; before Royal Commission, 148–50; denounces Royal Commission report at Dominion-Provincial Conference, 1941, 190–3, 194; fallout from failure of Dominion-Provincial Conference, 1941, 194, 195
Pearson, Lester, 134; on value of equalization, 288

Permanent Committee on Financial Questions, 116; only meeting, 119
Perry, J. Harvey, 60
Pickersgill, J.W., 186, 247, 272, 275–6, 286
Plumptre, A.F.W., 171, 211
post-secondary education, 6, 232, 263–4
Prang, Margaret, 156
Premiers' Plan, 33, 92, 134, 139, 163–4, 292
Price, W.H., 82
Prince Edward Island, 7, 32, 65; and equalization, 7, 276; ousts Liberal government, 65; joins Confederation, 42–3; at Dominion-Provincial Conference, 1934, 86; subsidy increase, 91; at Dominion-Provincial Conference, 1935, 109; before royal commission, 140, 146, 148; at Dominion-Provincial Conference, 1941, 192; and National Adjustment Grants, 257
Privy Council Office, 258; examines federal-provincial relations in United States and Australia, 258
Progressive Conservative parties, 5, 28, 54, 58–9, 65, 76–7, 83–4, 102–3, 106, 192, 209, 216, 247, 249, 254, 256, 277, 284, 286–7, 296
Purvis, Arthur, 143–5

Quebec, 8, 11, 18, 82–3, 126–7, 144–5, 174, 199, 214, 238, 244, 266, 277; and equalization, 3–4, 6–7, 275–6, 282–3, 285, 288, 290–1, 294–5, 297, 298; objection to tax rental deals, 10; and Confederation, 40–1, 43, 45, 47, 49; at

Dominion-Provincial Conference, 1934, 85, 87; at Dominion-Provincial Conference, 1935, 104, 107–8; Loan Council, 111; and Royal Commission, 26, 30, 35–6, 138, 150, 152, 156–7, 158, 169, 174, 179, 182; at Dominion-Provincial Conference, 1941, 190–1, 195; first tax-rental, 198; at Dominion-Provincial Conference, 1945–46, 215–16, 223–4; stays out of second tax-rental deals, 214, 216, 230, 237, 238, 240–1, 244; nationalism revives, 248, 251–2, 263–6, 267–8; stays out of third tax-rental deals, 264; and old-age security, 260–1; personal income tax, 264–6; Ottawa moves to end isolation, 271–6; generous equalization grants, 275–6; adapts Unemployment Assistance, 277; at Dominion-Provincial Conference, 1955, 277, 279, 281; rejects last tax-rental deals, 285–6
Quebec Conference, 42
Quebec Pension Plan, 270
Queen's University, 144, 213

Ralston, J.L.: budget of March 1940, 183
Randerson, Roger, 34
rationing, 193, 201, 228, 232–3; in the United Kingdom, 261
Reconstruction Conference 1945. *See* Dominion-Provincial Conference, 1945
Reinke, Carl, 31, 137
relief, 8, 18, 20–2, 23, 30, 77, 80–3, 85–6, 87, 94, 95–6, 98–9, 101–2, 105–6, 107–9, 112, 115, 117, 118, 126, 128–9, 142 145, 160, 178, 202, 209, 231, 251; and unemployed employables, 276–7; and Nova Scotia, 77, 84; and Prairie Provinces and British Columbia, 91, 149, 151–2; 1935 increase and 1936 cut, 116–17, 121; strikes, 118; Saskatchewan, 131, 140–1, 142, 229; Manitoba, 138–9, 192; in the United States, 12, 163; in Australia, 71, 75–6
Report on Social Security for Canada, 189
resources, transfer of control to Prairie Provinces, 68–9
revenues and responsibilities, 8, 13, 41, 114, 126, 256, 292, 293–4; at Dominion-Provincial Conference, 1935, 107–12, 159; Royal Commission approach, 134, 135, 181
Rhodes, Edgar, 65, 95
Richer, Léopold, 157
Riendeau, Roger, 118
Rinfret, Thibaudeau, 26
Robinson, Ian, 118–19, 144
Roebuck, Arthur, 116
Rogers, Norman, 143–5
Roman Catholic Church, in Quebec, 8, 11, 113, 148, 265
Roosevelt, Franklin Delano, 79, 93, 125, 200, 202, 204, 229, 236
Rose, Sir John, 45
Routley, T.C., 145
Rowell, Newton, 18, 24–8, 133, 137, 143, 146–7, 167; trip to Australia, 25; calls on William Aberhart, 151; and Mitchell Hepburn,

153–5; illness, 29, 34, 148, 153, 155–6, 163, 167–8, 182
Rowell-Sirois Commission. *See* Royal Commission on Dominion-Provincial Relations
Royal Commission of Inquiry on Constitutional Problems, 264–5; report, 267–8; calls for form of equalization, 267–8; assertion of Quebec as founding nation, 268
Royal Commission on Dominion-Provincial Relations (Rowell-Sirois Commission), 8, 13, 15, 18–19, 23, 50, 89, 135, 144, 145, 169, 171, 177, 212, 219, 255, 271–2, 277, 284, 293, 295; preparation for, 29; travels, witnesses and evidence, 18, 29–30, 142, 145; and fiscal change, 30; push to establish, 126–7; creation, 132; challenges, 135–7; in Australia, 31, 133, 169; frequent mention of Australia, 138; studies on Argentina, Australia, New Zealand, Sweden, Switzerland, United States, 161, 163–4; international experts, 162–3; report, 175–8; reception in wartime, 144, 175–80, 181, 184–5, 186, 189, 197, 214; at Dominion-Provincial Conference, 1945–46, 222; problems with report, 181–2, 263; St-Laurent salutes report, 278
Royal Commission on the Constitution, 51
Royal Commission on the Finances of Western Australia as Affected by Federation, 61–3; using Canada as a model, 62

Royal Commission on Health Services, 270–1
Royal Commission on Maritime Claims, 67–9, 86–7, 90–1, 147, 199; Australia's reaction to report, 69–71, 73
Royal Commission on National Development in the Arts, Letters and Sciences, 263
Royal Commission on the Finances of South Australia as Affected by Federation, 69–72; cites United States, 70–1; cites Royal Commission on Maritime Claims, 71
Royal Commission Provincial Economic Inquiry (Nova Scotia) (Jones Report), 87–90

Saskatchewan, 23, 35, 79, 102, 209–10, 227–9, 242, 244, 287, 290; economic troubles in 2019, 4; cites Australia, 141; Depression-era plight, 108, 141; accepts Loan Council, 122; on brink of default, 119, 122, 127–8, 130–2; at Royal Commission, 138, 140–2, 144, 178; health insurance, 221–2; hospital insurance, 255, 262; at Dominion-Provincial Conference, 1941, 192–3; tax-rental deal, 198; on National Adjustment Grants, 267; at Dominion-Provincial Conference 1955, 279–82; on equalization formula changes, 287
Saskatchewan Urban Municipalities Association, 141–2
Saunders, S.A., 184

Savard, Adjutor, 175
Saywell, John T., 107, 194
Scott, Frank, 132
Scott, W. Elwynne, 243
Scullin, James H., 72–3
Service, James, 51
Shah, Anwar, 296
Shapiro, L.S.B., 200
sharing: as a moral deed, 13; as a pragmatic solution, 127; Royal Commission view, 178; symbolic change in wartime to view social security as a moral right, 202–3; Australian premiers defend moral right to federal grants, 202
Shea, Ambrose, 42
Silver, A.I., 43–4
Simeon, Richard, 118–19, 144
Sirois, Joseph, 26, 31, 272; acting and then chair of Royal Commission, 35, 142, 156; reaction to D.A. Skelton's vacation, 172; timing of Royal Commission report, 168, 172, 175; does not issue minority report, 179; support for Quebec rights, 179; death, 179–80
Skelton, D.A., 25, 29, 31, 32–4, 125–6, 134, 144, 243; reconsiders Loan Council, 119–20, suggests voluntary council, 120–2; rejection of loan council, 124; support for Royal Commission and federal help for Manitoba and Saskatchewan, 126–8, 130–2, 133–4; with Commission, 135, 136–7, 139–40, 160, 162–5, 167–8, 172, 174, 176, 182, 184; to Dafoe, 165–7; vacation with O.D. Skelton, 172; timing of Royal Commission report, 172–3, 175; advocates implementation of Royal Commission report, 185–6; reaction to failure of Dominion-Provincial Conference, 1941, 194; planning postwar dominion-provincial conference, 1945–46, 211–12, 217; death, 180
Skelton, Isabel, 136
Skelton, O.D., 136, 167, 172; advocates implementation of Royal Commission report, 186
Slumkoski, Corey, 109
Smallwood, Joseph Roberts "Joey," 250; at Dominion-Provincial Conference, 1955, 277, 280
Smith, Sidney T., 132–3
Smith, J. Lavell, 259
Social Credit, Alberta, 121, 150–2
social rights, 231, 252–3
Social Security: slow expansion in Canada, 6, 10, 12, 85, 125–6, 96, 150, 160, 177, 181, 189, 214, 244, 253–4, 257–8, 288, 293–4, 297; in United States, 12, 202, 242; in United Kingdom, 242; advocacy during and after Second World War, 201–2, 203–4, 205–9, 212–13, 248–9, 253–4, 259–61, 262, 269, 276; momentum stalled after Dominion-Provincial Conference, 1945–46, 209, 215, 217, 218, 226; provincial demands for medical and hospital insurance, unemployment assistance, 221–2, 225, 229–31, 233–5, 237–9, 240–3, 251–2, 256–7, 259–61, 277–8; in

Australia, 227–8, 242, 248, 255; equalization allows expansion, 288, 297

Société Saint-Jean-Baptiste de Montréal, 157–8; asserts there are two founding nations in Canada, 157

South Africa, 73, 100; Baxter Commission of 1923, 62; 1935 agreement to exchange information with Canada and Australia, 97

South Australia, 17, 37, 46, 61, 69–72, 76, 76, 225

Southern States of America, petition, cited in Royal Commission on Finances of South Australia as Affected by Federation, 71

Special House Committee on Social Security, 205; examines two health insurance bills, 205, 210

Stalin, Joseph, 213

Steeves, Dorothy G., 150

Stevenson, Garth, 45

Stewart, Bryce M., 163

Stewart, James McGregor, 28, 31, 161, 179

St-Laurent, Louis, 5–7, 13, 26, 31, 133, 245; as francophone counsel, 139, 142, 146, 158, 167; as originator of equalization, 247–9, 282–6, 295–6; as King's successor, 190, 194, 245–6, 248–50, 252–3, 257–9, 285, 286; wins 1949 election, 254; pushed on social security, 257–60, 262–3, 264–6, 270; defends high defence spending, 262; at Quebec Reform Club, 265; pact with Maurice Duplessis, 263–6, 268; on tax-rental deals, 250–1, 271–6, 295; at Dominion-Provincial Conference 1955, 277–81, 283; in House of Commons on equalization, 283–4; 1957 election, 247, 286–7, 295–6

Struthers, James, 85, 118, 143, 177, 225

Stursberg, Peter, 137–8

Subcommittee on Financial Questions, renamed National Finance Committee, 109, 111, 127–8

subsidies, 7–8, 22, 36–7, 45, 54–5, 71, 74, 86–7, 88–90, 95–6, 104, 223–4, 279, 290–1, 293–4; complaints about amount in nineteenth century, 41, 45, 49–50, 64; Maritime increases, 68–9, 87, 91, 102, 108, 271; Royal Commission and NAGS, 134, 139, 141, 150, 152, 157–8, 160, 167, 181, 199, 257; post-Confederation difficulties, 291–2, 294

Supreme Court, Canada, 21, 26, 52, 104, 124

Sweden, 163

Switzerland, 9, 161, 163, 177

tariffs, Australia, 16, 41, 43, 53–4, 71, 73, 76

tariffs, Canada, 26, 40, 41, 44, 47, 74, 105; in the Maritimes, 65, 88–9, 147, 191; in the West, 120, 127, 139, 151–2

tariffs, in US southern states, 71

Taschereau, Louis-Alexandre, 104, 107–8, 144

Tasmania, 15–17, 35, 46, 60–1, 73–4, 171, 224

tax rental agreements, 10, 244,

293–5; first round, 10, 69, 189, 196–9; options in first round, 198; as Keynesian tool to promote economic and social security, 207, 211–12, 229, 239; renewal as goal at Dominion-Provincial Conference 1945–46, 213–14, 215–17, 219, 223–4; second renewal, 216, 230, 237–9, 241; third renewal, 247–50, 256–8, 264–6; fourth renewal and alternatives, 271–6, 278–82, 285–6

Taylor, K.W., 274
Taylor, Malcolm G., 262
Thomson, Dale C., 158, 284
Tilley, L.P.D., 86
Tilley, Samuel Leonard, 43–4
Toews, Travis: on fiscal stabilization, 4
Tolmie, Ross, opposes implementation of Royal Commission report, 186
Towers, Graham, 23–4, 33, 105, 164, 167; on Loan Councils, 100–1, 110, 112; support for Royal Commission, 126–32; timing of Royal Commission report, 172–3; advocates implementation of Royal Commission report, 185–6
Trades and Labor Congress, 145, 134; calls for comprehensive health insurance, 270
trade unions, 10, 211
Tremblay, Thomas, 264–5
Tremblay Commission. *See* Royal Commission of Inquiry on Constitutional Problems
Truman, Harry S., 213, 220, 261–2
Tupper, Sir Charles, 40, 42, 44–5

Underhill, Frank, 178, 181, 184–5
unemployment, 19, 76–7, 78, 79–80, 82, 96, 100–1, 117–18, 134, 143, 171, 204, 207, 218, 239–40, 241, 253–4, 257, 260, 262, 280; in Australia, 93, 227
unemployment assistance, 204, 218, 234, 238, 249, 253, 159, 272–3, 276–7, 297; provincial demand for, 257; federal cabinet rejects discussion in 1950, 259–60
unemployment insurance, 10, 12, 21–2, 76, 79, 82–3, 91, 96–8, 103–4, 125, 132, 135, 145, 169, 171–2, 179, 237, 246, 254, 259, 260, 297; in Australia, 124; in United States, 163, 202; demands for, 141, 147, 160, 231, 233, 249, 251
Union Nationale, 223
Union of New Brunswick Municipalities, 159
United Australia Party, 100
United Church of Canada, 259
United Kingdom, 54, 105, 114, 135, 170, 180, 188, 190, 222, 245; emigration, 46, 52, 236, 271; expansion of social security, 12; Canada examines its approach to treasury bills, 114; approach to social security, 202–3, 242
United States, 7, 9, 51, 66, 70–1, 73, 74, 98, 104, 125, 127, 158, 161–2, 163, 170, 177, 202, 229, 269; and social security, 12, 177, 202, 218, 242, 290; Civil War, 61; Privy Council examines federation, 258; variable grants as model for equalization, 275

veterans, 203, 211, 226, 231–2, 236–7; Charter, 232, 236–7
Victoria, 35, 37, 46, 51, 76
Villeneuve, Cardinal Jean-Marie-Rodrigue, 199
Visiting Homemakers Association of Toronto, 259

wage-and-price freeze, 200–1, renewed controls, 228
Walpole, Sir Robert, 245
Walters, Chester, 155
Ward, Russel, 70
Wardhaugh, Robert A., 136, 173
Warden, Mrs C.L. 81.
War Measures Act, 10, 189, 193
Watson, H.K., 16
Western Australia, 9, 16–17, 35, 37, 46, 60–3, 222, 227, 292; resisted federation until threatened, 52–4

Whelan, Edward, 42–3
White, Sir Thomas, 87, 104
White Commission, report, 90–1, 108–9, 147, 199
White Paper on Employment and Income, 106, 217–18
Wilson, John K., 70
Winer, Stanley L., 106
Winnipeg Board of Trade, 139
Winnipeg Real Estate Board, 139
women, in armed services, 189, 208–9, 261
Women's International League for Peace and Freedom, 121
women's organizations, importance to social security, 10, 201, 207, 233, 253, 256; in United States, 12
Woodsworth, J.S., 229
workmen's compensation, 84, 152